The Extended Stories of Guernsey County, Ohio

Volume 2

BY

WILLIAM G. WOLFE

Originally published 1943 – 1947

AS COMPILED, EDITED, AND REPUBLISHED BY

RICHARD L. BOOTH

Cambridge, Ohio
2024

The Extended Stories of Guernsey County, Ohio
Volume 2

The text of *Stories of Guernsey County, Ohio* by William G. Wolfe is in the public domain.

The text of historical newspaper articles written by William G. Wolfe is in the public domain.

Editor's preface and all-names index © 2024 by Richard L. Booth.

Library of Congress Control Number: 2024911852

ISBN 979-8-9906317-1-7

1st Edition, 1st Printing

Editor's Preface

On May 16, 1932, the Jeffersonian newspaper of Cambridge, Ohio, made the following announcement:

The Jeffersonian takes great pleasure in presenting its readers "One Hundred Stories of Guernsey County" written at its request by W. G. Wolfe, superintendent of Guernsey County Schools.

The writer is giving his services and The Jeffersonian presents the articles, because they hope, by doing so, to arouse a greater interest in Guernsey county by having people understand it better.

Six years and 313 published "stories" later, the "One Hundred Stories" series ended on August 13, 1938, having more than tripled its original article count goal. By that time, Mr. Wolfe had retired from the school system and had already begun working to revise and compile the long series of articles into what was to become his 1943 book entitled *Stories of Guernsey County, Ohio*. Yet, once his pre-1943 work was published in book form, Mr. Wolfe continued to write 171 more historical newspaper articles from 1944 through 1947. Many such articles contained references to related chapters and page numbers in the original 1943 book.

This two-volume *Extended Stories of Guernsey County, Ohio* reproduces the original, out-of-print, 1093-page *Stories of Guernsey County, Ohio* in Volume 1 plus the 171 later supplementary "sidelights" articles written by William G. Wolfe from 1944 to 1947, along with a new, extensive, all-names index to both volumes in Volume 2. Thus, these two volumes are meant to fully republish essentially all the historical writings of Mr. Wolfe, Guernsey County's best-known early historian.

This republication project started simply with the intent to make available in book form the last 171 articles Mr. Wolfe wrote, meant to supplement the original 1943 work. But the fact that the original book has been out of print, combined with the fact that many of the subsequently written articles made references to the original book, made republication of the 1943 book a necessary part of the project as well.

Volume 1

Volume 1 of this two-volume set contains a page-for-page reproduction of William G. Wolfe's 1943 *Stories of Guernsey County, Ohio* with the addition of four pages of historical maps for each of the last 19 chapters on Guernsey County's individual townships. The historical maps show land ownership in 1855, 1870, and 1902. For contemporary comparison, a fourth map of each township, derived from current United States Geological Survey offerings, shows terrain, roads, and land section identifiers as they exist today. Each map is accompanied by a QR code which can be quickly scanned by most of today's cell phones, linking to an online version of the same map which, when expanded, is usually much easier to read than the fine map text on the printed page. It is intended that the links will remain valid and active for many years to come. All of the maps can also be found online at *https://guernseydeeds.com/gcmaps.html*.

Though the page numbering of Volume 1 is identical to that of the original 1943 book, it is not a photographic reproduction of the original book, but rather a completely reproduced and digitally reformatted copy of the original text and images. This was deemed necessary so that a new all-names index could be accurately produced and placed in Volume 2. Volume 1, however, still retains the original book's index.

To be clear, there are minor differences between the original book and the Volume 1 reproduction. For ease of text search, all words which were originally broken in two and hyphenated across the end of a line of text have been restored to their unhyphenated form. As a result of this and other matters of minor text reformatting, on many pages there is a slight slippage of words from one page to another between the original book's layout and this reproduction. For instance, the last few mid-paragraph words of, say, original page 248 might appear at the beginning of reproduction page 249 instead. Likewise, the first few mid-paragraph words of, say, original page 839 might appear at the end of reproduction page 838. Obvious typographical errors in the original book have been corrected, and in some cases the spelling of the names of well-known individuals have also been fixed when it was clear that the spelling in the original was incorrect. For instance, the name of the controversial Ohio politician Clement Vallandigham has been corrected from Wolfe's "Valandigham" spelling in several places. Likewise, an early diarist incorrectly referred to as "M. Cummings" is now identified as Fortescue Cuming.

Volume 2

The second volume of this two-volume set contains the 171 articles published by William G. Wolfe in the Jeffersonian newspaper from 1944 through 1947. They are grouped into eight "extended chapters" numbered 40 through 47, as if to be natural extensions of the original 39-chapter 1943 book. The articles have been only lightly edited with punctuation corrections, spelling fixes, and some time-relative references such as changing "fifty years ago" in a newspaper article to a time-invariant "in 1894" where appropriate.

A very important additional feature of this second volume is an all-names index for both of the combined volumes of this set together. For ease of reference, page numbering in Volume 2 begins with page 2001 so that indexed name instances found on pages 1 through 1093 of Volume 1 can easily be distinguished from references found in Volume 2. In reproducing the 1943 book, it was found that fewer than ten percent of the names of individual people mentioned in the book could be found in the original index. This had no doubt been done because many pages of the original book were devoted to exhaustive lists of landowners within townships, soldiers within regiments, or members within social organizations. Such sections of name after name read like the phone book and would have severely bloated the original subject index. It is hoped that the new and vastly expanded all-name index will better serve future genealogists searching for a familiar name.

Historical Corrections

In our modern age of instant access to information over the Internet, it is possible to easily do research that William G. Wolfe could only have dreamed of in the mid-twentieth century. Guernsey County is particularly blessed in this regard by having nearly all of its Jeffersonian newspapers from 1860 to 1995 available for instant text search through subscription services available online. Thanks to these new research tools, it is possible to investigate further to elaborate more details about some of Wolfe's previously published stories, sometimes finding discrepancies or significant errors along the way. At this writing, therefore, there are some known errors in Wolfe's historical writings that are not corrected in this work of republication. To do so would have disrupted the page-for-page reproduction of the original book and would have been a haphazard attempt at best. Perhaps a future book will assemble more correct versions of some stories in need of adjustment.

The foregoing having been said, a few of the more significant errors deserving mention are the following:

- Ezra Graham, mentioned more than 20 times as the first pioneer resident of Guernsey County, serving as the original Wills Creek ferryman in 1798, in all likelihood did not bear that specific name. The first name "Ezra" has been traced to a copywriter's mistake in a 1910 booklet. A single faint memory of a possible "Mr. Graham" was attested in 1847, but the absence of any other records of a man named Graham in the Guernsey County area circa 1798 calls even that surname into question. The first pioneer Wills Creek ferryman was more likely a member of trailblazer Ebenezer Zane's extended family, possibly his nephew Ebenezer Ryan. Ryan was known to have helped blaze Zane's Trace through this area and lived his later life near Zanesville. The name of the first ferryman is, at best, a guess.

- Wills Creek was *not* named in memory of Wills Creek, Maryland, by Ebenezer Zane while blazing Zane's Trace circa 1798. It already bore that name on the famous John Fitch map made in 1785.

- Cambridge, Ohio, is probably *not* named after Cambridge, Maryland. The name origin statement in Wolfe's book, that ancestors of the town's founders came from Cambridge, Maryland, does not match genealogical records. Given that the founders of Cambridge built a government-authorized bridge over Wills Creek soon after their 1803 arrival at the future site of Cambridge, it is possible that wordplay—that they came to build the bridge—is the origin of the name.

- The rediscovery of an 1825 booklet entitled *"The Trial, Confession, &c. of John Funston"* has revealed that many of the details of the 1825 Postboy Murder case were garbled or even fabricated in historical retellings over the years. The more accurate true story, as given in the 1825 booklet published at the time and place of the crime, is just as fascinating. The booklet, produced as a documentary souvenir immediately after the murderer's execution, is available in reprint form online.

- The book's account of the 1865 murder of John B. Cook is relatively accurate but errs in some of its details. The entire 4,000-page trial transcript has been preserved on microfilm by the National Archives and serves as the definitive account of the case.

- A humorous story about local attorney William M. Farrar's Groundhog Day speech before the Ohio legislature turns out to be based on just a nugget of truth. A brief 1885 tongue-in-cheek proposal to change the date of Groundhog Day to March 4th somehow turned into a tall tale told and apparently believed decades later about a three-day speech on changing the date to January 2nd.

The point to be taken from the preceding corrections and clarifications is that historians often cannot verify the accuracy of stories they have been told and which they repeat when they regard them as credible. In fact, it is speculated that William Wolfe stopped short of calling his 1943 book a "History of Guernsey County," instead calling it "Stories of Guernsey County," because he was aware that much of the information he had amassed and been told was difficult or impossible to verify and could very well be wrong, as stories often are. As a matter of scrupulous honesty, he thought "stories" a more modest assertion than "history," which bears the implied weight of confirmed truth.

William G. Wolfe

William G. Wolfe was the much-beloved second great historian of Guernsey County, Ohio, the first having been Col. C. P. B. Sarchet who, like Wolfe, for many years wrote hundreds of historical newspaper articles before compiling those writings into his own 975-page *History of Guernsey County, Ohio* in 1911. Many of the stories within Wolfe's 1943 book are based on accounts previously published by Sarchet as the more original source. Col. Sarchet was born in 1828 and died in 1913, just two years after publishing his county history. At this writing, reprints of Sarchet's history are still in reprint publication and available online.

William G. Wolfe was born in the southeastern corner of Guernsey County at Quaker City in 1874. He attended Ohio Northern University and received his teaching certificate at the age of 23, then spent the next 43 years of his life working within the county's education system, first as a teacher for seven years, then 15 years as superintendent of the Quaker City Schools, followed by 21 more years as superintendent of all of Guernsey County's "county" schools outside Cambridge and Byesville.

At the time of his death in 1947, Mr. Wolfe was deeply involved in originating and planning the county's week-long sesquicentennial celebration scheduled for the following year. After his untimely death, others took over the planning of the great 1948 event and dedicated the celebration to Mr. Wolfe's memory. To this day, the phrase "the Wolfe book" is the way many lifelong residents of Guernsey County refer to the most comprehensive account of county history written to date.

It has been this editor's pleasure in recent years to take advantage of the many new technology-enabled research tools we now have, able to revisit and re-research many a Guernsey County story. Though occasionally delving into a good story's original sources turns up errors and exaggerations wrought through time, doing so often reveals new and equally interesting facts and other long-forgotten tales worth retelling along the way. Though the earliest written accounts of events are usually the most accurate, errors still continue to be made. Stories passed down through the grapevine will continue to be revised. The hunt for history continues.

Richard L. Booth, Editor
June, 2024

Photo by Griest

GUERNSEY COUNTY COURT HOUSE

Contents

	PAGE
Extended CHAPTER XL. Dramatic Tales.	2003

Early Days on Rocky Fork—The Courage of Pioneer Women—The First Criminal Court Case in Guernsey County—The Old Whipping Post—The Panther—How a School Got Its Name—The First Civil War Volunteer—The Patriotic Siens Family—The Spencer's Station Locomotive Explosion—Fateful Campbell's Station—Experiences of a Stagecoach Driver—Hess the Horse Thief—The Pleasant City Explosion—Actress Billie Burke's Cambridge Ancestry—Oliver Markle, A Father and Son in Two World Wars.

Extended CHAPTER XLI. Mysteries. 2031

The Hidden Pot of Gold—The Strange Story of Sophie Gibaut—Golden Guernsey (?)—A Lead Mystery—A Curious Freak of Nature.

Extended CHAPTER XLII. Some Chronological County History. 2042

The First Bridge in the Northwest Territory—Jacob Gomber's Powder Horn—How Cambridge Was Laid Out—From the Isle of Guernsey—The Hard Year of 1807—A Challenge, The Oldest Apple Tree—Where Cambridge Has Gone for Mail—The Laughlin Bees—The Old Town Pump—The United States Hotel—The First County Buildings—Linn's Mill—The Capitol of Pennyroyaldom, Fairview—Old Tavern Days—Old Stone Houses (1)—Birmingham—The Stone Bridges—Cost of the National Road—Why a Cumberland—McClary Row—The Evolution of a Pioneer Home—Old Stone Houses (2)—Old Stone Houses (3)—The First Library—The Siamese Twins—A Trip to Portugal—How Historical Records Are Lost—The Carlisle Cemetery—News Notes of 1843, 102 Years Ago Today—One Hundred Years Ago Today, October 22, 1845—One Hundred Years Ago Today, March 13, 1846—An Old Jeffersonian, February 24, 1848—Cambridge in 1849—County Officers of 1849—Lofland's Fish Trap—A Medical Course a Century Ago—The Beginning of Byesville—The Brown House—Making Sorghum Molasses—Guernsey County in 1860, 85 Years Ago—The Abolitionists—The Three Unknown Confederates—Sherman's Army Train—Return of the Boys of '61—The Cashmere Goat Company—Court Cases 78 Years Ago—Cambridge Schools in 1869—The Marsh Stogie Factory—The Fourth of July—The Old Farmer Coal Mine—Wills Creek Carp—First Pennyroyal Reunion—The First Automobiles in Cambridge—The Two Heaviest Snows—The Marietta and Lake Railroad—Mural Paintings of Pioneer History—Noted Writer Visits Pennyroyaldom—History in Street Names—Political Trends, Republicans, Democrats, and Whigs.

Extended CHAPTER XLIII. Noble County Stories. 2151

The Seneca Lake Country—Seneca Township, Noble County—The Beginning of Beaver Township, Noble County—The Beginning of Buffalo Township, Noble County—Early Days in Hiramsburg, Noble County.

Extended CHAPTER XLIV. The Cambridge Corner Stories. 2162

The Moose Home Corner—The Colonial Theater Corner—The Berwick Corner—The Woolworth Corner—The Style Center Corner—The Central National Bank Corner—The Old Red Corner—The Craig Corner—The Blue Corner—The Passing of a Wheeling Avenue Landmark—The Hood Corner.

CONTENTS

Extended CHAPTER XLV. Church Stories. 2190

    Some Early History—Senecaville Presbyterians, Some Early History—Some Early History—Early History of the Ninth Street Methodist Church—Antrim Presbyterians—When the Methodist Episcopal Church Burned—Rebuilding the Methodist Episcopal Church—The Oldest Church Building in Cambridge.

Extended CHAPTER XLVI. Individuals of Interest. 2205

    A Prominent Cambridge Attorney—Col. Thomas H. Anderson—Abraham Armstrong—"Arly" Aylor—Robert Boyd, The Circuit Rider—A Cambridge Boy Became Governor of Hawaii—Judge James W. Campbell—Finding a Name, Andrew Clark—Early School Days, The Samuel Findley Clark Story—Stephen B. Clark—A Fairview Pioneer, John Duncan—Rev. William M. Ferguson—Ezra Graham—John Gray—Former Citizen J. O. Grimes Recalled by Removal of a Building—Dr. William Rainey Harper—A Teacher of Other Days—Senecaville's Long-Time Doctor, Noah Hill—Col. Gordon Lofland—Judge Justus H. Mackey—A Versatile Citizen—Judge Edward W. Mathews—Jacob Gomber Metcalfe—Dr. Francis Rea—A Pioneer of Washington, David Robb—Forty-Five Years on the Stage, Charles T. Small—Addison Taylor Smith—Captain A. A. Taylor—Early Street Names, Turner Avenue—A Doctor of the Old School—Another Pennyroyal Senator—Dr. W. A. White—Pennyroyaldom in the U. S. Senate—Oxford Officials.

Extended CHAPTER XLVII. Family Stories. 2259

    The Jack Family—The Stockdales at Antrim—Pioneer Families, Broom—Pioneer Families, Burt—Pioneer Families, Dilley—Pioneer Families, Emerson—Pioneer Families, Ferbrache—Pioneer Families, Ferguson—Pioneer Families, Forney—Pioneer Families, Frame—Pioneer Families, Frye—Pioneer Families, Laughlin—Pioneer Families, McCullough—Pioneer Families, Meredith—Pioneer Families, Robins—Pioneer Families, Shriver—Pioneer Families, Spaid—Pioneer Families, St. Clair—Pioneer Families, Stiles—Pioneer Families, Thompson—Pioneer Families, Trenner—Pioneer Families, Warne—Pioneer Families, Weaver—Pioneer Families, Wyrick—Pennyroyal Families, Ables—Pennyroyal Families, Ault—Pennyroyal Families, Borton—Pennyroyal Families, Giffee, Merryman, and Arnold—Pennyroyal Families, Heade, Bell, Buchanan, and Barber—Pennyroyal Families, Henderson—Pennyroyal Families, Kennon—Pennyroyal Families, Morton—Pennyroyal Families, Rosemond—Pennyroyal Families, Wherry and Ferrell.

All Names Index 2315

EXTENDED CHAPTER XL

Dramatic Tales

Early Days on Rocky Fork
[Originally published 12/9/1944]

"Over on Rocky Fork" is a phrase often used in designating a particular section of Guernsey County. Rocky Fork is a creek that flows south through the western part of Monroe Township and empties into Sugar Tree. The latter stream flows into Salt Fork, whose waters join Wills Creek.

Rocky Fork, as the name implies, flows through a rocky section of the township. The pioneers found high hills, deep hollows, and caverns when they came here. The fertile soil produced mammoth trees, beneath which grew laurel and other shrubs. Pioneers found, too, that it was the kind of place in which wild animals loved to live, and it was many years before they had rid the valleys and adjacent hillsides of them.

Bears and wolves were the most troublesome. On Irish Ridge, above the creek, lived Archibald Little. One day, one of Little's sons tracked a bear into a large, hollow tree. He hastened home for an ax and, with two neighbor boys and axes, returned to the tree. It soon succumbed to their chopping, and they stood by with their axes to attack the bear, which they were sure would soon emerge. To their surprise, three bears rushed out and attacked them. The axes proved to be the proper weapons, and in the end, the boys won the fight.

The wolves "over on Rocky Fork" were exceptionally vicious. They not only killed the settler's stock but would occasionally attack the settlers themselves. On his way home one night, Benjamin Kennedy was attacked by two large wolves that seemed to be determined to conquer him or die in the attempt. Kennedy happened to be carrying an ax, which he used to good advantage. After one of them had been killed, the other slunk away.

So great a nuisance did the wolves on Rocky Fork become that a circular hunt was planned. One very large wolf, often seen, seemed to be the leader among all the wolves of that section. Nearly every family on Rocky Fork had suffered from his depredations. Time and again, he would succeed in eluding those set out to get him, only to lead a pack of his associates on a damaging marauding tour a short time afterwards. The chief purpose of the circular hunt was to capture this desperate animal.

On the day appointed for the big hunt, 1,000 people, it is said, came to take part. Several square miles of territory were surrounded, and the men and boys moved toward the center of the ring formed, which was on the Ralston farm. The animals within fled ahead and soon found themselves surrounded near the center of the ring. At the roundup, the big bad wolf was seen in the midst, along with many other wolves and wild beasts. He was easily recognized, as he had been an outstanding pest in the community for a long time and had been seen by many.

Notwithstanding the heavy cordon of men around the ring, the animal escaped by making a mighty leap over their heads. A hunter named Matthews fired his gun, breaking one of the wolf's legs. The dogs were let loose and gave pursuit. Although wounded, the wolf succeeded in keeping ahead of his pursuers until the Tuscarawas County line was reached. Here, it doubled on its track and returned to the ring where the men were assembled. Why this action on the part of an animal, supposed to be so sagacious, was never understood. It appeared to be a voluntary surrender. Jim Taylor, one of the hunters, grabbed it by the tail. It offered little resistance, and the dogs rushed in and killed it. Some of its teeth, it is said, were from four to six inches in length, and it had strength to kill a common-size dog at one bite.

The scalp, on which there was a bounty at that time, was given to Matthews. The hide was given to Ben Kennedy, who recognized the wolf as the one that slunk away the night he had the battle with the two wolves, when on his way home with an ax. For many years, he used it as a saddle cover.

The Courage of Pioneer Women

[Originally published 5/2/1947]

The women who braved the hardships and dangers of pioneer life in Guernsey County were, in most instances, heroic characters. We are apt to think of the part their husbands and sons had in transforming a wilderness into a place fit for habitation, and overlook the services of the mothers and daughters.

Courage and resolution were required of the women in the early days of this western country. As a rule, it was only the strong-nerved women who were willing to leave their comfortable and peaceful homes in eastern states to face the perils of frontier life, which were often greater than they had anticipated. But once here, however, their spirit and courage were strengthened by the trials they were obliged to undergo.

Eliza Wilson.—A typical pioneer woman of Guernsey County was Eliza Wilson. To illustrate what we have stated above, we here relate some incidents in her life, in each of which she displayed exceptional courage or presence of mind.

Near the beginning of the last century, Samuel and Eliza Wilson were living in Pennsylvania. Soon after Zane's Trace had been cut across Ohio, making a way to reach new land thrown open for settlement, the West beckoned them. On Zane's Trace, in the valley of Salt Fork Creek, a short distance east of the place where Frankfort (the Lost Town) was afterwards platted, they entered government land and built a cabin. Their coming here was prior to 1804, and their nearest white neighbor lived four or five miles away.

At that time, the Indians had not all left that section, and they resented the intrusion of the white settlers. Until matters quieted down, it was deemed best for Eliza to return to Pennsylvania for a time. Samuel remained at the cabin to clear the land. While back with the home folks, Eliza gave birth to a child whom she named Thomas. Receiving word that danger from the Indians had passed, she rode back on a horse to her home in the wilderness here, carrying the six-weeks-old Thomas in her arms. As the journey was beset with hardships and dangers, this showed the woman's fortitude and spirit.

Indian Squaws Take Thomas.—One day, when Thomas was about two years old, Samuel being away from home, some Indian squaws entered the cabin and made themselves disagreeable in many ways. Helpless to defend herself against so many, but knowing the Indians respected courage, Eliza went about her work as though unmindful of their presence. At length, the squaws picked up Thomas and started through the woods with him. Instead of showing alarm, Eliza pretended that she thought they were only playing with him and remained indoors. This so affected the squaws, who apparently admired the courage of the mother, that they returned the child before the arrival of the father.

Eliza Outwits a Bully.—In the course of a few years, the Wilsons had a number of neighbors. In nearly every community was a bully who would try to pick a fight with somebody, if for no reason other than to show that he was the better man. If he had a grudge against one, he would aim to find an occasion to fight him.

Such a one appeared at the Wilson cabin one morning and dared Samuel to step out and fight. The latter, knowing the bully's unfair method of fighting, wanted to talk it over, but the bully insisted on having it out then and there.

Most of the backwoodsmen wore their hair long in those days, often reaching to their shoulders. This bully was accustomed to grasping his opponent's long hair, twist it around something near at hand, and then pound the helpless victim to his satisfaction. Samuel was aware of this, and so hesitated to accept the challenge.

At this juncture, Eliza appeared on the scene with a sharp butcher knife in her hand. Instead of attacking the bully, as one might expect, she quickly grasped her husband's hair and cut it off close to the scalp. She then commanded Samuel to "wade into him." Deprived of the means for exercising his accustomed trick, the bully was helpless in the hands of Samuel, who soon had the better of him. Here we have the reverse of the Biblical story. Samson's strength was in his hair, and when Delilah cut it off, his strength was gone. In this case, Eliza cut off her husband's hair to give him strength.

Thomas Wilson.—Samuel and Eliza Wilson were the parents of five children—Henry, Samuel, Jane, Zachariah, and Thomas. Thomas located in Jackson Township, south of Byesville, entering government land there. When the National Road was built through, he was employed as a foreman of a group of laborers. While he possessed but little or no schooling, he had a great deal of natural ability and tact. In his business transactions, he could figure mentally as quickly and accurately as others could on paper. He died in 1884 at the age of eighty.

The late Henry H. Wilson of Byesville was a son of Thomas Wilson.

The First Criminal Court Case in Guernsey County
[Originally published 8/3/1946]

From the writings of Col. C. P. B. Sarchet, we have obtained the main facts in this story. He states that they were given him by an uncle, who, although but a young boy when the incident occurred, was present and remembered it distinctly. Such a trial today would be outlawed, but this one was at a time and in a place when and where, in the absence of a legally constituted court, it was deemed to be the proper procedure by the self-appointed authorities.

The Guernseyites.—As has been repeatedly told in our stories, Cambridge had two entirely different groups of pioneers. The first was the Beatty-Gomber-Metcalf group, originally from Maryland, coming here in 1803, buying the land, and establishing the town in 1806. The second group was composed of Guernseyites (folks from the Isle of Guernsey), who arrived in 1806, bought lots from the first group, and settled here.

Like the Pilgrims of Plymouth, the Guernseyites were dissatisfied with conditions across the sea and decided to come to America to find new homes. After a two-months' voyage on the Atlantic, mid calms, storms, and the attendant dangers, they reached Baltimore, Maryland. Here they procured horses, wagons, and provisions and began a land journey towards the West where they expected to settle. They had in mind a location near Cincinnati, Ohio. The number of persons in the group—men, women, and children—was twenty-six, or one-fourth as many as of Pilgrims who landed at Plymouth.

Their journey over the mountains was one of danger and hardship. It took them seven weeks to travel from Baltimore to Wheeling, and nearly a week to make the fifty miles over Zane's Trace from Wheeling to Cambridge. While it was not their original intention to settle in Cambridge, as indicated above, they were so tired of traveling when they reached here that it took but little persuasion on the part of the Beatty-Gomber-Metcalf group to convince them that this would be a good place to live.

The Criminal in the Case.—As they crossed the mountains on their westward journey, the Guernseyites came upon a young girl, fourteen or fifteen years of age, who was sitting crying by the wayside, far away from any habitation. She told them that her name was Betty Pallet, that she was an orphan with no relations, that she had run away from a Catholic institution, was penniless, and had no place to go. The sympathetic Guernseyites could not leave her alone in the deep forest, so they brought her along with them.

It was late on a Saturday evening when they reached Cambridge. Zane's Trace did not run west along what is now Wheeling Avenue, but came down between what are now Steubenville and Gomber to what is now Fifth Street where it turned squarely to the south, crossing Wills Creek near the present viaduct. The only improvements in the town at that time were a log house or two down by the creek, one where the A. Simon store is now located, and one on the site of the Montgomery Ward building. Here, where the trace made the sharp turn, was a good spring, and here the Guernseyites decided to camp for the night and over the Sabbath, on which day they would not travel.

Seeing smoke rising above the trees the next morning, some of the Beatty-Gomber-Metcalf group came out to investigate. Learning that the Guernseyites were looking for a place to settle, they pointed out the possibilities of their new town, Cambridge, and prevailed upon them to remain here. The Guernseyites bought lots up in town, and while erecting permanent homes on them, they lived together in a rude cabin which they hastily constructed, just as did the Pilgrims at Plymouth.

The time came at length when one of the new houses was to be raised. All the older members of the group, even the women, were needed to assist. Betty Pallet was asked to stay home to look after the small children. When the folks returned in the evening, they discovered that the chests and boxes they had brought from Guernsey Isle had been rummaged, and a sack of gold, which represented their wealth, was missing. Upon being questioned, Betty declared that she had seen no outsider about the place during the day, and that she herself had not opened the chests or boxes. The loss of the gold was a calamity, and few of the group slept that night.

The Only Clue.—The Guernseyites were Norman-French and could not speak English very well. They sent for Beatty, Gomber, and some others of the first group to come over and talk to Betty. She persisted in saying that she knew nothing about the theft. Somebody happened to notice that all the vessels about the place had been filled with water—for what reason, nobody knew. The water had come from the spring, and perhaps it had some connection with the matter. Thither they went, and there, sunk down in the water, was the sack of gold. Betty then confessed, saying that she had put it there, intending to get it that night and flee to the woods. She had carried in a lot of water so that nobody would have any reason to go to the spring that evening and perhaps discover it.

The Punishment.—So far as there is any record, this was the first crime ever committed in what is now Guernsey County. Today it would be a case for the juvenile court, but then there was no such court; in fact, there was no legally constituted court of any kind. Guernsey was then a part of Muskingum that had been organized but a year or two before. There was no jail in Zanesville and, of course, there was none here. Betty should be punished—but how?

The matter was left to Beatty, Gomber, and others of their group. It was a serious matter. After much deliberation the following decision was rendered: (1) she was to be lashed on the bare back with a hickory rod; (2) she was to be driven out of the town. Peter Sarchet, one of the Guernseyites, was appointed to do the whipping. Just at nightfall, she was led to the edge of the deep, dark forest and told to go. She was never heard of afterwards.

A cruel and unjust punishment you will say, and such it may seem, but—. Here was a girl who had been befriended and protected in time of great need, and by sympathizers who were little able to render such service. That she should betray this trust would make a whipping deserved. But that was the least to be considered. If she should remain here, her influence on the other children might prove to be a serious matter. Such a thing was unthinkable. There seemed to be nothing else to do.

Then she found herself in the same position she was in when picked up by the wayside after running away from an institution. The only difference was that she was here driven to that which she once voluntarily chose.

The Old Whipping Post

[Originally published 2/3/1945]

In the chapter on early courts in "Stories of Guernsey County," brief mention is made of the whipping post. A more detailed account of this early type of punishment for a crime is presented here.

It stood in the southwest corner of the courtyard. Nature placed it there, first in the form of an oak tree, two feet in diameter. One day a storm from the west came, broke the tree in two, leaving eight or ten feet of the trunk standing firmly rooted in the ground. This remaining part served a dual purpose—as a hitching post and a whipping post.

Long after the first courthouse was built, the yard around it was covered with the trees of the original forest. The underbrush was cleared away, and among the trees, folks who came to town hitched their horses and parked their wagons. It was the public parking lot—no meter charge.

In August, 1816, court was held in Cambridge, with William Wilson, president judge, and Jacob Gomber, Robert Speer, and Thomas B. Kirkpatrick, associate judges. Until 1851, there were three associate judges, not necessarily attorneys, in each county. Four times each year, a president judge, whose jurisdiction extended over several counties, came and sat in court with the associates.

A case coming before this session of court in 1816 was that of Samuel Timmons, who had been indicted on two counts for "uttering base coin," that is, passing counterfeit money. We do not know why such a case should have come under a state, rather than a federal, court.

The jury was composed of James Thompson, James Bratton, William Allen, Jesse Marsh, Andrew McCleary, John Huff, John Tedrick, William Pollock, Hugh Martin, Thomas Roberts, George McCleary, and James Lloyd.

Timmons was found guilty, and Judge Wilson ordered that he be whipped; that he be given nineteen lashes in one case on the following day, and twenty in the other on the next. To Elijah Dyson, the sheriff, fell the duty of administering the punishment.

The news soon spread abroad, and long before the appointed hour for the whipping, there had assembled about the aforesaid whipping post a vast crowd of people. A stranger entering the town would have thought it to be a holiday. The four judges were there, the grand jurors who had indicted Timmons, the petit jurors who had found him guilty, citizens of Cambridge, and many who had hurried in from the country.

Stripped to below the waist, Timmons was led to the post and placed facing it. His arms were stretched around the post and tied. With a heavy rawhide whip, Sheriff Dyson lashed him on the bare back nineteen times. One who witnessed it afterwards said that blood flew at every blow—probably an exaggeration. On the following day, the performance was repeated before the same audience. On account of the soreness resulting from the first whipping, this second one must have been exceedingly painful.

There are no records to show the reaction of the people to this barbaric type of punishment for a crime. We must not get the notion, however, that our Guernsey County forefathers possessed some of the savage instinct. They were not responsible for it. Judge Wilson ordered it done, and he lived outside the county and far away. While permissible under the law, whipping was not generally ordered by an Ohio court. Judge Wilson frequently handed out such sentences, for which he became widely known as the "whipping judge."

In Howe's Historical Collections of Ohio is an account of a whipping in Knox County. The details given are much the same as those in the Samuel

Timmons case. The victim was struck forty times and went off weeping and groaning, his back a pitiable spectacle. The same William Wilson who presided here was the judge in that case.

So great was the revulsion against whipping as a punishment for a crime that a law was passed by the General Assembly of Ohio in 1830 providing that thereafter it should be forbidden. James M. Bell, speaker of the lower house at that time, was a Cambridge man. It is said he opposed the bill. The records in the courthouse show but this one case of public whipping in Guernsey County.

The Panther

[Originally published 4/19/1945]

Among the wild animals of Guernsey County in early days, the panther was the most dreaded. Its haunts were the deep hollows back in the dark forest, especially places where there were caves under ledges of rocks. Sleeping during the day, it did its hunting at night. No more terrorizing sound was ever heard by the settlers in the nighttime than the shrill cry of the panther, which, they said, was like the scream of a woman in distress. Panthers were sometimes called painters.

The fur of the panther was a yellowish-brown, sometimes whitish underneath. Its tail was long. The soles of its feet were soft, enabling it to move silently. Its claws were long and sharp. The strength of the panther was extraordinary, and its fighting qualities proverbial. Unlike most wild animals, it did not attack its prey in a direct way, but would approach stealthily and spring upon it from a distance, unawares, with a force sufficient to bear a horse to the ground. With its claws, it would tear its victim to pieces.

On account of its large size—often eight or nine feet in length—it required much food and, being carnivorous, it preyed on the larger animals. Deer meat was its main diet, when such could be got; it was especially fond of horseflesh. The fact that it would lie concealed in trees, from which it would spring on its prey, unconscious of its presence, caused it to be feared by both man and beast. But, in a way, the panther was cowardly. Catlike in its nature, it had an aversion to dogs, and it would seldom attack a man if he displayed courage in its presence.

We have heard many stories told about the panthers that once frequented the deep forests of Guernsey County. To illustrate some of the characteristics mentioned above, we give the following incidents.

Isaac Oldham, who entered the land now occupied by the Fletcher General Hospital, lived in a log cabin which stood on the site of the old stone house a few rods north of the hospital ground. He had been clearing the land on which the hospital buildings are located when night came on, and he started home. Hearing a noise behind him, he turned and was horrified to see a large panther crouched in the attitude of springing upon him. He had no gun. He knew if he turned, the beast would make the leap. As long as he could face it, as if not in fear, he was safe. Keeping his eyes on those of the panther, he moved backwards, the beast creeping toward him at each step he made. He realized what would happen if he stumbled, but he dared not turn his head to see where he was going. Fortunately, he reached the cabin door, which was open. Backing in, he quickly threw the door shut and barred it. The panther left.

Nancy, wife of William Gibson, who in 1806 settled in what is now Liberty Township, had an experience with a panther that she often related. The Gibsons entered the land on both sides of the creek near the present Kimbolton. Their descendants now living in Guernsey County and elsewhere are numerous. For some time, William, Nancy, and their children were the only white persons living between Cambridge and Bird's Run. In the course of a few years, there were other settlers in that section, but living far apart. Nancy possessed considerable skill as a midwife, and her services were often called for. Whether day or night, she cheerfully and gratuitously answered the calls, which sometimes came from homes far away.

Once, summoned in the middle of the night, she mounted a horse and started alone. Riding along the trail through the depths of the dark forest, she heard a panther scream, and turning, she saw it was following her. She knew it was the horse in particular that the beast wanted, and the horse seemed to realize this, too. Then it became a race for life. The horse needed no spurring as this animal, for reasons stated above, was more easily frightened by a panther than by any other wild beast. Nancy and the horse won, but she almost collapsed when her destination was reached.

The Hosacks lived on the ridge near the present North Salem. The deep woods of that section and the caves beneath the ledges of rocks on the slopes were favorite haunts of panthers. Out one evening in search of his cattle, which were permitted to run at large in the forest, Mr. Hosack heard a fierce scream that chilled his blood. Crouched on a log ahead of him was a panther, ready to spring. Mr. Hosack carried no weapon except a stout club. He knew the consequences if he should turn and start to run. Instead of this, he moved toward the beast, looking it straight in the eyes and brandishing the club. True to its cowardly nature, it slunk off.

In the early 1820s, Joseph K. Black lived on what afterwards became the Culbertson farm in Adams Township. Living with him was William Strahn, a hired hand. One winter morning, there was a good tracking snow, and the two men decided to go deer hunting. Some distance from their cabin, they discovered the tracks of a panther and, in their desire to rid that section of such a pest, they followed the panther trail, forgetting deer for the time being. After traveling several miles in a sort of circuitous route, they saw where it had entered a cave beneath a ledge of rocks on the farm now owned by Ross Wells in the northwestern part of the township. Hoping to smoke it out, they started to build a fire. While arranging fuel for it, they happened to peer into the cave, and there saw two bright fiery spots. Believing these to be the panther's eyes, they aimed a gun between the balls of fire and pulled the trigger. When the smoke from the gun had cleared away, they looked in again but could see nothing. Had they killed the animal, or had it moved farther back in the cave?

After much consideration, Strahn proposed to crawl in to investigate. Black was to catch hold of his heels and follow to pull him out quickly if such action became necessary. Having entered, Strahn called for him to pull him back. Black did so and found that he was pulling out both his companion and the panther, the latter being dead. It was a large female, the last panther, it is believed, to be killed in Guernsey County. For many years, the Black family took pride in displaying the skin of the beast and telling the story of the adventure.

How a School Got Its Name

[Originally published 1/3/1945]

Why was a certain rural school in the southeastern part of Madison Township named Kansas? Every rural school had a name which was seldom given arbitrarily, as told on page 449 of "Stories of Guernsey County." It was usually suggested by its location or some characteristic of its environment. The name Kansas could not have been derived from either of these. A person might make a good many guesses before striking the reason why this school was so called.

Our curiosity prompted us to put the question to Attorney G. D. Dugan who received his early education in this institution. It was long after the school had been established and named, but when a boy he had often heard the story related by older folks. From what Mr. Dugan told us and from some old records that were available we are enabled to explain the origin of the name, which is probably one you never would have guessed.

Back before the Civil War, that community had many more people living in it than there are today. On nearly every farm were the owner and a tenant or two, each with a large family. The population of Madison Township was more than three times what it is at the present time. In the Kansas district there were nearly one hundred children to attend a one-room school. The building in use proving inadequate, both as to condition and size, it was decided to erect a new one. There was little or no objection in the district to this decision.

Those who have had much to do with schools know that in a majority of cases, when a new building is to be erected, there will be dissatisfaction on the part of some concerning its location. Every patron wants it near his home—something that cannot be. There are usually two factions, one wanting the building located in one place, the other in another. The members become bitter toward each other. Often the matter is taken into the courts. The controversy over the location of the schoolhouse in the Kansas district resulted in both of these, and in the superlative degree at that.

Two boards of education were elected, one by each faction. Each claimed to be the legal board. One got the start of the other and let the contract for a new building in a location that was satisfactory to its constituents. An injunction against paying for it was filed by the other board. The case was heard in the common pleas court and the enjoiners won. It was taken to the court of appeals, and they won again. Then it was carried to the supreme court with the same result.

In the meantime, the bad feeling between the two factions grew in intensity, sometimes resulting in blows. School went on, however, in both the old and new building, each faction having a schoolhouse of its own. When the contractor saw he could not be paid for his work, he attached the building, moved it two miles away, and sold it to Rev. Tannehill for a dwelling. All the pupils of the district went back to the old school.

But this did not end the trouble. The ill-feeling smoldered for a time and then burst out again when it came to hiring a teacher. The factions were still functioning. Two teachers were employed. Both were on hand the first morning, each claiming to be the rightful one. To show his authority, one began ringing the bell to call the children in. While this was going on, the other stepped to the desk and started the day's work by reading a chapter from the Bible. A member of each faction of the board was present to see that his man was installed. Both the bell-ringer and the Bible-reader made claim to open the school. One board member told this teacher to leave, and the matter would be settled later. When he did so, the pupils followed. But that's enough of the controversy. How did the school get its name?

While all this was going on in Madison Township, a similar but much bigger factional fight was being staged in another part of the country. By virtue of the doctrine of "squatter sovereignty," each territory, when seeking admission to the Union as a state, could decide for itself whether it would come in as a free or slave. Kansas was seeking admission and had to make the decision. There was a struggle between the pro-slavery and anti-slavery men. For three years the conflict raged. There was violence and bloodshed throughout the state. "Bleeding Kansas" became the topic of the hour all over the North.

To outsiders looking on, this struggle in the southeastern part of Madison Township bore some resemblance to the greater one in the West, and they referred to the district as "Bleeding Kansas." Time eventually healed the ill-feeling and today there are probably people living in the district who never heard how their school got its name.

MORE STORIES OF GUERNSEY COUNTY

The First Civil War Volunteer

[Originally published 12/6/1945]

Until his death in 1904, John T. Rainey claimed to be the first Guernsey County man to volunteer for service in the Civil War. Nobody ever disputed the claim. Whatever honor there may have been in being the first of some 2,000 Guernsey County men who left their homes to fight for the preservation of the Union belonged to John T. Rainey.

Fired upon by the Confederate General Beauregard, Major Anderson surrendered Fort Sumter in the harbor of Charleston, South Carolina, Sunday, April 14, 1861. On the following morning, a telegram sped on the wings of lightning to the nation; it was a call from President Lincoln for 75,000 men. Fuller particulars came immediately after this. The men were asked to enlist for three months; it was believed that the war could be ended in that time.

Having a telegraph office, Cambridge received the news that Monday morning. For a long time, war had not been considered improbable, yet it had been hoped that it might be averted. Within a very short time, everybody in town knew about it. Flags were soon flying from homes, and fife and drum were helping to kindle the flame of patriotism. It was a day of excitement in Cambridge. Arrangements were made for a great mass meeting to be held that night at the courthouse. (See page 255 of the book.)

It was decided at the meeting that Guernsey County should raise a company to go at once, and that other companies should be organized to follow as soon as possible. A recruiting committee was appointed, of which John Ferguson was made chairman. The word must be carried to every part of the county, but how? There were no radios, no telephones. John T. Rainey, a young man twenty-six years old, present at the meeting, called out that he would not only volunteer as a member of the first company, but that he was ready to give service at once by carrying the news to the remote parts of the county.

His offer was accepted, and, mounted on the fastest horse that could be procured at the moment, he was soon speeding out the Steubenville Road, informing the folks at every home he passed of what had happened and what was wanted. His mission was not unlike that of Paul Revere of old. He called upon the young men to come to Cambridge and enlist. Two things caused them to hesitate: the call was too sudden for immediate decision; then this was the planting season, the busiest of the year. Only one man returned with Rainey—Moses Stockdale, of Antrim.

Back in Cambridge, Rainey was given a fresh mount, and was soon ready for another trip, this time to the southern part of the county. He reached Cumberland late at night and rushed through the streets, crying "War, war, war!" He was more successful in finding recruits than he was over north, for fifteen men hastened back with him, seven of them from

Cumberland.

Within a week, a company, known as "Ferguson's Guards," was ready to start to war. Before leaving, the members chose their own officers — James W. Moore, captain, John T. Rainey, second lieutenant. Moses Stockdale, the Antrim recruit, was made first corporal.

At the end of the three-month period for which they had enlisted, all were discharged. But the war was far from being over, as had been expected. Meanwhile, Congress had voted 500,000 men, and President Lincoln had made another call, this time for an enlistment for three years. John T. Rainey immediately reenlisted as a member of Company H, Seventy-eighth Ohio Volunteer Infantry, of which he was made captain. He fought at Shiloh, Vicksburg, Kennesaw Mountain, Atlanta, and in other major battles.

For bravery in battle, Captain Rainey was commissioned a major, and before the close of the war, in which he remained, he was brevetted a lieutenant colonel. Notwithstanding this last and higher rank, he was afterwards commonly known as "Major" Rainey.

John T. Rainey was born in 1835 in Utica, New York, and came to Cambridge with his parents when he was six years old. He learned the printers' trade and afterwards studied law. Following the war, he formed a law partnership with Col. John Ferguson, the man who recruited the first company of soldiers.

The mother of Dr. William Rainey Harper, founder of Chicago University, was Major Rainey's sister. Major Rainey was a staunch Republican in politics and a lifelong member of the Cambridge United Presbyterian Church.

The Patriotic Siens Family

[Originally published 12/2/1944]

When the Civil War opened, Absalom Siens, Christina, his wife, and eleven of their thirteen children were living on the north side of Wheeling Avenue, between Sixth and Seventh Streets. The two oldest daughters were married and lived elsewhere. The boys were John, Leonard, Simon, William, Isaac, Peter, and George; the girls Mary, Emma, Susan, Melissa, Elizabeth, and Sadie.

Absalom Siens was 60 years of age and wore a long beard which was somewhat gray, as was also his hair. The grandfather had fought valiantly in the War of 1812, and when President Lincoln called for troops, Absalom felt the inherited patriotic urge, as did every one of his seven sons. Fearing that he would be rejected on account of his age, he dyed his beard and hair, presented himself for enlistment, and was accepted.

One by one, beginning with the oldest, the sons enlisted. Soon it was that the father and five sons were in the army. The next in line was Peter,

14 years of age. Having tried to enlist and having failed, he ran away from home, seeking acceptance elsewhere. By some means, not the best to be told here, he was successful. He became a member of the Ninety-seventh Ohio Volunteer Infantry under Major James W. Moore.

Absalom Siens and six of his sons were in the army—seven from one family. Left at home on Wheeling Avenue were the mother, four daughters, and George, who was a mere child. How the family managed to get along is not known.

Word reached Christina that Absalom had been killed in battle. A few weeks later, a message came that William had been killed. Then came another that told of the death of Isaac. And still later the news was borne to the grief-stricken wife and mother that Simon (familiarly known as Sy) had made the supreme sacrifice, too. The father and three sons were killed. John, Leonard and Peter returned home at the end of the war.

Rev. W. H. McFarland was the chaplain of Peter's company which participated in the Battle of Missionary Ridge. On the day following the battle, Peter wrote his mother a letter which has been preserved and which we present here.

Chattanooga, Tennessee, November 26, 1863.

Dear Mother:

I have just come through one of the most desperate fights of the war. I will commence and give you the details of the battle. On the 23d we got orders to have two days' rations in haversacks and prepare to move immediately. We moved out at two o'clock and attacked the enemy's lines at three, and drove them in. Our company was deployed as skirmishers. We fortified and lay there about twenty-four hours. About noon we were called to attention, and moved on about one-fourth of a mile and halted. The enemy was lying down, eagerly awaiting us. We had a wide valley to cross, and the enemy poured in their grape and canister shot thick as hail. We had to charge across the valley, as we had to go up Missionary Ridge. By this time they opened on us with musketry which was straight up and down. But the 97th and the rest of our brigade fought like veterans, never faltering an instant.

Onward we moved with our brave Colonel Barnes and Major J. W. Moore at the head of the regiment, crying, "Come on, boys, the day is ours!" And so we did. We followed them, pouring volley after volley into the rebel ranks. But they stood it well; they stood it until we were within five rods of them. Then they ran, leaving seventeen pieces of artillery behind them, which we turned on them and sent shells into their fleeing ranks. But finally Bragg got them rallied again.

By this time it was getting dark and we were ordered forward. We moved about half a mile, when the enemy fled, leaving behind artillery pieces, ammunition, caissons, commissary stores and ordinance stores, and throwing away their guns. I got one little touch on the back of the hand, a spent ball hit my arm, and one bullet went through my pant leg below the knee, but I was not disabled.

We are now in camp and have orders to go to Knoxville tomorrow. Our Regiment had ten killed and 116 wounded. Among the wounded was Major James W. Moore, in the hand; Captain Rosemond, in the leg; Captain Wiser, arm shot off

DRAMATIC TALES

(a mortal wound). Lieutenants Shutts, Brady and Eckelberry were wounded. Coon Clinesmith was killed.

Poor Sy is killed. I hate to give this sad news. My God! it's awful to think that three brothers and a father have been killed in this wretched war. Mother, take it as easy as possible, for it can't be helped. My heart is almost broken.

PETER R. SIENS.

All students of Abraham Lincoln are familiar with his letter to Mrs. Bixby, who lost five sons in the Civil War. Pronounced by the faculty of Oxford University, England, as being the "finest specimen of English ever written," a framed copy of this letter has been placed on a wall there. The letter follows:

Dear Madam:

I have been shown in the files of the War Department a statement of the Adjutant General of Massachusetts that you are the mother of five sons who have died gloriously on the field of battle. I feel how weak and fruitless must be any words of mine which should attempt to beguile you from the grief of a loss so overwhelming. But I cannot refrain from tendering to you the consolation that may be found in the thanks of the republic they died to save. I pray that our Heavenly Father may assuage the anguish of your bereavement, and leave you only the cherished memory of the loved and lost, and the solemn pride that must be yours to have laid so costly a sacrifice upon the altar of freedom.

ABRAHAM LINCOLN.

Such a letter might as well have been sent to Mrs. Siens. With a large family to support and with but little of this world's goods, she gave a husband and three sons. All fifteen members of the Siens family are now dead. Three grandchildren of Absalom and Christina—all children of Mary, a daughter—are living in Cambridge today. They are Mrs. Emma B. Davis, 745 Steubenville Avenue, and Fred, 113 N. Tenth Street, and John A. Foltz, a patient at Swan Hospital.

MORE STORIES OF GUERNSEY COUNTY

The Spencer's Station Locomotive Explosion
[Originally published 4/9/1946]

A kind of accident once occurring frequently, but seldom heard of anymore, is a boiler explosion. Contrivances for generating and utilizing steam as a mechanical energy had not reached the degree of safety they are today, and explosions were common. Due to better material and workmanship, boilers are stronger than they were in earlier days. Engineers used to fire too heavily or let the water get too low, resulting in a steam pressure that the walls of the boiler could not sustain, and it would explode with a force that was usually disastrous. We would often hear of an engine "blowing up" somewhere. Now, with the many automatic devices for control and the legal requirement that all engineers must be licensed, there is little or no danger.

Kinds of Explosions.—Steamboat boiler explosions often occurred, especially when speed was sought by heavy firing. There have been many stories written of such accidents on the Ohio and Mississippi rivers. The most common explosion, perhaps, was that of a sawmill boiler. The engineers were incompetent as a class, and frequently neglectful. In our early boyhood days, we would hear of so many sawmills "blowing up" that we were always nervous when near one. There have been several such disasters in Guernsey County.

There have not been so many railroad locomotive explosions, although we can now recall two that occurred in Guernsey County. One of these was so unusual in its effect and caused so much excitement at the time that we shall tell about it here. It happened at Spencer's Station, two miles east of Quaker City, on Monday evening, April 20, 1863. This was almost exactly three months before the Morgan Raiders went through.

Spencer's Station.—This little unincorporated town is situated in the southeastern part of Millwood Township and received its name from that of the man upon whose land it was platted. That one may visualize the setting of our story, we shall describe the place. It is now called Eldon.

Spencer's Station owed its existence to the Central Ohio (now the Baltimore and Ohio) Railroad. All the way between it and Barnesville, six miles east, is a grade of such proportions as at one time to necessitate the use of additional engines, called "helpers," by all heavy eastbound trains. Two or three of these were kept at Spencer's Station, "fired up" ready to ascend the hill at any time. Trains pulled by the powerful engines of today do not need "helpers." Here was a telegraph office with two or three operators to take and give orders for all trains. Trains took water here, the water being pumped from a dam on Leatherwood Creek, and this made employment for two or three men. The place was a refueling station, wood being used in those days. Spencer's Station was the center of a road section, the headquarters of several men who kept the track in repair.

There was a hotel near the station, used chiefly as a boarding house for railroad men. The town's importance as a shipping point should be mentioned, too. Livestock, tobacco, wool, and other agricultural products were brought here and loaded on cars for eastern markets. Spencer's Station was an active place and might have grown to be a town of considerable size had it not been that the owner of the land around it declined to sell any more for lots.

Happened on Pay Day.—Employees on the Central Ohio Railroad were paid once a month by a paymaster who traveled over the division in a "pay car." It was late Monday afternoon when the car, pulled by an engine named the "Reindeer," arrived at Spencer's Station. On the engine were William Reece, the engineer, and John H. Fowler, the fireman. William Price was the paymaster, and with him was an assistant. The engine took water at the tank and then moved up to the platform.

Having been notified in advance that they would receive their pay at this time, the employees had gathered there to await the arrival of the car. Playing on the platform were two little boys. One was the son of Samuel Fordyce, the station agent; the other, of E. V. Shipley, one of the telegraph operators. It was a beautiful, quiet spring afternoon, and the scene was one of contentment.

The men formed in line to receive their pay, and as Mr. Price called the amount due each, his assistant handed out the money. In the midst of this, the boiler burst with an almost atomic bomb effect. The sound was great and windows a half mile away rattled. The boiler was reduced to fragments, and pieces were driven into the sides of houses standing some distance from the scene.

Some Killed; Many Injured.—Among the killed were William Reece, the engineer, Samuel Denoon, and the little son of Samuel Fordyce, the station agent. Reece was cut about the body, scalded and thrown into the creek some distance away. The Fordyce boy was struck by flying metal. Denoon was scalded and otherwise injured, his death occurring shortly after the accident.

John Weir, keeper of the hotel, suffered burns and a broken arm; his son was also badly injured. E. V. Shipley, the telegraph operator whose little son miraculously escaped, was seriously hurt. John H. Fowler, the fireman, received scalds, but they did not prove fatal. William Price, the paymaster, was scalded; the assistant paymaster was blown far away. Samuel Fordyce and James Hart were also among those most seriously injured. There were many who escaped with minor cuts and bruises.

Money Blown to the Hillsides.—The money in the pay car, which amounted to approximately seven thousand dollars, was blown in every direction, some of it to a distance of nearly a half-mile. Most of it was recovered afterwards. There may yet be some of it sticking to the adjacent hillsides. When the writer was a youngster, he and other boys wandering around that section would look for it, but never found any.

MORE STORIES OF GUERNSEY COUNTY

Fateful Campbell's Station

[Originally published 1/8/1945]

Lore City used to be called Campbell's Station, the change of name being made in 1876. It had its beginning when the Central Ohio (Baltimore and Ohio) Railroad was built up the Leatherwood Valley in 1854. There had to be a railroad center eight or ten miles east of Cambridge, and this place was chosen. Train crews received their orders here from the telegraph office that was established. Engines were refueled and rewatered here. A section crew was stationed here for the maintenance of the track.

Campbell's Station became an important shipping point. Farmers over Senecaville and Mt. Ephraim way south, and those from Washington, Winterset, and the surrounding country north brought their agricultural products, such as wool, tobacco, and livestock, to be shipped out. Storekeepers came here for the merchandise they ordered. John Fordyce, the stationmaster, built a large warehouse for storage purposes.

Although no town was platted, a number of families built homes and moved into the settlement. Nearly all were employees of the railroad company. A post office was granted by the government and, as there was already one having a name similar to that of this station, it was called Gomber. Campbell's Station soon became a busy little town.

Some spots, like some men, seem to be plagued by fate. To the former, unfortunate events came rapidly—something to shock the people; hard luck follows the latter. Do these things come by chance, or are they destined by fate? The superstitious usually attribute it to fate. At any rate, Campbell's Station, in its early days, was beset by so many fatalities that the people became alarmed.

About sixty or seventy years ago, a citizen of the place compiled a list of these. It was published in several papers and attracted much attention. We here present a part of the list—we can't recall it all.

On July 24, 1863, Gen. John H. Morgan and his army entered Campbell's Station and proceeded to destroy property. They cut the telegraph wires, burned cars loaded with goods, tore up the railroad track, burned the bridge across Leatherwood Creek, and also the big warehouse, and the residence of John Fordyce. It is said that this was the only private property burned by Morgan anywhere on his raid through Ohio. (The probable reasons for this are given on page 306 of "Stories of Guernsey County.")

After four years of service in the Civil War, a happy soldier, returning home, was knocked from the top of a car at the bridge west of Campbell's Station and killed. A son of Mr. Campbell, after whom the town was named, was killed by a train just east of the station. After a year in school, a brilliant young man came home, went to work on a sawmill near the town, and was killed.

DRAMATIC TALES

A train drawn by an engine called the "Antelope" was approaching the station. The boiler burst, killing the engineer instantly and fatally injuring several others. A young Senecaville man came over to Campbell's Station and was killed at the crossing—hit by a train. At the same place, another young man was killed shortly afterwards.

A child fell into Leatherwood Creek and was taken out, supposedly dead. Means of resuscitation were resorted to, and its life was saved. Just outside of town, a portable sawmill engine exploded, killing two brothers. A shoemaker of the place drank heavily of strong liquor, took a walk to wear off its effect, and sat down on the railroad track to rest. A train came along, killing him. While coupling cars at the station, a brakeman was crushed between two of them, death resulting.

Near the town, a passenger and freight train collided. The conductor of the freight train met death, as did also a boy who was stealing a ride on the rear of the baggage car of the passenger train. A boy of the town was run over by a train. Although seriously injured, he eventually recovered. The boss of the section crew that worked out of Campbell's Station had his arm crushed while coupling cars. A boy accidentally shot himself in the arm. Lockjaw set in, and death resulted. One afternoon a grass fire broke out near the town. In trying to put it out, a young woman had her clothing to catch fire. She was burned to death.

So many fatalities in so short a time, in a community so small, caused the people of Campbell's Station to think they must be hoodooed. But the spell was broken, and luck changed. It would seem that it has swung to the opposite extreme.

Lore City is today the third largest village in the county, having four churches and a fine class of citizens. Seldom does anything unusual occur there to disturb the town. It appears to be a healthy community. There is not a dentist in the town, not a doctor, not a hospital, not an undertaker, and until just recently when a religious group laid out a burial ground for its own members, there was never a cemetery there. Is there any other town of the size in Ohio of which this can be said?

Experiences of a Stagecoach Driver

[Originally published 3/10/1945]

Since the publication of "Stories of Guernsey County" several sidelights to the stories have been brought to our attention from different parts of the county. Of some of these interesting incidents we had knowledge, but we could not embody them in the stories which necessarily had to be written in a somewhat general way.

An unusual incident of exactly eighty years ago should add special interest to the story, "Stagecoach Days on the National Road" (page 221).

It occurred on January 1, 1864, known in local chronicles as the "Cold New Year's". Never before and only once since (February 10, 1899) has there been recorded a colder day in Guernsey county. According to an unofficial report, on this "Cold New Years," the mercury was hovering around forty below at daylight and it continued to do so until darkness fell that night. That which made the cold harder to endure were an unceasing bitter wind and flying frost and snow. Unlike this, February 10, 1899, registered exceedingly cold in the morning only. By noon the mercury had climbed considerably.

Last of the Stagecoach Drivers.—From 1828 until 1854 when the railroad came through, there was much stagecoach travel on the National Road through Guernsey county. Even after the railroad was built some stage lines continued to operate for a few years for the accommodation of the towns not on the railroad and for carrying the mail. Among the last of the old-time stagecoach drivers were Thomas K. Pack whose home was in Fairview, and James Bayliss and Charlie Simms, of Cambridge. Bayliss was the son of Jack Bayliss, the noted driver on the Cumberland Road east of the Ohio River. Simms was the driver of the mail stage that unfortunately arrived at Washington at the same time Morgan's raiders did. He was held up there, the mail sacks were rifled, and his horses were taken by the raiders. Pack was the driver whose experience on the "Cold New Years" is here told.

Thomas K. Pack

A Cold Start.—The stage drawn by four spirited horses, made more spirited by the cold, left Wheeling for Cambridge on schedule time, due to arrive at the latter place about eight hours later. John Hargrave mounted the high seat on the outside as the driver. Only two passengers ventured a journey on such a day. Riding with them on the inside was Thomas K. Pack who was "dead-heading" back to make a return trip with another stage.

About five miles out of Wheeling, Hargrave called to Pack that he was freezing. Pack lifted him down and carried him to the inside of the coach, where he was given first aid by the two passengers, and took the driver's seat on the outside himself. At St. Clairsville, Hargrave was removed from the stage, given treatment, and soon recovered. Here the horses were changed and Pack continued on as driver. Another change of horses was made at Morristown, also at Fairview.

During all this time Pack remained in the driver's seat, the changes of horses being made by attendants at the stage terminals. At Fairview the two passengers left the stage—probably unable to endure the cold longer—, leaving Pack to journey on alone; the mail had to be taken through. The horses were changed again at Washington. Pack had not moved from his high seat outside since leaving St. Clairsville.

A Race With Death.—When the Four-mile Hill was reached, halfway between Washington and Cambridge, Pack began to feel comfortable. A sweet drowsiness settled over him, and consciousness was fading away. Realizing what this meant, he became alarmed. Exerting a supreme effort, he lashed the horses and urged them on.

As if sensing the situation, the four horses plunged ahead without a driver's hand to guide them, up hill and down, and around curves, but they held the coach to the road. They did not stop at the postoffice kept then by William McDonald, but continued on to Virtue's tavern where they stopped of their own accord. The unconscious Pack was slumped over on the seat.

Landlord Virtue and others in the big warm barroom ran out, lifted Pack from the seat and were carrying him inside when Dr. Tingle hurried across. "Don t take him to the fire," he called. "If you do, he won't live a minute." They laid him on the back porch and bathed him with cold water. He remained unconscious for several hours, and it was eight days before he could leave his bed at the tavern.

Thomas K. Pack was born in Fairview, an important stagecoach division terminal, in 1833. As a youngster he became interested in the activities on the Old Pike and aspired to be a stagecoach driver himself. As soon as he was old enough to drive, he entered upon the work and continued until the stages were taken from the road, dropping out for a time to serve his country in the Civil War. Fairview was always his home, his death occurring there in 1917. Mrs. R. H. Clark, Cambridge, is a daughter of Thomas K. Pack, and Ross C. Pack and Charles T. Pack, also of Cambridge, are sons Harry S. Pack; another son, lives in Chicago.

MORE STORIES OF GUERNSEY COUNTY

Hess the Horse Thief

[Originally published 11/23/1945]

Back in the horse and buggy days and long before we had buggies, the horse thief made news for the papers and work for the criminal courts; today it's the man who steals automobiles. Catching horse thieves was harder than automobile thieves, as there were then no radios, no highway patrols. News that a horse had been stolen could travel no faster than the horse itself, and the thief, having the start, could easily make an escape. Now a minute description of the car stolen is soon made known to authorities within a radius of hundreds of miles, and the automobile thief who can escape arrest is clever indeed. On account of the legal red tape necessary for the transfer of a car, it cannot be as easily disposed of by sale, as could a horse.

Horse thieves used to work in organized bands, much as bootleggers did in Prohibition days. Rendezvous were established along routes leading far away from the place of theft, and the horses were relayed from one to another. One such rendezvous was the picturesque ravine in Spencer Township known as Perry's Den. It was here that Walter G. Perry would conceal stolen horses until an opportune time came for passing them on (page 996 of the book).

In a later period than Perry's time, horse thieves became so numerous and active in Guernsey County that an organization, known as the Anti-Horse-Thief Association, was effected. Its object was to recover stolen horses and pursue and arrest the thieves. A constitution was adopted; a membership fee of one dollar was charged, and officers were elected annually. The headquarters were located in Washington.

A horse thief almost as notorious as Walter G. Perry was John Hess. Stealing horses was his business. He probably had confederates who disposed of the horses, but they were unknown. He worked in a fearless way, defying the officers and resorting to all kinds of strategy in eluding them. His very brazenness would throw them off the track. He stole a fine horse belonging to James McCleary of Center Township. Here, for once, the officers outwitted him, having him under arrest before he got the horse out of the county. He was placed in the jail at Cambridge.

It was the old jail, and not considered secure, as two prisoners had escaped from it within the year. Although aware of the condition of the jail, and conscious of the fact that he was holding a notorious and crafty criminal, William B. Barnett, the sheriff, neglected to take proper precaution. Somebody on the outside—probably a confederate of Hess—managed to slip him a saw. One night, he cut four of the iron gratings of his cell window, removed two of them, spread the other two apart, and made an opening through which he crawled and escaped.

Owners of horses had been breathing more easily since Hess had been placed behind the bars; now they were alarmed again. They criticized the sheriff and the commissioners, and efforts were made to have them removed from office.

Three days after Hess escaped, he arrived at his former home in Monroe County, riding a valuable horse that he had picked up on the way. He left the same night, telling the folks that he was making for the hills of West Virginia. A few days later, Sheriff Barnett received a letter, bearing the postmark of Louisville, Kentucky. We present the letter here just as it was written.

Louisville, April 30 1870

Mr. Sheriff sir—
in order that you may know that I still live by writing to you—you may think it strange: but you must know sir that this is a strange world in which we live, i come through your village friday night but had not the time to stop as the train would not waight. I would like to see you, please keep shirt till I call for it. I will write soon again, my destination is Omaha thence the Great West give my respects to all tell Mc. not to think hard of me as I will call some time and settle all claims, tell the Editors to go Hell the states Attorney likewise tell the Commissioners to build a new Jail against I get back any fool can get out of that one, so no more as the train starts in a few minutes, good by
Yours
   with respct
       JOHN HESS.

We find no records to show that Hess was ever heard of again. The commissioners seemingly acted upon the advice of Hess, for at their meeting a month later they unanimously voted to proceed to take the necessary steps for building a new county jail. Plans were drawn, the contract let, and the present county jail was ready for use in December, 1871. (See page 81 of the book.)

The Pleasant City Explosion

[Originally published 5/8/1947]

At 9:15 o'clock Friday morning, May 17, 1918, there was an explosion near Pleasant City that rocked the countryside for miles around. In the history of Guernsey County, there have been three outstanding explosions. The first was of steam, the locomotive explosion at Spencer's Station in 1863; the second, of dynamite at Senecaville in 1903 (page 980 of the book), and this one near Pleasant City, of nitroglycerine. Since the first two have been described, this authentic account of the third is here given for future reference.

Thought Town Was Being Bombed.—It was a quiet May morning, and Pleasant City folks were engaged in their usual daily activities. All of this was changed in an instant. There came a crash that shook every building in the town. The sound was deafening. Hundreds of windows were shattered, and many objects in homes and stores were jarred from their places.

The first thought that came to many people was that the town was being bombed. World War I was in progress at the time, and they believed that a German aircraft of some kind was responsible for what had happened. Rushing out of their homes, they first looked towards the sky as if expecting to see the cause there.

Explosion South of Town.—"What's happened?" was the question asked by everybody. Black smoke was rising to a great height above Jackson Hill south of town, which indicated that the source was in that direction, and thither people began making their way.

This is what happened. H. O. Hughey, an employee of the Marietta Torpedo Company, was transporting, in a motor truck, 320 quarts of nitroglycerine from that city to the oil fields near Wooster, Ohio, where it was to be used in shooting wells. The explosion did not happen on Route 21, which had not then been improved, but on the Pleasant City-Sarahsville Road, a short distance south of Pleasant City.

On the road ahead of Mr. Hughey and going the same direction as he, was a two-horse dray owned and driven by H. R. Phelps, who was accompanied by his son, Walter, aged sixteen. It is supposed that, in attempting to pass the dray, Mr. Hughey drove the truck off the end of a small culvert, and the wheel dropping down produced a jar that set off the nitroglycerine.

Story of an Eyewitness.—About 150 yards from the scene of the explosion was the home of E. A. Thompson. Churning on the rear porch, Mrs. Thompson heard the horn of the truck, blown by Hughey as a signal to Phelps that he was about to pass him, and glanced up just as the explosion occurred. There arose a cloud of thick black smoke that resembled a volcano, she said. At the same time, the air was filled with stones, pieces of dirt, fragments of the truck and wagon, that rained upon her. While the Thompson home was practically destroyed, Mrs. Thompson escaped injury, as also did her children who were with her. A piece of metal from the truck was driven through two walls of the house, passing a short distance over a sleeping baby, but leaving it unhurt. The next nearest building was an ice-storage plant which was blown to pieces.

Effect Was Terrific.—A hole thirty feet in diameter and twelve feet deep was made in the road. Hughey's body was blown to atoms. The mutilated bodies of Phelps and his son were lying on an adjacent hillside, stripped of their clothing. The horses were killed, and one was found hanging in a tree. Not only their harness, but even the shoes on their hoofs were blown off. Scarcely any part of the truck or dray could be found.

The explosion was heard as far north as Cambridge and as far south as Caldwell. Before evening, thousands of people had visited the scene.

Had the explosion taken place in Pleasant City, the effect would probably have been somewhat like that of the atomic bombing of Nagasaki and Hiroshima. The fact that Jackson Hill stood between the place of explosion and the town, serving as a sort of shock absorber, doubtless prevented much destruction.

Stored in 320 quarts of nitroglycerine is a force capable of indescribable effects under certain conditions. Since this explosion, a means of transporting this material with comparative safety has been found.

Actress Billie Burke's Cambridge Ancestry

[Originally published 7/23/1946]

It is generally known here that the ancestors of Billie Burke, the famous stage and screen actress, were Cambridge folks. Who these ancestors were and the order of her descent are not so well known. In fact, there are two lines of descent connecting her directly with the first two groups of Cambridge settlers.

The Two Groups.—In 1803, there came to what is now Cambridge the Beatty-Gomber-Metcalf group of settlers. Their ancestral homes were in Maryland, near the town of Cambridge on Chesapeake Bay. Three years after their coming here (1806), they laid out a town which, for obvious reasons, they named Cambridge. They were of the hardy colonial type, fitted by both nature and experience for meeting the dangers and enduring the hardships of this new country.

The same year Cambridge was laid out, there arrived another group of folks, coming from the Isle of Guernsey between England and France, commonly referred to as Guernseyites. They purchased lots in the new town and settled down alongside the original pioneers. In many respects, they were unlike the first group of settlers—in speech, dress, manner, and custom—but the two got along well together, even intermarrying. For instance, a son of the patriarch of the first group married a daughter of the leader of the second. These Guernseyites made good citizens, and when the Beatty-Gomber-Metcalf group formed a county four years later, they called it Guernsey in their honor. We thus see that the name of the town honors the first group; the name of the county, the second.

A Descendant of John Beatty.—John Beatty was the patriarch of the first group. Coming here with him was a son, Cyrus P. Beatty. John A. Beatty was Cyrus P. Beatty's son. Blanche B. Burke was the daughter of John A. Beatty. Billie Burke is the daughter of Blanche B. Burke. Therefore, it is seen that Billie Burke is the great-great-granddaughter of John Beatty, and thus a direct descendant of the first group.

A Descendant of Thomas Sarchet.—Thomas Sarchet was the leader of the second group—the Guernseyites. Coming here with him in 1806 was a daughter, Nancy Sarchet, thirteen years of age. In 1811, she and Cyrus P.

Beatty were married. John A. Beatty was their son. He married Cecelia C. Flood, and Blanche B. Beatty, their daughter, married William E. Burke. Billie Burke is their daughter. Therefore, it is seen that Billie Burke is the great-great-granddaughter of Thomas Sarchet, and thus a direct descendant of the second group.

Father A Showman.—William E. Burke, father of Billie, was a showman. The story is told that he wished for a son, but a baby born in 1884 was a daughter who was christened Ethel. Somewhat disappointed, he found satisfaction in giving her the pet boy's name of Billie, and by this name she became known to the world.

At a very early age, she began to display the essential characteristics of an actress, attracting the attention of Charles Frohman, the famous theatrical manager who lost his life on the torpedoed Lusitania in 1915. She was educated in France and London. In 1914, she was married to Florenz Ziegfeld, the great theatrical producer whose "Ziegfeld Follies" were noted all over the country for twenty years. Everybody interested in stage and screen is familiar with Billie Burke's brilliant career as an actress.

Claimed By Cambridge.—Although not born here, Billie Burke has an unbroken Cambridge lineage, aside from her father, for five generations. And more, too, it is evenly divided between the hardy colonials and the steady Guernseyites.

Some years ago, Billie was sent an invitation to attend a homecoming celebration here. On account of illness, she was unable to come. In sending regrets, her mother said that, when able, Billie would write to tell how proud she is of her Cambridge ancestors.

Oliver Markle — A Father and Son in Two World Wars

[Originally published 4/12/1945]

This is a sidelight to Chapter X of the book. Since the present World War opened, many incidents of human interest have been told. Friends meet each other unexpectedly in foreign lands; voices from home are heard by radio across the sea; in fact, unusual incidents are coming to light daily.

But here is a Guernsey County story that is not only unusual, but one with an exceptional human interest, and all who read it will, doubtless, agree with us in considering it a remarkable coincidence. The scene of the story is on two continents, and the time spreads over a whole generation. As a prologue to it, we offer the following paragraph.

From Guernsey County, 1,520 young men entered the First World War. All these returned except sixty. Of those who made the supreme sacrifice, thirty died in camp in this country, and thirty died overseas. Fifteen of the latter died in camp of disease, and fifteen sacrificed their lives in battle. After the war was over, the bodies of twenty who died overseas

DRAMATIC TALES

were returned to America. Ten bodies were left "over there" in cemeteries in France. Their graves may be easily located.

Now for the story we set out to tell, and which we shall relate clearly from the beginning. Oliver Markle married Nora Carpenter, and they established a home at Quaker City. A few months later, we entered the First World War, and Oliver was called into the service. A short time after he left home, a baby boy was born in the same house in which Oliver was born about twenty-five years before. Nora named the baby Oliver, after his father.

Pfc. Oliver Markle never saw his son. He was moved overseas to England and then across the Channel to France, and Nora didn't hear from him for a long time. Then one day, there came that dreaded message from the government: "We regret to inform you that your husband, Pfc. Oliver Markle, was killed in action at the Meuse-Argonne." His body was one of the ten from Guernsey County that were not returned. It was buried in the St. Mihiel American Cemetery, Thiacourt, Meurthe-et-Moselle, Block A, Row 8, Grave 35 (page 351 of the book).

Nora and little Oliver strove along together. The boy never saw his father, but his mother told him much about him. He attended the Quaker City Schools and then was employed in a store. Having reached the age his father was when he married Nora, he, too, married and established a home. A baby was born. The Second World War opened, and he was called into service just as his father had been about twenty-five years before. Again a Pfc. Oliver Markle was moved overseas to England, and then across the Channel to fight the Germans, whose fathers had killed his father twenty-five years ago. He wrote to his mother, telling her where he was. The emotion it occasioned was like that she had experienced just a generation ago. He was approaching the fatal spot. Were the histories of the two Pfc. Oliver Markles, that for a generation had been almost identical, to be ended in the same way? To the young wife, it was a reenactment of the same sad story she had heard so many times. There were reasons for forebodings. Nora wrote to Oliver, telling him the location of his father's grave. The other day, there came a letter to her, given here in part:

"Mother, today I went to see Dad's grave. I got a few postcard pictures and a folder, and I am going to find out whether or not I can send them home. I had my picture taken, standing behind the marker of Dad's grave. I don't know how soon I can get it developed, but I'll send it to you as soon as it is.

"I had quite a time finding Thiacourt, but after I did I had no trouble finding either the cemetery or the grave. It is a beautiful place and very well kept. Eight Frenchmen were working there as caretakers. With my limited knowledge of French I had one of them understand that my father was buried there and he gave me a diagram, a folder and some pictures.

"It is a good thing you sent me the letter telling the location of the grave or I would never have found it. All I knew was St. Mihiel, and there is a town by that name quite a distance from the cemetery. There was a register there and I wrote

my name in it."

This is a strange story—one that rivals the most unusual of the Ripley Believe-It-or-Not collection. We talked to Nora a few days ago, and she verified what we have written here. Father and son born in the same house, never saw each other, married at the same age, called to serve their country, said farewell to young wives at the same place, taken overseas bearing the same army rank and name, to fight the same enemy, on the same spot.

We can only imagine the emotion of the present Pfc. Oliver Markle as he stood at the grave of a father he had known only as his mother told him. The pilgrimage to his father's grave that he had long thought of making someday had been realized, but not in the way expected. May the parallelism in the lives of father and son end here, and may the latter soon be reunited with his mother, wife, and child anxiously awaiting his return.

EXTENDED CHAPTER XLI

Mysteries

The Hidden Pot of Gold

[Originally published 7/15/1946]

For a period of exactly 120 years, tradition of the hidden pot of gold has been told over and over in the Luzadder family, now reaching down to the fifth or sixth generation. And with the passing years, each successive generation has tried to locate the treasure, which the family knows with certainty exists and is rightly theirs. It lies somewhere in the hills of the northeastern part of Center Township. Two words of a dying man—"tree" and "spring"—are the only clue to the location.

In Edgar Allan Poe's "The Gold Bug," the forerunner of the detective story and now a literary classic, we have an account of the means employed in finding a treasure hidden on the coast of South Carolina by Captain William Kidd, the noted pirate. Figuring prominently in the clue were a scarabaeus and a tree. Here we have the tree, but not the bug; therefore, we suppose, until that essential instrument in our search is produced, the hidden gold may not be found.

Abraham Luzadder.—As this is intended to be one of the Guernsey County pioneer family stories, which we are writing as sidelights to "Stories of Guernsey County," we shall tell about the Luzadders, of which Abraham was the first. Of French descent, he was born in New Jersey, in 1757, where he spent his boyhood days, and then moved to Pennsylvania. When a young man, he volunteered to serve in the Revolutionary War, and under Gen. George Rogers Clark, he took part in the capture of Kaskaskia and the famous march against Vincennes. In this campaign, he did duty as a spy, scaling the walls of the fort and bringing back information to Clark that was of great value. In one of the battles in which he engaged, he received a bullet wound in the hip that made him a cripple for the remainder of his life.

Comes To Guernsey County.—In 1817, when 60 years of age, he came to Guernsey County, entering 160 acres of Military Land that had been set aside for soldiers of the Revolution, the deed given him being signed by President James Monroe. This farm was in the then-unbroken forest of Center Township, about three miles northwest of Washington. The journey over the mountains and over Zane's Trace from Wheeling to Washington was made in a wagon. With him came his wife, Leah (Hogue) Luzadder, and their three children, Isaac, John, and Patty.

Here they built a log cabin and began clearing away the forest. The cabin gave way to a more commodious hewed-log house which was afterwards weather-boarded and still stands, but is no longer occupied. Abraham died in 1826, leaving the farm to his two sons—80 acres to each—Isaac receiving the half upon which the home was located. Isaac married Deborah Lawyer, and they became the parents of nine children, one of whom was Jacob who succeed his father as owner of the farm.

Abraham, Isaac, and Jacob, good Old Testament names, and they were the possessors of the land in regular biblical succession. Jacob's heirs—Mrs. Laura Blume, Mrs. Nellie Enos, and David G. and William E. Luzadder—are now the owners. It always has been the Luzadder farm.

The Luzadder Gold.—According to the tradition, Abraham Luzadder, before coming to Guernsey County, had accumulated considerable wealth from various successful business transactions. In the form of gold coin and sealed in an iron pot, he brought this with him when he came here. There were no banks, and as did all others with money in those days, he kept it in the house.

Running through from Wheeling to the northwest was an Indian trail which passed the Luzadder home. It is said that traces of this trail through the farm may yet be seen. Bands of strolling Indians often went through, and while the settlers at that late date were not afraid that they would suffer bodily harm from them, they were anxious about their property, for the Indians did not hesitate to loot the homes and carry away with them everything of value they might want.

One evening about dusk, a band of whooping Indians came over the hill. Abraham seized the pot of gold and rushed to the woods to hide it; he then returned to protect the family. Believing the treasure safer in its hiding place than in the house, he left it there, not even telling his wife the place of concealment. Some time after this, Abraham became ill, and it was evident that death was near at hand. His wife begged him to tell where the gold could be found. All he could gasp was "tree—spring".

Not far away were numerous springs, and there were hundreds of trees. What spring did he mean, and what tree? In Poe's "The Gold Bug" a certain tree had to be located; then from that tree a certain distance had to be measured in a certain direction. How far from the spring was this tree, and in what direction? With nothing but the indefinite clue given by a dying man, a search was started that has continued through the successive generations. Unless somebody found the gold and kept the matter to himself, it is still there.

Old Soldier Buried On His Farm.—Abraham Luzadder and his wife, Leah, were buried on the farm near the home. A few years ago, the Anna Asbury Stone Chapter, Daughters of the American Revolution, of Cambridge, dedicated a monument erected at his grave, with fitting ceremonies that were attended by a number of interested people. Today, the only descendant bearing the family name, living in Guernsey County, is David G. Luzadder, of Cambridge, former teacher and retired city mail carrier. Mrs. Charles F. Gross, North Seventh Street, is a direct descendant of Abraham Luzadder.

The Strange Story of Sophie Gibaut

[Originally published 7/30/1945]

A few years ago, we were in the City Cemetery searching for a certain gravestone from which we hoped to find a date that would verify something we were writing. Assisting us was the late E. J. McIlyar, then the oldest citizen of Cambridge born here, a man whose clear memory of local history ran back farther than that of any other person. As we walked along, Mr. McIlyar pointed to a gravestone ahead, remarking, "There lies the most mysterious character Cambridge has ever known."

The stone was a plain rectangular slab, the style of grave marker in common use three-quarters of a century ago. On its face was inscribed the following:

Sophie Gibaut
Born
On the Island of Guernsey
A. D. 1812
Died
May, 1865

We told Mr. McIlyar that we had heard much about Sophie Gibaut, but those who had given us the information had heard it from others, and for our purpose we were not interested in hearsay stories. "Well I can give you the whole story first-hand," he said, "for I was a young man here when she died. I knew her well, talked to her many times, and I distinctly remember the sensation in Cambridge caused by her death. He then proceeded to tell us the story, which in substance was as follows:

One evening, long before the days of the railroad here, there alighted from the westbound stagecoach a strange woman who sought lodging at one of the taverns. Her height was more than the average; her features were fair; her dress was neat and of the style of that day, and she was not unattractive. She carried the usual traveler's baggage. Her name, she told the tavernkeeper, was Sophie Gibaut.

Cambridge, with its population of only a few hundred, was naturally curious about her. It was not a common thing for a stranger to sojourn in the town, and when that person was a woman entering alone, it was especially uncommon. Her arrival, and her reticence concerning herself, occasioned much speculative gossip over backyard fences and elsewhere in the village.

Everybody was anxious to know where she had come from, why she had come here, and how long she was going to stay. As the days passed by, the mystery surrounding the stranger deepened, but she either ignored or cast aside all questions about herself, other than to say that her name was Sophie Gibaut and that she was born on the Island of Guernsey. She seemed to have plenty of money, and she paid her tavern bills promptly.

At length, she sought employment. Whether she had become tired of the monotony of doing nothing, or whether she needed money, nobody knew. In those days, there was little for a woman to do, other than housework, and most families took care of that themselves. Sophie made it known that she was able to do any kind of odd jobs, and when it was seen that she could be so handy about a home, she had no trouble getting work, especially at house-cleaning time. Her physical strength occasioned wonder; her neatness, admiration. Sophie displayed considerable skill in papering rooms—it wasn't called "hanging paper" in those days. Folks did their papering as there were no professional paperhangers. If the ceilings were not the plain joists, they were usually whitewashed.

Another accomplishment was her skill in nursing the sick and caring for children. She was tender and kind and seemingly possessed some knowledge of medicine. As a midwife, she acquired quite a reputation, and to render service as such she was called to many homes. Although not mentioned by Mr. McIlyar in his story, an old record book of the Cambridge Township trustees shows that on November 7, 1857, an order for ten dollars was issued to Sophie Gibaut for keeping a certain indigent "during her confinement and childbirth."

Sophie left the tavern and established a home of her own. At one time she lived where the Colonial now stands; at another, in a little house on the northeast corner of Wheeling Avenue and Ninth Street. As the years passed by, people gradually ceased to wonder about Sophie; they seemingly had forgotten the mystery attending her arrival, and their curiosity had faded away. She had become a respected and useful citizen. In the meantime, however, she continued reticent as to her past, never dropping a word that might throw any light upon it. Twenty-five years, perhaps, passed away.

One day it was reported that Sophie was ill; a few days later that she was dead. Then came a report that rocked the town from one end to the other—Sophie Gibaut was a man!

After Mr. McIlyar had told us the story as above related, we sought the newspaper files of May, 1865. The Guernsey Times of May 11 carried the following:

"Sophie Gibaut, of this place, died at her residence on Monday last of Erysipelas fever after a short illness. Deceased was about 50 years of age."

Who was Sophie Gibaut? The name was doubtless an assumed one. Why did he come here in disguise and pose throughout the years as a woman. (We are now using the masculine gender.) It would certainly have been easier to get along here as a man than as a woman. Among some papers recovered from an old home here, Carl J. Rech recently found a receipt issued to Dr. Vincent Haines by Sophie Gibaut, acknowledging payment of 75 cents due the said Sophie for papering. It was signed "Her (X) Mark," indicating that he was unable to write his name.

"The report following the death produced the greatest sensation I have ever known in Cambridge," said Mr. McIlyar. People who had associated with him throughout the years tried to recall anything—word or action on Sophie's part—that might help to solve the mystery. But Sophie had played his part well. Everybody racked his brain over it. Some person happened to think of a remark once dropped by Sophie concerning something or other that he had been much at sea. This, together with some other things put with it, gave rise to the story that he had been a desperate pirate, and that certain death would be his fate if captured. Disguised as a woman, he had come into this little county-seat town where he would not likely be discovered. He had brought some of the booty with him and had hid it here in the woods. For many years following Sophie's death, search was made for the treasure, but like that of Captain Kidd, the greatest of all pirates, it was never found.

Another theory advanced that got a strong hold on the minds of many was that he was a political refugee over whose head a death penalty hung. There are some today who have stood high in authority who would probably like to hide themselves in that way, but it would not be as easy to do now as it was a century ago. The fact that Sophie couldn't write his name and had to make his mark would weaken that belief, it would seem. On the other hand, it would only tend to strengthen it. There would be no handwriting to be used as evidence against him, in case an expert in such should get hold of it; then there would be less suspicion if he posed as an illiterate.

According to many wild surmises afloat, Mr. Hitler may be playing a Sophie Gibaut somewhere at the present time. If he is, he is not establishing a precedent, for it may be that another notorious paperhanger tried it here successfully a hundred years ago.

Sophie Gibaut may have been nothing more than an eccentric person who chose to play the part he did as a way of life. For whatever purpose he assumed the role, he played it well. The mystery was buried with him in City Cemetery and will never be solved.

MORE STORIES OF GUERNSEY COUNTY

Golden Guernsey (?)

[Originally published 4/22/1947]

Don't take this story seriously. Although as a story it is true in itself, its import is not guaranteed, and it is not intended that it be given more than passing interest. I am submitting this as a sidelight to a statement made on page 17 of the book which, after publication, was questioned by a certain farmer in the county. If you read what follows, just forget it. Be it understood that I am not trying to start something.

In the book are listed the natural resources of the county. To one who reads the list, it would seem that the entire mineral kingdom is represented here. However, one exception is mentioned in these words:

"Guernsey County does not boast of having any gold mines. At any rate, no gold has been found amongst the many treasures concealed within the hills. It is hardly probable, though, that any other county in Ohio can show a richer, more extensive, and more varied line of mineral products than can Guernsey."

Statement Questioned.—Having read what is said above, a certain farmer, living within a dozen miles of Cambridge, called me to come out, and he would show me what he believed to be a deposit of gold. (For obvious reasons, I am mentioning neither names nor places.) He said he wanted my opinion as to whether he had gold on his farm that could be mined at a financial profit. Chiefly through curiosity, I went out, although I didn't know much about such things. My father was one of the early California gold-seekers. He made the trip from Oxford Township, Guernsey County, to the gold fields at a time when it took him six months to drive a mule team from the Mississippi River to California. (The other day an aviator made the journey from the Pacific, not only to the Mississippi, but on through to the Atlantic, in a little more than six hours.) After five years in the goldfields, my father returned by way of the Isthmus of Panama and New York.

Before going out to this Guernsey County El Dorado to advise the farmer, I tried to recall what my father had told me many years ago—how prospecting was done, what the signs of pay-dirt were, how the gold was mined, how it was panned, and such things. Then I went out to the farmer's home, feeling confident that I could put up a good bluff, and at least talk intelligently about the matter.

The Farmer's Story.—Finding the farmer at home, I inquired about the location of the prospective diggings, how the discovery was made, what proof he had that the substance was gold, and some other things that I thought would enable me to form an opinion. Following, in substance, is what I learned.

Out rabbit hunting one day, the farmer's brother and a companion chanced to cross a small stream on a remote part of the farm, at a place where there was an accumulation of sand and gravel. Glancing down, the men saw glittering particles of something that looked like gold. Upon investigation, they found some of the same substance embedded in small pieces of rocks that had been washed down the stream. They gathered up some of the rocks and brought them to a jeweler in Cambridge. After an examination, he reported that it appeared to be gold, but not being equipped with means for making a thorough test, he forwarded the samples to a wholesale jewelry firm in Cincinnati. The report came back that it was gold, and that the ore had been sent by the firm to the Mint of the United States at New Orleans to be assayed.

The Assayer's Report.—The farmer showed me the assayer's report, a copy of which is now before me. It was made to the Cincinnati firm of wholesale jewelers and signed by the official assayer for the government. It says that the ore submitted had been assayed and showed 15.4 ounces of gold to the ton, worth $539. This meant that every ton of such deposit in the hills was worth that amount.

A few months afterwards, the farmer himself sent some of the ore to the Mint of the United States at Denver, Colorado. There came back a report on a form similar to that from New Orleans, signed by the government assayer at Denver. He found, he said, that the ore submitted to him had assayed 9.69 ounces of gold to a ton, and was worth $339.15 at the then price of $35.00 per fine ounce Troy.

The Mysterious Visitor.—A short time after the report came from Denver, a stranger, driving a car bearing a Colorado license, called at the farmer's home, saying that he was out looking for a farm on which to settle, and he asked the farmer if he would sell his. Told that the farm was not for sale, he began making inquiries which indicated that he knew something about the gold. Given permission to look around, he returned in an hour or two and made the farmer a handsome offer for the place. This was refused, but a promise was given him that it would neither be sold nor leased until he was heard from again.

No Gold Is Found.—Having heard the farmer's story, I was really becoming interested. An emotion somewhat akin to that experienced by the "Forty-Niner" made me anxious to rush for the goldfield. I mentally rehearsed everything about mining gold that my father had told me, and with this secondhand experience, I was conducted by the farmer across a couple of fields to the edge of a woods that sloped down to a deep ravine. Here was a vigorous stream of water formed by the confluence of two smaller ones flowing down from the adjacent hillsides, one from the northeast, the other from the northwest. Below the junction was the accumulation of sand and small pieces of rocks referred to above. I clawed around in it for some time, but discovered nothing that to me looked like gold. My enthusiasm began to wane.

A few weeks after this, a friend and I slipped over to do a little prospecting, this time in a more thorough way, and over a wider area. We thoroughly explored the lower stream, then worked up the smaller ones and along the hillsides. We gouged into every likely-looking place, but all in vain. In the fields above were tons of boulders strongly impregnated with iron. We were looking for gold, not iron ore. We returned without staking off a claim.

Perhaps we didn't know enough about such things, notwithstanding my childhood training, for there were the jeweler's opinion, the wholesale jewelry firm's test, the assay of the United States Government (from two mints), and the visit of the mysterious stranger, which may or may not have had anything to do with the matter.

If the statement on page 17 of the book (quoted above) is found, without question, to be an error, it will be corrected. In spite of the apparently official documentary evidence, the writer is content to let the statement stand as written. There may be gold in "them thar hills," but neither my prospecting friend nor I could find any.

A Lead Mystery

[Originally published 9/4/1945]

This is a side light to the story, "Legend of the Lead Mine" (page 826 of the book). It should be read first.

C. C. Van De Mark, Madison Avenue, showed us some pieces of ore the other day that he had obtained from a couple of boys who had dug it out of a pit down on Second Street, not far from the mouth of Gordon Run. The ore was heavy, obviously rich in some metallic substance. Subjected to heat, it fused freely. The dross having been removed, there remained a bright metal that was soft and malleable. It had the appearance of lead, and its reaction to certain tests indicated it to possess all the properties of lead. Had the boys discovered a lead mine right here in Cambridge—or what?

Curiosity prompted Carl J. Rech and the writer to visit the place the ore was found, interview the boys concerning their discovery, look over the territory round about, and then try to arrive at some conclusion as to what it was and how it came to be there.

In their play, the boys had dug a hole three or four feet in diameter and four or five feet deep. From the bottom of it they had began to run a tunnel when they struck the ore. There seemed to be a good deal of it, but they had removed only a little when the ground began to cave in, compelling them to abandon their project. The ore did not appear to have been fused. Stone and metal were mixed together in it. We took some samples over to Muskingum College to be tested by Geologist Moses, and he pronounced it to be lead of a fair quality. Its identity having been established, we proceeded to consider how it came to be there.

Three theories presented themselves: first, it was a natural formation of lead in that place; second, it was some refuse from one of the mills once located in that part of the city; and third, it was lead ore brought from some other place for a purpose and hidden there.

Native lead ore, it is said, is seldom if ever found in areas where there are deposits of coal. Notwithstanding this, however, there used to be rumors of its discovery in various parts of Guernsey County. Excitement would follow, but that was all. We abandoned this theory to consider the second.

No mill had ever been located near the place the ore was found, and there was nothing in the surroundings to indicate that it had ever been used as a dumping ground for refuse from anywhere. This left us the third theory to consider, and, it being historical, it was the one we were especially looking for.

Lead for making bullets was prized by the Indians and white settlers. Hundreds of miles away to the northwest in the Lake Superior region, there was plenty of it and journeys were made there for it by the Indians. Obtained only through so much labor and danger, the ore—in which form it was carried back—was treasured and guarded carefully. Often it was buried in the ground, and the secret would be known to only a few.

In 1808, Eveline Tingle, seven years old, came to Cambridge with her parents. Before her death in 1886, she related a number of incidents connected with the early history of this section (page 551 of the book). She told about an Indian town down in Lofland's bottom. That section was a forest in her childhood. Before she died, it had become the Gordon Lofland farm and included the mouth of Gordon Run. The exact location of the Indian settlement is not known, but is believed to have been near the mouth of the run and not far from the elevation upon which the Lofland School stands. In their digging, the boys may by mere accident have discovered the town's treasury, the cache that was abandoned when the Indians left. This third theory is more than a guess, for there is reason to sustain it. If true, it is of interest historically, since it shows about where the Indian town was located.

A Curious Freak of Nature

[Originally published 7/10/1947]

Pictured here is probably the most curious freak of nature to be found in Guernsey County. It has been known locally since the earliest pioneer days, and with it have been associated a number of traditions that may or may not have had some foundation. But, strange to say, it has been given but little publicity. Not to our knowledge has a description of it ever been published or even attention called to it in print. It is possible for one traveling the public highway to pass beneath it without noticing it.

Located in Valley Township.—If you wish to visit this curiosity, you may reach it easily and obtain a good view of it from your car. It is located on the public road near the home of Clyde A. Roller in Valley Township. From Route 21, turn west near Derwent on Route 313 (the old Clay Pike). Follow this one and one-half miles, and then turn to the right on Route 323. It will be found one-half mile up this road.

An Arched Roadway.—On the west side of the road is a white oak tree, two and one-half feet or more in diameter at the base. Instead of growing erect and lofty, it swings over the road to the east side, in a remarkably symmetrical curve, and buries its trunk in the ground. Over the center of the road, it reaches its greatest height, and here the trunk is approximately two feet in diameter. At the place it reaches the ground on the opposite side, its diameter is approximately one foot.

This venerable white oak, as if ashamed of its abnormal physique and sensitive to the gaze of passersby, clears the road and hides its head in the ground. Apparently proud

Photo by S. W. Obenour, Jr., of Zanesville Times-Signal

of its strength, which has become proverbial, the majestic oak, as a rule, grows straight and tall. But here is one that, from some cause, met with misfortune in its youth. From the ground it arose, and to the ground it returned, yet it still lived on. Like some people who, with deformed bodies, display noble traits of character, so has this unfortunate tree apparently tried and succeeded in displaying a grace of beauty that attracts attention. From the upper side of the highest part of the curved trunk, it sends forth a symmetrical cluster of branches, as may be noted in the picture. These tree-like branches, rising erect, appear as proud as any oak.

Known to the Indians.—There used to be a junction of Indian trails near the site of the present Bethel Church. From here, one of the trails ran north to the Indian village of Old Town, which was located at the mouth of Trail Run. Whether the superstitious Indians designed the course at this place so that the trail should go under this arch, or whether it just happened by chance, is not known. Nevertheless, the public road that was established afterwards followed the trail, which took it beneath the tree.

On Farm of Henry F. Frye.—In pioneer days, the farm on which this tree is located was owned by Henry F. Frye. He owned several hundred acres of land and became one of the most prominent farmers of that section.

MYSTERIES

After marrying Sarah Trenner in 1826, he built his first home, which was located on the old Clay Pike where it was crossed by the Indian trail. Here he opened a store and kept a tavern. It was a busy place. Droves of stock and great loads of tobacco were taken by on their way to eastern markets.

We have been unable to find in the commissioners' records when the road that passes beneath the tree (Route 323) was opened. It is our opinion that Frye petitioned for it so as to make it easier for the people north to reach his place of business. It swings around towards Old Town as did the Indian trail.

EXTENDED CHAPTER XLII

Some Chronological County History

The First Bridge in the Northwest Territory

[Originally published 5/20/1947]

There is usually something about the first of anything anywhere that is fascinating. Especially is this true if it happens to be the first of something that becomes permanently established and common. We refer to the first settlement somewhere by a people, the first person to attain that which afterwards becomes commonplace, the first great achievement along a particular line, the first institution of some kind in some place, and so on in many things.

For an outstanding first, we need look no farther than our own community. Cambridge can boast of having had the first bridge authorized by the government in the Northwest Territory.

The Territorial Legislature.—For ten years after the settlement at Marietta, the government of the Northwest Territory was in the hands of Gov. Arthur St. Clair and three Judges. These four men exercised all the executive, legislative, and judicial powers of the Territory. Then representatives were chosen to make the laws, meeting at Cincinnati as the seat of government. This legislative body was composed of twenty-two members at first, representing a constituency scattered over 265,000 square miles. It was in force three years and held three sessions (1799-00, 1800-01, and 1801-02). The few laws enacted are recorded in Vol. 1 of Territorial Laws.

The most important act of the first session was the election of William Henry Harrison as delegate from the Northwest Territory to Congress, the population then entitling it to representation. At the third session, it was voted to appoint a committee to consider and report on the advisability of asking that Ohio be admitted as a state. Another act of this session was authorization for building two bridges in the Northwest Territory, "one across Wills Creek in Washington County, the other across the Muskingum River at Zanesville." This was the first and only action, relative to bridges, taken by the Territorial Legislature.

Then In Washington County.—It will be noted that two bridges were authorized at the same time, one across Wills Creek in Washington County, and the other at Zanesville. What afterwards became Guernsey County was then a part of Washington. Zane's Trace was the only road over which the Territorial Government had jurisdiction, and it crossed Wills Creek at what is now Cambridge.

Now, which of the two bridges was built first—the one here, or the one at Zanesville? It was at least ten years after this before a bridge was built at the latter place, and then by virtue of authority by the state legislature (Vol. 10 of Ohio Laws). Evidently, no advantage was taken of the Territorial law.

When Built Here.—In a story published the other day, we told that Ezra Graham began operating a ferry at the Wills Creek crossing in 1798, and continued alone to do so for two years; that George and Henry Beymer came here in 1800, bought an interest in the ferry, and they and Graham operated it together for the next three years; and that in 1803, the Beattys and Gomber took over the place.

Zaccheus A. Beatty, who, together with Zaccheus Biggs, had purchased the land on which the ferry was located, saw the advantage of a bridge over a ferry, and it was probably he who petitioned the Territorial Legislature for authority to build one. It would, of course, be a private project, and the date of building was between 1803 and 1807.

On October 17, 1805, Zaccheus Biggs sold his interest in the land to Jacob Gomber. It was conditioned in the deed that Biggs, or any member of his family, should at all times be privileged to pass over the toll bridge erected across Wills Creek on said land, toll-free (page 543 of the book). This would indicate that the bridge was then there, or that one was expected.

In 1807, a traveler by the name of Fortescue Cuming passed through here. He said he crossed Wills Creek on a wooden bridge which had become extremely dangerous, for some of the posts had been unplaced by floods, so that it was shelving, one side being a good deal higher than the other. Bad as it was, he said, he had to pay a toll of an eighth of a dollar for his horse (page 47 of the book). From this, it would appear that it was built some time before 1807, probably in 1805. Built of logs with a puncheon floor, it served as a crossing until 1828, when the National Road came through and it was replaced by the old covered bridge.

Both a Bridge and a Ferry.—Zaccheus A. Beatty evidently did not have an exclusive transportation franchise across Wills Creek. Eveline R. Tingle said that when she came here in 1808, there were a toll bridge and a ferry down on the creek. The ferry was kept by a man named Mahoney, who lived in one of the cabins that stood down near the bridge. He was a lanky, slim, slouchy-looking man, she said (page 552 of the book).

From the facts given above, there seems to be no question that the first bridge authorized by the government in the Northwest Territory was built in what is now Cambridge, about the year 1805.

MORE STORIES OF GUERNSEY COUNTY

Jacob Gomber's Powder Horn

[Originally published 10/31/1946]

We recently received from Mrs. Marguerite Metcalfe Watson, of Morristown, New Jersey, through her brother, Mr. S. W. Metcalfe, of Cleveland, Ohio, what we believe to be the oldest and most interesting existing relic connected with Cambridge history. Accompanying it was a statement in the handwriting of George Metcalfe, attesting to its authenticity. (The present generation of Metcalfs spell the name with an "e" added; hence the two spellings in this story.) This relic is the powder horn of Jacob Gomber, carried by him in 1803 when he first came to what is now Cambridge, and used by him here until his death.

The Beatty, Gomber, and Metcalf Families.—To make this little sidelight story plain, we repeat what we have already told many times. It won't hurt to do so, because, by our writings, we are trying to teach Guernsey County history, and we long ago found that frequent reviews are a very necessary part of the teaching process.

Zane's Trace—only a trail through the unbroken forest—was blazed through here in 1798. Down where it crossed Wills Creek, a man by the name of Ezra Graham built a log cabin—the first, it is said, between Wheeling and Zanesville, and operated a ferry. Two years later, two brothers from Pennsylvania came along, George and Henry Beymer, who either bought the place from Graham or joined with him in operating it. They enlarged the cabin, which stood near the site of the present Union station, and earned a little money by keeping occasional travelers overnight. They were squatters and had no title to the place, which was on government land.

In 1801, Zaccheus A. Beatty and Zaccheus Biggs bought four thousand acres of government land upon which a part of Cambridge now stands. In 1803, John Beatty, father of Zaccheus A., came out from an eastern state to settle upon this purchase. Coming with him were members of his family, including his son-in-law, Jacob Gomber, and Jacob Gomber's son-in-law, George Metcalf. They found the ferrymen on their land, down at the Wills Creek crossing, and they ousted them after they had paid them for their cabin and equipment.

Jacob Gomber.—As John Beatty was getting old, Jacob Gomber was the leader of the group. He bought Zaccheus Biggs's half interest in the four thousand acres and thus owned it jointly with his brother-in-law, Zaccheus A. Beatty, who did not come here to live until three or four years later. To Jacob Gomber the group of settlers looked for protection and advice.

This section was then a wilderness. For miles and miles in every direction stretched a dense forest in which were bears, panthers, wolves, and other wild animals. There were Indians around here, too, and their friendship was questionable. For protection against wild beasts and wild men, Jacob Gomber kept his flintlock musket close at hand at all times. Strapped over his shoulder was his powder horn, ever ready in case of need.

George Metcalf.—Next to Gomber in importance was George Metcalf who had married Susan, Jacob Gomber's daughter. In 1803, George was only twenty years of age. Like George Washington, he was a Virginian who learned surveying, and when but a boy was sent out to help survey some of the western country. The story is told that on one of his surveying trips through this section, he fell in love with the country, and when he returned home, he prevailed upon Beatty and Gomber to settle here.

George Metcalf may be considered the Guernsey County pathfinder. Three years after coming here, he laid out and platted what is now part of Cambridge. He was chosen the first county surveyor, and as such, he located the early roads. He established the township boundary lines. As a public official, he served as county treasurer, also as a judge of the county court. For many years, he kept a tavern. We have long wondered why a Boy Scout troop has not been named for him. A study of his life and activities in Guernsey County should afford much of the type of inspiration needed in Scout work.

Jacob Gomber died in 1820, at the age of sixty-one. Before his death, he presented to George Metcalf the powder horn he had brought here in 1803, the powder horn he had carried with him through the many years of danger and hardship.

The Two Jacob Gomber Metcalfs.—George and Susan Gomber Metcalf named their oldest son Jacob Gomber Metcalf. Susan died in 1820, the same year her father died. To perpetuate the Gomber name, a son born to Jacob Gomber Metcalf was called Jacob Gomber Metcalf, II. This boy became one of the most successful businessmen ever born in Cambridge. A few months ago, we wrote a story about him—his rise in life to such a height that at his death in 1916, the United Press referred to him as "one of the strongest figures in the railroad and financial world."

Before George Metcalf died in 1867, he passed the treasured powder horn over to his grandson, Jacob Gomber Metcalf, II, along with the following note of transmittal which, encased in cellophane, came to us with the relic: "Jacob Gomber's powder horn. You are the last one to have his name, and I feel you are the one to have it."

After the death of Jacob Gomber Metcalf, II, his daughter, Mrs. Marguerite Metcalf Watson, of Morristown, New Jersey, became the custodian of this family heirloom. Now it has been returned to Cambridge to remain permanently, if a Guernsey County Historical Museum is established.

The Metcalfes of Today.—We have no knowledge of any person in Guernsey County today who bears the name of Beatty, Gomber, or Metcalfe. Three children of Jacob Gomber Metcalf, II, (the railroad magnate) are living: J. G. Metcalfe, superintendent of transportation of the

Louisville and Nashville Railroad, Louisville, Kentucky; S. W. Metcalfe, a Cleveland, Ohio, businessman; and the Mrs. Watson referred to above.

Several weeks ago, Mr. and Mrs. S. W. Metcalfe came to Cambridge, remaining three or four days to visit the many places with which their ancestors were associated. Mr. Metcalfe told us he was here once before, when about six years of age, coming in a private train with his father to visit a relative.

So impressed was he with the story of the activities of his ancestors here—something, it seems, that the family had not known much about—that he indicated a desire for a reunion of Metcalfes in Cambridge at a later date. Noting our interest in the powder horn, he telephoned his sister, asking her to forward it here.

The Metcalf Pictures.—Another direct descendant of George Metcalf, Mrs. William H. Courtenay, II, is living in Louisville, Kentucky. However, she has not descended along the same line as the one about whom we have been writing, her great-grandfather being another son of George Metcalf. She has also become much interested in early Guernsey County history and has sent us silhouette pictures of George Metcalf and his wife, Susan Gomber Metcalf. She is planning a visit to Cambridge in the near future.

(EDITOR'S NOTE: The Jacob Gomber powder horn and the Metcalf pictures are now on display in the window of The Jeffersonian.)

How Cambridge Was Laid Out

[Originally published 6/1/1945]

One day, early in the summer of 1806, a little group of men might have been seen standing a few yards south of the present location of the Soldiers' Monument in front of the courthouse. One of these men was Jacob Gomber who, together with Zaccheus A. Beatty, his brother-in-law, owned the land, 4,000 acres of it, that surrounded them. Another was George Metcalf, who had married Susan Gomber, daughter of Jacob. George was twenty-three years of age, tall, and proportionally built, a young man of extraordinary physical strength and endurance, good judgment, and dignified bearing. As was George Washington, he was born in Virginia, and, like Washington, too, he became a surveyor when a mere boy. He had been a member of a party that surveyed the Military Land of which Guernsey County is a part. It is said that it was he who induced Jacob Gomber and Zaccheus A. Beatty to come here and buy land.

We can only guess who the other members of the group were. Zaccheus A. Beatty was living in Steubenville at the time and did not locate here until a year or two later, but he was probably here that day for an important work that was about to be started, as he had a special interest in

SOME CHRONOLOGICAL COUNTY HISTORY

it. His father, John Beatty, who lived in a cabin down at the Wills Creek crossing was probably one of the men, as were Wyatt M. Hutchison, his son-in-law, and Isaac Oldham, both of whom were living down by the creek, too.

This little group of men stood exactly midway between what is now the northeast corner of the building occupied by the Ohio Power and the northwest corner of the Craig building (Editor's Note—What was known as the "Craig" building for many years is now owned by Harry Atkinson. The Kresge store occupies the first floor corner.) Thousands of people walk over the spot every day. But how different it was then from now! They were standing in the midst of a dense forest. Excepting a small patch of cleared ground down by the creek, all was a wilderness extending in every direction. There were oak, beech, maple and walnut trees, with an occasional majestic poplar rising above them all. There was a thick undergrowth of shrubbery and vines clinging to the trees. Wild animals may have been peeping at the men from a safe distance, wondering what they were going to do.

If being born is the greatest event in a person's life, and if this applies to a city as well, this was the greatest event in the history of Cambridge. The men were there to lay out a town which Jacob Gomber said would be called Cambridge, after Cambridge, Maryland, where some of their forebears had once lived. "Drive a stake right here," he may have said to Isaac Oldham who, we have learned from some old records, was there to engage in that kind of work. This was the first public improvement in our city. Then George Metcalf stepped forward with his surveying outfit, a crude one-staff hoop affair with a compass about as big as a saucer, and planted it directly over the stake. "That's east," George may have said, after some sighting and adjustments were made. We might remark here that due to imperfect instruments and ignorance of accurate declinations in those days, he established a line a little off center, and this caused trouble in after years. George Metcalf was our first city engineer. Peter Sheehan, now holding that office, might do a better job than George, but that was then.

"Now start at the stake and measure forty feet along this east line," said Gomber, "and drive another stake." If this second stake is still there, it may be found exactly under the northwest corner of the Craig building. West from the first stake a distance of another forty feet was measured off and another stake was driven. Little did the man who drove this stake think, that he was marking the corner of a building that 140 years later would be housing offices of a company supplying thousands of people with power and light by means of a mysterious something, of which he had never heard.

This done, Jacob Gomber ordered Metcalf to locate a line running north from the first stake, and that on this line 576 feet be measured off, starting at the first stake. Those who carried the chain would today have to cross Wheeling Avenue, pass through the center of the Soldiers' Monument, through the front door and out the back door of the courthouse, through the jail and library and across Steubenville Avenue to a point halfway between the southwest corner of the McFarland property and the southeast corner of the Stella McCartney house. From the stake driven at the end of this line running north, a distance of forty feet was measured east and west as at the beginning, thus establishing the northern boundary of Steubenville Avenue, just as the first lines run marked the southern boundary of Wheeling.

But why the 576 feet? Jacob Gomber, Zaccheus A. Beatty, and George Metcalf had it figured out this way: eighty feet for the width of Wheeling Avenue, 198 feet for a lot facing south, twenty feet for an alley running east and west, 198 feet for a lot facing north on Steubenville, and eighty feet for the width of that street to the place of ending. These total 576.

Eighteen lots sixty-six feet wide and 198 feet deep were laid off on the south side of Wheeling Avenue, east of the second stake driven, and eighteen west of the third stake. After every third lot a space twenty feet wide was left for an alley, and after every sixth lot was left space for a street running north and south. There were thus thirty-six lots on the south side of Wheeling Avenue. These were numbered east from the one farthest west (southeast corner of Wheeling Avenue and Fifth Street) On the north side, thirty-four lots were laid off in a similar way, a space the width of two lots being passed over for the court square These were numbered down street from the northwest corner of Wheeling Avenue and Eleventh Street, that lot being thirty-seven and the last one (northeast corner of Wheeling Avenue and Fifth Street) being seventy.

On Steubenville Avenue, the lots were laid off in the same way, except that there were thirty-six on the north side and thirty-four on the south. The numbering began at the southeast corner of Steubenville Avenue and Fifth Street, which lot was seventy-one, and continued east to the southwest corner of Steubenville Avenue and Eleventh Street—lot 104. Passing down on the north side of Steubenville, they made the last lot 140 (northeast corner of Steubenville Avenue and Fifth Street). This completed the survey of the town proper. Some out-lots were afterwards laid out.

Many of the lines ran through trees, and it was necessary to survey around them. Some corners of lots, alleys and streets were marked by blazing the trees. Considering all the disadvantages, we must admit that George Metcalf did remarkably well.

The survey completed, Gomber and Beatty offered the 140 lots for sale. The price asked for the choicest was fifty cents per front foot. Today they might bring two thousand times as much. But this is now.

SOME CHRONOLOGICAL COUNTY HISTORY

From the Isle of Guernsey

[Originally published 7/14/1947]

Shown here is a photo of the deed executed on the Isle of Guernsey in 1597.

(This is a sidelight on the story, "Guernsey Island," page 41 of the book.)

Addressed to the "Guernsey County Historical Society," there have been received by Miss Mary A. Stone, president of the organization, a letter and two interesting relics from Mr. T. F. Priaulx of the Isle of Guernsey. Mr. Priaulx is a member of a family, some of whose members migrated to America in the early part of the last century and settled within and near Cambridge. They were included in the colony of Guernseyites from whom our county took its name. Some of their descendants are now living here.

Mr. Priaulx's Letter.—"From press clippings sent to me by my cousin, Mrs. E. M. Shoesmith of Maryland," Mr. Priaulx writes, "I have read of the interest you are taking in your namesake in the Channel Isles." Referring to the relics—an old newspaper and a deed—he says, "I thought you might find them worthy a place in your archives."

He states further in his letter that we here in Guernsey County should not hesitate at any time to ask for information concerning the Isle of Guernsey. He indicates a willingness to write an article or paper about the island or its families and says that any interest or pleasure it may give us will be regarded by him as ample compensation.

The Old Paper.—"Gazette de Guernsey," bearing the date of May 9, 1818, is the name of the old paper he sends. It has four pages, was published weekly, the only paper in Guernsey. Naturally, it is mostly in French, a small portion being in English. Mr. Priaulx says that copies as old as this are very rare, and we wonder why it was permitted to be sent from the island.

This paper was printed but a few years after the Guernseyites came to Cambridge. It is interesting to note that many of the family names appearing in it are the same as of those living here at the time. We find such names as Marquand, Podwin, Torode, Langlois, Martel, Blanpied, Robin, Le Page, Le Lacheur, Simon, and Thomas.

The Deed.—Of greater interest is the deed, bearing the date of November 24, 1597. If the old newspaper was rare on the Isle of Guernsey, this old deed must have been rare indeed. It was executed when Elizabeth was Queen of England, and ten years before Jamestown was settled. One would think that such a relic (exactly 350 years old) should be carefully preserved in a museum on the Isle of Guernsey. It is written with a pen in French, and on parchment. Attached to it is the green wax seal of the Royal Court of Guernsey.

Mr. Priaulx writes that he is sending it to us in order that the Guernsey Isle descendants in Cambridge may see the kind of deeds held by their ancestors in bygone days. He encloses a translation. Believing that its curious conditions and quaint style will be of general interest here in Cambridge, we produce it exactly as written.

To all whom these Letters may concern, Nicollas Martin, Lieutenant of Louys Devyck, Bailiff of the Isle of Guernsey for the Most Excellent Majesty of our Sovereign Lady, Elizabeth, Queen of England, etc., etc. Greetings in God, make known that before us in the town of Saint Peter Port in the said Isle, the XXIIIIth day of the month of November, the year of Grace One thousand V hundred ninety-seven, and in the presence of Jean de Sausmares and Jean Effard, Jurats of the Court of our said Lady, the Queen in the said Isle, There appeared Thomas de Putteron, son of Thomas, who in right of and by reason of Collette his wife, daughter of Thomas de Putron, son of George, of the district (contree) of Putteron the parish of Saint Peter Port, of his own pure and free will has confessed and acknowledged having sold, resigned, quitted, and totally transferred and transported from himself, from his said wife, and from her heirs, she being hereto present and assenting, and witnessed by the assembled parish and after having obtained leave and license from Justice so to do as has appeared to us under the signs of the said Lieutenant Bailiff and of seven Jurats, in perpetuity to Jeremye de Putteron, son of Collas of the said parish and district, and to his heirs, to wit— the whole and entire real estate which, as on this day and date, to the said wife may pertain and belong within the said Isle of Guernsey, as well as houses and land as rentes (i. e. wheat rentes) to receive and to pay, nothing excepted. For which said sale and transfer the said Thomas de Putteron and his said wife declare before us that they are well and truly paid and contented by the said Jeremye de Putteron, in respect of everything. And the said Thomas de Putteron in right of his said wife, and on behalf of her and of her heirs, promises and obliges himself to provide and guarantee at all times in the future to the said Jeremye de Putteron and to his heirs, the said sale and transfer free of all restraints and to permit him to enjoy it forever. And has the said wife taken oath and been sworn on God's Holy Gospels as is required in such cases, and declares that she has been neither beaten nor molested in any manner whatsoever to do this, but that she does it of her own free will, and she has promised that she will never go against, or contradict the above, under pain of perjury.

In Witness of which things the Seal of the Bailiwick of the said Isle of Guernsey is hereunto set the year and date before mentioned.

The Hard Year of 1807

[Originally published 9/10/1946]

We of today grumble a good deal because we can't get easily all the foods of certain kinds that we would like to have. Then, too, the housing situation is serious, so we think, because we can't find a place to live that just suits us, and at a cost that we would be satisfied to pay. For at least one year—that of 1807—the settlers of Guernsey County experienced a house shortage, a food scarcity, and other hardships that brought a suffering which we would think unbearable today, and we find no record of any complaint.

It was in 1806 that the settlers of Cambridge began arriving, and the next year was the "hard year." From our school histories, we learn that the year following the settlement at Plymouth by the Pilgrims was one of suffering, yet they bore it bravely, thus establishing an abiding illustration of pioneer fortitude. Right here in Cambridge was a parallelism that should be a lesson for us today.

The Housing Problem.—In the summer of 1807, a traveler passed through what is now Guernsey County and afterwards wrote about his trip (page 47 of the book). He said he found Cambridge to be a settlement of 12 cabins, finished and finishing, each of which contained two or three families. There wasn't room for all the furniture, utensils, and goods, he said, which were lying around promiscuously. Imagine a one-room log cabin as an apartment house.

Why Food Was Scarce.—The settlers who were gathering here brought a little food with them, but, until a crop could be raised, they were expecting to live upon whatever the forest might supply. They saved most of their corn for seed, and kept the livestock they had brought for propagating purposes.

In anticipation of plenty soon to come, they passed the first winter cheerfully, living on the game of the forest, together with some of the grain, which they used sparingly. The children were taught to call the white meat of the wild turkey bread. Salt was scarce and had to be doled out carefully. Of luxuries, there were none.

An Invasion of Squirrels.—Some small tracts of land having been cleared, they planted their corn in the spring of 1807, looking forward to a bountiful crop of grain. Just as the shoots began peeping through the ground, a horde of squirrels swept through the forest. Sometimes these little animals take a notion to migrate, and when they do, they go in bodies. In this year of 1807, myriads of them from somewhere in the South swam the Ohio River and overran the southern part of this state. When they reached here, they dug up every hill of corn in the clearings to get the grain which was in the process of germination, and then most of them passed on. Their devastations were somewhat like those caused by the locusts mentioned in the Bible, or the grasshoppers in some of our western states. So sweeping were the depredations of the squirrels that the state legislature enacted a law that year, entitled "An act to encourage the killing of squirrels." This law required all persons within the state, subject to the payment of taxes, to furnish a certain number of squirrel scalps in addition to the taxes he paid. One who failed to do so was subject to the same penalties and forfeitures as a delinquent taxpayer.

An Early September Frost.—It was necessary, of course, to replant the corn, and seed was scarce. The little grain that had been set aside until the roasting-ear season arrived was planted. There was little or no bread that summer.

As the result of the late replanting, the corn had not matured in early September when there came a killing frost. It froze the corn, which had not passed the roasting-ear stage. When dry, the grains were withered and black. Corn-pone and mush made from the meal were hardly fit to eat, but there was no good corn to be obtained elsewhere.

A Cold Winter.—To make matters worse, the winter of 1807-08 was one of the most severe ever known in Ohio. It was not only cold, but there was a deep snow. Colonel Sarchet says that, when a boy, he heard his uncle tell how they had two ways to keep warm. One was to chop and carry in wood to keep the fires going day and night; the other was to carry water from the distant springs to throw on the cabins to keep them from burning up. The situation was not altogether desperate. They had been able to raise a few potatoes and some turnips and cabbage. In one respect, the cold winter was a blessing. The squirrels that remained here after the main horde passed on nearly all perished with hunger. The following season was a normal one.

We of today may complain a good deal, but in at least one year of the past, things were about as bad in Guernsey County as they now are.

SOME CHRONOLOGICAL COUNTY HISTORY

A Challenge — The Oldest Apple Tree

[Originally published 7/15/1947]

Guernsey County believes it has the oldest apple tree in Ohio. To the end that it may be shown that it is wrong in its belief, if such be the case, it hereby challenges any or all other counties in the state to show an older one. The proof of all claims must be based upon authentic evidence and not something traditional.

140 Years Old.—Our entry in the contest was transplanted from Virginia to what is now Guernsey County in 1807, and has thus attained the remarkable age (for an apple tree) of 140 years. In fact, it is really older than that, as it was two or three years old before the transplanting.

It was in February, 1807, that Sarah Marling Oldham, a young bride, rode horseback from far-away Virginia to what is now Guernsey County, carrying in her hand a little switch, the sprout of an apple tree, which her father pulled up and handed her as she was leaving home, saying as he did so, "Sarah, the mare you are on may need a little touching up; use this as a riding stick."

Photo by S. W. Obenour, Jr., of Zanesville Times-Signal

"IN THE SHADE OF THE OLD APPLE TREE"

On her arrival here, she noticed some rootlets attached to the switch. There were then no apple trees in this part of the country. Hoping that it might grow, she stuck the switch in the ground below the cabin her husband, Isaac Oldham, had prepared for her. It may have been the first apple tree ever planted in Guernsey County. And it did grow, and has produced apples for six generations of Oldhams.

Near Cambridge State Hospital.—The cabin home was located on the farm that is now the site of the Cambridge State Hospital. At the time Isaac and Sarah Oldham located there, the country round about was a dense forest. The nearest white neighbor lived at Cambridge, which had been laid out the year before the coming of the Oldhams and consisted of only a few log cabins. Less than a mile northeast of the Oldhams was an Indian town whose inhabitants, with few exceptions, did not molest them.

When the cabin gave way for a substantial stone house (still standing), the apple tree, which had then been bearing fruit for several years, was not disturbed. Each year thereafter, it has borne its crop; there is no record to show that it has ever failed. At this time (July, 1947), there are apples on the tree.

Proof of Age.—Sarah Oldham died in 1869, at the age of eighty-six. Although that was more than three-fourths of a century ago, the tree was then more than sixty years old, and was attracting attention on account of its age.

Unquestionable proof of the tree's age was given the writer by Isaac J. Oldham a few years before his death in 1939, at the age of eighty-two. He was a grandson of Isaac and Sarah Oldham and was twelve years of age at the time of Sarah's death. He said that he had heard his grandmother relate the romantic story of the apple tree many times. She took pride in showing it to visitors and telling them about its great age. That was away back almost to Civil War days. And still the tree lives on!

Three Generations in Picture.—The children in the picture accompanying this article are Mary Ethel and Harry Edward Mason, great-great-great-grandchildren of Sarah Oldham. The man is the father, Edgar O. Mason, great-great-grandson of Sarah; the woman is his mother, Mrs. Clara Oldham Mason, a great-granddaughter. Her father was Isaac J. Oldham, son of Marling Oldham, who was the son of Sarah. All six generations lived in the old stone house (not shown in the picture), sat "in the shade of the old apple tree," and enjoyed its fruit.

(For the romantic story of Isaac and Sarah Marling Oldham, their early life in the wilderness, and the history and description of the old apple tree, see "A Cambridge Township Pioneer," page 795 of the book.)

Where Cambridge Has Gone for Mail

[Originally published 6/12/1945]

Beginning on page 624 of the book is the history of the Cambridge post office from the beginning to the present time. Postmasters are named in order, and the growth of the office and the improvements made from time to time in its service are shown. Not included in the article are the several locations of the office in the past. It is the purpose of this sidelight to tell where they were.

In 1807, Cambridge, then a year old, was granted a post office. Occasional letters had been received here before that time, brought in at first by travelers passing through on Zane's Trace, and later by a postboy who left mail at the taverns along the way where it was called for, the addressees paying the postage which was based upon the distance it had been carried. For a long time after it had been established, the Cambridge office served a territory about equal in area to that of today. But there were no rural carriers; folks had to come get their mail, or send for it. Files of old Cambridge papers—from 1824 and on—show that lists of letters in the office were published each week. One always knew when it was worthwhile to go to the post office. The announcement was a matter of general interest. Somebody was getting a letter from somebody, and there would be much speculation in the community as to whom it was from and what news it might bring.

The first postmaster was Cyrus P. Beatty, appointed by President Thomas Jefferson. He opened the office in a room in the house of his father, John Beatty, that stood on the north side of Wheeling Avenue, between Sixth and Seventh Streets, site of the M&K store. Here it remained until 1812, when Cyrus P. Beatty went to war, and was succeeded as postmaster by George Metcalf who took the office down the street to his tavern, site of the A. Simon drugstore. Beatty and Metcalf were the only appointed postmasters between 1807 and 1829 when Andrew Jackson became President. Jackson advocated and practiced "rotation in office." Post offices were for Democrats only, and George Metcalf couldn't qualify. Jacob Shaffner, who had a store where the Central National Bank building now stands, was a deserving Democrat, and he got the appointment, the salary being $219 a year. Five years later (1834), Shaffner resigned and was succeeded by William M. Ferguson who moved the office across the street to a little frame building that stood where the Firestone store is now located. Here it remained for about seven years.

When William H. Harrison became President in 1841, there was a change in postmasters, likewise in locations. Presumably, the owner of the building—now the Firestone site—was a Democrat, and the office had to be taken to one belonging to a Whig. This was found a short distance down the street, the site of Potter-Davis building. Three years later, with a year yet to go on the Harrison-Tyler administration, for some reason not now known, it was moved up to Peter Ogier's drugstore between Eighth and Ninth Streets, site of Commonwealth Loan. Then came Polk, another Democrat, and upon the appointment of a member of that party in 1845, the post office was taken down to a house that stood where the Grant store is now located. There it remained for two or three years, and then was moved back to where it started forty years before—the Beatty place.

The Whigs came into power again in 1849, and back up to Peter Ogier's drugstore went the office. Peter was a good Whig, ever ready to come to the aid of the party. In 1853, the Democrats were again in control, and down to the Beatty place the office was taken for the third time. We don't know who controlled that property then; it must have been a

Democrat, for the Beattys were Whigs. About the year 1860, it was moved up the street, same side, present location of the lower Kresge store.

Abraham Lincoln became President in 1861, and a Republican got the post office. He moved it to an old brick residence that stood where the Berwick Hotel now stands, and here it was kept until 1869. During Grant's first term (1869-73), C. L. Madison was postmaster, and for the third time, mail was handed out at the Peter Ogier stand. For the next 12 years—during Grant's second term and the administrations of Hayes, Garfield, and Arthur—David D. Taylor was postmaster, and the office was in the Taylor Block, between Sixth and Seventh Streets, north side. Here it was continued through the next 12 years, during eight of which the Presidents were Democrats.

Directly across the street from the Beatty place, the Odd Fellows completed their temple in 1897 with special rooms provided for a permanent home for the post office, and here it remained eighteen years. Then, in 1915, came the federal building, corner of Wheeling Avenue and South Tenth Street, the present location.

Cambridge has had a post office for 138 years. Before 1915, it was located above the courthouse three times, a total of nine years, always on the Peter Ogier lot. For nearly half the 138 years, it was located between Sixth and Seventh Streets. Never has it been off of Wheeling Avenue.

The Laughlin Bees

[Originally published 4/9/1945]

Guernsey County claims to have the oldest apple tree in Ohio. Brought from Virginia as a riding-switch in 1807 and planted within sight of the present Fletcher General Hospital, it still stands on the exact spot planted and is bearing apples at the age of 138 years (page 796 of the book).

Now we are going to claim the oldest hive of bees in Ohio. Strange to say, it bears exactly the same age as the old apple tree, as it was in the spring of 1807 that it came into captivity and today is producing honey. Of course, the bees in the hive are not 138 years old, but the occupants of the hive all these years have been the original swarm or their direct descendants. We can't liken this hive of bees to the proverbial Irishman's knife. Notwithstanding the fact that the knife had had two new handles and three new blades, he argued that it was the same old knife. Bees are animate, not inanimate like the parts of a knife, and their characteristics live on through the succeeding generations as the same colony.

One Sunday morning in the spring of 1807, John Laughlin who, with Deborah, his wife, had settled in the unbroken forest a short distance southwest of the present Lore City, after strolling around the little clearing he had made near his cabin home, sat down on a stump to rest. He noticed some wild bees gathering the sweet sap from maple trees he had recently cut, and he rightly surmised that they had a home not far away. He noted the direction they flew and, following the course, he soon located their place of abode, which was in a hollow tree.

In pioneer days, one would occasionally find a "bee tree," that is, a tree in which wild bees lived and stored honey. Such a discovery brought joy to the settler. There would be honey for the table—a change from the maple sugar and molasses—and perhaps the bees could be hived to supply sweet food for the future. Bears were especially fond of honey, and evidences of their futile attempts to reach it in a hollow tree often attracted the attention of the pioneer, who would usually succeed where the bear had failed.

A few days after locating the bees, John Laughlin felled the tree and, not having a hive in which to hive the bees, he cut the log off above and below the swarm, placed split boards over the ends of the section, carried it home, and set it up near the cabin. The bees seemed satisfied with their new environment, and each year they not only supplied the family with an abundance of honey, but sent out a colony for another hive.

Fourteen years after finding the bees, John and Deborah Laughlin moved into Center Township, two miles north of their original home, and they took the hive with them. Here the bees continued to supply the family with honey and send out a new swarm each year. There were eight children in the Laughlin family, to each of whom, when he or she married, a hive of bees from the original hive was given.

John Alexander Thompson, a grandson of John and Deborah Laughlin, located on a farm near that of his grandparents in Center Township, and came into possession of the bees. Interested in bee culture, he eventually had several hives, as he did not dispose of any of the swarms, in addition to the original colony. They were the wild black bees, somewhat belligerent in their nature. Regardless of Washington's admonition to keep clear of foreign entangling alliances, Thompson brought in some Italian queen bees, noted for their pacific tendencies, to rule over his savage colonies. In the course of time, a new type developed, but even down to the present day, the characteristics of the black strain predominate.

Today, the sons of John Alexander Thompson own their father's farm, located two and one-half miles northwest of Lore City, and James C. and Francis S. Thompson live upon it. While the Thompson Brothers specialize in Polled Hereford cattle, they are interested in bees as a sideline hobby, caring for fifteen hives. All of these sprang from the original swarm in the hollow tree 138 years ago, and at least one of them is as nearly the original as the Irishman's knife.

MORE STORIES OF GUERNSEY COUNTY

The Old Town Pump
[Originally published 4/23/1947]

One who passed up Wheeling Avenue back in the days of Zane's Trace or the early days of the National Road would notice a number of wells on each side of the street. These wells marked the location of taverns, and to the travelers through, no other sign was needed other than the name of the place.

Many Taverns in Early Days.—The heavy traffic on the highways necessitated many taverns. The westward movement of the pioneers, the stagecoaches going both ways, the Conestoga wagons eastward bound with farm products and westward with merchandise to be sold in stores, and the drovers with stock—all kept up a continuous line of travelers who would need meals and lodging along the way. Taverns sprang up like filling stations on the same highway today, and all did a good business.

For the accommodation of travelers, a well was found at nearly every tavern, and it was usually located in the most prominent place. In towns, this would be at the curb in front of the building—not in the rear. By being placed here, it would be convenient and would give notice to the world that here was a tavern.

The Old Pump.—The early pumps were homemade affairs, not especially artistic in design, but durable to a degree not surpassed by pumps today. An upright log hollowed out was attached to a wooden suction-pipe of smaller bore, that reached down into the water of the well. In the upper part was a piston rod with a leather "sucker." Valves were fashioned from leather. A handle and a spout having been added, the pump was ready for use.

In front of the pump was the log watering-trough where horses, oxen, and the stock of drovers were refreshed as they passed through. Fastened to the pump by a chain was a tin cup or gourd, for the use of the thirsty traveler.

Pumps Had Several Uses.—From Hawthorne's soliloquy of the Town Pump in McGuffey's Fifth Reader, one gets some notion of the services rendered by the old pump, aside from that of supplying water for the thirsty. It was the chief and most useful member of the fire department, when all water for extinguishing blazes had to be taken from wells. It served as the town crier by promulgating public notices tacked on its front. Sheriff sales, election notices, and announcements of public meetings were posted on the pump; in fact, it was the public bulletin board. Back in the days when kerosene was used to light the streets, it usually held a lantern over its head to keep pedestrians out of the gutter, who might be out late at night.

Wheeling Avenue Wells.—As late as Civil War days, there were not fewer than a dozen of the old wells along the sidewalks of Wheeling Avenue. Among the list of wells published in a local paper at that time was one in front of present A. Simon Drug Store, put there about the year 1806 by George Metcalf, proprietor of the Mansion House. At the Colonial Theater corner was another, that being the site of the Knowls, later the Holler, Tavern. Farther up the street, on the same side, where the Odd Fellows building now is, was the well in front of the Tingle Tavern. A little beyond, and on the opposite side of the street, present site of the J. C. Penney store, was the James B. Moore Tavern, afterwards the Eagle Hotel; there was a well here.

Although not a tavern corner, there was a well in front of the present Style Center, southeast corner of Wheeling Avenue and Seventh Street, put there by Shonfield Brothers to attract attention to their store. On the south side of Wheeling Avenue, between Eighth and Ninth Streets, was the Globe Inn, kept for a time by Andrew Metcalf, in front of which was a well. Across the street from this was the Hutchison Tavern, now the National Hotel. In front of this was one of the most popular wells of the town, dug in 1818.

Perhaps the last of the old wells to go, one that many of the older folks will recall, stood in front of the American House near the present post office. This well was dug in 1811, and it furnished water for the thirsty traveler for a full century. It once got into serious trouble, but not of its own fault. A traveler became ill east of town and stopped at the tavern for a drink of water, using the tin cup attached to the pump. It was learned afterwards that his sickness was smallpox, and the tin cup was so contaminated that persons drinking after him were affected by the germ, and an epidemic followed.

Wells Supplied Excellent Water.—The wells on Wheeling Avenue were dug to a depth of about forty feet. They were broad in diameter and walled with stone. Not only was there an inexhaustible supply of water in each, but it was of excellent quality. No doubt, each pump here would have fain repeated the words of Hawthorne's Town Pump in McGuffey's Reader:

"Drink, then, and be refreshed! The water is as pure and cold as when it slaked the thirst of the red hunter, and flowed beneath the aged bough, though now this gem of the wilderness is treasured under these hot stones, where no shadow falls, but from the brick buildings. But, still is this fountain the source of health, peace and happiness, and I behold with certainty and joy, the approach of the period when the virtues of cold water, too little valued since our father's days, will be fully appreciated and recognized by all."

MORE STORIES OF GUERNSEY COUNTY

The United States Hotel

[Originally published 1/18/1945]

For almost a century, a hotel stood on the site of the present Nicholson Building, East Wheeling Avenue. It was built when Guernsey County was a part of Muskingum, which was before 1810, and was torn away in 1897.

The first owner was Andrew Marshall, and he named it the United States Hotel, indicating that he was ready to receive guests from a wide area. When we consider that the westward movement had just then started, and emigrants from the eastern states were passing through on Zane's Trace to enter government land in the west, we can see that the name Marshall gave his hostelry was designed to catch the eye of the traveler.

To the east of the hotel, where the post office now stands, back of the post office, where the building used as the Service Center is located, and to the rear of the hotel itself was an open area. This was a part of the hotel property and was used by wagoners and drovers when they put up at the hotel overnight. Here they parked their wagons and penned and fed their stock. Wagoners with loads of farm products traveled east; with loads of merchandise, west. Drovers were invariably eastward bound.

There were two rooms in front with a hallway between. The west room, which had a wide wood fireplace, was the barroom. On its floor before the fireplace, when the hotel was crowded, as often was the case, the wagoners and drovers spread their robes and slept.

After the National Road was built, a number of stage companies operated their lines through Cambridge. One of the largest of these was the "Good Intent." This company changed horses at the Hutchison Tavern, which stood on the present site of the National Hotel. The company operating what was known as the "Old Line" made the United States Hotel its division point.

Marshall sold the hotel to Reuben Whittaker who some years later passed it on to Ebenezer Smith. William Ferguson was the landlord when the National Road was built through (1828). It was during this period that the place enjoyed its greatest prosperity.

In the winter of 1832-33 occurred an incident that caused the United States Hotel to be shunned for a long time. It was due to an epidemic of smallpox, the most dreaded disease of pioneer days. Means of inoculation were not then employed in this western country. Benjamin McNutt, who lived in Westland Township, was returning from a trip east where he had taken a load of farm products, when he became ill a short distance east of Cambridge. Unable to drive his team, he engaged a man to take him home. He stopped at the United States Hotel and asked for a drink of water, which Ferguson gave him in a tin cup. Upon reaching home, he went to bed and the neighbors round about called to see him. In a few days, it was discovered that his illness was smallpox. McNutt died from it, as did also the man who brought him home. The smallpox was soon raging in that community.

The cup from which McNutt drank at the hotel was contaminated. Ferguson and his entire family took the disease, but none of them died from it. The hotel business came to a standstill. Folks feared that smallpox germs might be clinging to the place, and it was a long time before the hotel regained normal patronage. One of the most popular landlords of the United States Hotel was John Woodrow who had charge before the National Road was built. He was in looks and demeanor an ideal tavernkeeper—portly and commanding, florid complexion, possessor of a shock of hair white as wool, and exceedingly congenial. At one time he managed the Bridge House down at the Wills Creek crossing; afterwards he was the keeper of the Endley Tavern at the Four Mile Hill.

In the palmy days of the National Road, the United States Hotel had much patronage. The coming of the railroad hurt the place, as it did most places along the highway in this section. This hotel passed from one management to another and finally underwent a change of name, to the Lofland House, by which name older citizens will remember it.

The First County Buildings

[Originally published 7/7/1947]

This is a sidelight on the stories, "The Old Court House" and "Guernsey County Jails," pages 64 and 81, respectively, in the book.

By an act of the state legislature on March 10, 1810, Guernsey County was formed from parts of Muskingum and Belmont, and on the same day, by the same body, Thomas B. Kirkpatrick, Jacob Gomber, and Robert Speer were appointed associate judges of the newly created county. The matter of choosing a seat of justice was left to a committee of three men named by the legislature. Cambridge wanted it, and so did Washington. The committee reported on April 20, 1810, that it had chosen Cambridge. It was influenced in making the choice, it is said, by the proposition of Jacob Gomber and Zaccheus Beatty that, if Cambridge were named, they would donate a site for the necessary public buildings; also, at their own expense, erect said buildings, ready for roof.

County Had No Funds.—In the forenoon of April 23, 1810, the three associate judges met at the Tingle Tavern and appointed the necessary county officers, the authority to do so being vested in them by law. In the afternoon of the same day, the three commissioners the judges had appointed—James Dillon, William Dement, and Absalom Martin met at the house of George Beymer to divide the county into townships, and consider means for raising funds for completing the public buildings after they would be turned over to them by Gomber and Beatty; also for meeting other county expenses. There was not a dollar in the county treasury.

The buildings Gomber and Beatty agreed to erect (in part, only) were a courthouse and a jail. There are no records to show whether they bore the entire expense themselves, or whether they just guaranteed it, depending upon subscriptions by others. If the latter, it was the first money-raising campaign in Guernsey County. We are apt to think, however, that they contributed all or most of it, as they would benefit from the sale of lots.

The Courthouse.—From the first records of the county commissioners, on file in the auditor's office, we are enabled to learn much about this first courthouse and its cost to the county. There is nothing to show what the part contributed by Gomber and Beatty (foundation and walls) cost them.

The building stood on the exact site of the present courthouse. It was a brick structure, forty feet square and two stories in height. On December 11, 1810, Gomber and Beatty reported that they had fulfilled their pledge; the building was now ready for roof. There remained the work of putting on a roof, erecting a tower and spire, and finishing the interior.

For completing the building, which was mostly woodwork, Thomas McClary was given the contract at his bid of $3,299. The finishing lumber had to be dressed by hand, and it was eight years before all the work was done and the building accepted from McClary. In the meantime, the county offices were located in various places in town. McClary had orders to finish the courtroom first, and it was ready for occupancy in August, 1813. For three years, most of the court sessions had been held at the Tingle Tavern. The commissioners appropriated sixteen dollars for chairs for the new courtroom, and two dollars to purchase stationery and candles for use the first four terms of court.

Before accepting the building from Thomas McClary on August 8, 1818, the commissioners appointed William B. Powell, Daniel Hubert, and Alexander Jamison to make an inspection of it to the end that it might be determined whether or not the work had been done in accordance with the specifications. They reported deficiencies amounting to $128.62½, and McClary agreed to a deduction of that amount, thus making $3,170.37½ the cost to the county of the first courthouse.

Court Square Full of Stumps.—Before work on the courthouse was begun, the trees, mostly oak and poplar, were removed from the square. This left the ground covered with stumps. While they may have appeared unsightly, they served a useful purpose. The courtroom and the court square constituted the community center. There was no other meeting place, not even a church building, for many years after the courthouse was built. In winter, the various religious denominations were permitted to hold services in the courtroom. Here, too, were held conventions, political rallies, and meetings of all kinds. In summer, the yard would be used. (It is assumed that some of the trees were left standing for shade.) On such occasions, the stumps were used as seats. When religious services were held in the yard, they served as both pulpit and pew. Lorenzo Dow, the noted pioneer

Evangelist, on his visit to Cambridge in 1832, stood on a stump in front of the courthouse while preaching.

The commissioners' records show that George Metcalf was awarded the contract for digging a well "for use of courthouse and jail." The water was to be lifted by a windlass and bucket. The location of this well is unknown today; it may be the well on the east side of the present jail.

The Jail.—Of more immediate need than a courthouse was a county jail. As stated above, places for holding court and housing the county offices temporarily could be found in the town, but no place for confining criminals. The population of the county was more than three thousand, and somebody was likely to go wrong. There had to be a jail.

Plans and specifications were prepared, calling for a hewn-log, one-story building to be used as a prison and a home for the sheriff. There were to be two cells, one for criminals, and the other for debtors.

The contract for building the jail was let to Andrew Marshall on July 9, 1810, for $590, this being the lowest bid. It was conditioned that the work had to be completed by February 1, 1811. Before this date, Marshall agreed to add a second story for $124, provided the time for completion be extended. One-half of this additional cost was met by public subscription, the other half by the county.

This first jail was not erected on the site of the present one, but to the left and a little in front of the courthouse. It stood partly on what is now East Eighth Street. In 1836 came a new brick jail, built where the present one stands. Jacob Shaffner took the contract for the work, burning the brick on his lot east of the court square, where the Carnes building now stands. Stone from the abutments of the old Beatty toll bridge were used for the foundation.

The front of the jail was on the west side as it now is in the present jail. The three cells were on the east side, and there was a dungeon for the worst criminals. The cells for the debtors were on the second floor.

MORE STORIES OF GUERNSEY COUNTY

Linn's Mill

[Originally published 6/12/1947]

The remnants of a dam, an old millstone, and a fast-fading memory are all that is left of the old landmark pictured above. For three-quarters of a century, Linn's mill ground grain and sawed lumber, often running both day and night. It was widely known.

Many communities take their names from a mill, because in early days it was the community center. It was the place to which folks from all the country round about would come to get their grinding done. While waiting their turn, they would exchange news which would be carried back home. The mills are gone, but the community name hangs on. As an illustration of this, we call attention to three such communities in Jefferson Township—Linn's and Armstrong's in the valley of Salt Fork Creek, and McCleary's in that of Sugar Tree.

There was something fascinating about an old mill. The dam, the humming machinery, the dusty miller—all were objects of interest. Connected with most of them were legends of romances, crimes, ghosts, or happenings of some kind that were handed down from one generation to another.

The Linn Family.—This old mill and the community got their names, of course, from the Linn family, one of the outstanding pioneer families of Guernsey County. In preparing to write this story, we gathered some conflicting data. From courthouse and war department records, and some handed-down traditions that seem to fit in, we have written and present the following, which we believe to be authentic.

Adam, the first of the Linns to settle here, came from Virginia in 1809 and entered Lot 18 in the southeastern part of what is now Jefferson Township. These lots of 100 acres each had been set apart by the government, when it made its survey, to be given away as a bonus to the soldiers of the Revolutionary War. Adam fought in the war, and it was probably the gift of a farm that had prompted him to come here.

Born in 1749, he entered the army in 1776 and served until the surrender at Yorktown in 1781. He fought in several of the principal battles, and according to the war records, he witnessed the execution of Major Andre.

Near the close of the war, he married Ann Hefelbower. Their eleven children were John, Joseph, George, Samuel, Aaron, Andrew F., Mary, Nancy, Sarah, Margaret, and Elizabeth. How many of these accompanied Adam and Ann to this section is not known.

On the farm he entered, through which passed Carpenter's trail (now the Steubenville Road), near the present Cross Road School, Adam opened a tavern, the first in Jefferson Township. He died in 1834, aged 85, and his body lies in an unmarked Revolutionary soldier grave somewhere in that section. Ann was still living in 1841, in which year she was allowed a widow's pension.

George Linn.—George, one of the sons of Adam and Ann Linn, born in 1790, did not come here with his parents, but remained in Virginia to teach school. However, the call of the West brought him in 1813, and he settled on a farm of 200 acres adjoining that of his father. Not having been a Revolutionary soldier, he had to buy the land, paying $400 for it. After coming to Jefferson Township, George married Pamelia Matthews, who became the mother of his eight children, namely, Harriet, Cyrus, Adam, William, Caroline, Rebecca, George, and Augustus. The last named succeeded his father as owner of the farm.

Builds a Mill.—On Salt Fork Creek, near the mouth of Brushy Fork, both of which ran through his farm, George Linn built a mill in 1814, the first in Jefferson Township. Near the mill, he built a house, and there he lived until his death. On the site now stands the home of O. M. Tedrick. George was not the first occupant of this farm, for prior to the War of 1812, there was an Indian settlement at the mouth of Brushy Fork. (See page 21 of the book.) In terms of present-day directions, the mill and home were located a quarter of a mile below the Salt Fork bridge on Route 22.

After seventy-five years of grinding and sawing, the wheels of the old mill ceased to turn about fifty years ago. The mill was torn away, but evidences of the dam, which used to back the water up the stream for a mile, and the old millstone still remain. The picture shown above came to us through the courtesy of Paul Crossen. We don't know when it was taken, but we assume not recently, judging from the style of the feminine dress.

This was always a water mill; steam power was never employed here. The saw used was one of the old up-and-down kind; it was continued even after the circular saw came into use. To cut a board from a large log took from twenty to thirty minutes. In its operation of three-fourths of a century, there were but two millers—George Linn and his son Augustus, familiarly known as "Gus."

Linn's Grove Picnic.—There came to be many Linns in Jefferson and adjoining townships, most of them descendants of George. In the course of time, the families scattered, some to sections far away. About sixty years ago, in a beautiful grove on the farm George had settled, there was held a Linn reunion which proved to be a marked success. It was decided to make it an annual affair, not only for Linns and their connections, but for the public generally.

For some years, Linn's Grove Picnic was almost as well known as the Pennyroyal Reunion. The attendance often reached as many as five thousand people, and this was back in the horse-and-buggy days. Governors, members of Congress, and other famous persons appeared on the programs. For some reason we do not know, this popular institution ceased to function about thirty years ago.

The Capitol of Pennyroyaldom — Fairview

[Originally published 7/6/1945]

Hundreds of automobiles, buses, and trucks pass through the town each day, but only occasionally does one of them stop. Their occupants see one long street and a few scattering houses back, the street lined on each side with buildings, most of them flush with the sidewalks. Some of these are stately brick residences of an architectural style in vogue a century and more ago. To a passerby, it is but another of the old Pike towns, somewhat like many he has seen along the National Road in Eastern Ohio, Pennsylvania, and Maryland, if he has traveled that far. Living here, according to the last census, are 206 people. This is Fairview, Guernsey County, Ohio, so close to Belmont that a house or two straddle the boundary line.

Fairview's claim to distinction is based upon its being the capital of the Kingdom of Pennyroyaldom, a domain of uncertain boundary, but including all of Oxford Township, of which the word Pennyroyaldom has become synonymous. Within this township once flourished an industry which, it is said, was the greatest of its kind in the world—the distillation of pennyroyal oil. This was made possible because after the forests had been cleared away, this little aromatic herb of the mint family sprang up spontaneously, and some of the first settlers had knowledge of its medicinal value. They were acquainted with the process of extracting an oil from it that commanded a ready sale and a good price in eastern markets. In a short time, most of the farmers either had distilleries of their own or were producing pennyroyal to sell to those who had.

Crossing Pennyroyaldom from east to west was Zane's Trace, which later took the name of the old Wheeling Road. On this thoroughfare, as a convenient center for pennyroyal oil and other products of the surrounding country to be brought and loaded in Conestoga wagons for hauling over the mountains to eastern markets, James Gilliland laid out a town in 1814. He platted 60 lots, each four rods wide and ten rods deep, thirty on each side of the street. In after years, the street was extended by the addition of more lots. Gilliland apparently had not thought of a name for his town until one day it was suggested to him that he call it "Fairview," because he had located it on a high hill and from it one could have a fair view of almost all of Pennyroyaldom.

A quarter of a mile east of the town was Bradshaw's Tavern, and a short distance southwest was Wherry's. Both of these were convenient stopping places for the pioneers who were continuously moving westward to seek homes in the new country thrown open by the government for settlement. Jesse C. Weir and James and Martin Rosemond opened stores. John Duncan moved in and started a carding machine, which he operated by a horse-power tramping-wheel. He also built a log schoolhouse and taught youth of the community.

William Bernard, who came to Fairview twelve years after it was laid out, told at the first Pennyroyaldom Reunion that he found it to consist of a few log cabins, of which three were taverns. There was no church in the town, but on a hill a quarter of a mile southwest was a small stone church founded by Dr. Samuel Findley, a preacher of the Associate Reformed denomination. A little group of Methodists, he said, were meeting in Duncan's Schoolhouse for worship. Women were spinning and weaving cloth for the family clothing. There were approximately 150 people living in the town.

In 1828 came the National Road, and Fairview awakened to activity. The new highway passed down Main Street, but missed the taverns of Bradshaw and Wherry. The former, by means of rollers, was brought into town and became a noted hostelry on the old Pike, a favorite stopping-place of Henry Clay, but Wherry's was closed. The log cabins gave way to brick residences, some that were considered palaces in their day. Within a few years, the town had a population of more than 400, and in 1846, almost a century ago, it was incorporated. Then it believed itself to be of such importance and to hold such possibilities for a brilliant future as to justify its becoming a county seat town. A new county with territory cut from Belmont and Guernsey, to be called "Cumberland," was petitioned for, but denied by the state legislature. Perhaps the greatest event the town has ever known was the Harrison and Tyler political meeting in 1840 (page 133 of the book), addressed by Tom Corwin. An estimated crowd of 12,000 was in attendance.

Like other old Pike towns, Fairview's glory began to dim when a railroad was built through a few miles away. No longer did the gay stagecoach, the massive Conestoga wagon, and the great drove of stock pass through. The distillation of pennyroyal oil was continued for a time, and then that industry faded away. Only a few persons are left to tell how this work was done. Only in memory does Pennyroyaldom exist today, a memory, which, for two-thirds of a century has been kept fresh by the annual Pennyroyal Reunions.

Old Tavern Days

[Originally published 6/25/1947]

This is a sidelight on the story, "The Hutchison Tavern", page 547 of the book. We obtained some of the data here used from the notes of Col. C. P. B. Sarchet.

Tavern Opened in 1818.—On the present site of the National Hotel, Wyatt Hutchison opened a tavern in 1818. The ground occupied by the tavern and wagon-lot had a frontage of 132 feet on Wheeling Street and ran back to the alley, a distance of 198 feet. Although not the oldest, it was the most commodious and best-known house of entertainment in Cambridge. On the same site came in succession the Brown House, the Noel Hotel, and the National. It is one of the oldest hotel sites on the National Road, having been established ten years before the road was built through here.

Much Help Employed.—In the Hutchison days, many persons were given employment within and around the tavern. Much food was prepared in the open wood fireplaces in the great kitchen. Here, Fanny Hutchison, a sister of Wyatt, presided, her assistants being colored women. Fanny herself was a famous cook; her biscuits, fried ham, eggs and coffee were praised by all the regular travelers on the old Pike.

Hutchison's wife and Matilda, a widowed daughter, were the hostesses. Every guest was made to feel at home, and this added to the popularity of the place. Many famous persons were entertained here. (For names of some of the guests, see story in the book.)

In the tavern was a bar that was open day and night. Whiskey could be sold to anybody, man or boy, drunk or sober, without let or hindrance. Here, too, was a barber shop with which was connected a cigar stand.

There was much work to be done outside the tavern. John Hutchison, Wyatt's brother, was stable boss. Along toward evening each day, the wagoners would begin driving in, and the parking space would be filled. Their horses had to be stabled and fed. Some of the stage companies made Hutchison's a division point and fresh horses had to be ready when the coaches arrived.

The Barber Shop.—Old Moman Morgan (colored) ran the tavern barbershop. As most beards were left uncut and many men wore their hair long in those days, Morgan's business was not pressing. He employed some of his spare time assisting at the bar and waiting on the table when meals were served. Moman was also the sexton at the old graveyard. He took pride in the burial ground, and near the southwest corner, he set out a sycamore tree (still standing). One night, he and a man named Sothern had a fuss about something or other. Found dead after it was over, Moman was buried under his sycamore tree. Years afterwards, from the effect of erosion, a fractured skull was exposed at the shallow grave. A belated post mortem examination was held, and the cause of his death was determined.

Eli Marsh (colored) succeeded Morgan as the tavern barber. A colored boy named Asbury worked in the shop to learn the trade. At the cigar stand, the famous Wheeling stogies were sold, three for a cent. Asbury let some of the wagoners have four. When this unfair business practice was discovered by Marsh, he grabbed Asbury by the collar and gave him a kicking. "I'll larn you how to sell four seegars for a cent," he said, "underminin' the rest of the merchants. Mr. Craig and Mr. Beymer are all complainin' about it."

Tempy Mitchell.—One of the long-time Hutchison helpers was Temperance Mitchell, familiarly known as Tempy, who worked in the kitchen. She was the mother of two children, Delitha and Asbury. Delitha married Sol Kimmey, who was employed at the tavern to dress chickens and cut meat. Back of the tavern was the smokehouse where large quantities of pork and beef were stored, and of this, Sol had charge. After she married Sol, Delitha helped her mother wash dishes. Asbury worked as a porter and "bell boy."

Peter Jackson, who had been employed around some of the taverns out the Pike, came in to Cambridge and attached himself to Hutchison's as a sort of roustabout. Although getting somewhat advanced in age, Tempy accepted Pete's proposal of marriage. They left the tavern and set up a home of their own. Pete wouldn't work, and Tempy took in washings. He would come home drunk, smash the dishes and furniture, and make life miserable for Tempy. She one day gave him a dime out of her wash money and told him to go down to Craig's store for a hog's jowl. Pete spent the money at Beymer's for whiskey and came home drunk late that night.

"Peter, whar's that jowl?" asked Tempy.

"Dat dime you give me was a bogus," Pete replied. "Mr. Craig, he put it right in the stove; you'd better look out how youse send me to Mr. Craig's with spurius money!"

Tempy finally applied for legal separation, which was granted. She returned to her old place at Hutchison's, and ever afterwards considered herself a lady of quality, taking great delight in telling guests about her "dee-vose."

The Yard Hands.—Among John Hutchison's assistants about the barn were the Ransome and King boys from Washington. Black Thornton was the wood hauler, driving two black horses owned by Hutchison. Old Sam Grimes, Ned Simpson, and Sam Dickens were the woodchoppers. It took much wood to keep the fires going in the big, open fireplaces. Black's wife, Maria Theran, and Pink Morgan were the washwomen and scrubbers.

As famous as Hutchison's Tavern was, with its no lack of guests, with its bar that was open to the public generally and going full blast day and night, Hutchison failed to make a success of it financially. His helpers imposed upon him, carrying away flour, meat, groceries, and whiskey from the storage rooms to which they had access. He sold the place to Basil Brown in the late 1840s. It then became the Brown House.

Old Stone Houses (1)

[Originally published 12/18/1946]

Considering the abundance and variety of good building stone in Guernsey County, one may wonder why there are so few stone houses here. Although we have traversed every part of the county hundreds of times, we can, at this moment, call to mind but few homes that are built of stone. We might mention in this connection, too, that there are comparatively few brick houses in the rural districts, although good brick clay can be found almost anywhere.

Timber Was Used by the Pioneers.—The pioneer found stone, clay for brick, and plenty of timber of various kinds from which he could build his home when he came into the county. As a rule, he chose the timber, for of it he could build in shorter time and at less expense. In respect to material for providing shelter, Guernsey County has been highly favored. We know of no like area in the United States that possesses greater natural resource for building.

Some of the first purchasers of lots in Cambridge found enough timber growing upon them to build a home. We are speaking literally and not figuratively when we say that some could have built their houses out of their cellars; that is, they could have used the excavated clay in making brick. Good stone for homes could be found on many farms. The courthouse in Cambridge was built of stone quarried in Guernsey County, and a good grade of stone, too. Back of the courthouse is the jail, built of brick that were made from a deposit of clay nearby. At one time, around the court square were log and frame buildings, and the timber used in their construction grew within or very near the town.

Stone Houses near Cambridge.—But we started to write about stone houses. The other afternoon, Carl J. Rech and the writer visited the ones in Cambridge Township, north of the city, and here we find more of them than in any other part of the county. We inspected five stone houses, or rather four and the site of one that is no longer standing.

Three of the five houses were built by men who came from the Isle of Guernsey. Over there, most of the homes are stone, as that material is plentiful, and timber and clay suitable for brick are scarce. It is only natural that the folks from the Isle of Guernsey would think in terms of stone when ready to build a home here. The first of these to build a stone house in what is now Guernsey County was Thomas Ogier, who came in 1808 and entered 160 acres of land a short distance north of the present site of Northwood cemetery. The stone home he built was torn away several years ago.

On the Isle of Guernsey, Thomas Ogier lived in a famous stone house (still standing), called Les Duvaux. He unintentionally killed a Russian soldier who was stealing his apples, and, frightened, he fled from home, carrying the family cradle (now in Cambridge) with him. He eventually reached Cambridge in his wanderings, and erected the stone home referred to above, probably to remind him of his beloved Les Duvaux, which he was never to see again. (For the complete story of Thomas Ogier and the famous cradle, see page 42 of the book.)

The Oldham Stone House.—In writing about the Oldham stone house, we are repeating what we have told before, but since it is one of the five referred to in this story, we mention it again. Erected by Isaac Oldham in 1822, it stands on the tract of land entered by him before there was a Guernsey County. Upon this tract of 150 acres, which he purchased from the government, there is now located the Cambridge State Hospital.

Almost lone-handed, Oldham first built a log cabin and then went back to Virginia for his wife. Fifteen years later, as he had prospered and facilities for building were better, he quarried stone from the hill back of the cabin and erected a new home. This old stone house has been made famous by the old apple tree that is associated with it. (For the complete story and picture of this house and the old apple tree, see page 795 of the book.)

(The history and description of the three other stone houses will be published tomorrow.)

MORE STORIES OF GUERNSEY COUNTY

Birmingham

[Originally published 12/23/1946]

Were you ever in Birmingham? To reach there from Cambridge, turn to the right from Route 21 at North Salem, and proceed eastwardly on Route 271 for eight or ten miles; or, turn to the left from Route 22 at Winterset and follow Route 16 north for five miles; or, turn to the right from Route 21, near Fish Basket, and follow the old Birmingham Road (Route 4) to Route 271, two miles east of North Salem. If these directions are not sufficiently plain, inquire of Pres, Orin, or Jim Johnston; they are products of this Monroe Township metropolis.

An Old Town.—Platted in 1826 by William Carson, Birmingham is 120 years old. Carson named it New Birmingham, but for an obvious reason the qualifying adjective was dropped long ago. We don't know what prompted him to plat a town on his farm, unless it was to attract attention to a mill he was operating there on Clear Fork Creek. He laid off thirty lots, each 3.64 rods wide and 9 rods deep, and offered them for sale at ten dollars per lot. The following were amongst the first purchasers of lots: George Anderson, Robert Adair, Henry Booker, Leonard Baum, Jonathan Cunnard, George Cresswell, Leonard Dallas, Henry Dixon, C. Fletcher, Jacob Hague, David M. Hill, Joseph Hill, John Johnston, Matthew Johnston, Joseph Morrison, Joseph McDaniel, Finley McGrew, Mary McConnell, William Rosamond, Martin Rosamond, Elizabeth Robinson, and J. M. Snyder.

Known As Brantown.—Operating the only grist-mill in that section, Carson enjoyed a wide patronage, and he took advantage of this lack of competition. According to an old record, for grinding one's wheat, he took half the flour, all the bran, and charged twelve and one-half cents a bushel in addition. Folks had to stand for it, or get no grinding done; they got to calling the place "Brantown."

As there was neither a post office nor free rural delivery, the citizens of the town had to go over to Washington (ten miles away) for their mail. After some years, they made application for a post office of their own. The government granted it, but declined to name it New Birmingham as there was already one with a similar name in Ohio. Honoring Jesse Milner, the first settler in that community, they called it Milnersville. With the coming of free rural delivery, the office was closed and the name changed back to Birmingham.

The Town in the 1870s.—Let's take a look at Birmingham in the 1870s; the place is a half century old. Main Street has been extended to the east by the addition of more lots, and running north and south is Cross Street. The population is 210. Among the family names in the town directory, we noted the following: Anderson, Boyd, Branniger, Browning, Carson, Clark, Dye, Dougherty, Edenburn, Engle, Foy, Grimsley, Grey, Hill, Hague, Hughes, Johnston, Keepers, Kimble, Little, Morris, Meredith, Moore, Mills, Price, Richards, Stephens, Tedrick, Vance, Willis, and Whitaker.

C. H. Price is a physician; Boyd and Johnston have a drug store; Thomas Foy has a general store; J. Vansickel is a carriage and wagon maker; and William Whitaker keeps a tavern. R. V. Dougherty makes and sells furniture, specializing in coffins. He is also the village undertaker. On the occasion of a death in early days, a cabinetmaker was called; he would measure the deceased, make the coffin, and take charge of the funeral. Cabinet making and undertaking went hand in hand.

As we walk up Main Street, we note a Masonic temple and are told that there is a strong Masonic lodge here. Down at the lower end of town, we see an industrial plant of some kind, and upon visiting it we are surprised to learn that it is an organ factory under the management of Dougherty and Son. We learn, too, that the Birmingham organ is being installed in many of the homes of that part of the county. Then there's the Birmingham Brass Band, led by W. W. McClelland, with a reputation in musical circles that is enviable.

We call at the municipal building and are there told by the Honorable Mayor that Birmingham is no longer a crossroads town, but is now a duly organized municipality. He says there was a bitter controversy when the matter of incorporation was being considered. A petition for incorporation, signed by thirty-nine electors, was presented to the commissioners. A remonstrance, signed by sixteen electors, followed, the objection being that the petitioners were not considering the future consequences or impropriety of having such a small village incorporated. Regardless of the remonstrance, Birmingham was incorporated December 10, 1874.

As It Now Is.—Accompanied by Carl J. Rech, we went over to Birmingham the other day to inspect an old stone house that any person who passes through the town is sure to notice. It is owned and occupied by Mr. and Mrs. William F. Tedrick. The first owner was Levi Branniger, a mason, who built strong and sure, as it was to be his home. The walls, twenty inches thick, are a good grade of sandstone that were quarried nearby. Within are six large rooms, originally heated from wide wood fireplaces. Its age is unknown, but claim is made that it is one of the oldest houses in Birmingham. For many years, it was the home of Dr. W. B. Rosamond, who practiced medicine there for almost half a century. On the occasion of our first visit to Birmingham many years ago, we met the old doctor, and for a full hour he discussed the community and a philosophy of life that apparently was peculiarly his own. We may get around to writing a story about him someday.

On our visit the other day, we missed our aged friend, Samuel Hazlett, the long-time village blacksmith, from whom we used to gather early-day history; his death occurred a year or two ago. However, Mr. Tedrick helped us make a brief survey of the town as it is now. The population is exactly sixty-seven (67). Three houses are now being torn away, and four others have been removed within the last three years. The business interests are represented by one store and one garage. The once-flourishing school has but one teacher, and some of the pupils are hauled in from the outside. For the spiritual welfare of the small population, two churches are yet supported; there used to be four.

The old mill is gone, as is also the old millpond, which was a quarter of a mile long and half as wide. One refreshing reminder of the old days still stands—the town pump, with its abundance of shade on the public square, and its water is just as good as ever.

The Stone Bridges

[Originally published 6/7/1946]

Many stone bridges were built on the National Road when it was run through Eastern Ohio in the latter 1820s. In Guernsey County were a half dozen or more, for a stream too large for a culvert was spanned by a stone bridge.

Wills Creek an Exception.—There was one exception—Wills Creek at Cambridge. Across it, a covered wooden bridge was erected because, on account of its width, a stone structure would have been too expensive. We recently discovered some old records, from which we learned that this historic bridge cost approximately $25,000. A century later, it was replaced by the present Viaduct at a total expenditure of $200,000.00. (For description and history of the old covered bridge, see page 203 of the book.)

SOME CHRONOLOGICAL COUNTY HISTORY

The Crooked Creek Bridge.—Next to Wills Creek, the two largest streams crossed by the National Road in Guernsey County are Salt Fork west of Middlebourne, and Crooked Creek west of Cambridge. Both were spanned by what is known as the "S" type of stone bridges. The bridges across the smaller streams were built straight. Neither the Salt Fork nor the Crooked Creek bridge is now on the National Road. When the highway was straightened a few years ago, they were left to one side, but not removed, and today they stand as monuments to the hardy pioneer bridge-builders of a century and a quarter ago.

Although the Crooked Creek bridge is not straight, it can hardly be called an "S" bridge. The fact that it has a turn in it made it a dangerous crossing, even in the days before the automobile. It was the scene of the first recorded accident on the National Road in Ohio (page 236 of the book).

The Salt Fork Bridge.—The Salt Fork bridge, on the E. B. Wallace farm, two miles west of Middlebourne, is perhaps the best example of an "S" bridge now to be seen along the National Road. There used to be a more unique one than this just over the line from Guernsey County, near Hendrysburg. The twists and turns in it attracted the attention of every passerby. To make the crossing safe for automobiles, it has been replaced by another kind of bridge, much to the regret of many who, for sentimental reasons, wished it to remain.

A Wheeling artist who sketched the Salt Fork bridge wrote recently that she will exhibit the picture at an art show to be held in that city. She is expected to remain with the picture during the exhibit, she says, to answer questions that will be asked. To be prepared, she desired more information than she possessed, and asked the following:

When was the bridge built?
Who built it?
What did it cost?
Why built in such a shape?

Unfortunately, we were unable to answer definitely any one of these questions. The contracts for building the National Road from Fairview to three miles west of Cambridge were let September 11, 1826, and the work on this part was completed in 1828. From this, it would seem that the Salt Fork bridge was erected about the year 1827.

On the stretch of road mentioned above, Jonathan Knight was appointed supervisor by the United States government, and it was doubtless he who directed the construction of all the bridges. On a tablet at the end of the old covered bridge at Cambridge was a statement that J. P. Shannon was the undertaker; L. V. Wernwag, architect; and J. Kinkead, the mason. It is probable that these men also built the stone bridges in the county.

We find no record of the cost of the Salt Fork bridge. As it was built entirely of stone quarried from the hillside nearby, the material cost nothing;

the only expense was for labor. A mason received sixty-two and one-half cents a day, and worked from sunup to sunset.

Why an "S" Bridge?.—This question has been asked hundreds of times, and many answers (all guesses) have been given. One of them—and it is most improbable, too—has been told so long and often that it comes to the mind first, was this: John McCartney, a stone bridge contractor, was drunk in the barroom of a tavern one night. He boasted that he could build a bridge of any shape any engineer could design. A National Road engineer happened to be in the barroom at the time, and hearing him say this, rapidly sketched a bridge that looked like the letter "S" and threw it across to McCartney, saying, "Let's see you build one like that." Not to be daunted, McCartney did build such a bridge. This gave him a reputation, and to show their skill, other contractors built bridges of shapes even more fantastic than this. They tried to outdo each other in artistic effect.

Another reason that has been given for building an "S" bridge is even less probable than the one above. Large trees would stand just where the bridge should cross the stream and it was easier to build around the trees than to remove them.

L. E. Carlisle, North Eighth Street, Cambridge, tells us that his grandmother kept a tavern a short distance from the Salt Fork bridge when it was built. When a boy, he often heard her tell why it was shaped like the letter "S". Coming west on high ground, the National Road would have plunged into a swamp after crossing the creek, if it kept straight ahead. To avoid the swamp, the contractors built a bridge that would turn the road to the left.

Another reason for "S" bridges was the belief of the engineers that they could withstand the force of floods better than straight ones. A study of the shape in relation to the course of the stream, even as it is today, would justify this view. It is our opinion that some were built as they were for one reason, and others for another. When the speed across them seldom exceeded eight or ten miles an hour, they were something to admire; with an automobile speed of sixty or seventy miles an hour, they became something to be feared. They had to go.

By making a detour a few rods to the north at Salt Fork Creek, a traveler on the National Road will cross the Salt Fork "S" bridge. It is one of the most curious relics of the famous highway that now extends from coast to coast. It should ever be preserved for its historical and architectural interest.

SOME CHRONOLOGICAL COUNTY HISTORY

Cost of the National Road

[Originally published 6/11/1946]

We are told that the project for improving the National Road in the western part of Guernsey County (from Cassell's Station to New Concord), a distance of approximately four miles, will cost a half million dollars, or $125,000 a mile. It will be financed by the federal government. This is thirty-seven times as much as it cost the federal government to build this same stretch of road 118 years ago.

Jonathan Knight Was Supervisor.—It was on September 11, 1826, that contracts were let for building the National Road (now Route 40) through Guernsey County, a distance of approximately 26 miles. The road entered the county from the east at Fairview, and was to continue west in as straight a line as practicable. Crossing the county from east to west, before this highway was constructed, was what was called the Old Wheeling Road, which was the successor of Zane's Trace. Its course was by no means straight, and the survey for the National Road deviated from it three or four miles in some places.

To supervise the work in Guernsey County, the United States government appointed Jonathan Knight. One of his associates was the youthful Joseph E. Johnston who afterwards became the famous Confederate general. Instead of one contract for the entire distance across the county, sections of about a mile each in length were let separately to the lowest responsible or competent bidders.

Width of 80 Feet Required.—While detailed specifications relative to grades, culverts, bridges, etc., were included in each contract, the following general requirements were common to all: First, the road had to be 80 feet wide. Farmers through whose lands it was to pass were so elated that they either donated right-of-way or asked but a nominal amount for it. In the course of time, many of them encroached upon the road, in some places crowding their fences in ten or more feet. They even placed buildings within the original limits of the highway. When asked to remove them many years later, for road adjustments or some other purpose, they either refused or demanded damages. The road had been turned over to the state, and what had it to show that it was entitled to a right-of-way 80 feet wide? There was nothing because, apparently deeming it unnecessary, the government had not recorded the deeds; at any rate, we have been unable to find any such in the Guernsey County courthouse. So many controversies arose in the state as to the location and width of the road that the General Assembly passed the following law on April 18, 1870:

"The proper limits of the road are hereby defined to be a space of eighty feet in width—forty feet on each side of the center of the graded roadbed."—Laws of Ohio, Vol. LVIII, p. 140.

Other General Requirements.—The survey established the central axis of the roadbed, and all trees and growth had to be entirely cleared away for 40 feet on each side of it. To a distance of 20 feet on each side of the axis, all stumps and roots had to be grubbed out. The roadbed had to be covered with stone to a depth of six inches, composed of particles of not more than four ounces in weight. The stone was broken by hand. The best quality of limestone was demanded, and bidders were required to submit samples of the material they would use. All along the route through Guernsey County was plenty of stone, which probably cost the contractors nothing.

The contractor of that day had no steam shovels, no stone crushers, no motor-trucks. Horses, oxen, and men furnished the power, and the equipment consisted chiefly of plows, mattocks, and shovels. Laborers were paid sixty-two and one-half cents a day, working from sunup to sunset. Each was given three "jiggers" of whiskey a day, if he was a drinker.

For the greater part, the contractors were men who followed the building of the road as it moved westward. While some of the laborers were of the same class, the majority were farmers who lived along the way. Here was afforded an opportunity to earn some real money, something that was scarce because there was little local market for their farm products, and the lack of a good road made it almost impossible to move them elsewhere. For their labor and the use of their teams, they received money to pay for the land, which they had purchased from the government; thus, some of the money paid for building the road went back to the United States Treasury.

Cost Was $3400 a Mile.—Work on the National Road began at Cumberland, Maryland, in 1808, and extended westward to Wheeling, which it reached in 1818. This division was known as the Old Cumberland Road. It had to be carried over the mountains, a stupendous undertaking. The average cost per mile from Cumberland to Wheeling was $13,000. Work on the 75 miles between Wheeling and Zanesville began in 1825, and was completed at an average cost of $3,400 per mile, which included culverts, bridges—everything.

Why a Cumberland

[Originally published 12/29/1944]

Cumberland, the only town in Spencer Township, once had a rival in the same political subdivision that might have outstripped it, had the proprietor of the latter worked as hard for its development as he who founded the former worked to develop his town. In fact, the site of the rival was a better one than that of Cumberland, and it had eight years the start of the town that eventually forced it off the map.

Among the first settlers of what is now Spencer Township was Col. Thomas Bay who arrived there in 1812. He entered government land and purchased more from the settlers who had preceded him; eventually he was the owner of a very large farm which was divided amongst his sons.

Benjamin, one of the sons, came into possession of 160 acres about a mile northeast of the present Cumberland, afterwards known as the Young farm. On it was a fine site for a town, and, there being no town near in those days, he had one laid out by a Zanesville surveyor, on March 9, 1820. He gave it the name of Zealand. There were two leading streets—Main, running east and west, and Cambridge, running north and south. The streets were four rods and the alleys two rods wide. Fronting on the streets were 50 lots, each four rods wide and ten rods deep. Proud of his town, which was destined to be a metropolis, Benjamin sat down (figuratively speaking) and waited for folks to move in.

Benjamin Bay had a brother, James Bay, who owned 160 acres of land about a mile up the creek. From an old record that fell into our hands, we learned that the two brothers had a dispute over a business matter that led to a lawsuit. Following this, considerable coolness and not a little jealousy existed between them.

To be even with Benjamin, James decided that he, too, must have a town on his farm. It seemed foolish to start a town only a mile from Zealand, but James decided to take a chance. He sent over to Zanesville for the same surveyor who had platted Zealand. When he arrived, James explained to him that he wanted a town with two streets—Main, running north and south, and Cross, running at right angles to it. He wanted 32 lots, each four by ten rods.

Before the work began, according to the record we have referred to above, a little party was thrown in honor of the surveyor. Among the refreshments served was a generous supply of liquor, of which the surveyor imbibed freely. As a result of this, his head was apparently swimming when he consulted his compass, for instead of running Main Street north and south as Bay had instructed, he got it turned around to run nearly east and west. This took place on April 24, 1828.

James named his town Cumberland. He didn't sit down to wait for folks to move in, but on the very day the town was platted, he set out to sell lots. Mrs. Bay, who was as enterprising as her husband, built the first house in the town. Four years later, there were several homes and some business buildings in Cumberland. To give it a municipal rating—something that Zealand had never attained—Bay had it incorporated on February 11, 1832. Washington was the first Guernsey County town to be incorporated (1829), Cumberland the second, and Cambridge the third (1837).

In those days, two towns only a mile apart could not both prosper. Incorporated Cumberland now had the advantage. Zealand began to decline, and in 1835 it appealed to the common pleas court of Guernsey County for the vacation of the town and the return of its lots to farmland. It thus has become one of the county's lost towns.

MORE STORIES OF GUERNSEY COUNTY

McClary Row

[Originally published 6/20/1947]

Did you ever hear of McClary Row? Probably not, for "Mac" Burgess says he never did, and he has lived within a stone throw of it more than three-fourths of a century. It was a row of houses on what is now East Eighth Street, extending from the First Baptist Church to Brown Avenue.

For many years after Cambridge was platted, there was no East Eighth Street, and these houses stood flush with the public square, fronting the courthouse. They were built by Thomas McClary, and as there was no street by which their location could be designated, they were given the name of McClary Row, which was dropped when the street was established. "Mac" says he can't remember that far back.

Thomas McClary.—About the year the county was organized (1810), Thomas McClary, an Irishman, came to Cambridge. He bought two lots, 88 and 89, paying Jacob Gomber $100 for them. These lots had a combined frontage of 132 feet on Steubenville Street and extended back along the east side of the public square to the alley, a distance of 198 feet.

On the corner (present site of the First Baptist Church), he built a home for himself. South of this as far as the alley, he built a number of substantial one-room houses, each with a basement. In later years, some of these cottages had second stories added. As some of the best families of Cambridge occupied the houses in early days, the row was looked upon as an aristocratic section.

Made Furniture.—McClary was a woodworker, and in the first house south of his residence, he opened a cabinet shop. He made most of the furniture used in the early Cambridge homes. If anybody here today owns a piece of this, he may consider it a rare antique.

Soon after his arrival in Cambridge, the building of the old courthouse was begun, and McClary was given the contract for the woodwork. The wooden tower extended a distance of eighty-seven feet above the ground. At the top of the spire was a large wooden ball. It used to be told that when the courthouse was completed, McClary was so proud of his work that he indulged in an Irish spree, climbed to the top of the spire, and stood on his head on the ball.

School Held on McClary Row.—In a room in one of the houses on McClary Row, the village school was held. In one of his articles, Col. C. P. B. Sarchet wrote that he was a pupil there when he was eight or ten years old. The teacher was Richard Hatton, who afterwards edited The Guernsey Times. His son, Frank Hatton, was Postmaster General of the United States when Chester A. Arthur was President (page 758 of the book).

On Friday, October 30, 1836, William Henry Harrison visited Cambridge. He was a candidate for President the first time, and his visit was, of course, a great event. After school had opened that morning, Hatton announced that it would recess until one o'clock. Traveling west, Harrison arrived in a private coach at ten o'clock, was escorted to the courthouse where he made a short address and met the people, and then to the Hutchison Tavern (now the National Hotel) for dinner (page 521 of the book).

A number of prominent Whigs decided to accompany their candidate to Zanesville. Hatton was one of these, and when the pupils reassembled at one o'clock, as they had been bidden to do, he told them there would be no more school until Monday morning. This was joyful news to the youngsters, and they all rushed up to Wheeling Street, hurrahing for Harrison.

The coach Hatton was in upset on the Norwich hill, and several of its occupants were injured. Hatton was one of these, and he appeared at school the following Monday morning with a bunged eye and one of his arms in a sling.

The Two Old Cronies.—In a cabin across the street (site of the present William Scott home) lived John Ferguson, the Irish weaver, and McClary and he became cronies. (The Ferguson story was published last week.) Tom and John spent much of their spare time together, and frequently engaged in celebrations in the Irish way.

At the corner above Ferguson's cabin (site of the present McFarland home) was the blacksmith shop of William McCracken who had married Margaret, daughter of Thomas McClary, in 1812. Here were three craftsmen living in the same neighborhood. It's not probable that McCracken participated in the Irish celebrations, as he was the main pillar in the Associate Church (now the United Presbyterian). (For the story of William McCracken, see page 563 of the book.)

Only a Remnant Left.—One by one, the buildings on McClary Row have been torn away. The first to go was McClary's own residence, razed in 1874 for a place for the old First Baptist Church. The last was torn away only a few months ago, and on its site, the Telephone Company will soon erect a new home. The basement walls, showing the type of masonry of the days of McClary, have not been removed. They yet stand as the last remnant of McClary Row.

The Evolution of a Pioneer Home

[Originally published 2/4/1947]

This story is designed to show the type of homes in which many of our Guernsey County forefathers lived, and how, by virtue of the sterling character and strenuous efforts of their owners, these homes were gradually transformed as time and conditions advanced. It will also serve to illustrate the unlimited opportunities America had to offer to the most humble of its citizens.

MORE STORIES OF GUERNSEY COUNTY

Through the courtesy of John W. Oliver, we have received a genealogy of the Black and Oliver families, Guernsey County pioneers, prepared by Dr. J. G. Black, formerly a professor in the College of Wooster, and a grandson of Samuel Black and John Oliver, patriarchs of the families. For our story, we are using the Black family, supplementing the outline and comments in Dr. Black's booklet with some other data at hand.

Irish Immigrants.—Born in Ireland in 1785, Samuel Black married at the age of 29, and in the year 1828, with his wife and four children—John, David, William, and Jane—set sail for America. Being unseaworthy, the ship was barely able to make the voyage, and when it landed at Philadelphia seven weeks later, the joy of the Blacks in escaping a watery grave was unbounded. They made their way to Baltimore, where a relative lived who had preceded them to this country. Although practically penniless, Samuel was able to obtain work, and they managed to get along for the next two years.

Much talk came to Samuel's ears about the West and its wonderful opportunities. With his family, he succeeded in making his way over the mountains to Wheeling, where he and the two older boys found employment. The National Road had just been extended west of the Ohio River. Samuel heard that out this road, in Guernsey County, Ohio, government land was still for sale at $1.25 an acre, but to get it, one had to go to Zanesville, 75 miles away, where the land office was located. He walked the entire distance, paid $100.00 (all the money he had) for 80 acres, got his deed, and started home by way of the farm, which was located about three miles northwest of Washington in Center Township.

It was February, 1831. He found his 80 acres a solid forest into which he would not bring his family—now larger than when he landed in America—until some improvements had been made. He engaged a man, living not far away, to clear a half acre, plant it in potatoes, and build a log cabin for him. It was his intention to return a year later with the family. The home would be ready, and there would be plenty of potatoes, a staple in Irish diet.

The Cabin in the Woods.—In March, 1832, Samuel brought his family and their few household goods to the new home. A Wheeling wagoner was engaged for the purpose. They came out the National Road to a point three miles west of Washington, then traveled north a mile and a half through the forest, cutting the brush that the team might get through. When they reached the 80 acres, they found a half acre of cleared ground and a small cabin of rough logs, with only the earth as a floor, with no chimney, no door. Back of the cabin was a "potato hole" in which the crop of the preceding year had been buried. They had no team of their own, no cow, no hogs. Wolves, whose rendezvous was the famous "Wolf Den" nearby, howled around the cabin that first night. There were yet deer in the woods, and Indians occasionally passed by.

The cabin was soon made comfortable with a stone chimney and fireplace and a puncheon floor and door. Samuel and the boys set to work to clear more ground, and until a crop could be raised, they managed to live out of the "potato hole," some game they killed, and a little food sent in by neighbors. All the family worked from sunup to sundown. They lost track of time. One day, Mrs. Black went over to call on the Brattons, a mile west on Endley Run. She mentioned what the men folks back home were doing that day. "Do they work on the Sabbath?" she was asked. Having been told that the day was Sunday, she rushed back as fast as she could. The Blacks were very religious, and that the Lord might not be cheated of what was rightly His, there was no more work done for the next twenty-four hours.

The Second Home.—After some ground had been cleared, an orchard was planted. Samuel and the older boys got work on the National Road and earned money to buy a team and some stock. Not far away, school was opened in a little log house, and this the Black children attended a few weeks each year, learning to read, write, and cipher.

A better home was built a few yards north of the old. It was of log, too, but it provided more room for the growing family. In all, there came to be thirteen children, seven of whom lived to mature years. One of the little girls was kicked and killed by a horse.

The Third Home.—In the course of time, a still better home was desired. This time it was of hewed logs, located near the second, and to the Blacks a veritable mansion. On the lower floor were two rooms, a big bedroom, and another known as "the room." The latter was used as a living room and a kitchen. At the middle of the north side was a capacious outside stone chimney. In the fireplace hung a strong iron crane. This wood fireplace was used for heating the room, cooking the food, and helping the candles supply light in the long winter evenings. In the corner of the room was a stairway leading to the one big room on the second floor where the boys slept. On the east side was a porch with puncheon floor and a roof.

Down by the spring was a log springhouse, and through a trough in it, water was made to run to keep crocks of milk and butter cool. The old second cabin was used as a loom house. Here, the mother and older girls kept spinning wheel and loom going to provide cloth for the family's clothing. They had but little money. Practically everything they ate and wore came off the eighty acres, and their other needs were few. Living conditions, after all, are largely a relative matter.

The Black Family.—Now, you may be wondering, what became of this Irish immigrant family. Samuel lived to be 82 years of age, dying on his old farm of 80 acres in 1867. Margaret, his wife, lived to be 90, her death occurring in 1883. Both were buried in the cemetery at Washington.

As devout members of the Washington Presbyterian Church, they reared their children in that faith. For many years, their second son, David, was one of the deacons there. The children were encouraged to take advantage of every opportunity for acquiring an education, that the conditions of the family would permit.

We have stated above that seven of the thirteen children lived to be adults. One by one, they married and established homes of their own. John married Mary Stewart and eventually located in Wisconsin. David's wife was Elizabeth Oliver, daughter of a prominent farmer on the National Road west of Washington; one of their sons became a Presbyterian minister and later a professor of mathematics in the College of Wooster. William, the third son, studied medicine, married Susan Frame of the well-known Wills Township family of that name, and located in Liberty (now Kimbolton). His second wife was Maria Luccock. Two or three of his sons became attorneys, one of them the mayor of Columbus, Ohio, and a distinguished judge. Jane, the oldest daughter, became the wife of John Oliver, sister of David's wife.

It is not necessary to tell more about the Blacks to show how, from a most humble beginning in Guernsey County, a family with strength of character and indomitable determination achieved marked success in spite of what seems to have been the most adverse conditions. A few of the Black descendants are now living in Guernsey County, at least one in Cambridge, Mrs. Ellsworth Scott, 814 North 7th Street, a great-granddaughter of the pioneer Samuel and Margaret Black.

Old Stone Houses (2)

[Originally published 12/20/1946]

The Peter B. Sarchet House

Photo by Van De Mark

Standing on a high hill one mile north of the Cambridge State Hospital, and commanding an extensive view in every direction, is a stone house that, according to an inscription over the front door, was built in 1831. For a just appreciation of this old landmark, one must go visit it; not try to imagine what it is like from a distant view.

Built By Peter B. Sarchet.—Thomas Sarchet came from the Isle of Guernsey to Cambridge, arriving in August, 1806. On the lot now known as the Central Drug Store corner, he built a home in which he lived the rest of his life. Four months after coming here, he bought 160 acres of government land in what is now the northern part of Cambridge Township, receiving a deed signed by President Thomas Jefferson.

Two of Thomas Sarchet's sons were David and Peter B., aged respectively nine and six years when the family arrived here. When these two boys reached manhood, Thomas passed the farm over to them, David receiving the western part and Peter B., the eastern. Upon his part, each built a stone house. There was plenty of timber they could have used, but there was also good building stone close at hand, and they chose that because stone houses would remind them of their early home across the sea. For sentimental reasons, perhaps, they modeled the houses after ones that stood on the Isle of Guernsey.

Description of the House.—Since the two houses are similar and were built about the same time, we shall describe but one of them, that of Peter B. It is said that the construction was supervised by a preacher who was paid fifty cents a day. The masons received thirty-seven and one-half cents a day, just one-fifth of what a mason now charges for an hour's work.

We have been unable to learn who the preacher was, but think he may have been Rev. William Wallace, who was then pastor of the Cambridge Presbyterian Church. It was near this time that William McCracken built the brick house on Steubenville Avenue, between Eighth and Ninth Streets, now owned by William Scott. The Rev. Wallace, according to McCracken's old account book, was employed on the job as a mason.

From foundation to roof, the walls of the Peter B. Sarchet house are two feet thick. So carefully were the stone dressed, and so neatly were they fitted together that now, after 115 years, they remain as originally placed and show but little effect of weathering. The frame joists are massive, hewed from oak logs, on one side of which the bark yet remains. The interior is finished in black walnut and wild cherry, all hand-dressed.

Now the E. B. Smith Home.—For the past twenty-three years, this farm of ninety-three acres and the stone home have been owned and occupied by Mr. and Mrs. E. B. Smith. They have made changes in the interior of the house and have added modern conveniences, but in doing so, they have endeavored to retain many of the original features that give charm to the place.

The David Sarchet House.—On the western part of the 160 acres Thomas Sarchet purchased of the government was a strong spring from which salt water flowed. Salt was made from this, and wells were afterwards sunk nearby that automatically flowed salt water, forced out by the accumulated gas below. Here, in 1815, were established the Sarchet saltworks. (See page 53 of the book.) It was near the saltworks that David Sarchet built his stone house.

In the woods above his house, we found David Sarchet's grave. Pushing aside the briers that cover it, we read on a stone that he died in 1883, at the age of 86 years, 8 months, and 13 days; and that Mary, his wife, died in 1888, aged 65 years, 5 months, and 14 days.

David had four wives and was the father of fifteen children. In 1817, he married Hester Hill (no children); in 1826, Sarah Britten (2 children); in 1835, Jemima Dehart (3 children); in 1840, Mary Torode (10 children). (For the story of David Sarchet's early life, see page 803 of the book.)

The Reed Stone House.—Our next visit was to the Reed stone house on the Birmingham Road. Hugh Broom built it in 1832. Ellen, Hugh's granddaughter, married John Reed, and this couple owned and occupied the house for many years. It came to be known as the Reed house and is yet often referred to as such. Now the owner is W. R. Braden, whose father was Daniel E. Braden and whose mother was Maggie Reed, a daughter of John and Ellen (Broom) Reed. It is thus seen that W. R. (Reed) Braden is a great-great-grandson of Hugh Broom.

Like the Sarchet houses, this one has withstood the ravages of time and is yet in excellent condition. The outer walls, twenty-two inches in thickness, are sandstone quarried from the farm. The interior finish is oak and walnut.

An Underground Railroad Station.—Hugh Broom was an ardent abolitionist, and this home, in his day, was a station on the Underground Railroad (page 712 of the book). Fugitive slaves were secretly carried here from the station in Cambridge. At an opportune time, Broom would pass them on farther north. He was a Baptist preacher and organized some of the churches of that denomination in this section. At the time he built the stone house, he was the owner of 400 acres of land.

(The Johnston stone house on Rocky Fork Creek in Monroe Township will be described next.)

SOME CHRONOLOGICAL COUNTY HISTORY

Old Stone Houses (3)

[Originally published 12/21/1946]

The Johnston House

Photo by Van De Mark

Early in the last century, a young Irishman, John A. Johnston by name, set sail from his native island, and a few weeks later, he landed in New York. A short time before this, some of his neighbors had come to America, and they had written back some glowing accounts of this land of opportunity. They had located, they said, in a newly-opened part of the country, in Monroe Township, Guernsey County, Ohio, five hundred miles from the eastern shore.

John A. Comes to Irish Ridge.—Inspired by these letters, John A. decided to come here, too. With difficulty, he made his way from New York to Ohio, to the very place his former neighbors had written about. Located on a ridge near each other were such families as the Littles, Kimballs, Clarks, Hazletts, Orrs, Smiths, and Baushfords. They, of course, were Irish, too—so many of them that the place became known, and is still known, as Irish Ridge. (See page 940 of the book.)

Although a poor Irish boy, John A. was strong and ambitious, and he was determined to succeed. By hard work, he soon earned enough money to buy some government land, which cost very little in those days. As the land on the ridge had been entered, he chose a farm at the foot of the northern slope, on Rocky Fork Creek. The next thing he did was to marry Catherine Johnson (spelled without the "t", and no relation), and settle down in a log cabin on the tract he had purchased. There, a son was born; their only child, they named him John A., Jr.

A New Home Is Built.—John A., Sr., and Catherine prospered. From time to time, they added more acres to their farm. Then they decided to build a new home. In Ireland, most of the houses were of stone, and it may have been sentiment that prompted Johnston to build a stone house here. There was plenty of good building stone on the farm. However, timber was not lacking, had he chosen to build of that; in fact, there is yet enough timber on the farm to build a town.

From outward appearance, the house yet stands much the same as it was a century ago. It is the largest old stone house in Guernsey County, and it attracts the attention of every passerby.

Ten Large Rooms.—For a family of only three, John A. Johnston built on a big scale. On each side of a wide hall were three large rooms. The two rooms in the rear have been removed. On the second floor, there were four large rooms and a hall. Beneath the entire house, he provided a basement with a high ceiling.

The stone of the walls were so smoothly dressed and neatly laid that they now show but little effect of weathering. A peculiarity is the way the walls were laid. They are double, two feet thick, tied together at certain intervals with an air chamber between. This method of insulation was employed to the end that there might be dryness and conservation of heat. Most of the interior finish was white oak. In some of the rooms were wide fireplaces for burning wood.

Stone Outbuildings.—By 1840, Johnston's farm had been enlarged to comprise 400 acres (page 938 of the book), and for his tenant on it, he built a stone house, too. This building no longer stands. The barn and other outbuildings were of stone. Evidently John A. was stone-minded, notwithstanding the fact that down on the creek he operated a sawmill. There was a tannery on the farm a hundred years ago.

Politics and Religion.—Many of the Irish over that way were Democrats, but John A. Johnston was a Whig, becoming a Republican when that party was organized. He was so much opposed to slavery that he sympathized with the abolition movement, and his home was a station on the Underground Railroad. Many a runaway slave was secreted in this stone house until he could be passed on towards Canada.

In religion, John A. and Catherine were Methodist Protestants. They were numbered amongst the founders of the church of that denomination, known as Hopewell, which still stands on Irish Ridge. They were buried in this church cemetery.

Next Owner Was John A. Johnston, Jr.—After the death of John A. Johnston, Sr., his son, John A., who had married Jane B. Smith, became the owner of the farm. They were the parents of nine children, only one of whom is living, W. B. (Beverage), the fourth to be born. Now in his eighty-seventh year, he lives at 207 North Tenth Street, Cambridge.

During his long ownership of the farm, John A., Jr., added more land to it. After the death of Johnston, the place was purchased by T. V. Foster, and it now belongs to the Foster estate. Mr. and Mrs. Frank Miller live in the stone house.

This farm of 665 acres is probably the largest farm in Guernsey County. A part of it remains much the same as it was the day John A. Johnston entered it more than a century ago. Half of the place, perhaps, is in timber, mostly white oak and poplar.

One may reach this farm by turning to the east at North Salem on State Road 271, following it about five miles to the Clear Fork Baptist Church, and there turning to the northwest on No. 68, which is the Irish Ridge Road.

The First Library

[Originally published 3/14/1946]

(Sidelight to Story Page 495.)

An organization providing for a Guernsey County Library was effected February 11, 1832, with fifty members. In the story in the book, we make the statement that there are no records to show how extensive this library was, how long it was continued, or with what success.

First Annual Report.—Since the story in the book was written, we found a report of the library made at the end of the first year; also, a copy of the rules and regulations governing its operation. Another find we made was a report in 1844 (twelve years after the library was established). From the last report, it would appear that the library was on its way out.

This first library was not public, as is the one we have today. It was maintained for its members only, but any person in Guernsey County could become a member by paying four dollars a year if he lived in Cambridge, or three dollars if he lived in the country. During the first year, there were fifty members, or stockholders as they were called. Included amongst these were the leading men of the county. The president of the organization was our representative in Congress; the secretary, our county clerk of courts; and the treasurer, our county treasurer. The report shows that the second year started off with only forty members, indicating that enthusiasm was waning.

At the end of the first year, the total number of books in the library was 223, of which 92 of them were donated and 131 purchased. Contrast this with the library of today, which, on January 1, 1946, had 46,625 volumes, including its branches in various parts of the county.

Some Library Rules.—No person except a stockholder could take out a book, and he was permitted to take but one at a time unless he held more than one share of stock; then he might take out as many books as he held shares. A borrower could keep a book one week, and if he retained it longer, he must pay a fine of twenty-five cents; if retained excessively long, the fine was the cost of the book. Stockholders living outside of Cambridge were granted some special privileges.

No person could borrow the same book oftener than once in a six-month period. If he failed to finish it within the seven days, he had to wait six months before he could get it again. It may be that the strict rules were partly responsible for twenty percent of the members dropping out the first year.

While the library room was open to its members at all times, books were let out on Saturday afternoons only. The member could take a book from the shelf and read it there, but if he failed to return it to its proper place, he was subject to a fine of twenty-five cents. A few periodicals were received by mail. Any member could get it at the post office, but he must take it to the library to read it.

The following officers were chosen for the second year: James M. Bell, president; Moses Sarchet, secretary; John Hersh, treasurer; and Nicholas Bailhache, William W. Tracy, Robert B. Moore, John P. Beatty, and Peter B. Sarchet, directors.

Library in 1844.—By 1844, the library had grown to include 900 volumes. In making the report, The Guernsey Times says, "The library is not patronized is it should be." M. Gaston was president; M. Thompson, treasurer; J. M. Bell, librarian, and N. Evans and John Hersh were the directors. So far, we have been unable to find anything further about this pioneer library.

The "Coonskin Library".—The most famous pioneer library in Ohio was established in Ames Township, Athens County, in 1804. A group of settlers organized what they styled the "Western Library Association." There was no money with which to buy books. It was proposed that stockholders pay for their stock in the association with coon and bear skins. These would be taken to Boston by one of the members and there sold, and the amount of money received would be used in buying books.

Bear and coon hunts were engaged in by the pioneers. Thomas Ewing, then fifteen years of age, who became famous in Ohio history, told in after years that he contributed ten coonskins—his entire wealth at that time.

The skins were hauled to far-away Boston by Samuel Brown and sold for $73.50. With the money, fifty-one books were purchased and brought back. "They were unpacked and handled as jewels of great price." In the list were "Bacon's Essays," "Addison's Spectator," "Pope's Poems," "Plutarch s Lives," "Shakespeare's Works," and other books that are read too little today.

As most of the money invested in the books came from the sale of coonskins, the collection was referred to as the "Coonskin Library." Fortunately, the original books and the case that held them have been preserved and may now be seen in the Museum of the Ohio State Archaeological and Historical Society in Columbus.

Where Are the Cambridge Books?.—Have any of the 223 volumes of our original library survived the 114 years since it was established? If so, they should be brought together, placed in a case to themselves, and preserved. Such books will bear copyright dates prior to 1832, and most probably will be marked as belonging to the library. It is not likely that any of them will be schoolbooks. They will bear titles similar to those in the "Coonskin Library."

The Siamese Twins

[Originally published 3/12/1946]

"The ladies and gentlemen of Cambridge and its neighborhood are very respectfully acquainted that the
Siamese Twin Brothers
will be at Mr. Metcalf's hotel, in that Town, on Tuesday and Wednesday next, the 4th and 5th of December.

"The Twin Brothers are in their twenty-second year, in the enjoyment of excellent health and have caused much surprise in this country, as well as in Europe, from the extraordinary manner in which their bodies are joined together.

"The price of admission will be Twenty-five Cents.

"Their room will be open from 2 o'clock till 4 in the afternoon, and from 6 to 8 in the evening.

"Pamphlets containing an historical account, and a likeness of the Twins, can be had in their room only—price 12½ cts."

There came into our hands the other day a copy of The Guernsey Times of the date of November 30, 1832. In it was the announcement appearing above. Concerning the matter is the following editorial in the same paper:

"By reference to an advertisement in another column it will be seen that the citizens of Cambridge and its vicinity will in the course of a few days have an opportunity of witnessing an exhibition which has attracted the notice of the learned and curious in various parts of Europe and America. The Siamese Twins have visited principal capitals of both countries, and wherever they have appeared their case has been looked upon as one of the principal curiosities of the age."

Description.—Everybody has heard of the Siamese Twins, the brothers who were joined together, yet each had all the faculties of a distinct individual. Their bodies were united by a short, cartilaginous band stretching from the end of one breastbone to the same place in the opposite twin. The left side of one was joined to the right side of the other. An attempt to separate them would have proved fatal. Notwithstanding this handicap, they grew to be five feet and two inches in height, and could walk, run, and swim.

History.—Their names were Chang and Eng, sons of Chinese parents. They were born on April 5, 1811, on the bank of the Siam River in Southeastern Asia; hence the name by which they were known.

Robert Hunter, an American touring China in 1829—the year the boys were eighteen years old—had his attention called to them. Sensing their value as an exhibit, he brought them to America. After they had been shown throughout the United States, they were taken to Europe, and later brought back here again. Everywhere, they created a sensation. Not to have seen the Siamese Twins stamped one as having missed something in life.

In the course of time, they had been seen nearly everywhere in this country and gradually ceased to be as much of an attraction as at first. Their coming to Cambridge was doubtless over the National Road as the railroad was not built for more than twenty years afterwards. In fact, the National Road itself was only four years old when they were here.

After their exhibition days were over, the boys married sisters and settled on a farm in North Carolina. They afterwards located in Mt. Airy, a town in that state. Here, in 1874, when sixty-three years of age, one of them died; the death of the other followed in less than two hours.

The World's Best-Known Twins.—This has not been the only case of united twins. There have been others, but none so well known as the Siamese. They were advertised everywhere. Eventually the term, "Siamese Twins," began to be used in describing any two organic bodies—plant or animal—that were alike and joined together by nature. "Siamese" is an English word for doubleness. Webster also gives it to mean "to join in manner suggestive of Siamese Twins."

A Trip to Portugal

[Originally published 12/16/1944]

Carl Rech and the writer recently spent an afternoon sightseeing in Washington Township's only platted town. It is located 24 miles northeast of Cambridge, a short distance south of the Tuscarawas County line. Two important roads intersect at the public square—one is the old Cambridge-Birmingham-Westchester Road; the other, the road running between Cadiz and Coshocton, which was much used by wagoners and drovers in pioneer days.

Although equipped with atlases and a map of the town, we became somewhat confused when trying to find our way around. After studying our maps carefully, we felt certain that we must be near the town, and we approached the only house in sight to make inquiry. Our rap at the door was answered by a pleasant, gray-haired lady who invited us in. After we had introduced ourselves, she told us that she was Mrs. Crouch, widow of Frank

Crouch, and then awaited our mission.

"Can you tell us the road to Portugal, which must be nearby?" we asked.

"Tell you the road to what?" was the reply. "I have lived here for a great many years, and I never heard of such a place.

We again consulted our plans and specifications, and decided without question that we were on the very spot. Seated before the fire, we proceeded to relate some local history—all new to Mrs. Crouch—which was substantially as follows.

Back in 1812, Levi Engle and his wife, Drusilla, entered the farm now owned by Mrs. Crouch. Two roads, then little more than trails through the forest, intersected on the farm, and at this intersection—the present site of Mrs. Crouch's home—they built a cabin. Within a few years, other settlers arrived. Many of them dressed like Indians and wore moccasins. That section became known as Moccasin Ridge. Across Atkinson Run was another settlement known as Boot Ridge, because a newcomer there wore leather boots. Between the two communities, a bitter feud arose.

In 1833, Levi and Drusilla Engle decided to lay out a town on their farm, with a public square at the intersection of the two roads. They called their town Portugal. The plat and description are recorded in the courthouse at Cambridge. The principal streets were Cambridge Street and Cadiz Street, and there were numerous alleys. The lots were four rods wide and ten rods deep.

When we told Mrs. Crouch that she was living on the public square of what was once a budding metropolis, she was much surprised. "And just to think," she said, "I always thought I was living in the country."

Strange to say, we were lost in a town having but one house. Where were the people? "Is there a graveyard near?" we inquired of Mrs. Crouch. "Just around the bend of the road," was the reply. And there we went.

We found it on the west side of the highway, with no fence between. Unlike many country burial grounds, it was fairly free from weeds and briers. It was carpeted, however, with a matted growth of the ubiquitous dark-green myrtle, whose presence, wherever it may be, invariably occasions a sort of funereal emotion. Some 50 or 60 graves are marked with stones. One stone bore 1810 as the date of the death of the occupant of the grave. The most recent date we noted was 1876.

We at length found that for which we were searching; in fact, the object that prompted our trip to Portugal. Mr. R. W. Hinds, Uhrichsville, Ohio, had written us that he was reading "Stories of Guernsey County," and that in the story about the oldest men who had lived in the county, no mention was made of one buried in an old graveyard in the northern part of Washington Township. He had noticed an inscription on a stone in this graveyard one day when passing by, he wrote, and wished information concerning the aged man.

We didn't know about it, but there it was. Chiseled distinctly on a well-preserved slab was—

> *"GEORGE READ*
> *Born February 27, 1727*
> *Died February 16, 1836."*

He was born five years before George Washington and lived to be 109 years of age. Who was this George Read? We went back to ask Mrs. Crouch, but she could tell us nothing about him. A mile or two south of the graveyard lives S. A. (familiarly known as "Amzi") Smith, who is the local historian. We crossed over to inquire of him, but he was unable to enlighten us further.

Returning to Cambridge, we searched through the records in the courthouse. Here we found that George Read entered 156 acres immediately south of the Engle farm in 1824. The deed received by him was signed President John Q. Adams, the compensation, as stated on the record, being "For Military Service."

The Military Lands, of which nearly all of Guernsey County is a part, were set aside by the federal government to compensate Revolutionary soldiers who had not been paid for their services in the war. Was George Read a Revolutionary soldier? He was 48 years old when the war opened, and 54 when it closed.

Searching through the record of wills, we found that of George Read, drawn in April, 1836, six months before his death. Set forth in the document, as in most wills, was "Being of sound mind and full age." The latter part of the established qualification was probably not questioned, as he was then past 108 years old. All his property was left to his wife, Susannah, for her use during her lifetime. At her death, it was to be divided equally amongst their children.

We had reached the end. George Read, like Portugal itself, had passed out of the picture.

How Historical Records Are Lost

[Originally published 12/15/1944]

Much recorded history is destroyed through a lack of appreciation of its value on the part of some into whose hands it falls. In many old homes are historical records, musty with age. When the last member passes out, a new generation takes possession and, along with the general run of junk, burns old documents and books of inestimable value to the historian.

Mary Galloway, a maiden lady, aged 82, recently died at Quaker City. For many years, she had lived alone in a large brick house that is 102 years old. In clearing the home of its contents after her death, G. G. Hartley laid aside a number of books and documents that otherwise would have been destroyed, as he thought we might be interested in them. And we were interested.

First, there was a complete file of almanacs, beginning with 1856 and running into the 1890s. Each, of course, was designed to announce to suffering humanity that a remedy was available for the very ailment by which one was afflicted. Among the almanac titles, we noted the following: Jaynes, Ayers (Cherry Pectoral), Radway (Ready Relief), Farmers and Mechanics, Walker, McLean, Wright, Clark, Green, Hostetter (Bitters), Burdock, Seven Barks, and others. These almanacs, which barely escaped the flames, should be of special interest to collectors of such literature.

One of the rare, printed books was a copy of Kirkham's Grammar, published in 1828. It was from this book that Abraham Lincoln learned to use the English language correctly. When clerking in a store in New Salem, Illinois, he heard of a man, six miles away, who owned a copy of Kirkham's Grammar. Lincoln walked the six miles, borrowed the book, and mastered it in six weeks.

The Galloway family record was also rescued from the junk pile by Mr. Hartley. Mary was the daughter of John Galloway, born in 1821. He was the oldest son of Enoch Galloway, who was born in 1798 and died in 1864.

Enoch Galloway was one of the old pioneers of Millwood Township, settling on a farm of 119 acres, two miles northeast of Quaker City. Here he operated a mill and a distillery. He was married three times—to Esther Coles, to Sarah Perego, and to Maria Perego. According to the record, he was the father of seventeen children whose names follow: John, William, James, Henry, Isaac, Samuel, Caleb, Enoch, George, Sarah, Harriet, Catherine, Mary, Elizabeth, Nancy, Esther and Lucinda. We wonder how many descendants of the seventeen are living in Guernsey County today. Enoch was a Democrat and took an active part in behalf of his party in the "Hard Cider" campaign of 1840. In determining party adherence, political heredity has long been one of the strongest factors. Have the present-day descendants been true to the political faith of their fathers?

Of special interest to us was a book of more than a hundred pages filled with writing, entitled "Enoch Galloway, His Day Book for 1836, Bought of Martin Roseman, Fairview, Price 75 Cents." It seems that Enoch had dealings with many people, mostly with employees and patrons of his mill and distillery. We here present a few of the entries.

The first entry is as follows:

"On Aprile (pronounce with long "i") the 18th Cornelius Dillehay sat in to Work for Enoch Galloway at Five dollars per month. Washing, Mending & Making his Every day Clothing in to the bargain."

Cornelius was to be docked for every day he did not work. During the first few months, he lost the following days:

> *"one day to hollands frolic*
> *"half day to fairview for goods.*
> *"one and a half days hauling plank for Meting house*
> *"one day to Barnesville to the store*
> *"one day to George Andersons frolic*
> *"one day Moving Carrothers*
> *"one day after he Came home*
> *"one day to Mercers frolic"*

Enoch paid Cornelius in money and service; also for goods bought by the latter at stores and charged to Enoch. Some of the items follow:

> *"to making one pair of pantaloons ... 25 cents*
> *"to 2 yards of linsey ... 75 cents*
> *"to making one Rapper ... 18¾ cents*
> *"to one slate ... 31¼ cents*
> *"to one pen knife for John ... 37½ cents*
> *"to one razor ... 25 cents*

To show prices of that day, we present some items from other parts of the book.

> *"to three quarts of Whiskey ... 37½ cents*
> *"to one chicken ... 6¼ cents*
> *"to one day shearing sheep ... 50 cents*
> *"to 7 lb of lard ... 35 cents*
> *"to 6 lb of butter ... 48 cents*
> *"to one umberelle ... $1.75*
> *"to one pair of fine Shoos ... $2.12½"*

The Carlisle Cemetery

[Originally published 8/1/1946]

Announcement of the burial of Mrs. Ida Carlisle in the Carlisle Cemetery, Wednesday afternoon, prompts us to write a short story about this unique burial ground. It is located in Wills Township, on the north side of the National Road, about one-half mile east of the crooked stone bridge that crosses Salt Fork Creek. It was opened in 1841 and is thus 105 years old. It received its name from John Carlisle, a pioneer of that section, upon whose land it was laid out.

A Community Burial Ground.—The Carlisle Cemetery is neither a church nor a public burial ground, nor, in a true sense, can it be considered private. Most rural burial grounds lie near churches, and a rural church without an adjacent yard for its dead is rarely seen. The decadence of rural churches in recent times, resulting in their abandonment, and eventually the disappearance of the church building, has left many graveyards without the care that was given them in other days. There are many such in Guernsey County whose neglect is to be regretted.

John Carlisle.—Early in the last century, John Carlisle settled in the eastern part of Wills Township, on one of the largest and best-known farms in Guernsey County. The value of his land was enhanced by the coming of the National Road, which passed through it. While the family worshiped at the Methodist Episcopal Church at Middletown, there was no cemetery there, and conscious of the need of a burial ground in the community, Carlisle took it upon himself to provide one, not only for his own family, but for all others who might care for burial space within it. There were about two acres in the original grounds.

So many took advantage of the free burial privileges that in the course of time, the cemetery became well-filled with graves. It was recently enlarged by a strip of land taken from the E. B. Wallace farm adjacent to it on the west side. This was laid out in lots which are sold, instead of given away, as were the original, and the funds so derived are used in helping maintain the whole ground.

The Carlisle Section.—When laying out the cemetery, John Carlisle provided that the southwest part should be held in reserve for the members of the Carlisle family of that time and their descendants of the future. Lewis E. Carlisle, Cambridge, is a grandson of John Carlisle, and Mrs. E. B. Wallace, east of Washington, is a granddaughter.

Since, as we have stated, it is not a church cemetery, it receives no church support for its maintenance. Likewise, not being public ground, there are no public funds for it. In past years, members of the Carlisle and Moore families, Mrs. Wallace being a member of the latter, and some others whose relatives are buried there, have given it their care.

News Notes of 1843, 102 Years Ago Today

[Originally published 10/30/1945]

Cambridge Mails.—The "Great Mail" from the east arrives at 4½ P. M. (by stage on National Road); from the west at 9 P. M. "Steubenville Mail" arrives Tues., Thurs., and Sat. at 3½ P. M. (by postboy on Steubenville Road); departs Mon., Wed., and Fri. at 6½ a. m. "McConnelsville Mail" arrives Tues., and Fri. at 6 P. M.; departs Wed., and Sat. at 6½ A. M. "Paris Mail" arrives Sat. at 6 P. M.; departs Sun. at 6 A. M. (Paris was a town in Westland Township.) "Senecaville Mail" arrives on Thurs. at 9 A. M.

—ISAIAH McILYAR, Postmaster.

Lots For Sale.—On the Steubenville Road, in the northwest corner of Center Township, David Kinkead platted a town in 1842, which he called Centreville. A year later, he advertises lots for sale. The town, he states, is located on high ground, has a commanding view, is well watered, has two first-rate mills, is healthy, and is desirable for mechanics and merchants. All that is left today of Kinkead's town are two churches, a burial ground, and the community name of "Center."

The Mansion House.—Announcement is made of the reopening of the Mansion House under a new manager, G. W. Honn. This noted tavern stood on the north side of West Wheeling Avenue, site of the present Stoner Building. It was erected by George Metcalf in 1806, the year the town was laid out, and he was its proprietor until 1842, when it was leased to Mrs. Eliza Greer, a widow. She was succeeded a year later by Mr. Honn, who had previously kept the Globe Inn, a temperance tavern that stood where the Hoge Building is now located.

Brick House For Sale.—Lot 123 Steubenville Avenue, on which is a brick house, is offered for sale by N. Evans, trustee. He states in his advertisement that it must bring at least $1,500. This house, still standing, is known as the Estella McCartney home. Built by either Jacob Gomber or George Metcalf (page 556 of the book), it was purchased from the latter by Robert B. Moore in 1842 for $1,000. A year later, Moore placed it in the hands of Nathan Evans, an attorney, to sell. Andrew Moore, younger brother of Robert B., purchased it for $1,600. The wing on the north side was added afterwards.

Town Officers.—R. D. Salmon, mayor; Allan W. Beatty, recorder (old name for town clerk); John P. Tingle, Z. C. Suitt, John P. Beatty, Joseph Stoner, and M. Atkison, members of council.

Other Items.—Col. James Bay, of Cumberland, visiting in the West and looking for a place to settle, dies there.

Richard J. Clark was married to Miss Ann M., daughter of Gen. Simon Beymer, of Washington, by Rev. W. G. Keil.

Fairview Light Infantry, composed of some of the best citizens of that place, paraded here, neatly uniformed.

Eleanor Rogers, wife of Samuel Rogers of Millwood, dies at her home there at the age of 76.

Eli Marsh, the "fashionable hair dresser and shaver", now has his shop at the Hutchison Tavern.

J. W. Potwin and Company advertise for 100,000 pounds of pork, 1,000 bushels of dried peaches, 1,000 bushels of small white beans, 1,000 bushels of dried apples, 10,000 bushels of wheat, and 10,000 pounds of butter.

One Hundred Years Ago Today — October 22, 1845

[Originally published 10/22/1945]

If your Cambridge newspaper of one hundred years ago today (October 22, 1845) is not lying around handy, you need not look it up, for below is what you would read in it. The general news pertained mainly to the annexation of Texas and the impending war with Mexico.

Whig Candidates.—Thomas W. Tipton, representative; John Crooks, treasurer; John M. Bushfield, prosecuting attorney; Abraham Anderson, commissioner; Thomas B. Cochran, poor house director.

Petitions for New Counties.—Petitions to be presented to next Legislature to establish a county to be called Noble with county seat at Sarahsville, from parts of Guernsey, Monroe, Morgan, and Washington counties. Another petition for a county to be called Chester, with seat of justice at Westchester, to be composed of parts of Guernsey, Harrison, Tuscarawas, and Coshocton counties.

Real Estate for Sale.—Ichabod Grummond offers to sell, on very reasonable terms, his tavern and 40 acres of good land on the National Pike, five miles west of Cambridge. Good tavern, two good wells of water, and a run through the meadow. (See page 1032 of the book.)

Jonathan Bye, Jackson Township, offers his property for sale, consisting of mill, store, and land. (See page 820 of the book.)

Marriages.—Abraham Armstrong, Jefferson Township, to Miss Elizabeth W. Walker, by Rev. H. L. Forsythe.

Andrew Nelson to Miss Matilda Talbert, by Rev. J. Nichols, pastor of the Methodist Protestant Church.

Francis Bell to Miss Martha Blair, by J. Black, Esq.

Noah Hyatt to Miss Ellen Grimes, by A. W. Beatty, Esq.

John Riley to Miss Rebecca Agnew, both of Cumberland, by Rev. William Wallace, pastor of the Presbyterian Church.

Robert McConahey to Miss Mary Gillett, at Winchester, by Isaac Bonnell, Esq.

Circus In Town.—Herr Driesbach's show exhibited in Cambridge. In the parade at 10 o'clock, four elephants pulled the band wagon. There were 20 cages of animals drawn by 70 horses. Admission to the tent, which could accommodate 5,000 people, was 25 cents; children admitted for half price.

Advertisers.—Cowen and Grimes, Kennon and White, Evans and Rainey, attorneys; C. L. Madison, clock and watch repairer; M. Zahnizer, blacksmith; Noah Cook, saddles and harness; Samuel M. Oldham, tanning; Israel Green, druggist.

County Temperance Society Organized.—In accord with the temperance movement sweeping the country at that time, a follow-up of the Washington Movement (page 658 of the book), a county temperance society was organized with the following officers: A. W. Beatty, Cambridge, president; O. Withrow, Washington, Henry Shadwell, Senecaville, J. C. Weir, Fairview, J. C. Cunard, Birmingham, and M. Atkinson, Cambridge, vice presidents; H. Skinner, Washington, recording secretary; M. Sarchet, Cambridge, corresponding secretary; and N. Kennon, Cambridge, treasurer.

Petition For a Road.—Notice is hereby given to the trustees of Adams Township that at their session in October, 1845, a petition will be presented praying for a road to be laid out and established as follows: Commencing at a dogwood post on the east side of John Priaulx's land, thence eastward to a black oak, thence to a black walnut on George Gallup's land, thence eastward to a dogwood post intersecting the Coshocton Road on the Widow Gallup's land. (From the description here given, can anybody locate the road today?)

Deaths.—Mrs. Washington Henderson, aged 30, died at her home in Millwood Township. She was a niece of Gov. Wilson Shannon. James Knox, Adams Township, is dead, aged 51.

Cambridge Township Officers.—J. G. Metcalf, Joseph D. Tingle, and William Bell, trustees; Allen W. Beatty, clerk: W. W. Tracy, treasurer; Moses Sarchet, assessor; James Turner, George T. Bryar, and Samuel Bratton, constables.

Public Library Poorly Patronized.—A public library was opened in Cambridge in 1832 (page 495 of the book). It seems that thirteen years later, interest in it had begun to wane. The officers then were M. Gaston, president; N. Evans and John Hersh, directors; M. Thompson, treasurer; and J. M. Bell, librarian. According to the librarian's published report, it was not too well patronized. The 900 books were kept in the law office of J. M. Bell, and for their use, each patron was required to pay two dollars a year.

SOME CHRONOLOGICAL COUNTY HISTORY

One Hundred Years Ago Today — March 13, 1846

[Originally published 3/13/1946]

In 1846 (exactly 100 years ago this spring), Henry Howe, the Ohio historian, seated on Tunnel Hill southwest of town, drew the above picture. The population of Cambridge was approximately 1,000.

The old covered bridge is seen in the foreground. Winding down to it is the National Road. This was before the day of the railroad. In the lower, left-hand corner is the Bridge House, site of Ezra Graham's cabin. The large house on the left as you ascend the hill is the Mansion House, now the site of the A. Simon drugstore. The third house above it is on the corner now occupied by the Berwick. At the top of the hill on the right is the Zaccheus A. Beatty house, now the site of the Moose Home. The old courthouse is prominent.

Imagine yourself in Cambridge exactly 100 years ago this evening. It will be Friday, March 13, 1846. You have just received your Guernsey Times—published each Friday—and are now sitting down to read it. It had not been delivered by a carrier, nor had it come through the mail. For it, you had to go over to Isaac Niswander's eating-place, where Alexander's shoe store now is.

Spread before us is a copy of the paper issued that evening, most probably the only one in existence. It consists of four pages, each with six columns. Richard Hatton was the editor, and he was living in a house that stood on the site of the Coney Island Restaurant. A few days after this paper was published, a son, Frank, was born, and he lived to become the Postmaster General of United States during the administration of President

Arthur. The subscription rate of The Guernsey Times was $2.00 a year if paid in advance; paid otherwise, $2.50.

Since you are not getting that paper this evening, we'll read it for you, and here present it in Reader's Digest form. We might say that the first page is devoted to foreign and general news, most of which has been copied from other papers brought here by stagecoach. There is but little local news in the paper, the assumption being that most persons already knew what was happening in the community.

Foreign News.—Statement is made that the steamer Cambria had arrived in Boston, bringing news of February 4th from London (five weeks old). "The news is gratifying in its nature," the paper says. "There is little of American interest except the debate on American affairs in the French chambers. Parliament was opened January 22 by the Queen."

James K. Polk was President, and the Mexican War was brewing: in fact, was on a few months later. We read the following: "Reports are afloat that Mexico is increasing her military forces, as if preparing for war. Resentment is being shown against the United States in keeping military forces on the boundary."

General Domestic News.—Fear is expressed that the Whig tariff bill, enacted in the Harrison-Tyler administration to protect American industry, "will be repealed by Democratic Party" then in power. It is pointed out that under the Whig law of 1842, the country had been lifted out of the 1837 depression and enabled to pay off most of the national debt.

The only banks in 1846 were state and some private banks. The state banking system had been established a year before, and our paper gives a brief summary of the first year's activities. There were sixteen branches, with a total capital of $1,769,000 and resources of $3,186,081.29. Two years after this, a branch was established at Washington, the first bank in Guernsey County.

Local News.—From the Cambridge market report, we note that wheat is selling for 70 cents per bushel, corn 25 cents, oats 19 cents, flaxseed 75 cents, butter 10 cents per lb., and eggs 6 cents per doz.

Three deaths are reported: David Bumgartner, a merchant, aged 31; Mrs. Anna Bonnell, aged 58, a member of the M. E. Church for 42 years; and Martha Wood, aged 47, near Birmingham, of Erysipelas fever.

We note that Rev. J. M. Henderson gave a lecture on slavery at the new Union (now East Union) Meeting-house, seven miles west of Cambridge, last Wednesday; also that Rev. Washington Maynard, pastor of the Cambridge M. P. Church, will lecture on Temperance at the M. E. Church next Friday evening, "beginning at early candle-lighting."

Advertisements.—Fully one-half the paper is taken up with advertisements. The biggest advertiser is Israel Green, a druggist, who carries a line of goods, in addition to drugs, that would lay a modern cut-rate drugstore in the shade. All his medicines are warranted pure. Among the toilet articles are French, German, and Italian cologne water, fancy soap, and bear's oil for men's hair. On sale for medicinal purposes is a complete line of wines and brandy. Carried in stock at all times are Dr. Lane's celebrated liver pills and worm specific, Dr. Eoff's anti-dyspeptic pills, Dr. Smith's improved Indian vegetable pills, and a compound syrup of sarsaparilla guaranteed to cure scrofula and all skin diseases. He advertises one remedy that has survived the century—Dr. Jaynes' Expectorant.

Craig, and Bumgartner have just received a fresh supply of groceries, such as N. O. molasses, Y. H. tea, Rio coffee, and saferatus. They carry a good line of calicoes, merinos, alpacas and silks. They would like to buy roll butter, lard, beef tallow, clover seed, timothy seed, shelled corn, oats, wheat, and white beans, for which they will exchange goods.

Jesse Snodgrass in Adams Township, six miles west of Cambridge, will have a public sale on March 26th. Samuel Swayne, of Millwood Township, offers to sell his farm of 112 acres, lying in the tobacco region and well adapted to the raising of that plant. M. Zahnizer informs all indebted to him, by note, account, or otherwise, that they "must come forward against the first day of April" or a magistrate will call upon them for collection. Samuel M. Oldham, at his tannery at the west end of Main Street, has leather on hand which he will exchange for wheat, corn, or oats. Samuel M. Neel is manufacturing gun barrels and can fill orders for any number or size.

Advertised are 36 sheriff's sales, mostly real estate mortgage foreclosures. The farms are located in all parts of the county. Why such a situation? We attribute it to the absence of banks. The purchaser of a farm would give a mortgage note with a high rate of interest to the seller. Often, he could not meet his obligation just when due, and the mortgagee would close in. As a rule, the latter would get the farm back at his own price, as there would be no other bidders, and the former would have to forfeit what he had paid on the farm. Many men became wealthy by this practice a century ago. Had there been banks where the debtor could have borrowed money to meet his payment, this situation would not have existed.

(Copies of "Stories of Guernsey County" (1093 pages) are on sale at Miller's News Depot, West Eighth Street).

An Old Jeffersonian — February 24, 1848

[Originally published 12/11/1945]

We have received from Mrs. Rose Byers, 130 East Eighth Street, Cambridge, a copy of The Guernsey Jeffersonian bearing the date of February 24, 1848. This paper, now almost a century old, was found by her husband a few years ago behind a mirror on an antique piece of furniture he was redressing. Its editor was W. H. Gill, and the place of publication was Washington, Ohio. For twenty-five years, The Jeffersonian and its predecessors were published in Washington. Unfortunately, the files of the papers of that period are seemingly lost, and this is one of the very few copies known to exist.

Established in 1824 by David Robb, the paper first bore the name of The Washington Republican. In the years following, there were frequent changes of editors, and some changes in the name. W. H. Gill became connected with it in 1844, at which time it bore the name of The Democratic Signal. Gill changed it to The Guernsey Jeffersonian. About the year 1850, he moved the plant to Cambridge, dropped the word "Guernsey," and since then it has been The Jeffersonian.

Gill was a staunch Democrat, and in 1848 he worked enthusiastically for the election of Lewis Cass, Democratic candidate, for the presidency against Zachary Taylor, the Whig. For his loyalty to and service for the party, he was appointed secretary of the Constitutional Convention of 1851, which was dominated by the Democrats.

The Jeffersonian in 1848 was a four-page paper of six columns to the page, published weekly. The subscription price was $1.50 per annum, and the advertising rate was $1.00 for one square (12 lines) for three weeks.

Fully one half the paper we hold is advertising matter, and most of the other half is political propaganda. There is very little general or local news. One item of general interest is the announcement of the critical illness of John Quincy Adams who was taken, in his seat in Congress, by a stroke of paralysis a few days before. Another is the report that a treaty of peace had been made with Mexico, virtually ending the war. The treaty gives to us the Rio Grande as the boundary, and also cedes to us New Mexico and Upper California for a pecuniary consideration.

An item of local news is the following:

Some workmen engaged in quarrying stone for the repair of the National Road, on the hill west of Cambridge, found, in a petrified state, what was supposed to be the body of an Indian child, which, perhaps centuries ago, was deposited in that spot. This extraordinary specimen of ancient remains was found embedded in a mass of solid rock, and has the appearance of a stone image, somewhat imperfect in its outward form, yet having the general outlines of the human shape. The material of which it is composed appears to be a species of limestone. In the same cavity was also found a small row of what appears to have been Indian heads, matted together.

The paper carries the following advertisement:

One Cent Reward

RUNAWAY from the subscriber living in Wills tp., on Wednesday, the 19th ultimo, William Ducker, an indented apprentice to the Farming business. All persons are forbidden to trust said boy on my account, as I will pay no debts of his contracting. The above reward and no thanks will be given to any persons returning said Ducker.

JOSEPH RHINEHART

SOME CHRONOLOGICAL COUNTY HISTORY

The leading mercantile advertiser is Albert G. Lawrence, the man who, ten years later, built for his home that which is now known as the Colonial Inn. Other merchants advertising are Craig Clark and Company, Stephen Potts, James Potten, William Lawrence, John Carey, Clements and Caldwell, and B. Borton. The following are some of the prices reported by the merchants:

dried apples,	62 cts. a bu.
butter,	12 cts. a pound
oats,	18 cts. a bu.
wheat,	75 cts. a bu.
corn,	25 cts. a bu.
eggs,	6 cts. a doz.
lard,	4 cts. a lb.
white beans,	62 cts. a bu.

Cambridge in 1849

[Originally published 10/23/1945]

Before us is a copy of the Cambridge Guernsey Times of January 1, 1849 (almost a century ago). In it is the local market report. Prices were somewhat different from those of today, and more, too, no points were required. Here they are:

Wheat (bu.)	.65
Corn (bu.)	.25
Oats (bu.)	.20
Apples (bu.)	.25
Dried Apples (bu.)	.40
Coal (bu.)	.05
Soap (lb.)	.03
Flour (lb.)	.02
Bacon (lb.)	.03
Butter (lb.)	.10
Beef (lb.)	.03
Lard (lb.)	.05
Eggs (doz.)	.06
Wool (lb.)	.20

A housewife, at a total cost of 57 cents, might bring the following home from the market: A five-pound roast or the same weight of the best cut of steak, five pounds of bacon, a pound of butter, a pound of lard, a dozen eggs, and a peck of apples.

Cambridge Advertisers.—
The population of the town was then about 900.
There were six general stores, each carrying a line of foodstuff as well as other merchandise:
>T. Naftel and Co.,
>Ogier and Clark,
>Samuel Craig,
>Rogers and Warren,
>Jacob G. Metcalf,
>and McCracken and Thompson.

The attorneys advertising were
>T. W. Tipton (afterwards the first U. S. Senator from Nebraska)
>and William M. Farrar.

D. Daniels and W. Maynard were wagon makers.
C. L. Madison was a watch maker.
Joel T. Irwin was a candle maker.
M. Zahnizer had a blacksmith shop.
Mrs. Rhoda Needham kept the Temperance Hotel (located on site of present Hoge building).
Oldham and Alter made harnesses and saddles.
A. E. Cook had an oyster saloon.
John Carey was a hat maker.
Joseph R. Johnson was a weaver.
Tracy and Beatty had a hardware store.
B. A. and F. W. Albright operated a foundry and manufactured plows, stoves, grates, salt kettles, pots, and plow points.

County Officers of 1849

[Originally published 10/24/1945]

President Judge	– Benjamin S. Cowen
Associate Judges	– Zadock Davis, Robert Reed, and Robert Marshall

(Before 1851, there was no common pleas judge, but instead there were three Associate Judges who would hold court four times a year, presided over by a President Judge whose district was composed of several counties. There was no Probate Judge; such work as is his today was cared for by the Associate Judges.)

Clerk of Courts	– Thomas W. Peacock
Prosecuting Attorney	– J. W. White

SOME CHRONOLOGICAL COUNTY HISTORY

Master Commissioner	– M. Gaston
Sheriff	– William Birch
Auditor	– William H. Endley
Treasurer	– William Abell
Recorder	– C. R. Moore
Surveyor	– William Dougherty
Coroner	– Charles Barnes
Commissioners	– James Stranathan, Richard Bell, and John Frame
Poorhouse Directors	– John Barton, Robert Leeper, and John Hastings

(The place provided for the care of indigents was at first called the poorhouse, and three directors were elected by the voters of the county for its administration. The term "poorhouse" became repulsive, especially after the publication of Will Carleton's pathetic poem, "Over the Hills to the Poorhouse," which was presented in an effective way by readers at literary societies and other public gatherings. This, more than anything else, brought about a change of the name to "county infirmary," which didn't sound so bad, then later to "county home," which had a still more softening effect. In this connection, we might add that those who lived in the poorhouse were called paupers; those in the county infirmary were inmates; those in the county home today are considered residents. And along with the improvement of the name of the institution have come conveniences, comforts, and treatment consistent with the change.)

Justices of the Peace

Adams Township	– Abraham Spear and James McGonagle
Centre Township	– John B. Heaton and William Parkinson
Jackson Township	– Elijah Shriver and John Stewart
Jefferson Township	– Cyrus Linn and David Jefferies
Knox Township	– Robert Duff and Robert Wagstaff
Londonderry Township	– Thomas Anderson and Edward Carpenter
Liberty Township	– Jesse Smith and Abraham Parrott
Madison Township	– James Stockdale and William Helm
Millwood Township	– Jonah Smith and Thomas Ruth
Monroe Township	– Jonathan B. Cunard and William Kennedy
Oxford Township	– John Morton, M. S. Maitland, and Reuben Borton
Richland Township	– James Rinehart and William E. Rose
Spencer Township	– David Needham and John Moore
Westland Township	– Robert F. Burt and Ichabod Grummond
Washington Township	– William Scott and L. B. Kingsbury
Wills Township	– James DeLong, P. B. Ankeny, and John McDowell

Wheeling Township — Alexander Mitchell and James Graham
Wright Township — Daniel Logee and Joseph Yakey

Mayors

There are eleven incorporated towns in Guernsey County today. In 1849, there were seven whose mayors were as follows:

Antrim — John Harrison
Cambridge — C. J. Albright
Cumberland — Russell Prouty
Fairview — James H. Rainey
Middletown — Robert Leeper
Senecaville — Henry Shadwell
Washington — Thomas Beaham

Of the above, Antrim and Middletown later surrendered their charters of incorporation. Incorporated since 1849 were:

Byesville
Kimbolton
Lore City
Pleasant City
Quaker City
and Salesville.

Lofland's Fish Trap

[Originally published 11/28/1945]

In time of flood at certain seasons of the year, fish will ascend streams tributary to the one which is their habitat. When the waters recede, they drop back to their original abiding place. Sometimes they get stranded far from home and will need to sojourn in the deeper holes of the smaller streams. We have known fish to ascend Leatherwood for a distance of twenty miles when there was a prolonged Wills Creek flood. Some of the fishermen on the upper course of the former creek used to give expression, to their delight, when the water remained high for several days, by remarking that it would bring the fish up. We recall that a school of redhorse suckers, many of them two and one-half feet long, apparently ignorant of the fact that, by virtue of the slope, Leatherwood goes down rapidly when it starts, couldn't make the return and had to take refuge in some of the deeper holes. It is needless to say that there was some fine fishing for several days thereafter.

Colonel Lofland's Home.—In these sidelight stories, also those in the book, reference has been made a number of times to Col. Gordon Lofland, one of the foremost citizens of Cambridge for nearly a half century. He owned a farm of approximately 500 acres which is now included in the northwestern part of the city. In his day, however, it was considered as being far out of town. To the residence, a footpath led diagonally through the woods and fields from Steubenville Avenue.

The home stood on an elevation near the center of the farm, now the site of the Lofland School on Fourth Street. On this knoll, it is believed, the three men killed by Indians in 1791 were buried (page 24 of the book). A large brick structure, the residence was surrounded by gardens and a well-kept lawn, beautiful with shrubbery and flowers and bordered with stately locust trees. Some distance back were ample barns, stables, and outbuildings for protecting stock and storing grain. Colonel Lofland kept the best breeds of horses, cattle, sheep, and hogs.

With his broad acres of tillable fields, pastures, meadows, and forestland, Colonel Lofland was looked upon as the outstanding farmer of this section. The stately mansion and its beautiful surroundings were an attraction. In many respects, the place was not unlike some of the plantation homes of the South. Colonel Lofland lived here until his death in 1869.

Gordon Run.—On the Lofland farm, a run that was fed by numerous strong springs near the present Taylor Pond, emptied its waters into Wills Creek. This little stream is known today as Gordon Run. It runs diagonally across the northern part of the city and frequently causes trouble by its overflowing. Many of the springs near its head have ceased to flow, and it does not now, outside of flood time, carry as much water as it did in early days. Before its waters became polluted by mines and mills, Wills Creek abounded in fish—pike, bass, red-horse suckers, catfish, and other kinds (no carp).

Colonel Lofland's Plan.—Colonel Lofland noticed that the Wills Creek fish would ascend the run in time of flood, and return as the waters went down. While, by fishing in the creek, folks might catch all the fish they wanted, they either did not have the time to fish or didn't care to do so. The civic-spirited Colonel conceived a plan designed to supply the whole town with fish the year round, and with but little cost. He would build a gate at the mouth of the run that could be raised and lowered at will. It was to be a complicated affair that required some machinery for its operation.

It was planned that when the water in the creek began to rise, the gate would be raised and kept up until the crest of the flood was reached; then it would be dropped. It was to be so constructed that the receding waters could pass through, but the fish could not. They would be trapped above and there would be plenty for everybody until the next flood came.

A Company Organized.—Lofland explained the project to a number of prominent citizens and sought their cooperation. A company was organized, composed of Colonel Lofland, C. J. Albright, C. L. Madison, Elza Turner, Moses Sarchet, and others. The gate was built, and everybody anxiously awaited a big rain.

At length the rains came, Wills Creek began to rise, up went the gate, and water backed up Gordon Run almost to its source. When it was seen that the flood had reached its highest, the gate was dropped. The water in the run gradually fell to normal. But there were no fish. The same result followed subsequent trials. The fish would not pass through, apparently wary of the new-fangled entrance to their erstwhile swimming pool.

A Medical Course a Century Ago
[Originally published 7/11/1945]

As a sidelight to the story, "Early Guernsey County Doctors," page 697 of the book, we here present some extracts from a diary kept by William George, a citizen of Pennyroyaldom, who graduated from the Cincinnati Medical college 90 years ago. The diary was handed to us by G. C. Borton, Steubenville Avenue, who found it stored away amongst the family records.

To practice medicine today, one must have a pre-medic college education before he can be admitted to a medical school, where he must spend at least four years in hard study, and much money, and time beyond that as an interne in a hospital. There were no such requirements a century ago. William George lived in Middletown, Oxford Township, and after "reading medicine" a few months in the office of a local physician, was admitted as a student in the Cincinnati Medical College. He entered the college January 3, 1855, and on February 1, less than a month later, he was given his diploma and licensed to practice medicine. With one of Stockwell's charts that cost a dollar, a medicine case filled with medicine, for which he paid $2.30, a pump and a set of cupping glasses which cost five dollars, and a skeleton salvaged from a corpse he himself had stolen from a grave, he started back to Middletown where he hung out his shingle, announcing that he was prepared to render efficient service to the physically afflicted.

The diary we hold in our hand covers the 33 days he was away from home, including the days of his departure and return. It is all interesting, but there is space here for only a few of the entries. His journey to Cincinnati was apparently his first "ride on the cars." The railroad had been completed through Guernsey County but a few months before.

January 1: Left home with James Likes for Washington, remained there until dark and took the stage to Cambridge, cost 50 cents. Staid all night at Cook's Hotel. Thought a good deal about home. Said my prayers, went to sleep and slept well.

January 2: Took the cars for Cincinnati. Got to Zanesville at 9 o'clock and was detained there two hours. Started to Columbus, cars broke down, missed our train to Cincinnati and we had to wait four hours. I went over and visited the penitentiary. Got to Cincinnati at 10 o'clock at night. I slept badly, but I was thankful my life was spared.

January 3: Got up much confused in mind. Went to college, heard one lecture, then went home and wrote a letter to my wife. Could not study after dinner, so went to see Professor Jones who was sick. At 3 o'clock I went to college again and heard Professor Baldridge lecture on the diseases of children. Went to bed early that night and slept well

January 4: Had a bad cold and a sore throat and did not feel very well. Went to lectures all day. Am learning very well. Felt some better at night, but head ached some. Went to bed and wished I was at home. After think awhile I went to sleep.

January 9: At college all day. Witt, Baldridge and Galloway lectured. Quizzed by Baldridge. Had a debate at night on the question, "Is it right to practice deception?" Weather cold and damp. Health pretty good. Want to be at home. Went to bed at 10 o'clock. Said my prayers and slept well.

January 17: Heard lectures all day. Bought a medicine case at Hill's drugstore and got it filled for $2.30. Bought a red dress for my wife; cost $1.50. Weather clear and cold. Would like to go home.

January 20: At lectures in the forenoon and in the afternoon I went to visit Professor Witt. Bought a pump and a set of cupping glasses for five dollars. Students all getting very tired and wanting to go home.

January 27: Stole the bodies of two dead men and got them into the dissecting room same night. Heard Dr. Williams lecture on dentistry today. Saw Dr. Wright amputate an arm. Want to go home very bad.

February 1: At lectures in the forenoon. In the dissecting room in the afternoon. Saw an operation for stones in the bladder. At night I got my diploma from the college, boxed up my skeleton and went to bed at 10 o'clock.

February 2: Started home at 6 and got there that night at 8 o'clock. Weather extremely cold. Six inches of snow on the ground.

The Beginning of Byesville

[Originally published 7/20/1946]

Byesville came into existence exactly ninety years ago this month. Puny at birth and for many years thereafter, it gave little promise of surviving at all; in fact, it appeared that sooner or later it would go the way of a dozen or more other Guernsey County towns whose very names are now forgotten.

Platted in 1856.—It was on July 1, 1856, that Byesville was platted. We find no record to show who founded the town or for what purpose. He evidently had little faith in its making a booming start, for he provided but eight lots, each 66 feet wide and 165 feet long, all in a row, fronting a street sixteen and one-half feet wide on the south. Today, this narrow street is Main Street and the eight lots are the ones beginning at the First National Bank corner and running east. Running north and south between lots No. 4 and No. 5 was an alley with a width of twenty feet. This was Byesville at the time of the Civil War, which began five years after the town was platted.

Jonathan Bye.—For about forty years before there was a Byesville,

Jonathan Bye, a Quaker who had come from Pennsylvania, lived on the creek a short distance below. Here he operated a saw- and grist-mill and kept a store. The place was widely known as Bye's Mill.

He was strongly opposed to slavery, as all Quakers were, and his home became a station on the Underground Railroad. Within it, many a fugitive slave found refuge in his flight from the South to Canada. A short time before the town was platted, Bye sold his property to William Grant and Isaac Hoopman and moved to Illinois. Although never a resident of Byesville, he was, in a sense, responsible for its location, and he left it a name.

Byesville in 1870.—We visit Byesville in 1870, fourteen years after it was founded. We find the mill and store down on the creek with William Grant as the proprietor. He has the post office in his store. Here the folks up in the town come for their supplies and mail; there is no other store in the community. Living on the eight original lots, which are yet the only ones in the town, we count twenty-five people—men, women, and children. We find no city directory, but had there been one, it would have listed just seven family names, as follows: Meek, Collins, Sayre, Shoff, Selby, Clark, and Secrest. On one of the lots is a blacksmith shop, the only industry in the town, owned by Jacob Collins. There is no school. Instead of the country children coming into town for their education, the Byesville children are going out into the country, to a one-room school called Oak Grove, located south of the village.

There is no church, but the twenty-five inhabitants are finding a way to worship on the Sabbath. The Baptists are going out to the old Brick Church on the Cambridge Road, of which Rev. J. G. Whittaker is the pastor; those of the Methodist Episcopal faith are worshipping over at Rainey's Chapel two miles northwest; and the Methodist Protestants are attending the Bethlehem Church on Trail Run.

Advent of the Railroad.—Three years later (1873), a railroad was built down the valley past Byesville. One of its main purposes was to provide an outlet for the coal which underlay all the surrounding country. However, it was not until 1877 that the mining industry got under way there. In the meantime, though, Byesville boasted of having a railroad even if the trains did come irregularly and far between. Some wag of the town, who afterwards described the service, said: "The first trains were run on a bi-weekly schedule; that is, they arrived one week and tried to get back the next." Out by the track, a store was opened which served as a waiting room, ticket office, and post office. Dr. Francis Walker, the first Byesville physician, not only kept the store, the depot, and the post office, but found time to administer to the physically afflicted.

Coal mines were opened near the town, the Pioneer and Old Farmer being amongst the first. Soon there were ten mines near Byesville, and eventually there were eighteen within working distance of the place. Miners began moving in, and it became necessary to lay out more lots and build more homes. Byesville had begun to move forward.

Incorporated In 1882.—We make another visit to Byesville in 1882. We learn that it was incorporated on February 7th of that year, and that on April 24th, T. J. Lee had been elected mayor; James Selby, clerk; L. W. Smith, treasurer; and George H. Dudley, marshal. There is no city building, and the council is meeting in a blacksmith shop. We register at the Red Cloud Hotel, kept by George Conner, and begin looking around. The population is 350 and increasing daily. There is now a school in town, and John A. Bliss, who is the principal, is also one of the county school examiners. James Selby is not only the town clerk, but he works at the cobbler trade and preaches on the side. David Burt has just started a livery and feed stable. William Grant, who succeeded Jonathan Bye down at the old mill, is still there, but living a retired life. John Seals is now the village blacksmith.

Byesville's Rapid Growth.—Eight years after it was incorporated (1890), the census showed a population of 789. In 1900, it was 1,267; in 1910, 3,156. By 1920, however, the coal industry had become weakened in that immediate section, and the population had fallen to 2,775; in 1930, it had dropped to 2,638; and in 1940, to 2,418.

In Byesville today there are many enterprising and progressive citizens who are aware of the wealth of natural resources of that community and have organized to the end that they may be developed. Aside from these resources, there are other great advantages. A realization of the possibilities has already resulted in a renaissance that promises a greater era of prosperity than any ever known in the past.

The Brown House

[Originally published 4/25/1947]

We have Brown Avenue and Brown High School, and we used to have the Brown House. They were not named for a man, but for a woman, Nancy Brown, one of the most enterprising women who ever lived in Cambridge. When the town was platted in 1806, an alley twenty feet wide was laid off between Wheeling and Steubenville Avenues, running from the present Fifth to the present Eleventh Street. To distinguish it from other alleys, which were afterwards laid off, it was given the name of Brown in honor of Nancy. As the term "Brown Alley" lacked dignity, it was officially named Brown Avenue. The Brown High School was built on a lot that Nancy Brown had owned

Predecessor of National Hotel.—On the site of the present National Hotel, Wyatt Hutchison built a log tavern in 1818, which he afterwards replaced with a two-story frame building. For nearly thirty years, Hutchison was the proprietor, and the place attained a reputation that reached far out on Zane's Trace, then on the National Road after it was built. When he became advanced in age, Hutchison decided to retire from active life. He advertised the tavern for sale, and it was purchased by Basil Brown. The old Hutchison Tavern then became the Brown House which, years afterwards, was torn away and the present National Hotel built on the site.

Basil Brown.—Basil Brown lived in Brownsville, Pennsylvania. In 1828, he married Nancy Johnson, and the couple opened a tavern in their home town. They afterwards engaged in tavern-keeping in Claysville and Washington, Pennsylvania. Learning that the Hutchison Tavern was for sale, they bought it and came to Cambridge.

One evening in 1849, after they had been here two years, a stagecoach stopped at the tavern and discharged a passenger whose trunk was strapped on top of the coach. In trying to remove it, Basil Brown fell and was killed.

Nancy Takes Charge of Tavern.—Left with nine children to support, Nancy decided to take over the tavern and carry on the work in the best way she could; in fact, there was nothing else for her to do. Osmond, the oldest son, was able to assist her some at first, then the next two older boys, Thomas and Robert, when they became old enough. Under her management, the Brown House, as it soon came to be called, was a signal success. In no other hotel in Ohio was a traveler more hospitably received, comfortably housed, and substantially entertained

To the boys on the road, Nancy became as a mother, and such she was called by all of them. In Civil War days, she was intensely loyal and manifested her patriotism in many ways. Soldiers passing through were taken in and entertained by her. If they had no money to pay for it, they were treated as though they had, and were then sent on their way with her blessing.

A Successful Business Woman.—Nancy profited by serving others, and her success in a business way was phenomenal. She was a woman of remarkable industry and energy. She reared her large family of children to be successful men and women. By industry and economy, she acquired much property within and near Cambridge. Her hospitality and generosity were widely known, and doubtless contributed much to the popularity and success of the Brown House. By her employees and servants she was revered.

Home on Steubenville Avenue.—After managing the hotel for many years, she leased it to others and retired to a home she built at the corner of Steubenville Avenue and North Ninth Street. This was a commodious and elegant brick residence and richly furnished for its day. It was torn away in 1926 and is now the site of the Ninth Street Methodist Church. She owned the property immediately west of her home, which was removed, in 1910, to give place for the high school that bears her name.

Nancy Brown died in 1888, and in the settlement of her estate, R. V. Orme purchased the Brown House. The old landmark was torn away, and in its place, Mr. Orme erected a modern, three-story, brick hotel. Bearing the name of Noel, the new hotel was opened in the early 1890s. This name was later changed to National.

Making Sorghum Molasses

[Originally published 5/28/1946]

While in conversation with S. M. (Sam) Smith the other day, there was brought to our mind a Guernsey County agricultural industry once extensively engaged in here, but little known anymore. That industry was the raising of sugar cane and the making of sorghum molasses. The scarcity of sugar in recent times, however, has been responsible for reviving sorghum-making a little, but it is hardly noticeable.

The Smith Family.—Sam, now 83 years old, lives on the National Road near Bridgewater, but he was born and reared on Pultney Ridge where his particular branch of the ubiquitous Smith family settled in very early days. His grandfather, William Smith, purchased 700 acres of land and opened a tavern called the Royal Oak at the intersection of the present roads 513 and 70.

Squire Smith, son of William, located on a part of his father's large farm, and became the father of five sons—William H., Jonah, George, Samuel M., and Charles. All these sons engaged in making sorghum. Sam began when he was twelve years of age and continued in the work for 50 years. Two members of the Smith family constituted a sorghum-making crew, and with one of their outfits, they toured the country for many miles around during the sorghum season in September and October.

Raising Cane.—Nearly every farmer had a cane patch of from one-fourth to one-half acre. About corn-planting time, the tiny seeds were dropped in hills three feet apart and in rows that were four. After the first hoeing, the stalks were thinned to five or six in a hill. For the remainder of the season, the cultivation was the same as that of corn, but more tedious because the young plants resemble foxtail, which always seemed to be growing amongst them and had to be pulled out by hand. In his boyhood days, the writer suffered from many a backache in a cane patch. The blades of cane are like those of corn. The seed head at the top of the stalk is short and dense, easily distinguished from that of broomcorn, which is long and loose.

By the time of early frost, the cane is supposed to be ripe. Before it is cut, the blades are stripped off. Strippers were usually made from tobacco sticks. They were shaved flat on two sides and the ends rounded for handles. Downward strokes from the tops of the stalks removed the blades. This was a work we really liked to do. The heads were clipped off and the stalk cut close to the ground. The cane was then hauled to the place where the sorghum was to be made, usually at a spring near the patch. Then two of the Smith boys would drive in with their outfit.

The Grinding and Boiling.—This consisted of a grinder and an evaporating pan. In the former were three metallic cylinders, probably two feet long and six or eight inches in diameter, which turned like the rollers of a clothes wringer, but vertically instead of horizontally. The cane stalks were run through these and the juice squeezed out. The power for turning them was furnished by a horse, sometimes two, that kept going round and round in a circular track.

The evaporating pan was a shallow affair, about twelve feet long and four or five feet wide. It was divided into narrow compartments opening into each other at alternate ends.

One of the Smith brothers would grind the cane while the other took care of the boiling. The juice was poured into one end of the evaporating pan and gradually worked to the other where it was drained off as molasses. En route from one end to the other, it lost about 95 percent of its volume through evaporation, as it took about twenty gallons of juice to make one of sorghum.

Smiths charged twelve and one half cents a gallon for the making. Most farmers kept their product for home use, occasionally selling some of it locally at the prevailing price of fifty cents per gallon.

Cane thrives best in a rich, sandy soil. A yield of 200 gallons per acre might be expected; however, most farmers planted no more than one-fourth or one-half acre. The juice is usually of a greenish color; sometimes, from the nature of the soil, it has a yellowish tint and is sweeter.

A Season of Social Events.—In other days, as some who read this may recall, there were no more enjoyable social events than the evening "frolics" at the cane mill. Young folks of the neighborhood, and sometimes older ones, would come together for an evening of pleasure. Occasionally, the number attending would reach from 50 to 100. There may have been lack of evening dresses and formality that characterize social gatherings today, but nevertheless they were enjoyed. Potatoes were baked, corn was roasted, and taffy was made. Near the evaporating pan was a pit dug in the ground into which the sorghum-maker threw the skimmings. It bore the name of the "soup-hole." Into this, somebody had to be shoved before the frolic ended.

Not Much Sorghum Today.—The Smith brothers don't make sorghum anymore. In fact, there are only a few persons in this part of the state who do, and they don't travel around from farm to farm. The cane must be hauled to the mill, perhaps many miles away, where they charge about fifty cents a gallon for making the molasses.

According to an agricultural report of sixty years ago (1885), 32,000 gallons of sorghum were made in Guernsey County in that one year, an average of more than a gallon for each man, woman, and child at that time. Now there is scarcely any made.

SOME CHRONOLOGICAL COUNTY HISTORY

Guernsey County in 1860, 85 Years Ago

[Originally published 11/27/1945]

Early in November of 1860, the eighth census was announced, showing that Guernsey County had a population of 24,475 and Cambridge 1,452. Since 1850, the county had lost 5,983 and the town had gained 411. The loss in the county was due to its yielding four of its townships to help form Noble.

The Courts.—Announcement was made that the Common Pleas Court, which would commence the following Monday, had 212 cases set for trial. Litigation seems to have been popular. The number of attorneys advertised in one issue of a local paper was fifteen (and there may have been others). With a population of about one-twelfth that of today, Cambridge then had as many or more attorneys. There was one for each one hundred people. Were there so many attorneys because there was much litigation, or was there much litigation because there were so many attorneys? In other words, have the people become more peaceful and agreeable toward each other now that there are fewer cases coming before the courts, or have the present-day attorneys found ways of settling difficulties outside. In addition to the attorneys in Cambridge, there were several in the villages in the county. We here list the ones in the county seat, who advertised:

William H. Farrar
E. W. Mathews
Milton Barnes
James DeLong
W. Wall
J. H. Norris
William Hillyer
J. T. Rainey
Vincent Haynes
M. Gaston
J. K. Casey
N. E. Evans
H. Skinner
J. M. Bushfield
J. Ferguson

Londonderry Fair.—The secretary of the Londonderry Fair, which was held a short distance southeast of that village, publishes his report. Large crowds were in attendance, and the number of exhibits was the greatest in the history of that institution; included in the entries were 74 horses, 25 head of cattle, 139 sheep, many hogs, much poultry, grain, vegetables, fruit, and fancy work. He reported no horseracing, but gave the results of footraces.

The Bible in the School.—Controversial as long as 85 years ago was the question of the use of the Bible in the schools. This is evidenced by the following announcement:

> *"Citizens are urged to assemble at New Concord Tuesday to discuss the propositions, 'That the Bible should be read in a class book in all our schools,' and 'That each teacher be recommended to open his or her school by reading the Scriptures and prayer.' Ministers of all denominations are urged to attend this mass meeting."*

Miller Academy.—Located at Washington, and under the jurisdiction of the Presbyterian Church, was Miller Academy. It stood on North Street, near the present Centralized School. In advertising the institution in 1860, the board of trustees state that Washington has a population of 1,000 and is a healthy community. The building is handsome and is equipped with a good library. There are literary societies, competent teachers, and religious influences. The course offered extends as far as the junior year in the best colleges. Vocal and piano lessons are taught. Ladies are admitted. Room and boarding in private homes may be obtained at two dollars a week.

Aerolites Found.—On May 1, 1860, the aerolites fell in the western part of Westland Township (page 1035 of the book). This phenomenon attracted the whole nation. The Guernsey Times of November 2, that year, says that a Mr. Buskirk had found two of the aerolites, one of which weighed nine pounds, and that he had sold it for $20.00 to the secretary of the New York Home Insurance Company.

Hogs Plentiful.—Within a period of three weeks in November, 1860, R. J. Clark butchered and salted between 4,000 and 5,000 hogs in Cambridge and Washington. The meat was shipped out to eastern markets at the rate of four carloads a day.

The Abolitionists

[Originally published 5/20/1946]

Passing out with slavery was a loosely organized party or society composed of men and women known as Abolitionists. There were people in both the North and the South who opposed slavery, but not all for the same reason or with the same degree of opposition. Some believed the institution of slavery to be morally wrong, and the question was taken up by the churches; some considered it an economic matter, and it became a political issue. Not all who opposed slavery were termed Abolitionists; it was only those who were most radical in their hatred toward it and activities against it.

Movement Started at St. Clairsville.—For many years, the sentiment against slavery had been growing in the North, but no organized effort had been made for its abolition. The question of its extension, however, had been a live issue almost since the beginning of the government. It fell to a St. Clairsville man, Benjamin Lundy, to start a movement that attracted the whole nation, one that eventually led to the Civil War and the emancipation of the slave. For our authority for making this statement, we quote from David Saville Muzzey, the American historian: "To (Benjamin) Lundy belongs the credit of organizing into a strong united movement the anti-slavery sentiment in our country. He was the first American to embrace the cause of negro emancipation as a life mission.

Benjamin Lundy.—Since Benjamin Lundy lived so near Guernsey County that his influence was felt here right at the beginning of his anti-slavery activities, it may not be out of place for us to write briefly about his life and work. He was a Quaker, born in New Jersey in 1789. When a boy, he came to Wheeling—then in Virginia—to learn the saddler trade, working as an apprentice. Here he married and moved out to St. Clairsville to engage in business for himself. Like most Quakers, he had an inveterate hatred of slavery which grew more bitter by his constantly seeing, when in Wheeling, gangs of slaves driven in chains through the streets to be loaded on boats for the cotton plantations of the deep South. That slavery was wrong was his belief, and something should be done about it other than mere talk, which had been about all that had been done before that time.

Organizes a Society.—In St. Clairsville, in 1815, Lundy organized what he called "the Union Humane Society", which grew to a membership of nearly five hundred. Its purpose was to arouse the people against slavery. Knowing of some others in different parts of the country who had anti-slavery views similar to his own, he wrote them, urging that they do what he had done. He sold his saddlery business at a sacrifice to devote his entire time to a cause that was obsessing him. He went over to Mt. Pleasant in Jefferson County to assist Charles Osborne, another Quaker, in publishing an anti-slavery paper.

Joined by William Lloyd Garrison.—From Mt. Pleasant, he went to several other places where he edited papers, even venturing into the South. He toured the country as a lecturer. In Boston, he was heard by William Lloyd Garrison, who became interested in the movement Lundy had started and joined him in his campaign for the emancipation of the slave. Lundy died when comparatively young, and Garrison carried on the work, becoming one of the greatest enemies of slavery the country knew. Joining in the work with Lundy and Garrison were such noted men as Wendell Phillips, Theodore Parker, Henry Ward Beecher, Elijah Lovejoy and James G. Birney. Whittier, Lowell, Emerson and others supported the movement by their pens, and Harriet Beecher Stowe was inspired to write "Uncle Tom's Cabin."

In his "Historical Collections of Ohio", Henry Howe says, "St. Clairsville is identified with the history of Benjamin Lundy, who has been called the 'Father of Abolitionism,' for he first set in motion those moral forces which eventually resulted in the overthrow of American slavery."

Abolitionists Considered Fanatics.—Abolitionists sprang up in many parts of the North. They were looked upon by many as fanatics who, if not checked, might injure the country. They flooded the South with their literature, which aroused a hatred and rage that knew no bounds. There was opposition to them in the North—by politicians who wanted the votes of the South; by manufacturers who were afraid they would lose the business of the South; by some who did not like the negroes.

An Abolitionist was not safe in either the North or the South. Lundy was driven out of Baltimore; Garrison was mobbed and dragged through the streets of Boston; Lovejoy was killed by a mob in Illinois; Birney had his newspaper wrecked in Cincinnati. In the South, rewards were offered for the capture of Abolitionists.

The Movement Spread.—In spite of the opposition, the Abolition Movement spread. Societies were organized throughout the country, many in places where it took courage to become a member. At least two such organizations were effected in Guernsey County, one at Washington, and one at Senecaville. We hold in our hand the record book of the Washington society, also a sheet of paper, yellow with age, upon which each of the thirty-three charter members affixed his name in his own handwriting. Without question, this document is one of the most interesting relics of the anti-slavery movement in Guernsey County. (For an account of this society and the names of the thirty-three daring members who doubtless realized that their action was unpopular, would brand them as fanatics in the minds of many other people, and perhaps injure their business, see story beginning on page 702 of the book).

The Liberty Party.—In 1840, the Abolitionists brought out James G. Birney as a candidate for the presidency. They called their party the Liberty Party. None but the most radical of the Abolitionists deemed it timely for making emancipation of the slaves a clean-cut political issue, preferring to work through the old-line parties. In Guernsey County, the Liberty Party polled only thirteen votes. Birney was again a candidate in 1844 and made a much better showing here.

SOME CHRONOLOGICAL COUNTY HISTORY

The Three Unknown Confederates
[Originally published 9/30/1946]

Side by side in the Washington Cemetery lie the bodies of three unknown Confederate soldiers. For eighty-three years, their graves have been pointed out to visitors to this burial ground, who have been told that they were three of Morgan's raiders killed on the streets of Washington on Friday, July 24, 1863, in what is known as the "Battle of Washington."

A Regular Battle.—It wasn't a great battle, 'tis true, but nevertheless it was fought between the armies of two generals of the Civil War, both of whom were present and commanding in person, and by regular soldiers on both sides—not members of the militia or guerrillas. And more, too, the armies were drawn up in battle array, and for a short time the fighting was fierce.

There is probably no eyewitness of the battle living today, that is, no one who was old enough at the time to recall it distinctly. The last of such persons was Elizabeth McMullen who died a few years ago at the age ninety-two. A few years before her death, she gave the writer a lengthy, detailed description of the battle and her own experience on that "terrible day." At the age of sixteen, she was living in Washington at the time of the battle, and just before it began, she waited on the table at which Morgan ate his dinner. During the firing, she took refuge in a cellar along with twenty other women and children. (For this story of Elizabeth McMullin, see page 318 of the book.)

Morgan and his men moved northward toward Winterset, and Shackelford, with his 2,000 Union troops, swept across the town in pursuit. Washington was the scene of carnage. Lying along the street were two dead and many wounded Confederates, one of whom died a short time afterwards. As for their bodily protection, many of the raiders fired from behind their horses; many of the latter were hit. Dead and wounded horses were stretched from one end of the town to the other.

Buried In Local Cemetery.—The three dead Confederates were buried in the village cemetery, their names unknown. Down in the South somewhere were loved ones, perhaps, who never knew their fate or burial place.

Most of Morgan's men came from some of the best Kentucky and Tennessee families. Cecil F. Holland, whose recent publication, "Morgan and His Raiders," a copy of which is in the Cambridge public library, says: "There was never another fighting command quite like this (Morgan's army), a band of gay, reckless men and boys. They included lawyers, doctors, merchants, newspaper men, and farmers."

It may truly be said that these are the graves of three unknown soldiers of the Confederacy. To one who visits them, there comes an emotion not unlike that occasioned when he stands at the grave of the unknown soldier at Arlington.

Northernmost Battle of Civil War.—Aside from what we have just stated, there is something else here of much historical importance. Nearly four hundred thousand Confederates were killed in the Civil War. It is believed that these three gave their lives for the "Lost Cause," in regular battle, farther north than any of the others. Two days after the battle, Morgan surrendered in Columbiana County, but there was no battle. Historians have placed Gettysburg as the most northern battle, but Washington is thirty miles farther north.

It thus appears that these graves are of much historic interest for two reasons: first, they are the graves of three unknown soldiers of the Confederacy; second, they are probably the graves of the three who gave their lives farthest north in regular battle. As such, they should be suitably marked. Is it not time that Guernsey County should give attention to a matter of such importance within her boundaries?

Sherman's Army Train

[Originally published 2/15/1945]

When the war is over what will be done with our great army equipment now scattered over the world? It has cost our government billions of dollars. Will it be sold, given away, or junked? Questions of that kind are being asked.

At the close of the Civil War, everything of value was saved and put to practical use in some way. There were no such things as bombers, tanks, and motor-trucks, but there were wagons, horses, and mules, and the government wisely decided to distribute them to the end that they might be of service in helping to restore to a normal condition a country that was suffering from four years of war.

With General Sherman on his march through Georgia, and subsequently through the Carolinas, were thousands of wagons, drawn by mules, that carried military supplies. These were brought to the North with the army at the close of the war. It was decided to send them to frontier posts in the West for government use and for settlers who might need such equipment. They were driven westward over the National Road.

The first contingent of "Sherman's Army Train," as it was called, reached Cambridge on Saturday afternoon, June 18, 1865, two months after the war ended. There were 250 wagons, each drawn by six mules, and attached to the rear of each wagon were from two to four extra mules. In all, there were more than 2,000, the greatest number of such animals ever seen in Cambridge at one time. But what attracted the most attention were the negro drivers, all ex-slaves who had joined the Union Army. There were two to each wagon, not riding within, but on the two wheel-mules. Before the war, colored men were seldom seen in Cambridge.

About a mile west of town, near the location of the present barracks of the Highway Patrol, they camped over Sunday, in order that drivers and mules might rest. It is needless to say that all day, the road between the town and camp was thronged with people who wished to see the battle-scarred wagons and mules from the deep South.

On Tuesday, June 21, 700 mules passed through Cambridge, with a full contingent of negroes in charge. In front was a bell mule that seemed proud of its position at the head of the procession. They did not display any of the proverbial stubbornness characteristic of the government mule. One who witnessed the procession said they actually kept step, almost with military precision.

On the following day came 750 more wagons, each having two negro drivers, six horses in front and from two to four in the rear. In the three contingents, there was a total of 1,000 wagons, approximately 10,000 mules, and more than 2,000 colored men.

In Volume II, Howe's "Historical Collections of Ohio," is a full-page frontispiece, from a photograph, showing "Sherman's Army Train" passing the courthouse in Zanesville.

Return of the Boys of '61

[Originally published 2/16/1945]

Lee's surrender to Grant on April 9, 1865, virtually ended the Civil War. The rejoicing over the event and the celebration in Cambridge that followed are described on page 272 of the book. The return of the boys to their homes was eagerly awaited.

Approximately 2,000 Guernsey County boys had joined the army. But not all of them would return, for about 400, or one out of five, had given their lives for the preservation of the Union.

The war having ended, the troops of Grant and Sherman were brought to Washington, D. C., where in triumph they marched through the streets for two days. Then, as rapidly as possible, they were mustered out and permitted to return to their homes.

Within a few weeks, nearly all the Guernsey County boys had returned. Plans for a great reception in their honor were made, and the date set for it was Tuesday, July 4. Committees were appointed and nothing was overlooked that might add to the success of the occasion. A country-wide invitation to be honored guests was extended to all soldiers and their wives or sweethearts.

On Tuesday morning at 11 o'clock, all assembled at the court square. Here, on behalf of the citizens, a formal address of welcome was made by the Rev. Mr. Ellison, pastor of the M. E. Church. To this, Col.

Milton Barnes responded on behalf of the soldiers. Milton Barnes was captain of Company G, Sixty-second O. V. I., which left Cambridge for service early in the war; he returned a colonel. An attorney and a Republican, he took an active part in politics, and was elected prosecuting attorney, serving two terms (1867-71). In 1876, he was elected secretary of state, the first Guernsey County man ever to be elected to an Ohio state office and served two terms.

Following the welcoming exercises, the honored guests formed in line and marched to the Town Hall where a free dinner had been prepared. Major J. K. Brown was marshal of the parade. He, too, had led a Guernsey County company in the war, Company B, Fifteenth O. V. I., and returned home a major. He afterwards served as county auditor (1874-77).

At 2 o'clock, the great crowd again assembled at the court square. Col. John Ferguson made the first address to the returned men. It was he who, four years before, recruited the first company to leave for the war from Guernsey County, bearing the name of "Ferguson's Guards," under the leadership of Capt. James W. Moore. He afterwards entered the service himself, as captain of Company F, Twenty-sixth O. V. I. The next to speak was Rev. W. H. McFarland, pastor of the United Presbyterian Church. Near the beginning of the war, he enlisted as a chaplain and served until the close in the Ninety-seventh O. V. I., in which James W. Moore was a major. The closing address was given by Gen. A. J. Warner, of Marietta.

This was a grand gala day in Cambridge. It was a happy day to the soldiers, for after four years of fighting, they were home again with their relatives and friends. It was a glad day to the citizens whose sincere greetings and words of appreciation were unbounded. Underneath it all, though, were sorrow and sympathy, for one out of five of those who left had not returned.

An effective feature of the reception came at the close, when the entire soldier body, as a mighty chorus, joined in singing,
"We'll Rally Round the Flag, Boys,
We'll Rally Once Again."

The Cashmere Goat Company

[Originally published 8/23/1946]

Designed to pay a high rate of dividend to its stockholders and turn the attention of the whole country towards Guernsey County as the first to engage in a unique industry, the Cashmere Goat Company was incorporated in 1866, the year after the close of the Civil War. It seems that for a long time, a lot of people here became goat-minded, and the topic for discussion everywhere was "goats." While it may not be good taste to give a hint as to the outcome of the venture this early in our story, we deem it not inappropriate to add to what we say in the preceding sentence that after the company had functioned a year or two, "goats" were still discussed, but this time in the figurative sense in which the term is frequently applied.

An Ideal County for Goats.—Early in the year 1866, a high-powered promoter by the name of White, representative of the United Cashmere Company of Tennessee, arrived in Cambridge with a sensational business proposition in which he soon succeeded in interesting a number of citizens. Much money was to be derived from raising Cashmere goats, he declared, and of all the places in the United States that he had surveyed, Guernsey County, by virtue of the blessings of nature, presented the greatest possibilities for success in this industry.

He had been looking for a suitable section of the country in which to organize a company, he said, and then proceeded to point out the reasons why he had chosen Guernsey County. Amongst these were the climate, surface, plant growth, and other natural conditions that made this an ideal county for raising Cashmere goats. It was a veritable goat Garden of Eden.

Meeting Is Called.—For the purpose of acquainting the people with the proposition, a meeting was held at the courthouse on January 13, Mr. White, of course, being the main speaker. He gave a description and history of the Cashmere goat, somewhat as follows: It is white in color and remarkable for its long, fine, and silky hair, from which the famous Cashmere shawls are made, which are in great demand at $1,000 each. A native of Kashmir, in India, it has been raised successfully in Tibet, but attempts to introduce it elsewhere met with little success until it was brought to America a few years before. The United States Patent Office had made a study of the matter, he said, and reported that it looked upon its introduction "as one of the greatest acquisitions of wealth ever brought to this country."

He announced that the natural conditions in Guernsey County were very similar to those in Kashmir, India, the long-time habitat of the Cashmere goat, and here the animal would feel at home. The climate was much the same. The rocky hills, springs of clear cool water, and the abundance of plant life were referred to. Possessing an omnivorous nature and a voracious appetite, the goat had to have a variety of vegetation in its diet. Never had he seen such a flora as that of Guernsey County. Goats thrived on the leaves and branches of trees and shrubs, a variety being necessary for their wellbeing. Here in Guernsey County could be found every kind of tree, shrub, vine, and herbaceous plant indigenous to the Temperate Zone.

There was a great demand for the hair of the Cashmere goat, he declared, and it commanded a very high price, being sold by the ounce rather than the pound. The parent company in Tennessee, formed primarily to propagate the animals, would market the product of a company organized here.

Officials Are Chosen.—So promising did White's proposition appear that before the meeting closed, a company was formed and subscriptions taken for stock to the amount of $10,000. The get-rich-quick spirit was in the air, and many wanted in on the ground floor.

At a stockholders' meeting held on Feb. 3, officers were chosen as follows: Hugh Broom, president; Robert Clark, vice-president; Thomas Frame, secretary; Stephen Potts, treasurer; Alexander McCoy, William Robe, and Thomas Perry, executive committee. Robert Clark was named to accompany Mr. White to Tennessee for the goats.

The Goats Arrive.—On February 22, Mr. Clark returned with forty-eight goats, for which he had paid $9,000. They were pretty little animals with long, silky, snow-white hair, just about ready to be clipped, and they attracted much attention.

Following the clipping a few weeks later, the hair was sent to the Tennessee headquarters to be marketed, according to agreement. Soon after this came a letter to the effect that the Guernsey County product was of a very superior quality, bearing out the prediction that the natural conditions here were such that this result would be obtained. This was encouraging, for the goats had been here but a short time—the climate and natural resources of Guernsey County were working wonders. Enclosed with the letter was a check for twice the amount expected by the stockholders.

Mr. White Returns.—A few days afterwards, Mr. White arrived in Cambridge again, ostensibly to congratulate the company on its good fortune. Incidentally, however, he announced that there were yet a few choice blocks of stock available, and he kindly offered to give the folks here the first chance. There was a scramble to buy.

More goats arrived and another clipping followed. As before, the fine, silky hair was forwarded to Tennessee. Something appeared to be wrong, for neither letter nor check was received. An investigation was ordered by the company. Although we have made a lengthy and careful search, we have been unable to find a recorded report of the committee appointed. Our guess is that, upon arriving in Tennessee, the committee discovered that the officers of the parent company, like Longfellow's Arabs, had folded their tents and silently stole away.

Now you may be wondering what became of the goats. We don't know. Were they Cashmere goats, or some other breed? We don't know that either. We recently made a study of the animal and learned that the Cashmere goat is unable to survive the climate of this country, and that probably there is not one in America today.

SOME CHRONOLOGICAL COUNTY HISTORY

Court Cases 78 Years Ago

[Originally published 1/27/1945]

A Guernsey County court docket of 1867 shows that 170 cases were set for the March term of court that year. Announcement was made that this number of regular cases would come before the court, and that doubtless several more would be assigned later. The common pleas judge was William Kennon; clerk of courts, E. C. Riggs; sheriff, William Stewart; prosecuting attorney, Milton Barnes.

From a study of the cases assigned, we find that they might be grouped as follows:

civil action, 66;
appeals—principally from the courts of justices of the peace—21;
violations of liquor laws, 25;
divorce, 11;
arson, 2;
burglary, 2;
partition, 10;
grand larceny, 1;
assault and battery, 2;
attachment, 8;
surety of the peace, 1;
stealing money, 2;
bastardy, 1;
forgery, 1;
replevin, 1;
keeping tavern without license, 6;
obstructing the highway, 2;
corrupting witness, 1;
alimony, 1;
dower, 1;
insolvent act, 2;
chancery, 1;
appeals from county commissioners, 2.

As many cases as are named above are not heard in a single term of Guernsey County court today. Were there more crimes 78 years ago than there are at the present time, and did more people take their troubles to court than do now? We shall answer the first part of the question by saying we still have crimes, but many of them are settled before they reach the Common Pleas Court. Then, too, many are settled between terms. Before 1915, we had common pleas districts, each district, perhaps, composed of several counties under one judge. He held court in each county of his district four times a year and was usually confronted with an accumulation of cases. Today there is at least one common pleas judge in each county, and his court is open at all times. He thus disposes of many cases between sessions

To the second part of the question, our answer is "yes." Court was more of an attraction seventy-eight years ago than it is today. It was not an uncommon thing for a courtroom to be packed with spectators every day of the session. In the South, even at the present time, the streets of a little county-seat town will be thronged with people on court days. It used to be here that a person apparently took pride in being pointed out as a litigant in a case. He felt important. It was customary for folks to take their differences to court to have them settled. An examination of the records shows that many of them were very trivial. We might register our opinion here that while many of the attorneys of the earlier days encouraged litigation, the tendency of most of them now, when prospective clients consult them, is to have the question in dispute settled outside of court.

The petit jury summoned to serve in the March, 1867, term of court was composed of George Frazier, John Montgomery, Isaiah Stout, M. Bumgardner, A. Sankey, William G. Walters, V. B. Cockins, Luke Barton, E. H. Webster, John Mack, S. Craig, and Lem Bonnell.

Cambridge did not lack attorneys in 1867. With a population of less than 2,000 the town had fifteen or twenty lawyers. A local paper carried the advertising cards of the following: Milton Barnes, James K. Casey, Francis Creighton, John Ferguson, William M. Farrar, M. Gaston, J. O. Grimes, E. W. Mathews, J. D. Taylor, J. B. Taylor, William S. Siens, Robert Savage, W. D. Shaw, B. F. Sipe, and Joseph W. White. There were probably several others, and so this meant much competition.

Cambridge Schools in 1869

[Originally published 11/26/1945]

Today we drop back three-fourths of a century for a look at the Cambridge Schools. As our guide, we have in hand a small manual, entitled "Rules and Regulations of the Public Schools of Cambridge, Ohio" bearing the date of August 31, 1869. We really do not remember how it came into our possession, but that doesn't matter. It may be the only copy in existence. It gives the course of study, the personnel, and the rules and regulations of the schools. For more data to aid us in writing this little story, we consulted the local papers of that year.

The Buildings.—At that time, school was held in an eight-room building that stood on the site of the present Park School at the top of the hill. This building burned in 1871, and following the fire, the Central School was erected on Steubenville Avenue. The bricks of the old school were given to the colored folks of the town, who cleaned off the mortar and used them in the construction of Shaffer's Chapel on Gaston Avenue. The Park School was not built until several years later. In addition to the school on the hill in 1869, there was a small, one-room building on the West Side in which pupils of the lower classes were taught.

The board of education, composed of Joseph D. Taylor (president), E. C. Riggs (clerk), E. W. Mathews (treasurer), Francis Hammond, Simeon Haynes, and John Stitt. The school term was nine months, the same as that of today, beginning on the first Monday in September and running five days a week from 9 A. M. to 12 M., and from 1:30 P. M. to 4:30 P. M.

Pupils and Teachers.—The schools enrolled 436 pupils. They were not classified by grades, as they are today, but by departments—high school, grammar, intermediate, and primary. In the high school were 50; in the grammar, 100; in the intermediate, 98; and in the primary, 126. In the one-room building on the West Side were 62.

Phebe E. Waller and Margaret Allison taught in the grammar department; Ella J. Betts and Anna M. Beatty, in the intermediate; and May Bell, Kate Bell, and Belle Riddle in the primary. Mattie Allison was the teacher of the one-room school on the West Side. John McBurney was the superintendent and teacher of the high school.

Course of Study.—The proverbial reading, writing, and arithmetic were stressed in all departments. Taught in the primary department were the alphabet, spelling, reading, writing, arithmetic, and language; in the intermediate department, spelling, reading, writing, arithmetic, language, and geography; in the grammar department, spelling, reading, writing, arithmetic, grammar, geography, United States history, and physiology.

While there were subjects in the high school curriculum not found there today, there are several today that were not offered then. These were taught: arithmetic, algebra, grammar, composition, rhetoric, philosophy, geometry, botany, trigonometry, mensuration, surveying, history, science of government, astronomy, Latin, and German.

Non-resident pupils were admitted to the high school for $2.00 a month, to the grammar for $1.50, and to the intermediate and primary departments for $1.00. The teacher was required to open her school each morning by reading a portion of the Scriptures. Prayer and singing were optional.

The Superintendent.—John McBurney, the superintendent, was then thirty-five years old. He was a graduate of Madison College, had taught a few years in the rural schools of Guernsey County, had served two years as a soldier in the Civil War, and had been superintendent of the Cambridge Schools for three years.

He alone was the high school faculty, teaching the fifty high school pupils the subjects named above. Among his other duties above, as prescribed by the board of education, he was to be the executive officer of the board, have supervision over the grounds, building, furniture, apparatus, and library, see that the janitor enforces neatness and proper ventilation and temperature in the building, examine all pupils and make promotions, visit all the rooms as often as his time permits and advise and encourage the teachers; hold teachers' meetings; see that the teachers report regularly; and a lot more which we haven't space to name here.

For all this work, Mr. McBurney received a salary of $600 a year. It is probable that many of the taxpayers thought it was too much. The board of education in the little manual called attention to the high standard of the Cambridge Schools, which was "equal to that of the best in Ohio."

The Marsh Stogie Factory

[Originally published 1/2/1945]

An important Cambridge industry back in the 1870s and 1880s was the Marsh Stogie Factory. The average annual output of this factory was three million six hundred thousand stogies. In 1881, Mr. Marsh reported that since going into business he had made one billion five hundred seventeen million five hundred thousand. This number probably included the product of the Wheeling factory.

Thomas C. Marsh, the Cambridge manufacturer, was connected with the Marsh family at Wheeling where the Marsh Stogie originated and where it is yet made. Every cigar store carries the Marsh brand.

There may be some old-time smokers who will recall the "long nines", packed in cylindrical pasteboard boxes. Their strength was outstanding and a simile for the day was, "As strong as a 'long nine'." Boys learning to smoke liked to boast of their progress by saying that they had managed a "long nine".

The Cambridge stogies were widely distributed. Mark Twain, in his famous book entitled "A Tramp Abroad," said that 1,000 Marsh Stogies formed a part of his outfit.

In "Stories of Guernsey County" (page 226), is told how the word "stogie" originated. Wagoners on the National Road received small wages and could not well afford to buy cigars. They were inveterate smokers. Marsh at Wheeling, for their special use, made a cheap cigar from homegrown tobacco which he called the Conestoga brand. This name was given because they drove Conestoga wagons. The name being too big for the wagoners, they got to calling them "stogies." Smokers who were not wagoners asked for them, and Marsh began to manufacture them for the general trade. Then the word "stogie" came into use all over the country as a colloquialism. In the course of time, it was adopted as a good English word and now it may be found in every dictionary, defined "a cheap cigar."

Thomas C. Marsh was born in Jefferson County, Ohio, began working in the Wheeling cigar factory when fifteen years of age, and came to Cambridge in 1861.

SOME CHRONOLOGICAL COUNTY HISTORY

The Fourth of July

[Originally published 6/25/1946]

Announcement that the Cambridge Band and American Legion Post No. 84 will jointly sponsor "an old-fashioned, rousing Fourth of July celebration" this year prompts us to write this story. Back a half century and longer ago, there was an observance of this anniversary in nearly every community in the country, and many of them would try to outdo each other in staging attractions that would draw crowds. The birthday of our nation is held as our greatest secular holiday, and is sanctioned by statute in every state.

Character of Celebrations.—The chief characteristics of a Fourth of July celebration in earlier days were spread-eagle oratory and unlimited meaningless noise. Since it commemorates the most joyous event in our nation's history, it has been deemed fitting to include fun-making features, such as callithumpian parades, chasing greased pigs, and climbing greased poles. Feats of strength, races, and games of various kinds were always a part of the day's activities. This was the day of unlimited patriotism. It was the day, too, as some seemed to think, for getting gloriously drunk. In such condition, they imagined themselves to be filled with the "Spirit of '76", and fights would follow.

Designed to arouse the spirit of patriotism, Fourth of July oratory has been of a character and style peculiarly its own. It was expected to show the justice of our Revolution, laud the brave deeds of our forefathers, call attention to the greatness of our country, and assert our determination to fight and die, if necessary, for its preservation and protection. In harmony with the general noise of the day, the oratory was usually of a bombastic type.

First Celebration in Ohio.—A few weeks after the arrival of the first settlers at Marietta, in 1788, came the twelfth anniversary of the Declaration of Independence. As busy as these pioneers were in erecting their cabins, clearing away the forest, and cultivating their first crops, they took a day off to celebrate the anniversary of the event they held as the greatest of the events that had led to their freedom.

Most of them were veterans of the Revolutionary War, and fresh in their minds were the hardships endured and sacrifices made to the end that they might enjoy the blessings of liberty that were now theirs in this new country. Their celebration began at daylight and continued until midnight. Like the Pilgrims at Plymouth in observing the first Thanksgiving, they made the day one of feasting and invited the Indians to the great common dinner that was prepared and served beneath the trees. According to a report that has been preserved, there were spread on the tables venison, buffalo and bear meat, wild turkey, and fish. On the day before the celebration, a pike had been caught in the Muskingum River that was six feet long and weighed over a hundred pounds.

There were toasts to George Washington, to Gov. Arthur St. Clair, and to Congress. When, towards evening, firing of cannon began as a feature of the celebration, the Indians became frightened and took to the woods.

Cambridge's Greatest Fourth of July.—Throughout the country, the Fourth of July of 1876 (the hundredth anniversary) was celebrated more enthusiastically than any before or since. Cambridge then had a population of approximately 2,500; July 4 fell on a Tuesday. The work of decorating the town began a full week before. In front of the old courthouse, a flag pole 110 feet high was raised. Where the soldiers' monument now stands, a platform was erected for the speaking.

It was a full twenty-four-hour celebration, as it began at exactly twelve o'clock Monday night and did not end until twelve o'clock Tuesday night. A cannon down on Wills Creek announced the opening. At this signal, every bell in town was started to ringing and kept ringing until daylight. Farm dinner bells, church bells, and school bells out in the country began ringing as soon as the ones in town were heard. The leading industrial plant in Cambridge in 1876 was the Simons Brothers foundry, whose chief product was bells. On hand were carloads of bells of various kinds, and every one was set ringing. A feature was a set of a hundred bells arranged to chime.

Early in the morning, folks came pouring into town, and the streets were soon thronged. Led by the Cambridge Band, then known as the Scott Band, came a mammoth patriotic parade in the forenoon, with Col. John Ferguson as chief marshal. In the afternoon, the people assembled at the court square for the program, which consisted of band music, singing, and oratory. John H. Sarchet led the singing. Attorney W. S. Heade read the Declaration of Independence; no Fourth of July observance was complete without it. The first oration was delivered by Hon. Ross W. Anderson, then the mayor of Cambridge; the second by Col. Milton Barnes, a local attorney who was that year elected Ohio's secretary of state.

Cambridge had never known so much noise as there was that day. Even above the bells could be heard the shouting of the people, which continued until the close of the celebration. It was the day before the giant firecracker, but a greater noise was made by means of anvils. There was no such elaborate and spectacular display of fireworks as we have today. Instead, they had what they called "illuminations," produced by placing candles or kerosene lamps in the windows of homes and business places, the burning of tar barrels, and the throwing of fire balls. From a patriotic standpoint, we believe the people held a little closer to the true purpose of the Fourth of July than they do today.

SOME CHRONOLOGICAL COUNTY HISTORY

The Old Farmer Coal Mine

[Originally published 4/21/1947]

At the southeastern edge of what is now Byesville was once a coalmine to which the community owed much for its early development. Although abandoned long ago, there are some who will remember it, and many there are who are more or less familiar with the traditions that have persisted through the years.

Opened in 1877.—It was opened in 1877—exactly seventy years ago—by three men, Messrs. Farmer, Anderson, and Cranage. Mr. Farmer was a Quaker and, being the most active member of the group, the mine became known by that name. By some, it was called the Central Mine. Notwithstanding the fact that it changed hands a number of times, and officially it bore different names, to the people generally, it was always the "Old Farmer Mine," and is referred to as such even today.

In 1873, the Cleveland and Marietta Railroad was built down the valley through Byesville, then a sleepy little hamlet of only a few houses. That coal underlay all the surrounding country was generally known, but its development was out of question because there were no transportation facilities. Now that there was an outlet for the product, the first step towards, opening the coalfield was taken by the three men named above.

Primitive Methods of Mining Used.—In order to reach the vein of coal, a fifty-six-foot shaft was sunk. This was one of the shortest coal shafts ever used in the county. Vein No. 7, which crops out near Cambridge, drops to the south and east, reaching a depth of two hundred feet at Senecaville. At the bottom of this shaft, a fine stratum of coal was struck, that had a thickness of five feet and ten inches. Unlike the veins of many mines in the county, this one was found to be uniform throughout and comparatively free from faults.

The work in the mine at first was the old-fashioned pick and shovel kind. With the advance of time, improved mining machinery was installed as soon as it made its appearance. Before Old Farmer was abandoned in 1904, after twenty-seven years of operation, it was up-to-date in every particular.

Many Changes of Ownership.—Farmer, Anderson, and Cranage operated the mine for some time and then sold it to the Manufacturers Coal Company. It afterwards was taken over by Anderson and Cope. They sold it to the Champion Coal Company of Pittsburgh. Next came the Ohio Coal Company, then the International Railway Fuel Company, and, when abandoned, it belonged to the Wills Creek Coal Company.

Following changes of ownership, usually came changes of mine superintendents. In its history, its work was directed by not fewer than fifteen men whose names follow: W. A. Smith, W. A. Davis, T. J. Lee, E. W. Smith, George Bancroft, David E. Evans, David Williams, David Cook,

William Sheehan, Gomer Lewis, John S. Holbrook, John Hood, Sr., James C. Orr, John Orr, and Benjamin Morris.

No Major Disasters.—Never in its operation of nearly a third of a century did Old Farmer experience a major mine disaster. It may be remarked here that Guernsey, one of the leading mining counties of the state, has never suffered a disaster of the kind that is common in most coalfields. This is attributed to a peculiar dampness in the Guernsey Valley that makes the mine dust impotent. The Senecaville mine explosion in 1903, in which several lives were lost, was an outside disaster caused by lightning (page 980 of the book).

Occasionally, a life was lost in the Old Farmer Mine, not from an explosion, but from falling slate, a premature blast, or other accident. Among those who suffered death in the mine were Eli Wilson, William Mackley, Thomas Allender, George Barnes, Hollis James, William Collins, John Hesse, Daniel Ables, Simeon Dickens, and James Davis.

Millions of Tons Mined.—During its long period of operation, thousands of men were employed in the Old Farmer Mine. It is estimated that if all the coal mined there and lifted up the single fifty-six-foot shaft had been loaded in cars of fifty tons capacity each, there would have been a number sufficient to form a solid train one thousand miles long. The value of this output, even at the low prices at which coal was sold a half century ago, would have been fully five million dollars.

A Maze of Passageways.—There were sixty-five miles of passageways in the mine, so intricately crossed and re-crossed as to form a labyrinth through which it was difficult for one to find his way. It reminds one of the labyrinth of King Minos of Crete, from which one who entered never returned, until his daughter, Ariadne, conceived a plan for the escape of Theseus, her lover, who was sent within. She gave him a ball of thread, which he was to unroll as he traveled from passageway to passageway, and this enabled him to retrace his steps.

Before it was abandoned, some of the early timbers had become decayed, and there were frequent fallings of slate. Air rushing through the intricate maze of passageways would produce weird sounds that preyed upon the minds of the superstitious. Then it was rumored that at certain times and at places where deaths had occurred in the mine, strange lights would be seen. There were many weird happenings that were never explained. Mystery may lurk in every abandoned coal mine. In this respect, Old Farmer stands out prominently. The greatest mystery in the history of Guernsey County coal mining, however, is that of Old Pete.

(See story on page 982 of book.)

SOME CHRONOLOGICAL COUNTY HISTORY

Wills Creek Carp
[Originally published 10/27/1945]

"Only a pesky carp!" or some similar expression of disappointment and disgust is very often heard over at Seneca Lake, occasioned by the landing of a fish of that lowly species. Following the anticipation incident to a strike, a quick jerk of the line, and the excitement while reeling in, out rolls a despised carp instead of the big bass or crappie that was expected. Back into the water it usually goes, to vex some other fisherman in a similar way. A carp, like a catfish, is active and tenacious of life out of water, and even if left on the bank, it is apt to find its way back to its accustomed place.

Multiply Rapidly.—Why, it is often asked, did those who stocked Seneca Lake with fish include the carp? They didn't; the carp were in the creek before the dam was built. When the waters came to cover the bottoms, out of the old channel went the carp to deposit their eggs on the grass and weeds of shallow places, each fish yielding several hundred thousand. June is its month for spawning. There are few fish that multiply as rapidly as the carp. They are a menace to other fish, too, as they tear up their nests and feed on their young.

Description of a Carp.—It is said that a carp may live for 200 years and attain a weight of 40 or 50 pounds. While there are several varieties of carp, that of Wills Creek is known as the German carp. Its scales are large and of a brownish hue. The dorsal fin is large; the mouth is small, and from its lips four barbels protrude. The flesh is soft and somewhat coarse; for this reason, it ranks low as a food fish, although there are ways of preparing it for table that make it pleasing to the taste. In Seneca Lake, it feeds chiefly on herbaceous matter, but will grab a worm and sometimes a minnow used as bait. We saw a fisherman over there the other day catching them with dough balls which he said he had made by mixing flour and cornmeal together, using vanilla to make a paste. Due to the fresh, clean water of Seneca Lake, the taste of the carp there is less disagreeable than that of those below, which feed on refuse matter in the channel.

A Native of Asia.—The carp is not indigenous to Wills Creek, or, for that matter, to any American stream. It originated in Asia and was brought from there to Europe, where it was prized as a food fish, especially in Germany. It possesses certain characteristics that adapt it to domestication. A hardy fish, it can be raised in sluggish ponds. In the winter, it snuggles down in the bottom of the stream or pond and hibernates.

Now we come to our question, "Why are there carp in Wills Creek?" They were not always there. James Gibson, who settled on the creek down by Kimbolton in 1806, names the kinds of fish found in the stream then, but does not include the carp (page 858 of the book). Some of the varieties he mentions are not there today; the carp seems to have possession, from mouth to source, as well as the lower courses of some of the smaller streams emptying into it.

Introduced Here in 1880.—About the year 1880, the U. S. Fish Commission, after studying the value of the carp as a food fish as considered by the Germans, its adaptation to domestication, and the inexpensive means necessary for its cultivation, introduced it into America and sent out bulletins urging people to establish fish ponds and raise their own fish for table use. Only a small space would be needed, it was pointed out, if supplied with running water. Farmers and many urban folks acted on the advice, and fish culture became a common thing.

David Daugherty's Fish Pond.—The first man to establish a fish pond in Cambridge was David Daugherty, the town street sprinkler. In those days, the streets were not paved, and to keep down the dust in summer an officer known as the street sprinkler was appointed. There was no city water system, and as much water was needed, the wells were inadequate. Where the Guernsey Laundry stands, on what is now North Eighth Street, was a strong spring. It is now the source of water supply for the laundry. To obtain water for sprinkling, Daugherty built a dam below the spring and a pond was formed, almost the size of a town lot. It occurred to him that this little body of water might serve a dual purpose and he stocked it with German carp.

The fish multiplied rapidly and grew. Frank Mahaffey, Steubenville Avenue, says he was but a small youngster then, but he recalls that this fish pond was a great attraction. The water was clear, and the carp—many of them as long as his arm—could be seen, so many of them that they could not swim around without bumping into each other.

Carp Escape To Wills Creek.—One day there came a heavy rain—a veritable cloudburst. Water poured into the pond from the slope at the east. The dam could not withstand the pressure. It broke, and out went the water into Gordon Run, fish and all. They soon reached Wills Creek where they found a home more nearly to their liking. The water was sluggish; the bottom of the creek was muddy, and there was much refuse matter upon which to feed. This explains why, after a half century, there are carp in Wills Creek and Seneca Lake. They are German immigrants and the descendants of the ones that were in Daugherty's pond.

SOME CHRONOLOGICAL COUNTY HISTORY

First Pennyroyal Reunion

[Originally published 7/3/1945]

On Wednesday and Thursday, August 22nd and 23rd, there will be a reenactment of the first Pennyroyal Reunion held in Gardiner's Grove near Fairview in August, 1880. Many are looking forward to this unique event, and Pennyroyalists now scattered widely are expected to return to enjoy it. They will meet beneath the same trees their forefathers gathered 65 years ago and established an annual institution that has continued to this day, and attracted nationwide notice.

At the first reunion 4,000 people were present. The crowds increased each year until in some years as many as six or eight thousand would attend. Interest in this pioneer of community gatherings has been less on the part of the general public in recent years, because there have come to be so many other gatherings of a like character. But the loyal Pennyroyalist is sure to be there.

Those taking part in the first reunion were pioneers of Pennyroyaldom, and their reminiscences covered the preceding 65 years; those who will participate this year will, for the greater part, be descendants of these, and each will assume the role of his ancestor. A complete stenographic report of the first reunion has been preserved, even to a description of the setting which will be reproduced. How many of the 4,000 who attended in 1880 are living today? All of these, of course, must be more than 65 years old. Wherever they may be living, they are invited to be present this year as honored guests.

According to the preserved report of this first reunion, "the stage was wreathed with the aromatic pennyroyal and in great letters of the herb the words 'Pennyroyal' appeared on the back of the stage and 'Welcome' in front of it." President J. O. Grimes, Esq., opened the meeting. Prayer was offered by Rev I. N. White. The Pennyroyal choir sang "Home Sweet Home". Hon. Newell Kennon gave the address of welcome, which was responded to by Dr. Paul, president of Muskingum College. Then came a selection by the Fairview Cornet Band composed of C. H. Giffee, Thomas Bratton, W. B. Lee, J. T. Morton, T. S. Rosengrant, Thomas Merryman, Charles Gleaves, Charles Hamilton, Eddie Stevens, N. H. Barber, Rufus Hunt, William Frost, William H. Kesselring, and Charles Tillett.

William Borton, Esq., gave the history of Pennyroyaldom, and Robert B. Buchanan presented an original poem, "Pennyroyal Holidays." A session was devoted to reminiscent talks by old pioneers, some of whom were amongst the first settlers of Oxford Township and far advanced in age. Amongst these were the Ables brothers, John and Bethuel, George Plattenburgh, William Bernard, William Morton, Hon. W. R. Wagstaff, Hon. Henry Kennon, Rev. Samuel Forbes, and Dr. S. L. Henry. Included amongst the others appearing on the program for talks were Hon. D. D.

Taylor, John Kirkpatrick, Col. J. D. Taylor, Hon. Joseph Ferrell, Col. John Ferguson, Baker Borton, W. S. Heade, Hon. William Lawrence, J. D. Henry, Hon. David C. Kennon, N. H. Barber, and Dr. J. T. McPherson.

The famous Pennyroyal Choir was organized at this reunion with the following as charter members: E. C. Morton, J. D. Talbot, W. B. Lee, J. T. Morton, Asa Van Fossen, W. C. Cowgill, Laura Hollister, Laura Gilliland, Carrie Holtz, Mollie Cowgill, Mrs. Capt. Rodecker, and Mrs. E. Hixon. This organization has continued to the present time, the personnel having changed through the passing years until today some of the members are grandchildren of the original ones. For many years, the late John H. Sarchet conducted the choir.

A feature of the reunions for many years has been what is known as the "Pennyroyal Play" in Fairview the evening of the first day. This is considered Fairview's greatest annual event and has become an established institution. The players are drawn from Oxford's best histrionic talent. There was no play in connection with the first reunion; instead of it, there was a big community dance at the Guernsey House, of which Thomas Smith was landlord.

At a business meeting on the second day, it was unanimously voted to organize a permanent "Pennyroyal Association" and hold annual meetings. It is hardly probable that these founders expected the organization to be functioning two-thirds of a century later. For the 1881 reunion, the following officers were chosen: J. O. Grimes, president; John Kirkpatrick, recording secretary and historian; D. D. Taylor, corresponding secretary; J. C. Beckett, assistant secretary; Newell Kennon, treasurer; and William Borton, Joseph Ferrell, Jonathan Rose, David C. Kennon, and Thomas Smith, members of executive committee.

The First Automobiles in Cambridge

[Originally published 5/18/1945]

'Twas very early in the present century that the first Cambridge-owned automobile appeared on the streets of the town. William Priaulx, a machinist here, was the owner. He obtained some parts of a Locomobile Steamer, and some other odds and ends, which he assembled, forming a crude affair in which he installed an engine he had on hand. When he first ran it out on the street, it occasioned about as much excitement as a submarine would today, moving up Wheeling Avenue under its own power.

This marked the beginning of a new transportation era in Guernsey County. Under favorable conditions, Priaulx boasted, he could attain a maximum speed of twenty miles an hour with his car, carrying two passengers. It happened that conditions were seldom favorable, and when they were not, it just wouldn't run at all. To make it around a square without having to get out to push and pull was an achievement of outstanding merit. In some respects, though, Priaulx was free from many of the disadvantages that confront modern motorists. Parking space was plentiful, and he needed it frequently; there were no traffic lights; no driver's license was required; no speed ordinance was in effect; points for gasoline hadn't been invented; and there was no danger of a head-on collision. He did have to submit to a lot of tongue-lashings, however, for scaring horses.

For a long time, Priaulx owned the only car in town. Then George Branthoover, of the Branthoover and Johnston firm, brought in a brand-new Pierce-Racine. William G. Urban and Charles T. Duffey began a study of its mechanism and managed to keep it in running order. Early in 1904, Cambridge was amazed to hear that Branthoover contemplated taking a trip to California in his automobile, that his wife and daughter would accompany him, and that William G. Urban had been engaged to do the driving. This was the year of the St. Louis Exposition, and the party would visit it en route. The trip was discussed for many days, and much advice was offered by well-wishers. Urban spent several days putting the car in condition.

The Hoyle Car of 1904
Ran from Cambridge to Wheeling in Five Hours

This car, now owned by C. T. Bundy of Barnesville, was photographed recently by his nephew, Robert Hoyle. The passengers are the original owner's son, Fred Hoyle, and his "bride" in 1904 driving costumes. This car will be on display in front of the Cambridge courthouse Saturday afternoon, May 19th.

They left Cambridge on a Thursday morning. A crowd of friends assembled to witness the start. After a period of cranking, Urban took his seat and the car glided off smoothly, the veils of the feminine passengers floating in the breeze. There was a mixture of emotions in the crowd, some declaring that the Branthoovers would never get back.

Just outside of town, something went wrong with the car, but Urban soon had it going again. Zanesville was reached without further mishap, but beyond, it began to rain. There was no top on the car, and all received a thorough drenching. The National Road was not then paved, and it became slippery. Chains were apparently not in use in those days; at any rate, they had none. By purchasing 150 feet of rope, cutting it into small lengths, and wrapping the wheels, they were able to proceed. They had neither spare tires nor innertubes. Gasoline stations were few and far between. At Springfield, Ohio, they broke down. An entire day was spent in trying to find a repair shop. Not finding one, they went to a blacksmith shop where they succeeded in getting the car in shape to run.

Eight days after leaving Cambridge, they arrived in St. Louis. Here the Branthoovers decided to make the remainder of the trip by rail. The Pierce-Racine was crated and shipped on to California by train. Urban came home. The car never returned to Cambridge. Branthoover sold it in California for more than it cost here.

Among other Cambridge folks who bought automobiles about this time, or shortly afterwards, were E. E. (Hub) Smith, Dr. Fred W. Lane, and William Hoyle who purchased an Oldsmobile while attending the St. Louis Exposition.

Mr. and Mrs. Hoyle planned a trip to New Jersey in their new car. They left Cambridge at 5 o'clock A. M., Monday, August 29th, and reached Wheeling at 10 o'clock, having traveled at an average speed of ten miles per hour. Their destination was reached on September 5th. It was about as hard to get gasoline as it is today, but for a different reason. Sometimes they would beg it at tin-shops and other places where a little could be spared.

At Hagerstown, Maryland, they experienced a modern-day vexation. An officer of the law signaled for Hoyle to stop and then informed him he was under arrest. "What for?" asked Hoyle. "For driving an automobile without a license plate," was the reply. Not being required in Ohio, Hoyle knew nothing about such things, but that didn't excuse him, and it was necessary for him to pay a fine of ten dollars. To avoid further arrest, he set out to buy a license, only to learn that they were not kept there and he would have to move on about twenty-five miles further to get one. "But how can I do this?" asked Hoyle, "I'll be arrested again before I get there?" "I'll fix it," said the officer of the law. He tore the top off a pasteboard shoe box, wrote "License Applied For" on it, and attached it to the car. Hoyle then proceeded on his journey. A one-way trip by automobile seemed to satisfy the travelers. They and the car returned to Cambridge by train.

Before the end of 1905, there were several automobiles in Cambridge, but they were still objects of attraction. When horns blew—and it seemed to be necessary for them to blow a good deal—folks would run to the door. To have "had a ride in an automobile" was something of which to boast. If one left town in his car, it was a matter for comment. On his return, he was usually asked, "Did you have any trouble?" Pleased was the returned motorist who could say, "Not a bit?"

William G. Urban and Charles T. Duffey did most of the repair work at first. In 1907, the Cambridge Motor and Storage Company, located on the site of the present Cambridge Dairy, was incorporated by W. F. Johnston, C. J. Rech, C. S. Turnbaugh, P. E. Gibson, W. H. Meek, and others. There were then nineteen automobiles in Guernsey County. This was the first of a Cambridge industry that leads in the activities of today, either directly or indirectly. All persons named above are now dead except C. J. Rech. He started with this pioneer company on its opening day and has remained in the automobile business to the present time—a full forty years.

The Two Heaviest Snows

[Originally published 2/12/1945]

In the story "Weather Extremes," page 756, reference is made to the two heaviest snowfalls on record in Guernsey County. Both came out of season, one in the late spring after cold weather was supposed to have ended, and the other in the fall before it was expected. Following is a fuller account of these phenomena than that in the book.

The spring of 1901 was normal. By April 19, on which day snow began to fall, the buds of some trees were ready to burst into leaf; wild flowers were in bloom; grass was green, and many gardens were planted. A heavy rainfall turned to snow, large flakes, which continued to come down unceasingly for about a day and a half.

As the snow was wet, it packed down, making travel through it difficult. Being about three-fourths water, it was heavy. It was reported that a quart of the precipitation weighed a pound and a half. Weighted down by the snow, many of the flat roofs in Cambridge began to sag, and frantic appeals went out for snow shovelers.

Some of the country roads were filled with snow to the tops of the fences on both sides, in some places from three to eight feet. Telephone and telegraph poles and wires were crushed to the ground. Trains on the railroad were abandoned. While the heavy rainfall extended from the Great Lakes to Georgia, the snowfall was somewhat local. In Pittsburgh, it was all rain, a steady sixty hours of it, and a great flood was expected.

The snow went off easily. The ground was warm, and there was no freezing. Much of the water formed from the melting sank into the soil and apparently did it good. Vegetation was not damaged. Grass seemed to grow beneath the blanket of snow. Fruit was not injured. Guernsey County had one of the biggest fruit crops in 1901, especially of peaches, that it had known for years.

In the spring of 1913, we had freakish weather. There were great floods that damaged many cities—Zanesville, Columbus, Dayton, and others. During the summer, the weather was normal. We had what might be called a late fall, no severe weather until Sunday, November 9. On that day, it began to snow, not a wet, sloppy snow of big flakes like that in April, 1901, but a dry, fine snow. There was much wind, and it became a regular blizzard. The snow was driven into every crevice and drifted into great heaps. It continued to snow throughout Sunday, Sunday night, and a part of Monday.

Business was at a standstill on Monday. Many people could not get away from their homes. Narrow lanes were cut through the streets, having walls five feet high on each side. Country roads were impassable. There was no delivery of mail, either rural or city. The coal mines in the Guernsey Valley did not operate, as the miners could not reach them. Trains on the railroad could not run.

Because it was early in the season, the ground was warm and the snow did not lie long. Within a few days, most of it had disappeared. There were many big drifts, though, that hung on till the following spring. Normal weather through the remainder of the fall and the winter followed the great snow.

The two snowfalls here mentioned have been the outstanding ones in the history of Guernsey County.

The Marietta and Lake Railroad

[Originally published 4/23/1945]

Washington, the oldest permanent town in Guernsey County, has experienced two great disappointments in its existence. It long hoped to be made the county seat, and it cherished the hope for seventy years, never relinquishing its efforts until a new courthouse was built in Cambridge in 1881. It long wanted a railroad, and time and again, its hopes were raised when surveys through or near the town were made, and rumors floated to the end that this cherished hope was about to be realized. Time and again, there was disappointment: another route taken or the project abandoned.

Then, at length, came material evidence of the thing hoped for. This became a reality one day when a locomotive was heard whistling in the south, and shortly afterwards came puffing up to the very back door of the town. And there was great rejoicing. The Central Ohio (Baltimore and Ohio), which was first surveyed through Washington, the old "Calico," which brought financial loss to many and became a project of derision, and two or three other roads that inspired hope but never materialized, had been disappointments. Now Washington had a railroad. It was the Marietta and Lake.

SOME CHRONOLOGICAL COUNTY HISTORY

The powers behind this project were Chicago capitalists. The promoter was W. H. Young. According to the plan announced, the road was eventually to extend from Marietta on the south to some point on the Great Lakes; hence the name given it. Its chief purpose was to afford an outlet for the rich coalfields through which it would pass. The first section, the promoter stated, would be built between Lore City and Washington, connecting with the Baltimore and Ohio at the former place. This would encourage the opening of mines between the two places at once. It was to extend north along the old "Calico" survey to Jewett to connect with the Wabash system. Beyond Lore City, it would parallel or absorb the Eastern Ohio to Senecaville, then push southward, crossing the Ohio River and Western near Whigville.

To build the seventy miles between Marietta and Jewett, a company was incorporated under the laws of South Dakota and a charter taken out in Ohio. It was capitalized for $3,500,000. As a condition for building the section between Lore City and Washington, the farmers along the survey were asked to donate 1,000 acres of coal to the company, which agreed to lease 1,000 acres more at twenty dollars an acre. The survey took the road through the Cale, Terrell, McCulloch, Coen, Criswell, Cook, and McDonald farms. The farmers near the route the road would take were so enthusiastic over the possibilities that lay ahead that they donated 1,500 acres and leased several thousand more than were at first asked by the company.

Work on the railroad was begun in March, 1908, a half mile west of Lore City. It connected with the Baltimore and Ohio at this point, rather than at the town, in order to obviate the necessity of a bridge across Leatherwood Creek. The grading was carried on rapidly, and soon a track was laid. A dream had become a reality.

Among the incorporators, in addition to Young, were A. Edward Ball and Robert A. Davis, of Chicago, who were expected to develop the coalfield. They did not do this, and there was little business for the railroad. For a few months, the one little train of the system made two trips a day between the two towns at its termini, and then left via the Baltimore and Ohio, never to return, and the company passed out with it. The rails were removed, and now, evidences of grading in some of the sod-covered fields are all that is left of the Marietta and Lake Railroad.

MORE STORIES OF GUERNSEY COUNTY

Mural Paintings of Pioneer History

[Originally published 11/2/1946]

In our last sidelight story, we reviewed the coming of Cambridge's first group of permanent settlers—the Beattys, Gombers, and Metcalfs. Three years after the settling of this first group here came the folk from the Isle of Guernsey—the Sarchets and some close relatives. In the "Pioneer Room" of the Berwick Hotel, recently decorated and equipped, have been placed murals depicting the trek of the Guernseyites after their landing in America, their arrival in Cambridge, and their being welcomed here by Jacob Gomber on behalf of the Beatty, Gomber, and Metcalf group. These pictures are attracting much attention.

The First Picture.—There are two pictures, each several feet in length. The first, entitled "From Guernsey Isle to Guernsey County," is a scene on Zane's Trace, somewhere east of here. The little group from Guernsey Isle are pushing westward—they hardly know where to find a place to locate in the New World. The difficulty of travel through the almost trackless forest is depicted. It took them seven weeks to travel from Baltimore to Wheeling, and nearly a week to make the fifty miles over Zane's Trace from Wheeling to Cambridge.

The Second Picture.—"Gomber Welcomes the Folk from Guernsey Isle", is the title of the second picture. In our last sidelight story, we told that the Beattys, Gombers, and Metcalfs settled down near the site of the present viaduct in 1803. When the folk from Guernsey Isle reached here in 1806, according to David Sarchet, a nine-year-old boy of the group, there were only two houses in Cambridge. One was a double log cabin down by the bridge over Wills Creek, and the other was Jacob Gomber's house on lot No. 67, now the site of the A. Simon store (page 803 of the book).

The Guernseyites reached Cambridge on a Saturday evening in August, and went into camp by a spring in the forest, near what is now the corner of Gomber Avenue and North Fifth Street. Here they planned to remain until Monday morning, for, being religious, they would not travel on the Sabbath. On Sunday morning, the settlers down by the creek were surprised to see smoke rising above the trees north of them. Did it come from a camp of Indians or white people?

Headed by Jacob Gomber, the men cautiously ventured out to investigate. Gomber carried his flintlock musket in his hand, ready for use, and strapped over his shoulder was a powder horn (now to be seen in the window of The Jeffersonian). Parting the bushes, he beheld a group of harmless-looking men, women, and children. The scene has been described by Col. C. P. B. Sarchet, and we here quote:

"They were strange-looking and strangely-dressed people, composed in all of men, women, and children to the number of twenty-six. The women, with short dresses and short gowns, belted around the waist, with large frilled caps on their heads, were busy about the campfire, preparing their frugal morning meal. The horses were hobbled and browsing among the bushes, and the men, with smock frocks, short breeches to which were attached long stockings, with heavy shoes, and white, broad-brimmed, wool hats, were moving about the wagons, talking a strange language."

Colonel Sarchet further says that John Sarchet, who was the most fluent with the English tongue, made Gomber to understand that they were Norman-French from Guernsey Isle, seeking homes in the new country. They were singing hymns of thanksgiving and rejoicing, as they would have been doing had they been back on their native island this Sabbath morning. For about three years, the Beattys, Gombers, and Metcalfs had been living down on the creek, almost isolated from the world. They were rejoiced to see the Guernsey people, the first to come Cambridge since their settlement in it, and the Guernsey people were pleased to find these strangers so friendly. Shown in the picture is Jacob Gomber extending a hand of welcome.

The Artist.—The decorations are the work of William E. Turner, whose life history is an interesting story in itself. Born in Athens County, Ohio, he began to display an artistic trait when a mere baby, grabbing for pencil and crayon whenever in reach. At the age of three, he was drawing pictures that attracted attention. Through high school and college, he continued to develop this talent. After a course in Ohio University, in which he majored in art, he entered the Academy of Fine Arts in Philadelphia. As staff artist on the publications of the institutions he attended, he acquired a practical experience.

His first commercial work was illustrating books and periodicals for various publishers. Such work requires a vivid and accurate imagination, something he apparently possesses. For five years, he was an artist in Hollywood, producing backgrounds for camera scenes. When the World War opened, he entered as a military artist and served eighteen months in an air base in England, making illustrations for posters and army publications. Here he became ill and was returned to America for treatment, to the Fletcher Army Hospital in Cambridge. While convalescing there, he did considerable art work for the hospital. After his discharge, he was engaged to make the mural paintings here described. It is his intention to continue his work in Hollywood.

MORE STORIES OF GUERNSEY COUNTY

Noted Writer Visits Pennyroyaldom
[Originally published 7/14/1945]

Grace Goulder, well-known staff writer of The Cleveland Plain Dealer, whose page appears each Sunday in the magazine section of that paper under the general head of "Ohio Scenes and Citizens," visited Pennyroyaldom a few months ago, and following is a part of her story that was published:

"I finally did get down to Pennyroyaldom. The headquarters of this realm of mint and memory is Fairview, Guernsey County. In this little old village and in the hills round about it all through the township which is called Oxford, one of the oldest institutions of the state is kept alive—in remembrance, that is—and a unique pioneer industry remains vivid to today's citizens, though it is nearly three-quarters of a century since the final remnants of the business closed down—the distilling of pennyroyal mint oil.

"Folks down here made tons of it and shipped it to eastern markets. The heyday of pennyroyal oil-making was about a century ago, and now even the plant itself, which once lay like snow over meadows, while it can be found in the hills, is scarce indeed. And the oil? Well, most people would tell you there is none to be had. But I found some, an ounce or two that is maybe 100 years old!

"Now, in the name of pennyroyal, every summer at the time when the herb in the old days was ripe for harvest and the pennyroyal stills were steaming, there is a reunion of the grandsons and granddaughters, the great-grandsons and the great-granddaughters of the old pennyroyal distillers. I know of no other such affair in Ohio. The Pennyroyal Reunion has been going on year after year and every year since 1880. I have wanted mightily to attend one of these gatherings, and this year laid all my plans to do so, but at the last minute I could not make it. On the very day of the reunion, our army son came home for one of those rare, joyful episodes so many families are experiencing now—a furlough—and of course of all the year this was not a time when I could leave home. So I missed the reunion in Gardiner's Grove, a beautiful stand of virgin forest on the edge of Fairview. I missed the speeches and the famous Pennyroyal Dinner of country-style chicken, ham, cakes, pies. I missed the pennyroyal masses that had been searched out to festoon the speaker's platform and that was worn in every buttonhole, and a corsage for every woman attending.

"But I did get to Oxford Township early in September. I visited with the folks of Pennyroyaldom, and I feel now as if I hadn't missed the reunion at all, so cordial was everyone, and eager to tell me about it.

"Up a winding dirt road, out in the country, remote and quiet, we stopped to see Frank Berry, one of the few people now living who made the oil. Mr. Berry, though almost 80, was on his roof, repairing a leak, but came down, and settling himself comfortably on the root of a giant elm in his dooryard, talked about the still that was 'yonder there, in the pasture.'

"They mowed the pennyroyal most of the time, he said, for it grew abundantly. Often they pulled by hand and stuffed it into bags. It grew everywhere, and many people distilled it. They stomped it tightly into vats, introduced steam at the bottom, and condensed the product to divide it, ultimately the water at the bottom, the oil coming to the top to be ladled off—the same process as for peppermint oil. They had cans made in Quaker City, shaped like log cabins with a roof for the top, a chimney for the spout. Crates of these cans, each of which contained a couple of gallons, were shipped from here to the wholesalers.

"But the pennyroyal does not grow as freely as it did—it likes new land, you see. I had trouble finding some. I found something that Mr. Berry said also was distilled-worm seed. They had me crush the seed and the leaf between my fingers, and then smell it. They made oil from this plant down here and gave it to their children to 'worm them.' And they sold this oil, too, to wholesale druggists in New York. They didn't make much of this, and for the sake of those who were children then, I am thankful.

"On our way home I stopped in Quaker City, which I want to discuss more fully in a later article, and there G. G. Hartley gave me the real oil of pennyroyal. He poured it from a good-sized flask into a little bottle which I now have here on my desk. It's thick and molasses colored, as it becomes with age, but it has its pleasant strong odor still.

"So while I missed the reunion I did get some pennyroyal oil, which is more than most people can say who attended."

History in Street Names

[Originally published 6/16/1947]

Did it ever occur to you that there is a lot of history in street names? As a rule, the name of a thoroughfare is not given it arbitrarily. There is usually a reason for it, based upon something that may be of historic interest. Names of streets will often indicate their age, or call persons or events to mind. To a certain extent, they may serve as mirrors of the past.

How Street Ages Are Indicated.—We can't imagine the pioneers calling their thoroughfares avenues, drives, roads, or boulevards. Such terms were not in their vocabularies. This stylish system of nomenclature indicates more recent additions to a town that opened with just plain "streets."

The name of a street sometimes shows the approximate date of its establishment. We don't know what year Blaine Avenue was laid out, but our guess is that it was near middle of the 1880s when Blaine was at his political zenith; and another guess is that a Republican had something to do with the street. McKinley Drive was doubtless opened in the 1890s, and by a Republican. Dewey Avenue is an exception; after the Battle of Manila in 1898, it was christened Dewey, having been commonly known for a long time as just National Road.

When. Col. Joseph D. Taylor's land north of town was laid out in lots and streets, one street was named for him. He evidently saw that some of his close political friends should be honored by street names—Gov. Charles Foster, President Benjamin Harrison, and Senator John Sherman.

The First Streets.—On the original plat of Cambridge (1806), nine streets were named, probably by Jacob Gomber, because it was he who named the town and the county four years later. Running east and west were Wheeling and Steubenville Streets (not avenues, as now). Wheeling Street was given that name because it became a section of the old Wheeling Road, which was formerly Zane's Trace. The other street led to Steubenville by way of Carpenter's Trail.

Running north and south between Wheeling and Steubenville Streets were six short streets which were given the names of trees. Many years afterwards, they were changed to numbers—Walnut to Fifth, Spruce to Sixth, Pine to Seventh, Chestnut to Ninth, Mulberry to Tenth, and Lombardy to Eleventh. What are now East and West Eighth Streets were not streets at all, but were included in the grounds of the public square. South Eighth Street to the bus station, which was the southern limit of the town, was called Market Street. It was afterwards continued down to Gomber's mill on the creek and called Mill Street.

Pioneers Honored.—The two proprietors of Cambridge—Jacob Gomber and Zaccheus A. Beatty—were justly honored by having their names given the first two streets running east and west, that were laid out after the two they had established. It is to be regretted that the next running parallel to these was not named Metcalf, the surveyor who platted the town, and the man, it is said, who influenced the other two to come here and found a town. This trio—Gomber, Beatty, and Metcalf—will ever be associated in Cambridge history. Aside from the names of the two streets we mention above, there is nothing to perpetuate the names of the three men to whom Cambridge owes more than to any others.

Stewart Avenue should bear the name of Metcalf. Back in 1872, William B. Stewart owned four acres between what are now North Seventh and North Eighth Streets. Although his land was somewhat remote from the town proper, he laid it out in twelve lots, and a street bearing his name. This street was afterwards extended east and west in a sort of zigzag, broken way.

Cambridge's Slow Growth.—A map of the town made in 1870 shows that there were but few more streets than there were in the original plat. Wheeling Street was extended from Lombardy to the top of the hill (the present Park School) in 1846; and Steubenville to what is now Highland, in 1847. Even as late as 1870, the country north of Steubenville Street was either open fields or woods.

SOME CHRONOLOGICAL COUNTY HISTORY

Mathew Gaston owned land south of Wheeling Street, and on it he laid out some lots and a street in 1846. He called the street "South," a name it bore until it became north of a considerable part of the town, when somebody suggested that it be changed to Gaston Avenue. Turner Avenue was originally the first alley south of Wheeling Street. Elza Turner laid out a row of lots fronting it on the south, and it became known as Turner Alley. Brown Alley, named for Nancy Brown, proprietor of the Brown House (now the National Hotel), ran between Wheeling and Steubenville Streets. There came a time when the council decided to improve these alleys, but found there was no law authorizing them to pave alleys. Thereupon they christened them avenues and proceeded in an unquestioned legal way.

Streets Named For Citizens.—Many men who platted additions to the town had streets named for them. Knowing when these men were active in civic affairs will enable one to form some idea as to the age of the street, and likewise when the oldest houses on it were built.

Clark Street gets its name from Stephen B. Clark, who owned the land through which it passes. Isaac Morton had a farm just outside the original town, which eventually became part of it. Morton's wife was a Carlisle; one of his daughters married a Campbell, and another a Murray; hence the names of these three streets. Some others who had land upon which streets were laid out were Dr. Andrew Wall, S. M. Burgess, John C. Beckett, and Alfred Weedon.

The South Side honored a few of the Presidents—Jefferson, Madison, Grant, and Garfield. It is not of great importance that one know how a street got its name, but to some it may be interesting.

Political Trends — Republicans, Democrats, and Whigs

[Originally published 3/5/1945]

Following the organization of the Republican Party in 1854, Guernsey County, in which the Democrats and Whigs had been running nip and tuck, swung heavily to the Republican side. Practically every Whig became a Republican, and many Democrats who were opposed to slavery crossed over to the new party.

Republicans have carried Guernsey County in seventeen of the twenty presidential elections since the Civil War. The first break came in 1916 when Woodrow Wilson, running for a second term, received 130 more votes than Charles E. Hughes. The next came in 1932; Franklin D. Roosevelt, running for his first term, had a lead over Herbert Hoover of 276. A candidate for a second term, he received 2872 more votes than Alfred M. Landon. But as a third-term candidate in 1940, he lost in the county, his vote falling 1415 short of Wendell Willkie's. In 1944 Thomas E. Dewey's lead was 2366. It will be seen that Roosevelt's combined vote of the four elections in which he came before the voters of Guernsey County as a candidate for President, was 636 less than the combined vote of his four Republican opponents.

To show the trend for the past eighty years we here give the Republican majority in each of the other presidential years: 1968, 794; 1872, 728; 1876, 636; 1880, 753; 1884, 882; 1888, 1040; 1892, 1339; 1896, 1117; 1900, 1894; 1904, 2969; 1908, 1760; 1912, 700; 1920, 1876; 1924, 5930; 1928, 8025. The large majority in 1924 may be attributed to the candidacy of Robert M. LaFollette, Independent, who drew more heavily from the Democratic Party than the Republican. In 1928, Alfred E. Smith was the Democratic candidate, and the fight against him was on religious and temperance issues, rather than political, and that accounts for the wide margin.

Since the Civil War (exactly eighty years) the Republicans have almost monopolized the Guernsey County offices. Within the past twenty years, however, the Democrats have been receiving a recognition that indicates a new trend. In 1936, every one of the seven Democratic county candidates on the ticket was elected. During the first sixty years after the Civil War, an occasional Democrat to county office was elected, usually due to some disaffection in the Republican Party.

Following is a table showing the number of years each party has held the county offices in the past eighty years, or since the Civil War. The numbers represent years.

	Repub.	Dem.
Representative	68	12
Probate Judge	69	11
Auditor	73	7
Recorder	76	4
Sheriff	64	16
Clerk of Courts	68	12
Prosecuting Attorney	70	10
Treasurer	70	10
Surveyor	58	22
Total	616	104

Always there have been three county commissioners. These, therefore, would represent a total of 240 years. Considered in this way, Republicans have held the office 214 and the Democrats 26 years since the Civil War.

EXTENDED CHAPTER XLIII

Noble County Stories

The Seneca Lake Country

[Originally published 5/4/1945]

Most of Seneca Lake lies in Wayne Township, and about one-fourth of Wayne Township is covered by the water of Seneca Lake. Noble was the last county to be formed in Ohio, and Wayne was the last township to be formed in Noble County. For the first forty years—until 1851—all of the Seneca Lake country was in Guernsey County, so it is proper to include its early history in the "Sidelights on the Stories of Guernsey County."

When Noble County was formed of territory cut from Guernsey, Monroe, Morgan, and Washington counties, it was divided into fourteen townships. Over in the northern part lived Joseph Burson who had a big farm, a store, and a mill, plus considerable political influence, and he wanted a township whose political affairs he could look after himself. It was deemed to be good politics, which was getting deeply rooted at the time, to please him, so it was ordered that a fifteenth township to be called Wayne be set off. To do this, it was necessary to take a slice off the western part of Beaver, another from the southern part of Richland, and so much of Wright Township in Guernsey County that it could not exist longer as a separate political subdivision, and thus passed off the map entirely. But Joseph Burson had what he wanted.

The new township was an awkward-shaped affair, having more than a dozen angles in its boundary. Seneca Creek flowed diagonally across it from the southeast to the northwest, having Beaver Creek from the east and 'Possum Creek from the south as tributaries. The residents were proud of their township, boasting that they had more bottomland and more fertile land than could be found in any other township of the county. An elevation that had long attracted attention was the Reeves Hill, later known as the Ward Hill. I used to visit my grandfather who lived on a ridge from which one could overlook the entire Seneca Lake country. Although five miles away, this hill could be seen towering above the surrounding land, a lone tree standing at its summit. I hoped that, at some time, I might climb to the top of it, but have never done so. Today, it is almost surrounded by water and may be seen from nearly every part of the lake.

Joseph Reeves, a veteran of the Revolutionary War, was the first white man to settle in the Seneca Lake country, coming there, it is traditionally stated, in the latter 1790s. But he didn't remain long because the Indians were hostile and troubled him a good deal. When more peaceful times came, he returned and spent the rest of his life near the hill mentioned above, dying at the age of 96.

The first of the Wards, who eventually added the Reeves land to that which they themselves entered, was Edward, who came from Pennsylvania in 1807. John, his son, was a lieutenant in the War of 1812. Edward Ward, Jr., son of John, was the first white child born in the Seneca Lake country. Edward Ward, Sr., died in 1818; John, in 1843, at the age of 83.

Other early settlers in the Seneca Lake Valley or on the adjacent hills included John Vorhies, who came in 1802 and may be considered the first permanent resident, since he was not scared away by the Indians, as was Reeves before him; Thomas and Andrew Richie in 1808, originally from Ireland; the DeLongs in 1805, from Pennsylvania; John Ferris, who settled on the farm afterwards owned by Amos Day; James Law in 1809, father of twelve children; Jacob Yoho in 1805; William Lowery from Pennsylvania; John Hague in 1812; Albert Strong from Ireland; John Thompson from Pennsylvania; Robert Carpenter, John Millhone, and John Stranathan.

When I was a youngster, I liked to listen to old Johnny Stotts tell about the hunting, trapping, and fishing in the Seneca Lake country when he was a boy. The beaver was trapped on the stream that bears that name, and opossums were plentiful along 'Possum Creek. Two of the Vorhies boys, John and Daniel, went coon hunting one night on the Reeves Hill, taking with them a dog and an ax. The dog struck a trail, and after while gave the bark that indicated he had treed the game. Hastening forward, the boys discovered that it was not a coon that the dog had treed, but a bear. One of the boys went to the Reeves home for a gun, while the other and the dog remained to watch the bear. The beast apparently noted the weakened besieging force and began to descend backwards, but the boy, with some withes he cut with the ax, together with the assistance of the dog, kept the bear in the tree until his brother returned and shot it.

Timothy Bates, who lived in the upper part of the Seneca Lake country, was noted in pioneer days as a hunter. Out hunting, he killed a bear, and having no way to convey it home, he removed its entrails and bent over a small tree to which he attached the body. When the tree resumed its upright position, it held the bear suspended in the air, head downward. Bates then went for a horse. Two small Reeves girls out hunting the cows came along, saw the bear looking down upon them from the tree, and were badly frightened.

Isaac Mendenhall was hunting deer. He suddenly came upon a large buck at which he fired, but only wounded it. The animal dashed forward. Mendenhall dropped his unloaded flintlock musket and began to climb the nearest tree. Not strong enough to hold him, the tree bent over and pitched him on the back of the infuriated animal. He clung to the buck and threw him down, and a fight for mastery followed. His cries brought a man to his assistance, who had accompanied him on the hunt, but not before his clothing had been torn from his body and he had been seriously injured.

Seneca Township, Noble County

[Originally published 5/15/1945]

Seneca Indians never lived in the Seneca Lake country as some have supposed. They were a tribe of the Iroquois, and their home was in Northern Pennsylvania and New York. They found an oil issuing from the ground, which they believed to possess medicinal qualities, and which became known as Seneca oil. It was nothing but common petroleum, which was afterwards obtained in great quantities in that section by drilling.

Some of the settlers in what is now the Senecaville Lake country discovered an oil that had oozed from the ground and was floating on the surface of the creek that flowed through the valley in which they had located. This oil had the smell and taste of the Seneca oil with which they were familiar, and they named the stream Seneca Creek. They didn't know that this same creek had been named Wills by the Zanes who reached it at the present site of Cambridge a few years before when they were blazing Zane's Trace. The Zanes had once lived on a Wills Creek in Maryland, and that suggested their giving name to this unnamed stream. Both names have been used ever since—Seneca for the upper, and Wills for the lower course.

Guernsey County was formed in 1810 and divided into five large townships. The southern one, through which Seneca Creek flowed, was called Seneca. Five years later, the first town in the original township was platted and named Senecaville. Then, more than a century later, came Seneca Lake. But the township was too large, and the Guernsey County Commissioners began to form others from it. The first set off was Buffalo, then Richland, then Spencer, then more. Seneca Township was eventually reduced to an area of twenty-four square miles. In 1851, Noble County was formed by the state legislature, and Guernsey no longer had a Seneca Township; she gave it to her new neighbor.

In our article about Beaver Township the other day, we mentioned Timothy Bates. By the shifting of township lines from time to time, he found himself geographically here and there, and he didn't move, either. He had settled so near the present boundaries of Beaver, Wayne, and Seneca that, in a way, he belonged to all of them. Seneca claimed him as her first permanent settler, as he had come there with his father, Ephraim, from Pennsylvania, in 1805. Born in 1778, he lived to be ninety-one years old. As we said in the Beaver story, Timothy farmed, kept a store and the post office, ran a mill, distilled whisky, and preached on Sunday. He bought hogs and drove them to the Baltimore markets, forcing them to swim the Ohio at Wheeling. He was a local preacher in the Christian Church and held services in the loft of his distillery. Stored there were barrels full of whisky, ready for the market. Timothy used these for both pulpit and pews.

Daniel Meade and wife were strong Methodists. It was customary for neighbors to join and harvest each other's wheat, the affair assuming the nature of a frolic at which whisky was used freely. Daniel was opposed to drinking, and when, one year, he invited his friends to his annual wheat harvesting frolic, the invitation carried the information that whisky would not be included in the refreshments. He didn't notice any unusual reaction to this, but when he arose early the morning of the big event, he was surprised to find that all his wheat had been harvested. The guests had come the night before, although it was Sunday, and by moonlight had done the work, stimulated by the beverage they had brought with them.

Following are the names of many of the pioneers of the twenty-four square miles comprising the present Seneca Township. Some of them have descendants living within the township or nearby today.

Abraham Rich from Pennsylvania, who farmed, operated a mill, and in 1826 built the first frame house in the township; Abraham Brown, who kept a small store on the farm of Abraham Rich; Levi Keller, born near Wheeling in 1795, came to Seneca Township in 1820, taught school, and operated a blacksmith shop; Jacob Thompson, who had a mill; John Casner, Daniel Craft, Thomas and Moses Campbell, Samuel and Hiram Danford, James Finley, Samuel Gibson, David Jennings, James Law, John Millhone, Aaron, Henry, and Jonathan Morris, John Miley, George Secrest, William Stranathan, John Stevens, Morris D. Spriggs, and Daniel Riggs.

A road, now State Route 147, ran through the township, connecting Barnesville and McConnelsville. The nearest trading point was Barnesville. Mail was received once a week. Levi Keller received the only newspaper coming into the township, The St. Clairsville Gazette. Among the early teachers were Enos Rhinehart, Isaac Q. Morris, Jeremiah Debolt, and James Mellon.

In 1838, on a high ridge, Ephraim Vorhies laid out the only town in the township. It was called Mt. Ephraim, its location and its founder's first name suggesting its name. Vorhies himself built the first house, a large double log cabin, known as the "Moss Tavern". It was so called because the cracks between the logs were chinked with moss instead of mud. Crawford Glover built the second house, in which he opened a store. Succeeding him at this business stand were Asbury Gardner, Bradfield and Barnes, and Isaac Q. Morris, in the order named. John Burnett, an evangelist, and Timothy Bates organized a Christian Church in 1839. James Tuttle was the first teacher in the town. Henry Steele had a tannery; he afterwards came to Cambridge and bought the McCracken tannery at the corner of Steubenville Avenue and North Ninth Street. Much tobacco was raised in Seneca and adjoining townships, which was packed at Mt.

Ephraim.

The chief source of water supply was the town spring, yet serving as such. Like many other little places with promising futures, Mt. Ephraim never grew. In celebration of its hundredth anniversary in 1939, a reunion, largely attended, was held, which occasioned many happy memories of other days.

The Beginning of Beaver Township, Noble County
[Originally published 5/14/1945]

Four Noble County townships were once a part of Guernsey—Beaver, Wayne, Seneca, and Buffalo. The history of each of these, for the first forty years, belongs to that of Guernsey County. We have told about the early years of Wayne in the story "The Seneca Lake Country." This is the story of the first forty years of Beaver. Those of Seneca and Buffalo will follow.

Beaver Township was cut from Oxford in 1816 and was much larger than it is today. In 1835, the northern part was removed to help form Millwood, and in 1851, a strip was sliced off the western side for Wayne, leaving the present area of thirty square miles. It took its name from Beaver Creek, which flows across it and empties into Seneca just outside the western boundary. Whisky Run, the next largest stream, flows into Beaver. The first settlers along this run engaged in distilling whisky, hence the name. Among them were Jacob Cline, George Peters, James Eagon, and John House. It was a lawful business in early days. Corn, in the form of whisky, could be transported to eastern markets more easily than the grain itself. The price of corn regulated that of whisky, which sold anywhere from twelve and one-half to thirty-seven and one-half cents per gallon. A bushel of corn was considered equivalent to a gallon of whisky.

John and James Reed, who came from Pennsylvania in 1804, were probably the first permanent settlers within the present boundaries of the township. They found the land heavily timbered and abounding in such wild animals as deer, turkeys, wolves, and bears, and a few panthers. Closely following the Reeds were other settlers, mostly from Pennsylvania, Virginia, and Maryland. The township lies in the Seven Ranges, and they received titles to their farms at the land office in Steubenville. They were an honest and hospitable people, strongly religious, but with little education.

Among the ones settling in different parts of the township were these: Thomas, John, and Joseph Carpenter in 1805, the last named being a soldier of the Revolutionary War; John House from Pennsylvania, in 1812; John Eagon, in 1811; James Lowery, a blacksmith from Virginia, in 1811; John DeLong, in 1812; John Mills from North Carolina, in 1812; John Ross, a soldier of the Revolutionary War; John Starr, in 1811; John Croy and

James Edgar, in 1812; William Deal, a strong anti-slavery man from Maryland; Isaac Cooper, who brought his family and household goods from Virginia in a two-wheeled cart drawn by two horses hitched tandem; William Williams, Robert Smith, William Murray, Edmund Gallagher, Francis Miller, John Jefferies, Philip and Daniel Wendell, and John Joy.

The Guernsey County commissioners ordered the township organized at the house of Philip Wendell. John House was named Justice of the Peace and served as such for eighteen years. He never kept any docket but recorded his transactions on slips of paper which he filed by sticking them between the logs of the walls of his cabin. He built a mill on Beaver in 1816, which was long a favorite place for getting grinding done.

Down in the western part of the original township lived Timothy Bates, hunter, farmer, miller, and local preacher. He had a mannerism and characteristics peculiarly his own. He was a strong Whig, and for many years kept the township post office, which bore the official name of Bates' Mill. When Jackson became President, he refused to serve under a Democrat and resigned the office. He was said to be a very homely man. The story is told that Ebenezer Zane, founder of Wheeling, once offered to give an iron kettle to the ugliest man in the country. The prize went to a Mr. Bartlett. On the way home with the kettle in his wagon, Bartlett met Bates. He looked him over, then jumped to the ground, saying, "I thought this kettle belonged to me, that I had won it fairly, but now that I have seen you, I know a mistake has been made: here, take it", and he handed it to Bates.

William Finley, father of eleven children, settled on the present site of Batesville. In 1828, a town was platted on his land and called Williamsburg after Finley's first name. His son-in-law, James Reed, opened the first store, hauling his stock of goods from Wheeling in a one-horse wagon. Nathaniel Pyles opened a tavern. Peter Cline was the village blacksmith. Jerry Brown made shoes. Adam Wiemer started a tannery. Henry Wehr was a tailor, and Nathaniel James Hendershot made hats. Robinson was a cabinet-maker. L. Fordyce taught the school. The town started off auspiciously. Down at the lower end, Daniel Wendell built the first brick house in 1830, a palatial residence for the time. It was afterwards known as the Harrison Wendell home and is still standing. When Timothy Bates resigned as postmaster at Bates' Mill, the office was moved up to Williamsburg and given the official name of Batesville. The town retained its original name, though, for a long time afterwards.

Samuel Wyscarver came from Pennsylvania in 1828 and settled on Beaver below Williamsburg. Jacob, his son, purchased a farm of seventy-three acres in 1843. By hard work and good management, he kept adding to it until he had 1,500 acres of the best land in the county. There were twelve children in the family, and on the farm at one time were five families of tenants. With the many barns, shops, and other buildings—even a schoolhouse, a racetrack, and a burial ground—it was a settlement within itself. Viewing the place from an adjacent hill the first time, we asked our grandfather what town it was. "That's Jacobsburg," was his reply.

Samuel Hastings, of Irish descent, came from Virginia and settled south of Williamsburg. He erected a cabin and moved into it before there was a floor or a chimney. He then laid a puncheon floor and built a chimney of sticks and mud. After paying for his land, he had $1.50 with which he bought three bushels of wheat to sow and lived the first year chiefly on cornbread and wild game. The farm was afterwards known as the Hiram Hastings place.

Beaver Township left Guernsey County in 1851 to become a part of Noble. Very soon thereafter, the people regretted the change and wanted back in Guernsey (page 686 of the book). They petitioned and threatened, to no avail. Then came a fight for the location of a county seat for the new county. Beaver was told that if it would vote for a certain location, the powers that would then be would see to it that it would be put back into Guernsey. Acting on this promise, it voted 262 to 27, only to learn afterwards that political promises are not always kept. Beaver Township is still in Noble County.

The Beginning of Buffalo Township, Noble County
[Originally published 5/23/1945]

We mean Buffalo Township, Noble County, and not the town of Buffalo in Valley Township, Guernsey. Both derived their names, though, from Buffalo Creek which flows across the township and empties into Seneca not far from the town. It is supposed that there were buffaloes along the creek at one time. We are apt to think of these animals as belonging to the prairie regions of the West, but there is evidence that they used to roam the forests of this section.

For its first forty years, Buffalo Township was in Guernsey County, set off by the county commissioners from Seneca Township on June 10, 1810. It was too big, the commissioners thought, so they cut a slice from the northern part to form Richland, and another later to help form Spencer Township. The state legislature created Morgan County in 1818 and asked Guernsey for a contribution of territory. The latter gave a liberal section from the western part of her big Buffalo Township. Then, in 1851, the state legislature formed Noble County, and Morgan was called upon to yield some of her territory. She gave what Guernsey had given to her a third of a century before. From this, Noble set off her Brookfield and Noble and parts of her Sharon, Center, and Olive Townships. Buffalo, that had once spread herself over Guernsey and Morgan counties, had been reduced to thirty-six square miles. Then, when Guernsey gave her to Noble, she retained twelve square miles to help from Valley Township, thus leaving twenty-four square miles, the present area.

MORE STORIES OF GUERNSEY COUNTY

This little story concerns the territory within the present limits for the forty years it was a part of Guernsey County. We might add, however, that after it left Guernsey, the Cleveland and Marietta Railroad was built through it, and the station of Glenwood was opened. It was in this township that the Shenandoah crashed in 1925.

One spring day, early in the last century, Abraham Rich and Abraham and John Miley came into the township, probably the first to settle there. They didn't take time to erect a cabin, but they threw up a few logs which they covered with brush, forming an open camp of the kind Daniel Boone and his companions had when they first came into Kentucky. They cleared a little patch of ground and planted some potatoes they had brought with them. This was their only crop, and the first winter they subsisted chiefly on potatoes and wild game, with which the woods abounded.

They managed to send word to John and George Rich, brothers of Abraham, who lived in Greene County, Pennsylvania, that they had found a location. They urged the brothers to come out, directing them to travel Zanes's Trace to Washington and informing them that they would blaze the trees to some distance from the camp to enable them to find it.

John Rich brought a couple of horses with him. One morning, they were missing. An extensive search was made for the lost animals, but all in vain. At length, he heard that two strange horses headed eastward were seen to swim the Ohio River near Moundsville. Rich took up the trail there and found them back at the old home place in Greene County, Pennsylvania. Their homing sense, horse sense—whatever you may wish to call it—had enabled them to make a journey through the trackless forest that their owner had made only with the aid of blazed trees.

Other settlers—mostly from Virginia—soon followed the Rich and Miley brothers: Jacob Gregg from Washington County, Pennsylvania; John, Samuel, and Isaac Kackley from Virginia; John and Jacob Larrick from Virginia, the latter establishing a horse-power saw- and grist-mill; Abraham Booher, veteran of the War of 1812; George R. Johnson, Thomas Nicholson, John Shriver, Andrew W. Clark, and John Drake. Coming a little later were Michael Crow, Robert Campbell, Samuel Findley, William Frye, Jacob and Henry Jackson, Levi Lyons, Amos Lazear, Hugh McCoy, George Spaid, Jacob and Elias Salliday, Jacob Secrest, Abraham and Jacob Thompson, Henry Trenner, and William Williams.

Many of these early settlers were Methodists, and they organized a society which met at first in each other's home and in the log schoolhouses. Abraham Rich was the first class leader. As a result of the great religious revival that swept over this western country in the early 1830s, several of the Buffalo Township Methodists became local preachers, including Abraham and John Rich, John Booher, William Lowery, Elijah Millhone, and John Thompson.

The first schoolhouse was built on the land of George R. Johnson in the southern part of the township. It was a round-log structure with a bark roof, clapboard door, greased-paper windows, and puncheon floor. John Kackley was one of the first teachers. Many of the family names we have mentioned are still to be found in Buffalo and adjacent townships.

Early Days in Hiramsburg, Noble County
[Originally published 4/18/1946]

Hiramsburg and Cumberland have always been in close relationship, and the names of the former's early settlers are familiar to residents of Cumberland.

First Families.—The Scotts were among the first families to settle in the Hiramsburg district, and Thomas Scott was secretary of the convention held in Chillicothe in 1802 to consider the forming of the state of Ohio. Ephraim Cutler, of Washington County, was the only person to vote against the new state. The most important thing decided at the convention was the defeat of an attempt to allow slavery in the new state, and Cutler helped to defeat this attempt. The constitution of the new state was never submitted to the people, but became a law solely by the act of the convention, which had been called by Congress without considering the opinion of the inhabitants.

Besides the Scotts, among the early settlers were the Jordans, Buckeys, Thorlas, Fowlers, Ganders, Gillespies, Erskines, McElroys and the Hamiltons.

Mrs. Emma Beckett is the oldest Cumberland resident from the Hiramsburg neighborhood. Her father was Sylvester Scott, whose home was about a quarter of a mile from Hiramsburg. She attended the Pleasant Ridge School, between the Thrap farm and the village, and to reach the school she had to cross a creek and climb 11 fences. Across the creek from the Scott home was the Scott Cemetery, which was also the burial place of many neighboring families. Mrs. John Thrap and Mrs. Betsy Combs were sisters of Sylvester Scott.

Mrs. Beckett recalls a visit she made to John Gray, a Revolutionary soldier, who lived with his relatives, the McElroys, about a mile and a half from Hiramsburg. She found him sitting on the porch; his long hair and beard were snow white, and so was his shirt, but the effect was marred by the tobacco stains around his mouth. The visit was made a short time before his death.

Laid Out Town.—Hiramsburg was named for Hiram Calvert, owner of the site of the place. In 1836, he employed John F. Talley to lay out 20 lots, to which additions were made in 1838 and 1858. Samuel Stevens had a store on the site long before the town was laid out, and a blacksmith was there in Jacob Stoneking, who sold the land to Hiram Calvert. Jacob Jordan was the first blacksmith after the village was laid out. He was a

Revolutionary soldier, and with his sons, Adam and Peter, was an early settler near the township line. Peter Jordan, also a Revolutionary soldier, married Rebecca Albin, daughter of another soldier of the Revolution, James Albin. Mrs. Jordan, who came to the Hiramsburg district in 1814, planted a willow sprout she had used for a riding whip. It grew into a tree with a circumference of 15 feet.

Township Officers Named.—Following a petition for the creation of a new township, Buffalo, in 1810, an election was held at the home of Jacob Jordan, near the site of Hiramsburg, for the selection of township officers. Buffalo Township then consisted of a large area. Olive Green Township was organized in Morgan County in 1819, but a few years later, because of political feeling in the township, the name was changed to Jackson. This was the only township whose boundaries were not changed after the creation of Noble County in 1851.

First House Built.—The first house in Hiramsburg was built by Harrison F. Larry, who kept a store there for a number of years. This building was torn down in 1886. Later storekeepers in this village were Wakefield & Shankland, Hiram Knight, Fortune Galbreath, Asa Burlingame, and Odel Squier from Cumberland, for whom Sylvester Scott clerked for a time.

Asa Burlingame was the first postmaster and hotelkeeper. The post office was started in 1845, and mail was brought from Cumberland once a week. Charles Lukens had a store there, and in 1847, John Stevens and George A. McClure engaged in mercantile business in the town. McClure was succeeded by his son, George, who afterward had a store in Cumberland for a short time. Business interests in Hiramsburg in 1886 included the general store of J. W. Murphy, Henry Shadwell's blacksmith, and Eli Covert's cabinet shop.

Notable Character.—A notable character in pioneer days was Reason Calvert who made potash from wood ashes he bought for five cents a bushel and sold it to refineries to make pearl ash. He also made linseed and castor oil. He was a lover of fine horses and rode a beautiful white steed, of which he was quite proud. To match the horse, he wore white trousers and coat.

A Baptist Church once stood on the hillside just above the town, but later the denomination withdrew, and the building was taken over by the Cumberland Presbyterian Church of Cumberland, and its preachers also served the Hiramsburg Church. This building is now gone, and there is a Methodist Church in the village, which is affiliated with the Methodist Church in Cumberland.

Early Physicians.—The first doctor in Hiramsburg was Dr. George, who came from Washington, Guernsey County, and remained three years. Dr. Nathan P. Cope, who came from Harrison County and belonged to the Society of Friends, practiced in Hiramsburg many years, coming in 1847. He married Jane Black, and they reared a family of eight children. He died in 1868. Another physician there was Dr. John Finley, who came in 1877. Dr. R. S. Conner, long a doctor of Cumberland, also had much practice in the Hiramsburg settlement.

Hoskinsville.—John F. Talley plotted the village of Hoskinsville in 1839, E. E. Parrish being the proprietor. The place was named for its first postmaster, Col. Erastus Hoskins, the post office being started before 1830, with weekly mail from McConnelsville and Barnesville. John Needham, a shoemaker, built the first house there. Ragan's chapel, at Hoskinsville, was organized in 1829 by the Methodist Protestant Church. At first, the congregation met at homes of the members or in the schoolhouse. In 1829, a brick building was erected where the present building now stands. The first Sunday School in that section, if not in the county, was started there in 1825 with Col. Erasmus Hoskins superintendent. This was under the Methodist Episcopal Church.

EXTENDED CHAPTER XLIV

The Cambridge Corner Stories

The Moose Home Corner

[Originally published 2/8/1946]

(This is the ninth in a series of stories on the leading corners of Cambridge. For his assistance in our research, we are indebted to Carl J. Rech.)

After Jacob Gomber and Zaccheus A. Beatty had completed platting the town of Cambridge in 1806, the latter looked the lots over and decided to reserve the first six of the 140 for his own personal use. These were the six lots on the south side of Wheeling Avenue, between Fifth and Sixth Streets. It was his intention to build a home for himself and family on lot No. 6, the one on the upper corner.

First Frame House in Cambridge.—When the town was platted, Beatty's family was living in Steubenville, and it was not until 1809 (believed to be the year) that he brought his wife and four children here to occupy the new home he had just completed. It stood on the site of the present Moose Home and was the only frame house in town; all the other fifteen or twenty houses were built of logs.

The First Frame House in Cambridge

Accompanying this story is a picture of the Beatty house, taken sixty or seventy years after it was built, and after an addition had been made to the south side. About the year 1881, Dr. J. T. McPherson purchased the corner and moved the house to the rear of the lot. It was remodeled and is now the residence and place of business of Harry E. Stahl. Without question, this is the oldest house in Cambridge, but it cannot be entered in any competition for the honor of being such, as it has been transformed and does not stand on the original foundation. In fact, it now bears little resemblance to the house shown by the picture.

The massive sills and lower joists, as may be seen in the basement today, were hewed out by hand. Some of them are black walnut of great length, indicating the height to which that tree once grew here. It is probable they were cut from the lots reserved by Beatty. The boards used for siding and interior finish were sawed at the Gomber sawmill, that stood just south of the present City Cemetery, and were dressed by hand. Peter Sarchet was the only carpenter in town at that time, of whom we have any record, and it was doubtless he who did the work.

Leading Citizen of Cambridge.—Zaccheus A. Beatty lived in this house until his death in 1835. During this time, especially after the death of Jacob Gomber in 1820, he was the leading citizen of Cambridge. He was the first representative to the General Assembly to be elected from Guernsey County; he afterwards served two terms as state senator from this senatorial district; he was county clerk of courts at two different times; he was active in every movement for the material advancement of the town, in which he was the recognized leader.

On the first three lots of Beatty's reservation (from Fifth Street to the alley east) he established a tannery, a much-needed industry at that time, and built a cabin at the alley corner in which his chief tanner, Christopher Duniver, lived. The material needs of the Cambridge pioneers had to be met here, as little or nothing could be brought in from the outside. Food, clothing, and shelter were necessities. There was plenty of game in the forests for meat. Every home had its truck patch in which vegetables were raised. Corn had to be ground for use, and Jacob Gomber established a mill. In most cabins were spinning wheels and looms for making clothing and other textile goods. Beatty saw the need of leather for boots, shoes, and harness, and he provided a tannery.

The Beatty Home.—The three lots above (from the alley to Sixth Street), a total of three-fourths of an acre, were Beatty's own private grounds. Around the house were shrubbery and flowers; back of the house was a garden; and on the two lots below, an orchard was planted. Here were apple, peach, and pear trees, the first to be brought to Cambridge. The apple trees, perhaps, were from one of the nurseries of Johnny Appleseed.

For twenty-five years this corner was the home of Zaccheus A. Beatty, and here six of his ten children were born, the last in 1822. (For the life story of this pioneer, see page 34 of the book.)

Nathan Evans Becomes Owner.—The next owner of the corner was Thomas S. Beatty, son of Zaccheus A., who, as was stated in a previous story of this series, failed financially, and all his property fell into the hands of Master Commissioner Moses Sarchet for liquidation. The corner was purchased by Nathan Evans, and for the next forty years, it was the Evans home. Evans was a prominent attorney, a Whig in politics, later a

Republican. While living on the corner, he served as mayor of Cambridge, prosecuting attorney, member of Congress for two terms, and judge of the common pleas court.

First Stone House in Cambridge.—After the death of Nathan Evans in 1879, Dr. J. T. McPherson purchased the corner, and moved the frame residence (then seventy years old) to the rear of the lot. On the site, he erected the first stone residence in Cambridge, which, for ten or twelve years, was the McPherson home. J. M. Ogier then became the owner of the property, selling it to S. W. Nicholson. From the latter, it was purchased by the Cambridge Loyal Order of Moose in 1916.

Today (2024) the old Moose Home Corner is occupied by Peoples Bank.

This picture, taken August 24, 1968, shows the Moose Home Corner on the right and the Colonial Theater Corner (then owned by the Scottish Rite) during the fire that destroyed the theater. Note the original McPherson stone house and Beatty home behind it. (Photo courtesy of the Guernsey County Historical Society)

THE CAMBRIDGE CORNER STORIES

The Colonial Theater Corner

[Originally published 1/15/1946]

(This is the fifth in a series of stories on the leading corners of Cambridge. For his assistance in our research, we are indebted to Carl J. Rech.)

Three buildings have stood at the southeast corner of Wheeling Avenue and Sixth Street. The first was the Holler Tavern, built in 1811; the second, a frame residence, in the late 1850s; and the third, the Colonial Theater, in the early 1900s.

The Holler Tavern.—Joseph Holler was the proprietor of the Holler Tavern until 1818, when he was killed by a horse he was leading, which jerked him off his feet and against a stump. On June 18, 1818, the following advertisement appeared in the Ohio State Journal:

"The public are respectfully informed that the Tavern in the town of Cambridge, Ohio, formerly kept by Joseph Holler, deceased, and distinguished by the sign of 'Hope, an Anchor,' is now conducted by Mrs. Holler, the surviving widow, in connection with James Turner, her son-in-law. The subscribers gratefully acknowledge past favors and assure the public in general, and the friends in particular, that their exertions shall be studiously devoted to the accommodation and entertainment of such as may please to call upon them.

"JAMES TURNER,
SARAH HOLLER."

Ten years after the death of Holler, the National Road was built through Cambridge, passing in front of the tavern, which was located on the crown of the hill. In order to establish a grade, it was necessary to make a cut which left the tavern several feet above the street. As a result of this, the place lost much patronage; the wagon and drove-lots provided were not as accessible as those of other taverns in town. Notwithstanding this, though, the tavern was continued for several years after the National Road was built.

Following its use as a tavern, the building was converted into a tenement house, or, as we might say today, an apartment house. Among the tenants living in it were Cyrus Wilson, a contractor, who conducted a boarding house, chiefly for his employees; Rev. John Burns, pastor of the Methodist Protestant Church; John Mehaffey, who made and repaired boots and shoes; Sam Wilson, who kept a store and also made chairs.

After the death of Mrs. Holler, the place was sold to Samuel H. Oldham for $1,100. The old tavern was torn away and upon the lot a frame residence was erected. This was removed very early in the 1900s for the Colonial Theater.

Tavern Described.—The old Holler Tavern was built of hewed logs (afterwards weather-boarded), two stories in height. The front was really two buildings, side by side, with the space between enclosed to make a wide entrance room. Opening into this was a large, circular-top doorway, paneled on each side with glass windows.

On the west side of the hall was a large barroom, the scene of many revelries. On the west side of the room was a wide fireplace in which wood was burned. On each side of the fireplace were three tiers of bunks in which wagoners and drovers slept. In the corner of the big room was the bar, at which all kinds of liquors were dispensed. The room east of the hall was the parlor.

Passing south through the hall, one came out on the lower floor of a large, two-story porch, on the west side of which were a dining room and a kitchen. Between the two was a double fireplace, one side to heat the dining room and the other to be used for cooking, all of which was done over the open wood fire.

The rooms on the upper floor were large. In each were two or more high-posted beds. For privacy, some of the beds were curtained and were let at a higher rate. This tavern was typical of most of the public houses of this section in pioneer days.

A Popular Tavern.—Before the National Road was built through Cambridge, the main thoroughfare was Zane's Trace, afterwards called the Wheeling Road. At certain seasons of the year, stagecoaches passed through before the days of the National Road, and the Holler Tavern became a stage office. This helped to advertise it. Competing with it in Wheeling Road days were the Bridge House down at the creek, the Mansion House on the site of the present Stoner Building, Tingle's on the site of Odd Fellows Building, Knowls' Tavern east of the Craig corner, the United States Hotel on the lot now occupied by the post office, and others.

The Holler Tavern was the scene of many wild parties. In his memoirs (page 1046 of the book), Jacob Banker, who lived in Wheeling Township, says, "I was often sent to Cambridge with grinding and would stay overnight at Holler's Tavern. This was a rough place—much drinking, swearing, and fighting—but they gave me plenty to eat."

Postcard circa 1905 showing the Colonial Theater Corner at right. Today (2024) it is a parking lot.

(Photo courtesy of the Guernsey County Historical Society)

THE CAMBRIDGE CORNER STORIES

The Berwick Corner
[Originally published 1/18/1946]

(This is the sixth in a series of stories on the leading corners of Cambridge. For his assistance in our research, we are indebted to Carl J. Rech.)

When Jacob Gomber died in 1820, the lot at the northeast corner of Wheeling Avenue and Sixth Street was deeded to Sarah McClenahan by Lloyd Talbott, administrator of the Gomber estate. A cabin was built on the lot, and, in 1832, John Clark became the owner for a consideration of $225. As it was deeded to James M. Bell the same year, Clark may have purchased it for him.

Bell Builds Brick Residence on Lot.—James M. Bell, prominent Cambridge attorney, entered Congress the year after he purchased the lot (page 675 of the book). On the lot, he proceeded to build a brick residence, patterned after the prevailing style in Washington City, and quite elaborate for that day. All the houses on Wheeling Avenue were built flush with the street, but he set his back near the center of the lot. With its large porch in front, it attracted much attention. This became the Bell home.

Seven years before Bell's death, which occurred in 1849, the property was deeded to Thomas Ewing and Henry Stanbery, both of Lancaster, Ohio, for a consideration of $2,676.43. Thomas Ewing was a prominent United States Senator and the foster-father of Gen. William T. Sherman. Henry Stanbery was Attorney General of the United States under President Andrew Jackson. Back of the transaction referred to above is a story which we shall not present here. It appears that Bell became financially involved, and Ewing and Stanbery came to his assistance.

Bell, it is believed, continued to live in the house until his death. In 1853, William K. Davis bought the corner from Ewing and Stanbery for $1,500, and in 1859, he sold it to Thomas Lenfesty for the same amount. Then came the Civil War.

Corner Purchased by Col. Joseph D. Taylor.—In 1866, Lenfesty sold the property to Col. Joseph D. Taylor for $3,000. Colonel Taylor was back from the war, was editor of The Guernsey Times, was Prosecuting Attorney of Guernsey County, and had just married Elizabeth A. Hill, of North Berwick, Maine.

Around his newly purchased property, he built a high brick wall and beautified the grounds with shrubbery and flowers. On certain days, the children of the town were invited to come there to play. Here, until the late 1870s or early 1880s, the Taylors lived. Then a new home was built north of town. It seemed to be far out in the country, but now it is within the city on North Seventh Street. (See picture on page 710 of the book.)

The Berwick Is Built.—On the site of the old brick residence, Colonel Taylor began the erection of a hotel, naming it The Berwick in honor of the town in Maine from which his wife came. The building was completed and formally opened on August 16, 1887, with a dinner and a grand ball. Probably never before in the history of Cambridge had a more elaborate social affair been known here.

Capt. W. M. Farrar was toastmaster at the dinner. The following toasts were given:

"Hotel Berwick—Its Builder," John M. Amos
"Hotel Berwick—Its Proprietors," Fred L. Rosemond
"Our Town," Dr. W. V. Milligan
"The People Who Live in Our Town," D. D. Taylor
"Hotel Berwick—Its Guests," Rev. I. A. Tannehill
(See picture of this first Berwick on page 587 of the book.)

The first proprietors of The Berwick were Mrs. T. B. Thrift, Columbus, Ohio, and T. H. Jewell and son, Lansing, Michigan, all experienced hotel people. In 1888, Lakin C. Taylor became manager, and in 1889, H. F. Hunt took charge.

Destroyed By Fire.—Lamented by all Cambridge was the loss of the four-year-old Berwick in the great fire of 1891, which burned everything on the north side of Wheeling Avenue from Sixth Street nearly to the alley east. But, undaunted, Colonel Taylor began at once to build a new Berwick. It was opened in 1894 by J. F. Murdough who came to Cambridge from Chicago where he had operated a hotel during the World's Fair, bringing with him furniture and other furnishings he had used there. Then came the fire of 1895, which swept away all the buildings Colonel Taylor had erected after the fire of 1891, except The Berwick, which had a firewall on the east side.

The Berwick Company.—In the latter 1890s, Charles Mast and H. V. Atkinson leased the hotel. Colonel Taylor died in 1899, but the corner remained as a part of the Taylor estate. A company, of which Mast and Atkinson were the principal stockholders, was formed in 1917 and incorporated. The Berwick was purchased by the company, and J. P. Johnston, another stockholder, became the manager.

Now the owner is Harry Kahn, who purchased the corner from The Berwick Company a few weeks ago, and James P. Peters is the manager of The Berwick.

The Hotel Berwick today (2024), now a senior housing facility.

The Hotel Berwick as seen on a 1930s postcard.

The Wheeling Avenue entrance to the Hotel Berwick. The presence of a hose cart in the background suggests this picture may have been taken just after the great fire of October 2, 1895, which destroyed many buildings nearby.

(Photos courtesy of the Guernsey County Historical Society)

MORE STORIES OF GUERNSEY COUNTY

The Woolworth Corner
[Originally published 1/30/1946]

(This is the eighth in a series of stories on the leading corners of Cambridge. For his assistance in our research, we are indebted to Carl J. Rech.)

One who notes the comparatively even grade on Wheeling Avenue from the Park School down to the Viaduct can hardly believe that crossing the street from south to north were once several deep ravines. Not only were bridges necessary in order that they might be crossed, but to some of the bridges there had to be corduroy approaches. If one tries to visualize Wheeling Avenue as it was during the first twenty-five years of Cambridge history, he need include the ravines and bridges in the picture.

Ravine at Seventh Street.—Running north down Seventh Street was a ravine over which was a bridge where it crossed Wheeling Avenue. The bridge was replaced by a big culvert when the National Road was built through, in 1828, and the ravine was filled with dirt removed from a crown that was lowered a short distance above. That it was not completely filled is evidenced by the dip in the street that may yet be noticed there.

The lot at the southwestern corner of Wheeling Avenue and Seventh Street is No. 12 of the original plat of the town. When, in 1806, the first sale of lots was made, the other three lots at this intersection were grabbed up at once. Thomas Sarchet bought the northeast and northwest corners, and his brother, John, the southeast. The fact that the ravine cut into the southwest corner made that lot less desirable; it did not sell for seven years.

John Dixon Purchases Corner.—John Dixon, the records show, paid Jacob Gomber and Zaccheus A. Beatty $100 for the corner in 1813. Upon it, he built a house. We here quote from the memoirs of Eveline Tingle (page 551 of the book) who came to Cambridge with her parents in 1808 and lived on the lot now occupied by the Odd Fellows' Temple. "On lot No. 12, John Dixon built a two-story house. I think it was the first frame house in town. It had a large room downstairs where elections were held and where I went to school for some time. Court was held here a few times after it left our house." (Eveline was wrong in recalling this as a frame house; there are records to indicate that it was built of logs.)

Home of Thomas Campbell.—Dixon owned the corner until 1817 when he sold it to David Humphrey for $560. During all or a part of the four years he owned it, it was occupied as a residence by Thomas Campbell and family. Campbell, a scholarly man, was born in Ireland, and was a Presbyterian preacher. He didn't come to Cambridge to preach, as there was no Presbyterian Church here at that time; probably he came to teach school, for we know of nothing else he did here. In the large east room of the Dixon house, he opened a subscription school, the first school of a scholarly character in Cambridge.

Alexander Campbell.—One of Thomas Campbell's sons was named

The Woolworth Corner's "Colley Block" building today (2024).

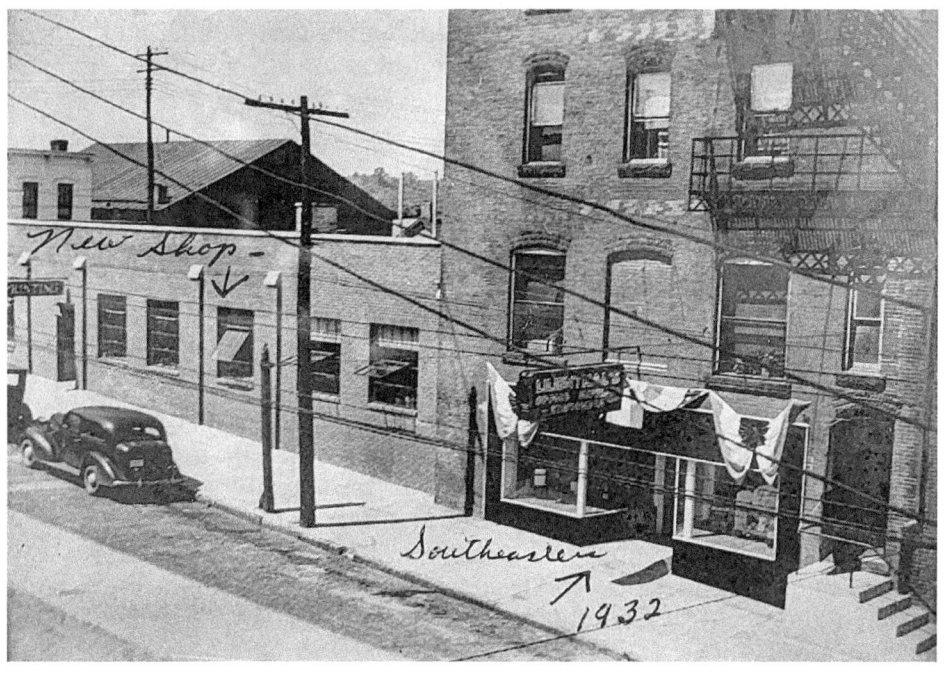

In the 1930s, the east side of the building was home to Southeastern Printing.

(Photo courtesy of the Guernsey County Historical Society)

Alexander. Like his father, he became a preacher. He was first a Presbyterian, then a Baptist. He translated and published the New Testament, immediately following which the Christian, or Disciples, Church was established with him as the great leader.

It has been said that Alexander Campbell attended the school taught by his father on the corner we are writing about, but it would seem that he was too old to attend such a school when his father moved here (page 396 of the book). He did stay with his parents here a part of the time, and he often preached in Cambridge.

Changes in Ownership.—This lot, like each of the others of the original town, had an area of one-fourth acre. It had a frontage of 66 feet on Wheeling Avenue and extended south along Seventh Street 198 feet. The records show that Humphrey sold it to William Kilgore, in 1822, for $321, and the next year Kilgore sold it to Jacob Shaffner for $300.

Shaffner either enlarged the original house, or tore it away and built a new one on the corner, for David Burt, Jr., paid him $2,000 for it in 1836. Here Shaffner had a store. He was a Democrat and worked hard for the election of Andrew Jackson. The latter rewarded him by appointing him postmaster at a salary of $219 a year. The office was kept on this corner.

David Burt, Jr., owned the property three years and then sold it to his brother, Ebenezer, for $1,900. Three years later, Jacob G. and Joseph A. Metcalf, sons of George Metcalf, the pioneer surveyor and tavernkeeper, purchased it for $1,600. The brothers kept a store here, selling all kinds of goods. In an old newspaper we found the following advertisement:

"*A good article of rectified whiskey received and for sale at 29 cts, per gallon.*

"*J. G. & J. A. METCALF*".

For a consideration of $1,200, Thomas W. Peacock became owner of the corner in 1847. In 1856, Peacock divided the lot and sold the east half of it (the corner) to John McFarren for $1,600. In 1868, Mr. McFarren sold it to Jacob Ferbrache for $3,000. Jane Moss bought it of Ferbrache in 1882 for the same amount he had paid, and in 1894 the ownership was transferred to John Colley for $5,000. It is now the property of the Colley estate.

Recent Occupants.—Having purchased the property, Colley erected the three-story brick building now on the corner. Since 1916, the entire first floor has been occupied by the Woolworth Company. For some years immediately prior to 1916, the Hub Clothing Company was located there.

This corner, as may have been noted, has been used for many various purposes: a residence, a school, a courthouse, home of the parents of one of the world's great religious leaders, a liquor store, a post office, an election place, a general store, and others.

THE CAMBRIDGE CORNER STORIES

The Style Center Corner

[Originally published 2/21/1946]

(This is the tenth in a series of stories on the leading corners of Cambridge. For his assistance in our research we are indebted to Carl J. Rech).

For $37.50, John Sarchet bought lot No 13, the southeast corner of Wheeling Avenue and Seventh Street, now known as the Style Center corner, when he arrived in Cambridge in August, 1806. At the same time, his brothers, Thomas and Peter, each bought a corner lot. The former chose the one now occupied by the Central Drugstore, and the latter, the one upon which the Central National Bank stands. These were probably the first lots to be sold in the newly-platted town.

Sarchet Brothers Build Homes.—John Sarchet's lot had a frontage of 66 feet on Wheeling Avenue and extended back 198. Immediately after making the purchase, he erected a one-story hewed log house on the east side of the lot, facing and flush with the street. Into this he moved his wife and three children. The children had been born on Guernsey Island; three more were born on this corner. John was a blacksmith.

Thomas Sarchet built a combined residence and store on his corner (For picture and description of this building, see page 569 of the book.) Peter, on his corner, built a two-story hewed-log house, and worked at the carpenter trade. All three brothers thus engaged in work that was necessary in the new settlement.

John had to have iron and steel to work into axes, mattocks, hoes, and nails. None could be obtained from any source of supply nearer than Pittsburgh, more than a hundred miles away. He made frequent trips to that place with packhorses and brought back as much metal as could be carried. His brother, Thomas, would often accompany him in order to obtain merchandise to be sold in his store.

John Builds a Brick Residence.—After living for a few years in the log house, John Sarchet built a brick residence exactly on the corner of the lot, into which he moved his family. This was probably the first brick house in Cambridge. Here the family lived until 1825 or 6, when John sold the lot to Peter Corbet for $1,200. Sarchet moved to Philadelphia, where he engaged in the manufacture of chain cables and anchors for ships. It is said that late in life, he returned to Guernsey Island and died there. Peter Corbet moved into the brick house and opened a bread and pastry shop. He had been a member of the second company of Guernseyites, coming here as a single man in 1807. A few years after purchasing the corner, Corbet sold it to David Burt for $1,500. From the latter, it passed into the hands of Benjamin A. Albright for a consideration of $2,000. It was in this brick building that Charles J. Albright, son of Benjamin A., published The Guernsey Times for several years.

Isaac Niswander's Place.—The hewed log house on the east side of the lot, which John Sarchet built in 1807 and which he lived in until he moved into the new brick residence, was torn away in 1847. For several years, it was the home of Isaac Niswander and his wife, "Peggy." Here they opened what was then called an oyster saloon where specially prepared foods and other refreshments were served. The place enjoyed the patronage of the best people in town, and parties would frequently repair there for refreshments after social events held elsewhere. Colonel Sarchet says that both Isaac and "Peggy" were noted characters in their day.

Two newspapers were published in the county—The Democratic Star (now The Jeffersonian) in Washington, and The Guernsey Times in Cambridge. These papers were neither sent through the mail nor distributed by carriers to local subscribers, but were left at Niswander's to be called for. This brought many people to the place, who would frequently buy something. "Peggy" was a relative of Peter B. Ankeny, publisher of The Democratic Star. Niswander was a staunch Whig, and members of that party expostulated with him for circulating a Democratic paper. He explained that it was not for political purposes, but out of deference to "Peggy," on account of her relationship. As a rule, partisan feeling was so strong in campaign times that Whigs and Democrats would not patronize each other.

The Shonfield Corner.—About the year 1856, the Shonfield Brothers came to Cambridge, bought the corner, made some changes in the first floor, and opened a store, specializing in men's and women's wearing apparel. In Civil War days, this was one of the leading mercantile establishments in town. For a long time, the corner was familiarly known as the Shonfield corner.

Joshua K. Brown was the next owner, purchasing the corner in 1872. He sold it to Samuel C. Carnes in 1889, and some years later, Carnes sold it to E. W. Mathews and Edward Eaton. Ever since the Shonfield Brothers entered the property, the first floor has been used as a business room, and the two above as office rooms or living apartments.

Now the Style Center Corner.—Harry E. Rosenberg came to Cambridge in 1921, bought Mathews' interest in the building, and opened the business in which he is now engaged there, under the name of the Style Center. A few years later, he became the sole owner of the corner and remodeled and enlarged the building. So many changes have been made from time to time in the John Sarchet brick residence that it now bears no resemblance to the original structure. Of the walls, only the east side remains. The front foundation and some of the hand-hewed sills are still there.

The walnut balustrade of the stairway leading to the third story and the flooring of this story remain as originally placed. In one respect, the building on this corner is one of the oldest in town; in another, it is one of the newest.

(The story of Joshua K. Brown, who owned this corner for seventeen years, will be published tomorrow.)

THE CAMBRIDGE CORNER STORIES

The Style Center Corner today (2024) is home to the Country Bits store.

The Style Center store circa 1950.

(Photo courtesy of the Guernsey County Historical Society)

MORE STORIES OF GUERNSEY COUNTY

The Central National Bank Corner
[Originally published 1/2/1946]

(Note: This is the second in a series of stories on the leading corners of Cambridge. For his assistance in our research, we are indebted to Carl J. Rech.)

At the northwest corner of Wheeling Avenue and West Eighth Street is lot No. 54, so designated by Jacob Gomber and Zaccheus A. Beatty when they platted the town in 1806. It is 66 feet wide and runs back 198 feet to the north. Its area is exactly one-fourth of an acre. As Gomber and Beatty paid $2,000 for the 4,000 acres of which it is a part, this lot cost them twelve and one-half cents.

Purchased By Peter Sarchet.—The year the town was platted, there arrived in Cambridge Thomas, John, and Peter Sarchet, and some others, from the Isle of Guernsey. Deciding to locate here, each of the brothers purchased a corner lot. Peter chose No 54, paying Gomber and Beatty $55 for it. At that time, there was no courthouse, not even a Guernsey County, and the deed for the lot was recorded in Zanesville, Cambridge then being in Muskingum County.

Great trees with underbrush beneath covered the lot. Peter Sarchet set to work to clear the ground and build a home on it. He probably cut enough timber from the lot for a house. Being a carpenter by trade, he built well. The house was of hewed logs and two stories in height. He built it near the center of the lot, facing east, about where the Branthoover-Johnston building is now located. Along the entire front was a wide porch. But looking across the street, he did not see a massive courthouse with landscaped grounds around; he saw nothing but the big woods.

Used For County Offices.—Three years after Peter Sarchet got settled, Guernsey County was formed, and he found himself facing the courthouse. In the course of a few years, it was found that the courthouse was too small to accommodate all the offices; then the commissioners rented two or three rooms in Sarchet's house and moved the offices of the recorder, clerk of courts, and sheriff over to them.

One night in 1826, a passerby saw that the house was on fire. He sounded an alarm and the building was saved. Had it not been for the timely discovery by this man out late at night, the official records of the first sixteen years of Guernsey County would have been destroyed. The advisability of safer storage was seen by the commissioners and they proceeded at once to erect a one-story addition on the west side of the courthouse. An addition was made on the east side in 1854. (For picture of old courthouse with the additions, see page 63 of book.)

Jacob Shaffner Buys the Lot.—Peter Sarchet sold the house and lot to Jacob Shaffner in 1828 for $280 and moved to Chandlersville, Muskingum County, to engage in manufacturing salt. Eight years later,

THE CAMBRIDGE CORNER STORIES

The Central National Bank Corner today (2024), now the home of PNC Bank.

The Central National Bank building as seen on a 1908 postcard.

(Photo courtesy of the Guernsey County Historical Society)

Shaffner tore away the log house and at the corner of the lot, fronting on Wheeling Avenue, he erected a two-story brick building which he used as a store and a residence. Shaffner was prominent in local Democratic politics, and during a part of Jackson's administration, he served as postmaster, receiving an annual salary of $219.

Sold By the Sheriff.—Jacob Shaffner was unsuccessful in business, and his creditors forced a foreclosure. The sheriff sold the property to Joseph Bute for $2,500. Bute remodeled the building, making of it a tavern which he called the American House. On the north end of the lot (site of the present Carnes Building) were the stables.

In the latter 1830s, Bute sold the building and lot to Elijah Grimes for $5,400. Grimes engaged A. E. and J. B. Cook to manage the hotel, and it became known as the Cook Hotel. In the years immediately preceding the Civil War, it was Cambridge's leading house of entertainment.

Near the opening of the war, the building was remodeled again, the lower floor being converted into storerooms, much as it was in Shaffner's days. Here, Maxwell and Glessner opened a general store, which they called the "Cheap Corner." The second floor was made into office rooms which were reached by an outside stairway on West Eighth Street. (For a picture of the building as it then was, see page 296 of the book.)

N. B. Long Becomes the Owner.—After the Cook Hotel had been closed, N. B. Long purchased the north end of the lot, tore away the old barns, and in their place he erected a hotel which David Jenkins managed for him. Long sold the hotel to Joseph Morton in 1873, and it was long known as the Morton House. After Morton's death, it was called the Park Hotel and changed ownership and managers a number of times. Now the Carnes Building, it is used as store and office rooms.

On lot No. 54 today are the five-story brick structure of the Central National Bank, erected in 1904, the Leyshon Building just west of it, and the Branthoover-Johnston and Carnes buildings north.

We see that this lot has changed hands a number of times. The amount paid for it 145 years ago was twelve and one-half cents. We'll not venture to guess what it might be bought for today, but if one is curious to know the amount at which it is appraised for taxation purposes, he can get the information at the county auditor's office. Cambridge property has risen somewhat in value and is still rising.

THE CAMBRIDGE CORNER STORIES

The Old Red Corner
[Originally published 1/7/1946]

(Note: This is the third in a series of stories on the leading corners of Cambridge. For his assistance in our research, we are indebted to Carl J. Rech.)

Now bearing a color that is a cross between a tan and a gray, the building at the southwest corner of Wheeling Avenue and South Eighth Street was once red, and was generally known as the Old Red Corner. Its name came naturally, since it was built of red brick and stood out in contrast with the colors of the other buildings on the corners at the public square. An application of red paint from time to time helped it to continue true to the original name. In later years, however, other colors of paint were used.

Oldest Building on Wheeling Avenue.—This is believed to be the oldest building on Wheeling Avenue, that has retained its original external form. It was built by Thomas S. Beatty in 1837, and is thus 109 years old. We might add here that it was built the year Cambridge was incorporated, and is thus the same age as the municipality. Beatty intended it for a tavern, and plans to that end were drawn. Before it was completed, he changed his mind and decided to make of it a building which he might rent for stores, shops, and offices. The bricks used in its construction were delivered on the ground for $3.50 per thousand.

This lot is No. 18 of the original plat of Cambridge. It belonged at first, of course, to Jacob Gomber and Zaccheus A. Beatty. For some reason, it was not sold by them immediately after the town was laid out, as were most of the other corner lots, and was still in their possession when Gomber died in 1820. Following the settlement of the Gomber estate, Beatty became the sole owner. In 1829, he passed the title to it over to his son, Thomas S. Beatty.

Thomas S. Beatty.—The third son of Zaccheus A. Beatty, Thomas S., was born in 1807, and was thus twenty-two years old when he came into possession of the lot. In some respects, he was a remarkable man, and mention may be made of it here. He learned to read, write, and cipher in the little subscription school that was held in Cambridge in his childhood days, and when William Sedgwick, the Baptist preacher, came here and opened a private school, in which were taught some of the higher branches, he entered it. His power of memorizing was his outstanding characteristic. It is said that he could read a whole chapter of the Bible or any other book, close it, and repeat the whole chapter verbatim.

In financial matters, Beatty's memory was not quite so retentive, or at least it did not seem to be. He failed to meet some of his obligations and eventually was closed out by the court. He then left Cambridge for a western state to begin life anew. Had his father lived, this financial misfortune might not have befallen him. Zaccheus A. Beatty, who died in 1835, was one of the most successful businessmen in the early history of Cambridge, and he doubtless would have advised Thomas S. in some of his financial dealings.

William Rainey Purchases the Red Corner.—Attorney W. W. Tracey, first mayor of Cambridge, was appointed receiver of the Thomas S. Beatty property. In 1840, he sold lot No. 18 to William Rainey. The latter opened a store in it, advertising it as the Red Corner. When purchased by Rainey, the building had a frontage on Wheeling Avenue of about two-thirds the width of the lot and extended back about half-way to Turner Avenue. He put an addition on the west side, making a building frontage of the full sixty-six feet. In the rear, along South Eighth Street (then called Market Street), extending to Turner Avenue, he erected a large warehouse.

Rainey's Red Corner was a complete department store. Here could be bought anything from notions to farm machinery. And it was a place where farmers could dispose of their products. They brought in everything from butter and eggs to wool and grain to exchange for merchandise.

Rainey suffered a great financial loss in the fire of 1873, although the original building did not burn. (See page 585 of the book.) The warehouses at the rear of the lot were destroyed, along with most of their contents. The merchandise in the store was removed to the courtyard when it began to appear that the Red Corner was doomed.

Succeeding Rainey as merchants on the corner were others, one of whom was W. H. H. McIlyar. In recent years, the Ohio Power Company has owned and used the east part of the original building for office purposes. Of the west part, fronting on Wheeling Avenue, there are two owners. Here are located a shoe store and a restaurant, with offices above.

This corner has had different names, but Red Corner stuck the longest. By many, it was always called the Red Corner. It was known as the Rainey Corner, then the McIlyar Corner. Now it is the Ohio Power Corner.

The Red Corner today (2024). The building's west side was demolished in 2023.

THE CAMBRIDGE CORNER STORIES

The Craig Corner

[Originally published 12/27/1945]

For exactly one hundred years, the southeast corner of Wheeling Avenue and South Eighth Street has been known as the "Craig Corner." The four-story business and apartment brick structure standing on the corner today is owned by H. V. Atkinson, but it was built by the Craigs in 1904, and is generally known as the Craig Building. Three generations of Craigs conducted business on this corner.

First of the Craigs.—Early in 1846, Samuel Craig, thirty-one years old, came to Cambridge from Washington where, for eight years, he had engaged in the mercantile business with his brother. He purchased the corner we are writing about, and upon it he erected a large two-story frame building, fronting on Wheeling Avenue and extending back towards Turner. This was planned for both a place of business and a residence. (For picture of the building, see page 614 of the book.)

In the building across South Eighth Street, now occupied by the Ohio Power, William Rainey had a store which he advertised as the "Red Corner." At the corner of Wheeling Avenue and East Eighth Street was McCracken's store, called the "Blue Corner." Not to be outdone by his competitors, and to complete the national colors, Craig named his corner the "White Corner." But that applied to the store only and not to the corner generally.

The First Chain Store.—An enterprising businessman, Samuel Craig was not content to confine his activities to Cambridge alone, but branched out, establishing the first system of chain stores in Guernsey County. It was a modest undertaking, but nevertheless it was the forerunner of what we have a century later. Among the stores he opened was one at Senecaville, which afterwards became the Brown store; another was at Birmingham, the Foy store.

Politics and Religion.—Samuel Craig was a man of great strength of character and positive convictions. He would never swerve the least from what he believed to be right, regardless of the effect it might have upon him in a business way. He never tried to shape his political and religious views to conform with party and church. He was born a Democrat, and as a young man, he was enthusiastic in promoting the interests of that party. But he was bitterly opposed to slavery on the ground that it was morally wrong, and when that question came to the front and the Democrats took a stand on it that he didn't like, he stepped out of the ranks and became a staunch Abolitionist. The Liberty Party, composed mostly of Abolitionists, was succeeded by the Free-soil Party, and Craig joined it. Then came the Republican Party with slavery views much in accord with his own, and he became a Republican. For the remainder of his life, he was a loyal member of this party, although never seeking any office.

Following in the faith of his fathers, he was a consistent Presbyterian until he began to think that his church generally was not taking as active a stand against slavery as it should. He therefore transferred his membership to the Associate Church which afterward, on joining with the Associate Reformed Church, became the United Presbyterian. He was a leader in the First United Presbyterian Church of Cambridge for many years.

An Underground Railroad Station.—At Washington, the Guernsey County Anti-Slavery Society was formed in 1841, with Samuel Craig as its secretary. (See page 702 of the book.) Fugitive slaves on their way to Canada and freedom via the "Underground Railroad" passed through Cambridge. Along the route were stations where they were fed and concealed until they could be carried on with safety. The Cambridge station was at the "Craig Corner," and Craig himself was the stationmaster. After the enactment of the Fugitive Slave Law, one who helped a runaway slave to escape was liable to a heavy fine and imprisonment. Samuel Craig's hatred of slavery was so great that he dared defy a law that was so odious in the North that some judges refused to enforce it. As the work had to be kept secret, it will never be known how many escaped slaves found refuge on the "Craig Corner." If it could speak, it might tell many interesting stories of slavery days.

Samuel Craig's Family.—To Samuel Craig and wife (Margaret McFadden Craig), eight children were born, five sons and three daughters. One of his daughters became the wife of David D. Taylor, long-time editor of the Guernsey Times. One of the sons, Samuel A., became associated with his father in the store, and after the death of the latter in 1891, he succeeded to the entire business, conducting it with the assistance of his brother, Cyrus F., and his two sons, Frederick G. and Samuel A., Jr. Following the death of Samuel A., Sr., the two sons took charge.

Most of the descendants of the original Samuel Craig have held to his last choice in politics and religion. They are Republicans and United Presbyterians. The only member of the third generation of this family now living in Cambridge is Mrs. S. C. (Elizabeth) Carnes, daughter of Samuel A., Sr., and granddaughter of the original Samuel Craig.

The Craig Corner today (2024).

THE CAMBRIDGE CORNER STORIES

The Craig Corner as seen on a 1912 postcard.

Looking east on Wheeling Avenue from the Craig Corner, 1912.

(Photos courtesy of the Guernsey County Historical Society)

MORE STORIES OF GUERNSEY COUNTY

The Blue Corner

[Originally published 1/9/1946]

(This is the fourth of a series of stories on the leading corners of Cambridge. For his assistance in our research, we are indebted to Carl J. Rech. See page 600 of the book for picture of the corner in horse-and-buggy days.)

Better known today as the DeFrance Drugstore, the building at the corner of Wheeling Avenue and East Eighth Street used to be called the Blue Corner. We said in our last story of this series that the building across the street, owned and occupied by the Ohio Power, was the oldest building on Wheeling Avenue that still presents its original exterior in every respect but color. The one we are now writing about was erected near the same time (in the 1830s), but, unlike the other, it does not appear the same, as its exterior has been plastered over.

Built by William McCracken.—The corner lot on which it is located is No. 53, which has a frontage on Wheeling Avenue of 66 feet and extends back to Brown Avenue, a distance of 198 feet. The records show that Jacob Gomber and Zaccheus A. Beatty, founders of the town, sold this lot to William Le Lecheur for $55, in 1815. It had cost them twelve and one-half cents. Little is known of Le Lecheur other than that he was a Frenchman who came here from Pennsylvania. He must have made some improvements on the lot, for in 1830, McCracken paid him $600 for it.

William McCracken, who came to Cambridge in 1809, was a blacksmith, a merchant, and a dealer in real estate. (See page 563 of the book.) In his time, he owned more lots on Wheeling and Steubenville Avenues than any other person except Gomber and Beatty. On the corner of lot No. 53, he erected the building that stands there today, and opened the McCracken and Hanna store. As the two stores across the street bore the names of the Red Corner and the White Corner, he called his the Blue Corner, probably to complete the national colors; at any rate, we know of nothing in the appearance of the building at that time that could have suggested the name.

McCracken and Hanna not only sold merchandise, but they bought or traded for all kinds of produce from the farmers, which wagoners hauled to eastern markets, bringing back manufactured goods to be sold in the store. On the rear of the lot was a large warehouse in which they stored wool, tobacco, flour, and cured meats. Between it and the store, fronting on East Eighth Street, was a large smokehouse in which fresh pork was cured. The meat brought in by the farmers had to be smoked before it could be shipped. Hams, shoulders, and sides were hung row over row in the building, entirely to the ceiling, and on the floor, a heavy smoke was produced by burning green hickory wood.

One afternoon, the building caught fire, and, for a time, all that part of town was threatened. The burning meat produced a heavy black smoke that could be seen for miles. Country folks hurried into town to learn the cause of it. The meat was damaged to the extent of not being marketable, but some of it was still edible. For many days, no home in the community lacked meat. This was one of the first great fires in Cambridge.

Known As the Davis Corner.—William McCracken died in 1872. At different times before his death, Matthew Thompson and A. J. Hutchison were associated with McCracken in the store. James Davis bought the property, and it became known as the Davis Corner

For many years, John H. Sarchet, son-in-law of James Davis, had a music store on the corner. After his retirement from business, the corner room was rented for a clothing store. For several years, there has been a drugstore in it.

This corner building, including the Davis Annex back of it, now belongs to the Davis-Sarchet estate. The northern half of the lot, with buildings fronting on East Eighth Street, is owned by Dr. C. A. Craig.

The Blue Corner and East 8th Street seen from the courthouse square circa 1910.
(Photo courtesy of the Guernsey County Historical Society)

The Blue Corner today (2024), now the home of U.S. Bank.

MORE STORIES OF GUERNSEY COUNTY

The Passing of a Wheeling Avenue Landmark
[Originally published 10/30/1946]

(For his assistance in checking the various owners of this building, we are indebted to Carl J. Rech.)

Soon to be torn away by John W. Little and Sons, general contractors, to make place for a modern business structure, is the building at the southwest corner of Wheeling Avenue and Ninth Street, whose ground floor is now occupied by the Jirles Corner Market and the Morrison Leather Goods. By the removal of this building, one of the last of the old Wheeling Avenue landmarks will have passed away.

Once Fronted by a Hollow.—Corner lots were amongst the first to be sold by Jacob Gomber and Zaccheus A. Beatty after they had platted the town in 1806. This corner, Lot No. 24, was an exception, because there was a deep ravine running north along the east side of it, and in front was a double log bridge with corduroy approaches. The records show that the lot was in the possession of the founders of the town until 1812 when they sold it to Daniel Naftel; no record of consideration found. Among the members of the second group of Guernsey Isle folk coming to Cambridge in 1807 was the Thomas Naftel family, but who was Daniel Naftel? It is our belief that he was a relative of Thomas, who never left Guernsey Isle but expected to come to Cambridge and purchased the lot in advance. Changing his mind, he sold the lot four years later to Charles E. Marquand, a Cambridge resident who had come here with the group of 1807.

Deed Made in Guernsey.—The deed conveying the lot from Daniel Naftel to Charles E. Marquand is one of the most interesting documents recorded in the Guernsey County courthouse. It was executed on Guernsey Isle in 1816. The quaint legal terms of that place at that time are employed, and it is written in the French language. What Marquand paid for the lot is not stated.

Like all the other lots on Wheeling Avenue, this one had a frontage of 66 feet and extended back 198. Marquand owned it for twenty years (until 1836) when he sold the east half of it to Jeremiah Jefferson for $250. Soon after buying the lot, Marquand built a cabin upon it in which he taught a subscription school. We have been told that this little log house was built to and around, from time to time, and is embodied in the present building. Mr. Little and the writer have probed the walls, but have found no logs. The razing of the structure will be watched with interest; perhaps the old Marquand School will be disclosed.

From 1836 to 1841, the cabin was owned by Jeremiah Jefferson. Here he lived and worked at his trade—that of a tailor. He was the grandfather of Dr. Charles E. Jefferson, the eminent preacher and author.

Purchased by Mathew Gaston.—The next owner of the coiner was

Mathew Gaston who paid Jefferson $500 for it. Gaston was a prominent Cambridge lawyer, a Methodist Protestant in religion, and a Democrat in politics. He served as prosecuting attorney (1839-41) and represented the county in the state legislature (1849). He laid out an addition to the town, and Gaston Avenue received its name from him.

In 1847, the property passed from Gaston to William W. Tracey for a consideration of $600. Tracey was also an attorney. When Cambridge was incorporated in 1837, he was chosen to be the first mayor. He resigned to serve as prosecuting attorney (1838-39).

In 1851, Tracey sold the corner to Josiah P. Smith for the same amount he had paid Gaston. From Smith, it passed to David Kyle, a monument dealer, who sold it to Samuel Burgess in 1857 for $900. It was here that Burgess's son, S. M. (Mack) Burgess, now living on Steubenville Avenue and approaching the age of 90, spent the first six years of his life.

Burgess deeded the property to William B. Stewart in 1863 for $1,000. Stewart owned and lived on a large farm near New Concord. He evidently purchased the corner as an investment and rented it to various persons.

Long Ownership of the Kirkpatricks.—When John Kirkpatrick purchased The Jeffersonian in 1872 and moved from Middlebourne to Cambridge to take charge of the paper, he rented the corner from Stewart for a residence. Kirkpatrick was a Democrat. Stewart was a Republican, so staunch that he would have no dealings with Democrats except in matters of substantial financial advantage. Once a month, he would come in to collect his rent. He would not enter the house, but demanded that the money be passed out to him through a window.

After renting the house for four years, Kirkpatrick purchased the corner from Stewart for $2,000. Following Kirkpatrick's death in 1886, the title was carried in the name of his heirs for some years; then his son, Roger Kirkpatrick, North Tenth Street, became the sole owner. Mr. Kirkpatrick sold it recently to Ed Allen who is having the building removed. The Kirkpatrick ownership extended over a period of exactly 70 years.

The southwest corner of Wheeling Avenue and Ninth Street today (2024).

MORE STORIES OF GUERNSEY COUNTY

The Hood Corner

[Originally published 1/25/1946]

(This is the seventh in a series of stories on the leading corners of Cambridge. For his assistance in our research, we are indebted to Carl J. Rech.)

Known as the Hood Corner for a half century, and before that as the Britton Corner, the northeast corner of Wheeling Avenue and Tenth Street is now the Sipe Corner by virtue of ownership. Upon the corner, three buildings have stood: first, a little log cabin; second, a two-story frame dwelling; and third, the present brick business and apartment building.

Sold For $100.—This corner lot, with a frontage of 66 feet on Wheeling Avenue and running back along Tenth Street 198 feet, was not sold for fourteen years after the town was laid out, but remained in the possession of the founders of the town, Jacob Gomber and Zaccheus A. Beatty. It was not a desirable lot because there was a hollow there that would need considerable filling to make it fit to be built upon. The hollow was lined with trees and a dense undergrowth. In 1820, James Clements purchased it for $100. Upon it, he built a small log cabin, in which, as the records indicate, he lived for several years.

Purchased by Joseph Britton.—In the early 1820s, Benjamin I. Briggs brought his large family from New England to Guernsey County and, as a tenant, located a short distance southeast of Cambridge, on a farm owned by Dr. Benjamin F. Bill, afterwards Joseph Britton. Briggs was a teamster, and while returning to Cambridge with a load of salt from the saltworks at Chandlersville, he met with an accident on Best Hill and was killed.

Joseph Britton was a man of considerable means for his day. The Britton family lived in a large, two-story, hewed-log house by the side of the Byesville Road. Joseph invested in town property, purchasing the lot we are writing about. He paid James Clements $275 for it, which would seem to indicate that the cabin had added $175 to its value. Britton died a short time after purchasing the lot in Cambridge, and James, his son, fell heir to the corner.

Briggs Family Moves into Town.—After Benjamin I. Briggs was killed, the widow saw that, as a tenant on the Britton farm, she could not support the big family of boys and girls. The boys were not interested in farming. They liked to come to town and hang around the stage stations where occasionally they would pick up odd jobs caring for the horses and such work. Years afterwards, some of them were stage drivers on the National Road. Mrs. Briggs brought the family to town and moved into the little cabin on the corner, which was then owned by the man on whose farm they had been living.

Mrs. Briggs was like the old woman who lived in a shoe with so many children she didn't know what to do. She managed to find places in the cabin for all of them to sleep, and then set to work to provide them with food. She baked and sold bread, pies, and cakes to travelers on the National Road, which ran past her door. In those days, there was much travel, especially westward. Families from the East were migrating to new homes in the West. They camped out at night and did their own cooking, but they had neither the time nor facilities for baking. Mrs. Briggs enjoyed a fairly good business.

The boys helped the family by earning a little now and then. Some of the girls learned to sew and were often given work by the neighbors. This was probably the most destitute family in Cambridge. There were no widows' pensions in those days, neither was there any public relief. It was a scant living, but they managed to get along.

(Believe it or not, one of the boys of this family became the first governor of the great state of Iowa. For the story of his life, see page 557 of the book.)

James Britton Builds Residence.—After the Briggs family moved out, James Britton tore the cabin away, and on the corner he built a two-story frame residence. The house was poorly planned and poorly constructed. This became the Britton home, and it became known as the Britton Corner. He sold the property in 1858 to Joseph Parks for $500; Parks sold it to James Sankey for $1,500 in 1867. In 1878, James Sankey sold it to John E. Sankey for $1,800.

Becomes the Hood Corner.—R. D. Hood purchased the corner from John E. Sankey in 1888. Time and the trend of business eastward on Wheeling Avenue had greatly increased its value. Upon the corner, Mr. Hood erected the building that stands there today, in which for fifty years he engaged in the merchandise business.

Upon his retirement from business a few years ago, the property was purchased by Charles H. Sipe, Jr. It is now the Sipe Corner.

The Hood Corner today (2024).

EXTENDED CHAPTER XLV

Church Stories

The First Methodist Church of Cambridge
Some Early History

[Originally published 12/3/1945]

The First Methodist Church of Cambridge, the first church of the Methodist denomination to be organized in Guernsey County and now the largest single group of any denomination in the county, is 137 years old. Organized in 1808 in a hewed-log house that stood on the northeast corner of Wheeling Avenue and Seventh Street, it did not have a home of its own for twenty-five years; its membership was too small, and its finances not sufficient to obtain and support one. At the end of the first twenty-five years, there were only about fifty names on the church roll, nearly all of them being members of families who came from the Isle of Guernsey. Today, this same church has a membership of almost 1,700.

Meeting Places.—Thomas Sarchet owned the house in which the church was organized. It was not only his residence, but in it he kept the only store in town at that time. Here the little group of Methodists met for five years (1808 to 1813). Sarchet, who had come from the Isle of Guernsey two years before, was a religious man, a licensed exhorter, and he led the services in the absence of a preacher, whose visits were by no means frequent. The courtroom in the old courthouse having been made ready for use, the commissioners permitted the Methodists to worship in it for the next ten or fifteen years. Then they moved over to the assembly room of the old academy that stood on North Seventh Street across from the Presbyterian Church. It was in 1833 that they erected a home of their own back on the alley now known as Turner Avenue. (For a picture of this church and a description of it, see page 379 of the book.) The board of trustees at that time, who supervised the erection of this little five-hundred-dollar structure, was composed of James Bichard, John Blampied, Joseph Cockerel, Nicholas Martel, Isaiah McIlyar, Joseph Neeland, Jacob Shaffner, Joseph W. White, and Joseph Wood.

Cambridge was twenty years old before there was a church building of any denomination in the town. The old courtroom was open to all religious groups. The Associates (now the United Presbyterians) built the first in 1826. The Presbyterian, Methodist Episcopal, and Methodist

Protestant churches were all built about the same time.

Early Preachers.—This little Methodist congregation had approximately forty pastors during the twenty-five years it was homeless. We here list them in the order they came:

1808, James Watts; 1809, James Watts and William Young; 1810, James B. Finley; 1811, John Strange and J. Mills; 1812, William Mitchell; 1813, John Clingan; 1814, William Dixon; 1815, Joseph Kinkead; 1816, William Knox; 1817, John Watterman and Thomas Carr; 1818, John Tivis and Samuel Glaze; 1819, Thomas A. Morris and Charles Elliott; 1820, S. R. Brockunier; 1821, James Hooper and Archibald McElroy; 1822, Leroy Swormstedt and M. M. Henkle; 1823, Burris Westlake and David Young; 1824, William Cunningham; 1825, Edward Taylor and Arza Brown; 1826, Zarah H. Coston and M. Ellis; 1827, Cornelius Springer and James Callihan; 1828, Joseph Carper; 1829, William B. Cristie; 1830, Alfred H. Lorain and Gilbert Blue; 1831, Jacob DeLong and William Young; 1832, John W. Gilbert and Levi P. Miller; 1833, Charles C. Leybrand.

Preachers Were Circuit Riders.—When organized in 1808, Cambridge was a preaching point on the Wills Creek Circuit, which extended over several counties in Southeastern Ohio, and the circuit-rider preacher had to travel 477 miles to make one round of his appointments. The most noted of these preachers was Rev. James B. Finley, whose home was on Leatherwood Creek between what are now Salesville and Gibson. (See story, "The Circuit Rider," page 413 of the book.) It will be noted from the list above that a circuit rider seldom held to a circuit longer than one year; it was a strenuous life.

In 1812, Cambridge was assigned to the Tuscarawas Circuit; in 1813, to the Zanesville. In 1834, the Cambridge Circuit was set apart from the Zanesville, and the preacher resided in Cambridge. His circuit included the following preaching places: Cambridge, Cumberland, Ross's, Salem, Gregory, McCoy's, Bethel, Bichard's, Liberty, Zion, Camp's, Claysville, and Rich Hill. He had thirteen congregations to look after.

By 1845, the Cambridge Church had so increased its membership as to justify the belief that it could stand alone, and it asked to be made a station. This request was granted, and such it became. But four years later, however, it dropped back to a circuit status. This time the preaching places were Cambridge, Washington, Antrim, Winchester, Allen's, and Middletown. In 1857, it again became a station and has thus remained to the present day.

Split in the Church.—Near the close of the twenty-five-year period about which we are writing, there came a dissension in the American Methodist Episcopal churches. Many members, although adhering to the doctrines of the church, became dissatisfied with the church government, which smacked too much, they believed, of those of the Episcopal and Catholic churches. A new denomination sprang up—the Methodist Protestant. When one of the dissenters, Rev. George Brown, came to

Cambridge in behalf of the new organization, the little Methodist Episcopal Church here split into two groups.

Rev. Cornelius Springer, one of the old circuit-riders, organized a society of Methodist Protestants and became its first pastor. Leading off in the break-away from the Methodist Episcopal Church were Thomas McIlyar and wife, Peter Corbet and wife, Zephima C. Suitt and wife, and Thomas Sarchet. Just twenty-five years before this, Thomas Sarchet had led in the organization of the church he was now leaving. As stated above, he furnished a meeting place for it for five years in his own home. Now he does as much or more for the new church in which he was a pillar for the rest of his life. He donated a lot on what is now Turner Avenue, and on it had a church erected, in a large measure at his own expense.

On account of this division, the loss of members by the original Methodist Episcopal Church became a matter of much alarm to those who could not see their way clear to go along with the dissenters. It had the effect, however, of arousing them from an apathetical state to one of greater church activity. A great revival followed, and the church was soon moving forward, stronger than ever before.

It may be mentioned here that almost exactly one hundred years after the split, the Methodist Episcopal and Methodist Protestant Churches came together again under the common name of "Methodist."

Senecaville Presbyterians — Some Early History

[Originally published 7/6/1946]

The destruction of the Senecaville Presbyterian Church by fire a few months ago, and the plans now under way for the erection of a new church, prompt us to write some early history of this congregation, one of the oldest in Guernsey County. Among the earliest settlers in what is now the Senecaville community were the Dilleys, Finleys, and some others, who had worshiped in accordance with the Presbyterian faith back in the eastern states from which they had come. When they came here, they found no church of their denomination; in fact, no church of any kind.

Church Organized by Rev. John Boyd.—Over at Washington, eight miles away, which could be reached by these people mentioned above only with difficulty over a road that was little more than a path through the forest, Rev. John Boyd organized a church either in late 1810 or early 1811. He was urged to come over to what is now Senecaville and organize a church; this he did the same year he came to Washington. There was no Senecaville until 1815, but there was a Seneca Creek, and Seneca was the name given the church. The one at Washington was called Leatherwood, because some of its leading members, especially the Frames, Robes, and Laughlins, lived in the Leatherwood Valley. One organized later in what is now the northern part of Noble County was called 'Possum. Many of the pioneer churches took the names of the creeks in whose valleys their members lived.

Sketch of Senecaville's First Preacher.—Rev. John Boyd was born in Ireland in 1768. When John was four years old, his father decided to migrate to America. Just before the ship was to leave, little John and his brother began to show symptoms of smallpox, and the captain refused to take them on board. But the illness, instead of proving fatal to the boys, really saved their lives, for the ship foundered at sea and all on it were lost. The Boyds sailed later and settled in Pennsylvania.

John studied for the ministry, and in 1801, he was licensed to preach. After preaching in Pennsylvania for ten years, he came to Guernsey County, hoping a change of climate would benefit his health, which was not at all good. He moved to the southwestern part of Ohio where he died in 1816, leaving a widow and eight children.

Next Preacher Was Rev. James Smith.—After Rev. John Boyd left, the Leatherwood and Senecaville congregations struggled along for a short time with occasional supply preachers. In 1815, Rev. James Smith, a Pennsylvania native, was installed as pastor of the two churches whose combined membership was forty-seven. He remained four years, during which time 38 more members were added.

Rev. James Smith was a frail man physically and predisposed to consumption. While delivering a discourse, he would often become so nearly exhausted that he could hardly proceed to the end. While here, he lived on a farm between his two appointments, which was near the present county home. His salary was small, and he tried to support his family by farming a little on the side, something he was scarcely able to do; in this, his neighbors generously helped him. His wife died and was buried in the old Presbyterian Cemetery near his home. In the spring of 1819, he went to Athens, Ohio, to attend a session of the Presbytery. While there, he suddenly became deranged and had to be put in a straightjacket to prevent him doing himself harm. A few days later, he died.

Rev. Thomas B. Clark Takes Charge.—For the next eighteen months, Seneca and Leatherwood depended upon supply preachers again. Then came Rev. Thomas B. Clark in 1821, who was engaged as pastor of the two churches, and 'Possum, which was added to the charge, at a salary of $400 a year. He gave one-half his time to Leatherwood and one-fourth to each of the other two. When he began, the combined membership of the three was ninety-four. In 1825, Rev. W. G. Keil came into the community as a missionary, and the 'Possum Church gave way to one of the Lutheran faith. This left Leatherwood and Seneca as one charge again.

Rev. Thomas B. Clark was a stout, heavyset man who was born in Pennsylvania. Before coming here, he had been preaching about ten years in his native state. He bought and lived on a farm about a mile southeast of Washington. Here he suffered the same loss as did his predecessor, Rev. James Smith; his wife died and was buried in the old Presbyterian Cemetery near his home. He was the father of ten children. Resigning as pastor in 1831, he moved to Logan County, Ohio, where he died twenty years later.

Church Declines.—After Rev. Thomas B. Clark left, the Senecaville Presbyterians, having no pastor, became discouraged and drifted away. A Cumberland Presbyterian Church was organized in the town, and some of the old Presbyterians joined it. Having no church building of their own, the Cumberland Presbyterians occupied the Presbyterian Church, which had been vacated, and afterwards claimed it. The Presbyterians who had remained true to the faith of their fathers resented this usurpation, but said little about it until they found need for the church afterwards.

During the winter of 1833-34, a great evangelistic meeting was held in Senecaville, conducted by Rev. Luke DeWitt, a meeting in which all denominations joined. There was a religious awakening that attracted wide attention. In the midst of it came Rev. David Polk who rounded up the old faithful Presbyterians and agreed to serve as their pastor. But the Cumberland Presbyterians had their church. They succeeded in showing that these usurpers had no legal right to the property and were thus able to recover it. Rev. David Polk was the pastor for two and one-half years. (In this article we shall not follow the line of preachers farther.)

The Church Buildings.—For thirteen years after their organization, the Senecaville Presbyterians had no church building, but worshiped around at the homes of each other. In 1824, they erected a church in what is now the southeast corner of the village cemetery. This was the building the Cumberland Presbyterians afterwards occupied. It was the first church building of any denomination in Senecaville.

From 1854 to 1862, Rev. William M. Ferguson was the pastor. During his ministry, a new church was built near the middle of the town, on the east side of Main Street, probably about the year 1860. For eighty-five years, this was the Senecaville Presbyterians' place of worship, although during that time there were many changes made in the building. It was the church that was destroyed by fire a few months ago.

The First Baptist Church of Cambridge
Some Early History

[Originally published 12/17/1945]

This is a sidelight on the history of the Cambridge Baptist Church, page 373 of the book. There, it is stated that Wyatt Hutchison, who came to Cambridge in 1803, may be considered the first of the Guernsey County Baptists. He was a faithful Baptist and was active in the interests of the local church until his death many years after his coming here. His wife was the daughter of John Beatty and a sister of Zaccheus A. Beatty, one of the founders of Cambridge. In announcing her death in 1844, a local paper said that she had never been a member of any church, although she was a firm believer in the fundamental doctrine of the Bible. It is said that some of the other members of the Beatty family leaned to the Baptist faith.

The Lone Baptist.—For some years, Wyatt Hutchison was, perhaps, the lone Baptist of Cambridge. The next, of whom we find any record, was Barton D. Holley, who entered land on Wills Creek just below the old steelworks. An Indian trail crossed the creek on his farm, and the place is known even today as Holley's Ford. Holley was a Baptist preacher and would come into town occasionally to hold meetings.

Church Organized in 1823.—It was not until 1823 that steps were taken to organize a church society. There came here in that year an itinerant teacher by the name of William Sedgwick who opened a private school to teach some subjects higher than the reading, writing, and arithmetic offered in the town school. He announced that he was also a Baptist preacher and would organize a church of that denomination if a sufficient number of the faith could be brought together. After a canvass of the town and community had been made, it was reported that seven had been found. They formed themselves into a church group with Rev. William Sedgwick as their pastor. This was the beginning of the First Baptist Church of Cambridge.

Services were held in the old courthouse. Most of the little congregation lived three or four miles south of town, too far away, they thought, to come here to meeting, so they decided to open a church nearer home. This was done in 1825. Now 120 years old, that place of worship is known as the Old Cambridge Baptist Church, sometimes called the Brick Church.

Having lost these members, the church in town didn't have the strength to continue. Rev. William Sedgwick got a preaching place elsewhere, and the few faithful joined the congregation at the Old Cambridge Baptist.

No Church for 25 Years.—For the next twenty-five years, there was no Baptist Church in Cambridge. Meanwhile, several families of that faith had moved here. Many of them found it inconvenient to attend a church so far away. Rev. William Mears, a Baptist missionary, came through here, saw the situation, and arranged for a meeting in the Methodist Protestant Church to make plans for a reorganization of the old church. On June 4, 1851, the reorganized Cambridge Baptists met with thirty-two consistent members.

They had no church home. It happened that at this time the Methodist Episcopalians had outgrown their little church on Turner Avenue, and were about ready to occupy their new building at the corner of Gaston Avenue and South Ninth Street. They offered to sell their old building to the Baptists for $300, and the offer was accepted. (For picture and description of this church see page 379 of the book.)

Pastor Paid $250 a Year.—Rev. William Mears was engaged as pastor at a salary of $250 a year, and he was to give full time to the work.

A janitor was employed for $15.00 a year. Wyatt Hutchison and David Meek were named as the first deacons, and T. T. Sarchet was chosen as the first clerk. An Englishman by birth, William Mears was a good man and an able preacher, but he lacked a winning way and failed to advance the church as rapidly as the members had hoped. After two years and three months of service, he resigned and was succeeded by Rev. B. Y. Siegfried. During the pastorate of Rev. Mears, thirteen new members were received.

Rev. B. Y. Siegfried Here Six Years.—Rev. B. Y. Siegfried was the pastor for six years (1853-1859), preaching here but half-time and receiving a salary of $225 a year. He had a revival the first year and baptized thirty. During the six years of his pastorate, he received 131 new members.

In 1860, Rev. C. H. Gunter took charge. He was young and energetic, and much was expected of him. But within a few months, the Civil War broke out, and many of the younger male members entered the service. Like churches elsewhere, this church suffered from the financial depression and found it hard to raise the $200 salary Rev. Gunter was to receive for half-time preaching. In 1862, it was decided to dismiss the pastor and discontinue the preaching services. The Sunday School was kept up, however, and prayer meetings were held regularly.

After the War.—The war over, Rev. Alfred Earl was engaged as pastor, coming here in 1866. He was not only a preacher, but a doctor of medicine as well. He agreed to serve as pastor for $300 a year, provided he be permitted to practice medicine on the side. It seems that he gave more attention to curing physical ills than to spiritual, and he only lasted six months.

Next came Rev. G. W. Churchill, who remained eight years and four months. It was during his pastorate that the Baptists built a new church. They bought a lot at the corner of Wheeling Avenue and Eleventh Street and were about to start work on the building when many objected because they thought it too far uptown. This lot was sold and the site of the present church, corner of Steubenville Avenue and East Eighth Street, was purchased. Here a new church was erected in 1874. (See picture on page 374 of the book.)

The little old frame church on Turner Avenue that was used for the Methodist Episcopalians for twenty years, and the Baptists for another twenty, was sold to Simons Brothers, to be used as a storeroom for their foundry that was located nearby. It was destroyed by the fire of 1873, which burned that section of the town.

Some Early Baptists.—Deacons: Wyatt Hutchison, David Meek, John B. Ambler, David Marshall, Jonathan Deets, John Simons, Peter Mears, A. W. Halliday, Ezekiel McCollum, Frank Mathews, Jacob Smith, Joseph Keepers, John Huffman, and E. F. Green.

Clerks: T. T. Sarchet, M. McPeek, Jeremiah Reynolds, William Rollins, C. R. McCarty, Mrs. Samuel Moore, George Dillon, W. K. Gooderl, and Robert McKahan.

CHURCH STORIES

Wyatt Hutchison served longest as a deacon, and C. H. McCarty as a clerk, the latter for seventeen years.

Early History of the Ninth Street Methodist Church
[Originally published 6/7/1947]

The First Methodist Protestant Church
Erected in 1833

For a little more than a century, that which is now the Ninth Street Methodist Church was the Methodist Protestant Church of Cambridge. The men and women who organized it had been members of the Methodist Episcopal Church here, but becoming dissatisfied with certain principles relating to the government of the denomination, they withdrew to form a society in accordance with a movement that was then getting under way in many parts of the country.

The New Movement.—In November, 1830, a convention of dissenting Methodist Episcopalians was held in Baltimore. Many in attendance had been expelled from the church of their fathers, not because they had violated anything in the creed of that denomination, to the principles of which they, believing in, had been faithful, but because they had refused to comply with certain Episcopal forms of government in the organization.

They were especially opposed to the power exercised by the bishops. Presiding elders, they claimed, should be elected by the members of the churches instead of being appointed by a higher authority. Then they had various other objections to the church machinery.

They formed a new denomination at the convention and gave it the name of Methodist Protestant. Instead of having bishops, they provided for presidents whom they would elect. They gave to the members of the churches the power of choosing their own presiding elders and pastors. The new denomination started off with eighty-three ministers and 5,000 members. The movement spread and soon reached Cambridge.

Thomas Sarchet's Letter.—There recently fell into our hands a copy of The Guernsey Times, of April 6, 1831, in which we found a letter written by Thomas Sarchet, setting forth the reasons why he had just left the Methodist Episcopal Church to join the Methodist Protestant. As it contains an unquestionably authentic account of the earliest church activities in Cambridge, we here quote the first part of the letter:

"I am now an old man and have lately been excommunicated from the Methodist Episcopal Church of this place by the Rev. John Gilbert, preacher in charge, contrary to rule and without even being notified by his Reverence to come to trial.

"I was born in the Island of Guernsey, January 29, 1770. About 1794, I joined the Wesleyan Methodists of that place. Having obtained a testimonial of my religious and moral deportment, I came to America and arrived in this place in July, 1806. There being no religious worship established here at that time by any denomination, I wrote to the Baltimore Annual Conference of the Methodist Episcopal Church to send us a preacher. The Rev. J. Watts was accordingly sent on.

"From that time, my heart and my house have been open to receive the preachers, and my wife and myself have done all we could to render them comfortable and to open their way to be useful among the citizens.

"A class was raised, principally of the French. For ten or fifteen years, we struggled, pretty much alone, without being joined by many of the Americans. Ultimately, they came in, and Methodism began to take hold upon the community; and in time there came to be a pretty considerable society in Cambridge."

Mr. Sarchet goes on to tell why he became dissatisfied with the Methodist Episcopal form of government, which resulted in an accusation being made against him of neglecting class-meeting and openly showing a sympathetic attitude towards the reformers. For this, he was expelled from the Methodist Episcopal Church.

A New Organization.—Holding views similar to Sarchet's, a half dozen Methodist Episcopal members got together and organized a Methodist Protestant Church, under the directions of Rev. Cornelius Springer. The charter members were Thomas McIlyar and wife, Peter

CHURCH STORIES

Corbet and wife, Zephima Suitt and wife, and Thomas Sarchet.

In 1833, they completed and dedicated a church home on Turner Avenue, the present site of the home of the Fraternal Order of Eagles. Thomas Sarchet, who, twenty-five years before, had established a Methodist Episcopal Church in Cambridge, now took the lead in organizing a church for the Methodist Protestants.

A Brick Church.—Thomas Sarchet not only contributed much money towards the fund needed to build a church, but, lone-handed, he solicited and obtained the rest. It was a small brick structure. John Clark laid the brick and Zephima Suitt did the carpenter work. For forty-four years, it was the place of worship of the Cambridge Methodist Protestants.

In 1876, a second church was erected on the same site at a cost of $7,000; in 1898, a third, which cost $13,000. In 1926, the present church which, including grounds, cost $182,000, was erected.

Growth of Church.—The first members were principally folks from the Isle of Guernsey. Others, such as some of the Beattys and Metcalfs, soon joined with them. When the second church was erected, the membership had reached 230, only one of whom, Thomas LePage, belonged when the first was built.

Among the pastors in the first church were Jacob Myers, A. H. Bassett, J. W. Ragan (died and buried here), John Burns, John Herbert, William Marshall, William Ross, Jacob Nichols, Israel Thrapp, John Rowcliffe (died and buried here), E. S. Hoagland, Walter Moore, C. J. Sears, J. W. Call, T. H. Scott, J. M. Woodward, and S. A. Fisher.

Methodist Protestants and Methodist Episcopalians are now together again as "Methodists."

Antrim Presbyterians

[Originally published 5/12/1947]

After 111 years of activity, the Presbyterians at Antrim are now disorganizing and offering their church property for sale. This has been deemed advisable because removals from the community have reduced the number of members, and the few remaining, by virtue of present-day traveling facilities, can conveniently attend the church of their choice elsewhere.

Organized in 1836.—This church had its beginning in 1836, six years after Antrim was platted. It was the third church to be established in that community, the first being the Associate Reformed (United Presbyterian) in 1824, and the second the Methodist Episcopal, about 1830. A burial ground was laid out at each church, and interments are yet made in all three.

Rev. Samuel Crowles organized the Antrim Presbyterian Church and served as its pastor for several years, with Rev. John Hattery as supply. There were twenty-one charter members. Included amongst them were the Meredith, Anderson, and Eaton families. Active in the work of the church in a later period were such prominent families of the community as the Williams, Stockdales, Downerds, Hardings, Pulleys, Thompsons, Cunninghams, Beggs, Tannehills, Tuttles, and Barretts.

Two Church Buildings.—Soon after the church was organized, a plot of ground was obtained and a small frame house of worship erected in the northeast corner of it, not far from the place chosen three years later for the location of Madison College. Although an Associate Reformed Church institution, this college had students of other denominations in attendance, some of whom were Presbyterians. The membership grew until the little building could no longer accommodate the congregation.

In 1859, a larger frame church was erected in the southwest corner of the grounds, and it is this building that is now being offered for sale. The Antrim Presbyterian Church enjoyed its greatest prosperity in the decades immediately following the Civil War.

Pastor for Twenty-Five Years.—Rev. Robert Tannehill was the long-time pastor at Antrim, from 1867 to 1892. Since the Tannehill family became prominent in that community, a brief sketch of its leader is in order here.

The son of William Tannehill, Rev. Robert Tannehill was born in Belmont County, Ohio, in 1814. With a medical career in view, he prepared for that profession and practiced medicine for a while. Then came the call of the ministry.

In the family coming to Antrim were three sons and two daughters. Lyle, one of the sons, became a Guernsey County teacher and prepared for the ministry at Allegheny Seminary. William H. (father of Deputy County Auditor R. P. Tannehill) graduated from Muskingum College and Allegheny Seminary, studied for the medical profession, and then entered the ministry. At the time of his death in 1903, he was pastor of the Antrim Presbyterian Church. I. A., the youngest son, was a teacher, served as a member of the Guernsey County board of school examiners, studied law, and was admitted to the bar, and practiced in Cambridge and Wisconsin.

Rev. Robert Tannehill was a man of broad and liberal views and stood high amongst his ministerial brethren in the Presbytery. He was revered by the people of his community, and his counsel was sought by the ablest men of his denomination because they had confidence in his integrity and ability.

The twenty-fifth anniversary of his pastorate at Antrum was observed May 11, 1892, on which occasion he tendered his resignation because of his advanced age. His death occurred three months later.

CHURCH STORIES

When the Methodist Episcopal Church Burned
[Originally published 1/16/1945]

(In "Stories of Guernsey County" will be found the local history of each church denomination represented in the county. For reasons that should be obvious, many incidents of interest had to be omitted. Some of these will be published in The Jeffersonian from time to time as sidelights to the church stories).

When members of the Cambridge First Methodist Episcopal Church arrived at their place of worship, corner of Steubenville Avenue and North Seventh Street, Sabbath morning, November 28, 1897, they found their church building in ruins. Many wept as they stood on the streets and looked upon the scene before them, and all of them were not women who did so.

Instead of the beautiful stone edifice erected only eleven years before at a cost of $32,000, the pride of every member of the church, there stood nothing but blackened walls surmounted by a tower. The interior of the building and all the furnishings had been destroyed by flames. The beautiful pipe organ that had been installed at much cost was now but a pile of twisted metal. Aside from the blackened walls and spire, everything of practical value was lost.

On the afternoon preceding this darkest of all Sabbaths in the history of the Cambridge M. E. Church, a fire broke out in the basement and spread with such rapidity as to be beyond control of the firemen when they arrived. About noon, a fire had been placed in the furnace to heat the building for the services of the following day. Some defect in the heating plant, it was believed, was responsible for what followed.

The last meeting that had been held in the church was the general Thanksgiving service two days before. Participating in it were all the pastors of the city. According to the report following, it was the most largely attended and the most impressive service that had ever been held in the city.

Before this building was erected, the congregation worshiped in the old church that stood on the site of the present American Legion home. That was the place of worship from 1854 to 1886. During the eleven years the church that burned was used, there were five pastors: James R. Mills, John Brown, Sylvester Burt, J. M. Carr, and R. B. Pope who had been serving for about two months. He was in the church at the time the fire broke out and gave the alarm. Awaiting a parsonage not then ready for occupancy, Dr. Pope had stored household goods and other personal belongings in the church. These were mostly destroyed, as was also his rare and valuable library.

Dr. R. B. Pope held high rank in the ministry, being one of the best-educated men in the Conference. He attended the public schools of Cleveland and graduated from Baldwin University. Before coming to Cambridge, he held preaching appointments in Toledo, Delaware, Ann Arbor, Michigan, Chicago, Cleveland, Coshocton, and Steubenville.

Only $12,300 insurance was carried on the church. This meant that to replace it, a large amount would have to be raised. Within ten days after the fire, steps to that end had been taken. The officials voted unanimously to rebuild on an improved and larger plan, and also to build a parsonage. The work was begun in April.

In the meantime, the other churches of the city tendered the use of their buildings to the unfortunate congregation. Their kindly offers were accepted until arrangements could be made for occupying Hammond's Opera House. On November 29, 1899, two years and two days after the fire, the present church was dedicated.

Rebuilding the Methodist Episcopal Church
[Originally published 1/23/1945]

The fire that destroyed the First M. E. Church of Cambridge on Saturday afternoon, November 27, 1897, an account of which was given in The Jeffersonian the other day, was a sad blow to the members, but they did not yield to despair. Gathered about the ruins the following morning, the congregation received an invitation from the Presbyterians diagonally across the street to come over and make use of their church for their morning worship. There they assembled, and while smoke was still pouring forth from the ruins, they held their usual Sabbath service.

On the following day, the trustees met and voted unanimously to rebuild the church, also to build a parsonage. They decided that the new church should be built on a larger and more improved plan. S. R. Badgley, a Cleveland architect, was engaged to plan the new structure. While the old building was ruined for practical purpose, the foundation, walls, and tower were found to be serviceable, and this lessened the cost to a considerable extent.

The contract for rebuilding was let to Vansickle Brothers, Cuyahoga Falls, Ohio, who were the lowest bidders, and they began work in April, 1898. One morning in May, it was found that they had thrown up their contract and left the city in the night. This caused a delay, attended with much anxiety.

It was then decided to have the work continued by a different method altogether. Separate contracts were let, most of them to local contractors and firms. There were twenty or thirty of them. W. C. Carlisle, Cleveland, Ohio, was employed by the church as superintendent of construction. The building was ready for dedication on Sunday, November 29, 1899.

On the old building which cost $32,000.00, including grounds, there was an insurance of only $12,300.00. Not including the grounds, parts of the foundation, walls and tower, and some materials salvaged from the ruins, the cost of the new was $36,500.00.

Efforts were made to have this amount raised before the day of dedication, so that the service could be conducted on a clean slate. "This will be done," was the assurance of Col. Joseph D. Taylor, who headed the committee to raise the necessary money. But Colonel Taylor died two months before the dedication, and the day arrived with a shortage of $1,500.00 The Ladies Aid Society, that had previously pledged $2,000.00, announced that it would also assume the amount of the shortage.

Participating in the dedicatory service were the following: Dr. R. B. Pope, pastor of the church; Dr. J. R. Keyes, presiding elder of the Cambridge district; Dr. A. L. Petty, pastor of the church in the 1860s; Dr. Riker, president of Mt. Union College; Rev. C. W. Smith, editor of the Christian Advocate; Rev. J. J. Jackson and Rev. J. L. McIlyar, Pittsburgh, both former pastors. A feature of the service was the playing of the new pipe organ by Dr. Miner C. Baldwin, Chickering Hall, New York City. Dr. C. W. Smith had charge of the service.

The Oldest Church Building in Cambridge

[Originally published 11/24/1945]

Seventy-six years ago this fall, the oldest church building in Cambridge, the First United Presbyterian, was dedicated, the exact date being Sunday, September 26, 1869. The dedicatory sermon was delivered by Dr. J. B. Clark, of Allegheny, Pennsylvania. Attending the services were approximately 900 persons.

At that time, the church organization was forty-seven years old, and had attained a membership of 300. Before the organization was effected in 1822, there had been a church society here for several years, under the leadership of William McCracken, but with no regular preacher. This little, unorganized group worshiped at each other's home for a time, in accordance with the faith of the Associate Church which, joining with the Associate Reformed Church some years later, became the United Presbyterian Church. The homes not proving to be suitable meeting places, they erected a tent out by Fish Basket and would gather there. Their first regular pastor was Rev. Daniel McLean who came in 1824 and remained with them for thirteen years.

William McCracken and Rev. Daniel McLean took the lead in a movement for a permanent church home in town. In 1826, a lot on Steubenville Street, between Tenth and Eleventh, was purchased (now the site of the rectory of St. John's Episcopal Church), and upon it, a small brick structure capable of seating about one hundred persons was built. Here the members worshipped until 1842.

Succeeding Rev. Daniel McLean as pastor in 1837 was Rev. James McGill. The little brick structure could no longer accommodate the growing congregation. The lot occupied by the present church was purchased, and a frame building to seat 350 was erected. Rev. James McGill was succeeded by Rev. Thomas Brown in 1849, and he, in turn, by Rev. W. H. McFarland in 1860.

Seven years after Rev. W. H. McFarland came to Cambridge, three of which he had spent as a chaplain in the Civil War, the need of a better and larger church was seen. The United Presbyterians were proud of their record in the war, for, following the lead of their pastor, fifty of their members and fifty of their adherents—a total of one hundred—had entered the service. The returned soldiers were especially active in the movement for a new building, which began in 1866.

Not including the material and labor donated by the loyal and enthusiastic members and adherents, the structure cost $18,000.00. It was designed to seat 1,000. At that time, it was the largest and most attractive church in Cambridge, although the interior decorating was not completed.

Six years later (December 5, 1875), the church was rededicated, following the completion of the interior decorating and the making of a number of external improvements. The entire interior was renewed by professional decorators, and the glass in the windows changed. The grounds were enclosed by an iron fence to match that around the adjoining Central School Building that had been erected in the meantime.

EXTENDED CHAPTER XLVI

Individuals of Interest

A Prominent Cambridge Attorney

[Originally published 2/20/1945]

A prominent Cambridge attorney of the last century, of whom mention is made in the book a number of times, was Ross W. Anderson. As his death occurred more than forty years ago, there are not many who will recall his various and valuable services in behalf of the community. For the information of those who did not know him, this sidelight to the stories is written.

The son of Abraham Anderson, he was born in Washington Township, Guernsey County, in 1838. When eight years of age, the father, of Scotch descent, had come to that township from Maryland, in 1811. Thus, the Andersons were amongst the earliest settlers of that section of the county.

Ross W. attended the one-room log school of his district, which had but little to offer in the way of educational advantages. Eager to acquire higher education, he entered Franklin College at New Athens, from which he graduated in 1860. Like most all other educated young men of his day in this part of the country, he taught a district school for a time; then, with a legal career in mind, he went to Columbus and entered a law office to prepare for that profession.

The Civil War opened; there was a call for volunteers, and Anderson enlisted in the Eighty-fifth O. V. I., and was afterwards transferred to the One Hundred Twenty-fifth. He offered himself as a private, was made a lieutenant, then a captain. Captured in battle, he was thrown into Libby Prison, where he suffered untold hardships for twenty-two months. He was taken to Andersonville, in which conditions were worse than at the former place.

After the war, he entered the Cincinnati Law School and completed his legal education. Coming to Cambridge, he formed a law partnership with Col. Milton Barnes, who, in 1878, was elected Ohio's Secretary of State. In 1868, Anderson was elected to represent Guernsey County in the General Assembly, and was re-elected in 1870, serving both terms with distinction. Rutherford B. Hayes was governor at that time. From 1874 to 1878, he was mayor of Cambridge. He was a Republican and did much work for the success of his party, although he seldom aspired to an office for himself. He was chairman of the Republican County Committee for several years and was outstanding as a political speaker.

Ross W. Anderson was naturally endowed with a keen mind. Through much reading and study, he became well informed. His ability as an attorney was widely recognized, and as a counselor, his services were in demand. In civic affairs, he took much interest and gave much time and effort for the welfare of the community. In religion, he held to the Presbyterian faith and was a staunch member of the local church of that denomination.

His wife, Martha Hunter Anderson, was the daughter of James Hunter, a Cambridge cabinet-maker, who exactly a century ago established what is now the Bair Furniture Company at its present location. Ross W. Anderson died in 1902. Of his six children, the following are living: Mrs. W. P. Devore, Cambridge, O.; Warren R. Anderson, Milwaukee, Wis.; Mrs. Alice Hanna Roselle, New Jersey; Mrs. Irene Potter, of New York City; and Hunter Anderson, Phoenix, Ariz.

Col. Thomas H. Anderson

[Originally published 12/19/1944]

A prominent attorney in Cambridge in the 1870s and 80s was Col. Thomas H. Anderson. His residence was on Steubenville Avenue, between Eighth and Ninth Streets; it is now the Presbyterian home and occupied by Rev. Lester S. Evans. Colonel Anderson was not a veteran of any war. He was given the rank of colonel by Gov. Charles Foster, on whose staff he served as aide-de-camp.

Thomas H. Anderson attended school at Fairview, Guernsey County, and Mt. Union College, and he taught school in the rural districts of the county and the Cambridge High School. He read law under Col. Joseph D. Taylor, and after his admission to the bar in 1871, he entered the law office of Colonel Taylor as a partner.

In 1880, Anderson was attorney for the defense in a trial that attracted wide attention. It marked a step in his legal career, as it showed his skill as a defense attorney. The trial lasted an entire week, and while the case was not important in itself, it went to show that a skillful attorney may sometimes get justice for his client in spite of overwhelming evidence against him. As an example of such, it has often been referred to as an outstanding trial in the Guernsey County court. From the records of the courthouse and from published reports of the trial, we have gathered the following:

On the night of June 18, 1880, when Albert and Jennie Caldwell were away from home, their dwelling was broken into forcibly, and much personal property was taken. The burglary caused considerable excitement, and in the course of time, suspicion rested upon Harvey Swan as the guilty one. Having procured the necessary warrant, officers searched the Swan home, and therein concealed, they found a part of the stolen goods. Swan was arrested and indicted for burglary and concealing stolen property. When arraigned, Swan pleaded "not guilty"; the case was set to be heard at the November term of court.

William H. Frazier was the judge of the Common Pleas Court; James O. Grimes, the prosecuting attorney; J. M. McKitrick, sheriff; and J. P. Mahaffey, clerk of courts.

Swan stated that he was unable to furnish counsel, and Judge Frazier appointed Thomas H. Anderson to defend him. Anderson was reluctant to take a case in which he was sure to lose. Judge Frazier insisted, and he asked a few days to think it over. In the meantime, he visited the prisoner in the jail, then reported to the court that he would accept the appointment.

At the trial there was an avalanche of testimony against the accused, and nothing offered in his defense except his own plea of "not guilty." It was shown that Swan began to act in a strange way immediately after the burglary, and this led to a searching of his home. The officers testified to finding a part of the stolen property concealed in his home, and this led to his arrest. But the leading prosecuting witness testified that that left no doubt as to Swan's guilt. He said that late one night after the burglary and before Swan's arrest, he met Swan on the road carrying a load of the stolen property. He asked for an explanation. Swan broke down, he said, and confessed the crime. He explained in detail how at one o'clock in the night, he had broken the lock and entered. He told him that he knew he was suspected and, fearing his house would be searched, he was taking the property back to the Caldwell home, intending to leave it on the outside. He planned to carry the remainder over the next night. But before this was done, the officers had searched the Swan home, found the remainder of the stolen goods concealed there, and had arrested him. A man who was with the leading prosecuting witness that night testified to the same thing.

In the minds of the jury and the people who packed the courtroom during the trial, there was no doubt of Swan's being guilty. The evidence against him was overwhelming. Anderson alone believed him innocent. In his argument in behalf of the defendant, which was of exceptional power and eloquence, he showed that the defendant was innocent and that the leading prosecuting witness himself was the guilty man.

It was the leading prosecuting witness who had broken into the Caldwell dwelling at the hour and in the manner described. He took the stolen goods over to the Swan home and asked that they be left there for a few days. To accommodate him, Swan accepted them, perhaps not knowing they had been stolen. Then came the excitement attending the burglary, and he realized that he had the stolen property in his possession. He was much worried about it, and this caused him to act in a strange manner before his arrest. He deemed it advisable to get rid of the goods and had adopted the plan of taking them back to the owner as being the most honorable.

It took the jury but a few minutes to consider the case and render a verdict of "not guilty." The leading prosecuting witness was then arrested for burglary and perjury. But that was a case for another attorney. The Swan trial gave Anderson much prestige as a defense lawyer.

Politically, Colonel Anderson was a Republican and an active worker in his party. He was especially strong as a speaker, and in the presidential campaign of 1880, he was called upon to make political speeches in Ohio and other states in behalf of Garfield and Arthur.

Colonel Anderson was the only Guernsey County man who ever reached a high place in federal diplomatic service. In 1889, President Benjamin Harrison appointed him as the United States Minister to Bolivia. Following a four-year term as such, he practiced law in Washington City for six years. In 1899, he was made United States District Attorney, and in 1901, he was appointed an Associate Justice of the Supreme Court of the District of Columbia.

Abraham Armstrong

[Originally published 12/28/1944]

Exactly one hundred years ago, Abraham Armstrong was Auditor of Guernsey County; today his great-grandson, Willard Patton, holds the same office. Armstrong has been a familiar name in Jefferson Township since the very beginning of that political subdivision.

John Armstrong, the father of all the Jefferson Township Armstrongs, was born in Green County, Pennsylvania, in 1781, married Susannah Henderson in 1809, and came to what is now Jefferson Township, Guernsey County, Ohio, in 1813. Running through the land he entered was Salt Fork Creek, and on this stream, in 1815, John Armstrong erected a dam and built a mill that became widely known and gave to the community a name it still bears. John Armstrong died in 1852.

After his father's death, Abraham, the oldest son, born in 1810, took charge of the farm and mill. When six months old, Abraham lost the use of his right leg by an illness (probably infantile paralysis), and ever afterwards used a crutch when walking. He availed himself of the meager educational advantage of that day and prepared to teach school. In politics, he was a Whig until that party passed out; then he became a Republican. In religion, he held to the United Presbyterian faith and was one of the organizers of the Pleasant Hill Church of that denomination, located near his home.

Abraham Armstrong was the Whig candidate for County Treasurer in 1839 but was defeated by Newell Kennon. In 1843, he was elected County Auditor. In 1871, he was chosen to represent Guernsey County in the state General Assembly. For twenty-two years, Abraham Armstrong was a justice of the peace in Jefferson Township, and for seventeen years he served as township treasurer.

In addition to operating the mill and a large farm, he kept a general cross-road store. The post office in the store, closed many years ago, was called Clio, a name that is still often used in referring to the Armstrong community.

Abraham Armstrong died in 1890, leaving three sons. Mrs. Ward Johnson, North Tenth Street, Cambridge, a granddaughter, has in her possession a number of diaries kept by her grandfather. Both local and general events of each day are recorded. Following are a few of the entries, which will enable one to form some notion of the character of the man.

July 2, 1881:
A very clear morning and a little cool. It may be a fine day for the farmers to pursue their various occupations of the season. Jeremiah is taking a load of flour to Washington.

The heart-rending news was received this evening that President Garfield was shot by an assassin at 9 A. M. The wound is thought to be fatal.

July 4, 1881:
The President is still living, but little hope of his recovery.

The comet still makes its appearance in the evening, west of north. It is said that a second comet is seen in the early morning, in the northeast. It is the same comet.

August 4, 1881:
The boys arose this morning shortly after 4 o'clock to make ready to go to Cambridge to see the Free Mason show of usurping the authority of laying the cornerstone of the new courthouse. It is said a great crowd was present to see the stone laid, but very few went out to the grove to hear the addresses.

September 20, 1881:
Cool air but clear and nice. We received the very sorrowful news this morning that President James Abraham Garfield died last night about 1 o'clock—a great calamity to the nation.

September 21, 1881:
James went to Cambridge with Walker in the afternoon. He brought papers home giving a fuller account of the President's death. He died at Long Branch, N. J. The remains will be removed today to Washington City and lie in state in the Rotunda of the Capitol Thursday and Friday. They will then be taken to Cleveland and lie in state till Monday at 2 o'clock, and then be interred in Lakeview cemetery.

January 1, 1832 (Sunday):
On account of cold weather, cannot go to church. I adhere to my long-adopted resolution of not writing on the Sabbath unless some urgent necessity requires it. I make my notes of Sabbath always on Monday.

I am thankful that I have been permitted to see the beginning of the year 1882, and thankful for the blessings I have enjoyed during the past year of 1881.

MORE STORIES OF GUERNSEY COUNTY

"Arly" Aylor

[Originally published 1/21/1947]

Charlotte Aylor, familiarly known as "Arly," was born a slave on a Virginia plantation, May 25, 1797, and died a beloved colored Cambridge woman, July 11, 1876, aged 79. Her passing was mourned by the white family with whom she lived, as if she had been one of its own members. While her life was uneventful in respect to special incident, a brief story of it is worthy a place in Guernsey County history, serving as it does as a continuous outstanding example of faithfulness to a benefactress. Arly died more than seventy years ago, and only a few, now living, will remember her.

Left at Home of Andrew Moore.—On Zane's Trace, a few miles southeast of Washington, was laid out the first town in this part of the country, Frankfort, now known as the "Lost Town." Here, before there was a Guernsey County, Andrew Moore and Elizabeth Bines Moore, his wife, kept a tavern known for its good cheer and hospitality. In this home were their nine children, Robert B., William, James B., Andrew, Thomas, Jacob, Maria, Harriet, and Eliza.

One evening in the fall of 1809, there arrived at the tavern a family of father, mother, and some small children, traveling westward in a wagon. With them was one of their slaves, Charlotte Aylor, 12 years of age, whom they had brought along to care for the children. They were from Virginia, they said, and were on their way to some destination, and for some special purpose not now known. Supper, lodging, and breakfast were engaged by them.

The slave girl became ill in the night, and in the morning, she was tossing with a high fever. As she was unable to be moved, and the travelers could not remain back with her, they left her at the tavern and continued their journey. It was evident that they expected her to die, but they said that they would return later for her, something they never did.

For a long time, Arly lay in a serious condition. Notwithstanding the fact that in the household there were many children to be looked after, Elizabeth Bines Moore nursed the slave girl as if she were one of her own children, and eventually she recovered. Why a white woman, a total stranger, should give a slave girl such treatment was beyond Arly's comprehension. She had never heard of anything like it. Her appreciation was boundless, and she vowed she would be a faithful servant to Mrs. Moore, if she would let her, as long as she lived. To this vow, she religiously clung, and when Mrs. Moore died, she transferred her loyalty to a daughter, thence on, even to the third generation.

Goes To Middletown.—In 1827, the National Road was built through a few miles north of Frankfort, and Zane's Trace was seldom traveled anymore. The town was abandoned, and the old tavern was closed. Meanwhile, Andrew Moore had died. Mrs. Moore went over to Middletown to live with one of her sons, Andrew, Jr., who had opened a tavern there. Arly went along. The wife of Andrew, Jr., died, and Mrs. Moore, her youngest daughter, Eliza, and Arly located in Cambridge. After a time, Eliza married Col. James M. Bushfield, and Mrs. Moore, now far advanced in age, went to make her home with another son, William, out on the National Road, east of town. Arly, of course, went along to care for her. (The Eliza here mentioned was the grandmother of U. S. Senator Harlan J. Bushfield, former governor of South Dakota).

Enters the Scott Family.—Elizabeth Bines Moore died, and Arly turned her affection to the one who had been closest to her benefactress, Mary A. Moore, only daughter of William, with the vow that she would serve her. Mary A. married Elza M. Scott, who lived out the East Pike and operated the Scott Salt Works and the Scott Coal Mines. (See pages 54 and 473 of the book.) In 1872, the Scott family purchased and moved into the McCracken property on Steubenville Avenue, between Eighth and Ninth Streets, now owned by William Scott, a grandson of Elza M.

To Elza M. and Mary A. Scott, ten children were born. Arly took care of all of them, and her influence upon them was ever for good. She was not of the "black mammy" type that we read about in fiction, indulgent to an extreme and extravagant in her manifestations of affection, but she treated the Scott children sensibly, in such a way as to win their love and obedience.

Respected By Everybody.—By her quiet demeanor, dignified bearing and versatility in household activities, Arly won much respect in Cambridge. In the preparations for entertaining, the Scotts would depend upon her. She was a wonderful cook, and she prepared many delicious dishes of her own invention. Often asked by a guest for a recipe, she would name the ingredients to be used. "But how much of each?" she would then be asked. "Oh, just as much as you need," she would reply. Arly had little or no education.

As One of the Scott Family.—In 1850, Arly joined the Cambridge Presbyterian Church, of which the Scotts were devout members. Every Sabbath day, she would accompany the family to the services and sit with them in their pew. And this was before the Civil War. In some parts of the country, it would have attracted attention, but here where everybody knew of the reciprocal devotion, there was little or no comment.

The time came when Arly, by virtue of lifelong hard work and advanced age, could no longer care for others, but needed to be cared for herself. She became as helpless as she was the day, years before, when Elizabeth Bines Moore became her nurse. The Scotts gave her the attention they would have given one of the family. And when death came to her later, they mourned as if she were one of them, and laid her body to rest in their own lot in the cemetery. We were shown the family Bible, now possessed by William Scott. Along with the records of the members, coming in order of their deaths, is that of Charlotte Aylor, with dates of birth and death, but no comment as to her having been colored or at one time a slave.

MORE STORIES OF GUERNSEY COUNTY

Robert Boyd, The Circuit Rider
[Originally published 7/10/1945]

Through the courtesy of G. G. Hartley, of Quaker City, there recently came into our hands a small volume entitled "Personal Memoirs, or Hardships and Sufferings of Itinerant Life." He had found it amongst the books of an old home that was being dismantled. It was of especial interest to us because, when we were young, we had heard much about this local Methodist circuit rider from some of his descendants who were our neighbors, and because it vividly describes the hardships endured by the Methodist preachers of this section a century ago.

Robert Boyd, the writer of the book, preached in nearly every part of Guernsey County. He was born in Westmoreland County, Pennsylvania, in 1792 and was a circuit rider for almost 50 years. During these years, he moved 35 times, traveling a circuit out of each place that often took several weeks for a single round. Unable to own a horse part of the time, he would sometimes walk eight or 10 miles a day to fill a preaching appointment, which might be in a private home or schoolhouse. He had to travel all kinds of weather over miserable roads, and he experienced many narrow escapes. For all this, he was allowed a mere pittance as a salary, some of which he would be unable to collect.

In Guernsey County, he was stationed first at Fairview, then at Washington. The Fairview circuit included Barnesville and the western part of Belmont County. When living in Washington, he had charge of the Cambridge Methodist Church and all others in a good part of the county. He was there in 1841 and helped to organize the Anti-Slavery Society (page 702 of the book). At other times, he was stationed at Summerfield and Norwich.

In his memoirs, he mentions several narrow escapes while traveling on his circuit. Once he was riding horseback to a cabin where he was to preach, over a trail through the forest. The cold was extreme, the wind was strong, and the snow was two feet deep. He became so cold that he fell into a sleepy condition and could move neither his eyelids nor his mouth. The horse reached the cabin, at length, and Boyd fell off at the door. Carried inside, he fainted and was ill for three weeks.

At another time, in crossing a stream, his horse sank into the mire. He jumped off and soon sank as deep as the horse, which had then sunk to the back. By pulling the bridle reins and raising his voice, he succeeded in having the horse make a desperate effort, and both were miraculously saved.

Many of the parsonages were miserable affairs. He describes the one at Summerfield as being "an old hewed log house, small size, one story high, and in two rooms. When I came to it, the roof was much decayed, the walls crooked, doors and windows greatly out of order. Much of the enclosure around the lot had fallen down, and the balance stood crooked.

An old log stable, or rather the lower part of one, was there; all the roof and upper part were gone. The well was filthy and in a state of ruin."

At Norwich, he found the house provided for him and his family to be a dilapidated concern, with cracked walls, broken windows, doors, no stable, no water, and near a drunkard's tavern. The inside was worse than the outside. The rooms were too dirty to be cleaned. His wife and daughter made an effort to clean one room, which they occupied until something better could be found.

But perhaps the most unpleasant experiences were those connected with the entertainment furnished him while making the circuit rounds. Practically every night brought a change in lodging place. His stomach often rebelled at the food set before him, but in order not to offend, he tried not to dodge it. "In some families," he said, "the food was about as clean as cats, dogs, and small children would make it. I have, in some instances, known all these creatures diving in and getting the first bite or sup."

He was once a guest at a home presided over by a sore, red-eyed woman who prepared the dinner before going to the forenoon service in an old log schoolhouse. The chief dish on the menu was buckwheat cakes. These she baked—a great stack of them—and placed them in what was called the stock-hole, in the back wall of the cabin chimney. The cats, left in the cabin, discovered them, ate their fill by gnawing around the edges, and then climbed to the top, curled up on the stack, and were contentedly sleeping where it was soft and warm when the folks returned. The old lady drove them off, remarking that she believed they had the "worst cats in the country." The slab table was set, the stack of cakes, nicely escalloped all around, was placed on it, together with some dirty-looking butter in an old pewter plate, and some milk in hard-looking tins. The Rev. Boyd was asked to set in and help himself. He waited until the stack had been lowered somewhat by other members of the family, and then taking a cake for himself, he managed to eat a little without disturbing the erose margin.

As hard as was the eating, he says, the sleeping was worse, since there was less chance to dodge it. In some places, he was provided a small feather bed for a cover, with tick too dirty to ascertain whether it was composed of woolen or linen, and when he got warm, the odor was so strong that he found it necessary to muffle his mouth and nose with his handkerchief. Sometimes he was put in a bed with the children; at other times with a horde of small bedfellows that persisted in disturbing his rest.

Rev. Robert Boyd's health broke under the strenuous efforts made and hardships endured in carrying the gospel to the pioneers of this section of the country. Many here today do not realize the debt owed to such preachers as he. In many respects, the services of Rev. Robert Boyd resembled those of Rev. James B. Finley, one of the greatest of the Methodist circuit riders (page 413 of the book).

Forced to retire, on account of his health, before he desired the superannuation relation, he spent his last days in Barnesville. In closing his memoirs, he says, "I feel glad that I was spared and enabled to do effective service. I am sorry that I lost three years in location and two years in untimely superannuation. I feel that I am now living where I shall die and be buried, and I feel a solemn nearness to the spirit-world and a good hope, through grace, of a heavenly home."

A few descendants of Rev. Robert Boyd are living in Quaker City; a great-grandson in Cambridge.

A Cambridge Boy Became Governor of Hawaii
[Originally published 2/22/1946]

(This is the eleventh in a series of stories on the leading corners of Cambridge. For his assistance in our research, we are indebted to Carl J. Rech.)

We here present a sidelight to our yesterday's story, entitled Style Center Corner, in which we stated that Joshua K. Brown owned the corner from 1872 to 1889. Older Cambridge residents may remember Brown; also his son, Raymond C. The careers of both father and son were outstanding, and they merit permanent recording in Guernsey County history. The father was the first United States officer to be sent to Hawaii after its annexation in 1898, and the son was the acting governor of that territory for three years.

Joshua K. Brown.—Joshua K. Brown came to Cambridge from Martins Ferry, where he was born in 1839. When the Civil War opened, he raised a company of Guernsey County soldiers, known as Company B, Fifteenth Ohio Volunteer Infantry, of which he was the captain. At the end of the war, he returned to Cambridge as a major. He married Anne Tingle, daughter of Dr. J. P. Tingle and granddaughter of George R. Tingle, of Tingle Tavern fame. (See page 549 of the book.)

Their home at first was on North Seventh Street, between Wheeling and Steubenville Avenues; in 1872, they moved into the brick residence at the corner of Wheeling Avenue and Seventh Street, now the site of the Style Center, which Brown had purchased from the Shonfield Brothers. From 1874 to '77, Brown was auditor of Guernsey County. For a few years, he was editor of The Cambridge News, a paper that was afterwards called The Herald. In 1879, the great National Soldiers' Reunion was held in Cambridge (page 299 of the book). Major Brown was chief marshal of the parade, and while riding in it, he was thrown from his horse. He was so seriously injured that he lay unconscious for several weeks.

The Brown family moved to Columbus. Here, Joshua K. became prominent in politics, serving as secretary of the State Republican Committee in the presidential campaign, in which Blaine and Logan were defeated by Cleveland and Hendricks. The defeat of Blaine, his idol, was a severe blow to him.

President McKinley sent him to Hawaii in 1898 to administer the

INDIVIDUALS OF INTEREST

Chinese Exclusion Act. This law, which had been effective in the United States for several years, would now apply to Hawaii, since we had accepted the islands through annexation. Prohibited from entering the United States, the Chinese had been settling down on the Hawaiian Islands in swarms, but now this had to be stopped.

Major Brown had a difficult task assigned him. His health broke under it, and he was granted a leave of absence. Cambridge would be the place to recuperate, he thought, and, with his wife, he started on the long journey here, where he had expected to live after ending his public service. But he never reached Cambridge alive; he died on the train between San Francisco and Chicago. His body came through and was buried in the City Cemetery. His wife, who died a few years later, was buried by his side.

Raymond C. Brown.—But few of Cambridge's native sons have reached higher stations in public life than Raymond C. Brown. Living in Honolulu, Hawaii, a few years ago, he was asked for a brief account of his career. His reply was in the form of a brief sketch of his life, which is here given.

"The son of Joshua A. and Anne Tingle Brown, I was born in Cambridge, Ohio, just opposite the old Presbyterian Church of Dr. Milligan, in 1867. When I was five years old, we moved over to a brick house which father had bought on the southeast corner of Main and the street we had been living on. The school I attended was on Steubenville Street, and Mattie Allison was my first teacher.

"There were five boys in our family: Charles G., deceased; Orlof F., now in Cleveland; Frank G. in Baltimore; and J. Kelley and I in Honolulu. My boyhood ambition was to become a telegrapher. The telegraph office was diagonally across the street from our house, in the upstairs of a brick building. Billy Green was the operator, and he gave me lessons. I well recall being in the office with Billy on Saturday afternoon, July 2, 1881, when it was flashed over the wire that President Garfield had been assassinated. Billy handed me the message and told me to rush out and post it on the bulletin board on the street. As I ran downstairs with it, the thought occurred to me that it would be a wonderful scoop for father, who was then publishing The Cambridge News. He could have an "Extra" on the street before either The Guernsey Times or The Jeffersonian even knew of the assassination. No time was lost in carrying the bulletin to him and telling him what I had in mind. But he didn't think it would be practical, and, to my disappointment, it was not done.

"After we moved to Columbus, I became a clerk in the office of Gov. J. B. Foraker, afterwards in the office of the secretary of state. My next position was with the Railroad Commission. In 1901, I came to Hawaii, of which I have since been a loyal resident.

"My first position here was that of special agent of the Department of Labor. Then I entered the immigration service and was sent to Europe as the representative of Hawaii in recruiting laborers. I spent two years there, and after my return I served seven years as secretary of the Hawaiian Chamber of Commerce.

"Following the election of President Warren G. Harding, I was appointed Secretary of State of the Hawaiian Islands. I served through his term and the terms of Coolidge and Hoover, also one year under President Roosevelt. For three years, I was the acting governor of the Hawaiian Territory. President Roosevelt discovered I was a Republican—then I had to go. I am now retired from active service."

(Mr. Brown died a year or two ago.)

Judge James W. Campbell

[Originally published 3/20/1945]

In this series of sketches of common pleas judges between 1851 and 1915, we stated that there were four from Guernsey County: Nathan Evans, a sketch of whom is given on page 102 of the book; Edward W. Mathews, whose sketch was recently published in The Jeffersonian; James W. Campbell, whose sketch follows, and J. H. Mackey, whose sketch will appear later.

James W. Campbell was born in Oxford, the township that has produced so many office-holders, in 1847. His father was the village doctor at Middletown, but died when James W. was only five years of age. His death was caused by a fever he contracted from a patient passing through on his way to California. Although he knew the deadly nature of the disease, through kindness of heart, like the Good Samaritan, the doctor went to the aid of the stricken man whom others had shunned, with the result here stated.

Young James W. attended the district school until 1861 when the Civil War opened. He was not quite fourteen years of age, but he wanted to fight for his country. He tried to enlist, but was rejected on account of this age. He tried a second time with the same result. Then he did what many other boys of that period did under like circumstances: he ran away from home and managed to enlist in the One Hundred Twenty-ninth O. V. I. where he remained until the end of the war, participating in many bloody engagements.

After the war, he entered Wittenberg College at Springfield, Ohio. Here he met James A. Garfield, then a member of Congress, who told him he should go over to Williams College in Massachusetts, from which he himself had graduated. Following this advice, he was soon on his way to Williams, carrying with him a letter of recommendation from Garfield to Mark Hopkins, president of that institution.

After his graduation in 1869, James W. Campbell came to Cambridge and began the study of law under Capt. William M. Farrar. The

INDIVIDUALS OF INTEREST

Cambridge News, afterwards known as The Herald, was established that year by Captain Farrar, and Campbell worked in the newspaper office, reading law at the same time. In 1874, when twenty-seven years of age, he was admitted to the bar. The preceding year he had married Miss Martha, daughter of Hon. J. W. White, a prominent Cambridge attorney who represented this district in Congress in Civil War days. James W. Campbell entered into a law partnership with his father-in-law, and after the latter's retirement from the firm, Mr. Campbell became a partner of Fred L. Rosemond.

In 1884, W. H. Frazier, who had served as judge of this common pleas court district for fourteen years, was named to the court of appeals, and Edward W. Mathews was appointed to serve on the common pleas court bench until the next general election. At this election, James W. Campbell was chosen to serve the remaining two years of Judge Frazier's term, and at the expiration of the term he was elected for a full term of five years.

Not only was Judge Campbell eminent in legal circles, but he was prominent and successful in a business way. He was an officer in the National Bank of Cambridge, special counsel for the Baltimore and Ohio Railroad and the United States Steel Company, general manager of the Eastern Ohio Railroad, and attorney for various corporations.

Judge Campbell's home stood at the northwest corner of Ninth Street and Wheeling Avenue. It was afterwards moved back and, until recently, was the home of the Knights of Columbus. Judge and Mrs. Campbell were members of the Cambridge First Methodist Church. He died in 1917 and was buried in the City Cemetery.

Finding a Name — Andrew Clark

[Originally published 9/18/1945]

Many persons from different parts of the country write us, asking for something or other about somebody who lived in Guernsey County in the distant past or supposedly lived here. Sometimes we have the information at hand, and sometimes we have to resort to research. Sometimes, we neither know nor are able to find an answer.

From a lady in Nebraska came a letter a few months ago, asking for the first name of her great-great-grandfather whose last name was Clark; also, if handy, to forward her the first name of her great-great-grandmother. She advanced the information that her great-great-grandfather owned a farm of 320 acres in Guernsey County in the very early days, upon which he operated a mill. It didn't take us long to decide that we couldn't answer the question offhand, and with so little to start from, we hardly knew how to conduct a research. There had been several pioneer Clark families in Guernsey County. We were to find one with 320 acres and a mill. It might not be hard to find such a one among the Clarks in the county today, but we would have to search amongst the Clarks of at least 125 years ago.

We turned to our accumulation of historical data. Whether it would be better to try to find a Clark with a mill or a mill owned by a Clark was our first thought. Fortunately, we chose the latter, and brought out our list of pioneer mills. There we found that an Andrew Clark owned a mill in Jefferson Township very early in the last century. This was a starter. Now, did this Andrew Clark own 320 acres of land? Consulting our list of Jefferson Township farm owners of that day, we found that he did, and that it was located on Sugar Tree Creek. So far, we had met all the specifications sent us, and we were pleased with the progress we were making. But was this the great-great-grandfather Clark sought, and what was the first name of his wife?

Perhaps there was a will that would throw some light on the matter, but none was recorded. There was, however, a record of the transfer of this land on March 25, 1841, by Andrew Clark and his wife Nancy, to James, William, Alexander, and J. L. Clark, for a consideration of $6,341. These four purchasers were evidently his sons.

James took over that part of the farm upon which the mill was located and continued its operation. Our political data showed that James was an ardent Whig, as were his father and brothers. In the Harrison and Tyler campaign of 1840, he was one of the most enthusiastic Whig workers in Jefferson Township.

Adam Clark, another son, had gone over to Zanesville to take charge of a mill there, and had become involved in debt. To help him out of his financial difficulties, his father had mortgaged the farm for $2,000, and it evidently carried this encumbrance when sold to the four other sons. Then Andrew died before the mortgage was paid. The four sons did not have a clear title.

On April 9, 1852, the farm was offered for sale at public auction by the Guernsey County sheriff, "to satisfy creditors." Henry McCleary's bid of $3,663.25 was the highest. From that date, the Clark mill was known as "McCleary's." It was closed down many years ago, but the name still clings to that community.

We learned further that William Clark, one of the sons of Andrew and Nancy, had a son whom he named Samuel Findley Clark. This was an additional clue. He must have been named for Dr. Samuel Findley, president of Madison College at the time, and the leading preacher in the Associate Reformed Church of that day in Guernsey County. Evidently the Clarks were members of the Associate Reformed Church.

By uniting with the Associate Church, this denomination became the United Presbyterian Church. Almost without exception, the descendants of members of the early church have been true to the faith of their fathers and are today United Presbyterians.

The Clarks were Whigs. Most Whigs became Republicans when that party was formed. Political heredity has long been the strongest factor in determining one's party affiliation. The descendants of Andrew Clark would most probably be Republicans today.

We had what we believed to be the answer to the question asked us—namely, the first names of great-great-grandfather and great-great-grandmother Clark, but one thing more was needed to make our findings conclusive. We wrote to the Nebraska lady, asking her politics and religion.

Her reply made further research unnecessary.

Early School Days — The Samuel Findley Clark Story
[Originally published 10/18/1945]

Kate Graham writes us from Alliance, Nebraska, that the Samuel Findley Clark mentioned in a recent story, "Finding a Name," was her grandfather, a United Presbyterian preacher. He was the grandson of Andrew Clark who built and operated the mill known as McCleary's on Sugar Tree Creek in Jefferson Township.

Long before his death, Samuel Findley Clark wrote a sketch of his early life, a copy of which Kate Graham sent us. How he succeeded in acquiring an education under adverse conditions is of special interest, and we here present, in part, what he said about it. The district in which he started to school is now known as McCleary's and the building he describes stood near the present one in which school is yet held. He was born on his grandfather's farm across Sugar Tree Creek, a half mile from the school. Not infrequently, the water covered the bottom between, and the school could not be reached.

The schoolhouse was twenty-four feet long, sixteen feet wide, and one story high. It was built of logs ten or twelve inches in diameter, hewn on two sides to bring them close together, and the cracks between were daubed with mortar made of tough clay and short-cut straw. From the square to the comb, the end logs were cut shorter so as to give the roof the proper slant. The building was covered with clapboards about four feet long, held down by weight poles. The floor was made of puncheon dressed smooth on one side and laid flat upward.

Windows were made by cutting out sections of logs and putting in vanes of glass instead. The seats were backless slabs on legs. Writing desks were slabs on wooden pins, driven into the wall. When writing, the pupils sat with their backs to the room; there were no other desks. When not writing, they had to sit facing the room, as it was a breach of discipline to turn the back to the teacher.

Little Samuel Findley Clark started to school at a very early age. His teacher was Rebecca Stewart who was remarkably kind to the little folks. It was a summer term. Men teachers were always employed for the winter terms, for it was then that the big boys attended, and a woman was not supposed to be able to discipline them.

The only textbook he had from which to study was a little board on which the letters of the alphabet were pasted. There were no school readers and, until the McGuffey Readers came out, the pupils read from the Bible. Spelling was taught from the United States Speller. Little Samuel Findley advanced rapidly, and erelong he was ready for the higher branches, that is, for studies beyond reading and writing. He began the study of arithmetic under James Robinson, who was severe as a disciplinarian, but considered a good teacher. It was one of his rules that there should be no playing before school hours. One morning, while waiting for school to be called, nearly all the boys engaged in a little sport on the grounds. They were called in and made to stand in line. Robinson commenced at the end of the row and proceeded to administer punishment with a heavy rod. Strokes fell thick and fast, and one victim after another was sent to his seat with smarting limbs. Being at the far end of the line, Clark escaped, as the teacher's strength was spent before he was reached.

When Samuel Findley Clark was twelve years old, his father died, and the boy went to live with a brother four miles east of Washington and attended a school two miles away. He says, "The teacher was poor, the school was poor, all was poor, and it was almost impossible to make any headway." His arithmetic was the Western Calculator, his grammar was Kirkham, and his reader was still the Bible. At the age of fifteen, he went over to Norwich to live with two other brothers and a sister who had moved there. A man by the name of Tudor taught the school, and young Clark studied arithmetic, grammar, and geography, paying his tuition by hearing some of the lower classes. The next year, he worked in a tanyard and earned enough money to pay his tuition at Muskingum College for the following spring term. He walked back and forth, six miles each day. Five months of such and his pocketbook collapsed, he says, and he dropped out of college to earn more money.

From Dr. Samuel Findley, president of Madison College and county school examiner, he received a certificate and was employed to teach the McCleary School at eighteen dollars a month. At the age of eighteen, he went to Iowa to live with a brother who was a preacher there and who taught him Caesar in Latin, Greek grammar, and the New Testament. His brother was killed by lightning, and he was again thrown on his own resources. He wanted to become a minister in the Associate Reformed Church. A wealthy member of his brother's congregation lent him two hundred dollars, and he returned to Muskingum College where he studied more Latin and Greek, and tried to master geometry, but flunked out. The two hundred dollars all used up, he began teaching at Northfield in Knox Township, and boarded with a family named Coulter.

Following this term of school, he entered Madison College at Antrim, remaining there a year and a half, when he suffered another pocketbook collapse. He was employed to teach the Crab Orchard School, and while doing so, he boarded with the Edward Carpenter family. In the meantime he kept up his studies at Madison College and was enabled to graduate with his class, another member of which was the late Dr. John McBurney, of Cambridge.

Stephen B. Clark

[Originally published 12/7/1944]

In "Stories of Guernsey County," frequent mentions are made of Clark Street, Clark's Grove, and Clark's Addition to Cambridge. But who was Clark?

He was Stephen B. Clark who, for more than half a century, was one of Cambridge's most progressive citizens. His activities here were varied, and his influence was outstanding.

Born in Maryland in 1810, he came to Guernsey County with his parents in 1825. John Clark, his father, was a brickmaker and worked at that trade when he first came to Cambridge. He afterwards moved to Antrim where he engaged in the mercantile business for many years. Having retired from this, he located in Washington where he died. Both he and his wife are buried in the Cambridge City Cemetery.

At the age of sixteen, Stephen B. began teaching school. While teaching, he "read" medicine in the office of Dr. Thomas Miller in Cambridge. In those days, it was the custom for a medical student "to read medicine" in a practicing physician's office. Anatomy, materia medica, and chemistry were the required subjects. Having passed an examination in these, Clark hung out his shingle as a Cambridge doctor. He later attended the Philadelphia Medical College and formed a partnership with his brother, Dr. John T. Clark.

Peter Ogier was the Cambridge druggist. Pharmacy appealing to Stephen B., he entered a partnership with Ogier, and for a long time the place was known as the Ogier & Clark Drug Store.

At the corner of Wheeling Avenue and South Eighth Street, William Rainey had a mercantile store known as the "Red Corner." Dropping medicine, Clark became a partner of Rainey, the firm bearing the name of Rainey & Clark. The building occupied by them still stands and is the home of the Ohio Power.

Stephen B. Clark made money, and when the National Bank of Cambridge was organized in 1863, he became one of its largest stockholders. He was chosen as its first president and held this office for thirteen years.

In 1859, he purchased a large farm, known as Oak Grove, northeast of Cambridge. This farm is now a part of the city. On it were laid out Clark's

Addition and Clark Street. The commodious brick residence on the farm, in which the Clark family lived, is now the older part of the Swan Hospital. On the farm was a beautiful grove in which there were many notable gatherings. Both the Republicans and the Democrats held their great rallies in this grove in the Vallandigham campaign of 1863.

In 1839, Stephen B. Clark married Jane McCracken, daughter of William McCracken, the pioneer blacksmith, who taught "Fighting Bill" Reed, of Perry Victory fame, his trade. The McCrackens lived on the north side of Steubenville Avenue, between Eighth and Ninth Streets, and at their home, Stephen B. and his wife lived until they purchased the farm. They were the parents of nine children.

William McCracken was the founder of the Cambridge United Presbyterian Church. When Stephen B. married into the McCracken family, he, too, became a United Presbyterian, or an Associate Presbyterian as the denomination was called in those days. For the rest of his life, he was active in church work, being a ruling elder for thirty-five years.

Politically, he was first a Whig, then a Free-soiler. The latter party, which was active back in the 1850s, was strongly opposed to slavery. When the Republican Party was organized, Clark became a member of it, and was the first Republican Committee Chairman in Guernsey County. Although he took an active part in behalf of his party in all political campaigns, he was never elected to office himself.

Stephen B. Clark died in 1894; his wife, in 1902. Both are buried in the Cambridge City Cemetery.

A Fairview Pioneer — John Duncan

[Originally published 9/8/1945]

We find that in the early development of a Guernsey County community—and we presume that it is generally true everywhere—some one person has taken the lead. He may have been one gifted with an enterprising nature, who, sensing possibilities of material gain, has been actuated through a somewhat selfish motive; or, as less frequently has been the case, he may have been one who felt the need of a moral, religious, or intellectual uplift in the community and directed his time and efforts to that end. In our research and study of the beginnings of Guernsey County communities, we have not found many who lead off in all of these.

An exception was John Duncan, a pioneer of Fairview. He was born in Scotland in 1789. When fifteen years old, he came with his parents to America and located in Pennsylvania, where, a few years later, he married Elizabeth Harvey, a young woman of English descent. In 1816, John and Elizabeth decided to migrate to the newly opened land west of the Alleghenies. They followed Zane's Trace until they came to a little settlement called Fairview that had been platted two years before. They found that thirty lots had been laid off, fifteen on each side of the road, upon some of which cabins had been built. Near one end of the town was Wherry's Tavern; near the other was Bradshaw's. There were two stores kept by Jesse C. Weir, and James and Martin Rosemond, respectively. There was no industry, no school, no church.

In those days, there were no public schools. Unless they received a little instruction in reading, writing, and ciphering in the home—and very few of the parents were able to give it—the children would grow up in ignorance. Duncan, twenty-five years old at the time, possessed some education. The fact that the children were denied it grieved him. At his own expense, he built a little log schoolhouse, perhaps fifteen or sixteen feet square, with puncheon floor, slab seats, and an open wood fireplace, and opened a school. He himself became the teacher. It was a subscription school, and the parents paid him a little for his service, according to the number of scholars furnished. Money was scarce, and payments were often made in meat, flour, potatoes, or whatever they had to offer.

John Duncan then turned his attention to the religious needs of the settlement. To him came the thought that a town without a church would never prosper. Duncan was a religious man, true to the faith of his fathers back in Scotland, which was Presbyterian. He called the folks together and organized a Presbyterian society, offering the use of his schoolhouse as a church. A regular place of worship was afterwards built, and he served as a ruling elder for forty years.

School and church having been established, he began to consider the material interests of the community. There were no industries other than the ones in the homes. Clothing was needed. The cloth was made by the women by a slow process of carding, spinning, and weaving that necessitated much hard work. Duncan started a carding mill, operating it by horse-power on the tramp-wheel principle. This was the first industrial plant in Fairview. Some years later, this mill was struck by lightning and burned.

By virtue of his activities, Fairview became a good town in which to live, and to it were attracted many new families. The thirty lots were soon occupied, and more were needed. Duncan met the emergency by laying out "Duncan's Addition," which extended Main Street westward.

John Duncan was a sincere Christian for sixty years, and his religious influence reached to many. To him and Elizabeth, three sons and three daughters were born. Two of the sons became Presbyterian ministers. Mrs. Mary L. Tracy, of Cambridge, is a great-granddaughter. John Duncan lived to be ninety years old, dying in St. Clairsville in 1879.

MORE STORIES OF GUERNSEY COUNTY

Rev. William M. Ferguson

[Originally published 11/29/1945]

As a long-time preacher in the Presbyterian Church of Washington, Rev. William Ferguson held the record. His term of service extended from 1854 to 1874—a period of twenty years. During the first eight years of this time, he was also the also the pastor of the Senecaville Church. When called to Washington, he received a call from the Presbyterians at Newark, Ohio, but declined it to accept the one here.

Early in the history of Washington, Presbyterians led off in church activities. They not only established the first church, but they were the only denomination there for several years. Most of the early settlers in the community were Presbyterians. Numbered among them were the Robbs, Frames, Lawrences, Robes, Scotts, Laughlins, Hawkins, Cochrans, Engleharts, Smiths, Reas, Edies, Robinsons, Sawhills, McCollums, McCrearys, Thompsons, McCurdys, Pattersons, Dugans, McCrackens, Leepers, Caldwells, Moores, and others.

At first, they worshiped in a little log church on the hill southeast of town. Around it there came to be a burial ground, which may be seen to the right of the road leading south from Route 40 past the County Home. Here lie many of the early Presbyterians of the Washington community. Next came a brick church down in town, which served until the present one was built.

The Washington Presbyterian Church, now 135 years old, probably enjoyed its greatest prosperity during the two decades that Rev. William M. Ferguson was its pastor. His activities in behalf of the church attracted wide attention, and he became one of the best-known preachers of the Presbyterian denomination in Ohio. In 1858, he conducted a revival in Washington, at one meeting of which, fifty new members were added to the church roll. In 1868, another revival was similarly successful.

It was while he was the pastor at Washington that the present church was built. As it was in 1861 that it was completed, the structure is now eighty-four years old. Work on it was begun in 1859, just after the three Lawrence homes had been completed. At about the same time, the old Union School (still standing) was built. The brick used in the construction of all these were burned in a field east of town, that is now a part of the county fairground. Aside from the Friends Church in Quaker City, which dates back to 1821, this Washington Presbyterian Church is the oldest church building yet in use in Guernsey County. It was while the Rev. Ferguson was preaching at Senecaville that a new Presbyterian Church was erected there.

In addition to his services as pastor of the church, Rev. William M. Ferguson directed Miller Academy, which stood back of the church. It was an educational institution that would be considered a junior college today, as the course covered the first two years of colleges of the higher rank. Incorporated in 1849 by the Presbyterian Church, a charter was granted it by the state legislature. Miller Academy was closed a short time after the Civil War. Rev. William M. Ferguson taught mathematics and languages in the academy. As a mathematician, he held an enviable reputation. Washington-Jefferson College, Washington, Pennsylvania, conferred a high honorary degree upon him.

It has been said that Rev. William M. Ferguson was the "pride of the Presbyterian Church." He was a learned religious counsellor and an eloquent pulpit orator. He wrote much for the public press and denominational journals, and lectured extensively. Much to the regret of his congregation, he resigned as pastor of the Washington Church to become Chaplain of the Ohio Penitentiary. His death occurred at Plymouth, Ohio, in 1895.

Ezra Graham

[Originally published 5/9/1947]

The Chamber of Commerce has under consideration an observance next year (1948) of the Sesquicentennial of the opening of Zane's Trace and the beginning of Cambridge. If plans proposed are carried out, it will be the greatest event ever held in Cambridge, and one of the greatest in Southeastern Ohio. Zanesville, which was reached by Zane's Trace and had its beginning the same year as Cambridge, is planning a similar observance.

Zane's Trace.—In 1796, George Washington being President, Congress authorized Ebenezer Zane to cut a road through the wilderness from Wheeling, Virginia, to Maysville, Kentucky. A small group of men with Jonathan Zane, Ebenezer's brother as foreman, did the work. They probably did not start the project before 1797. Beginning at Wheeling, they worked westward and passed through the present sites of Cambridge and Zanesville in 1798.

This was the first federal road to be built in the Northwest Territory. In the opening and development of the West, it was a factor of much importance. Over it, settlers began pouring into Ohio. Connecting with the Maysville Pike, and the latter with the Wilderness Road at Lexington, Kentucky, a way of travel was opened through to Natchez and New Orleans. Thirty years after it was cut through, it gave way to the National Road through this section.

Was Only a Trail.—At first, Zane's Trace was only a trail or bridle path. Trees were blazed to show travelers the way; underbrush was cut out where necessary; a little grading was done in a few places, and that was about all. As travel increased, it was gradually widened, and came to be known as the Wheeling Road before the National Road was opened.

Ferries on Zane's Trace.—One of the conditions of the contract was that Zane must establish ferries at the crossings of the three rivers on the route—the Muskingum, Hocking, and Scioto. All the other streams, it was supposed, could be forded. When the present site of Cambridge was reached, the pathfinders came to a stream that apparently had been overlooked. They gave it the name of Wills Creek, because the Zanes had once lived on a stream by that name back in Virginia. It was too wide and deep to be forded, and they were not equipped for building a bridge. But Wills Creek had to be crossed, or the whole project would be a failure. What could they do?

The Problem Is Solved.—At this juncture, a man by the name of Ezra Graham appears on the scene. Nobody knows today where he came from. He may have been one of the group of men who were blazing the trail. He may have just happened to come along at that time. He may have been engaged by Zane and sent here. At any rate, he agreed to make a log raft and pole travelers across when they arrived at the creek, they paying him a small fee, of course. This was our first public utility.

On the north side of the creek, very near the place the Union Station now stands, he built a cabin in which to live. It was said to be the first house between the Ohio and Muskingum rivers. Without question, it was the first house in Cambridge. Ezra Graham was our first citizen.

Little Known of His Life.—No amount of research has enabled us to know more about Ezra Graham than that he lived in the cabin down on the creek and operated the ferry for two years from 1798 to 1800. For a time, his nearest neighbor on the east lived on the Ohio River; on the west, the Muskingum. Whether he had a family here with him, or lived alone, nobody knows. His first name prompts us to visualize him from a picture of the Biblical character we recall—past middle age, broad face, gray hair and beard.

His two years here alone are a blank in our history. In 1800, George and Henry Beymer came out from Pennsylvania and bought a part interest in the ferry. These two brothers and Graham became partners. Travel on Zane's Trace was increasing, and the three men opened a tavern. The ferry and the tavern together made them a good business. But they were only squatters with no right to be here at all.

In the meantime, Beatty and Gomber purchased the land and came here in 1803. They took over the ferry and tavern. The Beymer brothers bought land and settled near. Ezra Graham passes out of the scene.

INDIVIDUALS OF INTEREST

John Gray

[Originally published 1/29/1945]

In that part of Noble County which, until 1851, belonged to Guernsey, a short distance south of Cumberland, is a grave that has long attracted much attention. Inscribed on a stone at the head of the grave is the following:

> JOHN GRAY
> DIED
> March 29, 1868
> AGED
> 104 years, 2 months, 23 days.
> The last of Washington's companions.
> The hoary head is a crown of glory.

There are two things inscribed here that attract attention: first, the great age of the man, which was half as many years again as allotted by the Psalmist—an age that is seldom attained; and second, the statement that the one lying there beneath the sod was the last to die of all the soldiers who fought in the Revolutionary War. Naturally, the observer will be curious to know something of the life of this John Gray.

He was born in Fairfax County, Virginia, in 1764. The Revolutionary War opened when he was eleven years old; his father enlisted and was killed in the Battle of White Plains in 1776. Although but a mere boy, John shouldered his father's musket, marched to the front, and asked to be taken in his father's place. For the remainder of the war, he fought valiantly under Washington and was at Yorktown at the final surrender. Mustered out at the close of the war, he returned home and accepted work as a field hand on Washington's Mt. Vernon estate.

When Ohio was admitted to the Union, he came to what afterwards was Guernsey, then Noble County. Here he lived until his death, in moderate circumstances, the last few years almost in poverty. His condition was called to the attention of "Private" J. M. Dalzell, Caldwell, who reported it to Hon. John A. Bingham, our representative in Congress at that time. The latter visited John Gray, gave him money from his own pocket, and sought for him a pension, something, it seems, that had been due him for a long time. On February 22, 1867, the old veteran was made happy when he received word that Congress had awarded him a pension of five hundred dollars a year. But he only lived to receive it one year.

By the death of John Gray, so the newspapers of the time of his death say, the last veteran of the Revolutionary War passed from earth. A plain slab, inscribed as above, was placed at his grave which was located in a family burial ground a few yards north of the modest home he had lived in for many years and in which he died.

John Gray was married two times in Virginia and once after coming to Ohio. He survived all his wives and children except one daughter who lived with him in his last days. He was strongly religious, holding membership in the M. E. Church for eighty years. His friends were many, and at his funeral, which was presided over by several clergymen, more than a thousand persons were present to pay their respects.

We would rather not feel it proper to write the following, but in justice to all, we believe it should be done. We have no wish to disparage the claims of those who accorded John Gray the honor of being the last soldier of the Revolutionary War, a distinction in which this section has long shared. But the real facts should be known.

The Veterans Administration at Washington City was asked recently to give any information available concerning the last veteran of the Revolutionary War. The Administration replied that the last pension check to a soldier of the Revolution was issued April 5, 1869, to Daniel F. Bakeman who died at Freedom, New York, aged 109 years. As authority for the statement, reference was made to the Annual Report of the Pension Bureau for 1911, page 31.

Daniel Bakeman lived a year longer than John Gray and was five years older when he died.

Like Gray's, Bakeman's pension may have been a belated one. There may have been no record of it when Gray died, and this may have given rise to a justified belief that John Gray was the last soldier of the Revolutionary War. Without this technical distinction, however, John Gray was a true patriot whose memory will always be revered.

Former Citizen J. O. Grimes Recalled by Removal of a Building

[Originally published 1/10/1945]

Last April and May, an old frame dwelling on East Eighth Street, adjacent to the Cambridge First Baptist Church, was torn away. We watched the work of razing the building as it was carried on from day to day, because we wanted to see if it had been constructed at the time thought and in the way thought, and if there might be some papers or letters found that had slipped into crevices of the walls or beneath the floors. The contractors promised to be on the lookout, but they found nothing that appeared to be of historical value.

As we supposed, the house had been built in sections at different times. From the material used and the way it was put together, one could fairly determine the time each section was added.

It was one of three or four one-story houses that once stood on that side of the street. The first stood on the corner and was removed in 1874 when the old Baptist Church was built. When this church building was razed

INDIVIDUALS OF INTEREST

in 1911 in preparation for building the present edifice, the one-story cottage next to it south was taken away. The church later purchased the property, which is the subject of this article, and removed the building last year in order that the grounds might be made more attractive and be used exclusively for church purposes.

There was originally a wide wood fireplace on the north side. The heavy frame timbers had been hewn out by hand from oak logs and put together with wooden pins. The flooring, which had afterwards been overlaid with another, was the kind used a century ago. The laths had been split from oak with a frow and fastened to the studding with cut nails. The original house had but two rooms and was probably built in the 1830s.

Some years afterwards, a room was added to the south end, a hall cut from the original north room, and a second story placed over both rooms. This change was easily distinguished from the material and type of workmanship. Afterwards came an addition on the east side, making a large house.

The removal of the dwelling called to mind a former owner, James O. Grimes, who lived in it for many years. For almost half a century, he was one of the leading citizens of Cambridge, taking a prominent part in the social, civic, and political affairs of the town and county.

Born in Pennsylvania in 1821, he taught school for a time, and came to Cambridge in 1844. He read law with Attorney W. W. Tracey, first mayor of Cambridge and prosecuting attorney (1837-39) and was admitted to the bar. At that time, Grimes was a Whig in politics, becoming a Republican when that party was formed. He became not only a member of the party, but a party leader. He did much political work in Civil War days, especially in the Vallandigham campaign and the campaign for the second election of Lincoln.

He was elected to public office a number of times. With him it seemed to be in again—out again. His first office was that of prosecuting attorney to which he was elected in 1849. In 1853, he was appointed postmaster of Cambridge and served three years. For nine years, he was a justice of the peace, receiving his first election in 1855. He resigned this office to become mayor of Cambridge in 1865. Then in 1871, he was again elected prosecuting attorney. Having completed his term, he was a second time chosen mayor. But the office of prosecuting attorney apparently held some attraction for him, as he was a third time a candidate for it and elected in 1879. While many of our prosecuting attorneys have held the office more than one term, Grimes is the only one who served at three different times. He was one of the few persons, too, who served as mayor in terms that were not consecutive.

When not holding public office, James O. Grimes engaged in the practice of law. As a lawyer, he was one of the leading members of the local bar. In religion, he was a Methodist and was active in church work. His death occurred in 1890.

MORE STORIES OF GUERNSEY COUNTY

Dr. William Rainey Harper
[Originally published 12/10/1945]

Since the publication of "Stories of Guernsey County", we have been asked by a number of people why the book carries no story about Dr. William Rainey Harper. The stories, as the title of the book indicates, concern people and events inside the boundaries of Guernsey County, and since Dr. William Rainey Harper was born a few rods over the line in Muskingum County, that county claims him.

Closely Connected with Guernsey.—For certain reasons, we feel justified in making him the subject of one of our sidelight stories. In fact, we are not sure that he did not deserve a major story in the book. Samuel Harper, his father, was born and reared in Adams Township, and had crossed over the line to keep a store in New Concord only a short time before William Rainey was born. His mother, Ellen Elizabeth Rainey Harper, was a Cambridge girl. She was a sister of Major John T. Rainey, the first Guernsey County volunteer of the Civil War, concerning whom a story was published the other day. Samuel Harper and Ellen Elizabeth Rainey were married in Cambridge in 1854, two years before William Rainey Harper was born. Then, as a further claim Guernsey County might have on William Rainey Harper, when he decided to marry, he chose Miss Ella Paul for a wife, daughter of Dr. David Paul, president of Muskingum College. Dr. Paul was born and reared in Oxford Township, Guernsey County, and was a thoroughbred Pennyroyalist. Even though Dr. William Rainey Harper cannot be claimed by Guernsey County, he had a lot of close connections here.

A Precocious Boy.—Samuel and Ellen Elizabeth Rainey Harper went to housekeeping in a log house on the south side of Main Street, New Concord, which still stands and is fittingly marked to attract the attention of travelers through the town. Here, William R. was born in 1856. In early childhood, he was healthy, docile, and intellectually precocious. At a very early age, he began to display a noticeable degree of intelligence. In the fall of 1864, when he was only eight years old, he might have been seen one morning on his way up the hill to enter Muskingum Academy, an institution of high school rank. At the same time, his boy playmates had completed the second reader, would now start in the third, and try to learn the multiplication tables. There was a four-year course in the academy, but William R. completed it in two years. Thus, at the age of ten, he was given an academy (high school) diploma. Other boys of his age received certificates of promotion from the fourth to fifth grade.

An A. B. Degree at Fourteen.—In the fall of 1866, he entered Muskingum College—a ten-year-old freshman. He might have completed the course in a couple of years, but he took his time, and also a number of subjects not required of him. He graduated as a member of the class of 1870, an honor student, delivering his oration in Hebrew. An A. B. degree was conferred upon him. His boy friends received promotion to high school that same spring.

Here was a boy of fourteen, who had taken all Muskingum College had to offer and was yet too young to go over East for further study in one of the great universities. He worked around his father's store, played with the other boys, and learned to blow a cornet. He and Ella Paul furnished music on various occasions, she playing the piano, and he the cornet. Then he learned to play the piano, too, becoming quite proficient. He was made leader of the New Concord Band, and frequently he would come over to Cambridge to play in the Sarchet Band here.

Enters Yale University.—Reaching the age of seventeen, he went over to Yale University to enter as a graduate student. Pretty young, they must have thought, yet he might have applied for admission three years earlier. A year later, they sent him home with a Ph. D. degree. Now we have Dr. William Rainey Harper, aged eighteen.

Becomes a Professor at Nineteen.—In 1875 (he was then nineteen), he became a professor of languages in a college in Macon, Ga. A college professor should be old enough to marry, but Dr. David Paul, president of Muskingum College, did not think all of them were. Notwithstanding parental objection, the Dr. William Rainey Harper (aged nineteen), professor of Hebrew and other languages in a Georgia college, and Ella Paul, found a way, and as husband and wife they went to the South together.

He remained at Macon one year; then he accepted a professorship in Denison University, Granville, Ohio. Three years later (he was then twenty-three), he became a professor in the Baptist Theological Seminary in Chicago. After two years' service there, he received a call from Yale University.

At Yale, he did a prodigious amount of work. He not only held one of the most important chairs in the great institution, but he lectured throughout the country, wrote books, and engaged in various other activities. It is said that his daily mail was sometimes greater than all the rest of the mail together coming to the University.

First President of Chicago University.—John D. Rockefeller called Dr. Harper to head the University of Chicago, an institution then contemplated. He met the trustees and told them he would accept only on condition that he be given the full privilege of carrying out his own conception of what such an institution should be—not just another ordinary American college, but a great university, a leader in education and research. The trustees consented, and thereupon Dr. Harper began to make plans for one of the most largely endowed collegiate institutions in the world. He went to work in his own way, and it was not long until he was recognized as one of the greatest educators in America, if not in the world.

As he did at Yale, he worked hard at Chicago. He continued to write books, to lecture, even to teach classes in the institution he headed. He had a remarkable memory and became proficient in many languages. He was said to be the greatest Hebrew scholar in the world. The inductive method of teaching did not originate with him, but he was a strong advocate of it, and many college and high school textbooks, designed to be taught by that method, bore his name as author or co-author.

A lifelong student of the Bible, he was a devout and professing Christian. Although aware of a cancerous affliction, for which, he was told, there was no cure and would soon end his life, he continued his hard work almost to the very last. He died in 1906, when but fifty years of age. His monument is the great University of Chicago, and in it his spirit will ever be embodied.

A Teacher of Other Days

[Originally published 2/2/1945]

A beautiful eulogistic editorial on E. L. Abbey, superintendent of the Cambridge schools fifty years ago, written by Harry W. Amos, who was one of his pupils here, was published in The Jeffersonian the other day. In the editorial, reference was made to "the 'Bill' Hawkins type of teaching," which has suggested the writing of this sidelight to the chapter on schools in "Stories of Guernsey County."

For a full half century William, familiarly known as "Bill," Hawkins was a teacher in the one-room rural schools of Guernsey and Noble Counties. Some of the older men and women of these counties today will remember him. The schools in which he taught were numerous and widely scattered, as he seldom remained in the same district longer than one term. This tendency to itinerate was sometimes due to a call from a board of school directors to come into a district where physical, rather than mental, attention was considered an immediate necessity, for in giving, the former Hawkins was an adept; more often, however, it was too much display of the art in which he was so proficient that was responsible for his brief tenure in a school.

"Readin' and 'Ritin' and 'Rithmetic, taught to the tune of a hick'ry stick" was the motto of "Bill" Hawkins. His code of rules, laid down on the first morning of the first day of every school he taught, was "Do right, tend to your own business, and obey me."

The writer, in his school days, never sat at the feet of this old pedagogue of long ago, but he has heard a lot about him. He remembers that before he was old enough to attend school, he visited his grandparents in Noble County at a time when Hawkins was teaching in their district. Passing the school one afternoon with his grandmother, he noticed "Bill" on the outside peeping into the window. Curious to know the reason for this, he inquired of his grandmother, and was told that the teacher was looking to see if there were any of the children acting naughty while he was out; if so, he would go in and punish them. This was the writer's first lesson in pedagogy, one whose soundness he questioned even in that early period of his life.

Although he carried it to an extreme, Hawkins was not alone in employing this method of disciplining a school. In the era of his teaching in this section, a teacher's worth was often evaluated in terms pertaining to corporal punishment. It was the common belief that obedience to authority could best be secured by means of the rod. But "Bill" lacked tact, especially in dealing with parents whose children he had punished severely and who called to complain about it. With such persons, he had no patience. The grievance would be carried to the school directors, and the next year, "Bill" would be looking for a school elsewhere.

Hawkins was a giant in physical strength. One of his former pupils told the writer that "Bill" weighed far more than two hundred pounds and had muscles like a prizefighter. Stern and unyielding, he would soon have the most rebellious school under control. He would brook no interference from the outside. He had it understood that he would lick every man in the district, if necessary, to establish his authority.

Hundreds of boys and girls of the last century, in the two counties named above, were his pupils, and many of them afterwards thankful that they had been. Discipline was needed in many of the schools he taught, but his method of securing it would not be employed today, for much better ways have been found.

When not teaching school, Hawkins farmed a little and engaged in horse-trading. In the latter, he was an expert. He lived to be eighty-four years old, dying at his home near Claysville, Westland Township, in 1905. He was buried in the cemetery at the Harmony Church on the Clay Pike.

Senecaville's Long-Time Doctor, Noah Hill

[Originally published 5/31/1945]

From 1834 to 1894, a full sixty years, Noah Hill was a Senecaville doctor. For the greater part of this time, his practice was not alone confined to the village, for he was called upon to administer to the afflicted in all the country around. Both day and night, in all kinds of weather, he might be seen riding far out to homes where such service as he could render was needed.

Dr. Noah Hill was born in Westmoreland County, Pennsylvania, in 1809. At the age of nineteen, he came to Senecaville to teach the village school. This was about the time Rev. William G. Keil, the Lutheran preacher, came there, and Keil afterwards wrote that he found it a shabby-looking place with houses built of logs. The population was approximately 100.

When Hill arrived, the village doctor was John Baldridge, brother-in-law of young Hill (page 128 of the book). It was he, perhaps, who influenced the young teacher to study medicine. He entered Baldridge's office to study for the profession, and in the meantime, he continued to teach. He afterwards entered the Cincinnati Medical College, from which he graduated in 1833. Returning to Senecaville, he married Mary Dilley, daughter of Abraham Dilley, the village blacksmith, formed a partnership with Dr. Baldridge, his former preceptor, and settled down to practice his chosen profession for the next sixty years.

After the death of Dr. Baldridge in 1844, Dr. Hill practiced alone until 1862 when he formed a partnership with his oldest son, Dr. John Hill, which continued for ten years. Dr. Hill again practiced alone until 1879, in which year he took in Dr. Winfield Scott, his son-in-law, as a partner. Dr. Noah and Mary Dilley Hill were the parents of thirteen children, and all but one of them lived to be adults.

In 1833, a great religious revival swept over this section. Dr. Noah Hill was converted and became a member of the Methodist Episcopal Church. For fifteen years, he worshipped with this denomination and then transferred his membership to the Senecaville Wesleyan Methodist Church. Through his associations with Dr. John Baldridge, Rev. William G. Keil, David Satterthwaite, and others he had come to hate slavery, and he did not think the Methodist Episcopalians were taking as aggressive an opposition to the institution as they should. The Quakers excepted, the Wesleyan Methodists were the most bitterly opposed to slavery of all the religious groups. They even had organizations within their church pledged to assist the fugitive slaves. Here Dr. Hill found an opportunity to do work in connection with the Underground Railroad system, something that he thoroughly enjoyed.

Dr. Hill was at first an ardent Whig. When that party began to straddle the slavery question, he became a Free-soiler, and in 1848, he supported Martin VanBuren for President. Then he turned to be an abolitionist, and at a time when the members of that radical party were in danger of being mobbed, even in many parts of the North. He was one of the first three abolition voters in Guernsey County. Upon the organization of the Republican Party, he joined it because he believed it to offer the only hope for the emancipation of the slaves. After slavery had been abolished, Dr. Hill turned his attention to the temperance question and, not satisfied with the Republicans' stand on the issue, he became a Prohibitionist and voted for that party's candidates the last eight years of his life.

Dr. Noah Hill lived what we might term an aggressive and positive life. He hated slavery; he hated intemperance; and he fought both vigorously and courageously. Apparently heedless of the effect it might have on his profession, he was outspoken in advocating what he believed to be right. With him, there was neither surrender nor compromise in questions of conscience.

INDIVIDUALS OF INTEREST

For almost a half century, he was a pillar in the Senecaville Wesleyan Methodist Church. His house was a veritable preacher's home. In his earlier days, he was remarkably successful in his practice of medicine. An inveterate reader, he kept versed in current affairs. As a counselor, especially in church matters, his advice was sought to the very close of his life.

Col. Gordon Lofland
[Originally published 12/20/1944]

From the title of this article, several familiar Cambridge names have been derived; as, Lofland Addition, Lofland School, Gordon Run. One hundred years ago, Gordon Lofland owned and lived on a farm of nearly 500 acres a short distance northwest of the village of Cambridge. On this farm, the Lofland Addition to Cambridge was later laid off; on this farm the Lofland School was built; and on this farm Gordon Run empties into Wills Creek.

It was on this farm that three white men were killed by Indians in 1791 (page 24 of "Stories of Guernsey County"). These men, so far as there is any record, were the only white persons ever killed by Indians in what is now Guernsey County.

We stated in our book that the exact place of the attack was not known. From what we believe to be authentic sources we have since learned that it was near the mouth of Gordon Run. Four white men in the party attacked escaped to Wheeling. A few days later, Capt. John McCullough and a party of men returned and buried the bodies of the victims on the knoll which is now the site of the Lofland School.

Born in Virginia in 1794, Gordon Lofland came to Cambridge in 1816, and this was his home until his death in 1869. In 1824, he married Mrs. Sarah P. Metcalf, widow of Thomas Metcalf. She was a daughter of Jacob Gomber, one of the founders of Cambridge.

In checking through the files of Guernsey County newspapers from 1824, the year Gordon Lofland married, until the year of his death, a period of 45 years, we find frequent mention of him. It seems that during these years, there were but few activities, that had for their purpose the material growth and prosperity of Cambridge, in which he did not have a leading part. He was, in truth, a public-spirited man.

An outstanding characteristic of Gordon Lofland was his patriotism. For this he was given recognition on October 9, 1826, by Gov. Jeremiah Morrow who commissioned him Colonel of the 1st Brigade, 4th Regiment, 3rd Division, Ohio Militia. Carl J. Rech, of this city, has the original commission, presumably preserved by the late Mrs. A. J. Hutchison, daughter of Colonel Lofland.

When the Civil War opened, Colonel Lofland was 67 years of age, too old to enlist. His unbounded patriotism prompted him to serve his country in other ways. He raised recruits and endeavored to keep active the spirit of patriotism in every way in his power. Governor Tod sought his counsel in many matters pertaining to Ohio's activities in the war. In 1863, Governor Tod appointed him as Ohio's Commissioner for the Gettysburg Cemetery, and Colonel Lofland was on the platform with President Lincoln at Gettysburg when the latter made his immortal address. In 1867, Colonel Lofland was chosen as Ohio's Commissioner at the dedication of the cemetery at Antietam.

In politics, he was first a Whig, then a Republican when that party was formed. He was never a candidate for office. During his 45 years in Cambridge, no man's counsel was valued more highly than Colonel Lofland's.

Judge Justus H. Mackey

[Originally published 3/26/1945]

The last of the four judges of the court of common pleas from Guernsey County between 1851 and 1915 was Justus H. Mackey. He served a full term of five years (1902 to 1907) as judge of the first subdivision of the eighth district, composed of Guernsey, Noble, Morgan, and Muskingum counties.

The Constitution of 1851 provided that Ohio be permanently divided into nine common pleas court districts, that these be divided into three subdivisions each, and that a judge for each subdivision be elected by the electors thereof for a term of five years. As stated in a previous article of this series, an amendment became effective in 1915 that provided for at least one judge of the court of common pleas in each county. In the sixty-eight years under the district and sub-district plan, Guernsey County furnished but four of the judges of this subdivision. Sketches of the first three of these have been published.

Justus H. (familiarly known as Howard) Mackey was born in Claysville, Westland Township, in 1857. The family moved to their ancestral farm in the Bunker Hill School District, Spencer Township, where Howard received his early education. A precocious boy, he passed the teacher's examination at the age of sixteen and began teaching in the Blue Bell School, Valley Township. He entered Scio College but left there and went to Muskingum where he became the roommate of W. O. Thompson, afterwards the president of Ohio State University. Young Thompson, like young Mackey, was working his way through college by teaching. In order to keep together, the two boys would seek schools in neighboring districts. One winter, they taught in Oxford Township, and they managed to find a boarding place convenient enough to the school of each to enable them to continue to room together. In 1878, they graduated from Muskingum College in the same class.

Mackey chose the law for his profession, and Thompson the ministry. Mackey came to Cambridge and began the study of law in the office of Attorney J. O. Grimes, and while doing so he taught two years in the Cambridge High School, Dr. John McBurney then being the superintendent. He was admitted to the bar in 1880 and went to Missouri where he opened a law office. Not satisfied with the West, he returned to Cambridge to practice and, except a year of practice in Cleveland, this was ever afterwards his home. For two terms, he served as a member of the state bar examination board.

Justus H. Mackey was an ardent Republican and active in political circles. He was a forcible speaker and much in demand by his party, as such, in state and national campaigns. For some years, he was chairman of the county committee of his party. In 1887, he was elected prosecuting attorney of Guernsey County, and he was reelected in 1890. He was a fearless prosecutor, and he vigorously enforced the law. In 1902, as stated at the beginning of this article, he was elected judge of the court of common pleas.

Judge Mackey was married twice; first, in 1880, to Miss Belle Conner who died in 1887, and second, in 1892, to Mrs. Laura Hobbs. By the first marriage, two children were born—Glessner (Mrs. Carl J. Rech) and Frank C. Mackey.

An outstanding characteristic of Judge Mackey was his decisive manner. Keen and alert, he would quickly arrive at the point he was aiming. He loved a legal battle and was at his best as a trial lawyer. He was always loyal to his clients and courteous to his associates in the legal profession. A public-spirited citizen, he gave much time and effort in behalf of the community.

Trained in the Presbyterian faith, he was a member of the local church of that denomination. His death occurred in 1916. The speaker at the funeral service was Dr. W. O. Thompson, his boyhood schoolmate and lifelong friend.

A Versatile Citizen

[Originally published 1/11/1945]

In 1833 Andrew Magee, who was born in Pennsylvania in 1807, came to Cambridge which then had a population of about 550. He asked to be employed as the teacher of the village school. The school directors were Joseph Bute, John B. Thompson and John Hersh. Having examined Magee's credentials which appeared to be satisfactory, they employed him for a term of three months. We happen to have in our possession the original contract signed by all parties concerned. It provided that Magee should teach seven hours per day for five and a half days a week, school closing on Saturdays at noon. At his own cost he was to provide a school room, all seats and desks, all necessary fuel and all janitor service. For all this he was to receive $25.00 a month.

How long he continued as the village schoolmaster is not known. He read law, was admitted to the bar, and became a Cambridge attorney. Noting the need of doctors in the town, he began the study of medicine and received a license to practice. He next prepared for the ministry and was ordained as a preacher in the Methodist Episcopal Church.

This teacher-lawyer-doctor-preacher was probably Cambridge's most versatile citizen a century ago. Old newspapers of that period mention him frequently, indicating that he was ever ready to practice any one of his professions when the service of such was needed.

He eventually devoted most of his time to the ministry and became a prominent preacher in the M. E. Church, having the D. D. degree conferred upon him. His first pastoral work was here in Cambridge, in the little frame building that stood on Turner Avenue. The Cambridge charge then included Washington.

It was while Rev. Andrew Magee was pastor here that the second M. E. Church was erected, in 1853. Built of brick at a cost of $8,000.00, it stood at the corner of Gaston Avenue and Ninth Street. The Rev. Mr. Magee not only preached the last sermon in the old church, but also the first in the new.

Andrew Magee was a substantial citizen, and his work was highly regarded, whether in teaching, in law, in medicine, or in the ministry. He was a man of great fervency and deep piety. He was strong in his convictions, and when he believed that he was right, nothing would induce him to change. Strongly opposed to slavery, he was one of the first abolitionists in the county and supported James G. Birney for President. And this was at a time, too, when to be an abolitionist meant to be ostracized from society. It made no difference, however, to Magee. When the Civil War opened, he was denied enlistment as a soldier on account of his age. He rendered valuable service for the Union, though, in other ways.

In 1888 he died in Illinois.

Judge Edward W. Mathews

[Originally published 3/16/1945]

From 1851 to 1915, we had common pleas court districts, each presided over by one or more common pleas judges. Since 1915, each county has constituted a district within itself, a constitutional amendment providing such having become effective that year.

INDIVIDUALS OF INTEREST

From 1851 to 1879, Guernsey County was in a common pleas district with Belmont and Monroe Counties; and from 1879 to 1915, it was in a district with Noble, Morgan, and Muskingum. During the first period of twenty-eight years here mentioned, the district had five judges, of whom one, Nathan Evans, was elected from Guernsey County (page 102 of book). During the thirty-six years of the second period, three of the judges were chosen from our county—Edward W. Mathews, J. W. Campbell and J. H. Mackey.

Edward W. Mathews was an appointee and served for a few months only. W. H. Frazier, of Caldwell, was elected to the court of appeals in 1884 after serving as our common pleas judge for fourteen years (page 1015 of the book), and Gov. George Hoadley appointed Mathews to serve until the next general election. Judge Mathews was a candidate to succeed himself, but being a Democrat and the district normally Republican, by 4,000, he was defeated by J. W. Campbell. (A sketch of Judge Campbell will be published later.)

Edward W. Mathews was born on the Isle of Guernsey in 1832. That same year and the one following, the cholera swept over Asia and Europe and across the Atlantic to America, even into Guernsey County, Ohio, where it took several lives (page 757 of the book). The father of the baby Edward Mathews was a victim on the far-away Isle of Guernsey. Some relatives of the widowed mother were coming to America, and she and her children accompanied them, arriving in Cambridge in 1833. Here she found friends who had left her and their native Isle of Guernsey in years past.

Edward attended the Cambridge School, such as it was in that day when the town had about 600 people living in it, and then entered an academy, which then took the place of a high school. John Mahaffey, a brother-in-law of Edward, was a shoemaker, and for three or four years, the boy worked with him. In the excitement following the discovery of gold in California, the Cambridge-California Mining Company was organized, and Mathews, then eighteen years of age, joined it and left for the goldfields in 1850. He returned to Cambridge two or three years later, somewhat enriched by his venture, and bought an interest in the drug business of E. R. Nyce.

With a legal career in mind, he read law under Attorney Mathew Gaston, while working in the drug store, and then entered the Cincinnati Law School, from which he graduated in 1860. He returned to Cambridge and began to practice with his former preceptor here.

Except the few months he served as common pleas judge, he practiced law in Cambridge the remainder of his life. For several years, he was a partner of J. W. White, who represented this district in Congress in Civil War days. He afterwards was the senior member of the law firm of Mathews and Heade, which, when his son, Edward W. Jr., became a member, was known as Mathews, Heade, and Mathews, and later as Mathews and Mathews.

Judge Mathews was a Democrat of the old school. He was chosen delegate from this district to the Democratic National Convention in 1888, which nominated Grover Cleveland for a second term. In the campaign that followed, he did much public speaking in behalf of his party in this and other counties. From 1872 to 1874, he was mayor of Cambridge, and he served two terms as a member of the board of education.

With Gen. A. J. Warner, he was active in promoting and building the Cleveland and Marietta Railroad through Guernsey County in 1873. He was appointed attorney for the company soon after its organization, and continued as such for thirty-six years. At the organization of the Central National Bank, he became a member of the board of directors, and later its president.

Judge Mathews was married twice, first to Amelia Haynes, who died in 1877, then, in 1879, to Anna Means. In religion, he was a Presbyterian, and he served as a trustee of the local church for eighteen years. At the age of twenty-one, he joined the Cambridge Masonic Lodge, and before his death he had advanced to the thirty-third degree. Judge Mathews died in 1911.

Jacob Gomber Metcalfe

[Originally published 7/16/1945]

That a Cambridge-born boy who received his early education in the local schools rose to such heights in the business world that his fame attracted the attention of three continents, is not generally known here. He became, and here we quote the United Press—"one of the strongest figures in the railroad and financial world."

All students of local history are familiar with three names—Zaccheus A. Beatty, Jacob Gomber, and George Metcalf. We may say that to these three men we are indebted for our county and our town. Without question, they were the outstanding characters in our early history. These three men were related.

But how many know about Jacob Gomber Metcalfe? (Note that an "e" is added to the original spelling.) He got the name from his ancestors, being the grandson of George Metcalf, the great-grandson of Jacob Gomber, on his grandmother's side, and a great-great nephew of Zaccheus A. Beatty. He was born in Cambridge, Ohio, June 28, 1849, in a house (still standing) immediately west of the Foursquare Gospel Church on Steubenville Avenue, between Fifth and Sixth Streets.

Jacob Gomber Metcalfe bore the same name as his father, except that the latter spelled it without the "e". Five years after he was born, the Central Ohio (Baltimore and Ohio) Railroad was built through here. It had special fascination for young Jacob, and the station being near his home, he spent most of his time down there when he was not in school. He watched the trains come and go, and he dreamed of someday directing traffic on a great railroad himself. He was intrigued by the mysteries of the telegraph. An accommodating operator showed him how to manipulate the keys, and, in the course of time, he was able to send and receive messages. He sought and obtained a position as operator on the Central Ohio, between Bellaire and Zanesville.

His next connection was with the "Panhandle" line, also as operator and train dispatcher at Dennison, Ohio. With this same road, he became chief dispatcher at Logansport, Indiana. Accepting the position of train dispatcher at Louisville, Kentucky, with the Louisville and Nashville Railroad, he continued in the employ of this road for a number of years in posts of increasing responsibility, serving from 1883 to 1888, successively, as superintendent of the Louisville and Cincinnati division at Louisville, and superintendent of the St. Louis and Henderson division, at Evansville, Indiana. In the last named year, he became superintendent of the South and North Alabama and the Birmingham Mineral Railroads, owned and controlled by the Louisville and Nashville, and was promoted in 1889 to the office of general manager of the entire Louisville and Nashville system at Louisville.

In 1900, he was chosen general manager of the Denver and Rio Grande Railroad, and two years later accepted the same position with the Evansville and Terre Haute Railroad. He next became president of the Mexican International Railway with headquarters at Durango, Mexico. When, in 1905, the Mexican International Railway and the Mexican National Railroad were merged, he assumed the office of first vice president of both lines, with headquarters in Mexico City, and continued in that capacity until the properties were taken over by the Mexican Government. Mr. Metcalfe then resigned and returned to the United States.

He then became connected with the banking house of Speyer and Company, of New York, as consulting railway expert. He became interested in the development of the railways of the Philippines and Bolivia, and of the railway and transportation situation in such Latin American Republics as Peru, Chile, and Ecuador. He became vice-president and a director of the Bolivia Railway Company; vice-president and a director of the Manila Railway Company, a director of the London Underground Railway Company, and a director of the Missouri Pacific Railroad.

Little did little Jacob think, when he watched the trains come and go down at the station here, that his railroad ambition would carry him to such heights over so much of the world. He mastered his profession by actual experience, covering almost every grade of railway service. Here, truly, was a Cambridge boy who made good in a business way. The town should be proud that it gave him birth. Jacob Gomber Metcalfe died in 1916.

Our attention was called to the remarkable career of this man recently upon receipt of a letter from S. W. Metcalfe, Cleveland, Ohio, a son of Jacob Gomber Metcalfe, stating that a few days before, while in the

Cleveland Public Library, he had contacted a copy of "Stories of Guernsey County" from which he had learned much he had not hitherto known about his ancestors here. He ordered a book, wrote to a brother, J. G. Metcalfe, Superintendent of Transportation of the Louisville and Nashville Railroad Company, Louisville, Kentucky, and a sister Mrs. H. E. Watson, Morristown, New Jersey, who also sent for books. They expect to visit Cambridge as soon as convenient, to see the birthplace of their father and learn more about their ancestors.

Dr. Francis Rea

[Originally published 11/9/1946]

In Old Washington are several spacious brick residences of a style in vogue a century ago. They attract the attention of the passers-by who will often make inquiry about them. Three of these houses were built by the Lawrences in 1857 and are described on page 1072 of the book. Next to these in elaborateness, perhaps, and built about the same time, is what was long known as the Rea (now the Paisley) residence on the north side of Main Street, immediately west of the Presbyterian Church. It was built by Dr. Francis Rea who lived in it and practiced medicine for fifty years.

Son of a Preacher.—Dr. Francis Rea's father was Rev. John Rea, D. D., who was born in Ireland in 1773. When a lad he came to America with his parents and settled in Pennsylvania. After his marriage, he located in Harrison County, Ohio, and here Francis, his seventh child, was born. April 17, 1808.

Francis attended Franklin College near his home, then entered Miami University, from which he graduated. He received his professional education at the Jefferson Medical College of Philadelphia, graduating with the highest honors in his class.

Comes To Washington in 1839.—In 1839, eight years before his marriage, which was to Mary H. England, of Steubenville, in 1847, Dr. Rea came to Washington to practice medicine with Dr. John McFarland as a partner. His reputation as a successful physician extended far and near. He was highly educated in the profession, and for a small-town doctor of that day, he displayed a skill that was outstanding.

A Presbyterian and a Democrat.—During his fifty years in Washington, he was an active member of the local Presbyterian Church. Twenty years after he located there (1859), work was started on the present church building by the side of his home, and the edifice was completed for occupancy and dedicated in 1861. Dr. Rea was a member of the church building committee, and for many years, he served as a trustee of the church.

In politics, like the Lawrences, his neighbors, he was an uncompromising Democrat, ever steadfast to his party. For some years,

INDIVIDUALS OF INTEREST

Guernsey County was entitled to two members in the General Assembly. Along with Hugh Broom, he represented this county in that body for two terms (1856-60).

In addition to practicing medicine, Dr. Rea engaged in various commercial activities, one of which was the purchasing, packing, and shipping of leaf tobacco. It is said that he was the largest tobacco dealer of his time in Eastern Ohio.

The Rea Family.—To Dr. and Mary H. Rea, two sons and four daughters were born, all in Washington. The sons were William P. and David E., the daughters, Elizabeth J., who married Alfred Day, Mary F., wife of Harry Haines, Sarah J., who married William H. Ledlie, and Ada, who became the wife of M. G. McMahon. The only one of these now living is Mrs. McMahon, 503 North Tenth Street, Cambridge.

Dr. Francis Rea died in Washington, February 9, 1890. He was buried in Steubenville.

A Pioneer of Washington — David Robb

[Originally published 2/23/1945]

In 1805, two brothers, Henry and George Beymer, platted a town in what was then Muskingum County, which they named New Washington. They laid out 80 lots and reserved two of the choicest for a courthouse, expecting a new county to be formed later with their town as the county seat. The county was formed, but Beymerstown, by which New Washington was best known in early days, lost in the contest to become the seat of judgment. Cambridge was chosen instead.

The Beymers advertised their lots for sale. Two inducements to settle there were offered. First, the town was on Zane's Trace, the main thoroughfare into Ohio at that time, about a day's journey from either Wheeling or Zanesville. Travelers each way would stop there for lodging; hence it was a good location for taverns. One who passed through the town in 1807 described it as a settlement consisting of twelve cabins, four of which were taverns. The second inducement offered prospective lot-buyers by the Beymers was the prospect of its being made a county seat.

Among the first to buy lots was David Robb who came from Pennsylvania. He apparently saw the possibilities of tavern-keeping, for he bought the lot on which the Presbyterian Church now stands, and on it he erected a large log tavern. This was probably one of the four taverns mentioned by the traveler.

Most of the settlers within and around Beymerstown were of Scotch-Irish descent. They were confronted by the task of clearing away the forest before they could raise their crops. Although rough in appearance, they were men of great physical and moral strength and bore the mark of noble character.

Among these sturdy pioneers, David Robb was undoubtedly the far best educated. Possessing a commanding presence and military bearing, he became a leader in community affairs. He was, in truth, a valuable asset to the budding town. Many like him are often forgotten in the very communities that profited from their work. David Robb deserves this belated recognition.

One evening in 1809, a lone traveler, who gave his name as Mr. Lenington, stopped at Robb's Tavern and engaged supper, lodging, and breakfast. Mr. Robb, learning that he was a Presbyterian preacher, invited him to remain over Sunday and preach to the settlers. The traveler consented, and the news was carried to the surrounding country. The service, largely attended, was held in the tavern. A Presbyterian organization was effected, and the society met frequently in the tavern or in the yard at the rear. When David Robb died years afterwards, in a distant part of the state, it was found that he had willed to the church the ground on which the tavern had stood.

David Robb was a great admirer of Andrew Jackson, and to promote locally his candidacy for the presidency, he founded The Washington Republican, now The Jeffersonian. He was a vigorous and fearless writer, especially on political subjects, and he once wrote and circulated a document against a political enemy that led to a suit being brought against him for libel, which attracted much attention (page 70 of the book.). He worked enthusiastically for the growth and welfare of Washington, and he laid out what is known as Robb's Addition to the town.

In politics, he was a strong Democrat. He served as sheriff of the county from 1816 to 1818. He was elected state senator from this district in 1819, and served two terms. Again, in 1826, he was sent to the state senate and served two more terms. His admiration and enthusiastic support of Andrew Jackson, as manifested through his paper and political speaking, brought him, as his first reward, the appointment of Receiver of the General Land Office at Zanesville, where he had charge of the sale of the government lands in the Military District. This necessitated his removal from Washington to Zanesville.

A treaty was made with the Indians whereby they would give up their lands in Ohio for territory west of the Mississippi River. Their removal was a work requiring much tact. Robb's second reward for his work in behalf of President Jackson came when the latter appointed him Indian Agent to supervise the removal. He performed his duties with honesty and integrity, and afterwards wrote and had published an account of this important event in our state history. His death occurred in northwestern Ohio where he moved after receiving the second appointment.

INDIVIDUALS OF INTEREST

Forty-Five Years on the Stage — Charles T. Small

[Originally published 3/18/1946]

(Sidelight to the Story, "Guernsey County's Colored Population," Page 668 of the book.)

For the past thirty years, a colored man has been living in Cambridge who, for the forty-five years immediately preceding his coming here, was on the stage as a musician and an actor. He used to be seen on the streets daily, but due to his advanced age of ninety-three years and a failing eyesight, he now seldom leaves his room at 210 Gomber Avenue.

We became acquainted with this veteran star of the stage several years ago, and have often enjoyed hearing him talk about his theatrical experiences. He went on the stage before he was twenty years old as a bass soloist in a colored chorus, and afterwards became an actor in a number of white theatrical companies, a kind of work he liked better.

Charles T. Small is his name. In stature, he is somewhat below the average. His hair and pointed chin beard are snow-white. One who converses with this quiet-mannered man soon discovers that he is well educated. His broad knowledge and culture may be attributed to lifelong study, travel and contacts with intellectual people. That which impresses one most is the tone of his voice, which is not only soft and melodious, but of a quality that is unusually pleasing. Back in the days when "Uncle Tom's Cabin" was a popular play, one of the leading theatrical companies chose him to act the part of Uncle Tom. One who has seen and talked with Mr. Small, and who is familiar with the play, can readily understand why he was sought for this prominent part.

Charles T. Small

At our request, Mr. Small gave us a brief outline of his career which, in his own words, was substantially as follows:

Born In Kentucky.—"I was born in Maysville, Kentucky, March 29, 1853. At that time, my father was a steward in a hotel there, and my mother was the chief cook. When I was ten or twelve years old, we moved to Cincinnati. There, father was employed as head steward in the Merchant Hotel, and mother was employed to do the baking. I attended school and became interested in music, both vocal and instrumental. When a mere boy, I was invited to sing in the choir of one of the Cincinnati A. M. E. churches.

"One day, before I was twenty years old, the manager of a colored chorus and concert company which was being organized in Cincinnati, who had been visiting the various churches to listen to the singers, came to me and asked me to become a member. He said he wanted me as a bass soloist. It was then, back in the early 1870s, that I began my stage career. We traveled widely over the United States. After making the tour, I joined the Hyers Sisters Musical Concert Company, of which, in addition to my singing, I was stage director. This, too, was a colored organization, and I remained with it for thirteen years.

Becomes An Actor.—"The next offer I received came from a large, white theatrical company in need of a colored actor to play a certain part. I had long wished for this kind of work and was glad to make the change. The company was presenting "Coon Hollow," and I was wanted to take the role of an old colored man. This was a popular play, and after touring America, we went to England where we appeared in all the larger cities. Portraying American country life far back amongst the hills, as it did, it produced a sensation across the sea.

"When I was a member of the first musical chorus, the manager one day made known his need of a colored pianist. I told him I had recently seen the advertisement in a paper of a Miss Nellie V. Ransom, Cambridge, Ohio, who was seeking such a position. He asked me to write her, which I did. A few days later, she joined us and became a member of our company. Not long after this, we were married, and for nearly forty years, we worked together on the stage. She was a sister of Bishop Reverdy Ransom who became one of the most eloquent and best-known colored preachers in the United States.

"In the role of Uncle Tom in "Uncle Tom's Cabin", I probably attained the heights of my acting career. This was once the most popular play in America, and there were scores of troupes presenting it. It was not shown in the South, as every state had a law prohibiting it. The company I was with was one of very high order, the actors and actresses, for the greater part, being stage stars of much renown. I, a colored man, was honored in being chosen to play the part of Uncle Tom. A colored girl with much successful stage experience was our Topsy.

"The Simon Legree of our company was a noted tragedian who had starred in some of the Shakespearian dramas. He was a large man with a heavy voice, and so absorbed in his art would he become that he sometimes forgot himself and his lashing me became too realistic for my comfort. He didn't mean to hurt me, but he would forget, and I found it necessary to wear a heavy pad on my back. As you know, one of the most affecting scenes in the play is Legree's beating Uncle Tom to death. Once, when I was being lashed with a blacksnake whip in the hands of Legree and the scene was about to reach a climax, back in the breathless audience a woman jumped to her feet and screamed, 'Don't you hit that man again.' It broke the spell and spoiled the entire act.

"Another touching scene was the death of Little Eva. It would be hard for me to describe my own emotions at this particular place in the play. To me, the act became more real than pretended, and I would almost break down under it. Perhaps it was better to be that way, but the audience never knew how I suffered. The audible sobs coming from the audience always made it harder to bear. By means of a system of invisible wires operated by machinery behind the scenes, Little Eva was lifted up and made to float heavenward with wings appearing as she ascended.

Traveled Extensively.—"During my forty-five years on the stage, I appeared before audiences in every large city in every state in the United States, with probably one exception, in every province in Canada, in Mexico and Europe. I appeared before many noted persons, one of whom I recall at this time was the Prime Minister of Canada at Ottawa. Our audiences were often large, sometimes reaching ten or twelve thousand.

"Often the members of colored companies to which I belonged in the early years of my stage career would find it difficult to get hotel accommodations. This was not only true in the South, where memory of the war was still fresh, but even in some sections of the North. Many times, we lacked conveniences on account of race prejudices. It was different when I was a member of white companies as an actor.

Cambridge Became His Home.—"Upon retiring from the stage thirty years ago, I came to Cambridge to live, as this was the girlhood home of my wife, who is buried in Northwood Cemetery. I married again, this time to Jennie A. Jackson, of Virginia. She, too, is deceased. I hold membership in Shaffer's A. M. E. Church in Cambridge, but am no longer able to attend services there."

Addison Taylor Smith

[Originally published 7/27/1946]

When we were a small boy, we first came to know Addison Taylor Smith who was then working in a furniture store in Quaker City, our hometown. Now, at the age of 84, he is living a retired life in Washington, D. C. From a letter he wrote us not long ago, it is evident that he has never lost interest in and love for this, his native Guernsey County. He left here sixty years ago to engage in government work, became a brilliant lawyer and statesman, served twenty consecutive years in Congress, and won national distinction.

Born In Adams Township.—Addison T. Smith was born in Mantua, Adams Township, September 5, 1862, his parents being Isaac and Jane (Forsythe) Smith. When he was a mere child, the family moved to Oxford

Township where he attended the old Center School.

In previous stories, we have mentioned the virtues of pennyroyal oil and its apparent effect politically on the Oxford Township people. From little Oxford Township, which has never had more than a small population, have come, either directly or in directly, three U. S. Senators, several members of the U. S. House of Representatives, and a host of district and county officers. While living there, Addison T. doubtless imbibed this product of Pennyroyaldom, and from it received the inspiration that led to his political success.

The family moved to Cambridge when Addison T. was eleven years old, and here he attended the old Central School, graduating in 1882. After completing a course in business college, he was employed in Quaker City.

Goes To Washington City.—Col. Joseph D. Taylor (also a product of Pennyroyaldom), having been seated in Congress, sent for Addison T. Smith to come over to Washington, D. C., to serve as his secretary, and to bring along with him the Taylor team of white horses. They were loaded on a freight train which Smith boarded in order that he might feed and water them on the way. Long afterwards, when Addison T. had become nationally known, a Washington paper published a story telling how this prominent member of Congress had entered the national capital the first time in a boxcar.

In Washington, he took up the study of law and received the degree of L. L. B. from Georgetown University; later the degree of L. L. M. from the National Law School. After Colonel Taylor retired from Congress, Smith was engaged as secretary to George L. Shoup, the territorial representative from Idaho. When this territory was admitted to the Union as a state, Shoup was elected a U. S Senator, and Smith continued with him. Shoup died in office, and Weldon E. Heyburn was elected his successor. Smith then became his secretary and was serving as such when, in 1913, he himself was elected to Congress. Here he remained until 1933. After retiring from public life, he practiced law in Washington City.

A Republican in Politics.—He has always been a thorough Republican. In his adopted state, he was known as the "Clean Man in Idaho Politics." In the Taft-Roosevelt campaign of 1912, where the Republican Party was split in two, Idaho, as a state, jumped on the Roosevelt bandwagon. Addison T., a candidate for Congress, followed the Taft banner, and because of his personal, rather than his political influence, he polled the largest vote in the state, winning over his nearest opponent by 17,000.

During his political career, he was secretary to two U. S. Representatives, two U. S. Senators, and was himself a U. S. Representative for twenty years. It was once said of him that he was the schoolmaster of more Congressmen than any other man living.

Aside from his political activities, he found time to engage in work that pertained to the affairs of his state. His efforts in promoting the interests of Idaho were outstanding. He was especially active in establishing towns and promoting irrigation projects.

Living here today are a nephew and a niece of Addison T. Smith—Samuel T. Smith, east of the city, and Mrs. S. O. Grant, 222 North Fourth Street

Captain A. A. Taylor

[Originally published 12/21/1944]

The writing of this article has been prompted by a letter from Mrs. John L. Howerton, Greensboro, N. C. She states that she is the daughter of Byron Taylor and that she lived in Cambridge when a small girl. She requested that a copy of "Stories of Guernsey County" be mailed her, as she had learned that it contained stories concerning three of her uncles—Joseph D., David D., and Alexander A. Taylor.

There is much in the book about the first two named, but not much about the last; hence this sidelight concerning the Taylor family, which was one of the best-known families in Guernsey County during the latter half of the last century.

The father was Alexander D. Taylor, and the family lived in Oxford Township, on the National Road, near the present Center Consolidated School. There were nine sons—William P., J. Clarkson, Joseph D., J. Byron, Wilson Shannon, David D., G. Kennon, T. Corwin and Alexander A. (familiarly known as "Ad".)

Both the father and mother were intellectually inclined, and they encouraged all their sons to acquire the best education possible. All became teachers, and at one time, six of them were teaching in the schools of Oxford Township.

Alexander A. attended the district school in his home township, and Madison College at Antrim. In 1862, he enlisted in the 85th Ohio Volunteer Infantry for service in the Civil War and was mustered out in 1865. The greater part of his three years of service was spent in Confederate prisons—twenty-one months in Libby at Richmond, eleven months at Macon, Georgia, and two months at Charleston, South Carolina. Before the war closed, he had been commissioned a captain.

After the war, he became prominent as a Cambridge citizen, taking a leading part in many of the city's activities. He was the first commander of the Cambridge G. A. R. post, and he worked indefatigably to the end that a soldiers' monument might be erected in front of the courthouse.

For thirty-six years, he was connected with the Guernsey National Bank. In 1870, he was elected County Auditor. As were all the Taylor boys, he was a Republican in politics. In religion, he was a Methodist.

In 1870, Captain Taylor married Ella McCracken, daughter of

Alexander McCracken and granddaughter of William McCracken, the pioneer blacksmith. Their home was on Steubenville Avenue, between Eighth and Ninth Streets, the building now occupied by Dr. Naldo Moss.

Captain Alexander Addison Taylor was born in 1832 and died in 1908.

Early Street Names — Turner Avenue
[Originally published 1/20/1945]

Cambridge streets derived their names from various sources, and several of these are mentioned in "Stories of Guernsey County." There is a narrow street, named for a prominent citizen of the last century, that at one time had reason to be proud of its prominence. This is Turner Avenue.

The boundaries of the town, when laid out by Gomber and Beatty in 1806, were as follows: Fifth Street on the west; an alley, 20 feet wide, running east and west to the rear of the lots on the south side of Wheeling Avenue, on the south; Eleventh Street on the east; and an alley running east and west to the rear of the lots on the north side of Steubenville Avenue, on the north. Fifth and Eleventh Streets were then known as Walnut and Lombardy, respectively.

Turner Avenue today is the alley that marked the southern boundary of the original town. Long before it had a name, the alley came into prominence. Bordering on its south side, near its center, the first burial ground was laid out. On the same side of the alley, west of the burial ground, the first church in Cambridge was completed, the M. E. Church; later the Baptists used this building as their place of worship. A few rods west of the M. E. Church the Methodist Protestants erected their first church in 1833, another on the same spot in 1876, and still another in 1898. After the old Town Hall had been torn away, Robert Hammond built Hammond's Opera House (1885); he located it on Turner Avenue. This was the place to which politicians came from every part of the county to hold their conventions, and the scene of many spirited political meetings; here, too, came many famous lecturers, actors, and actresses, for Cambridge had many high-grade entertainers to come here a half century ago.

On Turner Avenue was located the first great industry of Cambridge, the foundry of Simons Brothers. It was on this alley that the first town prison was built. One of the three greatest fires in the history of Cambridge, that of 1873, originated on and did its most damage on this alley.

Elza Turner was the man for whom the street was named. His parents, James and Mary Turner, came from Virginia to Cambridge in 1816 and took charge of the Holler Tavern on West Wheeling Avenue, and here Elza was born in 1823. When he was eight years old, his mother died and he was taken into the home of David Sarchet to be reared. He attended the town school and learned the tailor trade. As soon as he had acquired sufficient means, he opened a shop of his own.

For twelve consecutive terms, he was elected justice of the peace, and thus became familiarly known as 'Squire Turner. In 1870, he was elected mayor of Cambridge and served two terms. For several years, he was one of the township trustees. Before the Civil War, he was a member of the National Guard, and during the war he served under Col. John Ferguson as Sergeant Major.

Having purchased the land south of the alley we have here described, as far east as Eighth Street, he laid out what is known as Turner's Addition a short time before the Civil War. The alley was widened ten feet and given the name of Turner Avenue. It was necessary to take a strip ten feet wide from the north side of the old graveyard. Some of the bodies were removed, it is said, but others remain buried beneath the street.

Elza Turner was a faithful member of the Presbyterian Church. His residence, still standing, was on the street that bears his name, and here he died in 1899.

A Doctor of the Old School

[Originally published 1/19/1945]

During the latter half of the last century, the name of Dr. Andrew Wall was a household word in nearly every part of Guernsey County. Although his home and office were in Cambridge, his practice was not confined to the city, as he was called upon to alleviate physical suffering over a wide surrounding area.

No journey was too long, road too bad, or weather too disagreeable for him to answer a call, if he felt that he could render a needed service. He often answered calls at the sacrifice of his own health. He was a man of remarkable endurance, and, it is said, he was known to go for a week at a time, day and night, without sleep other than a little napping as he journeyed along from one stricken home to another. It was this trait of Dr. Wall, of giving service above self, that endeared him to the people—rich and poor, high and low. As to the class of people to whom he ministered, he made no distinction.

Andrew Wall, born in Pennsylvania in 1829, came with his parents to Guernsey County when sixteen years of age and settled in Westland Township, near Claysville. Muskingum College was near his home, and he enrolled there as a student. He afterwards taught school for a few terms and then began the study of medicine under Dr. Vincent Haynes in Cambridge. Following a medical course in the University of Michigan, he was licensed to practice, returned to Cambridge, and opened an office. The Ohio Medical

College at Cincinnati conferred an M. D. degree upon him in 1862.

The Civil War opened, and Dr. Wall enlisted as a surgeon in the Seventy-seventh Ohio Volunteer Infantry. Inclined towards surgery in his practice, he here found an opportunity to employ his skill and ability to the fullest extent. The experience along this line acquired in the army hospital was a valuable asset when he returned to private practice. Although he treated every type of illness, his skill as a surgeon was outstanding, and he was called to all parts of Guernsey and adjoining counties when special surgical attention was needed.

He remained in the army as a surgeon until 1866, when he returned to Cambridge and became a partner of Dr. William Clark.

In 1868, this partnership was dissolved, and for the remainder of his life, Dr. Wall practiced alone, conducting a drugstore at the same time. On account of his skill in surgery, he received the appointment of division surgeon of the Baltimore and Ohio Railroad, and that of chief surgeon of the Cleveland and Marietta, positions he held until his death.

Dr. Wall died in 1898 at the age of sixty-nine. More than forty years of his life had been given to the alleviation of the sufferings of humanity, much to the detriment of his own health. His last illness was brief, and he was aware of his serious condition, but himself he could not cure.

At the time of his death, a local paper said: "Dr. Andrew Wall was the most eminent physician who ever practiced medicine in Guernsey County—so stated by old present-day doctors who knew of his life work."

He was truly a doctor of the old school.

Another Pennyroyal Senator

[Originally published 8/7/1945]

Our article in The Jeffersonian the other day, relative to the Wherry family, has indirectly brought to light another U. S. Senator with a Pennyroyal background. Hon. Kenneth S. Wherry, of Nebraska, asks to be adopted into the Pennyroyal family.

In the article referred to, we stated that in 1901, David Wherry, a Revolutionary War veteran, brought his wife, Ann, and their small children from Pennsylvania and settled a short distance southwest of the present site of Fairview. This, we believe, was the first white family to establish a home in Pennyroyaldom.

Wherry opened a tavern on Zane's Trace, and when Oxford Township was organized nine years after he settled there, he suggested the name for it and became its first treasurer. Until his death in 1838, he was one of the township's leading citizens. There came to be several Wherry families in Pennyroyaldom, but by deaths and removals, the name gradually passed out of that section.

INDIVIDUALS OF INTEREST

Postmaster H. E. Frost of Fairview sent Senator Wherry a copy of the Jeffersonian containing the article, together with an announcement of the coming Pennyroyal Reunion. The Senator wrote Mr. Frost that the family referred to was his family, and that the article had been filed with the family records, and if it could be arranged, he was going to come to represent the Wherry family at this homecoming of descendants of Pennyroyalists. A few days later another letter came, which in part was as follows:

"Whether you like it or not, this is to tell you that I trace my ancestry back to the Guernsey County, Ohio, Wherrys. David and Ann Wherry were the parents of James Wherry who was my grandfather. He married Mary Jane Moore, a daughter of another pioneer family of Guernsey County, and then settled near Wyoming in Jones County, Iowa. My grandfather, James Wherry, and my father, David E. Wherry, migrated to Liberty, Nebraska, and later to Pawnee City, Nebraska. Pawnee City has been my home.

"We have a son, David, who is now in Annapolis, and a daughter, Marilynn. We expect sometime to visit Fairview, Ohio, and inquire into our ancestry, and also visit the old homestead if we can locate it, and go to some of the cemeteries where members of the pioneer Wherry family have been buried.

"We understand that the famous Pennyroyal Reunion will be held around August 23. We would like very much to attend one sometime. It just so happens that the Senate adjourned last night, and we will not be in the East to attend the reunion this year. However, we will consider it an honor if you will adopt us into your family of Pennyroyalists."

Pennyroyaldom now lists three United States Senators, two of them members of pioneer families, and one a descendant of a pioneer family. Nebraska became a state in 1867. One of its first two U. S. Senators was Thomas W. Tipton who had formerly lived in Pennyroyaldom. Now Nebraska's last Senator is Kenneth S. Wherry, whose great-grandfather was the first white man to settle in that realm.

Secretary of Commerce Henry A. Wallace writes:

"Mrs. Wallace's grandmother's maiden name was Maria Bratton, and she was born about two miles from Fairview, Ohio, in Guernsey County in an inn on what, in the days before the Civil War, was known as the 'Old American Pike'. Her parents and grandparents, I believe, kept an inn on the old Pike. The Brattons came to Guernsey County, Ohio, from Pennsylvania in the early 1800s."

(For a history of this family, see the story, "Brattons, the Pioneers of Madison Township", page 894 of the book.)

Pennyroyal oil is powerful stuff!

MORE STORIES OF GUERNSEY COUNTY

Physician Has Practiced Over Two-Thirds Century
Dr. W. A. White

[Originally published 10/15/1946]

Babies brought into the world by Dr. W. A. White, when he entered upon his professional career two-thirds of a century ago, are probably great-grandparents today. You will not think this to be unusual, for such may be said of many a doctor who long ago retired from the profession; but during all these years, Dr. White has continued to practice medicine, although not much of late except to prescribe for members of his own family and close friends. And more, too, he has had his office all these years on almost the exact spot he opened it sixty-six years ago.

Dr. White, who is now ninety-six years of age, while still maintaining his office stocked with medicine at Salesville, since the death of his wife, which occurred recently, has been staying at the home of his son-in-law and wife, Mr. and Mrs. H. L. Thomas, 1200 Blaine Avenue, Cambridge. He is alert and keen of mind and, as in his younger days, is keeping well informed on current affairs.

Son of a Doctor.—Dr. W. A. White's father, Dr. J. W. White, practiced medicine in Middlebourne, Guernsey county, where W. A. was born November 29, 1850. When the latter was nine years old, Dr. J. W. moved to Salesville and lived there until his death in 1913, at the age of ninety. W. A. received his first schooling at Middlebourne, his teacher there being William Morton, a well-known educator of Oxford township before the Civil War. One of his teachers at Salesville was the noted Bill Hawkins.

Becomes a Railroader.—Built through Salesville five years before W. A. went there to live was the Central Ohio (Baltimore and Ohio) Railroad. The passing of the trains through the village was a great attraction to the boy, and he resolved that when he grew up, he would be a railroader. At the age of seventeen, he became a brakeman on a freight, and for a few

Dr. W. A. White

years, he ran on trains between Bellaire and Columbus. A serious accident incapacitated him for such work for a time, so he returned home and began the study of medicine under his father. After an academic course in Muskingum College, he entered the Eclectic Medical College at Cincinnati, from which he graduated in 1880. He married Miss Emma Martin, of Fairview, the same year and settled down in Salesville to practice with his father.

A Country Doctor for 66 Years.—Practicing medicine two-thirds of a century ago was quite different from what it is today. There were no telephones; the roads in winter were almost impassable, and many of the things considered indispensable by the modern physician were unknown. Still, the people would get sick, and the doctor was called out for long trips in the night as well as day. Many nights, Dr. White would almost lose his way while traveling through the dark forests; many times, he would get stuck in the mud.

Interested in Civic Affairs.—In his long residence in Salesville, Dr. White has served his village and community in various civic ways. He was a member of the Salesville village and the Millwood township boards of education, and for sixteen years, he was a member of the Guernsey County Board. For several years, he served as a justice of the peace. While mayor of Salesville, back in the 1880s, he took it upon himself to exercise police authority after the duly elected officers had failed to capture "Dory" Taylor, the notorious outlaw who was terrorizing that section. Heading a posse of volunteers, he personally took the desperado at the point of a revolver when he attempted to escape from a house. (For the story of "Dory Taylor" see page 919 of the book.)

The Oldest Mason.—Dr. White holds another record, one that may be unparalleled in the state. In 1878, he joined Quaker City Lodge No. 500, Free and Accepted Masons, and has held membership in this one lodge for sixty-eight years. He was master of it sixty years ago, and as far back as eighteen years ago he received the prized medal for fifty years of continuous service. He is still a member in good standing.

MORE STORIES OF GUERNSEY COUNTY

Pennyroyaldom in the U. S. Senate

[Originally published 7/9/1945]

Two United States Senators were former citizens of Guernsey County, one a native, and the other a resident for several years. Both lived in Pennyroyaldom, whose leading product in the old days—Pennyroyal Oil—seemed to arouse political aspiration, for more prominent officeholders have come out of Pennyroyaldom than any other part of the country. One of these men was Nathan B. Scott, a native, who represented West Virginia in the U. S. Senate for twelve years (page 952 of the book). The other was Thomas W. Tipton, a brief sketch of whose life follows.

Living in Nebraska in 1880, he was invited to attend the first Pennyroyal Reunion. Being a candidate for governor of that state at the time, he could not leave in the midst of his campaign, but he sent a letter to be read at the reunion from which we here quote.

"In September, 1840, having graduated at Uniontown, Pennsylvania, I hastened to Fairview in order to hear that marvel of popular eloquence, Thomas Corwin, then candidate for governor of Ohio, and reached there on Saturday before the election. In Fairview I commenced my political life, and advocated the claims of Clay in 1844, of Taylor in 1848 and of General Scott in 1852, for President. In 1845 I was nominated and elected to the legislature of Ohio (as a Whig from Guernsey County), commencing my canvass on the day of the birth of my first son whom I named Thomas Corwin for political luck and personal esteem.

"To Oxford Township I look back to my starting point as a temperance lecturer and could instance churches and schoolhouses in which my youthful enthusiasm had vent, and remember many devoted men and women, who cheered me with kind words and sympathetic demonstrations.

"There, too, I commenced professional life in magistrates' courts. To Oxford Township I brought my young wife of thirty-eight years ago, when the households of the Rosemonds and Jeffersons and Lanes, of Fairview, were adorned with amiable and beautiful girls. There, too, rests the sacred remains of my mother and two sisters, so that by pleasant memories and sad recollections I am ever bound to Oxford Township."

Mr. Tipton was born in Cadiz, Ohio, in 1817, the family later moving to Fairview. After his admission to the bar in 1844, and while practicing law here, he studied for the ministry and was ordained as a Methodist minister. In 1859, he moved to Nebraska, which territory had been organized five years before. He served in the Civil War from 1861 to 1865 as chaplain of the First Regiment, N. V. I. Following the war, he was appointed internal revenue collector for his territory.

Nebraska was admitted to the Union as a state in 1867, and Tipton was chosen a member of its constitutional convention. His work in this attracted attention, and he was elected one of the first U. S. Senators and reelected at the end of his term. In Guernsey County, he had been an ardent Whig; in Nebraska, he became a Democrat and was elected to the Senate by that party. He died in Washington City in 1899 and was buried in Rock Creek Cemetery there.

Oxford Officials

[Originally published 2/6/1945]

Is there something in pennyroyal oil that arouses political ambition? Oxford Township, widely known as Pennyroyaldom, has produced more pennyroyal oil, it is said, than any other spot of like area in the world. Then, too, that same little political subdivision has sent out far more national and local officeholders than any other township in Guernsey County, Cambridge excepted. Not satisfied with holding just one office, some have afterward climbed to another, and still another. And so far as the records show, all proved to be efficient and faithful public servants.

Following is a list of public officials Oxford has furnished. Not all were natives of the township, and not all were living in the township when elected to office; but all were residents of the township at some time in their lives, apparently long enough to be affected by the politically inspiring liquid, or whatever influence it was that existed there.

Then there have been many officeholders throughout the country who, though they never lived in the township, have had ancestors who did. From them they seem to have inherited this office-holding tendency, which they either followed for themselves or transmitted to others.

It was reported here that Former Vice-President Henry A. Wallace traced his ancestry back to Guernsey County. A Cambridge citizen recently wrote him, asking if this were true. He replied that it was not, but added that his wife's folks came from Pennyroyaldom. Now you see how it is—pennyroyal oil has had a far-reaching and potent effect, even by remote control.

U. S. Senate: Nathan B. Scott (West Virginia) and T. W. Tipton (Nebraska).

U. S. House of Representatives: William Kennon (1829-33 and 1835-37), Joseph D. Taylor 1883-85 and 1887-93), C. Ellis Moore 1918-33), and Addison T. Smith (Idaho).

Ohio State Senate: William Armstrong (1843-44) and D. C. Kennon 1898-99).

Ohio House of Representatives: J. W. Tipton (1845), Joseph Ferrell (1862), David D. Taylor (1890-92), and N. H. Barber (1894).

Common Pleas Judges: Thomas B. Kirkpatrick (Associate) (1810-16), Thomas Henderson (Associate) (1816-23), William Kennon (President Judge) (1841-48), James W. Campbell (1884-92), and Charles S. Sheppard (1939-).

Probate Judges: Newell Kennon (1877-82) and N. H. Barber (1888-94).

County Auditors: A. A. Taylor (1868-70), John C. Beckett (1880-66), and Thomas Smith (1886-90).

County Treasurers: Newell Kennon (1840-44), Stephen Pott (1852-56), William Borton (1856-60), and T. M. Bond (1897-01).

County Commissioners: James Dillon (1810-20), James Gilliland (1826-31), Jonathan Rose (1863-78), and L. P. Moore (1902-08).

County Recorders: C. S. Stockdale (1909-13), G. F. Henry (1913-17), and W. F. Bryant (1917-21).

Sheriff: Thomas E. Gracey (1931-35).

Clerk of Courts: Earl Henry (1921-25).

Prosecuting Attorneys: Joseph D. Taylor (1863-67), Charles S. Sheppard (1906-11), C. Ellis Moore (1915-19), and Earl Henry (1945-).

County Surveyors: John Kennon (1832-33), John Morton (1850-56), and Joseph D. Taylor (1856-62).

EXTENDED CHAPTER XLVII

Family Stories

The Jack Family

[Originally published 6/28/1946]

Called to mind by the approaching Fourth of July are the Mecklenburg Resolutions and the connection with them that Cambridge was once thought to have. In May, 1775, more than a year before the Declaration of Independence was adopted, a committee of Mecklenburg County, North Carolina, citizens met at Charlotte, the county seat, and drew up a set of resolutions somewhat similar to the ones embodied in the immortal document, the anniversary of the adoption of which we celebrate. Charlotte has claimed that she, and not Philadelphia, is the birthplace of the nation, and on the street of the former city is a memorial marking the spot where the convention was held.

Capt. James Jack Bears Resolutions to Congress.—History says that immediately following the adoption of the Resolutions, a copy was dispatched to the Continental Congress, then meeting in Philadelphia, together with an urgent appeal that they be adopted by that body. The bearer was Capt. James Jack, a member of the Mecklenburg convention. His dramatic ride with these important papers, through a section of country that at the time was largely Tory, is recorded in American history along with some other rides that are famous. While the Continental Congress did not, at the time, take the action hoped for, the Resolutions doubtless helped to create a sentiment for the adoption of the Declaration of Independence the next year.

The Capt. James Jack of Cambridge.—In the early part of the last century a Capt. James Jack resided in Cambridge. Long afterwards, there were some reasons to think that he was either the bearer of the Mecklenburg Resolutions or a member of the family of the Capt. James Jack who was celebrated as such. The writer, who has checked carefully all the files of old Cambridge newspapers in the library of Western Reserve Historical Society in Cleveland, dating back to 1824, found a number of references to Capt. James Jack, but nothing that would throw much light on his past history. Even the announcement of his death gives little of his past, other than that he was a captain in the War of 1812. From the age given, it would appear that he was too young to have been a member of the Mecklenburg Convention.

MORE STORIES OF GUERNSEY COUNTY

Seventy years ago (1875), which was then long after Capt. James Jack's death, Ross W. Anderson, mayor of Cambridge, received the following letter from Dr. C. L. Hunter, of Lincoln, North Carolina:

"During the Revolutionary War there resided in Charlotte N. C. an old citizen named Patrick Jack. He had five sons and five daughters. Capt. James Jack, the eldest son, was the bearer of the celebrated Mecklenburg Declaration of Independence on the 20th of May, 1775, to Philadelphia.

"Soon after the war, two of the sons, Samuel and Robert, settled in Chambersburg, Pa. One of the descendants, James Jack, went West about 1833, and settled in Cambridge, Ohio.

"Will you be so kind as to inform me if any of that name of near relatives are now living in Cambridge, and if so, I would like to know from which branch of the family—Samuel or Robert—they may have sprung. I am now writing a sketch of this distinguished family of Revolutionary fame."

Kept A Store Here.—Mayor Anderson set to work to gather all available information possible about the Capt. James Jack who had lived and died here many years before. His reply to the letter of inquiry was substantially as follows:

Capt. James Jack moved to Cambridge in 1829, and accompanying him were William Gibbs and the latter's two sisters, Rachael and Mary Gibbs. Both Jack and Gibbs were bachelors, and neither of the Gibbs sisters ever married. The father of Jack had married the mother of William Gibbs and his sisters. (According to another account, one of the women was Sarah Jack, sister of James, instead of Rachael Gibbs, sister of William.) The four lived together as one family in a little frame house that stood on the north side of Steubenville Avenue, between Eighth and Ninth Streets.

Jack and Gibbs bought and kept the store at the northeast corner of Wheeling Avenue and Seventh Street that had formerly belonged to Thomas Sarchet. Business being slack one evening, Jack, who was alone in the store, lay down on the counter to rest. A customer calling later found him dead. Capt. James Jack, William Gibbs, and the two women are buried side by side in the Old Founders' cemetery. The inscriptions on their gravestones are entirely obliterated.

It is our opinion that the Cambridge Capt. James Jack was a nephew of the famous Revolutionary War Capt. James Jack.

FAMILY STORIES

The Stockdales at Antrim

[Originally published 12/23/1944]

There is an Antrim in Ireland, also an Antrim in Madison Township, Guernsey County, Ohio. As may be supposed, the latter Antrim gets its name from the former because it was settled by Irish folk. On the old Steubenville Road, six miles northeast of Antrim, there settled another group from Ireland, and they honored their former home across the sea by calling their town Londonderry, a good old Irish name.

One of the first from Ireland to come to what is now the Antrim community was John Stockdale, born in 1750. With his wife and young children, he crossed the Atlantic in a sailing vessel, landing on the eastern coast of America. Far to the west, he learned, land was being opened up for settlement, and westward he made his way. The long journey to the present Antrim, where he had decided to enter land, was one of hardship and danger, but he eventually reached his destination, built a cabin for his family, and began clearing a patch of ground.

There were six sons in John Stockdale's family, and their names were Robert, John, James, Moses, Hugh, and William. The last two here named were sons of a second wife. We find that in 1840, the four older sons were large landowners in Madison Township and leading citizens of the community. As an illustration of the Stockdale progressive activities, we shall follow the career of James.

He was but a mere child when he crossed the wide ocean with his father and made the long trek to Antrim. Although reared in a cabin in the backwoods with scarcely any educational advantages, James did succeed in learning enough to enable him to teach in the kind of school that was provided at that time. In a log school building with puncheon floor, greased paper in the windows in lieu of glass, and a wood fireplace taking up one side of the room, he would sometimes, on a cold morning, seated on one end of a backlog, hear pupils recite, who were perched on the other end.

When James reached young manhood, there was still government land in Madison Township that had not been entered. Being in the Military District, this land was sold at the Government Land Office in Zanesville. James long had his eye on a certain unsold tract and was saving his money to purchase it. Knowing that James had saved a little money, but not knowing the purpose, a neighbor came to him one day for a loan. From a remark made, James began to suspect that the neighbor wanted the money to purchase the very piece of ground he was hoping to buy, so he declined to lend it.

The neighbor succeeded getting the money elsewhere and prepared for a horseback journey to Zanesville. Young Stockdale had no horse to ride, so he set out on foot a little in advance of the other and reached there first. To this tract, he added other land from time to time until it became one of the largest farms in the township.

James married Phebe Lening in 1825 and they became the parents of eleven children whose names follow: Lydia, Moses, Mary, Sylvanus, Elizabeth, Jane, James, Martha, Thomas, Margaret, and Elias.

For more than thirty years, James Stockdale was a justice of the peace in Madison Township and so well did he serve as such that it was seldom that one of his decisions was reversed in a higher court. He was a man of excellent judgment, and folks came to counsel him on many matters. For ten years he engaged in the mercantile business in Antrim. James, one of his sons, was the proprietor of the old United States Hotel in Antrim for many years.

James Stockdale, Sr., died in 1889. In politics he was a Whig until that party passed out; then he became a Democrat. He was a member of the Presbyterian Church. The Stockdale name still lingers in Madison Township. The descendants of John Stockdale, the old pioneer from Ireland, are many and widely scattered.

Pioneer Families — Broom

[Originally published 5/2/1946]

Hugh Broom and wife (Helen Swan Broom), both natives of Scotland, came to Guernsey County, Ohio, in 1816. They located on a farm of 81 acres, three or four miles northwest of Cambridge, that they purchased from George R. Tingle. To this tract, Broom added land from time to time, until 1840, when he was the owner of 400 acres.

Hugh Broom Was a Baptist Preacher.—In addition to farming, Hugh Broom did considerable preaching. For several years, he was pastor of the Old Cambridge (Brick) Baptist Church between Cambridge and Byesville. He was actively engaged in ministerial work for more than half a century, during which time he aided in the organization of many congregations. Established near his home in 1832, the Center Baptist Church was most probably organized by him.

Rev. Hugh and Mrs. Broom were the parents of eight children—four boys and four girls. The Rev. Broom died in 1863; his wife had died nine years before.

Daniel Broom.—Born in 1820, Daniel Broom succeeded his father on the home farm; in fact, he had the management of it long before the latter's death. His wife was Mary Kimball, daughter of a Guernsey County pioneer.

Daniel Broom had one ever-abiding hatred—that of slavery. During the Underground Railroad days, the Broom home was one of the principal stations on the line in this section. Escaping from the South, slaves would enter Guernsey County at Senecaville where they were concealed and cared for by such anti-slavery men as Rev. W. G. Keil, Dr. Noah Hill and Judge William Thompson. From here, they were secretly taken over to Jonathan Bye's at Byesville; thence to the care of Alexander McCracken and Samuel Craig at Cambridge, who would manage to get them out to Broom's. The latter would move them to the next station, and in such manner they were carried on and on northward until they eventually reached Canada.

Originally a Whig in politics, as was also his father, Daniel became a Free-soiler when that party was organized to oppose the further extension of slavery. Then came the Republican Party, and he joined it. With a lot of the reform spirit in his nature, he became interested in temperance movements and joined the Prohibitionists after slavery was abolished.

Adam K. Broom.—Adam K., born in 1843, was a son of Daniel Broom. He was only 18 years old when the Civil War opened, yet he enlisted at the very beginning and continued in the service even beyond the end in 1865. After returning from the war, he worked on his father's farm for a few years, then came to Cambridge to engage in the meat and grocery business.

Adam Broom's Drum Corps.—A Cambridge musical organization that had its beginning a short time after the close of the Civil War was Adam Broom's drum corps. It continued active until recent years, and there are but few of the old-time residents of Guernsey County who will not remember it. While the personnel changed a little in its long existence, the four members first coming to mind as composing it were Adam K. Broom himself, Samuel C. (Craig) Knouff, Clay Phipps, and Charles Adamson.

Phipps was the fifer, Broom the bass drummer, and Adamson and Knouff the snare drummers. As a bass drummer, Broom used two sticks, striking both sides of the head at the same time.

This drum corps was originally intended to be the official musical organization of the local post of the Grand Army of the Republic, but so much attention did it attract that it was called upon to appear on occasions of various kinds, far and near. No patriotic parade in Cambridge was complete without it. To such tunes as "Yankee Doodle," "Dixie," and "The Girl I Left Behind Me," a step was set that carried the procession along. At most Republican political meetings in which there were parades, Adam Broom's drum corps was a feature. Being a staunch Republican, Broom would not play in Democratic parades. When Cambridge chartered a special train and went to visit McKinley in the 1896 campaign, Adam Broom's drum corps led the parade in Canton.

MORE STORIES OF GUERNSEY COUNTY

Pioneer Families — Burt

[Originally published 4/29/1947]

Around and within Byesville, the name Burt used to be heard so often that it was almost a household word. Although there are fewer Burts and their connections in Guernsey County now, the influence of those who have passed on is still felt here.

Luther, the Original Burt.—Some of the county's pioneers came here from the Isle of Guernsey, one of the Channel Islands between England and France. The Burts came originally from Jersey, another island of the same group. The immigrant was Luther Burt who, after arriving in America, first settled in the state of New Jersey.

Very early in the last century, Luther Burt came from New Jersey to what is now Guernsey County, Ohio. The journey was made over the mountains, and out Zane's Trace from the Ohio River, in a one-horse cart. In this vehicle, the scant household goods were carried; most of the family walked. Having reached Cambridge, they turned to the south and selected and settled on 200 acres of land that is now the grounds of the Cambridge Country Club.

Daniel Burt.—There were nine children in the Luther Burt family, all of whom may not have accompanied him here. One who did, however, was Daniel, his fifth son, and as he succeeded his father as owner of the farm referred to above, we shall follow his line.

Daniel was born in New Jersey in 1793. He married Catherine Waller, who was born in Virginia in 1805. They became the parents of nine children, three sons and six daughters, the sons being John, Eli, and William. Daniel died on the old farm in 1870, and Catherine died there in 1879.

Eli Burt.—After the deaths of Daniel and Catherine, their second son, Eli, succeeded to the ownership of the home place. His wife was Nancy Smith, who was born and reared near Washington, this county. To this couple eight children were born, namely, John, Sarah, Nancy, Roland, Jennie, William, David, and Rhoda.

Eli added land to the original Burt farm until he became the owner of 600 acres. By dint of hard work and successful management, he became wealthy, owning property in Byesville and Cambridge, in addition to the farm.

David S. Burt.—In recent years, the name of "Dave" Burt, as David S. was familiarly called, was the best known of the Burt clan. One of the younger sons of Eli and Nancy Burt, he was born on the farm of his forefathers and continued to live there until he was twenty-two years old. With a desire to be a dentist, he came to Cambridge and took up the study with Dr. Jefferson (father of Dr. Charles E. Jefferson) and Dr. Cooper. After a few months of study, he decided not to follow that career and went back to the farm and worked as a blacksmith near Byesville. He married Lucinda A. Hoopman, and they settled down on his father's farm. A short time later, they moved into Byesville, which was ever afterwards their home.

From the time David S. Burt located in Byesville, until his death, his business activities were many and varied. In the development of communities, there will invariably be some enterprising citizen or citizens as leaders. One such in Byesville was "Dave" Burt.

When he settled in Byesville, the Old Farmer Mine had just been started, and the little town that had erstwhile been lying dormant was beginning to show life. A love of horses prompted him to open a livery barn. His next activity was the operation of a sawmill. Although he continued to reside in Byesville, he opened a sales barn in Baltimore, and one later in Cleveland. He took the contract for transporting the mails between the Cleveland post office and the trains and the boats, and had thirteen wagons in the service.

Appointed postmaster of Byesville, he served as such for nine years. He erected what was known as the Burt Block which, up to that time, was the largest building in the town. He became interested in the coal industry, purchased considerable coal land in the Guernsey Valley, and operated some of the mines. Mules and ponies were once used in the mines for hauling coal to the foot of the shaft. Burt supplied these for the various mines, selling as many as one hundred fifty thousand dollars' worth in a single year.

As a contractor, he engaged in many projects. Among these were the building of the glass plant in Cambridge, the brick and tile plant in Byesville, the Lincoln School building in Byesville, the rolling mill and the pottery plant in Cambridge, and the rolling mill in Marietta. He also took contracts for building public roads and bridges. He engaged in so many different activities and built so many houses in his home town that he was sometimes called the "Father of Byesville."

David S. Burt was a staunch Republican. He apparently didn't care to hold office himself, but he was alert and ever ready to come to the aid of the party with whatever service might be needed.

Pioneer Families — Dilley

[Originally published 10/17/1945]

Ever since its very beginning, the Senecaville community has carried the name of Dilley amongst its family names. For a long time, the Dilleys were numerous, both there and elsewhere in the county, but there are only a few of them anymore. Their connections under other names, however, are still many.

For our start on the Dilley family, we drop back two centuries and find Aaron Dilley and his wife, Hannah, living on a farm in New Jersey. The French and Indian War came on, and Aaron enlisted. He returned home safely. We know little about the family of Aaron and Hannah, other than that they had at least three sons, one of whom was Samuel, and another, Ephraim, born in 1755.

When the Revolutionary War opened, Aaron again shouldered his musket and went out to fight, and with him this time went Ephraim. Hannah tried to carry on the farm work, as did many wives and mothers while their husbands and sons were fighting for freedom. On June 28, 1778, she was plowing in the field. Borne to her ears from a distance were sounds of guns. The Battle of Monmouth was being fought, and her husband and son were in it. She plowed on all day, too distressed to eat her dinner.

Ephraim had spent the preceding winter with Washington at Valley Forge. On a monument there, marking the spot where his regiment was quartered, his name is inscribed. He crossed the Delaware with Washington the night of the Battle of Trenton, and in 1779, he was with Wayne at the capture of Stony Point.

The war ended in 1781, and Ephraim came home and married Lucy U. Ayer, who was 18 years old. It is said that she was connected with the Ayer family of patent medicine fame. A half century and more ago, Ayer's Almanac was considered a household necessity, supplying, as it did, much astronomical data and various statistics, besides proclaiming the virtues of "Ayer's Cherry Pectoral" and "Ayer's Hair Vigor." The children of Ephraim and Lucy Dilley were Joseph (1782), Abraham (1785), Hannah (1787), Anna (1789), Robert (1793), William (1796), Ephraim, Jr., (1799) and Samuel (1802).

The Military Lands of the Northwest Territory were opened for settlement, and farms were given free to Revolutionary soldiers who had not received all their pay for service in the war. It may have been the allurement of a free farm that brought Ephraim, Lucy, and the children to Ohio. They settled on land a short distance north of what is now Senecaville. When the sons grew older and purchased farms of their own, there came to be a little settlement of Dilleys there. According to our list of real estate owners in 1840 (page 974 of the book), Ephraim, Sr., owned 80 acres; Robert, 160; William, 60; and Ephraim, Jr., 100. Abraham and Robert owned lots in Senecaville. Ephraim, the old Revolutionary patriot, died in 1844, at the age of 89, and was buried in the Senecaville Cemetery.

Joseph, the oldest son of Ephraim and Lucy Dilley, married Sarah Burkley and settled on a farm near that of his parents. As he died in 1833, his name does not appear in the list of Dilley farm owners above. Two of his descendants bearing the Dilley name are living in Cambridge today—Ephraim M., a grandson, and Samuel M., a great-grandson. Another great-grandson was Otho E. Dilley, the well-known musician whose stage name was "Herbert Dillea." He was directing the orchestra in the Chicago Iroquois Theater at the time of the great fire in December, 1903, in which nearly 600 persons perished, and a nervous breakdown followed. from which he did not recover. There seemed to be a strain of music running through the Joseph Dilley family. James L. Dilley, a grandson, served the entire length of the Civil War as a member of an army band. James V. Dilley, a great-grandson, a skillful cornet player, organized the present Cambridge band in 1898, and was its leader for several years. Charles Morrison, composer of the popular piano selection, "Meditation," was also a great-grandson of Joseph Dilley.

Abraham, the second son, married Jane W. McCleary, an Irish girl, in 1808. Four years later the War of 1812 opened, and he enlisted in Capt. Simon Beymer's company. After the war, he engaged in blacksmithing in Senecaville.

Robert, the third son, married Hannah McDonald and located on a quarter-section of land near the farms of his father and brothers. Clara Dilley, granddaughter of Robert, is the only person bearing the original Dilley name, who is living in Senecaville today. William, the fourth son, married Elizabeth Lowery and settled immediately north of the others. In the early days of the National Road, he teamed between Zanesville and Wheeling. Ephraim, Jr., married Rachel Henry. Although but a mere youth, he served in the War of 1812, it is said. About the year 1857, he and his brother William moved their families to Minnesota. Samuel, the youngest of the six sons of Ephraim and Lucy Dilley, left the Senecaville community when he was 25 years old, going to Mississippi where he engaged in the nursery business and preached some. During the Civil War, four of his sons were with the Confederate Army.

In early days, there were no schools in the Senecaville community (page 426 of the book). William and Robert Thompson engaged a teacher from Philadelphia to teach their own children and invited all the parents to send their children to the school, which would be free. The several Dilley families accepted the invitation but insisted that they bear a part of the expense. This is said to have been the first free school in Guernsey County.

The pioneer Dilleys were Presbyterians, and it was largely through their influence that the church of that denomination was established in Senecaville. In politics, most of the descendants of Ephraim and Lucy Dilley have been and are Republicans.

MORE STORIES OF GUERNSEY COUNTY

Pioneer Families — Emerson

[Originally published 5/13/1947]

Emerson was a prominent family name in the southeastern part of the county a century ago. In one community, in 1840, were listed six farms for taxation, each owned by an Emerson, namely, Ezekiel, Sr., Ezekiel, Jr., John, George, Scott, and Thomas. The six landowners held a total of one thousand acres. In addition to the Emersons in that community, there were others owning farms not far away.

Came From Rhode Island.—The Emersons came to Guernsey County from Rhode Island, but not all at the same time. Ezekiel, Sr., who came in 1816, was the first. He and his wife, formerly Patience Burlingame, were typical New Englanders, belonging to the same branch of that family name as Ralph Waldo Emerson. They were the parents of twelve children—six boys and six girls.

A Long Journey.—Thomas, one of the sons of Ezekiel, Sr., and Patience Emerson, was six years old when the family migrated to Guernsey County. Many years afterwards, he told about the long journey, which made such an impression on his childish mind that he remembered it well; also, the condition of the country near Senecaville at that time, where they first located.

To make the journey from Rhode Island to Guernsey County, in the way they traveled, required nine weeks. They came by wagon and lodged in taverns or camped out at night. Of special interest to the young Thomas were the rivers they crossed: the Connecticut at Enfield, the Hudson at New York City, the Delaware at Easton, the Monongahela at Williamsport, and the Ohio at Wheeling.

From the last crossing, they followed Zane's Trace through St. Clairsville to Smithtown (the Lost Town) where they spent the last night on the way at the Moore Tavern. The following morning, they turned south through the forest and traveled a few miles to their destination, the Robert Thompson farm near Senecaville.

The New Home.—Thomas said that Senecaville had just been platted the year before (July 18, 1815) by David Satterthwaite, and at the time of their arrival consisted of only three log cabins in a clearing of stumps. Soon after this, others came and were employed at the saltworks on the creek below, which were operated by David Satterthwaite and William Thompson, who lived west of the town.

Meat was never lacking, he said, for there was plenty of game, especially deer, bear, and turkeys, and the creek was full of fish. "Many a time," he said, "did I stand at a trough where the horses were eating to keep the wild turkeys from getting the grain." There were wild hogs in the woods, and when fresh pork was wanted, one was shot and dragged home by a horse.

Three miles east of the Emersons lived Joseph Reeves who had a horse mill where they got their grain ground. (The Reeves farm was afterwards known as the Ward farm and is now partly covered by Seneca Lake.) On the creek above the mill, some Indians were living when the Emersons arrived. They were friendly, however, and devoted their time chiefly to hunting and fishing.

Move to Leatherwood Valley.—After living near Senecaville for six years, Ezekiel Emerson, Sr., purchased land in the Leatherwood Valley, southwest of the present site of Salesville, and moved there. In the course of time, there came to be so many Emersons around him that the section was known as the Emerson community.

In politics, the early Emersons were Democrats, and in religion they held to the faith of the Congregationalists—a New England heritage. Broad-minded, public-spirited, and progressive, they ranked among the prominent pioneers of the county.

The Emersons gradually moved from the county. We know of but one here today, who bears the name. George Emerson, a great-grandson of Ezekiel, Sr., retained a part of the old farm, built a modern bungalow on it, and spends his summers there.

Don E. Weaver, editor of the Columbus Citizen, is a descendant of Ezekiel Emerson, Sr.

Pioneer Families — Ferbrache

[Originally published 11/18/1946]

One of the very earliest families to settle in what is now Guernsey County bore the name of Ferbrache. Like that of many other pioneers, this family name is rare here today, yet there are a few Ferbraches left in the county, and there are several Ferbrache connections.

Daniel Ferbrache.—The patriarch of this Guernsey County pioneer clan was Daniel Ferbrache, born on the Isle of Guernsey in 1772. He married Judith Sarchet, a neighbor girl who was two years younger than he, and the young couple established a home on their native island. In this home, six children were born to them, namely, Daniel, Judith, Thomas, Mary, John, and James.

In 1806, when Daniel was thirty-four years old and Judith thirty-two, they decided to migrate to America along with three brothers of Judith and their families, these brothers being Thomas, John, and Peter Sarchet.

They left the Isle of Guernsey on a sailing vessel bound for Norfolk, Virginia, at which city they arrived on June 3, 1806, after a two months' voyage on the ocean. The Isle of Guernsey belonged to England, and England and France were at war with each other at the time. As the ship upon which our friends embarked flew an English flag, it was convoyed to what was believed to be a safe distance from land by an English man-of-war and then left to go on alone. A few days later, a French cruiser was sighted in full pursuit. An American flag was quickly raised on the English vessel, and the cruiser, believing it had made a mistake, turned back.

An Unpleasant Voyage.—Col. C. P. B. Sarchet, grandson of the Thomas Sarchet named above, said in an article published in The Cambridge Herald, in 1902, that the voyage was an unpleasant one. When in mid-ocean, there was a calm of eight days' duration, during which time there was neither wind nor wave. The sails were tacked in every direction, but to no avail. The ship became becalmed. His description reminds us of a couple stanzas in Coleridge's "Ancient Mariner."

> "Down dropt the breeze, the sails dropt down,
>   'Twas sad as sad could be;
> And we did speak only to break
>   The silence of the sea!
>
> "Day after day, day after day,
>   We stuck, nor breath nor motion;
> As idle as a painted ship
>   Upon a painted ocean."

Following the calm came a violent storm, lasting for several days and nights. Matters were made worse by the captain's becoming beastly drunk. Riding the bridge in his delirious condition, he permitted the ship to drift at the mercy of the waves, far out of its proper course. A meeting of crew and passengers was called, at which it was voted to ask him to give up the command of the ship. Upon his refusal to do so, he was caught and handcuffed, and John Sarchet and the mate took charge.

Ferbrache Child Dies.—A distressing incident of the voyage was the death of one of the six children of Daniel and Judith Ferbrache. The body was wrapped in a sheet and given an ocean burial after an impressive Episcopalian service that was read by the captain of the vessel.

Arrive at Cambridge.—When Norfolk was reached, the captain was put ashore and the vessel was taken on to Baltimore with the Sarchets and Ferbraches still aboard. Here they procured horses, wagons, and equipment for a long journey to some place in the West where they had it in mind to locate. Eight weeks later (August 14, 1806), they reached Cambridge. In a recent sidelight story, we told about their arrival and the welcome extended them by Jacob Gomber on behalf of the Beattys, Gombers, and Metcalfs, who had settled here three years before. (This welcome is pictured on the walls of the Pioneer room of the Berwick Hotel.)

Colonel Sarchet wrote that they erected two cabins in which to live until more permanent homes could be provided. In one of these, during the winter following, lived the families of Thomas and John Sarchet, fourteen members in all; in the other were housed the Peter Sarchet and Daniel

FAMILY STORIES

Ferbrache families, the two numbering twelve persons.

Meanwhile, Thomas, John, and Peter Sarchet were engaged in building permanent homes for their families—respectively located on the present sites of the Central drug store, the Royal Cloak, and the Central National Bank.

Ferbrache Buys a Farm.—Although he apparently remained in the settlement for a time, we find no record to show that Daniel Ferbrache purchased a lot and built a home in the town. We do find, however, that sometime after his arrival here, he entered 160 acres of government land in the northern part of Cambridge Township, and the deed he received was signed by President James Madison.

First Male Child Born in Cambridge.—After coming here, three more children were born to Daniel and Judith Ferbrache—Jacob N., Nancy, and David. Born in 1808, Jacob N. is said to have been the first male child born in Cambridge. When nineteen years old, he married Elizabeth Underhill, and they became the parents of nine children. His second wife was Mary Estep, who bore him eight more children, thus making him father of seventeen in all.

And Jacob N. was only one of Daniel and Judith Ferbrache's six sons. There came to be many Ferbraches here in the early days, most of whom lived in the northern part of Cambridge Township. Now, as we stated at the beginning of this story, there are very few persons in the county who bear that name.

Pioneer Families — Ferguson

[Originally published 6/10/1947]

In the late 1700s, there lived a family in Donegal County, Ireland, consisting of John Ferguson, his wife, and their four children, namely, Margaret, William, Andrew, and June. Chafing under the harsh treatment of England, to which Ireland was subject, some of the Irish revolted in 1798. One of these was John Ferguson. After the rebellion had been suppressed, he was compelled to flee from his native land in order to save his life

Escapes to America.—A vessel named the Serpent, commanded by an Irish sympathizer, was leaving for America. Ferguson managed to make his way to the place of sailing, and the captain secretly stowed him in the hold and a few weeks later, landed him in Baltimore. Here he was, widely separated from his family and with no means for getting them to this country.

In Ireland, he was a weaver, and for eight years, he worked at that trade in Baltimore, saving every penny possible out of his wages. After eight years of hard work and sacrifice, he had accumulated a fund sufficient to bring his wife and children over, and the family were reunited.

Comes to Cambridge.—Learning that there were opportunities in the West for such as he, the family moved to Jefferson County, Ohio, but remained there for only a year and then came to Cambridge. John Ferguson decided that this place should be their permanent home. From Jacob Gomber, he purchased a lot, on which there was a cabin, for $150. It was on the north side of Steubenville Avenue, between the present Eighth and Ninth Streets, and on the lot now stands the brick residence of William Scott.

For the support of his family, John worked here at his trade of weaving. Everybody wore homespun clothing in those days, and weaving was a necessary occupation. He died in 1831, aged eighty-eight years. Mary, his wife, had died in 1826. Both were buried in the old cemetery on South Eighth Street.

Born in Ireland in 1792, William, son of John and Mary Ferguson, married Jemima Schaffer. Their first home was a cabin near a big spring in the woods north of town. The Guernsey Laundry on North Eighth Street stands today on the exact spot the cabin stood. William became a successful citizen and at one time owned a half-section of land a short distance north of Cambridge. He died in 1876.

Col. John Ferguson.—In the cabin mentioned above, John Ferguson, son of William and Jemima, was born in 1816. Until his death in 1886, he was a man of much prominence and influence in Cambridge. After a course in college, he entered the practice of law. Always active in politics, he was a staunch Democrat until the beginning of the Civil War when he united with the Republican Party and afterwards worked enthusiastically for its success. When a Democrat, he was elected Prosecuting Attorney of Guernsey County (1843), and to represent this senatorial district in the General Assembly (1852).

During Civil War days, he was one of the most active and influential patriots of the county. He recruited the first local company, "Ferguson's Guards," to enter the service (page 256 of the book). After assisting in the organization of several other companies, he recruited one of his own, Company F of the Twenty-sixth Regiment, Ohio Volunteer Infantry, and went out as its captain. He rose to the rank of colonel in the war.

Colonel Ferguson was a man of striking appearance. He was a fine horseman and would attract much attention when riding in parades. No local patriotic event was complete without an address by Colonel Ferguson. He married Louisa E. Bute in 1841, and they became the parents of nine children.

Captain Joseph B. Ferguson.—The oldest son of Col. John and Louisa E. Ferguson was Joseph B., who was born in 1844 and died in Cambridge a few years ago. "Cap" Ferguson, as he was familiarly called, was a well-known figure on the streets for many years. Like his father, he attended college and then took up the study of law. He was a student at Muskingum College when the Civil War began, and he laid down his books to take up arms in behalf of his country. He came out of the war a captain. He joined the regular army after the war, and for seventeen years, he served as a commissioned officer on the plains, participating in a number of battles with the Indians. Following this service, he began the practice of law in Cambridge.

Pioneer Families — Forney

[Originally published 5/14/1946]

For our today's story of a pioneer Guernsey County family, we drop down into Wheeling Township, in the neighborhood of the present little town of Guernsey. Here came Abraham Forney in 1811, the year after the county was organized, who entered 400 acres of government land. He was not the first settler in that township, though, for families by the name of Atkinson, Shoff, Fuller, and some others had located in that section ahead of him. We choose to write about the Forneys, rather than some of the others, because they grew in number and great influence in the community, and now, after 135 years, you will still find a few of the name there. Most of them, however, have scattered to various parts of the world.

Family Came from Maryland.—Abraham Forney was born in Frederick County, Maryland, the son of Abraham and Mary Forney, also natives of Maryland, but both of German descent. In 1801, Abraham, Jr., married Mary Curtis, and the couple located in Baltimore, coming to Guernsey County ten years after their marriage. The story is told that Mary, when a small girl, was kidnapped, carried far away, and sold. She was afterwards ransomed and returned to her native city of Baltimore. Mary was an intelligent and cultured lady whose influence was an important factor in the intellectual and social development of Wheeling Township in early days.

Country Was Wild.—Upon their arrival here, Abraham and Mary found the country in its primitive state, but they set to work clearing away the forest and placing under improvement the large tract they had entered. They kept adding land to their original entry, and as a result of their prudence and energy, the wide productive acres of the Forneys attracted much attention.

At the mouth of Bird's Run, a short distance from their home, was an Indian town whose chief was the notorious Doughty. (See page 1049 of the book.) Although not hostile to white settlers, the Indians annoyed them at times, and there was much relief when, during the second war with Great Britain, they began leaving that section.

Forney liked to hunt and, as the woods abounded in game, he had ample opportunity to engage in the sport when duties in his clearings did not require all his time. In his later years, he used to tell how, near his home, he had killed 400 deer, also many bears and wild turkeys.

A Successful Pioneer.—To Abraham and Mary Curtis Forney, nine children were born—five sons and four daughters—Joseph, Elizabeth, Mary A., Solomon, Frederick, John, Sophia, Eli, and Susan H.

Abraham died in 1855. Before his death, he had the satisfaction of looking over his broad acres of cultivated land with the consciousness that they had reached their high state of development through his own hard work and that of his large family. Mary, his wife, died in 1862 at the age of 82.

Joseph Forney.—Joseph, the oldest son of Abraham and Mary Curtis Forney, was born in Maryland in 1802, and thus was nine years old when the family moved here. Like all pioneer boys, he was soon put to work and was of much help to his father in clearing away the forest. He married Susan Miskimen, daughter of a neighboring settler, and in 1826, they moved across the line into Coshocton County. Thus, the Forneys over there, even to this day, may trace their lineage back to Abraham and Mary through Joseph.

John Forney.—John, the sixth of the children of Abraham and Mary, probably did more than any of the others in developing further the Forney interests in Wheeling Township. Being the father of fifteen children, he took pride in his part in keeping the Forney name alive. Born in 1816, he lived at home and worked on his father's farm until 1840, when he married Eliza J. Wilson. The young couple established a home in an old, abandoned tobacco house in the woods, which they made habitable by cutting doors and windows and daubing the crevices between the logs with mud. They remained here, however, only long enough to erect a brick residence across the road into which they moved.

He opened a store, operated a sawmill, and farmed. To him and Eliza J., nine children were born. Eliza J. died in 1867, and in 1868, John married Ellen Walker. By this union, he became the father of six more children. He kept adding land to his farm until he was the owner of 1,300 acres in one tract.

John Forney cast his first presidential vote for Harrison and Tyler, the Whig candidates of 1840, and when the Republican Party was organized, he became a strong believer in its principles, as have the Forneys generally since that day. In religion, the early members of the family were Methodists.

The name has been variously spelled, as "Furney" and "Forni" and "Forney." In Guernsey County today, it is "Forney."

FAMILY STORIES

Pioneer Families — Frame

[Originally published 2/27/1945]

For several years, the Frame Reunion was held in the southeastern part of Guernsey County. It grew yearly until the crowds attending reminded one of those at the Pennyroyal Reunion in its more palmy days. Not only were the Frames there, of whom there were many, but there were hundreds of Frame connections and others who were attracted by the entertainment offered.

The Frames were amongst the earliest settlers in Guernsey County, and when they came here, they seemed to come en masse. This early start of a large group of them will account for the many Frames and Frame connections in the county today.

It is not our intention to enter into the genealogy of the family in this article. One who does that, even if he starts no farther back than the coming of the Frames into Guernsey County and follows their numerous ramifications to the present day, would have enough material for a big fat volume. Our purpose here is merely to tell who the Frames were and are.

The ancestors of the Guernsey County Frames had their beginning in Scotland. They moved over to Ireland where they intermarried. This made them true Scotch-Irish. There was a persecution in Ireland and the Frames were amongst the victims. Of one family, all were killed except George Frame and two of his children, and he was left for dead. He escaped and recovered, and from him have descended all the Frames of Guernsey County.

Near the beginning of the last century, Thomas Frame, a descendant of the persecuted George Frame, was living in Fayette County, Pennsylvania. He was the father of seven sons, all with families; namely, Moses, William, Jacob, David, John, James, and Thomas. The westward migration movement had started, and the father and seven sons decided to move to the newly organized state of Ohio. They came to what is now Wills Township, Guernsey County, not all at the same time, but all between 1805 and 1811, and located near each other.

These pioneer Frames had large families. Besides the seven sons, Thomas Frame had four daughters. One of the sons had eighteen children. It is plainly seen that multiplying at that rate, there would be a host of Frames in the course of a few generations, with degrees of relationship hard to figure. They clung to the original family names until it became confusing. For instance, if one mentioned James Frame, he would not be understood until he told which James he meant. This was clarified somewhat when, for identification purposes, it became the custom to speak of "Big Jim", "Little Jim", "Captain Jim", "Jim of William", "Jim of Dave" and "Jim of Jim". Then there were "Long John", "Short John", "Colonel John", "Big Tom" and "Little Tom".

The Frames were substantial and progressive citizens. The value of their services in the development of Wills Township cannot be estimated. Outside of Washington itself, they were the true pioneers. They entered an unbroken forest, but undaunted by the immensity of the task, they felled the trees and laid out fields that were soon blossoming under cultivation. Much of the best land of the township was theirs. To show the extent of their holdings a hundred years ago (1840), we present the following: William D., 328 acres; James of William, 160 acres; John, 200 acres; Moses, 187 acres; William of David, 209 acres; James of David, 279 acres; James, Sr., 273 acres; James of James, 152 acres; James, Jr. 117 acres. By 1840, some of the family had crossed over into adjacent Richland Township where they owned large farms, and some as far away as Liberty.

In politics and religion, the early Frames were Democrats and Presbyterians, but many members of the succeeding generations departed from the political and religious faith of their fathers. We know practically nothing as to how any of the present generation are inclined, either politically or religiously. William Frame, one of the original seven sons and a Democrat, was an associate judge in Guernsey County for seven years (1816-23). William D. Frame, a Democrat, was a county commissioner for two years (1825-26). John Frame, a Democrat, was a county commissioner two years (1849-50). But farther down the line came Roland S. Frame, grandson of the original Moses, who, as a Republican, represented Guernsey County two terms (1881-85) in the General Assembly.

Some member of the Frame family, with time and inclination, may write its history. It will be obvious from the little general sketch we have here given that such a work would be of interest to many who would have reason to be proud of the record of their forefathers.

Pioneer Families — Frye

[Originally published 4/23/1946]

At one time, there were many families of Fryes living in the southern part of the county—especially in Valley and Jackson Townships. Like many others of that section, their forbears had come from Virginia, and they possessed many characteristics that truly belonged to the South.

Family of German Descent.—Through marriage, the Fryes were closely tied up with the Trenners. Both families came from Germany. Before the Revolutionary War, in which he fought, Henry Frye came to America and settled in Virginia. After the war, he became wealthy, owning a large plantation in the Shenandoah Valley. He left a large family, one of his sons being Henry Frye, Jr.

John Frye was the son of Henry, Jr., thus a member of the third generation of Fryes in America. Learning of the opportunities the new state

FAMILY STORIES

of Ohio offered, he migrated to Guernsey County about the year it was organized and entered land near the present site of Byesville; in fact, a part of the town is located on this farm. He was the first of the Fryes to settle here.

Home in the Backwoods.—Surrounding his cabin home was an unbroken forest. Two miles up the creek, at the mouth of Trail Run, was an Indian village called Old Town (pages 26, 825, and 826 of the book). The only roads were trails for packhorses that had been blazed through the woods. After other settlers arrived, they banded together and cut a road through to Cambridge. John Frye died of typhoid fever about the year 1826. His wife lived to be more than 90 years old.

Henry F. Frye.—John Frye brought with him to Guernsey County his little son, Henry F., who was born in Virginia in 1803. The name "Henry" was seemingly a Frye favorite, for this was the third in line in the four generations in America. Coming from the wide-open areas of the Shenandoah Valley, the big woods appealed to little Henry F. They abounded in game, and he persisted in going hunting, causing his parents much concern, who were afraid he would get lost or be attacked by wild beasts.

One day, when Henry F. was about 12 years old, his father was called from home. Before leaving, he cautioned the boy not to go far from the cabin and not to take the flintlock musket down from the wall. But he disobeyed. Hardly was the father out of sight before little Henry F. was slipping back into the woods with the gun. Near the place that is now the busiest section of Byesville, he unexpectedly came upon a group of seven bears. At such a juncture, an old experienced hunter would have been cautious and probably have done some thinking and planning before making an attack. But Henry F., thrilled at the sight, immediately aimed at a vital part of the largest, and fired, expecting to see it roll over dead. The shot only wounded the beast and, enraged, it made for the boy. He dodged around here and there, in the meantime reloading the gun. He fired again and killed it.

(As we have no records by which we can verify this incident, we are giving it here just as it was handed down in the Frye family. It has more adventure in it than the wildest bear stories in the Life of Davy Crocket that we used to like to read when a boy. We are sorry we can't tell you what became of the six other bears.)

Henry F. Marries Sarah Trenner.—In 1826, Henry F. Frye married Sarah, daughter of Henry Trenner, a neighbor. Trenner had come from Virginia to Guernsey County. His father was named Henry, and like Henry Frye, Sr., he, too, was of German birth and fought with the Colonists in the Revolutionary War.

The many Frye families in Guernsey County were mostly the descendants of Henry F. and Sarah Trenner Frye, who were the parents of thirteen children. A few years after they were married, they bought a farm on the Clay Pike, two miles northwest of the present Derwent. Here they farmed and kept a store. It was a busy place. Countless droves of stock and great loads of tobacco were taken by on their way to eastern markets. Frye kept adding land to his farm until it comprised 400 acres. Some of his sons, after marrying, became prosperous farmers in Valley and Jackson Townships.

A Lutheran and a Democrat.—In religion, Henry F. Frye was a Lutheran. He was one of the organizers of the Harmony Evangelical Lutheran Church in Hartford (Buffalo) in 1848, and until his death, he served as one of its trustees. In politics, he was a Democrat. His descendants have not all adhered to belief of their ancestor in either religion or politics.

He died in 1887 at the age of 84. Sarah, his wife, had preceded him, having died in 1874.

Pioneer Families — Laughlin

[Originally published 3/12/1945]

Laughlin is a Guernsey County family name dating back to the earliest years of the last century, when John and Deborah Laughlin came from Pennsylvania and entered land in what is now Richland Township, a short distance southwest of the present Lore City. John Laughlin was born in 1777 and married Deborah Wilson in 1804. He came here in 1807, built a cabin, and cleared a small patch of ground, went back to Pennsylvania, and returned in the spring of 1808, bringing with him Deborah and their two small children, Alexander and Hugh.

The land they entered in the unbroken forest was then in Muskingum County, and their deed for it was recorded in Zanesville. Two or three years after they came here, Guernsey County was organized with Cambridge as the county seat. The county was much larger than it is today, as the southern part was afterwards cut off to help form Noble, and the Laughlin land was near the center. Traveling facilities were poor in those days, and many wanted the county seat moved to a location more convenient to all than Cambridge was. Laughlin believed that his farm would be the most suitable place for it, and in 1812, he and Elijah Lowery platted a town which they called Union, setting aside lots for a courthouse and other public buildings. But their town never grew (page 966 of the book).

John and Deborah lived on this farm for fourteen years, and there five more children were born—Mary B., Margaret, Thomas W., John, and Deborah. Then they moved into Center Township, two miles north, and here James, their youngest son, was born. In 1840, John and Deborah Laughlin owned a farm of 532 acres in Center Township, upon which they lived the rest of their lives.

As this is not a genealogical article, we shall not follow the family farther than the second generation. In 1877, seventy years after John

FAMILY STORIES

Laughlin entered his land, all eight of the children were living. Alexander, the oldest son, was living on the original farm. He was seventy-three years old and had been married fifty years. To celebrate the event, his seven brothers and sisters returned to the old home. They came to Cambridge and were photographed together. James, the youngest son, was then fifty-six. If, on this occasion, each of the eight gave an account of himself, it would be about as follows:

Alexander and John remained upon or near the old home place, each owning large adjoining farms. Alexander was politically inclined, and in 1840 he was elected county commissioner and held the office for six years.

Hugh and Mary B. married into the family of Thomas B. Clark, pastor of the Washington Presbyterian Church from 1821 to 1831. In 1834, they moved to Logan County, Ohio, where Rev. Thomas B. Clark, their father-in-law, had located after leaving Washington.

Thomas W. settled on a farm north of his father's in Center Township. From the age of nineteen, he was an elder in the Washington Presbyterian Church. John W., a son of Thomas W., served as a first lieutenant in the First Ohio Volunteer Cavalry in the Civil War. In 1874-76, he represented this senatorial district in the General Assembly.

When the Civil War opened, James recruited a company of cavalry which, as its captain, he led to the front. This company fought valiantly in a number of bloody battles (page 265 of the book). In it were four of James Laughlin's nephews and a future son-in-law. James returned home as a lieutenant-colonel.

Margaret married James McCreary, and Deborah became the wife of William Thompson. Both the McCrearys and the Thompsons became prominent citizens and wealthy landowners in Center Township. The farm William and Deborah Thompson settled upon is still owned by their descendants.

In 1907, the Laughlins and their connections again assembled at the original Guernsey County home to celebrate the hundredth anniversary of John Laughlin's coming here. A large crowd attended, coming from almost a dozen different states. The oldest persons present were of the third generation, all of the second having passed away. There were representatives of six generations there. It was announced that direct descendants of John and Deborah Laughlin were then scattered over more than half the states in the Union and some foreign countries.

In political matters, the early generations of Laughlins were Democrats; in religious matters, they were Presbyterians. John and Deborah were buried in the old Presbyterian graveyard, a mile southeast of Washington.

For courtesies shown in our preparation of this article, we are grateful to Miss Emma E. Laughlin, of the Barnesville Public Library; also to Mr. Charles C. Laughlin, 110 North Ninth Street, Cambridge, who is eighty-five years of age and the only surviving member of the third generation of Laughlins in Guernsey County.

MORE STORIES OF GUERNSEY COUNTY

Pioneer Families — McCullough

[Originally published 3/27/1945]

McCullough has long been a familiar name in Guernsey County. It appears first in the record of marriage licenses in the courthouse, according to which the forty-fourth license in the county was issued to John McCullough and Jane Forsythe on April 7, 1812. Three years later, we find the young couple located on a farm of 240 acres in the northwestern corner of what is now Jefferson Township.

John McCullough, who was twenty-five years old when he married Jane Forsythe, had crossed over into Guernsey from Belmont County where he was born, the son of Robert McCullough. It is not known why he came into this new county, or how and when he first met his future wife. He became a prominent citizen, farming and owning and operating a mill on Rocky Fork Creek, which ran through his land.

John and Jane McCullough became the parents of eleven children, David, the oldest son, being born in 1816, and Robert, the youngest, in 1831. The sons became heads of McCullough families, and now, after a century and a third, their descendants and their descendants' connections in the county have become numerous. John died in 1860 and was buried in the Bell Cemetery near his home.

It is not our intention in this article to follow the family forward from John and Jane. There are so many ramifications and connections through marriage, embracing so many familiar Guernsey County family names, that we would soon be lost. These descendants, if interested, may do this for themselves. Of more general interest is the McCullough background. It is that of the McCulloughs who were famous as frontiersmen in the Ohio Valley and whose deeds of daring are recorded on the pages of pioneer history.

According to the family history, four McCullough brothers, Abraham, Samuel, George, and John, together with the Zanes, Wetzels, and other frontiersmen, came over the mountains and settled within or near what is now Wheeling. Elizabeth, sister of the McCullough brothers, was the wife of Ebenezer Zane. Here they built cabins and erected Fort Henry, in which all could take refuge in case of Indian attacks.

Two attacks were made on the fort, one in 1777 and the other in 1782. No two stories of heroism in border warfare have been told oftener than those of Major Samuel McCullough and Betty Zane. The latter was the sister of Ebenezer Zane. Her daring deed, when the fort was besieged in 1782, has been told over and over in both history and romance. The most romantic account of it may be found in the novel, "Betty Zane," written by Zane Grey, a descendant of the Zane family.

No less thrilling than the deed of Betty Zane was that of Major Samuel McCullough. This was "McCullough's Leap," an incident of the

FAMILY STORIES

attack of 1777. On August 31 of that year, nearly 400 Indian warriors of the most bloodthirsty type, led by the notorious Simon Girty, appeared before the fort and demanded its surrender. Although there were only thirty defenders within the fort, including women and boys, they resolved to fight and perish, if need be, rather than yield to a savage army. For several days, they withstood the siege, the women molding bullets and shooting with fearless intrepidity.

When it appeared that they could not hold the fort longer, that all was lost, there came rushing to their defense forty mounted horsemen from up the river, under the command of Major Samuel McCullough. The gate was quickly thrown open, and all reached safety within except McCullough himself, who, anxious for his men, held back to the last. Cut off from entering, he fled to the adjacent hill, the Indians in pursuit. They could have shot him, but they wanted him alive so they might burn him at the stake, as he was known to them as one of the greatest fighters on the frontier.

When McCullough reached the top of the hill, he was confronted by a band of Indians coming from the other direction, and he was soon surrounded on all sides but one. Here was an almost perpendicular precipice 300 feet in descent. Knowing the fate that awaited him if captured, he put the spurs to his horse and made a leap to what he himself must have thought would be certain death. The Indians stopped in amazement, then rushed to the brink only to see him galloping off safely below and waving defiance to them far above.

This ended the siege. McCullough bore a charmed life, the enemy believed. The defenders in the fort had been reinforced. The Indians departed, but before doing so, they burned the cabins in the settlement and wantonly killed upwards of 300 head of cattle and hogs. On the side of the National Road, at the top of Wheeling Hill, one may today see a monument marking the spot from which Major McCullough made his famous leap.

The incident related above belongs to the McCullough history. Here, as we believe, is the authentic background of the Guernsey County McCulloughs. John, who married Jane Forsythe in 1812 and located in Jefferson Township, was the son of Robert of Belmont County. Robert was the son of John, one of the four noted fighting McCulloughs, a brother of Major Samuel McCullough who made the famous leap, and of Elizabeth, the wife of Ebenezer Zane. This group of four brothers and their sister were the sons and daughter of another John McCullough, whose family came to America from Ireland about the year 1730. The McCulloughs had formerly lived in Scotland.

MORE STORIES OF GUERNSEY COUNTY

Pioneer Families — Meredith

[Originally published 5/21/1947]

Guernsey County Merediths date back to 1819 when George Meredith came here from Virginia, to which he had moved from Pennsylvania, and entered a quarter-section of land in Londonderry Township. He bought it at the Government Land Office in Steubenville, and the deed given him was signed by President James Monroe. The quarter-section he bought, at probably two dollars an acre, was the northwest one-fourth of Section 24, Twp. 10, Range 7.

Of Welsh Descent.—The Merediths originated in Wales and went over into England to live. They were in sympathy with the Quaker movement, which started in England about the middle of the seventeenth century, and when William Penn founded a colony in America, they came to Pennsylvania.

Here in this country, according to their family traditions, some of the Merediths became distinguished. In his Autobiography, Benjamin Franklin mentions a Meredith (a member of this particular branch of the family, they say) who furnished him money to enable him to get started in the printing business. A Meredith was Attorney General of Pennsylvania, and another was the first Treasurer of the United States under the Constitution.

Thomas Meredith.—The first of the Guernsey County branch of Merediths, of whom we have an authentic record, was Thomas. Born in Chester County, Pennsylvania, in 1750, he was twenty-five years old when the Revolutionary War began. On January 23, 1776, he enlisted and served as a private under Capt. John Reese and Col. Arthur St. Clair. (This Col. St. Clair afterwards became the first governor of the Northwest Territory.)

In 1782, the war being over, Thomas Meredith married Eleanor Thomas, born in 1754. This couple became the parents of six children, all born in Pennsylvania, as follows: Thomas, Owen, George, Jonathan, Sarah, and Lettice. All six children married and reared families.

The records in the pension office at Washington show that Thomas Meredith applied for and was granted a pension in 1818. He died in 1844, aged ninety-four.

George Meredith.—As stated above, George, the third son of Thomas and Eleanor Meredith, came to Guernsey County with his family in 1819. Until his death, which occurred in 1868, he continued to live on the Londonderry Township quarter-section of land which he entered. His 7 children were Thomas, George W., John, Robert, Isabella, Eleanor, and William, who died at the age of twenty-five. As was the custom in early days, the Merediths seemed to hold to family names.

George provided in his will (on file in the office of the Probate Judge) that from his estate his wife should have all that she needed for her maintenance during the remainder of her life. Within three years after her death, according to the will, two-thirds of the farm should be divided equally between his two oldest sons, Thomas and George W., and the other third equally among the other four children. It was conditioned, however, that the two-thirds left to Thomas and George W., should ever remain in the Meredith family; at least this desire was expressed.

Many Merediths.—The descendants of George Meredith became numerous in Londonderry Township and elsewhere. Each year, for many years preceding the late war, family reunions were held on the original home farm, which yet carries the Meredith name, being owned and occupied by Georgia and Frances Meredith, great-granddaughters of George Meredith.

Notwithstanding their Quaker background, most of the early Merediths of this section were Presbyterians. In politics, they were Republicans.

Pioneer Families — Robins

[Originally published 3/7/1945]

The Robins family is one of the oldest in the county. The first group of immigrants from the Isle of Guernsey, composed of about a half dozen families, arrived here in the summer of 1806. A year later there came a second group—seven families and eleven single men. One of the latter was John Robins. It may have been adventure, or it may have been the hope of finding better opportunities for the future in the New World than the Isle of Guernsey had to offer, that prompted him to come. Whatever it was, he remained until his death, establishing a family name in Guernsey County that has been carried down to present day. And it is a family name that has ever ranked high amongst those of the most substantial and progressive citizens.

Cambridge, but one year old in 1807, had little in the way of employment to offer an energetic, ambitious young man like John Robins. Over at Coshocton, four years older than Cambridge, salt was being manufactured. This article was in much demand in pioneer days, and, believing the salt industry had a promising future, young Robins went to Coshocton to engage in that business. He did not remain there long, however, but returned to Cambridge. There may have been a special reason for this.

One of the seven families coming from the Isle of Guernsey when John Robins came was that of Widow Hubert, who had a daughter named Mary. As John Alden of Plymouth, a lone young man in a new country, wanted a home of his own and married Priscilla who had crossed the Atlantic with him, so John Robins, similarly situated, married Mary. Just as the marriage of the two Pilgrims was one of the first in Plymouth, so this was one of the first in Cambridge, taking place in 1810, the year the county was organized.

The year they were married, John and Mary began looking around for a farm upon which to settle. They chose eighty acres of fertile land on Buffalo Creek in what was then Buffalo, but now Valley Township. This was what was known as Congress Land and sold for two dollars an acre.

Few of our county pioneers were more anxious to succeed than was John Robins, and Mary was a valiant helper. Coming from a Norman-French country, he had only a little knowledge of English, but he did have much common sense and practical ability. He was a good mathematician and a good penman, two accomplishments that were of value to him in his business transactions. Within a short time, he added another eighty acres to his farm. He continued buying adjacent land until he was the owner of 800 acres. Then he began buying land south of Cambridge and eventually owned 400 acres there. He became a wealthy man.

To John and Mary Robins, eight children were born, of whom the oldest was Peter D. Like his father, he, too, became a large landowner. At least three sons of Peter D. became interested in the coal industry and were among the pioneer operators in the Guernsey Valley coalfield. They opened the Buffalo Coal Mine which, for several years, was the largest mine in the county; also Guernsey Mine, just east of Cambridge. They platted a town here and named it Guernsey. It was settled largely by a high-class group of Irish Catholics. Two sons of Peter D. opened King's Mine. Here they platted a town and named it and the mine for a colored man (page 672 of the book). A son of Peter D. erected a home at the corner of Wheeling Avenue and South Tenth Street. To make a site for the post office, this was moved back and is now known as the Service Center. Robins (Trail Run) in Jackson Township was named for other descendants of John and Mary Robins.

John Robins was an earnest Christian, a member of the Methodist Episcopal Church. He helped organize the Bethel Church near his home in 1833, and gave the society a site for a church and cemetery (page 1009 of the book). He died in 1840, his wife in 1845. Both are buried at Bethel, as is also the Widow Hubert who lived to be ninety-nine years old. The farm entered by John and Mary Robins in 1810 has always remained in the family name, and it is now owned by two of their great-granddaughters.

FAMILY STORIES

Pioneer Families — Shriver

[Originally published 4/25/1946]

To one familiar with Guernsey County history, the name Shriver suggests Jackson Township. The family was established there before there was a Jackson Township, even before there was a Guernsey County.

The First Shriver.—Adam Shriver, Sr., was the first to arrive, coming alone from Greene County, Pennsylvania, in 1808. Although immediately before coming here he was living in Pennsylvania, he was a native of Maryland and had fought in the Revolutionary War. Three miles southwest of the present Byesville, he entered a large tract of government land which was then in Muskingum County. This tract was a part of the Military District, which was set aside for soldiers of the Revolution and given to those who had not received full compensation for their services in the war. Adam Shriver, Sr., may have come out to claim and get possession of the land that would be his for the asking, but with no intention of settling here. At any rate, he went back to his old home the same year and we find no record of his ever returning here, although he may have done so. It would appear that he came to secure the land for his son, Adam, Jr., to whom he deeded it in 1809.

Adam Shriver, Jr.—We now drop down to the next generation of Shrivers, the real pioneer Guernsey County family of that name. Adam Shriver, Jr., was born in Maryland in 1787, and moved to Greene County, Pennsylvania, with his father. When Adam, Sr., entered the land in Ohio, Adam, Jr., was just of age and ready to strike out for himself. This may account for his father's coming here just at that time—Adam, Jr., would need a farm. Adam, Jr., married Delila Gordon, born in Virginia, in 1790, and thus was 18 years old at the time of her marriage. Immediately after the wedding, they started for their new home far away in the wilderness.

The Journey.—To make such a journey in those days was not an easy matter. They brought with them all their worldly belongings—a horse, a colt, and a few household goods, the latter including a feather bed, the bride's usual dowry. Delila rode the horse, and Adam, Jr., walked, leading the colt. On the colt's back were strapped the feather bed and the few other goods they possessed. Their route, after reaching Wheeling, was over Zane's Trace to Cambridge, thence south five or six miles to the land the father had entered.

The New Home.—A cabin was raised in the woods, perhaps as rude as that in which Abraham Lincoln was born. One hole, made by cutting out a section of a log, served as a window; another hole in the wall served as a door. Over the one used as a door, a quilt was hung at night. There were so many wild animals in the great forest that surrounded them that it was not safe to go far from home without a gun. One morning, when Adam, Jr., was on his way to his clearing, he was confronted by a bear. He shot, but only wounded it, and the animal kept coming on towards him. Fortunately, however, the wound was fatal, and before reaching him the bear dropped dead.

Elijah Shriver.—The first son, whom they named Elijah, was born in 1810, the year after their arrival here. His birth occurred on January 23, exactly three months before Guernsey County was organized. Elijah grew to manhood on his father's farm and, in 1840, married Margaret Witten. They were the parents of six children. Margaret died in 1872, and in 1875, Elijah married Jane Shaw, a widow. At his death, Elijah Shriver was one of the wealthiest men in Jackson Township.

Michael Shriver.—Michael Shriver, second son of Adam, Jr., and Delila, was born March 18, 1812. In 1843, he married Martha Woodson, and to them, six children were born. The oldest of these was Adam G., who, in the Civil War, was killed at Atlanta, Georgia.

In 1840, Adam Shriver, Jr., was the owner of 360 acres of land in Jackson Township, which included the original entry of his father. Elijah had 242 acres, and Michael 82. Adam, Jr., died in 1861, aged 74. Delila lived ten years longer, dying in 1871.

Pioneer Families — Spaid

[Originally published 6/19/1945]

In the southern part of Guernsey County, there have been and yet are many Spaid families and their connections, all of whom have sprung from one progenitor—George N. Spaid. A few years ago, the late A. T. Secrest, a Spaid connection, wrote a comprehensive history of the family, which is our authority for a part of what follows.

In Revolutionary War days, England, being short of men to fight the colonists, arranged with the ruler of Hesse, a small German state, that for thirty-six dollars a head, he furnished soldiers to fight in the British army, the money going into the treasury of Hesse. Notwithstanding the fact that these Hessians had no grievance against America, and most of them had no desire to enter the British army, about 30,000 of them were forced into the service by an autocratic ruler.

One April morning in 1776, George N. Spaht, a boy 17 years old, whose home was in the Grand Duchy of Hesse, was happily swinging along the road on his way to school. Two soldiers seized him and took him to prison, for what reason he did not know. He was not permitted to communicate with his parents; in fact, he never saw them again. He was taken over to England and told that he was to be sent to America to fight the colonists. He wondered why he had to fight them, since they had never injured him or his country.

A few months later, George was in America, stationed at Trenton,

FAMILY STORIES

N. J. with more than a thousand other Hessians under Colonel Rahl. On Christmas night, 1776, Washington crossed the Delaware, surprised the Hessians, killed a number of them, and took 1,000 prisoners. George N. Spaht was one of the latter. He was sent to a prison camp near Winchester, Va., where he was held until the end of the war.

There is a tradition that, after a short time in the prison, George, who had been forced to fight for England and hated the country on that account, volunteered to fight for the Continental Army, took the oath of allegiance, was released from prison, and fought under Washington until the surrender of Cornwallis at Yorktown.

Whichever it may have been, as soon as the war was over, George N. Spaht changed his name to George N. Spaid, married Elizabeth Cale, daughter of a Revolutionary soldier, and settled down near the prison camp in Virginia. Here they remained for 37 years, and here to them nine children were born—John, Frederick, Elizabeth, Mary, Michael, Christina, William, Nancy, and Richard who died in childhood. By 1819, the older children were married and had families of their own. All had settled in the same Virginia community.

Out in the state of Ohio, in a new county called Guernsey, they heard, was land in the valleys of two creeks called Seneca and Buffalo, much better than where they were living, which could be purchased at a low cost. Four of the Spaid families decided to migrate here, those of William, Michael, Mary, who had married George Hillyar, and Elizabeth, whose husband was Henry Secrest. We might remark here that this was the beginning of the Secrest family (direct descendants of George N. Spaid) in Guernsey County, the story of which will be written later as a sidelight to the many Secrest references in the book. The four farms of these brothers and sisters lay in a row. On one of them, the town of Buffalo is now located. Nancy, who married William Frye, came later and settled up Buffalo Creek about three miles from the others.

The families of John, Frederick, and Christina remained in Virginia. Although advanced in years in 1819, George N. and Elizabeth chose to migrate to Guernsey County with the five families coming here. Two years later, Elizabeth died and, after a time, George N. married Barbara Albin, widow of a Revolutionary soldier. George N. lived to be 75, dying suddenly in 1833. His body was taken back to Virginia for burial.

It is thus seen that there were two settlements of Spaids and their connections, one in Virginia and the other in Guernsey County. In the course of time, the descendants of the Hessian schoolboy became numerous. Through the years, the Virginia and Guernsey County Spaids kept in close touch with each other, visiting frequently. Then came the Civil War. Like Robert E. Lee, the Virginia members of the family felt it their duty to follow their state into the Confederacy. On the other hand, the Guernsey County members were loyal to the Union. Now they were to fight each other in a great war. An outstanding incident in this connection is given on Page 1007 of the book.

There lives in Buffalo today a lady whose grandfather fought in the Confederate army, making her eligible for membership in the Daughters of the Confederacy. This same grandfather fought in the Union army, so she can claim membership in the Daughters of Union Veterans. She is a great-great-granddaughter of George N. Spaid and is thus eligible to join whatever organization there may be in England (if any) of descendants of their Revolutionary soldiers. If it is true, as tradition has it, that George N. Spaid was released from prison to fight for the colonists, she may join the D. A. R. Even if he remained in prison till the close of the war, she is eligible for membership in the latter, as her great-great-great-grandfather fought in the Revolutionary War.

A. T. Secrest has estimated that there are now more than 6,000 descendants of the Hessian boy who was kidnapped in April, 1776, and sent across the sea to fight against a country of which he afterwards became a loyal citizen. Mr. Secrest has listed more than 4,000 of these descendants, those whose forebears came to Guernsey County.

Pioneer Families — St. Clair

[Originally published 4/17/1946]

When William St. Clair, aged 92, died on his farm a mile west of Salesville, March 13, 1871, he left 133 direct descendants. Many of them were living near the home of their venerable ancestor, whom they honored and whom the entire community esteemed. It was truly a St. Clair neighborhood.

This patriarch of the St. Clair clan had settled there 46 years before his death, which occurred exactly 75 years ago. We thus see that the St. Clair family has been rooted in Guernsey County for 121 years.

Had the increase of the 133 direct descendants of three-fourths of a century ago approached, in number, that of his revered ancestor, there would have been a host of St. Clairs by this time. After the death of the patriarch, the families scattered widely, and today there are only a few, living near Salesville, who bear the name.

Stories Not Genealogical.—In our occasional stories of Guernsey County pioneer families, we attempt to keep clear of genealogy. The purpose of the stories is to show in an historical way who the families were, something of their background, and why they came to locate here. To do this, however, it is sometimes necessary to drop down farther than the first generation in the county. In the story of the St. Clairs, we do not do so.

Of Quaker Descent.—William St. Clair was born in Loudoun County, Virginia, May 24, 1779. His parents were Quakers. In 1801, he married Miss Alice Smith, also of Quaker parentage. Two years after they were married, they migrated, with their infant child, to Belmont County,

FAMILY STORIES

Ohio. The journey was made in a wagon, which also carried their few household goods, over the mountains to Wheeling, thence by way of Zane's Trace to a farm near the present Lloydsville where they located. A short time before this, William's father had settled in that same section, and he had urged the son to come there, too. His eagerness to leave Virginia was probably due to slavery. Being a Quaker, he hated the institution and was only too happy to have a home in the Northwest Territory where slavery was forbidden by the Ordinance of 1787.

Prominent in Belmont County.—In his new home, William St. Clair became a prominent citizen. He lived there for 22 years. He served several terms as a justice of the peace, and, in 1813, he was elected to represent Belmont County in the state legislature. After he had taken his seat there and entered upon his duties, his opponent contested the election and St. Clair was ruled out. For the next term, he was a candidate again, but lost in the election by one vote.

Although a Quaker, he did not hesitate to fight when he felt that his services were needed by his country. Near the close of the War of 1812, he raised a company of Belmont County volunteers, trained them, and, as their captain, waited a call to go to the front. The call came and the company started. His men became discouraged before the scene of action was reached, and one by one they deserted. Only a mere remnant of that gallant army that marched from Belmont County with fife and drum and flags flying was left. However, St. Clair pushed on with the few of his men who stuck by the colors. Before they reached the front, a message was delivered to them, stating that the war was over. The loyal remnant hurried home, arriving there about as soon as the deserters. It is needless to say that the latter, thus branded for life, regretted their action.

Comes to Guernsey County.—In 1825, William St. Clair moved to the Leatherwood Valley in what is now Millwood Township, Guernsey County, and purchased 160 acres of land from Jonah Smith, the founder of Quaker City. As Smith was a Quaker who had come from the same locality in Virginia as the St. Clairs, he may have been a relative of Mrs. St. Clair, and it may have been on his account that they settled here. This was 20 years before Salesville, one mile east of the St. Clair farm, was platted. His coming marked the beginning of the St. Clairs in Guernsey County.

On Leatherwood Creek, he built a dam and erected a mill for grinding corn and sawing lumber. St. Clair's mill was widely known. It was always operated by waterpower. The mill burned in the 1880s, supposedly set afire by "Dory" Taylor, the outlaw (page 919 of the book).

Three years after St. Clair settled in the Leatherwood Valley, the Leatherwood God made his appearance there. The excitement caused by his coming and claims became intense. (See page 729 of the book.) Among the neighbors of St. Clair at the time were the Williams, Brills, McCormicks, Pulleys, and others. Much of the excitement centered about the mill. When the self-styled celestial, to prove his supernatural power, announced that on a certain night, at a certain hour, he would walk on water across the St. Clair dam, a large crowd of both the "flock" and the "lost" gathered to witness the miraculous feat, but the pretender failed to appear. Again, he invited all to assemble at the mill one night where they would behold his performance of a miracle, namely, the making of a seamless garment from a bolt of cloth. The brethren and others were there, but the Leatherwood God was absent.

Wife Died in 1861.—Alice Smith St. Clair died in 1861, the couple having lived together for 60 years. William lived 10 years longer. Both lived to see the Central Ohio (Baltimore and Ohio) Railroad come up the valley through their farm, cutting close to their house. A son afterwards built a large brick residence farther back from the railroad. This is now the Little place.

Twenty years before his death, St. Clair divided his large estate amongst his children. He was buried in the old Joseph Williams burial ground near his home.

Pioneer Families — Stiles

[Originally published 3/23/1946]

In many sections of Guernsey County were once families bearing the same name, so many of them that the community was named for them. The school there, and often the church of whatever denomination it might be, would be known by the same name. The members of these families, being more or less related, would possess traits and characteristics common to all, and generally they were of one mind in politics and religion.

A study of community history shows that often a family once densely settled in a place, and apparently deeply rooted, will, in the course of time, have disappeared, leaving little more than the name. One who visits the old burial ground near the church will learn where many of them are, but this tells only a part of the story; others have gone elsewhere to live and are now widely scattered.

We received a letter recently from Miss Jessie V. Stiles, Dayton, Ohio, saying that she had discovered a copy of "Stories of Guernsey County" in the public library there, and in it mention was made of the Stiles family. She wished to know whether persons of that name are still living in the county, where the original Stiles came from, and most especially the maiden name of her great-grandmother who was the wife of Jonathon Stiles.

A half century or more ago, over in Jefferson Township, one would meet a Stiles at almost every turn of the road. Today we know of but one person in the township whose name is Stiles. There may be others. Undoubtedly, there are Stiles connections whose names have been changed through marriage. There are some Stiles families in Cambridge, but most of the members of this once-numerous clan of Jefferson Township have gone farther away.

FAMILY STORIES

Jonathon Stiles.—The patriarch of the Stiles clan was Jonathon Stiles, a man of English descent, who settled in what is now Jefferson Township in 1806. The first to settle there were William Launtz and Martin Stull, coming from Green County, Pennsylvania, in 1805. Jonathon Stiles, whose wife was a daughter of William Launtz, followed them from the same county in Pennsylvania to Ohio the next year. He entered the southeastern quarter of section 17, a short distance northwest of the present Allen's Church.

The wife of Jonathon Stiles was a sister of George Launtz, a hero in the War of 1812, who was wounded in the Copus Battle and who killed the last Indian of Jefferson Township (pages 250 and 835 of the book).

Fourteen Children.—Jonathon Stiles and wife were the parents of fourteen children—ten boys and four girls. Three of the children were born in Pennsylvania, and eleven after the family settled in Jefferson Township. We here give the names. Note the regularity of their births:

John, 1800; Stephen, 1802; William, 1804; Andrew, 1806; Thomas, 1808; Simon, 1810; Mary, 1812; Jacob, 1814; George, 1816; Margaret, 1818; Jonathon, 1820; Deborah, 1822; Lewis, 1824; and Eliza; 1827.

All these Stiles children lived to become adults in Jefferson Township, and, as the ten boys doubtless became heads of families there, the Stiles name began to multiply. To meet the needs of his growing family, Jonathon added more land to the original 160 acres he had entered until, in 1844, he was the owner of 372, and four of his sons—Andrew, Thomas, Simon and Jacob—had farms of their own.

Deeds Land to Children.—In 1844, Jonathon Stiles, then seventy years of age, deeded his farm to seven of his children, mostly for nominal considerations only. To Lewis and Jonathon, he deeded 160 acres each; to George, Deborah, and Eliza, 80 acres each; and to Jacob and Stephen, six acres each. The records in the courthouse do not show that his wife signed the deeds; hence, we infer that her death occurred before 1844.

Dies In 1860.—Having disposed of his land, Jonathon went to live with one of his sons near Sugar Tree Creek, and here he died. From a gravestone in the cemetery at the Clear Fork Baptist Church, we learn that he was born July 18, 1774, and died November 15, 1860, aged 86 yr. 3 mo. and 27 da. If his wife was buried there, her grave is unmarked. Not far from the original Stiles home in Jefferson Township is an old burial ground that has been neglected and the gravestones destroyed. It is probable that this was her burial place.

The inquiry of Miss Jessie V. Stiles set us on the trail of the Stiles family, not in a genealogical, but an historical way. With the aid of Mr. George L. Stiles, this city, we were able to supply all the desired information except the first name of her great-grandmother.

In a later letter, Miss Stiles writes that she is a granddaughter of Jonathon Stiles, Jr., who, with his brothers, Thomas, George, and Lewis, migrated to Indiana near the close of the Civil War.

MORE STORIES OF GUERNSEY COUNTY

What was once known as the Stiles Schoolhouse in the northern part of Jefferson Township was later called Sugar Tree; it has been abandoned. Except the gravestones in the burial grounds, there is little to show that the name of Stiles, which was almost synonymous with the name of the township itself, ever existed there.

Pioneer Families — Thompson

[Originally published 5/23/1947]

The selling of a farm near Senecaville recently has suggested our writing this story of a pioneer family. By the sale, the name of Thompson that the deed for the property carried for more than 130 years has given place to another.

Came from Pennsylvania.—William Thompson, the first of this particular family to settle in Guernsey County, was born in Fayette County, Pennsylvania, in 1783, married Betsey Finley there in 1806, and came here with his family in 1810. Finley entered land in that part of Guernsey County which is now Noble. On his farm, he erected the first mill in that section.

In 1815, David Satterthwaite laid out a town, which he named Senecaville. On the creek below were saline springs, and here Satterthwaite and Thompson engaged in making salt, employing a number of men as woodchoppers and boilers. To be near the salt works, Thompson purchased and moved to a farm a short distance southwest of the town.

Had Numerous Business Interests.—For the accommodation of the salt-workers and other settlers who were coming in, Thompson opened the first store in Senecaville. In a four-horse wagon, he would haul tobacco and other farm products to Philadelphia to exchange for merchandise to sell in his store. The road passing his home (afterwards known as the Clay Pike) was traveled a good deal, as this was in the days before the National Road. For the accommodation of wagoners and drovers, he made a tavern of his home.

There were no public schools in those days; in fact, no person in the Senecaville community who would teach a subscription school. On one of his trips to Philadelphia, William Thompson engaged Isaac Woodard, a lame teacher, to come here to teach the Thompson children. He provided a schoolroom at his own expense, and invited the salt-workers and settlers to send their children to it. This was the first free school in Guernsey County (page 968 of the book).

Opposition to Slavery.—The Wesleyan Methodists, of which church William Thompson was a member, were bitterly opposed to slavery. His home was a station on the Underground Railroad, which passed through Senecaville, and he helped many fugitive slaves along their way to freedom.

A Colonization Society, in which Thompson was a leader, was

FAMILY STORIES

organized in 1829. Other Senecaville citizens who were active in the anti-slavery movement were David Satterthwaite, Rev. William G. Keil, Dr. John Baldridge, Dr. Noah Hill, and Dr. David Frame. The opposition to slavery was stronger in this community than elsewhere in the county.

A Victim of Cholera.—William Thompson was elected to represent Guernsey County in the General Assembly in 1825. In 1829, he was chosen one of the associate judges of the county and was serving as such at the time of his death in 1833. This was the year of the cholera (page 757 of the book).

Of all the epidemic years in Guernsey County history, 1833 was the worst. The disease attacked persons regardless of age or rank, and there seemed to be known no cure for it. Thompson died within seven hours after he was stricken. He was buried in the Senecaville cemetery. His widow died in 1860.

William Thompson's Family.—William and Betsey Thompson were the parents of seven children—Ebenezer, James, Jane, Harriet, Betsey, Evan, and William. Soon after the family located in Guernsey County, two of William's brothers, Robert and John, came here from Pennsylvania. In 1840, there were eight Thompsons owning farms near Senecaville, having a total of approximately 1,500 acres.

On his farm of 266 acres at the southwest edge of Senecaville, William Thompson built a brick house (still standing), which has long been a familiar landmark in that community.

Ebenezer Thompson.—The descendants of William Thompson have been many, and we shall not attempt to trace any of them except the family of Ebenezer, the oldest son, who occupied the old home after his father's death.

He was born in Fayette County, Pennsylvania, and came to Guernsey County with his parents. With a business career in view, he succeeded his father in the management of the Senecaville store. At the great religious revival of 1833-34 (page 972 of the book), he became converted and decided to enter the ministry. After a course at Ohio University, he was ordained by the Cumberland Presbyterian Church. He married Louisa Halley in 1845, and they became the parents of two sons and three daughters.

On account of poor health, he retired from the ministry to farm. Like his father, he was a public-spirited citizen and had a wide influence. His death occurred in 1884. William H. (Halley), his son, became owner of the old farm and occupied the brick house, from whose family it recently passed.

MORE STORIES OF GUERNSEY COUNTY

Pioneer Families — Trenner

[Originally published 4/24/1946]

Trenners were many and prominent in the early days of Valley and Jackson Townships. The original Guernsey County Trenner family came from Germany to Virginia, and from Virginia here.

Came as a Hessian Soldier.—Going back to the days of the Revolutionary War, we find Henry Trenner living in Hesse Cassel, a province of Germany. The ruler of this province, who was needing money, hired out several thousand of his Hessian subjects to the British to help them in the war they were waging against the Colonists. Henry Trenner was one of these, and much against his will, he was brought to America. When he reached here and saw that the Colonists were fighting for a just cause, he deserted the British army, swore allegiance to the Americans, and cast his lot on the side of those against whom he had intended to fight. In one of the battles, he lost a part of his foot.

Settled in Virginia.—The war over, Henry decided to stay in America; in fact, it would not have been safe for him to return to his native country where he would have met the fate of a deserter. He married and settled in the Shenandoah Valley, not far from Winchester.

Here, in 1790, a son was born who was named Henry, Jr. When the War of 1812 opened, Henry, Jr., enlisted, and, when about ready to start for the front, he took down with the measles and could not go with the company that was leaving. As evidence of his patriotism, he sent a substitute at his own expense, although it was not required of him to do so.

Henry Jr. Comes to Ohio.—A number of neighboring families in the Shenandoah Valley had moved or were contemplating moving to the newly organized Guernsey County, Ohio. Henry, Jr., felt the urge to migrate, too, and with his aged father, the old Revolutionary soldier from Hesse Cassel, he came to what is now Valley Township, entering 260 acres of government land a short distance northwest of the site of the present Derwent. Until his death, which was not long after his coming to Guernsey County, the old veteran made his home with his son.

Life in the Woods.—Henry Trenner, Jr., married Sarah Frye, who was born in Virginia in 1800. They were the parents of eight children—all boys—seven of whom grew to manhood in Valley Township: Noah, John, Isaiah, William, Henry, Caleb, and Benjamin. This explains why the name of Trenner became a common one in the Guernsey Valley.

The first home of Henry, Jr., and Sarah Trenner was the usual log cabin in the woods. It was a crude affair, typical of the homes of most of the pioneers. Nearly all their food was game from the forest or grain and vegetables raised in their own clearing. They kept a few sheep in order to have wool for clothing; they grew flax, which they made into cloth. In the home, they spun the wool and flax, wove the cloth, and made all garments for the family. When boots or shoes were needed, they killed a beef, took the hide to Cambridge, and had it made into leather. The tanner was given half of the leather for tanning it. Footwear was made by itinerant cobblers who would come through occasionally.

Members of the Lutheran Church.—Both Henry, Jr., and Sarah Trenner were charter members of the Harmony Evangelical Lutheran Church which was founded by Rev. William G. Keil in Hartford (Buffalo) in 1848. They continued as devout worshipers at this church the remainder of their lives. Their descendants, for a great part, have held to the same faith. Like most of the other pioneers of the southern part of Guernsey County, who came from Virginia, the early Trenners were Democrats. They voted in accordance with their inherited political principles but were not active in politics.

Pioneer Families — Warne

[Originally published 5/17/1945]

Out the Steubenville Road, six miles northeast of Cambridge, is a place known as Warnetown. It is really not a town, and never was such, but at one time, there were several homes clustered closely together there, a tavern, a distillery, a store, a blacksmith shop, and perhaps some other business or industrial establishments. A census of the community would have shown that nearly every family bore the name of Warne. Today, there is little to indicate that this was once an important community center, but the name is still in use, especially in directing inquiring travelers to turn to the right or left on roads leading from Warnetown when they want to reach certain places. The farm is still owned and occupied by a descendant of the Warne who entered the land.

It was in 1802 that Thomas Warne, Anne his wife, and their small children came from New Jersey to what is now Wills Township, Guernsey County, Ohio. Apparently dissatisfied with their new location, they did not remain long, but moved on into Muskingum County. Here they lived until 1811 when they returned to Guernsey County and entered land on Carpenter's trail, later called the Steubenville Road, now Route 22 or the William Penn Highway. Warnetown is on this farm, which today is owned by D. C. Warne.

Thomas and Anne Warne built a log cabin for themselves and their children. Game was plentiful, and they did not lack for food. The children afterwards said that they could step out of the cabin door at any time and kill a deer or wild turkey. But all was not pleasant. Not far away were camps of Indians who troubled them a good deal. The cabin was on low ground, which was occasionally flooded. Once the water rose so high that the family had to be removed from the cabin on horses.

One day, Thomas received word that he had fallen heir to a part of a large estate in New Jersey, which was then in litigation. To prosecute his claim, he decided to make a trip back to his early home. This meant some money for the journey, and this he did not have; neither was it to be got in the community. Learning that it might be obtained over on Stillwater Creek, he started there in quest of it and was drowned on the way.

Leadership of the Warne family then fell upon Jonathan, the oldest son, who was born in New Jersey in 1791. When the War of 1812 opened, he joined the company organized by Capt. Absalom Martin. Soon after the close of the war, he married Martha Luzadder, born in Pennsylvania in 1799, daughter of Abraham Luzadder, a soldier of the Revolutionary War, who had entered land near the Warne farm.

To Jonathan and Martha, nine children were born. As patriarch of the Warne clan, Jonathan was an influential citizen. His farm comprised more than 300 acres. It was he who directed the various activities at Warnetown. Politically, his leaning was toward the Whig Party, but he was a great admirer of Andrew Jackson and worked for his election. Most of the Warnes since his day, we believe, have been Republicans. His death occurred in 1855.

After the death of Jonathan, his son, DeWitt Clinton, became owner of the Warnetown farm and added to it until he controlled more than 900 acres. The names Jonathan and DeWitt Clinton have seemingly been fixtures in the Warne family, there having been three or four of each in successive generations. The Warnes and their connections, the descendants of the pioneer Thomas and Anne, are widely scattered. Many of them, though, may be found in or near the Warnetown community.

Mrs. Mary C. Allen (Mary Catherine Warne), 137 South Twelfth Street, Cambridge, now in her ninety-first year, is the oldest of the Warne family now living in Guernsey County. Mrs. Eliza Voorhies, a sister, ninety-three years old, is living in Coshocton, and another sister, Mrs. Martha R. Bratton, aged eighty-nine, lives in Columbus.

Mrs. Allen was born near the Steubenville Road, west of Warnetown, and attended the Slaughter Hill School. Exceptionally keen of mind, and spry of body until recently, when she met with a slight accident from which she is recovering, she delights in talking about events of the far-away past. Clearly remembered are incidents connected with the Civil War, Morgan's Raid, and the Vallandigham campaign.

"Morgan did not come past our place," she said, "but we were afraid he would, and father hid the horses back in the woods—all but one, which he rode over towards Washington to see what was happening there, and it was taken from him." The Vallandigham campaign (page 146 of the book) impressed her most, as she took an active part in it. "We were strong Unionists," she said, "but out the Steubenville Road there were several Copperheads who persisted in wearing butternuts, the emblem of their party. We would snatch them from the boys whenever we had a chance, and there were some bitter and fierce struggles. On the day of the great Brough meeting in Cambridge, the young girls of our community, all dressed in white, rode in the parade, standing in a big wagon. We waved flags and cheered for Brough and the Union. It was one of the proudest days in my life."

Pioneer Families — Weaver

[Originally published 5/3/1946]

Traveling east on State Route 265, one will pass through the original Weaver farm, three-fourths of a mile beyond Gibson Station. On the hill north of the house, he will see a little fenced-in burial ground. Here are buried the Weaver pioneers.

Of Irish Descent.—Hans Weaver, the patriarch of the Guernsey County clan of that name, according to a record set down in his own handwriting in an old Bible owned by one of his descendants, was born December 10, 1776, in County Down, Ireland. Susanna, his wife, was born August 16, 1787. To them, in Ireland, five children were born: Robert, who never married; Judith, who married James Gibson; Nellie, who died in childhood; Grace, who never married; and Hans, Jr., who married Harriet Bigham.

To Guernsey County in 1820.—America, the land of promise, appealed to this Irish family and, in 1820, they set sail for this country. They came to Guernsey County, Ohio, and settled on the farm mentioned above. It then comprised 300 acres, mostly a virgin forest. Upon the tract, Hans built a log cabin in which genuine Irish hospitality was always found. He set to work to clear away the woods, and to his already large farm, he added 135 acres more. He engaged in raising wheat, which he hauled over to the canal at Newcomerstown; there were no railroads in this section at that time.

Here five more children were born: John, whose descendants became numerous; James and William, who never married; Edwin, who married Anna Duncan; and Carlisle, who died in infancy. To accommodate his growing family, Hans supplanted the log cabin by a large hewed-log house, and this, in turn, by a frame residence that still stands.

John Weaver.—Of the ten children of Hans and Susanna Weaver, we shall trace but one of them farther, John, the first to be born in this country. He was born in 1821 and lived on the farm with his parents until 1851, when he married Deborah Williams, who lived on a farm nearby. They became the parents of four children—Hans, Preston, Grace and Dora. Hans, the older son, married Mary La Rue. Don E. Weaver, a grandson of Hans and Mary La Rue Weaver, is now editor of The Columbus Citizen. From the standpoint of descent, he is the great-great-grandson of the original Hans and Susanna Weaver.

Hans Weaver's Will.—Hans Weaver was an adherent of the Democratic Party, but not all of his descendants have inherited his political faith. No other Guernsey County pioneer was more respected than he. In addition to rearing a large family, he accumulated considerable of this world's goods, as considered in his day. He was a progressive citizen and active in civic affairs. The first Guernsey County bank was established in Washington in 1848, with Hans Weaver as one of the stockholders. When, in 1854, the present Baltimore and Ohio Railroad was built up Leatherwood Valley past the Weaver home, he became a stockholder in that, too.

In the office of the Probate Judge may be seen the will of Hans Weaver, made in 1854 and probated in 1866. It is a curious document, evidently drawn by himself. Characterized by Irish wit, the document makes known the maker's wish in no uncertain terms. A part of it we quote here verbatim:

To my wife, Susanna Weaver, I bequeath the upper or south room above the cellar, and bedroom adjoining; the use of one-half the milk cows during her life; 200 lb. of beef; 200 lb. of pork, 5 or 6 cwt. of flour if she needs it, as much cornmeal as she needs, as many eggs and chickens as she wants, as much wood and coal as she requires, and all the furniture in said room. I also allow her $10 a year for close, if she needs them.

To my son, Robert Weaver, I bequeath the $1000 I have in the Washington Bank, also the $750 I have in Central Railroad stock; a horse, a saddal and a bridal; his bed, board and washing in the house, as he formerly had in the times past. He may either work or go idle, as he pleases.

To my son, John Weaver, I bequeath the land he now possesses in the south side of the creek, also three pieces cut off this tract I now live on by the Railroad.

I bequeath to my son, William Weaver, the whole of my estate I now live on and possess, together with all and everything on the place. As to furniture, let Mother and Grace have all they can claim as their own. I prohibit William or any of his heirs, administrators or assignees from selling or otherwise disposing or dividing the estate I now bequeath to him, for 100 years after my decease. William, you are here put under great obligations to take care of your Mother and Grace, and allow them sufficient tallow to keep them or her in candles; also plenty of soap to keep themselves clean.

To my son, James, I bequeath $500; to my son, Edwin, $200; to my daughter, Judith, $200; to my daughter, Grace, $563, provided she never marries, but if some freak should induce her to marry, the $563 shall be void and of no effect.

To all my grandchildren of my name, I leave each $100. I bequeath the desk I have to William, the clock to Robert, and the stove to be family property amongst all of you.

I nominate John Frame, my brother-in-law, and my sons, John and Robert Weaver, executors.

Hans Weaver died January 20, 1866; Susanna, his wife, April 10, 1872.

FAMILY STORIES

Pioneer Families — Wyrick

[Originally published 4/24/1947]

A pioneer family name once common in Guernsey County, but now seldom heard here, was Wyrick. Most of the families bearing this name lived in Madison, Jefferson, and adjoining townships. The patriarch of the clan was Peter Wyrick, a veteran of the Revolutionary War.

Came from Pennsylvania.—Our attention was recently called to the Wyrick family by a letter of inquiry from the Genealogical Society of Salt Lake City, Utah. The letter stated that the Society possessed a few facts about Peter Wyrick, namely that he was born about 1743, married Catherine Sunon, sold his property in Northumberland County, Pennsylvania, and, at the age of 76, when applying for a pension, was living in Guernsey County, Ohio. More information concerning the man and his family was wanted.

In our book, "Stories of Guernsey County," page 244, we had Peter Wyrick listed amongst the Revolutionary War soldiers of Guernsey County, as follows:

"Born 1744—enlisted 1776—residing in Guernsey County in 1818, when applying for a pension—died in 1823."

Settled in Jefferson Township.—From the record of deeds in the courthouse, we learned that Peter Wyrick purchased lot No. 33 (100 acres), Township 3, Range 2, from George Beymer for $250.00 on May 26, 1810. Guernsey County was then but a month old. This tract of land is known as the Tedrick farm today. It lies in the southern part of Jefferson Township, adjoining Center, and is crossed by Federal Route 22.

History in Wills.—We next sought the record of wills. A will is often the source of much history. Many makers of wills, especially in early days, would take care to explain why a bequest was made or withheld certain members of the family, thus revealing some family history not obtainable elsewhere. Each member of the family would be named, usually in order of age. By checking the record of deeds and the record of marriage licenses, further information concerning this second generation and those that followed can be obtained.

It is often necessary, however, to construct much of the family history from the documentary data obtained. This necessitates one's exercising both imagination and reason, but as a rule, the history formulated is as reliable as most hearsay family traditions. There being an absence of the latter in the Wyrick families we contacted, we drew up the history of Peter Wyrick from his will and passed it on to the Salt Lake City Genealogical Society, but not guaranteed.

Peter Wyrick's Will.—It was written by Peter Umstott, justice of the peace at Washington, February 26, 1821, and was probated February 15, 1825. These dates define that of his death, which we had given as 1823. To his wife, Sarah, he leaves his farm for her use as long as she lives or is not married to another. Should she get married again, she must leave the place. In case of her death or remarriage, the farm was to be divided amongst four of his sons—David, William, Thomas Jefferson, and George Washington—each to receive twenty-five acres.

To each of three daughters—Betsey, Fanny, and Sarah—likewise to Polly Johnson, his wife's daughter—he bequeaths a bed and bedding and one cow, to be given them when they marry or reach the age of twenty-one.

To two sons—Michael and Peter—and two daughters—Mary and Susanna—he bequeaths five shillings each.

And lastly, he orders that all the rest of his estate, of whatever kind, be given to his wife, Sarah, for her use during her lifetime, or until her marriage again, after either of which it shall be divided equally amongst his sons—David, William, Thomas Jefferson, and George Washington—his three daughters—Betsey, Fanny, and Sarah—and Polly Johnson.

Conclusion Reached.—From the will and the meager data obtained elsewhere, we thus construct the story of Peter Wyrick. He was born in 1744 and entered the Revolutionary War in 1776. He first married Catherine Sunon, and to them four children were born—Michael, Peter, Mary, and Susanna. His second wife was Sarah Johnson, a widow with a daughter named Polly. Peter and Sarah became the parents of a second set of children—David, William, Thomas Jefferson, George Washington, Betsey, Fanny, and Sarah. It is evident from the will that there were two sets, and that one was favored more than the other. Since Polly Johnson was favored along with one set, its members must have been her half-brothers and half-sisters.

Michael and Peter Wyrick served in the War of 1812, one being a member of Captain Beatty's company, the other of Captain Martin's (page 246 of the book). They evidently belonged to the first set, as the other boys would not have been old enough to fight. There is nothing to indicate why Peter discriminated between the two sets.

Peter was nearing eighty years of age when he died. His second set of daughters were young, as they were not to come into their inheritance until they reached the age of twenty-one, or married. He was probably older than Sarah, since he twice mentions the possibility of her remarrying, and wished her penalized if she did so.

The numerous Wyrick families in Guernsey County a number of years ago were, doubtless, descendants of the sons of Peter Wyrick. Some of them spelled it Wirick. Although we have not been able to locate his grave, it is believed that Peter was buried in the Culbertson graveyard in the southeastern part of Jefferson Township, as this was originally the Wyrick burial ground.

FAMILY STORIES

Pennyroyal Families — Ables

[Originally published 8/21/1945]

Speaking at the first Pennyroyal Reunion, Bethuel Ables said, "In 1806, I was born within a mile of this spot, amongst the wolves, Indians, and snakes, and am the oldest person living who was born in Oxford Township." His father was John Ables, concerning whom the following tradition has been handed down in the family:

John Ables was born in Amsterdam, Holland, in 1778. His father owned a ship and sailed the seas. In 1783, he started on a voyage to America, taking with him his little son, John. While the ship reached America, the skipper never did. According to one story told, the crew mutinied and threw him overboard; to another, the ship was captured by pirates and its owner was killed; and to another, the skipper died on the voyage and was buried at sea. Whatever happened, the ship eventually landed at Philadelphia, bearing a homeless orphan five years old.

It happened that Dr. Thomas Thorne came along, saw the plight of the child, and took him to his home. The thought occurred to the doctor that some farmer might be willing to adopt him. On the first market day following he took him over to the stalls where farmers were selling produce and found there an old Quaker farmer by the name of Dillon who lived across the line in New Jersey. "Yes, I'll take him", said Dillon, and it was in that Quaker home that little John was reared.

In an article the other day, we said that Benjamin Borton came from New Jersey to Pennyroyaldom in 1804 and was the first to distill the oil. It would appear that the Dillons and Bortons were neighbors in New Jersey, for, in 1802, John Ables married Ann Borton, daughter of Benjamin; she was born in 1782. It also would appear that John and Ann, also members of the Dillon family, came here with the Borton family. So far as we can learn from available records, the Bortons, Dillons, and Ables were the first families to settle in Oxford Township after the Wherrys.

(NOTE.—The writer of these Guernsey County stories has, since the beginning, aimed to keep clear of any mention of himself or family, other than to say that he was born in Guernsey County and has always lived here. He trusts that he will be pardoned for mentioning here parenthetically that he is a direct descendant of the aforesaid Dillon family, coming to Pennyroyaldom in 1804. His grandmother, Eleanor Dillon—his mother's mother—was born in 1818 within two miles of Gardiner's Grove. She was the granddaughter of James Dillon, one of the first three commissioners of Guernsey County, who helped to organize the county on April 23, 1810. Pardon him, please, for saying here that he is proud of both his Quaker and Pennyroyal descent.)

When John and Ann Borton Ables came to Pennyroyaldom, they brought with them their infant daughter, Mary Ann, who died when young. Three sons and a daughter were born here, two of the sons being Bethuel and John. Both spoke at the first Pennyroyal Reunion, and they will be represented this year by their great-grandsons, Attorney Earl Henry, Cambridge, and Rev. Thomas D. Ables, Portsmouth, respectively. State Director of Education Kenneth Ray is a great-grandson of the daughter. Benjamin, the other son, died in youth.

Ann Borton Ables died in 1812, and the next year, John married Alazannah Cochran, daughter of Alexander Cochran, a veteran of the Revolutionary War. John Ables first settled with the Bortons and Dillons near the Fletcher Church, but after his second marriage, he entered 160 acres of land north of Middlebourne, near the present Kansas School.

To John and Alazannah Cochran Ables, eleven children were born. Thus, John, it will be noted, was the father of sixteen. These children and their children began to scatter, some going to California at the time of the early gold excitement and remaining there. Today, scattered over the country are thousands of descendants of the little five-year-old orphan picked up at the boat landing in Philadelphia in 1783. There are more than 200 descendants in Guernsey County. Following are some of the families or their connections:

Ables, Henry, Marlowe, Cunningham, McMillen, Heskett, Rigby, Williams, Stottsbury, Boyd, Forney, Stockdale, Suitt, Tedrick, and others. Mrs. Vera Ross, wife of Mayor Vern Ross, is a great-great-great-granddaughter of John Ables. Once each year, an Ables reunion is held; it is one of the largest established family gatherings in the county.

For much of the data used in this article, we are indebted to Mrs. H. O. Morrison, Stewart Avenue, Cambridge, a great-granddaughter of Bethuel Ables.

Pennyroyal Families — Ault

[Originally published 7/27/1945]

AULT

Charles M. Ault, 81 years old, is living in the house in which he was born, and he has never lived in any other place. Another record he proudly mentioned to us was that he had attended all the 65 Pennyroyal Reunions but one.

The house, one of the most pretentious, commodious, and conspicuous residences in Fairview, stands flush with the street at the far end of the town. It was built 100 years ago by Daniel Ault, father of Charles M. In the century of its existence, it has had but two owners—father and son.

Today the house is apparently as solid and plumb as when it was built. The brick of which it was constructed was made a few rods away, and the stone trimmings were quarried from the hills nearby. The oak lumber in which it was finished was cut from logs with one of the old up-and-down

FAMILY STORIES

saws, operated perhaps by Daniel Ault himself, as he was the owner of a mill.

Not long ago, a newcomer to Guernsey County, who had been traveling over it, inquired of us about the many old brick houses here and there that he had noticed. They were built long before we had railroads. "How could they transport the brick here?" he asked. We told him that Guernsey County has, in almost every part of it, a clay that is admirably suited for brick, and he would find that the brick in the houses were local products. It was possible for a man to build his house out of his cellar—that is, he could make the brick for the walls out of the clay from the excavation. Some of the first settlers of Cambridge bought lots on Wheeling and Steubenville Avenues for a mere song, and then proceeded to build their houses out of the timber growing on them. Truly, Guernsey County has wonderful resources!

But we are getting away from the Ault house we started to describe. It has a frontage of about 55 feet, is two stories high in front and three in the rear. There are five basement rooms, seven rooms on the first floor, and seven on the second, making 19 in all. Two of the first-floor rooms are each 18 feet square, and the two bedrooms above are the same size. All, as we have stated, are finished in oak. The only change made in the house in the century was on the roof—shingle at first, now slate.

John Ault, father of Daniel, was of German extraction. He settled across in Belmont County, where Daniel was born. Coming into Fairview, Daniel at first operated a large tannery and was very successful, until there came to be a scarcity of oak bark necessary in the tanning process. He then entered the mercantile business, and also engaged extensively in other enterprises. He was married three times, his first two wives being sisters by the name of Bratton. His third wife was Mary Cranston, mother of Charles M.

Since the beginning, the Aults have been ardent Democrats. They were Lutheran in religion as long as there was a church of that denomination in the Fairview community; now they lean to the Methodist faith.

The Ault family will be represented on this year's Pennyroyal Reunion program by Mrs. Elizabeth Reed Carter, a granddaughter of Charles M. Ault.

MORE STORIES OF GUERNSEY COUNTY

Pennyroyal Families — Borton

[Originally published 7/18/1945]

BORTON

This is the first in a series of short articles on the pioneer families of Pennyroyaldom. We start with the Borton family because it was one of the very first to settle there, the first to distill pennyroyal, and the family to engage in the industry for a longer time than any other. And more, too, the Bortons were amongst the leading participants in the early Pennyroyal Reunions.

It was in 1804 that Benjamin Borton, together with his wife and small children, made the long overland trek from New Jersey to Ohio. Having crossed the mountains, they reached Wheeling, and then followed the newly-blazed Zane's Trace until they came to a place a short distance southwest of the present location of Fairview, which pleased them. They decided to enter the land and make it their future home. Their neighbors at first were few; in fact, we have record of but one other family living near at that time—the Wherry family.

Benjamin erected a cabin for his family and began clearing a piece of ground. He raised some corn, potatoes, and other vegetables. The forest abounded in wild game, and the family had plenty of meat. But a little ready money was needed to pay for the government land, the taxes on it, and some necessaries that the wilderness did not provide. He could not sell any of his farm products as there was nobody near to buy them, and to transport them to eastern markets was out of the question, because they were too bulky to be hauled so far over the kind of roads there were at that time. The situation became serious, and Benjamin became greatly discouraged.

To the discouraged and suffering Israelites in the wilderness, God sent relief in the form of manna, which came and covered the ground. In a similar way, but in another form, He sent it to the Bortons. A year or two after he had cleared away some of the forest, Benjamin was surprised to see that the new ground was covered almost entirely with a spontaneous growth of a low, aromatic herb of the mint family, which he recognized as pennyroyal. He recalled that the same plant grew in New Jersey, but not so profusely as here. Over there, an oil was distilled from it that had a ready sale and brought a good price. And over there, he had learned how to distill it. His rejoicing knew no bounds; his financial problem was solved. He could manufacture the oil and have it transported to the eastern markets without much difficulty, as it would be neither bulky nor heavy.

A still was set up, and soon in operation. Benjamin continued to distill the oil as long as he lived. His sons engaged in the same work, as also did his grandson and great-grandsons after him. Pennyroyal sprang up on the land of Benjamin's neighbors, and he taught them how to distill the oil. It is said that here came to be the greatest pennyroyal-oil industry in the world. When the season of the year came that the little plant was ripe, the air of all the country around was scented from the steam of the distilleries.

There were eight children in the Benjamin Borton family, and so the Borton clan got off with a good start. We can't follow them all here. James, the fifth child of the eight, was born in New Jersey in 1801, and was a mere baby when the family came to Ohio. In 1821, he married Maria Williams, and to them were born nine children. One of these was William, born in 1826. He married Charity Dillon, and they became the parents of eight. William engaged in the pennyroyal-oil industry on the old home place, and sold his product to New York druggists, realizing several hundred dollars from it each year. He studied law, was admitted to the bar, and practiced his profession in Quaker City and Cambridge.

At the first Pennyroyal Reunion 65 years ago, William gave a brief history of the Kingdom of Pennyroyaldom. This year the speech he made will be presented by his grandson, G. C. Borton, of Cambridge.

Pennyroyal Families — Giffee, Merryman, and Arnold
[Originally published 7/25/1945]

GIFFEE

Benjamin, first of the Giffees, entered a quarter-section of land a short distance south of Fairview. He was a native of Maryland, and had married Hannah Gilliland in 1804.

Benjamin and Hannah became the parents of ten children: Benjamin, Elizabeth, James, Sarah, Susanna, Josiah, Mason, Perry, Ruth, and Hannah. Several of the children died when quite young.

Benjamin, Jr., born in 1821, married Eliza L. Kennon, daughter of James and Rose A. Kennon, who lived near the Giffee farm. After the deaths of Benjamin, Sr., and Hannah, Benjamin, Jr., and Eliza took over the place his father had entered, erected a commodious brick residence and began adding land to the original farm. It eventually grew to be the largest farm in Pennyroyaldom, comprising 1,437 acres. Two of their children are living—Mrs. B. Frank Sheppard, Cambridge, and J. B. Giffee, Barnesville.

The Giffees have been loyal and enthusiastic Pennyroyalists since the beginning of the reunion. In religion, they have been Methodists; in politics, Republicans. The home and a part of the original farm are yet owned by the family.

MERRYMAN

James Merryman settled on the National Road, a mile and a half west of Fairview, in 1833, five years after that highway was built through Guernsey County. Ever since then, the farm he purchased has been owned by the Merryman family. He was born in Maryland in 1794, and married Margaret Etzlar, born in the same state in 1793. James Merryman died in 1869, his widow in 1870.

To James and Margaret Merryman, five children were born; James E., Rachel, Margaret, Kile E., and Jane. James E., the older son, married Hannah Stevens, and they became the parents of twelve children. After the deaths of his parents, James E. and Hannah occupied the home his father had owned. After their deaths, one of the sons became the owner, and it is still possessed by the Merrymans.

ARNOLD

A family name known throughout Pennyroyaldom in early days was Arnold, but by death and removal, there are only a few of the name left. Not long ago, an Arnold descendant living on the Pacific Coast wrote us that he had recently passed through here on the National Road and tried to find some of his ancestors, but was unable to do so. He appealed to us to locate for him their early homes in Oxford Township, as he wished, as soon as it might be convenient, to make a return trip to visit them.

William Arnold, the first of the name to settle in Pennyroyaldom, came from his native state, Maryland, back in the Zane's Trace days, making the journey by wagon. He entered a half-section of land about two miles northwest of Fairview. Here, he and his wife lived until their deaths. The farm then came into possession of their son, Anthony, who was born on it in 1826. Anthony married Keziah Watkins, and they became the parents of nine children. One of these was John W. Arnold who was proprietor of the Guernsey House in Fairview for many years. His son, Charles M. Arnold, Belmont, Ohio, has the distinction (along with A. C. Saltsgaver, Cambridge, Ohio,) of never having missed one of the 65 Pennyroyal Reunions that have been held.

Pennyroyal Families — Heade, Bell, Buchanan, and Barber

[Originally published 7/31/1945]

HEADE

The original Heade farm lies a short distance south of the present Oxford Consolidated School. Here settled in pioneer days James Heade and his wife, Sarah Dillon Heade. James was born in Maryland, and Sarah in New England. Both had accompanied their parents to Oxford Township. The Dillons were Quakers.

Two children of William and Sarah were Levi and Wilson Shannon. After the deaths of the parents the former continued to live on the home farm for many years. Wilson taught school, studied law, was admitted to the bar, and opened an office in Quaker City. He afterwards moved to Cambridge and formed a partnership with the late Judge E. W. Mathews. He married Margaret H. Clark, daughter of Stephen B. Clark who was prominently connected with many Cambridge activities.

The Heades had prominent places on the program of the first Pennyroyal Reunion, and will be represented this year by E. C. Heade, of Salesville, grandson of James and Sarah Dillon Heade. E. C., we may add here, was born on the second day of the first reunion, almost in sight of the reunion grove.

BELL

The Bell family came from Ireland. The ancestors there were Thomas Bell, born in 1777, and Isabella Hetrack Bell, born in 1780. One of their sons, Thomas H. Bell, came to America and located in Fairview to engage in blacksmithing, the same trade his father followed in Ireland. He married Henrietta Clark, and they became the parents of five children: William C., Lydia A., Dora, Charles H., and John A.

BUCHANAN

Members of the Buchanan family first settled across the line in Belmont County, but some of them afterwards located in Fairview. The head of this family was George Buchanan, born in York County, Pennsylvania, in 1785. He married Margaret Henry, and to them were born thirteen children. They moved to this section in 1800, and George died in 1841.

Wilson H., their son, born in 1799, married Elizabeth Bryan in 1818, and they established a home in Fairview. Their seven children were Margaret J., Cassie, Nancy H., Martha, David, George W. and John W.

At the first Pennyroyal Reunion, Robert B. Buchanan presented a poem he had written especially for the occasion, entitled "Pennyroyal Holidays." The same poem will be recited this year by Miss Mary Jane Gracy, of Cambridge.

BARBER

Since the Kingdom of Pennyroyaldom includes the western part of Belmont County, the Barbers, who settled there at first, may be considered Pennyroyal pioneers, although they were not Oxford Township residents until more recent years.

William and Ann Hammersley Barber were natives of Antrim, Ireland, the former born in 1792, and the latter in 1793. They came to America in 1817, landed in New York, and immediately joined the procession moving westward over the Cumberland Road and Zane's Trace, and settled east of Fairview. William died when only 35 years of age, but

Ann survived until she was nearly 89, dying in 1881. They were the parents of six children.

Mathew, the oldest son, born before the family came to America, was the father of the late Nathan H. Barber, a well-known Guernsey County attorney who served two terms as probate judge, and represented the county in the General Assembly afterwards. Nathan H. was a member of the Fairview band that played at the first Pennyroyal Reunion, and he also spoke at this and many succeeding reunions. Mrs. H. R. Lloyd, of Cambridge, a granddaughter of Nathan H. Barber, will represent the family on the program this year.

Pennyroyal Families — Henderson

[Originally published 7/20/1945]

Going back a century ago, we find that eight Henderson families owned farms in Pennyroyaldom, ranging in size from 80 to 400 acres each. At an Oxford Township election held in 1813, four of the officers chosen were Hendersons. It would seem that the Hendersons, both in numbers and influence, were outstanding in the pioneer days of Pennyroyaldom. All these families were related to each other.

The family had its beginning in Scotland, but went over to Ireland with many others at the time of the political disturbance in the former country. In 1758, William Henderson came with his wife and children to America and settled in what is now Juniata County, Pennsylvania. They were truly Scotch-Irish, a mixture of blood of which many of our best American citizens have liked to boast of possessing. The children of William and Agnes Henderson were James, John, Agnes, and Isabella

John, born in Ireland in 1747 and coming with his parents to Pennsylvania, married Martha Long and moved to Ohio in 1804, locating in the northern part of Belmont County. Their children were William, Thomas, John, Robert, David, Andrew, Margaret, Martha, Sallie, and Nancy. The older sons were married and had families of their own when their parents left Pennsylvania, and they remained there for a while.

William, born in 1774, had married Nancy Clendennon in 1797, born in 1780. They, with their four small children, came to Ohio in 1806, entering land on Zane's Trace in what is now the southeastern part of Guernsey County, Ohio. At his death, William was the owner of more than 400 acres of land. Nancy, who was educated in Harrisburg, Pennsylvania, was the first teacher in what is now the Pleasant Valley, Oxford Township, School. An adventure with Indians a short time after they had settled in the forests of Pennyroyaldom, in which Nancy was the heroine, is told on page 959 of the book.

The children of William and Nancy Clendennon Henderson were

FAMILY STORIES

John C., Sarah, William, Rachel, Margaret Ann, Maria Jane, David, Simpson S., Thomas, George Washington, and two others who died young. Most of the sons reared families in Pennyroyaldom.

About the same time William and Nancy migrated from Pennsylvania to Ohio, two or three of his brothers brought their families here. One of these was Thomas, who became the first justice of the peace in Oxford Township, and officiated at the first Guernsey County wedding (page 945 of the book). Thomas represented the county in the General Assembly from 1813 to 1815, and served as an associate judge from 1816 to 1823.

On the roster of Guernsey County soldiers in the War of 1812 is the name of Andrew Henderson, a member of Captain Beatty's company. He was probably the brother of William and Thomas. We have been told that William engaged in the war, too, making his own sword, which is yet preserved in the county. The roster, however, does not include his name.

Once numerous in Pennyroyaldom, only a few Hendersons are to be found there now. The family has become widely scattered.

Pennyroyal Families — Kennon

[Originally published 8/13/1945]

In 1806, the Kennon family, consisting of John, the father, Elizabeth, the mother, and six children—Nancy, Margery, William, Ruth, Abner, and John—came into Pennyroyaldom and entered 160 acres of primeval forest in what is now the southeast corner of Oxford Township. John, of Scotch descent, was born in Ireland, his ancestors having migrated to that island along with many other families at the time of the persecutions of Charles II.

John Kennon came to America about 1792, and located in Fayette County, Pennsylvania. In 1794, he married Elizabeth Withney, daughter of a Revolutionary soldier. Twelve years afterwards, with wife and children as stated above, he started for Ohio. Having reached the Ohio River, the family followed the Pultney Road to the Grier Tavern near the present boundary of Belmont and Guernsey Counties. The land he had chosen lay two miles due north, and there was not even a path to it. He cut a trail through the dense forest, and near a spring, he erected a rude hut. This was done by driving four stakes into the ground, laying poles across the top, covering with brush, and using bark for siding. Here the family lived for several months, protected from panthers, wolves, and bears by a dog that guarded a hole left in the bark siding for an entrance.

After a little land had been cleared and a crop raised, a rough log cabin 12 feet square was built. It had a real roof—clapboards weighted down by poles—and a puncheon door that swung on wooden hinges. In the course of time, another and larger log house was built a short distance away, and here John and Elizabeth reared their family of ten children, four more having been born—James, Thomas, Newell, and Henry.

There were no schools. This brought grief to Elizabeth. In addition to the work that fell upon this pioneer mother, the household head of a family of twelve, she tried to teach her seven sons and three daughters to read, write, and cipher a little. Some other families settled nearby. A little log schoolhouse, 16 feet square, was built, and Elizabeth became the teacher. We know of no other example in our local history as outstanding as this of a mother's efforts, under adverse conditions, to educate her children. We hear much about a mother's influence. Elizabeth was intensely anxious that her boys succeeded in life; she spared nothing that she could contribute to that end. It is said that when John and she left Pennsylvania for a new home far away in the wilderness, her folks thought it a foolhardy venture, of which she would soon regret, and asked her when she would be back. "Not until my son, William, passes through on his way to Washington to take his seat in Congress," was her reply. And there is no record to show that she failed to keep her word.

William Kennon, after acquiring all the education the little log school had to offer, went over to Franklin College where he spent two years. He read law in St. Clairsville and was admitted to the bar in 1824. Four years later, he was elected to Congress and served two terms (1829-33). He was a member of the convention that framed the second Constitution of Ohio. In 1854, he was appointed a member of the Supreme Court of Ohio to fill a vacancy and was afterwards elected to a full term of five years.

John Kennon, Jr., became a surveyor at the age of 16, made the first true map of Guernsey County, and served as county surveyor for six years (1832-38). (For a fuller account of this member of the family, see page 953 of the book.)

Henry Kennon left home in 1828 and went over into Licking County, Ohio, where he was elected probate judge. He moved to Illinois. His address at the first Pennyroyal Reunion showed high scholarly attainments.

Newell Kennon served as Guernsey County treasurer (1840-44); was elected to the General Assembly in 1846 and served as probate judge from 1877 to 1882.

James Kennon became a surveyor, a profession that seemingly ran in the family, due, perhaps, to the mother's insistence that her boys learn to cipher. David, son of James, became a surveyor, too. He was elected county surveyor of Belmont County, was appointed by Governor McKinley to survey the state lands along the old canal between Cleveland and Marietta, and was elected state senator of this district in 1898. His son, James H. Kennon, Pittsburgh, Pa., who, with his sister, Miss Verna Kennon, Barnesville, Ohio, will represent the Kennon family at the Pennyroyal Reunion next week, is resident engineer of the Pittsburgh Water Works system. He owns the farm upon which his great-grandparents, John and Elizabeth Kennon, settled in 1806.

The Kennons, in the main, have always been Democrats. Their nearest church in pioneer days was the "Old Stone Church" (page 962 of the book) on the hill above Fairview. This was of the Associate Reformed denomination. Most of the descendants today are either United Presbyterians or Presbyterian.

Pennyroyal Families — Morton

[Originally published 7/24/1945]

William Morton, the first of the family in Oxford Township, came there in 1816 from Chester County, Pennsylvania. He was then 50 years of age, having been born in Antrim, Ireland, in 1766. His father, James Morton, was of Scotch descent.

William came to America and married Mary Girtler, a Pennsylvania girl who was born the same year as he. When a young girl, Mary had a thrilling Revolutionary adventure. The Battle of Brandywine was fought near her father's home. The British burned the house, but the family escaped, and Mary hid under a tree nearly all night.

The children of William and Mary—all born before the family moved here—were Jacob G., Sarah, Margaret, Annie, Mary, William, David, Isaac, Lydia, and Robert B.

Two years after coming to Oxford Township, William, the father, was accidentally killed while chopping ice from the water-wheel of a mill he had built on Salt Fork Creek. Mary, the mother, died in 1837. The children married and settled in Pennyroyaldom.

William, the son born in 1806, farmed and taught school for 30 years. As one of Pennyroyaldom's pioneers, he spoke at the first reunion. We here quote from his speech:

"When I came into Oxford Township, there was here but a wild, unbroken forest—an expanse of tree and leaf. There were not more than fifteen persons in the township. Those who followed were from New Jersey, New York, Delaware, Maryland, Pennsylvania, and Virginia. All went to work to carve new homes in the forest. The old fathers are entitled to the credit.

"The boys had to hunt the cows from ridge to ridge, and sometimes come home without them. They braved dangers, too. The hogs in the woods, wild as they were, were more dangerous than the bears. When cow-hunting, the dogs would scare up the hogs; the hogs would charge in battle array upon the dogs; the dogs would fall back upon the boys, who would have to stand the battle from great fallen trees or from the saplings. The boys had to go to mill. The milling was done by horse-power at first, then came the water-mills.

"Our cabin homes were not dreary. They were made lovely by the women, who planted their little parterres of flowers about the doors, and the vines trained by their lovely hands wreathed about the chimneys and clambered over the roofs—and all the houses were dwelling places of home happiness and of love. Whatever of happiness we now enjoy, the foundations for it all was laid by the pioneers who toiled in the primeval forest and wrought out into destiny the victories over adversity which we today so fittingly celebrate."

Isaac, born in 1810, another son of William, Sr., and Mary Morton, became a prominent citizen of Cambridge. He was identified here with different business enterprises, such as milling and the building of the Cleveland and Marietta Railroad. One of his daughters married Charles L. Campbell, who was connected with the Guernsey National Bank, and another married A. R. Murray, who for many years was with the National Bank of Cambridge.

Pennyroyal Families — Rosemond

[Originally published 8/1/1945]

This family name has been variously spelled in Guernsey County—Rosemond, Rosamond and Roseman. Somebody traced the name as far back as the fifth century and found it then to be "Hrosmond." In Pennyroyaldom the first spelling was adopted, since it most nearly approached the original, and it will be thus used in this article.

The first Rosemond to locate in Pennyroyaldom was Philip who, with his wife and children, came from Ireland to America in 1795. After sojourning in Philadelphia, then Brownsville, Pennsylvania, then St. Clairsville, Ohio, he came here in 1810, the year the county was organized, and settled on a quarter-section of land two miles southwest of the present site of Fairview, which was laid out four years afterwards.

Through his farm, which he subsequently enlarged until it comprised more than 600 acres, ran Zane's Trace. Over this, there was getting to be much travel as the western movement increased immediately following the War of 1812. Rosemond enlarged his house, making of it a tavern, and it became well known to travelers as a stopping-place. His neighbors—some of them somewhat remote—were the Wherrys, Kennons, Hendersons, Bortons and others. Mail addressed to Fletcher, Ohio, was left for them at the Rosemond Tavern. Nearby were the Fletcher Church and the Fletcher burial ground. The National Road came through two miles north, and traffic was diverted from Zane's Trace to it. A once active community has passed out. The name has been preserved by the Fletcher Church, practically abandoned—and the old burial ground in which lie buried many of the pioneers of Pennyroyaldom. Philip Rosemond died in 1831 after 21 years on this land as a progressive farmer and businessman.

Soon after Philip came here, other Rosemond families settled in Pennyroyaldom. Among these were two of his brothers, and some sons of brothers who did not come. A century ago, there were several Rosemonds owning farms in Oxford Township and lots in Fairview. At the first Pennyroyal Reunion (1880), William Bernard, an old pioneer, said that when he came to Fairview in 1826, there were two stores there, one of which was kept by James and Martin Rosemond. Together with John Gibson and John Davenport, Philip Rosemond platted an addition to Fairview in 1825 and another addition in 1827.

In the course of time, the Rosemonds became scattered. Some located in the Cumberland community, spelling the name "Roseman"; some in Monroe Township, spelling it "Rosamond." All of them, however, sprang from the same Irish stock. Fred L. Rosemond, of Columbus, formerly a leading Cambridge attorney, is a great-grandson of Philip Rosemond, the original pioneer. His wife was Miss Ella Grimes, daughter of Attorney J. O. Grimes, a Pennyroyalist and president of the first reunion.

Representing the Rosemond and Grimes families, Attorney Fred L. Rosemond will speak at this year's reunion, Thursday, August 23rd.

Pennyroyal Families — Wherry and Ferrell

[Originally published 7/23/1945]

WHERRY

David Wherry, Ann, his wife, and their small children, were the first white persons, it is believed, to settle in what is now Oxford Township. David, whose parents came to America from Oxfordshire, England, was born in Pennsylvania in 1756. He was a soldier in the Revolutionary War, entering the service in 1778. After the war, he lived in Washington County, Pennsylvania.

In 1801, three years after Zane's Trace had been cut through, David, Ann, and the children came over to Wheeling and took the new trail, which they followed until they reached a spot a short distance southwest of the present site of Fairview, which pleased them. Here they decided to enter this government land, located in the seventh of the Seven Ranges, and establish a home. This was thirteen years before there was a Fairview, and nine before Guernsey County was formed.

In the course of time, there came to be much travel on Zane's Trace, and David opened a tavern which was familiarly known as "Wherry's." A Philadelphia man made a trip over Zane's Trace in 1807 and afterwards wrote a book about it (page 46 of "Stories of Guernsey County"). He was traveling east. Telling that he ate breakfast at Frankfort (the "Lost Town"), he then says "The country now become better settled, but still continued very hilly. I walked on, passing Wherry's Tavern where the stage was to sleep at five miles." The National Road, built through Oxford Township in 1828, passed several rods north of "Wherry's," and the tavern was closed.

It was David Wherry, it is said, who suggested the name for Oxford Township when it was formed in 1810. He intended it to honor his ancestral home in England. He died in 1838 and was buried at Fairview. Although we know of no persons in Pennyroyaldom, today, who bear the name of Wherry, descendants of this pioneer family may be found there.

FERRELL

The Ferrells settled two one-half miles west of Fairview. The head of the family was William, born in Mercer County, Pennsylvania, in 1781, the last year of the Revolutionary War. His father, Joseph Ferrell, had come to Pennsylvania from England after marrying Mary Paxton, an Irish girl.

William, the seventh child of Joseph and Mary Paxton Ferrell, served in the War of 1812. In 1815, a bachelor of 34 years of age, he came to Pennyroyaldom and entered 160 acres of land in Sections 13 and 14. The farm was far back from Zane's Trace and somewhat inaccessible. The year after his arrival, he married Sophia Anderson, of Maryland. They became the parents of eight children.

Thirteen years after locating in Oxford Township, the Ferrells were made happy when they learned that the great National Road that was being built would run through their land. Like many others along that famous highway in early days, Ferrell opened a tavern, and it enjoyed a good patronage. He died in 1830, his wife in 1869.

Joseph, the oldest son of William and Sophia Anderson Ferrell, became prominent in Guernsey County political affairs. He married Mary Morton, member of another pioneer family of Pennyroyaldom, read law, and was admitted to the bar in 1848. For a short time, he practiced his profession in Washington, and while there he served as mayor of the village.

Returning to Oxford Township, he was chosen a justice of the peace, an office he held for thirteen years. In 1881, he was elected to represent Guernsey County in the General Assembly and was re-elected in 1863. Politically, he was first a Whig, then a Republican. Prominently connected with the early Pennyroyal Reunions, he contributed much to their success.

ALL NAMES INDEX

This "All Names Index" covers both Volume 1 and Volume 2 of *The Extended Stories of Guernsey County, Ohio*. Page numbers are interpreted as follows:

- Page numbers **below 2000** refer to Volume 1.

- Page numbers **above 2000** refer to Volume 2.

- Page numbers in **lowercase Roman numerals** refer to the Editor's Preface found in both Volume 1 and Volume 2.

In an attempt to make every individual and family name in this two-volume set easy to find for historical and genealogical research purposes, this index has been compiled from the more than 23,000 separate given name and surname references across both books. These references include cases where the name of a school, church, or other placename appears to refer to a family surname, in which case a general family name entry has been included.

A

Abbey
   E. L. 444, 2232
Abbott
   William B. 601
Abel 951
   William 996
Abell
   H. P. 463
   William .. 95, 695, 2107
Abels
   Bethuel 278

Harry C. 352
James 352
William E. 352
Ables 957, 2301, 2302
Alazannah Cochran
   2302
Ann Borton 2301, 2302
Benjamin 2302
Bethuel 945, 953, 954,
   2137, 2301, 2302
Clarence 352
Daniel 2134
Elzie M. 352

John 953, 954, 956,
   2137, 2301, 2302
John J. 746
Mary Ann 2301
Rev. Thomas D. 2302
Absalom
   William C. 352
Acheson 426
   R. V. 169, 653
   T. V. 95
Ackley
   Samuel 924
Adair 1036

ALL NAMES INDEX

Arthur 246
Emma 502
George .. 115, 127, 892
Isaac 674
James ... 261, 276, 281, 302
John 112, 198
John (Heirs) 892
John S. 277
L. B. 502
Michael 884, 892
Morris 241
Rebecca 938
Rev. Joseph Paregoy 1010
Rev. Ross C. 1010
Rev. Ross Wesley 1010
Robert .. 938, 939, 976, 2072
Thomas 352, 370
W. J. 501
Waldo K. 352
William 502
Adams 305, 505, 678
David 1060
George S. 352
Jane 832
Jesse E. 352
John 786, 799, 834
John Q. 111
John Quincy 786
Mike 352, 369
President John Q. . 132
President John Quincy 112, 135, 460, 461, 519, 720, 2094, 2104
Seth 229
Adamson
Charles 2263
David A. 275
Isaac 275
Addison
Albert 509
Harlan E. 352, 368
John 919
Joseph A. 352

Mary E. 512
Addy
Anderson 276
John 848
William 844, 848, 1050
William, Jr. 848
Ader
Andrew 265
Andrew M. 280
Benjamin 265, 280
George 265
Aduddle
Charles 610
Thomas 279
William 277
Agho
Zaro 723
Agnew
G. D. 770
Isaac 994
J. 129
John 989, 994
Rebecca 2099
S. 504
Agricola 439
Ahrendts
A. O. C. 770
Richard 500
Richard A. 498, 499
S. B. 499
Aiken
Martha 934
Robert 746
T. R. 390
Aikins
John 822
Aitkin
J. 456, 458
Akens
James 231
Aker
Joseph 639
Alban
Lyda 1007
Albaugh 887, 951
Cecil D. 352
Albert

Lee 352
Albin
Abraham 400
Barbara 2287
Elizabeth 402
James 1004, 2160
Martha J. 402
Rebecca 2160
Thomas 402
Albright 569
B. A... 56, 73, 232, 495, 2106
Benjamin 275, 281
Benjamin A... 646, 797, 2173
C. J. 379, 630, 782, 2108, 2109
Charles 621
Charles J. 102, 103, 105, 108, 120, 131, 143, 144, 458, 646, 651, 758, 2173
F. W. 2106
Hon. C. J. 81, 210
Jacob 275
W. A. 491, 608, 610
Walter B. 352
Albrite
Bengemen 805
Alcock
Samuel E. 352
Alden
John 2283
Alexander 2101
A. 127
Alexander 198, 682, 886, 887, 894
David 279, 281
Elizabeth 965
James 115
James R. 180
John 277, 281
Matthew G. 279
Mrs. 1038
Rev. John E. ... 381, 972
Robert 277
Rollin E. 352

ALL NAMES INDEX

Thomas 866
William G. 894
William L. 279
Alford
  J. E. 412
Alger
  Horatio 881, 882
Allbritain
  Charles L. 352
Allen 10, 377, 595, 767, 831, 832, 2191, 2291
  B. C. 498, 499
  David 833
  Ed 2187
  Emma A. Harford .. 892
  F. B. 124
  Francis 834
  Francis B. 703, 832
  Frank 833
  Governor William .. 65, 462, 1073
  Harvey H. 350, 352
  J. M. 833
  James B. 277
  John 506
  John A. 352
  John T. 277
  Joseph 258, 262
  Mary Catherine Warne
    2296
  Otto 606
  Samuel 822
  Will 616
  William. 112, 522, 829, 830, 832, 833, 834, 2009
  William M. 892
Allender
  Clyde 352
  Dova 512, 513
  George M. 349, 351, 352
  Margaret 1016
  Thomas 2134
Alley
  Walter B. 352
Allison

Alva P. 281
Bill 1028
Dales W. 507
Donald M. 352
E. C. 488, 655
F. M. 601
Golda 507, 508
Hannah 508, 509
Howard Clayton 366
J. L. 936
James 603, 695
James M. 276
John 276, 508, 1013
John A. 755
John M. 495, 894, 1062
John M. (Heirs) 646
Margaret 2129
Mattie 2129, 2215
Mayor R. M. 421
Philp Linkhorn 366
R. M. 629
Richard M. 625, 639
Robert 646, 797
Thomas 1029
W. R. 458
Will 618
William 89, 90, 112, 457, 626, 797
Allman
  Clyde 88, 186, 630
  Clyde H. 185, 517
Alloway
  Marvel J. 499
Alter 2106
Alters
  Clarissa 375
Always
  Henry 281
Alwood
  Lewis 281
Ambler 559
  Bathsheba 375
  John B. 375, 799, 2196
  Lewis 375
  Mary Ann 375
  Mrs. John B. 799
  Nancy 375

Sarah A. 375
Thomas 1060
Amos
  Frank B. 466, 518
  H. E. 652
  Harry W. 6, 177, 335, 464, 466, 639, 839, 2232
  Herbert E. 464, 466, 639
  Herbert M. 352
  J. M. 498, 499
  John 613
  John M. 164, 166, 175, 463, 464, 465, 466, 496, 499, 527, 611, 2168
  Thomas E. 464, 466
Amspoker 1036
  J. 1025
Anderson. 8, 55, 431, 433, 435, 449, 670, 2073, 2133, 2200, 2205
  Abarham 954
  Abraham .. 1060, 1062, 2099, 2205
  Aldes O. 352
  Alice 511
  Andrew 892, 894
  Arthur E. 352
  Charles 150
  Col. Thomas H. 2206, 2207, 2208
  Colonel T. H. 623
  Dr. 1043
  Dr. J. M. 258
  Dr. William 462
  Geo. S. 433
  George ... 87, 129, 866, 894, 921, 939, 1012, 1016, 2072, 2096
  George S. 142
  Hon. Ross W. 2132
  Hunter 2206
  J. M. 258, 281

James. 869, 976, 1012, 1016
James C. 281
John 279, 391, 649, 822, 924, 973
Major 2014
Major Robert 506
Marlie M. 352
Martha Hunter....2206
Mary 510
Mayor Ross W.....2260
Mrs. Alice 2206
Mrs. Ann 268
Mrs. Irene 2206
Perry W.................281
R. W. 81, 155, 656
Reba......................510
Rev. John 728, 963
Ross W. 106, 161, 629, 2205, 2206
S. H........................506
Samuel 994, 996
Sarah.....................934
Sophia 2314
Stephen P. 279
T. H. 81, 164, 379, 623
Thomas 866, 2107
W. 1038
Warren R. ... 605, 2206
William.. 246, 671, 892
Andre
 Major 2065
Andreasen
 Captain Alfred........411
 Mrs. Alfred............411
Andrews
 M. R. 468
 William..................892
Angle
 Cleo............... 507, 508
 G. H. 507
 George H...... 352, 368, 504, 505
Angus
 Richard.......... 124, 811
 William..................447
Ankenny

Peter B. 1060
Ankeny 231
 P. B.54, 125, 462, 2107
 Peter B. 107, 2174
Anker......................557
 Charles R. 352
 Harry....................352
 Levi D. 176
Ankrum
 Walter R...............352
Annon
 James 989
Ansley
 William.................921
Antigone 439
Antill
 Arthur 352
Antony 452
Apperson
 Aletha 513
Applegate..................215
Appleseed
 Johnny 9, 750, 751, 752, 2163
Arbenz
 Ward J..................367
Arbothnot
 Samuel B. 280
Arbuckle
 Alexander.............278
 James 819, 822
Arbuthnot
 Rev. 1031
 Samuel 834
Archer
 Anna 507, 508
 George 994
 Henry 994
 Henry C. 352
 James 994
 Jennie.. 998, 999, 1000
 John 980
 John M. 278
 Joseph........... 246, 252
 Michael 247
 Rev. John..............972
 Rev. W. G. 470

W. D. 652
Wilson S. 279
Arden
 Enoch 951
Ariadne....................2134
Arick
 Andrew 277
 Jacob....................970
 John 921
 Mabel....................655
Armbruster
 William..................296
 William, Jr. 515
Armor
 Charles 696
Armstrong ... 10, 449, 830, 832, 833, 834, 1043, 2064
 A. 84
 Abraham 106, 123, 126, 649, 830, 833, 834, 2099, 2208, 2209
 Billy 229, 230
 Elizabeth W. Walker 2099
 Henry C. 352
 Hon. Abraham.........80
 James 62, 2209
 James M. 832
 Jeremiah 2209
 John 649, 746, 829, 830, 833, 834, 855, 2208
 John W. 352
 Robert..................866
 Samuel 674, 675
 Susannah Henderson 2208
 William. 107, 115, 125, 258, 748, 954, 956, 2257
 William H. H. 279
Arndt
 Charles 797
 H. W.87, 180, 181, 654
 Henry 279

ALL NAMES INDEX

Nancy 965
Arneal
    Alexander 73, 869, 894, 1062
    Hugh 892
    John 1016
    Thomas 799
    William 894
Arneel
    Thomas ... 95, 123, 124
Arnold 2305, 2306
    Albert H. 352
    Anthony 279, 2306
    Charles M. 2306
    David. 747, 1028, 1029
    Dr. G. L. 81, 157
    Fanny 954
    Frank P. 88, 89, 517, 629, 630
    Fred 639
    Fred W. 572
    G. L. 508
    H. J. 507
    John W. 279, 2306
    Keziah Watkins ... 2306
    Lizzie 510
    Mary 516
    Rev. 399
    Robert 352
    Roy Y. 352
    Susannah 919
    W. A. 258
    William 866, 954, 2306
Arrick
    Joseph 924
Arthur
    Chester A. 161
    James C. 276
    John 797
    President Chester A. 523, 524, 625, 758, 759, 2056, 2080, 2102, 2208
Asbaugh
    Frederick 956
Ashbaugh
    Frederick 954

Ashwood
    Dr. J. W. 422
Askins
    John 1062
    John (Heirs) 1060
    Robert 811, 1062
    Samuel 1060
    William 1062
    William, Sr. 1060
Astor
    Mrs. John Jacob 535
Atchinson
    David 848
    John 848
    Robert 848
Atchison 989
    Dales Webster 366
    John 789
    Olive 512
    Reuben ... 24, 752, 985
    Wilmer Reed 366
Aten
    John 866
Atha
    Leo B. 352
    Milford L. 352
Atherington
    Benjamin 954
Atherton
    Daniel 1047
    David 866
    Gibson 105
    James 866
Athey 833
Atkins
    Jonathan B. 1062
    Robert H. 586
Atkinson 871, 1013, 2093, 2273
    A. A. 489
    H. V. ... 518, 656, 2168, 2181
    Harry 2047
    James 746
    Jonathan 1022
    M. 2099
    Mitchell 646

Robert 246, 1037
Walter C. 509
Atkison
    M. 2098
Atwell
    John H. 976
Atwood 149
    A. D. 674
Aubmire
    Michael 919
Aududdle
    Eli 747
    Elias 747
    Thomas 281
    William 279
Aududle
    Alexander 954
    Charles 954
    Elias 867
    Thomas 954
Augustus
    A. A. 479
Ault 2302, 2303
    Charles M. . 2302, 2303
    Daniel 2302, 2303
    John 2303
    Mary Cranston 2303
Austin
    Laura 509
    Samuel G. 514, 518
Ax
    J. 696
Ayer
    Lucy U. 2266
Ayers
    Rosemond 352
    William 339
Aylor
    Arly 2211
    'Arly' 670, 2210
    Charlotte 670, 2210, 2211
Ayre
    C. 588, 589
Ayres
    Thomas 833
Azarovitz

ALL NAMES INDEX

Andrew 352
Joseph 366

B

Bacon
   Linas 988
Badenelle
   Clyde 366
Badgley
   S. R. 2202
Baer
   John 1016
Bagent
   Anna 511
   Harvey 610
Bailey 310, 701
   Henry 910
   James C. 1069
   Jared 241
   Jarrett E. 275
   Jesse 746, 921
   Miss Anna 399
   Sydney 811
   William 1031
Bailhache
   Nicholas 458, 495,
     2090
Bainum
   Hannah 690
Bair 2206
   J. G. 498, 499, 568, 653
   James 500
   James G. 499
   John 395
Baird 449, 1056
   Abraham 279
   Forrest R. 350, 351,
     352
   James 811
   James H. 848
   John 241, 649, 829,
     832, 1047, 1060
   Joseph 834
   T. F. 115
   Thomas 830
   Thomas F. 127, 834

Wm. F. 434
Bakeman
   Daniel F. 2228
Baker
   Alexander 280
   Calvin 280
   G. T. 127
   George 869
   George W. 280
   Hannah 869
   Harry C. 352
   Harry W. 352, 367,
     517, 639
   Henry 247
   Ida 508
   J. L. 377
   Jacob 865, 867
   John 973
   Laird C. 352, 368
   Lewis 463
   Lewis W. 352
   Maggie 508
   Robinson 954
   William 606
Baldridge
   Alvin W. 279
   Dr. 56, 968
   Dr. John .. 97, 115, 128,
     129, 713, 720, 969,
     973, 2234, 2293
   J. 699
   John 121, 123, 128,
     495, 976
   M. D. 675
   Mary 965
   Milton D. 713
   Professor 2111
   Rev. 385
Baldwin
   Christopher C. 237
   Dr. Miner C. 2203
Balentine
   H. Dwight 639
Bales
   Clarence O. 352
Ball
   A. Edward 2143

Benjamin 275
Ernest C. 352
Ford S. 368
William 277
Ballantine
   David 198, 520, 546
   R. G. 88
   Ray 185
Ballard
   Stephen .. 87, 113, 746,
     973
Ballou 523
   Eliza 523, 1028
   Joseph 994
   Welcome 994, 996
Balloue
   Dr. W. 129
   L. L. 501
Baltzell
   J. 646
   Jacob 797
Bancroft
   George 2133
Bane
   John 987
Banker
   Jacob 1038, 1046,
     1047, 2166
   Mary Good 1047
   Mrs. Jacob 1038
   Selvon 280
Banner 480
Baptist
   John the 533
Barber ... 605, 2306, 2307,
   2308
   Abraham 867
   Ann Hammersley 2307,
     2308
   C. A. 498, 499
   H. O. 608
   Judge N. H. 530
   Mathew 2308
   N. H. 94, 106, 161, 164,
     166, 169, 2137,
     2138, 2257, 2258
   Nathan H. 2308

Samuel.. 279, 603, 799
William...... 2307, 2308
Wilson M. 277
Barclay
 Catherine 510
 John 280
Barcus
 Jesse 789
Bargar
 Major G. H. 158
Barishford
 Isaac..................... 940
Barker
 Edie 921
 Jacob........... 748, 1047
 John (Heirs)...........921
 Wharton 168
Barkey
 Jacob.................... 954
Barkhead
 Thomas 867
Barkhurst
 Daniel................... 973
 James 867
 William.......... 954, 956
Barlow
 William.................. 270
 Zachariah 867
Barnes ... 9, 746, 848, 863, 2154
 Abraham 802
 Abram 787
 Amos..................... 921
 Charles 996, 2107
 Col. Milton . 669, 2124, 2132, 2205
 Colonel Milton 302, 2016
 Ford 57, 112, 245, 747, 994, 1025, 1026, 1031
 Francis 802
 Francis A. 802
 George 2134
 Henry 956
 Israel 121
 James 834

Jennie....................504
John W. 802
M. 261
Milton 93, 158, 262, 276, 629, 2117, 2127, 2128
Nathan 894
O. O.......................989
Tobias 69
William....................278
William A. 835, 837
William H. 279
Barnet
 Thos 805
Barnett 1028
 Anna 511
 C. N. 507
 Ephraim 1025, 1029
 George 277, 1029
 George W.............. 278
 Golda M. 513
 J. B. 258
 Jacob..................... 277
 John B. 276
 John J. 621
 Mary 1025
 Nancy.................... 513
 Riley 621
 Samuel C. 275, 281
 Sheriff William B.2024, 2025
 Walter 258
 Walter B................. 278
 William B................. 90
Barnum
 P. T. 534, 535
Barr
 Forest W. 352
 J. M. 81
 J. R..................81, 515
 James 798
 James R. ... 76, 91, 107, 178, 179, 467, 468, 526, 529, 625, 629
 Mabel.................... 504
 Mayor J. R. 166
 Mayor James R......588

William.. 352, 369, 370
Barrett
 Fred C................... 352
 Joseph 867
Barretts 2200
Barron
 Josiah 245
 Thomas 245
Barry
 Benjamin... 9, 723, 724
 Joseph 703
Barthalow
 Benjamin Grady 366
 Robert L. 352
Bartlett
 Lawrence W. 352
 Mr. 2156
 S. M. 499
 Samuel H............... 498
Bartley
 Governor............... 254
 Mordecai........ 254, 813
Barton 487, 492
 A. A. 447
 Alex 245
 Alexander............ 1060
 Billy 678
 Herman S. 352
 J. J. 275
 John 144, 247, 461, 567, 1060, 1062, 2107
 Luke 1059, 1062, 2128
 Richard................. 994
 Robert 988, 989
 Robert H................ 280
 Thurston R. 352
 W. 258
 William.......... 674, 704
 William H. 279
Bartrug
 Ivan 377
Basford
 Leslie C. 352
Bassett
 A. H. 2199
 C. 696

ALL NAMES INDEX

Bate
- Maggie 510

Bately
- John 258

Bates 2156
- Alice 513
- Beatrice 370
- C. 178
- Calvin 180
- Daniel 245
- Elisha 702
- Ephraim 2153
- Ezekiel 245
- George 894
- Harold 371
- Harold Herschel 366
- Harry E. 352
- Hobart 370
- James 280
- John 247
- Joshua 352
- Lorren Ogier 366
- Timothy 649, 2152, 2153, 2154, 2156
- Vera 371, 501
- William 834, 988

Baughman
- William 798

Baum
- Leonard 128, 2072

Baumgardner 646
- Daniel 1062
- Henry E. 280

Baumgartner
- Benjamin 673
- David 123
- Nicholas 245
- William 277

Baun
- Leonard 939

Baushford 2087

Baux
- General J. 292

Baxter
- A. M. 491
- Hugh 673
- J. A. 629

John 1062
Robert 869
William 870

Bay ... 721, 722, 989, 1026
- Andrew 522, 921, 932, 954
- Andy 721
- Ann 741
- Archibald 987
- Benjamin 987, 988, 989, 2079
- Charles 604
- Col. James 2098
- Col. Robert 70
- Col. Thomas 987, 2078
- Helen 501
- Homer T. 352
- James ... 247, 682, 987, 989, 990, 994, 996, 2079
- Jane 988
- John 129, 987, 992
- Mary 513
- Miss Grace 990
- Mrs. 2079
- Mrs. James 989
- Nathan 921, 932
- Robert .. 115, 241, 987, 994
- Samuel 247, 987
- Susan 721, 913
- Thomas 247, 385, 987, 990, 1029
- W. W. 402
- William. 721, 752, 921, 932, 954, 956, 987
- William C. 994

Bayliss
- Jack 2022
- James 2022

Bayly
- Ada 502
- Andrew 502
- J. L. 502
- Joseph L. 502
- Nellie 502

Beabout

Andrew J. 276, 282
John 258, 276, 282

Beach
- Albert V. 352
- Arthur 629
- Arthur L. 352, 498
- David 987, 994
- Julius 987, 994

Beadling
- James 276
- Lieut. William 281
- Samuel 258, 278
- William 258, 276

Beaham
- John 811
- Thomas 2108

Beal 943
- Abraham R. 275
- Edward 844
- Elias 938
- Elijah 66
- George 830, 1047
- Isaac 832, 834, 934, 938
- Isaac of George 938
- Nicholas 114
- William 938

Beall 409, 663, 910
- Charles 892
- Edward 276
- Elijah 71, 85, 112, 258, 276, 282, 921
- Elizabeth B. Moore .34
- Glenn R. 352
- Hamilton 276
- Henry 646
- James 601, 921
- James P. 994
- John 34, 601, 695
- Sarah 913

Beam 836
- Christian 867
- George 799
- Homer E. 352
- John 279, 282

Bean
- Andrew A. 353

ALL NAMES INDEX

Daniel 277
Frank 353
Russell 90, 186
W. E. 515
Bear 1019
   Andrew 353
   John W. 132
Beard
   Ambrose 636, 637
   Moses 245
   Robert 280
Beaton
   John 601
Beattie
   Mr. 47
Beatty 29, 31, 373, 576, 611, 795, 895, 2006, 2007, 2027, 2043, 2044, 2045, 2055, 2056, 2063, 2106, 2144, 2145, 2162, 2195, 2199, 2270
   (Heirs) 646
   A. W. 140, 143, 577, 579, 2099
   A. W., Esq. 2099
   Allan W. 2098
   Allen Metcalf 36
   Allen W. 2100
   Allen Wilkins 36
   Ann 646
   Anna M. 2129
   Blanche B. .. 2027, 2028
   Capt. Cyrus P. 564, 574
   Captain Cyrus P. .. 2300, 2309
   Cecelia C. Flood .. 2028
   Col. Zaccheus A. 552
   Colonel Z. A. 540
   Cyrus P. 36, 67, 88, 90, 91, 106, 244, 246, 458, 546, 624, 2027, 2028, 2055
   Cyrus P. (Heirs) 646, 789, 798
   Cyrus Parkinson 713

John 30, 31, 32, 34, 35, 38, 39, 47, 86, 90, 95, 110, 111, 124, 201, 203, 373, 425, 426, 545, 548, 551, 554, 576, 580, 668, 976, 2027, 2044, 2047, 2055, 2194
John (Heirs) 646
John A. 458, 646, 2027, 2028
John P. . 495, 540, 797, 2090, 2098
John Parkinson .. 36, 37
John, Jr. 552
John, Sr. 425
Margaret Malinda ... 36
Miss Ann 441
Mr. 51
Mrs. Cyrus P. 458
Nancy Sarchet 2027
Rachel 646, 799
Robert 675
Sarah 34
Susanna 32
Thomas 892
Thomas S. .. 495, 2163, 2179, 2180
Thomas Swearingen 36
'Tobe' 668
Washington 954
Z. A. 568
Zaccheus 520, 646, 695, 2061, 2062
Zaccheus A. 30, 32, 33, 34, 35, 36, 37, 38, 39, 47, 60, 63, 64, 67, 68, 75, 78, 79, 81, 88, 91, 105, 106, 107, 110, 111, 113, 203, 425, 542, 543, 544, 545, 546, 548, 550, 566, 567, 569, 572, 573, 574, 577, 740, 796, 805, 875, 1066, 2007, 2008, 2043, 2044,

2046, 2047, 2048, 2101, 2148, 2162, 2163, 2170, 2176, 2179, 2184, 2186, 2188, 2194, 2226, 2240, 2250
Beauregard
   General 2014
Bebout
   Charles E. 353
Beck
   John 126, 811
Beckett 595
   Earl R. 353
   J. C. 80, 656, 2138
   John C. 76, 84, 160, 379, 634, 636, 2149, 2258
   John, Jr. 185, 655
   Mrs. Emma Scott 2159
   Walter 604
Beecher 914
   Henry Ward 2119
Beeham
   Thomas 696
Beem
   Richard 887
Beer
   Ella M. 469
Begg 630
Beggs 2200
   James 651, 852, 855
   James M. 839
   John 87, 834
   Morris 892
   Robert 855
   William 867
Begham
   James 87
Beham 232
   James 110
   John 67, 232
Behrent
   Flora 513
Belcher
   William E. 353

ALL NAMES INDEX

Bell .. 449, 574, 859, 1043, 2167, 2306, 2307
  Amelia 649
  Amuell 66
  Atty. James M. 56
  Aura Leone 501
  Benjamin 511
  Bertha 501
  Capt. John 63
  Charles H. ... 353, 2307
  David 1047
  Dora 2307
  Edward. 153, 261, 272, 606
  Elijah 944
  Ernest A. 353
  Francis 2099
  Fred J. 186
  G. E. 447
  Gen. James M. 118, 130, 131
  'General' 101
  'General' James M. 676
  George . 337, 789, 853, 855
  George (Heirs) 834
  George D 353
  George W 629
  Gilbert W. 353
  Henrietta Clark ... 2307
  Isabella Hetrack .. 2307
  J. Albert 498
  J. M. ... 560, 629, 2090, 2100
  J. W. 337, 342
  Jacob F. 282
  James ... 282, 852, 855, 1000
  James M 54, 56, 66, 69, 70, 71, 73, 101, 102, 105, 106, 107, 112, 113, 114, 115, 457, 495, 555, 567, 568, 574, 646, 658, 675, 676, 720, 2010, 2090, 2167
  James R. 279
  John 56, 145, 501, 822, 855, 954, 956
  John A. 2307
  John F. 90
  John G. 272
  John T. 265, 280
  Joseph 87, 245, 822, 834, 852
  Kate 2129
  Lydia A. 2307
  Martha Blair 2099
  May 2129
  Milton T. 353
  Moses A. 265
  Mr. Ira 433
  Mrs. G. P. 1074
  Orvill J. 353
  Ralph Lee 366
  Richard.. 87, 892, 2107
  Robert .. 748, 787, 798, 853, 855, 867, 892
  Robert (Heirs) 789
  Russell B 353
  Thomas 2307
  Thomas H 2307
  Walter 129, 1029, 1031
  William 798, 2100
  William C. 2307
  William H. 651
  Willis C. 353
Belmont
  August 535
Bemis
  Jonas 994, 996
  Martha 988
Benam
  Lemuel 279
Bendure
  Delbert R 353
  G. R. 515
  Orville M. 353
Bennett 449, 1028
  A. J. 337, 342, 343, 345
  Arthur J. 706, 707
  Daniel 276
  David 282
  Emmett S. 839
  Harold E. 353
  Harold F. 350
  J. 269
  James Gordon 535
  James, Jr. (Heirs) ... 789
  James, Sr. 789
  John 606, 954, 1029
  Mont 366
  Mr. A. J. 405
  Mrs. 965
  Mrs. A. J. 405
  Porter 353
  R. King 729
  Ralph 353
  Ransom 669, 670
  William. 276, 494, 649, 973
Benns
  Samuel 996
Benson
  John W. 277
  Levi 921
Benton
  Thomas H. 117
Bera
  Adam 353
Beresford
  Andrew 1028
Bernard
  Thomas R. 353
  William 949, 2067, 2137, 2313
Beros
  Father 408
Berra
  Kazick 353
Berry 505, 678
  B. F. 479
  Benjamin 884, 892
  Dr. 913
  Eli 855
  Father 408
  Frank 2146, 2147
  James ... 180, 185, 277, 339, 353, 412, 669, 996
  James A. 353

John N. 275
John S. 90, 174
Richard 276
W. T. 447
William H. 924
Best 1032, 1034, 2188
Mr. 1025
Bethal
Walter E. 353
Bethel
John 973
Russell 276
Betts
Drewry 1068, 1069
Ella J. 2129
Fred D. 1070
Joseph D. 1070
Judah 1068
Margaret 503
Margaret A. Turner
.... 1070
Nicholas 1068
Peter 1068
Silky 1068, 1069
Stewart 1070
Tempy 1068
Will 1068
Bevard
Samuel 938, 1047
William 954, 956
William, Jr. 1060
Bevington
Richard 608
Bevis
Etta 513
Beyers
Augustus 634, 635
Beymer .. 7, 29, 31, 36, 48,
49, 228, 254, 580, 678,
763, 800, 1057, 1059,
1064, 2069
Ann 32
Ann M. 2098
Bateman 32
C. C. 652
Capt. Simon 2267

Captain Simon .. 70, 71,
786
Conrad 32, 673
Earl H. 809
Eleanor 1074
Ellanor 32
Frederick 29, 245
Gen. Simon 1056, 2098
General Simon 194
George . 24, 29, 30, 31,
32, 35, 37, 38, 49,
85, 91, 110, 111,
128, 195, 201, 425,
544, 545, 580, 740,
794, 807, 1024,
1056, 1057, 1058,
2043, 2044, 2061,
2226, 2243, 2299
H. M. 166
Henry ... 29, 30, 31, 32,
35, 38, 49, 201,
231, 245, 545, 580,
740, 1056, 1057,
1058, 1062, 2043,
2044, 2226, 2243
John ... 32, 89, 90, 115,
122, 123, 135, 139,
231, 246, 558, 649,
650, 869
John of Simon 113
Joseph 32, 142, 144,
673, 703
Julia 32
Mary 32
Mr. 2069
Nancy Webster 31
Noah 32, 276
Peter 29
Philip 29, 32
Richard 32
Samuel 32, 246
Sheriff John 69
Simon . 29, 31, 32, 231,
232, 244, 245, 250,
646, 717, 1060,
1062, 1064, 1066,
1074

William 29, 31, 32, 245,
280, 673, 798, 869,
1062
Wilson 32
Bichard 41, 574, 2191
Charles J. 278
Daniel 798
James 41, 2190
Nicholas 41
Peter 41
Peter S. 277
Bickford
Charles H. 353
Bickham 887
John 245, 866, 870
Bidwell
John 165, 166
Bierly
W. F. 402
William T. 656
Biers
Susanna 818
Bigger 693
Col. Samuel 762
Colonel Samuel 139
Samuel ... 56, 106, 113,
114, 115, 122, 129,
566, 692, 1060
Biggs
L. B. 1059
Thomas 24, 25
Zaccheus 30, 32, 33,
35, 36, 37, 38, 196,
543, 544, 740, 794,
805, 875, 2043,
2044
Bigham 762
Alex 789
Harriet 2297
James 246, 789
Jane 1060
John 789
Sarah 1060
William 747, 1060
Bigley
Alfred 270, 281
Bill

ALL NAMES INDEX

B. F. 457, 568
Benjamin F. 567
Dr. B. F. 697
Dr. Benjamin 566
Dr. Benjamin F. 557, 2188

Bilyeu
Mrs. L. E. 182

Bines
Elizabeth ... 2210, 2211

Bingham
Eli 115, 246, 987, 994
Hon. John A.. 439, 612, 899, 2227
John A. ... 65, 103, 105, 133, 152, 153, 154, 155, 590
Margaret............... 787

Birch
Charles 245
John 90
William................. 2107

Bird 1037, 1046
C. C....................... 185
Parker C. 275
Rebecca 504
Rev. Milton 972
S. A....................... 501

Birkheimer
Helen 507
Leota............. 507, 508

Birkhimer
Misses Helen M. ... 497

Birney
James G. 135, 138, 140, 2119, 2120, 2238

Birtcher
Fred B. 499

Bishard
Clarence................ 353
James.................... 353

Bishop
Eli 994
Governor Richard M. 301, 1000

Bittsberger
E.   279

Bixby
Mrs. 2017

Black............. 2082, 2083
Bernard O. 353
C. W. 507
Cliff 353
David 814, 2082, 2083, 2084
Dr. J. G. 2082
Elizabeth Oliver... 2084
J. R........................ 261
J., Esq. 2099
James ... 127, 494, 844, 848
James H................. 277
Jane. 2082, 2084, 2160
Jeremiah 157
John .. 696, 2082, 2084
Joseph K. 2011, 2012
Joseph R............... 277
Margaret............ 2084
Maria Luccock..... 2084
Mary Stewart 2084
Mrs. Margaret..... 2083
Owen W. 353
Samuel . 270, 281, 798, 811, 1060, 2082, 2083, 2084
Stephen................. 353
Susan Frame 2084
William....... 651, 2082, 2084
Zachariah 1038

Black Hawk.... 9, 532, 533, 548

Blackburn
Alvin..................... 604
E. O. 605
Emmett......... 604, 606
Iola 504
Ray F. 353
W. A..................... 499
William.. 115, 126, 811
William P............... 621

Blackford
Charles Edgar 366

Blackiston
Ebenezer 956
Vincent................. 989
William........ 954, 1060
William P.............. 957

Blackston
Elijah 994
Michael 994
Thomas, Jr............ 994
Thomas, Sr. 994

Blackstone
Elijah 988
Ernest................... 353
Harry Holmes 366
James 1031
Nancy 988
Rebecca................ 988

Blackwell
J. L. 412

Blackwood
Robert................... 865

Blaine 2147, 2214
James G.... 8, 160, 162, 163, 173, 525, 598, 599

Blair
Alexander............. 277
Alexander, Jr. 798
Alexander, Sr......... 798
F. B. 155
Harry 349
Henry 353
James ... 120, 127, 798, 811, 869, 1062
John 798, 811
Martha 2099
William (Heirs) 789
William H. 277

Blake 833
Harry 502
J. W. 515

Blampied
Elisha.................... 799
John 2190
Mrs. Elisha 799

Blanpeid
Elisha.................... 798

ALL NAMES INDEX

Blanpied 2050
   Thomas 282
Blantied
   John H. 279
   Thomas 279
Blazier
   Peter 954
Bliss
   J. A. 160
   John A. ... 95, 165, 166, 447, 821, 2113
   Washington 822
Blocker
   Corbin J. 279
Blue
   Gilbert 2191
   Rev. Gilbert 1009
Blume
   Mrs. Laura 2032
Bluster
   C. H. 412
Bly
   Nellie 512
Boales
   John 789
Boals
   J. A. 1028, 1029
Boden
   S. E. 173
   W. E. .. 63, 81, 84, 652, 656, 754, 755
   William E. 106, 160, 845
Boetcher
   G. H. 81
   George H. 300, 653
   George W. 278
Bofford
   William 279
Bogle
   John 495
   Samuel 848, 855
   Walter 651
Bohal
   Elizabeth 512
Bold
   Lucy 500

Bollen
   John 246
Boller
   Alexander 144
Bollon
   John 574
Bologna
   John 606
Bolon
   Wilma 501
Bomesberger
   W. N. 479, 480
Bomsberger
   Walter 657
Bonar 760
Bonchonsky
   Father 408
Bond 449
   Charles 867
   Henry F. 353
   John M. 279
   Joshua 867
   Larkin 867
   Resin 281
   Rezin 275
   T. M. 95, 2258
   W. P. 842
Bonham
   J. P. 517
   Jess P. 639
Boniphant
   Bert H. 353
   Joseph H. 353
Bonnell 884
   Albert 832
   Billy 903
   C. J. 508
   Catherine 892
   Charles 299
   Daniel 894
   Emma 832
   Ervil R. 353
   Foster R. 353
   George 621
   Isaac 241, 887
   Isaac, Esq. 2099
   Jesse 834

   John 833, 894, 1060
   John P. 279
   Jonathan 71
   L. T. 145, 261
   Lem 2128
   Lemuel L. 601
   Mrs. Anna 2102
   Paul 629, 630
   Paul D. 514
   Roy Irvin 366
   Sarepta 45
   T. A. 94, 106, 174, 447, 514
   William 575, 894
Bonom
   C. A. 503
   Charles 504
Booher
   Abraham 2158
   Captain 263
   Harold L. 353
   John 2158
   Rev. J. R. 402
   William A. 280
Booker
   Henry 939, 2072
Boomer
   Father 406
Boone 875
   Daniel 2158
Booth .. 1038, 1043, 1044, 1046
   Charles H. 353
   George 1047
   Henry 976
   John 1047
   Levi 894
   Orrin B. 491
   William 696
   William Samuel 366
   William W. 279
Boothe
   Effie 511
Borrows
   John 153
Borton 873, 957, 2301, 2302, 2304, 2312

ALL NAMES INDEX

Ann 2301
B. 887, 2105
Baker 2138
Benjamin 833, 945, 2301, 2304, 2305
Bethuel 649
Charity Dillon 2305
G. C. 2110, 2305
J. W. 498, 499, 569
James 954, 2305
John W. 169, 171
Maria Williams 2305
Reuben 834, 954, 2107
William ... 95, 161, 606, 669, 748, 954, 2138, 2258, 2305
William R. 279
William, Esq. 2137
Boswell
James R. 353
Botkin
Frank 353
Friend 353
Botts
John 822, 973
John, Jr. 973
Boughton
Rev. F. G. 528
Bouler
James 954
Bouton
Lieut. A. L. 760
Bowen
Albert Eugene 366
B. F. 716
Bower
Joseph 839
Bowers
George W. 280
Glenn A. 353
H. H. 887
Hugh 886
Hughie 903
James 892
Joseph ... 245, 892, 894
Josiah 67, 867
Ralph Wyrick 366

Sallie 268
Bowersock
Clarence 339, 353
Bowles
C. A. 502
Charles 503
Frances 503
Homer D. 353
Ross K. 353
Boyce
B. 678
Francis ... 799, 834, 938
Boyd .. 559, 595, 833, 887, 951, 1028, 1056, 2073, 2302
A. W. 518
Andrew W. 639
Benjamin 867
Bernard F. 353
Cecelia 703
Dr. A. W. 817
Edward 515
Elizabeth 807
Frank 370
Frank B. 353
Fred D. 95, 181
Fred L. 353
G. Roy 652, 707
George .. 509, 954, 973
J. R. 391
J. S. 272
James 789, 811, 853
James R. 965
John 80, 695, 811, 966
John E. 69, 129, 996
John L. 276
John R. 353
Jonathan 892
Joseph 675, 797
Kate 510
Lyde 510
Matthew 867
Melton ... 93, 185, 450, 472, 496, 597, 677, 815, 845, 1040, 1041
R. H. 390

Ralph C. 353
Rev. J. A. 410
Rev. John 380, 381, 385, 413, 971, 2192, 2193
Rev. Robert 2212, 2213, 2214
Robert .. 509, 703, 787, 789
Samuel 1028
Samuel (Heirs) 1029
Sidney R. 353
Susan 1060
T. S. 507
Thomas 370, 892, 1047
Walter 275
Walter W. 281
Wilber B. 353
William 789, 867
Boyer 1021
Abraham 822
Levi 275
William 395, 748, 1016, 1020
Bozigar
Mike 353
Bozzaris
Marco 452
Bracken
John 833, 834
John L. 278
Thomas 747, 1016
William S. 278
Bracker
Dr. 128
Bradbury
Clifford 369
Raymond 353
Braden
Clyde 353
Daniel E. 2086
Ezekiel 265, 280
Jewel 513
Maggie Reed 2086
W. R. 2086
Bradfield 2154
Bradford

ALL NAMES INDEX

Boyce E. 353
Dr. W. N. 491
John 789
W. N. 629
Brading
   Ezekiel 811
   Joh 811
Bradley 989
   Cyrus 989
   F. 696
   John 206
Bradshaw 10, 49, 50, 101, 113, 115, 121, 229, 233, 625, 631, 632, 669, 696, 961, 962, 2067, 2223
   James 855
   Major William 961, 962
   Thomas 232
   William 949
Brady. 670, 767, 785, 833, 840, 843
   Enos 669, 822
   George 353
   John I. 278
   Lieutenant 2017
   Michael 921
Braesock
   Fred 608
Bragg
   General 313, 314, 2016
   John (Heirs) 798
Braniger 934
   Frederick 940
   Jessie 500
   Ospane E. 353
   R. 936
Braninger
   Frederick 275
Branniger 2073
   Levi 2074
Brannock 663
Brannon
   Harry P. 498
   Thomas 245
Branthoover 538, 2140, 2176, 2178

G. W. 508
George 2139
Harriett 508
Brashear
   Mrs. Otho 1013
   Otho 115, 121, 129, 1012, 1016
Bratton 10, 889, 894, 895, 2083, 2253, 2303
   E. A. 66, 601
   Edward ... 87, 567, 762, 832, 894, 895, 896
   Elizabeth 838, 895, 896
   Jacob 892
   James 86, 241, 386, 798, 838, 839, 884, 887, 889, 894, 895, 2009
   James, Jr. 892
   John 115, 245, 838, 889, 892, 895, 896
   John E. 278
   Maria 2253
   Martha R. Warne 2296
   Ned 570
   Rachel 895
   Robert 895
   Sam 149, 671
   Samuel . 127, 798, 865, 866, 2100
   Samuel D. 353
   Sarah 895
   Thomas 2137
   William ... 69, 126, 829, 834, 895, 896, 938, 956
Breckinridge
   John C. 145
Breidenthal
   Henry 966, 976
   J. W. 174
   William 176
Brenan
   Carl L. 605, 606
Brewer
   Samuel, Esq. 206
Bricker

Gov. John W. 74
Governor John W. 186, 187
John W. .. 184, 185, 186
Bridge
   Rev. W. E. 340
Briggs 558, 2189
   Ansel 495, 557, 558, 565
   Benjamin 275, 557
   Benjamin I. ... 557, 2188
   C. A. 515
   Charles 337
   Charles C. 353
   Electa 557
   Henry 865
   Mrs. 2188, 2189
   Mrs. H. 865
   Nancy M. Dunlap .. 558
Bright
   Jonathan 822
Brill 917, 2289
   Benjamin F. ... 275, 277, 282
   Bethel 277
   C. O. 95
   Clifford O. 176
   Clyde 515
   Clyde H. 514
   David 921
   Eli 276
   Elizabeth 919
   Emanuel 275
   Francis M. 275
   George .. 917, 921, 924
   George W. 277
   Harry M. 353
   Henry 921
   Irwin O. 353
   Jacob B. 277
   Jacob G. 921, 924
   Jacob S. 919
   James B. 281
   James E. 275
   John 921
   John L. 353
   L. E. 502

ALL NAMES INDEX

Mary 919
Michael 1060
Miss Marie 489
Salathael 282
Salathiel 279
Samuel 921
Solomon 924
William 277, 976
Brindley
   Adjutant William ... 411
   Henry 275
   Mrs. William 411
Brinton
   James 921
Brister
   Grover C. 353
Bristol
   Fred 1038
Britten
   Sarah 2086
Britton 2188, 2189
   Bertha 512
   J. H. 678
   J. K. P. 277
   James . 559, 646, 1047, 2188, 2189
   James H. 353
   John 1047
   Joseph 2188
   Joseph, Jr. 798
   Robert 277, 1047
   Walter R. 353
Brockunier
   S. R. 2191
Brodhead
   Col. Daniel 804
   Gen. Daniel 22, 23
   General 895
Brokaw
   Dorothy 510
Brookes
   William 280
Brooks
   Phillips 642
Broom 570, 595, 2262
   A. K. 298
   Adam 295, 511

Adam K. 2263
Daniel. 128, 712, 2262, 2263
Elder H. 373
Helen Swan 2262
Hugh 57, 143, 566, 798, 848, 855, 2086, 2126, 2243
Hugh, Jr. 106
Judson 277
Mary Kimball 2262
Miss Mollie 623
Rev. Hugh 2262
Broomhall
   Eli 128, 924
   Jacob 921
   John 921
Brough 420, 591
   Gov. 2297
   Governor John 287
   John 148, 149, 150, 155
Brour
   David 848
Browder
   Earl 185
Brower
   Emanual 867
   John 867
   William 834
Brown 175, 444, 445, 454, 678, 833, 1023, 2068, 2070, 2113, 2114, 2149, 2181, 2214
   Abraham 2154
   Albert M. 280
   Anne Tingle 2214, 2215
   Archie B. 350, 353
   Arthur W. 634
   Arza 2191
   Augusta 512, 513
   B. Gratz 156
   Basil 2070, 2114
   Bazil 231
   Bernard . 651, 954, 956
   Charles G. 2215
   Columbus 880

Colvin 879, 880
Commissioner 83
David 245, 855
Dorcas 880
Dr. F. A. 394
Dr. Oscar S. 880
Edward A. 353
Frank G. 2215
G. H. 502
G. W. 269, 972
General R. B. 298
George W. 277
Govey 811
Henry M. 279
Hon. Turner G. 879
Hugh 381, 1060
J. A. 412
J. K. .. 84, 157, 272, 300, 498
J. Kelley 2215
James 127, 867, 869
James H. 277
James W. 278
Jerry 2156
Joel 1038
John 127, 747, 799, 848, 1031, 1060, 2201
John (Heirs) . 789, 1016
John M. 265, 280, 649, 894, 973
Jonas 848
Jonathan 277
Joseph ... 862, 863, 954
Joseph H. 277
Joshua A. 2215
Joshua K. 275, 2174, 2214
Judge Turner G. 880
Levi 880
Levi C. 441
Lewis H. 353
Major J. K. 2124
Major Joshua K. .. 2215
Mary 880
Mattie McClelland 952
Michael 703

ALL NAMES INDEX

Miss Jennie 268
Miss Margaret T.... 491
Mrs. 832
Mrs. Maria 799
Mrs. T. G. 81
Nancy 2113, 2114, 2149
Nancy Johnson 2114
Nicodemus 115
Orlof F. 2215
Osmond 2114
R. E. 508
R. O. 161
Ralph E. 353, 502
Raymond C. 2214, 2215, 2216
Rev. George 393, 2191
Rev. M. M. 385
Rev. Philip M. 405
Rev. Thomas 389, 2204
Robert 789, 2114
Robert (Heirs) 789
Robert H. 277
Robert J. 275
Roy T. 339
S. W. 270
Samuel 799, 880, 2090
Samuel M. 277
Sarah 880
Simeon 887
T. G. 106
T. J. 262
Thomas .. 10, 135, 391, 439, 522, 832, 833, 834, 878, 879, 880, 2114
Turner .. 227, 662, 879, 880
Turner G. 54, 66, 67, 87, 127, 649, 865, 867, 878, 1016
Turner G., Sr. 879
W. H. 335, 657
W. R. 299
Walter 353, 880
William 80, 83, 87, 157, 674, 675

William J. 281, 282
Browne
  Arthur W. 635
  Vasco D. 469
  William C. 634
Browning 2073
  Presiding Elder Wesley 1009
  Rev. William 579
Brownlee
  Ebenezer 811, 973
  J. C. 391
Brugh
  Thomas W. 353
Brumbaugh
  D. W. 887
Brumley 1019
  Clarence 353
  Peter 747, 1016
  William D. 280
Brush
  Daniel 1047
  E. F. 514
Bryan
  Charles W. 179
  Elizabeth 2307
  G. T. 56
  Thomas 110, 111, 235, 696
  William 247, 1029
  William Jennings .. 167, 168, 170, 171, 172, 173, 175, 599
Bryant 586, 678
  David 747, 1016
  Frank 176
  G. W. 157
  W. F. 88, 2258
Bryar
  George T. 2100
Bryce
  Robert J. 353
Bryson
  Abraham 797
Buchanan 2306, 2307
  Cassie 2307
  Clinton C. 966

  David 1012, 2307
  Elizabeth Bryan ... 2307
  George 855, 2307
  George W. 2307
  James 63, 965, 966
  John 649, 789, 848
  John W. 2307
  Joseph 696
  Lucretia 965
  Margaret Henry .. 2307
  Margaret J. 2307
  Martha 2307
  Nancy H. 2307
  President James ... 143, 625, 846
  Robert B. 2137, 2307
  T. J. 675
  Thomas 93, 938
  Thomas J. T. 94
  W. R. 66, 713
  Wilson H. 2307
Bucher
  Abram 522
  Asa 994, 996
  George 994
Buck
  Edna P. 513
Buckey 2159
  J. B. 369
Buckingham
  Alvah ... 834, 848, 1047
  John 515
Buckley
  John 811
Buckner
  Simon Bolivar, Sr. .. 167, 168
Buckstone
  Daniel J. 258
Bucy
  John 522
Buford
  Oss 671
Bugher
  Walter E. 353
Buker
  Margaret 512

ALL NAMES INDEX

Mrs. Marda 896
Bulger
   Reuben 954, 956
Bulkley
   Robert J 184
Bumgardner
   H. E. 265
   Jacob 1060
   John 856
   M. 2128
   Michael 1060
Bumgartner 55, 2103
   Cynthiana 649
   David 2102
Bundy
   C. T. 2139
   Hallie 503
   Ross D. 503
   Walter R. 498, 500, 639
Burch
   Catherine 834
   Ephraim 921
   Mrs. 833
   William 834
Burcher
   Lewis Harvey 366
Burdett
   Elias 884
   James 957
   John 270
Burdette
   Robert J. (Bob) 759
Burge
   Everett 353
   Howard 353
Burgess 555, 556, 557, 595
   Alf 270
   Alfred 281
   E. A. 444
   Homer 617
   J. S. 507
   'Mac' 2080
   Mack 616, 617
   S. 262

S. M. 299, 498, 499, 541, 549, 556, 569, 652, 2149
S. M. (Mack) 555, 2187
Samuel 556, 2187
W. O. 299, 556, 581, 606, 614, 617
Burke
   Billie 2027, 2028
   Blanche B. Beatty 2027, 2028
   Ethel 2028
   Robert 789
   William E 2028
Burkhead
   John W. 279
Burkley
   Sarah 2267
Burles 670
   Martha 412
Burlingame 840
   Asa 2160
   C. E. 510
   Ferdinand 275
   Justin 275
   Patience 2268
Burnett
   John 2154
   William 822
Burns 718
   Congressman James T. 180
   Davis 245
   Jackson 278
   James 822
   John 621, 2199
   Joshua 277
   Jospeh 278
   Rev. 263
   Rev. John 2165
   Robert ... 235, 353, 625
   Thomas H 280
Burnside
   Gen. A. E. 147
   Gen. E. A. 151
   General 313, 314
   William 867, 894

Burnsworth
   G. H. 124
   James 839
Burnworth
   John 892
   Rebecca 934
Burr
   John 994
   Mrs. 989
Burris 473
   Andrew 272
   Charles W. 503
   Fred 353
   Listen 69, 90, 142
   Mary 1013
   Robert 169
   Sheriff L. 713
   Zacariah 522
Burrough
   Zachariah 994
Burroughs
   Miss H. 268
Burrows
   Hugh 1016
   James 1016
   John 789
   Liston 1031
Burson 435
   Alvin 276
   Emma 507
   Isaac A. 892
   John 973
   Joseph .. 277, 649, 689, 2151
   R. 887
Burt 262, 819, 2264
   Albert 621
   Andrew 353
   C. B. 1026
   Catherine Waller . 2264
   Cyrus 1031
   D. S. 469, 656
   Daniel .. 651, 822, 2264
   David 115, 246, 822, 973, 996, 1029, 2113, 2173, 2264

David S. 'Dave' ... 2264, 2265
David, Jr. 495, 720, 2172
David, Sr. 495
Ebenezer 2172
Eli 2264
Frank 616
James Walker 366
Jennie 2264
John 746, 799, 2264
Lieut. David 574
Lucinda A. Hoopman 2265
Luther 2264
Mrs. John 799
Myrtle 511
Nancy 2264
Nancy Smith 2264
Paul 353, 369, 370
R. F. 121, 1026
Rhoda 2264
Robert F. 651, 2107
Robert Fletcher 505
Roland 2264
Sarah 2264
Sylvester 2201
Vern W. 353
William 269, 822, 2264
Burton
  Daniel 27, 696
  Daniel (Heirs) 798
  Harold H. 187
  John 110, 111
  Joseph (Heirs) 798
Burwell
  G. W. 265
Busey
  Richard 258
Bush 534
Bushala
  Charles J. 353
Bushfield
  Captain 309
  Col. J. M. 630
  Col. James M. 2211
  Colonel W. M. 662
  Eliza Moore 2211
  Harlan J. 630
  J. M. ... 66, 81, 93, 155, 255, 261, 289, 560, 601, 629, 630, 2117
  John 616
  John M. 278, 2099
  Senator Harlan J. .. 2211
  William 275
Bushnell
  Asa S. 958
Buskirk
  Mr. 2118
Buson
  Charles 265
Bute
  C. D. 695
  John 54, 601, 811, 973
  Joseph 89, 90, 115, 123, 124, 430, 495, 626, 762, 801, 802, 2178, 2237
  Louisa E. 2272
Butler 1062
  Charles 595
  Charles T. 621
  Ora Y. 353
  Rev. C. E. 405
  William L. 353
  William Orlando 141
Butt
  William 376
Buxton
  Daniel I. 275
Bye 687, 863
  Jonathan 10, 115, 123, 126, 128, 566, 649, 712, 720, 746, 820, 822, 2099, 2111, 2112, 2113, 2263
  Joshua ... 121, 126, 135
  Maria 820
Byer
  Rev. 528
Byers
  Mrs. Rose 2103
Byrer
  Rev. C. E. 405
Byron 612

C

Cady
  William 617
Caesar 443
Caffery
  Donaldson 168
Cain
  Samuel 353
Cajni
  Anna 513
Calbert
  Francis 834
  John, Jr. 834
Caldwell 2105, 2207, 2224
  A. H. 390
  Albert 2206, 2207
  David T. 277, 282
  J. K. 649
  James 105
  James C. 280
  Jennie 2206, 2207
  John 381
  John H. 125
  Joseph 1060, 1062
  William 353, 855
Cale 1004, 2143
  A. H. 510
  Elizabeth 2287
  George 822
  John (Heirs) 822
  Lambert R. 353
  Maggie 510
Calhoun
  Fred Richard 366
  John 145
Calihan
  Moses 822
Call
  J. W. 2199
  Roy L. 353
  William H. 353
Callahan

ALL NAMES INDEX

    Clara 510
    Rolland 353
Callendine
    Jacob 892
Callihan
    Ben S. 353
    C. C. 585
    Chester 604
    E. W. 171
    Gab 514
    James 2191
    John 818
    Julian Hooks 818
    Ray W. 353
    Walter D. 353
    William H. 277
Calvert
    A. J. 157
    Alfred 276
    Francis C. 265, 280
    Grover B. 183
    Hiram 2159
    J. J. 514, 629, 630
    Reason 2160
    T. J. 169
    William 270, 275
Cameron
    Alexander 800
    H. E. 480
    James Alexander ... 353
    Malcolm 662, 800
    Mrs. Alexander 800
    Mrs. S. 800
Camp 2191
    Albert A. 276
    C. F. 258
    Chauncy 295
    Corwin F. 275
    Etta 511
    John W. 277
    Thomas 1030
    William E. 275
Campbell ... 208, 305, 306, 595, 755, 808, 978, 2020, 2021, 2149, 2170
    Alex 125

    Alexander 396, 397, 398, 938, 979, 980, 1019, 2170, 2172
    Alexander J. 502
    Alfred S. 43
    Archibald 822
    Archie 397
    Archie N. 353
    Attorney J. W. 992
    Brice Finley 354
    Carrie 302
    Charles 491
    Charles L. 511, 636, 2312
    Charles S. 88, 186
    Eleanor 934
    Ellen 268
    Fred 366
    H. G. 499
    Herbert 354
    Hobart A. 354
    Homer 913
    Hubert T. 354
    Hugh 354
    Hugh G. ... 95, 185, 186, 639
    J. T. 391
    J. W. .. 74, 81, 980, 2239
    James 696, 1031
    James E. 958
    James M. 354
    James W. 162, 2257
    Jane 892
    Jay W. 755
    John 746, 867
    John O. 351, 354
    John S. 288
    Judge J. W. 590
    Judge James W. ... 634, 2216, 2217
    Kate 268
    L. R. 498, 508
    Leonard E. 88, 183
    Lillian 508
    Luther 623
    Martha White 2217
    Morton 354

    Moses 2154
    Mr. 2020
    Mrs. C. W. 178
    Mrs. W. S. 491
    R. F. 865
    R. L. 610
    R. Leonard 186, 498
    Rev. Alexander 426
    Rev. Thomas 397
    Robert 87, 106, 810, 822, 865, 884, 1031, 2158
    Robert F. 867
    Robert, Jr. 867
    Robert, Sr. 867
    Sarah A. Harford ... 892
    T. W. 66
    Thomas 397, 426, 2154, 2170
    U. G. 28
    Victor L. 354
    W. A. 500
    W. S. 491, 498, 499
    W. T. 964
    Willard D. .. 74, 93, 107, 183, 185, 186, 514
    William . 124, 811, 867, 1060
    William E. 354
    William S. 500
    William Y. 349, 351, 354
Canaday
    James 993
Canann
    Caleb 832, 833
    Hannah 832
Carbonnier
    Theodore E. 354
Carey
    Isaac R. 265
    John 127, 548, 867, 2105, 2106
Carleton
    Will 2107
Carlisle 589, 595, 884, 888, 2096, 2097, 2149

ALL NAMES INDEX

Carrie 268
George B. 649
Hannah M. 260
Harry R. 354
Ida 500, 508
John 230, 747, 894, 2096, 2097
John (Heirs). 834, 1060
John H. 277, 278
Joseph 956
L. E. 2076
Lewis E. 2097
Mrs. Ida 2096
W. C. 2202
William. 649, 892, 894, 974

Carlow
John 41, 110, 889

Carman
David E. 491

Carnal
Archibald 921, 932
Kelley 605
Mrs. W. K. 516
W. K. 498, 629
W. Kelly 500

Carnegie
Andrew 496, 497

Carnes 589, 595, 632, 2063, 2178
Anna 511
Charles 494
Craig 629
Ella 511
Fred 606
J. O. 653
James 270
James P. 275
John 834, 994
Mrs. S. C. (Elizabeth) 2182
Robert.. 194, 670, 808, 1012
S. C. 497, 514, 518
Samuel C. 74, 639, 2174
Samuel Jacob 366

Carney
John 1016

Carpenter 10, 197, 775, 873, 878, 883, 1015, 2065, 2148, 2295
Aaron 870
Clifford C. 498
Crum 349, 354
Doyle 354, 370
Edith 370
Edward. 196, 197, 288, 416, 746, 762, 800, 864, 865, 867, 871, 875, 876, 878, 881, 882, 1043, 2107, 2221
Edward (Heirs) 867
Edward, Jr. 872, 876
Edward, Sr. 873, 876
George 762, 867, 1047
George D. 881, 882
Hillary 354
John 869, 870, 871, 872, 873, 874, 875, 876, 1043, 2155
John R. 354
Joseph 2155
Josiah V. 354
Loyd 354
Malissa 513
Massy Stewart 1043
Mrs. C. 865
Nancy ... 874, 875, 877, 878
Nora 2029, 2030
Robert 2152
Thomas 2155
W. A. 81, 161, 870, 876
William 354, 1043

Carper
Joseph 2191

Carr
Charles F. 354
Elizabeth 1038
Eva 508
F. I. 335
J. C. 499
J. M. 444, 460, 2201
James 282, 1060
John 1047
Thomas 258, 2191
W. T. 492, 610
Walley 619

Carrel
Henry 245

Carrell
Charles 822

Carrick
George 279

Carroll
Charles 54, 100, 703
David 867
George 252

Carrothers 2096
Abraham 68, 69, 70
G. W. 621
James 954

Carruthers
Willis 354

Carson 2073
Andrew 1016
Charles 585
Charles W. 354
Ebenezer 1029
F. M. 473
J. M. 84
James M. 145, 156, 1030
James N. 98, 99
John 1016
William. 746, 936, 938, 939, 2072

Carta
John 412

Carter 376, 1036
Clayton J. 354
Earl C. 354
Edward 282
Ella 510
Frank 354
James 956
John 258, 924
Levi 748, 959

ALL NAMES INDEX

Mrs. Elizabeth Reed 2303
Philip 954
Richard 994
Samuel .. 919, 921, 924
Warren J. 354
William A. 1047
Cartmel 1053
Cartner
   James 513
Caruthers
   Dr. John 696
Carver
   H. M. 272
   J. C. 511
Cary 718
   Samuel F. 157
Case
   Myron L. 706
   Peter 747
Casey 618, 619
   C. L. 346
   Charles L. 177, 769, 770
   Francis Gerald 366
   Frank S. 618
   George 338
   J. K. 88, 261, 2117
   James K. 2128
   M. B. 504
   Matthew B. 90, 144
   Richard V. 354
   Samuel A. 277
Cash
   H. L. 447
Caskey
   Frank E. 354
   Samuel 280
Casner
   John 2154
   William 156
Cass
   Lewis 140, 141, 675, 813, 2104
Cassel 787
Cassell . 47, 196, 232, 680, 1025, 1028, 2077

Cassidy
   Robert 354
Casterline
   James 892
Castner
   Joseph V. 354
Castor
   John 650
   Ralph R. 84
Cater
   Frank 354, 369
Cavender 670
   Henry 412
Caygill
   Andrew 354
   George 366
   Hugh 606
   Jennie 514
Cervera 295
Chafin
   Eugene W. 174
Chalfant 377
   Jesse 921
   Orville M. 354
   Othar R. 354
   Othar Revere 350
   Wilbur R. 354
Chamberlain
   N. 1038
Chambers
   David 696
   Frank 354
   John 954
   Robert ... 110, 241, 574
   Samuel 370
   William 855
   William (Heirs) 1048
Champion
   R. E. 262
Chance
   Benjamin 275, 282
   Benjamin H. 276
   George 695
   Mary 1062
   William 245, 674
Chandler
   Caleb 970

   Elizabeth Keil 970
   Isaac H. 1047
   Levithin 867
   Spencer 748, 1016
   W. M. 972
   William W. 279
Chang 2092
Chans
   Alfred C. 275
Chapman 1027
   H. P. 204
   James 279
   John . 26, 27, 110, 111, 495, 566, 750, 751, 752, 807, 825, 826, 827, 828, 889
   John (Heirs) 798
Chappelear
   Albert S. 498
   Albert S., Jr. 499
Charles
   King, II 58, 2309
Charlesworth
   Colonel 310
   James E. 160
Charlott
   Calvin 996
   Stephen 994
Charlotte 747
   Stephen 989
Chase 593
   Bishop 404
   Chief Justice Salmon P. 156
   Hon. Salmon P. 879
   Senator 65
Chatham
   Thomas 740
Cherry
   Moses P. 747
   William 247, 822, 1029
Chervenak
   Andrew 354
Chesser
   Alva 504
   Samuel 822
Chester

ALL NAMES INDEX

M. R. 506
Oscar D. 499
Chick
   William 295
Chickering 2203
Chiesa
   Lawrence 354
   Victors 354
Chrisman 833
   Rev. 150
Christian
   Mildred 508
Church
   John 600
Churchill
   Rev. 991
   Rev. G. W. 375, 2196
Churchman
   Morland D. 354
Cicero 439, 443
Clabaugh
   John 198, 869
Claggett
   C. C. 515
Clancy
   Rev. George 579
Clark 56, 150, 151, 570, 670, 671, 886, 1004, 1056, 2073, 2087, 2105, 2106, 2112, 2217, 2218, 2219, 2221, 2222
   A. 601
   A. B. 296
   A. D. 438
   A. J. 494
   Adam 73, 89, 90, 2218
   Alexander ... 277, 2218
   Alexander, Jr. 646
   Amanda 551
   Andrew 746, 830, 855, 2217, 2218, 2219
   Andrew W. 2158
   Ann M. Beymer ... 2098
   Arthur T. 463
   Barnabas 921
   Benjamin 1009

   Bryan J. 354
   Captain 262
   Catherine 511
   Charles 621
   Daniel 834, 934
   David 246
   Dr. J. B. 2203
   Dr. J. T. 698
   Dr. John T. 2221
   Dr. William 2252
   Dwight M. 354
   Elizabeth 934
   Frank 412, 671
   Gen. George Rogers 2031
   George 679, 680
   Henrietta 2307
   Henry 495
   J. B. 1005
   J. L. 2218
   J. Reid 499
   J. T. 698
   James ... 121, 127, 832, 834, 2218
   Jane 819
   Jane McCracken .. 2222
   John 73, 258, 495, 574, 601, 673, 695, 763, 844, 847, 849, 855, 2167, 2199, 2221
   John B. 110
   John L. 434
   John R. .. 275, 651, 652
   John S. 1000
   John T. 106
   Jonas 670
   Joseph 822
   Joshua 245
   Levi 375
   Lewey 805, 806
   Lydia 965
   Margaret H. 2307
   Mary B. Laughlin . 2279
   Matthew 279
   Mina 508
   Mrs. Elizabeth 180
   Mrs. R. H. 2023

   Nancy 2218
   R. 269
   R. J. 594, 673, 2118
   R. P. 412
   Ray 354
   Rev. James H. 405
   Rev. Thomas B. 381, 383, 971, 2193, 2194, 2279
   Rev. Walter 941
   Richard 495, 1060, 1062
   Richard J. 2098
   Robert 729, 2126
   S. B. 651, 698
   Samuel 940
   Samuel Findley ... 2218, 2219, 2220
   Stephen B. 651, 652, 2149, 2221, 2222, 2307
   T. C. 81, 508, 886
   Thomas M. 277
   Tom C. 594
   W. H. 269
   William .. 80, 568, 2218
   William (Heirs) 811, 1062
   William F. 601
   William H. 848
Clarke
   Charles 662
Clary
   Benjamin 1060
   Carl 354
   Edward 337
   Enoch 921
   Frank 621
   Frank R. 354
   Henry E. 354
   Howard 921
   Jared 956
   John 924
   Nathan 275
   Plummer 924
   Raymond 354
   Washington 919

ALL NAMES INDEX

William 621, 867
Claudy
   Robert 650
Clay
   Cassius M. 146
   Henry ... 111, 112, 113, 114, 117, 131, 132, 136, 139, 140, 198, 216, 217, 234, 460, 519, 534, 630, 674, 675, 676, 742, 813, 950, 962, 2067, 2256
   Hon. Henry 548
Clayton 559
   Joseph 265, 280
Cleary
   Henry 944
   Rosalie 656
Clegg
   Thomas . 115, 127, 848
   William C. 343
Cleland
   E. E. 391
Clements . 231, 254, 1056, 2105
   Abraham 67, 254
   Abraham (Heirs) . 1062
   Charles B. 514
   Hezekiah 252, 253, 254, 1060, 1062, 1067
   James 798, 2188
   Mary 1060
   Mrs. 253
Clendennon
   Nancy ... 959, 960, 961, 2308, 2309
Cleveland
   Grover 598, 599
   President Grover . 162, 163, 164, 165, 166, 167, 525, 625, 759, 2214, 2240
Cline
   Abraham 921
   Jacob 2155

John 970
John H. 350, 354
Peter 2156
Sadie 503
W. O. 503
Clinesmith
   Coon 2017
   Coonrod 278
Clingan
   John 2191
Clinton
   DeWitt 110, 111
   General 906
Clipner
   David 277
   John 276, 277
Clippenger
   Bishop A. R. 400
Clippinger
   Elizabeth Ann 814, 815
   George .. 807, 811, 813
   Israel 811, 814, 815
   John 277
   Joseph 811
   William 811
Clodfelter
   John 822, 1029
Close 833
Cloud
   William 321
Cloyd
   James 889
Clubs
   Political 145
Clutter
   Matthias 956
Coates
   Charles 855
Coburn
   Dr. D. C. 394
Cochins
   Vincent 994
Cochran 502, 509, 537, 2224
   A. 917
   A. C. 262, 499, 652
   Alazannah 2302

Alex 914, 916
Alexander 381, 502, 789, 799, 2302
Basil 601
Charles Avard 366
Clarence 354, 370
Col. William 128
J. W. 1005
James 697
Mrs. Alexander 800
Mrs. Julia 497
Richard Hugh 354
Thomas 277, 811
Thomas B. 2099
William. 115, 123, 746, 954, 956
Cockerel
   Joseph 2190
Cockerell
   B. 601
Cockins
   Robert A. 276
   Simeon 276
   V. 269
   V. B. 2128
   Vincent 278, 988
   William H. 276
Coder
   Rev. W. S. 399
Coe
   John W. 265
Coen 2143
Coffey
   Charles F. 354
Coffield
   James 954
Coffman
   Henry 511
Cogan 618, 619
Cogle
   Lewis 270
Cole
   Hon. Ralph D. 298
Coleman
   J. A. 272
Coleridge
   Samuel Taylor 2270

ALL NAMES INDEX

Coles
  Benjamin....... 649, 921
  Isaac...... 649, 746, 921
  Jesse 919, 921
  John 921
  Solomon 921
Colfax
  Schulyer 155
Collart
  Celistene 350, 354
Collentine
  Henry 1047
Colley 508, 515, 937
  John 2172
  Lydia 934
  Peter 230
  Solomon 934
  William................... 674
Collins 2112
  Allen J. 354
  Attorney W. C. 528
  Captain E............... 411
  Findley 245, 994
  Finley 987
  Jacob................... 2112
  John 279, 822, 994
  Mary 511
  May............... 371, 501
  W. C. 169, 172
  W. H. 371, 501
  William................. 2134
  William B. 747
  William R. 974
Colson
  Desire G. 354
Columbus
  Christopher........... 238
Colvin
  Edward J. 349, 354
  M. L....................... 621
Combs
  Alice 513
  Mahlon 173, 1016
  Mrs. Betsy Scott.. 2159
Comin
  John 391
  Robert................... 272

Comstock
  Edgar P.................. 368
Conan
  Caleb..................... 834
Condon
  John 994
Cone
  B. L. 579
Conger
  Elias...................... 973
Congleton.................. 892
  James.................... 892
  William, Jr. 892
Conkle
  Jacob..................... 988
  Rev. J. H. 586
Conkling
  Senator 759
Conn
  G. F........................ 265
  George 761
  Neva...................... 508
Connelly
  Bessie.................... 367
  John 567
  Miss Bessie 337
Conner 819
  Ada........................ 510
  Belle 2237
  Catherine Reasoner
    1024
  Dr. R. S. 2161
  E. W. 91
  Earl......... 349, 354, 370
  Edra....................... 369
  Edra W. 354
  Edward L. 354
  Elizabeth 1024
  Ernest W. 498
  George 2113
  James.................... 994
  John 246, 994
  John, Jr.................. 994
  Joseph (Heirs) 1029
  Katy Reasoner.... 1018, 1019
  Lucy....................... 501

  Mary C. 988
  Nancy 988
  R. S. 989
  Robert 69, 1029
  Samuel 258
  Thomas E. 1024, 1025, 1029
  William E. 276
Conrad
  Abraham 695
  Wesley H. 354
Conrath
  Walter C. 498, 499
Conroy
  James W................ 354
  John 354
Consky
  D. P........................ 124
Conway
  General T. W. 158
  John 649
  Samuel 1060
Conwell
  Josiah 494, 1059, 1060, 1062
Cook .. 48, 232, 632, 1056, 2110, 2143, 2178
  A. E.... 695, 2106, 2178
  Alfred 695
  Allen..................... 921
  C. B....................... 618
  Capt. Thomas 574
  Capt. Thomas B..... 241
  Captain Thomas ... 232, 804, 805
  David................... 2133
  Elizabeth 811
  George 461
  George (Heirs)..... 1060
  Isaac................ 62, 601
  J. B...................... 2178
  John 762
  John B. .... vi, 277, 285, 286, 287, 288, 289, 302
  Joseph 889
  Josiah 494

ALL NAMES INDEX

Laura Haines 623
Milton 621
Mrs. John B. ... 287, 288
Noah 601, 2099
Provost Marshal John
    B. 8, 68, 99, 709
Sarah 908
Thomas 9, 110, 111,
    635, 771, 804
Thomas, Jr. 805
Thomas, Sr. ... 804, 805
William 245
William G. 956
Cooke
    Thomas 67, 495
    Wm 806
Coolidge
    President Calvin ... 177,
      179, 180, 181, 625,
      2216
Cooney
    John 354
Cooper
    Abraham 747, 994,
      1031
    C. W. 377
    Charles 500
    Charles F. 354
    Charles L. 354
    Cloma 500
    Dr. 2264
    Dr. C. W. 380
    Francis 282
    Isaac 2156
    James 494
    James K. 153
    John 822
    Lozia 509
    Lozie 513
    Myers Y. 181, 182
    Peter 158
    Ralph K. 354
    Stanton 509
    Thomas 938
Cope 2133
    Dr. 56
    Dr. Nathan P. 2160

Jane Black 2160
Samuel 954
Copeland
    Jacob (Heirs) 974
    James 884
    Joseph 276
    Lizzie 268
    Thomas 1016
Copick 409
    Isaac 910
Copus ... 8, 835, 838, 2291
    James 250, 251, 836
    Mrs. 252
Corbet 41
    Peter 41, 393, 566,
      646, 849, 2173,
      2192, 2199
Corbett
    Charles R. 354
Coril
    Abner 279
Cornelius
    Ben H. 354
    Cora 509
    Hayes A. 349, 354
Cornell
    John 839
    Richard 834, 839
Cornwall
    Albert 354
Cornwallis
    General Charles .. 2287
Corson
    O. T. 444
Cortelyou
    George 528
Corvin
    Mr. 494
Corwin
    Benjamin S. 67
    Kathrine 508
    O. G. 507
    Ora 508
    Senator Tom 65
    Sumner O. 354
    Thomas 121, 137, 568,
      602, 813, 2256

Tom 131, 132, 133,
    134, 139, 146, 593,
    2067
Corwyn
    Peter 230, 950, 954,
    956
Corzine
    John 272, 974
Cosgrave
    Henry 279
    Henry E. 279
Cosgrove
    Augusta 989
    C. C. 335, 653
    Henry 988
    J. 100
    James 934
    John 275
    W. 989
    W. B. 81, 989
    William .. 753, 754, 989
    Wilson ... 501, 993, 996
Coston
    Zarah H. 2191
Coulter 1028, 2220
    David 1029
    Elijah 849
    Elizabeth 1029
    James 848
    James M. 276, 282
Coultrap
    David 956
Couplin
    J. O. 499, 502
    James O 95
Courtenay
    Mrs. William H., II2046
Courtney
    Dr. H. W. 380
    H. W. 377
Courtwright
    Rev. C. W. 972
Couts
    Ikey 942
    Isaac 941, 942, 943
    William 941
Covert 985, 987

ALL NAMES INDEX

Eli 2160
Cowan
  Alex 129
  Alexander 1031
  Andrew 696
  Andrew M. 276
  John 996, 1029
Cowden 431
  David 124, 432, 433, 649, 921, 924
  Dr. D. L. 606
  James 610
  Paul 606
  Russell 606
  W. N. 654, 783
  William .. 115, 932, 957
  William, Jr. 921
  William, Sr. 921
Cowen 70, 2099
  B. S. 66
  Benjamin S. 56, 105, 121, 122, 133, 137, 2106
Cowgill
  Acquilla J. 649
  Clarence A. 354
  Jennie Bonnell 511
  Joseph 115, 129, 1037, 1048
  Lewis 276
  Mollie 2138
  Philip 227
  Ralph 947
  W. C. 2138
Cox
  Alexander 867
  Chester 604, 605
  Church 124, 867
  Clarence H. 354
  David 176, 488
  Ephraim 129, 1016
  Gov. James M. 337, 346
  James M. 175, 176, 177, 178, 522
  Joseph 822
  Peter P. 994, 996

Raymond G. 354
Roy A 354, 369, 370, 503
Russel I. 503
Russell 369
Russell I. 178, 354, 370
S. S. 151
Samuel S. ('Sunset') 151, 152
Coxe 55
Coxey
  Jacob S. 958
Coyle 559
  John 1062
  Joseph 245
  Ross 282
Coyne
  Otis G. 354
Crabbe
  Attorney General C. C. 180
Craft
  Daniel 2154
  H. H. 655
  Howard 501
  William H. 276
Craig 55, 164, 262, 586, 614, 646, 678, 808, 1036, 2047, 2069, 2103, 2105, 2181
  Arthur 617
  C. A. 106
  Cyrus F. 2182
  Dr. C. A. 2185
  Elizabeth 2182
  Emily 500
  Frederick G. 2182
  John 106, 115, 277, 649, 650, 703, 1062
  John Kackley 366
  Lydia 302
  Margaret 703
  Margaret McFadden 2182
  Martha 302
  Mary 703

Miss Martha 268
Mr. 2069
Mrs. C. A. 186, 516, 517
Mrs. Fred C. 516
Robert F. 276
S. 2128
S. A. 518, 583
Samuel . 128, 586, 649, 651, 662, 702, 703, 712, 820, 2106, 2181, 2182, 2263
Samuel A. 354, 2182
Samuel A., Jr. 368, 2182
Samuel A., Sr. 2182
Sarah 502
V. D. 494
William 696, 1028, 1029
Cramblet
  John, Jr. 1048
Cramblett
  Eli B. 276
  Ray M. 354
  Samuel 354
Cramer 46
  Elizabeth 890, 891
  Henry 892
  Mrs. E. 884
Cramford
  G. W. 602
Cranage 2133
Cranston
  Archibald 954
  James 954
  John 945, 954
  Mary 2303
  Miss A. 268
  Thomas 71, 954
  William 954
Crause
  William 921
Craven
  Major 271
Crawford
  Bertha 501

ALL NAMES INDEX

Hugh 1047
James 988
John 834
Maude 508
Rebecca 833
Robert 938, 1029
Robert B. 276
Thomas 988
W. B. 1025
W. H. 111, 112
William B. 994
William C. 258
William H. 460
Crayton
 Alfred 354
Creighton 230, 787
 Christopher 954
 E. M. 492, 1059
 Elias 621
 Francis ... 93, 144, 261, 289, 625, 2128
 Frank R. 173
 James 1060
 John 1060
 Michael 919, 921
 Mrs. E. M. 492
 William 848
Crepps
 William A. 276
Cresswell
 George 939, 2072
Crisman
 Rev. 272
Cristie
 William B. 2191
Criswell 2143
 D. A. 508
 H. H. 517
 R. C. 391
Crock
 Father 407
 Father Clement H. .. 408
 Rev. Clement C. 515
Crocket
 Davy 2277
Crofford
 John 703

Cronebaugh
 C. L. 444
Crook
 Jackie 672
 John 651
Crooks
 Henry 789
 John 121, 123, 789, 2099
Cropper
 Dallas S. 337, 354
 Harold M. 354
Crosby
 Miss Marie E. 439
Cross 833
 Robert L. 354
 Samuel 691
Crossen
 J. C. 265
 Jason S. 280
 John C. 88, 169
 Joseph M. 279
 Paul 2065
 Thomas 980
Crouch
 Frank 2093
 Joseph C. 276
 Mrs. 2092, 2094
Crouse
 Jacob, Sr. 892
 William 703, 919
Crow
 Alexander 1029
 Annie Williams 510
 H. K. 501
 Homer J. 752
 Isaac 852, 855
 Michael 2158
 William 994
 William J. 752, 994
Crowles
 Rev. Samuel 2199
Croy
 John 2155
Croyle
 Daisy 510
Crozier 989

J. A. 989
Cruiser
 Henry 867
Crum
 Rev. John 399
Crumbacker
 J. H. 887
Crume
 F. J. 761
Crumton
 William D. 279
Cruser
 Henry 522
Crusoe
 Henry 865
Crusser
 Alexander L. 865
Cubbison
 John 354
Culbertson 2011, 2300
 Attorney Samuel 67
 Benjamin 934, 938
 Hugh 834
 J. 124
 Jacob 924
 James .. 277, 282, 1029
 John 834
 Joseph 849
 Margaret 832
 Mary E. 508
 Mr. 851
 Robert 834
 Robert F. 282
 Samuel 66
 Thomas 834
 William 166, 789
Culhan
 John 354
 William J. 354
Cullen
 James 848, 855
 William 848
Culler
 E. J. 623
Culver
 John 994
 John J. 276

ALL NAMES INDEX

Listen B. 276
Cumberland
    Emanuel 412
    Greenleaf 412
    Rev. Greenleaf 671
Cuming
    Fortescue ..... iv, 46, 48, 49, 50, 228, 580, 2043
Cummings
    William H. 279
Cummins
    Joel B. 276
    John 241
    William 956
Cunard
    J. C. 2099
    Jonathan B. 2107
Cunnard
    Jonathan 939, 2072
Cunningham 873, 884, 1056, 2200, 2302
    Andrew 892
    David 492, 674
    Edward 811, 1060, 1062
    J. 269
    James . 811, 892, 1016, 1060
    James L. 282
    James T. 265, 280
    John 747
    John, Jr. 1016
    John, Sr. 1016
    Mattie 268
    Mr. 884
    Russell J. 354
    Samuel 1016
    Thomas 278, 1060
    William. 270, 867, 903, 2191
    William C. 276
Curran
    George 515
Currell
    Benjamin 924
Current

John 270
Westley 270
Curry
    Jacob L. 279
    James 921
    Otway 129
Curtis
    Charles E. 181, 182, 183
    Daniel 996
    George W. 697
    Mary 2273, 2274
    Miss Josephine 497
Cusac
    R. A. 258
Cusic
    M. 989
Cusick
    Michael 988
Cutler
    Ephraim 2159

D

D'Yarmett
    Daniel 568
Dainfer
    Harrison 275
Dallas
    Estam M. 354
    Leonard 939, 2072
    Sadie 511, 512
Dalzell
    James M. 299
    'Private' J. M. 165, 2227
Danford
    Abraham 87, 649
    Harold B. 354
    Hiram 2154
    Ira E. 354, 502
    J. E. 510
    Lorenzo . 105, 156, 157
    Samuel 2154
    Virgil H. 354
Daniel
    E. 988

Daniels
    D. 2106
    Eleanor 509
    G. H. 989
    J. H. 989
Danielson 55
Danley
    Arthur 789
Dante 722
Darby 833
Darling
    Mrs. M. 268
Darr
    Conrad 938
    Philip 1048
Dart
    Harold 369
Dartt
    Roy E. 354
Daubs
    John 1009
Daugherty 1019
    David 2136
    Edward 1012, 1016
    Harry M. 171
    J. T. 1014
    James 994
    John 833, 1014
    Joseph 635
    Robert 354
    W. S. 279
    William 94
    William S. 157
Daughterty
    Edward .. 122, 123, 129
Davenport
    John 105, 892, 948, 2313
Davey
    Gov. Martin L. 74
    Martin L. 181, 182, 184, 185, 186
    William A. 280
Davids
    Ben 95
Davidson . 871, 872, 1015, 1019

ALL NAMES INDEX

A. J. 502
B. 865
John B. 354
Margaret 512
Rev. 261, 263, 399
Rev. T. 257
William 278
Davis 538, 589, 678, 2055, 2185
   A. C. 265
   Alexander C. 280
   Bessie 504
   Carson B. 100, 173
   Clarence 354, 369
   Clyde. 354
   Darius 621
   Edward 245
   Elijah 604
   Elza Z. 276
   Ensel L. 354
   Francis 507
   Fred 653
   G. W. 258
   George H. 498, 499
   H. O. 515
   Harry L. . 178, 179, 180
   Henry 245
   Henry G. 171
   Henry O. 354
   James ... 258, 262, 601, 617, 781, 2134, 2185
   James E. 354
   James V. 696
   Jeff 151, 152
   Jefferson 532
   Jeremiah G. 278
   John 151, 355, 798, 976
   John C. 355
   John N. 695
   John W. . 173, 179, 180
   John, Jr. 502
   Jonathan 646
   Joseph 819, 824
   Joshua ... 231, 278, 646
   Josiah 269

   Manlove 696
   Mrs. E. 865
   Mrs. Emma B. 2017
   Nathan M. 279
   Nehemiah 996
   O. H. 696
   'Quaker John' 566
   Raymond R. 355
   Robert A. 2143
   Theodore N. 355
   Thomas 498
   Thompson 974, 976
   W. A. 2133
   W. K. 697
   William. 280, 285, 286, 289
   William K. 696, 2167
   Wm. 434
   Zadoc 67, 800
   Zadock ... 69, 646, 798, 811, 2106
   Zedoc 805
Dawes
   B. G. 105
   Beman G. 104, 170, 171
   Charles G. 179
   General R. R. 165
Dawson
   Clancy W. 355
   Harry A. 355
   James 277
   Levi 1048
   May 510
Day
   Alfred 2243
   Amos 73, 2152
   Amrah 568
   Arura 1062
   Elizabeth J. Rea ... 2243
   Levi 412
   Lewis 834
   Phebe 1062
   Walter 1062
Daymuth
   Steve 355
Dayton

   Delmar T. 355, 368, 498
   Jacob 279
De Francis
   Daniel 803
De Joinville
   Prince 548
De Long
   Florence 501
   J. W. 507
De Witt
   Rev. Luke 972
Deal
   Charles M. 503
   Gertrude 503
   Richard 503, 921
   William 2156
Dean
   Alexander 279
   F. W. 677
   Harvy G. 355
   Henry 994
   Horace S. 355
   Joseph 197
Deardorff
   Christian 70
deBaurenfeind
   Frank E. 639
Debbs
   Eugene V. 168
Debolt
   Jeremiah 2154
DeBritner
   Thomas 245
Debs
   Eugene V. 173, 174, 175
Deck
   Nicholas 974
Decker
   John 867
   Joseph 867
   Mrs. 865
   Theodore A. 280
Deeble
   J. E. 258
Deeran

ALL NAMES INDEX

Thomas 994
Deeren
   Cora 512, 513
   John 1005
   Raymond C. 355
   T. D. 510
   Thomas 822
Deets
   Benjamin............... 282
   John 822
   Jonathan 2196
   Nancy 375
DeFrance 2184
   Daniel.................... 825
   DuQuesne 825, 826
Degenhart
   Charles, Sr............. 515
Dehart
   Cornelius............... 855
   Jemima 2086
   William 855
DeHart
   W. P. 84
   William 853
Delaney
   Roy 514
   Stewart R. 355
Delano
   Columbus 153
Delarne
   John 822
Delehanty 618
   Joe 619
Delilah 2006
Delong
   James 974
DeLong 2152
   David 245
   Isaac 247
   Jacob 2191
   James 66, 94, 145, 246, 258, 261, 2107, 2117
   John 128, 2155
   Judge James 713
Dement

William 67, 85, 87, 2061
Demosthenes 439
Dempsey
   Rev. D. L. 77
Demyon
   Michael 355, 369
Denfenbach
   Isaac 279
Dennis
   Adam 974
   David 277, 994
   Fletcher J. 278
   Harvey 276
   Howard H. 355
   Jacob 747, 988, 994
   James 696
   John 1030, 1031
   Peter 275
   Rev. I. 399
   Thomas 246, 1037
   William 275
   William, Sr............. 994
Dennison
   A. S. 375
   Elias 822
   Governor William . 146
   Henry (Heirs) 822
   J. W. 697
Denniss
   John 822
   William 822
Denny 619
   Artie Erven 511
   Ralph 339, 355
   William L. 639
Denoon
   S. 972
   Samuel 2019
Dent
   George H. 123
Depew 559
   Abraham 649
   James 974
Derby
   Joe 355
   Steve 355

Desallums
   John 849
Deselm
   B. F. 84, 204, 515
   Blanche S. 516
   James 279
   John 844
   Jonathan 279
   Mrs. T. R. 556
   Robinson 282
   T. R. 169, 515, 518, 656
   Thomas 848
   W. D. 84, 173
   W. Kirk 185, 639
   Wilbur D. 639
   Wilbur K. 355
Desmond
   Countess of 723
Devault
   William 938
Devine
   M. F. 656
Devinney 833
   Aaron 892
   James 1062
   Joseph 833
Devolld 231, 810
Devore
   Fred R. 355
   Mrs. W. P. 2206
   Odessa 512, 514
   W. P. 515
Dew
   David 849
Dewey 477, 2148
   Thomas E. 2149
DeWitt
   Bernard 245
   Paul 247, 1037
   Rev. Luke 2194
Deyarmet
   Daniel 691
Dick
   Johnson 869
Dickens
   John 811
   Jonah 669

ALL NAMES INDEX

Sam 2070
Simeon 2134
Dickerson 819, 1003
  Asa 142
  Eliza 1006
  Frederick 747, 889
  Joshua 822
  Kinzie 24, 25
  Mary 956
  Oliver 355
  Richard 819
  Simon 819
Dickinson
  Joshua 277
  Seth J. 696
Dickson
  Francis 70, 1030
  John .. 567, 1028, 1030
  Joshua 282
  Peter 849
  Samuel 277
  Thomas 277, 282
Diehl
  Clem L. 295
  Jennie A. 629
  William C. 514
Diggins
  W. A. 444
Dillahay
  John 277
Dillea
  Herbert 2267
Dillehay
  Cornelius ... 2095, 2096
Dilley 435, 2192, 2266, 2267
  Aaron 2266
  Abraham 245, 971, 2234, 2266, 2267
  Abraham, Sr. 976
  Abram .. 566, 966, 968, 972
  Anna 2266
  Ayer 2266
  Clara 2267
  E. M. 125, 629
  Elizabeth Lowery 2267

Ephraim 966, 971, 2266, 2267
Ephraim M. 2267
Ephraim, Jr. 974, 2266, 2267
Ephraim, Sr. . 241, 974, 2266
Florence 367
Hannah 2266
Hannah McDonald
  2267
Helen 511
Ichabod 245
J. H. 630
J. R. 502
James L. 276, 2267
James M. 355
James V. 605, 2267
Jane W. McCleary 2267
Joseph 968, 2266, 2267
Joseph B. 279
Lucy 2267
Lucy U. Ayer 2266
Mary 2234
Mayor J. H. 424
Mr. 605
Otho E. 2267
R. H. 509, 511
Rachel Henry 2267
Richard H. 276
Robert .. 115, 965, 974, 976, 2266, 2267
S. M. 972
Samuel 2266, 2267
Samuel M. 499, 965, 2267
Sarah Burkley 2267
William 279, 974, 2266, 2267
Dillie 930
Dillon 957, 2301, 2302, 2306
  Charity 2305
  Christopher 955
  Eleanor 2301
  George 2196
  Henry 867

Herschel L. 355
James . 67, 85, 87, 112, 800, 2061, 2258, 2301
James (Heirs) 954
John 1048
Mr. 2301
Nathan 277
Paul F. 355
Samuel 944
Sarah 2306, 2307
Sidney H. 355
William .. 277, 944, 955
Dinga
  John 366
Dissirms
  James 275
Dithridge 618
  Will 619
Ditto
  Norman W. 355
Dix
  Ralph M. 185, 639
Dixon
  Frank 355
  Henry 939, 2072
  John 73, 114, 129, 552, 1048, 2170
  John (Heirs) 646
  William 2191
Doakley
  Thomas 646
Doal
  Rev. W. 438
Dobbins
  William C. 886
Dobbs
  John 994
Dodd
  Clarence E. 355
  Lawrence 355
Doddridge
  Dr. Joseph 65, 403, 404
Dodds
  Archibald 566, 798
  William A. 277
Dodshon

ALL NAMES INDEX

Archdeacon J. H. ... 405
Dodson
  Byron N. 355
Dolan
  Mark 355
  Mike 355
Dollison
  Edith 370
  Frank S. 514
  J. B. . 90, 169, 172, 657
  J. H. 509
  James M. 355
  Jasper 917
  John 824, 965
  Lucinda 965
  M. E. 507
  Sheriff J. B. 169
Dollman
  Cyrene J. 278
  William 994
Dolman
  John 989
  Samuel 989
  William 501, 989
Donahey
  Governor Vic 94
  Vic 109, 178, 179, 180, 522
Donahoo
  John 1060
Donaldson
  Rev. Newton 972
  William S. 275
Donaway
  Widow 1020
Donchonchett
  Dr. Francis 697
Donley
  James 849
  John 834
Donover
  C. 245
  Christopher, Jr. 574
  Christopher, Sr. 242, 574
Dornon
  Clarinda 500

Thomas E. 339, 355, 498, 499
Dorsey
  G. V. 150
Dosin
  James 434
Dotson
  G. C. 509
Doty
  Carl W. 355
  Rev. 403
  Rev. R. W. 403
  Thomas A. 355
Doudna 409
  Carl B. 355
  Cynah 654
  F. B. 491
  Francis S. 355
  J.   269
  J. W. 499
  Jesse 654, 923
  John 923, 929
  Noas 910, 923
Dougherty 2073
  Andrew 245
  Anna M. 512
  David 245
  Edward 69
  H. A. 936
  R. V. 2073
  W. 100
  William 2107
Doughty 1049
  Betty 552
  Chief 11, 20, 21, 28, 552, 1043, 1049, 1050, 1051, 2273
  H. C. 610
Douglas 859
  Albert 924
  David 272, 277, 924
  David D. 282
  David, Jr. 855
  David, Sr. 855
  J. C. 441, 459, 708
  J. L. 506
  James 277

Jane 923
John C. 651
Joseph 270
Mrs. J. L. 741
Richard 131
Samuel 855
Stephen A. 145, 146
Walter 503
William .. 106, 277, 855
William H. 275
Douglass
  J. C. 447
Doup
  Henry 1060
Dow 663
  Lorenzo 9, 65, 533, 534, 2062
  Neal 161, 162
Dowdell
  W. W. 509
Dowell
  Frank 507
Downard
  Daniel 867
  David 867
Downer 864
  Andrew 275
  Benjamin 800
  David 870
  Jake 806
  James 295
  Mrs. Benjamin 800
  Nathan 258
  Newton 275
  Sarah M. 508
  William 275
Downerd 2200
  Earl M. 355
  Glenn B. 355
  John S. 355
  William F. 355
Downey
  Catherine 1009
  Merryman 996
  Miley F. 355
  Mr. 120
Downs

ALL NAMES INDEX

Eliza Potts 293
Upton 293
Doyle 1056
John 1060
Matthew 1060
Miss Ina 497
Draher
Earl H. 368
Drake 481, 743
John 2158
Widow 230
William 855
Drakely
Thomas 856
Draper
C. 989
George 279
John 988
Drew
David 1057
Driesbach
Herr 2099
Driggs
W. H. 626
Drummond 559
Rev. James 138, 521
S. B. 262
Samuel B. 646
Drury
John H. 355
Dryden 1019
Robert 867
Samuel 1016
DuBois
Homer L. 355
Ducher
Abraham 811
John 957
Ducker
William 2104
Dudley
Alice 510
Belle 504, 510
Elsie 502
George H. 821, 2113
Guy A. 355
H. E. 515

Lawrence 355
Linnie 508
Ray 355
Ray G. 180
Rex F. 355
Duensing
Christopher 892
Duff
Alexander 849
Andrew 849
David 603, 746
Frank N. 355
Fred 299
Fred R. 605, 606
George .. 115, 126, 789
James 849
John 278, 849
Oliver E. 849
Robert 844, 2107
Samuel 621, 746
Samuel D. 603
William 849
Duffey
A. C. 652
C. T. 515
Charles T. ... 639, 2139, 2141
George 856
Thomas J. 184
William 621, 855
Duffie 10
George 833, 834
Duffy
Alice 509
W. C. 506
Dugan 1056, 2224
Attorney G. D. 2012
G. D. 93, 169, 204
George D. 91, 172, 180
H. M. 166
Henry M. 91
James 494, 807, 811
John 515
Mrs. James 807
Norma 369
Robert 381
Thomas 280

W. K. (Kenna) 337
William K. 355
Duhammel
Amos 956
Duke
Col. Basil W. 314
Colonel 303
Dull
David 856
Dumbruski
Henry 355
Dunbar
Dr. 150
J. 261, 629
John 282
John, Jr. 867
John, Sr. 867
Marcellus 355
Duncan 873, 2223
Adam 867
Anna 2297
C. C. B. 441
Dr. James .. 9, 788, 789
Elizabeth Harvey 2222, 2223
J. M. 391
James 391, 867
James (Heirs) 867
John 892, 947, 948, 949, 954, 956, 2067, 2222, 2223
Rev. James 728, 787
Rev. John R. 385
Dunfee
Carrie 511, 513
Mrs. Cecelia 186
Dunheifer 559
Dunheiffer
Jacob 798
Dunifer
Edward R. 277
Harrison 258
John 277
L. A. 467
Duniver
Christopher 2163
J. O. 621

ALL NAMES INDEX

W. H. 464
Dunlap
  A. J. 601
  Charles K. 355
  James 56
  Joseph 919
  Major James 124, 520, 557, 558, 574
  Marshal 560
  Nancy M. 558
Dunlevy
  Joseph 994
Dunn
  Samuel 144
  Thomas 227
  William 227, 1060
Dunning
  Mural 514
  Robert 278, 824
Durbin
  Dr. 65
  Howard L. 355
  Rev. 570
Durm
  Samuel 129
Durner
  Abner 921
Dusouchet
  Capt. Francis 762
  F. 457
  Francis 567
Dusouchett
  Francis 73
Dusz
  Charles 355
  Mary 502
Dwiggins
  James 1012
  John 1014, 1016
  Robert 834
  Sylvester 834, 1012
  W. A. 202, 539, 600
Dye 2073
  Firnean 996
  George .. 245, 250, 251
  James 247, 856
Dyer

Capt. James B. 289
David C. 498
Hugh 811, 844
James C. 350, 355
Dylks
  Joseph C. 730, 731, 732, 733, 734, 735, 736, 737
Dyson 507, 970, 1003, 1004, 1006
  Aquila 913
  Aquilla 923, 924
  Christina 400
  Christina M. 402
  Elijah 67, 81, 86, 90, 426
  John B. 73
  Joseph .. 69, 123, 1005, 1007
  Lawrence 924
  Maggie 510
  Mary 400, 502
  Property Lister Elijah 68
  Sarah 402
  Sarah M. 402
  Sheriff Elijah 2009
  Squire 1005
  Thomas A. 402
  Worthy 94, 174, 447
Dzubay
  Father 408

E

Eads
  Superintendent of Construction 608
Eagleson
  Alexander 807, 811
  Freeman T. ... 106, 107, 676
  Hon. Freeman T. ... 298, 817
  James 807
  Joseph 807
  Katherine 807

Martha 807
Rev. A. G. 381, 972
Thomas 494
Eagleton
  John 811, 813, 814
Eagon
  Florence 503
  James 974, 2155
  John 2155
  William S. 279
Eakin
  J. G. 269
  J. H. 503
  James 504
  James H. 503
  Leitta 504
  Vincent H. 278
Earich
  Austin E. 511
Earl
  Ernest 355
  Rev. Alfred 2196
Earle
  Grace 369
Earley
  Francis L. 355
  George A. 355
  Roger A. 355
Early
  Chauncey 355
  John .. 515, 1044, 1045
  Jordan 669
  Joseph 669
  Rev. 1045
Eastman
  Jonathan 246
Eaton 2200
  Edward 2174
  J. W. 1059
  James 494
  James H. 1059
  Joel H. 265
  Joel M. 280
  Joseph 242, 808
Eberle
  Adelia 503
  C. W. 656

ALL NAMES INDEX

Harry M. 355
Margaret 370
Pauline 503
Eberly
Rev. 399
Eckelberry
George 844
Lieutenant 2017
Eckler
Samuel 1031
Eddy
Almon E. 355
Frank 350, 355
Govenar R. 355
Edeary
Saline 833
Edenburn 2073
Ederley
George 970
Mary Ann Keil 970
Edgar
James 2156
John R. 277
Edie 2224
Catharine 1048
Joseph 113
William 57, 381
William, Jr. 1048
Edinburn
Miss 1013
Edmonds
Wilbert C. 355
Edson
Dan 229
Edwards
Beryl F. 355
Isaac 1016
James 245, 649
Joseph 938
Lewis 649
Louis 1012
Nathan 105
Sarah 936
Effard
Jean 2050
Egbert
Jerome 277

Eggar
C. C. 355
Egger
Clifford 369
Clifford C. 370
H. C. 656
Eichbaum 46
Eichelberger 646
Eisenhart
Captain Merritt 411
Eldon . 377, 701, 917, 927, 2018
Elery
J. M. 491
Elizabeth
Queen 2050
Ellenwood
L. W. 169
Ellicott 724
Elliott
Charles 2191
Robert W. 355
S. L. 502
Simon 278
Ellis
Homer C. 355
John F. 697
M. 2191
Seth 168
William T. 56, 437
Ellison
Rev. 272, 294, 2123
Ellsworth
Isaac 956
James W. 479
Leroy Wesley 675
Elsworth
Isaac 682
Eltringham
Ira 355
Elwood
Abel 183
Embree
Auldy 924
Emde
Harry W. 514
Emerson . 974, 2268, 2269

Ezekiel 71, 112
Ezekiel, Jr. 2268
Ezekiel, Sr. ...974, 2268, 2269
George 919, 2268, 2269
John 974, 2268
Noah A. 160
Patience Burlingame
.......................2268
Ralph Waldo 904, 2119, 2268
S. S. 649
Scott 965, 974, 2268
Sewell 123, 125
Thomas 974, 2268
William G. 703
Wm. G. 703
Emery
James, Sr. 913
William, Jr. 480
Emler
Clyde P. 355
Emmons
Stephen 994
Endley . 48, 114, 231, 669, 807, 825, 826, 833, 2061, 2083
George A. 650
J.   269
J. R. 507
Jacob 113, 195, 808, 811, 1060, 1062
William 84, 144
William H. 2107
Eng 2092
England
Mary H. 2242, 2243
Engle 1023, 2073, 2094
Asa 1016
Drusilla 1013, 2093
James E. 355
Levi.. 1013, 1016, 2093
Mary 936
Moses F. 276
Englehart 2224

ALL NAMES INDEX

William......... 245, 381, 1059, 1060, 1062
English....................... 884
   Howard E. 180
   John 924
   John (Heirs). 892, 1062
   Kinsey O. 355
   Richard.......... 913, 924
   William H. 161, 523, 524
Enoch 712
Enos
   B. F. 93, 174
   John 974
   Mrs. Nellie 2032
Enot
   Michlos Gejza 366
Enslowe.................. 46, 47
Enty
   Elias....................... 798
   John 646
Entz
   John 498
Eoff
   Dr. 2103
Erbes
   Pete 355
Ernest
   Augustus 198
Ernsberger
   Dale D. 355
Errington
   Thomas 265, 280
Erskine 2159
   Frank..................... 337
   Frank R. 355
   J. F. 515
Erven
   George 337
   George B. 355
Ervin
   Ella 511
   Harve 616, 617
Ervine
   Harve 621
Erwin
   Ben 315, 316

Manuel................... 662
Mrs. 315, 316
Robert................. 1031
Eschbaugh
   Carlos 370
Esely
   S. H. 652
Estep
   George .. 787, 844, 849
   J. M. 154
   Mary 2271
   Mrs. 787
   Walter J. 355
Eston
   Frank..................... 355
   Stephen P. 355
Etzlar
   Margaret............. 2306
Eubanks
   Frank P. 355
Euga
   F. J. 491
   Mrs. F. J. 491
Evan 55
Evans 655, 2099, 2163
   Alfred H. 258
   Ashabel 994
   Atty. Nathan 56
   Benjamin............. 1048
   David E. 2133
   Dr. Lester S. ... 381, 385, 497
   Elisha..................... 245
   H. H. 698
   Henry 1060, 1062
   Henry H. 567, 649, 650
   Hon. N. 206
   Lester S. 639
   Major 131
   Mrs. R. 399
   N. 139, 2090, 2098, 2100
   N. E. 2117
   Nathan . 34, 66, 69, 70, 74, 93, 102, 123, 131, 135, 140, 143, 261, 495, 557, 560, 561, 629, 630, 646, 2098, 2163, 2164, 2216, 2239
   Rev. Lester S. 490, 2206
   Rev. William B. 1019
   Susan M. Metcalf Lofland................ 34
   Thomas W. 275
   William J. 994
Everett
   Edward.................. 145
   James 245
Evilsizer
   John 824
   Jonathan 824
Eviston
   George 892
Ewalt
   Robert Morrison ... 366
Ewers
   Miss Clara 623
Ewing......................... 593
   Cyril M. 355
   General Thomas.... 301
   Jemima............... 1027
   Leroy Vincent 366
   Mrs. Paul D. . 396, 438, 541
   Paul D. 549
   Ruth C. 549
   Senator Tom 65
   Thomas 131, 139, 2090, 2167
Ewings
   Robert 245
Eynon
   Harry B. 355
   Percey R. 355
Ezekiel
   Emerson., Jr. 974

F

Fackiner
   C. J. 500, 502, 518
   Dr. C. J. 514

ALL NAMES INDEX

Fairbanks
- Charles W. 171

Fairchild
- J. T. 173, 174, 176
- John 606
- Mrs. 832
- Mrs. Elizabeth 46
- P. T. 46
- Thomas 833, 834
- Walter 606

Fairhurst
- Peter 355

Faltys
- James 355

Family
- Scott 2211

Faris
- Herman F. 179

Farley
- Archibald 279
- Leal E. 355
- Levi 279
- Melville G. 279

Farmer 2112, 2265
- J.   936
- Mr. 2133
- Rev. Roy I. 395

Farnsworth
- Madison 355

Farrar
- Andrew 994
- Capt. W. M. 2168
- Capt. William M. ... 551, 2216, 2217
- Captain 263
- Captain W. M. 945
- Captain William M. 592, 593, 594
- Hon. W. M. 80
- James 994
- Joseph 996
- Mayor W. M. 524
- W. M. 79, 155, 261, 629
- William H. 2117
- William M. ..... vi, 9, 91, 106, 157, 161, 255, 466, 590, 591, 592, 651, 2106, 2128

Faught
- Arthur 480
- Arthur G. 498
- Howard E. 93, 186

Faulkner
- R. R. 509

Feaster
- Gabriel H. 277

Featherstone
- Joseph 276

Fehrman
- Delbert Foster 366

Felker
- Rev. A. C. 402

Fell
- Conductor 257

Felton
- Rev. A. R. 402

Fenwick
- Alice 513

Ferbrache .. 41, 600, 2269, 2270, 2271
- Code 600
- Daniel 39, 698, 798, 803, 2269, 2270, 2271
- David 2271
- Elizabeth Underhill 2271
- Isaac 854
- Jacob ... 798, 849, 2172
- Jacob N. 2271
- James 800, 2269
- James D. 276
- John 2269
- John W. 279
- Judith 2269, 2271
- Judith Sarchet 2269, 2270, 2271
- Mary 2269
- Mary Estep 2271
- Mr. 840
- Nancy 2271
- Thomas 800, 849, 2269

Ferguson 574, 2015, 2271, 2272
- Andrew 2271
- Capt. John 263
- Captain 262
- Captain Joseph B. 'Cap' 2272
- Carrie 595
- Col. John 271, 273, 2015, 2132, 2138, 2251, 2272
- Colonel John 524, 662, 999, 1000
- David McKinley 355
- Emory 653
- Everett 355
- H. C. 695
- Hall 616
- Hayes 355, 368
- J.   2117
- J. B.. 81, 161, 300, 335, 339
- Jacob 601, 695
- James 849
- Jemima Schaffer . 2272
- John 66, 81, 88, 93, 107, 114, 115, 124, 144, 255, 256, 258, 261, 272, 275, 495, 558, 713, 892, 2014, 2081, 2124, 2128, 2271, 2272
- Joseph B. 275
- June 2271
- Lemen 1060
- Lemon 649
- Louisa E. Bute 2272
- Margaret 2271
- Mary 2272
- Mrs. J. B. 491
- Rev. 320
- Rev. William 972
- Rev. William M. 381, 2194, 2224, 2225
- Samuel 649
- Samuel (Heirs) 955
- Thomas 955

V. 699
William 54, 73, 95, 461, 798, 2060, 2061, 2271, 2272
William M. 56, 624, 2055
Ferrall
　Clyde L. 498
Ferre
　J. 989
　Joel 989
Ferree
　John 1030
Ferrell 230, 2313, 2314
　Hon. Joseph 2138
　Joseph 106, 2138, 2257, 2314
　Mary Morton 2314
　Mary Paxton 2314
　Mrs. Anne 884
　Sophia Anderson 2314
　William 2314
　William (Heirs) 955
Ferren
　Harry 618
　W. H. 174, 176
Ferris
　John 2152
Ferryman
　John 279
Fess
　Senator Simeon D. 182
　Simeon D. 109
Field
　James G. 165
Fields
　Addison D. 355
　Leona 501
　Vincent 923
　William 355
Fiester
　John W. 198
Fife
　Jacob L. 280
　Walker 95
　Walker C. 174
Fillmore 608

President Millard .. 143
Finch
　Thomas 923
Findley
　David 899
　Dr. 440
　Dr. Samuel . 10, 96, 97, 98, 413, 437, 438, 470, 564, 658, 680, 873, 896, 897, 898, 899, 900, 952, 963, 964, 1015, 2067, 2218, 2220
　Dr. Samuel, Jr. 439
　Joseph 974
　President Samuel .. 902
　Rev. Samuel . 385, 386, 901, 949
　Rev. Samuel, Jr. 438, 439
　Rev. Samuel, Sr. 439
　Samuel . 389, 390, 798, 893, 894, 2158
　Samuel, Jr. 899
　William 896
Fink 810
　Dale H. 355
　George 806
　George W. 811
Finley 2192
　Arthur R. 355
　Bert 355
　Betsey 2292, 2293
　Catherine 988
　Cephas 279
　Charlie 604
　Dr. John 2161
　Ebenezer 81, 824
　H. 725
　James 87, 649, 824, 965, 2154
　James B. 2191
　Jeremiah 282
　John 649
　John H. 402
　John R. 355
　Joseph 965

Joseph D. 966
Lee 605
Lester M. 355
Lynn W. 355
Mabel 503
Milton 280, 656
Paul 606
Paul L. 356
R. L. 503
Ray L. 356, 370
Ray M. 356
Rev. 570
Rev. J. B. 376
Rev. James B. 378, 413, 414, 415, 416, 417, 990, 2191, 2213
Robert 834
Roy 350, 356
Samuel .. 402, 974, 988
William 568, 970, 2156
Finn
　Owen 276
Finnefrock
　Jacob 675
Finnegan
　Aunsford E. 356
Finney
　Thomas 894
Firestone
　Ruth 500
Fish
　Samuel 495
Fishel 970, 1003, 1004
　A. P. 1010
　Rebecca 1009
　Sarah 1009
Fishell
　Philip (Heirs) 824
Fisher 934
　David 940
　Jacob 938, 1062
　James 913, 924
　Rev. 524
　Rev. S. S. 528
　Richard S. 279
　S. A. 2199
　Stephen 356

ALL NAMES INDEX

Fisk
- Oran J. 356
- Robert J. 356

Fitzgerald
- Edward 279
- Pearly 356
- Samuel E. 356
- Wilbur 356

Fitzpatrick
- Custer 356

Fitzsimmons
- Catharine 974

Flaherty
- Earl J. 356
- R. J. 515
- Roger 356

Flanagan
- C. A. 1007
- Emma 510
- H. D. 470, 507, 510

Flegor
- Jacob 955, 956

Fleming
- Alexander 811
- B. F. 379
- Bertha 512
- James E. 277, 282
- Russell D. 356
- Thomas 824

Fletcher 416
- A. E. 173
- C. 939, 2072
- John F. 356

Fligor
- Jacob 746

Flood
- Cecelia C. 2028
- Harry J. 356
- John H. 279
- Thomas 923

Floto
- Rev. A. K. 402
- Rev. C. F. 402

Floyd 932
- Allen W. 503
- B. F. 503
- C. E. 509

Fluhart
- Catherine 510

Fogle 262
- Frank 370

Foley
- Delano R. 356

Folkert
- John 276

Foltz
- Fred 2017
- John A. 2017

Foraker 597, 598
- F. R. 370
- Fred R. 356
- Gov. J. B. 2215
- Governor J. B. 164
- J. B. 527
- John 649
- Mary A. 965
- Senator Joseph B. 169, 171

Forbes
- Boyd 955
- Henry 277
- R. S. 272
- Rev. Samuel 2137
- Samuel A. 275, 282

Ford
- Bertom G. 356
- D. C. 621
- George 834
- George B. 91, 174
- John 94
- John C. 145, 261
- Mildred 652
- Robert ... 278, 790, 798
- Russell P. 356
- Seabury 140, 141
- Thomas 869
- William E. 356
- William M. 356

Fordyce 678
- David D. 894
- J. 269

- John 128, 209, 305, 306, 557, 577, 894, 969, 976, 1017, 2020
- John D. 370
- John M. 507
- John W. 508
- Joseph 651, 800
- L. 2156
- Lieut. S. W. 306
- M. 81, 595
- Melville J. 356
- Russell K. 356
- S. W. 265, 304
- Samuel 156, 649, 2019
- Samuel W. 280

Foreacre
- George 974
- Isaac 974
- John 974, 1060

Foreaker
- James 923

Foreman
- John 867
- William H. 279

Forest
- Paul 432

Forney .. 2273, 2274, 2302
- Abraham 762, 1038, 1048, 2273
- Abraham, Jr. 2273, 2274
- Eli 2274
- Eliza J. Wilson 2274
- Elizabeth 2274
- Ellen Walker 2274
- Frederick ... 1048, 2274
- John 1048, 2274
- John R. 356
- Joseph 1048, 2274
- Mary 2273
- Mary A. 2274
- Mary Curtis 2273, 2274
- Solomon 2274
- Sophia 2274
- Susan H. 2274
- Susan Miskimen .. 2274

ALL NAMES INDEX

Forni 2274
Forrest
   Archibald 867
   Gabrill 893
   General Nathan
      Bedford 308
   James 867, 955
Forsythe 368, 479, 508,
   640, 809
   D. W. 989
   David 1030
   David W. 277
   Elijah 790
   Emmitt C. 356
   George 994
   Hugh 389, 390
   James 1028, 1030
   Jane . 988, 2247, 2280,
      2281
   John 893
   John R. 153
   Mary 511
   Mrs. 589
   O. C. 989
   Porter..................... 106
   Porter H. 186, 356, 505
   Preston H. 277, 282
   Rev. 294
   Rev. H. L. 2099
   Rev. Hugh L. ... 963, 964
   Robert 852, 1043, 1060
   Robert H. 282
   Stella Bruce 507
   Thomas 800
   Thomas B. 849
Foster 608
   Benjamin 938
   Charlie 598
   Christian 1048
   Gov. Charles 2148,
      2206
   Jesse 923
   John 129, 987, 994,
      996
   John M. 990
   Josiah 339, 356
   T. V. 176, 2089

   William Z. 179
Fotheringham
   James 956
Foulke
   Judah 923
   Rev. Henry C. 385
Fowler 2159
   Henry 356
   James 356
   John H. 2019
   John W. 277
   Thomas C. 277
   William H. 356
Fox 1028
   George 409
   George K. 919
   Isaac 746, 824
   John 819
   Marion 369
   Marion W. 356
Foy 262, 2073, 2181
   Daniel 811
   Michael 762
   T. 269
   Thomas 992, 2073
   William 798
Fracker
   George 650
Frakes
   Unora 512
Frame 917, 1072, 2192,
   2224, 2275, 2276
   Abraham Raymond 366
   'Big Jim' 2275
   'Big Tom' 2275
   'Captain Jim' 2275
   'Colonel John' 2275
   Daniel 380
   David. 380, 1056, 2275
   David A. 649
   Dr. David 704, 711,
      969, 2293
   Floy 356
   George 2275
   Hon. R. S. 80
   Howard S. 349, 356
   J. 125

   Jacob 1056, 2275
   James ... 247, 381, 974,
      1056, 1060, 2275
   James M. 280
   James of David ... 1060,
      2276
   James of James .. 1060,
      2276
   James of William 1060,
      2276
   James, Jr. 2276
   James, Sr. ... 1060, 2276
   'Jim of Dave' 2275
   'Jim of Jim' 2275
   'Jim of William' 2275
   John 87, 124, 855, 889,
      965, 1048, 1056,
      1060, 2107, 2275,
      2276, 2298
   John, Jr. 974
   'Little Jim' 2275
   'Little Tom' 2275
   'Long John' 2275
   Moses 649, 1056,
      1060, 2275, 2276
   R. S. 106, 157, 447,
      492, 494
   Roland S. 2276
   'Short John' 2275
   Susan 2084
   Sylvester 270, 276
   Thomas 492, 1056,
      2126, 2275
   William ... 66, 112, 461,
      855, 856, 862, 863,
      1048, 1056, 1062,
      2275, 2276
   William D. 87, 461,
      769, 1060, 2276
   William of David. 1060,
      1062, 2276
Francey
   William 867
Francy
   Mrs. J. 865
   William 515, 865
Franklin

ALL NAMES INDEX

Benjamin............ 2282
Dr. Benjamin...... 1032, 1033
Franks
  Mary Jane Leeper 292, 293
  Robert L. 292
Fraser
  Laura 500
Frazey
  D. V. 231
  Samuel (Heirs) 1062
Frazier 47, 196, 767
  Alex 302
  Alexander 126, 275, 790
  David..... 258, 790, 800
  Emma 302
  George 265, 280, 1012, 1017, 2128
  James A. 275
  John 258, 275, 282
  Judge 99, 999, 1000
  Judge W. H. 992
  Judge William H. 1016, 2207
  Mrs. Mary 992
  Mrs. Nancy.......... 1013
  Thomas 291, 292
  W. H. 2217, 2239
  W. T. 258
  William C. 992
  William H. 74, 1015
  William T. 275
Fred
  John D. 1059
Free
  J. N. 536, 537
Freeland
  George 1017
Freeman
  James 824
  Joseph A. 356
  Thomas 974
  Thomas J. 1025
  Truman A. 356
Fremont

John C. 143, 144
French
  Charles R. 356, 499
  Dr. 721, 723
Fresh
  George 867
Frew
  Alexander.. 1060, 1062
Friel
  Clarence E. 356
  Robert E. 356
Friend
  James R. 356
Frisbee
  Betty 501
Fritter
  Eldon 63
Frizzle
  Lloyd 889
Frohman
  Charles 2028
Frost
  Clyde M. 349, 356
  Herman E. 356
  Levi 282
  Postmaster H. E. ..2253
  William 2137
Fry
  Noah S. 650
  Peter 245
Frye 819, 970, 1004, 2276, 2277, 2278
  Dwight 502
  Elizabeth R. 400
  Henry 2276
  Henry F. 400, 824, 2040, 2041, 2277, 2278
  Henry, Jr. 2276
  Henry, Sr. 2277
  Isaac J. 923
  John ... 157, 272, 2276, 2277
  Mary 400
  Nancy Spaid 2287
  Noah 824
  Peter 747, 1060

Sarah 2294, 2295
Sarah Trenner 2041, 2277, 2278
William....... 2158, 2287
Fulk
  I. L. 369, 503
  Ira L. 370
  Mary 504
Fuller 2273
  Andrew 646
  G. T. 725
  Jacob 938
  James 246
  James H. 1048
  Johial 746, 748
  Johiel 938
  Joseph 1048
  Thomas 1037, 1048
  William 855, 856
Fulton 989, 1028
  Bessie 507
  Charles P. 356
  Ebenezer 824
  George 356
  J. D. 635
  James 509
  John 277
  John D. 278
  Joseph 1030
  Marcus 280
  Mary 501
  Rev. William R. 385
  Robert 238
  Samuel 1031
  Walter E. 356
  William 276, 501
  William T. 350, 356
Funk
  Hosea 824
  Hosea B. 798
  Lemuel 696
Funston
  John vi
Funstone 1053
Furney 2274

ALL NAMES INDEX

G

Gabel
  Eugene 356
Gadd
  George A. 356
  Isaiah 938
Gage
  C. S. 657
  Rilla 504
Galbraith
  James 279, 867
  John 1017
Galbreath
  Clarence 356
  Fortune 2160
  James L. 400
Gallagher
  Edmund 2156
  George A. 356
  Hugh 849
  J. M. 503
  James 1060
  John 650
  John M. 503
  Lottie 503
  Robert 649
  William 811
Gallentine
  Abraham 834
  Jeremiah 994
Gallienne
  John 790
Galliger
  Floyd 356
Galligher 435, 680, 787
  Floyd 349, 351
  George W. 509
  John 798
Gallihan
  James 275
Gallintison
  Jeremiah 746
Gallop
  John 805
Galloway 2095, 2111
  Benjamin 824

Caleb 2095
Catherine 2095
E. 601
Elijah 1030
Elizabeth 2095
Enoch ... 124, 746, 923, 2095, 2096
Esther 2095
Esther Coles 2095
George 2095
Harriet 2095
Henry 2095
Homer P. 356
Isaac 2095
James 2095
John 2095
Lowden 811
Lucinda 2095
Maria Perego 2095
Mary 2094, 2095
Nancy 2095
Richard 606
Samuel 155, 2095
Sarah 2095
Sarah Perego 2095
Susan 1025
William 2095
Gallup
  Charles 621
  E. S. 514
  George 2100
  J. 126
  John 288, 571
  M. E. 583
  Widow 2100
  William 279
Gamble 833
  Clark 629
  John 356, 956
  Joseph 504
  William 867
Gander 473, 2159
  David 994, 1009
  Harold 366
  J. S. 821
Gang
  Conrad 514, 630

Mayor Conrad 334
Tillie 508
Garber 435
  Anson D. 349, 356
  H. B. 503, 654
  Harry B. 503
  Jonathan W. 76, 100, 160
  L. S. 169
  Lillian 503
  May 510
  Samuel 974
Gardin
  Wm. 434
Gardiner 957, 2137, 2146, 2301
Gardner
  Asbury 2154
  Frank 509, 621
  Harley Otho 366
  Howard Amazon ... 366
  James 955
  John A. 275
  Ralph V. 356
  Robert L. 356
  Thomas 867
  Thomas, Jr. 867
  Thomas, Sr. 867
  Wilbur 356
  William 955
Garey
  Edward Darlington 366
  Olive 512
  Olive Cameron 511
Garfield
  Abram 523, 1028
  Eliza Ballou .. 523, 1028
  Gen. James A. 591
  General James A. .. 301
  James A. 1028
  James R. 529
  President James A. 8, 65, 78, 161, 162, 521, 523, 524, 525, 527, 598, 625, 711, 2056, 2149, 2208, 2209, 2215, 2216

ALL NAMES INDEX

Garford 175
   A. L. 175
Garland
   Isaac 276
Garner
   John N. .. 182, 183, 184, 185
Garretson
   David 824
   Joseph .. 426, 427, 428, 429
Garrett
   Charles M. 498
   George 515, 976
   Henry H. 280
   James 955
   John 95
   John W. 356, 499
   Joseph 974
   Ray 356
Garrison
   William Lloyd 702, 2119, 2120
Garvin
   John 994
   Moses D. 1048
   William 754, 755
Gary
   Sumner 498, 515
Gaskill
   Abraham 800
   William 356
Gass
   William 856
Gaston 140, 471, 618, 746
   Alexander J. 280
   Attorney Mathew 2239
   Atty. 56
   Charles W. 279
   John W. 279
   M. 261, 577, 579, 2090, 2100, 2107, 2117, 2128
   Mathew 54, 69, 93, 106, 115, 124, 498, 500, 782, 2149, 2186, 2187

Matthew 646
Miss Mollie 257
Shepherd M. 279
Welcome 619
Gatchell
   Jacob 955
Gates
   A. C. 882, 883
   Albert C. 10, 880
   Albert Carpenter ... 882
Gatwood
   Albert Lawrence 366
Gauley
   Robert 571
Gavula
   Father 408
Gay
   Benjamin 1031
   Elizabeth 974
Gazzam
   Joseph P. 956
Gear
   Rev. H. R. 524
Geary 231
Gebhart
   S. 502
Gee
   Charles S. 412
Geese
   Hugh W. 356
   Walter E. 356
George 937
   Alexander 790
   Cyrus P. 277
   Dr. 2160
   Isaac 1017
   James 924
   Jonah 1013, 1017
   Lloyd 640
   Simpson 127, 265, 280, 867
   Western 1017
   William 996, 2110
Gerrick
   John M. 356
   Mike 356
Getchel

Jacob 747
Getz
   Albert 882
Geyer
   Mrs. George H. 421
   N. A. 460
Gibaut
   Sophie 2033, 2034, 2035
Gibbons
   Dr. 913
   John 412
   Miss Laverna 264
   Peter 974, 976
Gibbs
   D. S. 501
   Fred 356
   G. W. 265
   George W. 280
   Harry B. 356
   Mary 2260
   Rachael 2260
   William 2260
Gibeaut
   Captain 263
Gibson 400, 406, 435, 701, 766, 769, 852, 2191
   Abel 858
   Anderson 860
   Angeline 860
   Beyer A. 356
   Boyd T. 356, 370
   C. I. 635, 637
   C. T. 502
   Charles I. 639
   Charlie H. 356
   E. E. 509
   Elizabeth 198, 858
   Elsie 503
   Esther 370, 503
   F. M. 621
   Fred 356
   General W. H. 155
   General William H. 300, 301, 596
   George 858, 923, 1038

George of George 856, 1048
George R. 356
George, Jr. 855, 856
George, Sr... 855, 1048
Harry M................ 356
Henry 858, 1048
Hiram 800, 858
Hugh 955
J. J. 629
J. O. 370
J. T. 503
James... 762, 855, 856, 857, 858, 859, 974, 1062, 2135, 2297
James M................ 860
Jimmy 860
John 247, 356, 853, 854, 855, 856, 858, 859, 923, 948, 956, 1017, 2313
Josie 503
Judith Weaver.... 2297, 2298
Kenneth 356
Leroy 860
Lucinda 858
Margaret J. 860
Marion 621
Martha 858
Mary 504, 858
Matilda Morrison.. 860
Millard H. 356
Milton 860
Mr. 719
Mrs. Jane 1038
Nancy 859, 2011
Nancy M. 860
Naphtah L. 860
P. E. 2141
Porter.................... 270
Porter W. 860
R. O. 503
Robert................. 1048
Robert P............... 282
Rodney.................. 370
Rodney O. 356

Samuel 965, 2154
Samuel A............... 275
Samuel B. 280
Thomas 858
Thomas D.............. 860
Verna R. 503
William. 246, 270, 566, 775, 853, 855, 857, 858, 859, 1037, 1043, 2011
William E............... 356
William H. 621, 860
William, Jr. ... 246, 855, 1048
William, Sr..... 855, 856
Giddings
  Joseph R................. 65
Gidos
  George 356
Giffee 2305
  Benjamin..... 956, 2305
  Benjamin (Heirs) ... 955
  Benjamin, Jr. 2305
  Benjamin, Sr........ 2305
  C. H. 2137
  Eliza L. Kennon.... 2305
  Elizabeth 2305
  Hannah 2305
  Hannah Gilliland . 2305
  J. B. 653, 2305
  James 2305
  Josiah 955, 2305
  Mason 2305
  Miss M. A. 268
  Perry 2305
  Ruth 2305
  Sarah.................... 2305
  Susanna 2305
Giffen
  James G................. 356
  John W.................. 356
  Joshua 1031
Giffin 619
  Thomas 278
Gilbert
  John W................ 2191
  Rev. John............. 2198

Gildea 435
  Daniel.................... 282
  Dr. G. W. 406
  Dr. George W. 977
  Justin J.................. 356
  Paul 356
Gildow
  M. 507
  M. E..................... 507
Giles
  David B. 368
  James W................ 356
Gill
  Barnabas 893
  Elijah 277
  James 855
  Joseph 277
  Mordecai............... 955
  Thomas 279
  Tom....................... 325
  W. H. .. 462, 463, 2103, 2104
  Wesley 884
  William H. 108
Gillespie 589, 2159
  Blaine J. 356
  Byron K. 350, 356, 839
  F. W...................... 504
  Hugh 277
  James 834
  John 834
  Paul S. 356
  Richard 784
  Richard C....... 498, 499
  William.................. 277
  William D. 356
Gillett
  Comfort................. 798
  Horace 893
  J. E. 258
  Jacob 824
  James E. 276
  Jedediah................ 893
  Joseph 649
  Mary 375, 2099
  Oliver P. 894
  Wheeler 893, 894

ALL NAMES INDEX

Gillette
    Charles 356
Gilliland
    Hugh 946
    James .. 87, 2067, 2258
    Laura 2138
Gilmore
    A. A. 377
    Hugh 974
    Ralph Y. 356
Gilpin
    Daniel J. 275
    Elijah 1048
    James 811
    John 806, 957
    John, Jr. 811
    John, Sr. 798
    Matthias 811
    Samuel 811
Gilson
    Nero 807
Ginnis
    John F. 277
Girtler
    Mary 2311, 2312
Girton 655
Girty
    Simon 1049, 2281
Gist
    Thomas 790
Gitchell
    Ferdinand 277
Gitshell
    Jacob 944
Gladstone 477
Glaser
    Mrs. John 492
Glasgow
    Arthur 867
Glasner
    Thomas C. 966
Glass
    David E. 356
    Davis 994
    Joseph 356
    Thomas 71, 938
Glaze
    Samuel 2191
Glazener
    Eli 974
    Jacob 956
    James 955
Glazier
    Marian 512
Gleason
    Charles 280
Gleaves
    Charles 2137
    Isaac 123, 128, 229, 956
    Samuel 955, 956
Gledhill 833
Glenn 1028
    Alexander E. 505
    Donald W. 356
    Gabriel 1030
    George 277
    H. G. 505
    Isaac 277, 282
    Ivan 356
    John H. 356
    Josiah B. 277
    Josiah D. 282
Glessinger
    George W. 278
Glessner 262, 2178
Gleur
    Joseph 787
Gleves
    Alfred C. 282
Glover
    Crawford 2154
    Fred 356
Goddard
    C. B. 66
    General 129
Goff
    John F. 601
Goldsmith
    Thomas 976
Gollop
    Charles 356
    Griffith 369
    Griffith E. 356

Gomber 29, 576, 611, 1066, 2006, 2007, 2020, 2027, 2043, 2044, 2045, 2144, 2145, 2270
    (Heirs) 646
    Catherine 611, 626
    Catherine B. 34
    Jacob 7, 32, 33, 34, 35, 36, 37, 38, 39, 41, 42, 60, 63, 64, 66, 67, 68, 75, 78, 79, 81, 85, 91, 106, 110, 111, 373, 425, 542, 543, 544, 545, 546, 550, 552, 554, 556, 557, 561, 562, 569, 572, 573, 574, 577, 580, 794, 795, 796, 803, 1047, 2007, 2008, 2009, 2043, 2044, 2045, 2046, 2047, 2048, 2061, 2062, 2080, 2098, 2144, 2145, 2148, 2162, 2163, 2167, 2170, 2176, 2179, 2184, 2186, 2188, 2226, 2235, 2240, 2250, 2270, 2272
    Maria A. 34
    Mr. 51
    Sarah P. 34
    Susan 32, 34, 2045, 2046
    Susanna Beatty 32
Good
    Mary 1047
Gooden
    Mrs. F. 965
    Tamar 965
    William 974
    William F. 649
Gooderl
    George .. 649, 965, 966
    Miss Della 623

ALL NAMES INDEX

Mrs. George 965
W. K. 81, 153, 157, 441, 447, 656, 1059, 2196
William K. 142
Goodey
　Joseph 272
Goodhart
　D. C. 654
Goodrell
　George 974
　Stewart 976
Goodrich
　Warner 670
Goodsell
　George D. 277
Goodwin
　Joseph Wiley 366
Gorby
　B. Y. 504
Gordon
　Albert G. 938
　Delila 2285, 2286
　Ebenezer 277
　James 974
　Jarus 971
　Rev. Thomas P. 385
　Thomas 996
Gorley
　Floyd C. 357
Gorman
　O. G. 180
Gorrell
　John S. 357
Gorsuch 819
Goulburn
　Mary 510
Gould
　Daniel W. 278
Gouldborn
　Walter 357
Goulder
　Grace 2146
Gowdy
　G. W. 390
　J. B. 964
　Mrs. G. W. 268

Grabham
　George H. 357
Gracey
　Jackson 279
　Thomas E. 90, 2258
Gracik
　Father 408
Gracy
　Jackson 865, 955
　Miss Mary Jane ... 2307
　Richard 955
　Thomas E. 183
Graham 833
　A. W. 712, 713
　Alice 511
　Belle 511
　Charles V. 498, 500
　Christopher 938
　D. L. 211, 212
　Ethel 511
　Ezra ...v, 13, 14, 24, 30, 32, 35, 36, 37, 38, 49, 91, 196, 201, 425, 544, 545, 550, 554, 580, 700, 740, 800, 985, 1024, 1054, 2043, 2044, 2101, 2225, 2226
　Francis 272
　James 125, 1048, 2108
　Joseph ... 115, 127, 748
　Kate 2219
　Leonard 357
　Lewis I. 357
　O. C. 367
　R. B. 504
　Rev. John 830
　Richard R. 505
　Thomas 809
　Walter H. 357
　William. 798, 923, 932, 955
Grandstaff
　Adam 996
　Cyrus 994
　Jeremiah J. 282
Granger

　Francis 114
　Judge Moses M. ...1015
Grant 593, 819, 2055
　General 2123
　General Ulysses S. 155, 160
　Mrs. S. O. 2249
　President U. S. 625
　President Ulysses S. 155, 156, 157, 158, 160, 462, 521, 530, 2056, 2149
　Richard 849
　William 820, 821, 2112, 2113
Graves
　John 494
　John W. 87, 166
　Winfield S. 357
Gravina
　Charles E. 357
　Willis S. 357
Gray 618
　Alex 125
　Alexander 938
　Andrew 696
　Asa 277
　Claire 377
　Gail 357
　George 867
　James 258, 798
　James N. 276
　John ... 867, 994, 2159, 2227, 2228
　Perry H. 351, 357
　Robert 811
　Roger 619
　Sarah 936
Grear
　Joseph C. 357
Greathouse
　Leonard 279
Greeley
　Horace . 156, 157, 535, 878
Green 576, 833
　Billy 2215

ALL NAMES INDEX

Charles R. 669
Davis 698
Dr. M. 139
Dr. Milton 56, 143
E. F. 655, 2196
Edgar 501
Elmer 173
Elmer E. 469, 821
General 988
George 989
Harry 183, 606
Harry A.. 100, 185, 186
Herbert D. 350, 357
Isaac 276
Israel 2099, 2102
Jacob 798
James 698
James L. 1062
John 192, 988
M. 695
Milton 34, 122, 123, 135, 142, 438, 698, 699, 893, 894
R. M. 1029
Sarah 758
Susan Moore 34
W. B. 594
William.. 175, 177, 178
Greene
General 804
Greeneltch
John 279
Greenland
Thomas 499
Greenow
John M. 73
Greer
Mrs. 547
Mrs. Eliza 2098
Gregg
Andrew 824
Barr 956
Burr 955
C. H. 656
Ellis 357
Ernest W. 88, 185, 186
Harley M. 357
Israel 275, 276
J. M. 656
Jacob 2158
John 95
Joshua 95, 261, 662
Leo F. 357
Samuel 258
W. H. 93, 94, 169, 170, 178, 447, 460
Gregory 2191
George 369
George R. 357
John 57, 1048
Gresham
Postmaster General Walter 759
Gress
John 357
Grey 2073
Joseph C. 357
Zane 2280
Grier 931, 2309
Ezekiel 160, 932
H. E. 503
H. R. 370
Homer E. 357
Isaac 125, 955
John 1030
Otho B. 277
Thomas 746, 955
Wilson S. 265
Griest .... ii, 12
Milton 506, 924
Griff 75
Griffin 947
C. L. 503
Lady 43
Samuel 798
Sir Charles 43
Thomas 1048
Griffith 231
Abel 1017
George 867
Joseph.. 124, 807, 811, 893, 1062
P. J. 105
Reason 492
Rezin 1059
Robert 504
Wesley 279
Grimes 589, 2099, 2313
Attorney J. O. 2237, 2313
Catherine 938
Col. E. 261
Col. Elijah 522
E. 559
Ed 604
Ed.603
Edward 621
Eli 412, 671
Elijah ... 522, 646, 2178
Ella 2313
Ellen 2099
Francena 938
George 1048
George, Sr. 938
Hut 618
J. J. 66, 139, 685
J. O. ... 80, 93, 143, 153, 155, 256, 629, 2128, 2138
J. O., Esq. 2137
James 955
James O. 625, 2207, 2228, 2229
Jesse 302
Jesse L. 275
John 302, 994
Sam 230, 2070
William 955
Grimsley 2073
Delphi 936
S. L. 81, 992
T. M. 1014
Grindstaff
William W. 357
Grizelle
Mrs. 884
Gross
C. F. 652
Mrs. Charles F. 2033
Grossman
Benjamin 369

Benjamin S. 357
Marvin 366
Grouch
Wesley 824
Groves
Belle 514
H. F. 447
Harry F. 88, 180
Grubb 534
Smith 923
Grubbs
Abraham 277
Alva J. 357
George D. 357
Mansel N. 357
Gruber
Earl 356
Isaac 277
Grudier
Olive 511
Peter 399
Walter C. 357
Gruen
Henry 498
Gruetter
Rev. Alexander J. J. 405
Grummon
Ichabod 1030
Isaac 1030
Grummond ... 11, 47, 129, 196, 232, 1028, 1034, 1035
Ichabod.. 69, 115, 129, 1032, 1033, 2099, 2107
Isaac 67, 106, 112, 676, 747, 1025, 1028, 1032, 1033, 1034
Gudgen
D. L. 972
Gudgeon
Sarah Laird 375
Guegold
Walter 498
Gueysott 326
Guille
N. B. 133

Napoleon B. 659
Gumbar
Mr. 47
Gunn
Delight 832
John 834
Gunsaulus
Frank 642
Gunter
Rev. 261, 524
Rev. C. H. 375, 2196
Guthridge
Capt. A. J. 289
Earl M. 357
Guthrie
Bert 640
Burt M. 357
Joseph 790
Lena 369
Thomas 790
Gwynn
Elmer 357
Elmer E. 368
Gyer
Lena 511

H

Hackley
Kenneth Ray..........357
Hacock
William 1017
Hagan
Joseph 893
Hagar
Kileon 649, 650
Hagerty
James 439
Hague 370, 2073
Dallas C. 357
Frank B. 357
Fred L. 357
Friend J. 357
Hannah 919
Harry 357
Jacob 939, 2072
Jehu 919

John 974, 2152
John T. 357, 370
Joseph 650
Haig
William 913
Hail
Rev. A. D. 991
Haines
Charles 924
Dr. Vincent 2035
Fred L. 499
Harry 2243
Jake 232
L. G. 594, 623, 662
Mary F. Rea 2243
Miss Laura 623
Nathaniel 1061
Thomas 198
W. G. 184
William 1059
William R. 956
Hair
Rev. Samuel 381
Hakey
Joshua 277
Hale
Alfred 357
Irwin L. 357
John P. 142, 143
William Lawrence . 366
Haler
William V. 357
Hales
H. W. 377
Hall 449, 718, 784
A. B. 91, 447, 498, 499, 515
Albert M. 357
Alva B. 91, 502, 509, 514
Basil C. 357
Beatrice 512
Benjamin 923, 924
Benjamin, Jr. 649
Blanche B. 419, 503, 654, 655
Bonner H. 357

ALL NAMES INDEX

Caleb 923
Capt. W. 206
Carl 357
Clarence W. 610
Cyrus 128, 427, 448, 654, 920, 924, 925, 926, 927, 929
E. H. 265
Edward 277
Edward H. 265
Edwin L. 280
Eli 651, 654
Emma 503
F. J. 654
F. W. 106, 377
Forest W. 183
Fred D. 357
Fred J. ... 419, 488, 503
George 955
H. F. 504
Henry 919, 923
Henry T. 629
I. A. 503
I. C. 160
I. W. 269
Isaac 205, 923, 924
Isaac A. 419, 503
Isaac W. .. 80, 357, 651, 654, 706, 909, 911, 913, 917
J. C. 502
James 955
Joel 419, 503, 654
John 10, 123, 128, 205, 409, 418, 419, 427, 649, 650, 775, 849, 908, 909, 911, 913, 923, 924, 925, 926, 927, 956, 957
John D. 919
John P. 651, 923
John R. .. 205, 418, 419, 420, 654, 909
John W. 265, 277
Joseph 923
Joseph K. 1044
Lizzie 508

Mary 512, 919
Maude 503
Milton 504
Minnie L. 503
Nathan 919, 923
Oscar 277, 283
Paul 357
Paul C. 368
Phebe Webster 909
R. Elvira 419
Rev. Frank 375
Robert 955
Russell 370
Russell G. 357
Sade K. 503
Samuel 1060
Stephen 923
Thomas 651
Thomas C. 654
Veda 503
W. E. 503
William 923, 956
Hallam
  Lewis 265
Halleck
  Jeremiah 73
  Jeremiah T. 66
  Judge 73
Halley
  Edward 824
  Louisa 2293
  Mary 965
Halliday
  A. W. 507, 2196
Halterman
  Rev. 399, 400
  Rev. W. S. 400
Hamer
  Thomas L. 131
Hamilton 670, 2159
  Alexander 759
  Amanda 1038
  Andrew 787
  Charles 2137
  Clyde O. 349, 357
  Hazel 513
  J. M. 964

John 955
Joseph 867
William. 357, 369, 579, 893
Hamlin
  Hannibal 145
Hamline
  Rev. 570
Hamme
  H. S. 621
  Seymour 616, 617
Hammerly
  Isaac 855
Hammersley
  Ann 2307, 2308
  Henry G. 283
Hammond 9, 166, 170, 188, 380, 527, 619, 620, 621, 623, 2202, 2250
  Benjamin 994
  Boyd 606
  Charles 120, 275
  David 278, 800
  David P. 798
  Francis 84, 145, 153, 261, 586, 697, 2129
  George C. 350, 357
  H. A. 507
  Harry W 755
  J.   124, 272
  J. C. 391
  James 447, 697
  John 787, 790, 987, 1025
  Johnston 275
  Mary 507
  Miss Rebecca J. ... 1010
  Mrs. David 800
  Mrs. J. 787
  Rezin 974
  Robert 63, 81, 91, 157, 275, 511, 620, 2250
  Shandy 247
  William H. 275

ALL NAMES INDEX

Zoath 994
Zoth 988
Hanberg
   William S. 357
Hancock
   George 276
   John 1030
   Loretta 500
   Winfield S. ... 161, 162, 523, 524
Haney
   Catherine 988
   Thomas 988
Hanglin
   E. J. 480
Hanlon
   Ann 552
Hanly
   Governor 421
   Hon. J. Frank 421
   J. Frank 177
Hann
   Thompson 976
Hanna 55, 262, 2184
   Andrew . 278, 695, 811
   F. C. 605
   Frank 605, 606
   Henry 894
   Herbert F. 357
   Hon. Thomas 718
   John 67, 283, 746, 798, 855, 884, 889, 893, 894, 1061, 1062
   Mrs. Alice Anderson 2206
   Ruth 504
   Senator M. A. 171
   Sheriff 166
   Thomas 106, 107, 112, 127, 128, 135, 457, 814, 894, 1059
   W. H. C. 165, 166, 300, 335, 511
   William... 63, 245, 746, 811
   William H. C. 89, 90, 157, 265, 280
Hannah
   Joseph G. 357
Hannan 1028
   W. M. 518
Hannum
   Alpheus 370
   Alpheus M. 357
   David 1061
   Walter C. 357
   William 265, 280
Hansom
   Isaac 277
Hanson
   Capt. Thomas N. . . 1028
   Myrtle 510
   Thomas 1030
   Thomas N. 283
Happs
   John 316
Hara
   Charles 650
Hardesty
   Fred P. 357
   Henry 278
Harding 2200
   Bennet 886
   Bennett 893
   Capt. James 574
   Clyde L. 357
   G. B. 504
   Guy L. 357
   J. H. 447
   Jeremiah 894
   John 893
   John D. 1012, 1017
   Joseph 315
   Lindsay N. 357
   President Warren G. 177, 178, 521, 625, 2216
   W. 887
Hardy
   Reuben 357
Hare
   Charles 649
   John W. 502
   Joseph 956
Walter D. 357
Harford 10, 884, 891
   Alexander 891, 892
   Charles N. 892
   Emma A. 892
   F. L. 886
   Freeman L. 891, 893
   George M. 891
   Mary E. 892
   Mary M. 891
   Sallie 268
   Sarah A. 892
   Wade 892
Hargrave
   Jeremiah 669
   John 2022, 2023
Harkness 505
   John 662
Harman
   Mike 357
Harme
   Rev. D. M. 402
Harmer
   Rev. D. M. 402
Harmon
   Judson 172, 173
Harper 435
   Alex 66
   Alexander 105, 110, 111, 139, 246
   Dr. William Rainey ... 2015, 2230, 2231
   Ebenezer 965
   Edwin J. 357
   Ella Paul 2230, 2231
   Ellen Elizabeth Rainey 2230
   J. 886
   Judge 129
   Nancy 988
   Robert 279
   Samuel 651, 790, 2230
   Thomas A. 357
   William, Sr. 110
Harriette 473
Harris 670
   C. A. 698

ALL NAMES INDEX

Eliza 1068
George 1068, 1070
Governor Andrew L.
   .... 172, 173
Isaac 855
Israel 923
Jacob 1048
James A. 412
John 601, 696
Mrs. H. 800
Mrs. James A. 412
Mrs. R. 886
Mrs. W. H. 268
Robert 498
Russell K. 357, 368
Thomas 357
William .. 290, 291, 798
William E. 357
Willis 370
Zela 369
Harrison 476
Benjamin 598
Daniel 270
Gen. William H. 248
General 1054
General William H. ... 65
General William Henry
   .... 118, 520, 521
J. 886
John 270, 2108
President Benjamin
   163, 164, 165, 166,
   521, 625, 2148,
   2208
President William H.
   . 65, 114, 115, 116,
   129, 130, 131, 132,
   133, 134, 135, 137,
   138, 142, 163, 164,
   187, 2055
President William
   Henry 8, 56, 57,
   117, 118, 119, 125,
   458, 520, 521, 624,
   625, 2042, 2067,
   2080, 2081, 2102,
   2218, 2274

Thomas 894
William 270
William Henry 548, 758
Harshman
   Anzoetta 508
   O. F. 508
   Rev. O. F. 403
Hart
   Jacob 57, 245, 1048
   James 2019
Hartell
   Vivian 511
Hartgrave
   William 865
Hartill
   Joseph 637
Hartley 409, 910
   Bishop 407
   Captain 310
   David B. 923
   Dora 500
   G. G. .. 931, 2094, 2147,
      2212
   G. M. 419, 503, 654,
      655
   Garrett M. 503
   H. S. 419, 654, 657
   Hallie 503
   Ira 657
   Ira W. 506
   J. B. 87, 176
   James 435, 436
   John 923
   Joseph 923
   M. E. 509
   M. L. 336, 337, 656
   Mahlon 924
   Milton L. 499
   Mrs. M. L. 341, 516
   Noah 919, 923
   Russell 357
   Sarah 919
   William 432, 498
   William P. 90, 157,
      158, 310
Hartman
   Christian 867

Christopher 1014
John 995, 1007
John, Sr. 995
Margaret 1007
Hartong
   John 811, 1061
Hartshorn
   M. V. 270
   Thomas 277
Hartup
   James 965, 974
   John W. .. 286, 289, 290
   John Wesley 68, 99,
      709
   Joseph H. 279
   Russell 981
   Samuel 981
Harvey 540
   Ann F. 919
   Elizabeth ... 2222, 2223
   Theodore L. 834
   Thomas 923
Hase
   Ben Linton 806
   John Harmon 805
   William wood 806
   William Wood 805
   Wm Adams 805
Hastings 1019
   G. S. 509
   Hiram 2157
   James 1013, 1017
   John 142, 2107
   John, Jr. 1060
   John, Sr. 1061
   Mrs. William 1013
   Samuel 970, 2157
   William 395, 1017
Hatcher
   John 1048
   Obadiah 938
Hathaway 989
   Mary McClelland ... 331
   Miss Eva 331
   Mr. 989
   Mrs. T. M. 331
   T. M. 655

ALL NAMES INDEX

Hatters
  Samuel 247
Hattery
  Rev. John 2200
Hatton
  Frank .. 758, 759, 2080, 2101
  James H 95
  Jas. B. 703
  Lizzie Snyder 759
  Richard. 120, 139, 458, 758, 759, 2080, 2081, 2101
  Sarah Green 758
Hatwell
  John 128
Hauk
  Rev. A. J. 402
Hawes
  Harry 295
  John 988, 994
Hawk
  Elizabeth 1027
Hawkins 1056, 2224
  Andrew 824
  Andy 969
  C. W. 655
  Charles W. 501
  Esther 501
  James 245, 748
  Philip 242
  Samuel .. 73, 114, 1061
  William 209, 381, 1060
  William 'Bill' 2232, 2233, 2254
Hawley
  Lamech 495
Hawn
  George 547
Hawthorn
  Benjamin 849
  James 849
Hawthorne 405
  Capt. Edmund 368, 369
  Charles M 357
  D. M. 621, 653, 662
  David M. 847

Dr. 913
Edmund 173, 174, 176, 357, 367
John 844, 849
Mrs. D. M. 497
Mrs. Julia Cochran 497
Mrs. Virgil (Young) 491
Nathaniel .. 2058, 2059
Stella 511
Hay
  Bessie 503
  Cecil L. 498
  R. S. 503
Hayes 593
  Asa 279
  Bailey 746
  Benjamin 128
  Bessie 507
  Blanche 503
  Charles W 265, 280
  Cyrus 913
  Gov. Rutherford B.
  1015
  Governor Rutherford
  B. 521, 522
  H. H. 503
  Harry R. 171
  J. H. 503
  Jasper 503
  Joseph 279
  Michael 1017
  President Rutherford
  B. .. 8, 65, 158, 159, 160, 462, 521, 522, 523, 625, 711, 2056, 2205
  S. E. 505
  Samuel 746
  Sylvester 279
  W. H. 1059
  Walter 357
  William H. 649
Hayhurst
  Enos 515
Hayman
  Jacob 494
  Orval K. 357

Roy A. 357
Hayne 452
Haynes 678
  Amelia 2240
  Dr. Vincent .. 651, 2251
  Ed 623
  H. C. 623
  Raymond H. 357
  Samuel 687, 688
  Simeon 262, 2129
  Theodore 623
  V. 143, 261
  Vincent 2117
Hays 69, 230, 742, 743
  Ann Bay 741
  Bailey 923
  Edmund 923
  John 992
  Joseph 923
  Michael 938
  Nelson 741
  Tacy 742
  Thomas 741, 742, 743, 746, 811, 955, 956, 957, 1060
  William. 668, 950, 956, 957
Hayward
  Henry 834
Hazard
  T. R. 652
  Thurman R. 639
Hazlett 934, 2087
  Capt. J. C. 206
  J. 854
  James 940
  Samuel 2074
Head
  Amy 511
  James 955
Heade 2239, 2306
  Attorney W. S 2132
  E. C. 2307
  James 2306, 2307
  Levi 2306
  Margaret H. Clark 2307
  Mrs. W. S. 81

Revere 518
Sarah Dillon 2306, 2307
W. S. 81, 161, 623, 662, 2138
Wilson Shannon. 2306, 2307
Headley
  A. B. 657
  Dr. A. B. 339
  John 1060
  Mrs. A. B. 517
Heakin
  Albert 366
  Charles 357
Heald
  W. R. 66
  William A. 265
Heaney
  C. C. 370, 507
  Charles C. 357
  Irene 370
  John T. 278
  Minnie 507
  Robert 278
Heaston
  Dr. W. D. 380
Heaton
  John B. 2107
Heaume
  David 279, 283
  John 653
  Peter 824
Hecker
  Guy 619
Hedding
  Rev. 570
Hedge 859
  Aaron 123, 849, 855
  George M. 855
  Israel 849
  John 1037
  Joseph 849
  Samuel 1017
Hedges
  Aaron 245
  Israel 247

Joseph 24, 25
Samuel 1014
T. B. 761
Heed
  H. H. 503
  Harry H. 503
Heery
  Father 406
Hefelbower
  Ann 2065
Hefferman
  R. J. 498
Heffernan
  Reginald J. 357, 499
Heidelbach
  Charles 972
  Geo. W. 649
  Washington 972
Heidelback 435
Heidlebach
  Charles 974
  G. 974
  George W. 974
  Rosemond 654
  Theresa 974
Heinbeck
  Charles W. 357
Heinlein
  A. J. 501
  Edward 1009
  James D. 283
Heinlen
  Rev. Aaron H. 1010
Hellstern
  Agnes 369
Hellyer
  M. 261
Helm
  Madison 893
  William 2107
Henden
  Joshua 1048
Hendershot
  Cyril S. 357
  M. 686
  Nathaniel James.. 2156
  Nettie 511

Hendershott
  C. S. 370, 503
  Reba 370
Henderson 2308, 2309, 2312
  A. 269
  Agnes 2308
  Albert 277
  Andrew 246, 651, 834, 2308, 2309
  David 2308, 2309
  Ebenezer 849
  G. W. 932
  George 923
  George W. 917
  George Washington 2309
  Isabella 2308
  J. M. 391
  James 955, 2308
  John 127, 829, 834, 839, 944, 955, 1017, 2308
  John (Heirs) 955
  John C. 955, 2309
  Maggie 832
  Mahlon H. 357
  Margaret 2308
  Margaret Ann 2309
  Maria Jane 2309
  Martha 2308
  Martha Long 2308
  Mrs. Washington 2100
  Nancy 2308
  Nancy Clendennon 959, 960, 961, 2308, 2309
  R. 269
  Rachel 2309
  Rev. J. M. 2102
  Rev. James 410
  Robert 955, 2308
  Sadie 503
  Sallie 2308
  Sarah 2309
  Simpson S. 2309
  Susannah 2208

Thomas .. 66, 106, 944, 946, 2257, 2308, 2309
Tom 944
U. G. 491
Washington 932
William. 127, 746, 944, 959, 961, 2308, 2309
William, Jr. 955
William, Sr. 955
Willis 357
Hendricks 2214
Grand Chief Flora .. 509
Thomas A. 158, 162, 599
Henkle
M. M. 2191
Henman
J. W. 989
Henry 2302
Attorney Earl 2302
Captain Everett 411
Dr. R. H. 494
Dr. S. L. 2137
Earl 91, 178, 368, 2258
Fred A. 357
G. Earl 630
G. F. 174, 2258
G. H. 88
George Earle 367
Gustavus 824
J. D. 2138
Joseph 811
Joseph Beymer of . 703
Margaret 2307
Michael 867
Morris 834
Mrs. Everett 411
Nadine 508
Patrick 452
Peter 955
Rachel 2267
Stewart 955
Herbert
John 2199
Joseph E. 357

Mrs. Jacob 1045
Herlan
G. H. 656
George H. 504
Gladys 502
Harold H. 503
Herpko
Terezia 513
Herrick
Governor Myron T. 171
L. D. 506, 657
Samuel . 66, 67, 71, 93, 105
Shirley 370, 507
Herring
B. S. 262, 507, 511
Benjamin S. 278, 505
Herron
Andrew W. 706
Rev. J. D. 405
Hersh
John . 54, 84, 115, 120, 122, 240, 574, 626, 646, 720, 2090, 2100, 2237
John, Jr. 430, 458, 495, 801, 802
Hershey
Edith 369
Heskett 1036, 2302
Elam 995
Everett 276, 999, 1000
James 938
John H. 824
John M. 276
Landon 824, 974
Logan F. 90, 176
William J. 277
William L. 276, 283
Heslep
Joseph 1048
Hess
John 2024, 2025
Hesse
John 2134
Rev. William 402
Hessen

William 994, 1031
Hester
W. J. 100
Hetherington
Christopher 974
Hetrack
Isabella 2307
Hevlow
Rev. 399
Hewitson
Rev. 264
Heyburn
Weldon E. 2248
Hibbs
Benjamin 867
Lacy S. 279
Valentine 746
Valentine, Jr. 867
William (Heirs) 867
William of Val 867
William, Jr. 867
William, Sr. 867
Hick
Hugh R. 497
Hickey 203
Hickle
George 276
Hannah 402
James C. 357
John 400, 824
Stephen 276, 824
Timothy 400, 402
Hickman 1019
James 1017
John 1017
Joseph R. 357
Hicks
Amanda 514
Capt. R. C. 289
Hobart M. 357
Thomas 283
Hickson 1019
Dr. 913
Higgin
Jess 697
Higgins
Thurman A. 357

ALL NAMES INDEX

Hill 2073, 2111
- A. B. 469
- Charles B. 976
- Clarence P. 357
- David M. 938, 939, 1017, 2072
- Dr. John 2234
- Dr. Noah 711, 969, 2233, 2234, 2263, 2293
- Elizabeth A. 2167
- Hester 2086
- J. W. 469, 509
- James 357
- James (Heirs) 798
- James M. 357
- John 811, 972
- John E. 357
- Joseph 939, 2072
- Lou 440
- Margaret 867
- Mary Dilley 2234
- Matthew 923
- Noah 699, 976
- Noah Leon 357
- Richard 127, 798, 1062
- William 110

Hilles
- Charles D. 166

Hillier
- Captain Henry 411

Hillman
- John 621
- William P. 276

Hillyar
- George 2287
- Mary Spaid 2287

Hillyas
- George 974

Hillyer
- Gen. 157
- William 2117

Hilton
- Joseph 923
- Morris 955
- William 357, 674, 675

Himes

Rev. A. M. 403

Hinds
- Abraham 798
- James 1017
- Moses 1017
- R. W. 2093

Hineline
- Asa 994
- Edward 994, 996

Hines
- Captain 311

Hinton
- David 994
- Donice E. 357, 639
- Ed 604
- Fred T. 357
- General Otho 234, 235
- Moses 994

Hipkins
- George S. 357, 368

Hipsley
- E. L. 507
- Elmer 180

Hiscox
- Peter (Heirs) 867

Hite 718
- Henry 245
- Stewart 675

Hitler
- Adolf 2035

Hiveley
- George 502
- Janet 502

Hively
- Carl 357, 501, 502

Hixon
- Mrs. E. 2138
- William 894

Hixson
- Della 511
- Dr. G. W. 339
- Joseph H. 357
- Matthew 893
- Mrs. G. W. 497
- Ralph S. 357
- Ward V. 358

Hoadley

Gov. George 2239
Governor 74

Hoag
- Garnet 504

Hoagland
- Captain 302
- E. S. 2199
- Rev. 272, 294, 524
- Rev. E. S. 940

Hobart
- Garret A. 167

Hobbs
- Henry 1017
- Mrs. Laura 2237

Hoben
- Patrick 279

Hobson 329
- H. Z. 444, 491

Hockenberry
- Mary 504
- Orah 504
- Ross 503
- Ross W. 358, 370

Hodder
- Ralph D. 358

Hodges 1028, 1036
- Charles 1030

Hoey
- Francis J. 358
- O. B. 412

Hogan
- Timothy S. 175

Hoge 126, 141, 505, 548, 2098, 2106
- Dr. W. 81
- James D. 207
- M. 261
- O. M. 166, 498, 499, 514, 656

Hoggerty
- Nicholas 976

Hogue 833
- Leah 2031
- O. M. 100
- Ossie M. 639
- Rev. 263

Hokar

2370

ALL NAMES INDEX

Henry 265
Holbrook
    John S. 2134
Holdren
    Charles A. 358
    Florence 504
Hole-in-the-Ear 10, 20, 807, 825, 826
Holland
    'Arsenic' 671
    Cecil F. 2121
    James 923
    Nelson 411, 670
    Nelson Lincoln 671
Hollen
    Henry 824
Holler 574, 1047, 2059, 2165, 2166, 2250
    Joseph 2165
    Sarah ... 646, 798, 2165
Hollett
    George 867
Holley 24, 2195
    Barton D. 2195
Holliday
    George W. 277
Hollingshead
    Rev. 642
Hollingsworth 937
    Dr. J. B. 783
    Homer 370
    Homer G. 358
    J. 936
    James 1017
Hollins
    Adam 412
    H. 412
    Viola 412
Hollis
    David 247, 994
Hollister
    Laura 2138
    Nathan 142, 143
Holloway
    Aaron 867
    Robert 867
Holmes

A. 989
John 923, 932
Mr. 304
Oakley O. 339, 358
Holston
    J. G. F. 698
Holt
    Jacob 996
    James 923
Holtz
    Carrie 2138
    Jacob 227
Holtzman
    William 976
Homer 414, 439
Hommer
    J. K. 514
Honn
    G. W. 2098
Hood 2188
    Charles F. 265
    Elizabeth 500
    Ill. Willard J. 500
    James 115
    John, Sr. 2134
    Lawrence Robert ... 367
    Mrs. R. D. 421
    R. D. 2189
    Willard J. 639
Hook
    Captain G. 411
Hooker
    General 289
Hooks
    Julian 818
    Robert 645
    Susanna Biers 818
    William 645
    William F. 824
    William Frazier 818
Hooper
    James 2191
    Thomas 110
Hoopman 177, 819
    Anna 504
    Isaac 819, 820, 824, 2112

J. A. 504, 656
Jacob 923
Lucinda A. 2265
M. B. 653
W. E. H. 269
Hoover 669
    John 278
    President Herbert 625, 2149, 2216
    President Herbert C. 181, 182, 183
    William 492
    William H. 157
Hope
    Joseph 278
    Richard 834
Hopkins
    I. Y. 501
    Jared 955
    Mark 2216
Hopper
    Rev. C. Arch 405
Hopps
    Marie 502
Horace 439
Hornbrook
    H. C. 588, 589
Horr
    Wilbert R. 358
Horton
    Emerson 509
    George A. 277
Hosack 859, 2011
    John 855
    Mr. 2011
    William 834, 855
Hosiach
    William 247
Hosick
    L. P. 81
    Lot J. 847, 848
    Lot P. 94, 1000
    William 847
Hoskins
    Abbie 511
    Col. Erasmus 2161
    Col. Erastus 2161

ALL NAMES INDEX

Harry 358
Hostetler
   M. E. 507
   Merritt E. 505
Hotchkiss
   Castle 127, 867, 894
   William.. 121, 893, 894
Hote
   James 932
Hough
   John 24, 25
Houk
   George A. 508
House
   John .. 970, 2155, 2156
   Lofland 2061
   Mead 279
   R. C. 509
Householder
   Albert 358
   Frederick 923
   Polly 974
Houseman
   Albert R. 358
   C. S. 156
   Jacob 996
   Johnson 1030
   W. 972
Houston
   General Sam 531
Howard
   Joshua 66
   O. L. 656
Howe
   Father 406
   Henry ... 592, 715, 716, 717, 1058, 2009, 2101, 2120, 2123
   Rev. Lyman 405
Howell 989
   Amanda 274
   Andrew 358
   David K. 358
   George 849
   Henry F. 358
   Herman 275
   Hiram 358

John 275
John C. 358
Raymond 501
Robert L. 358
Howells
   William Dean 716, 736, 737
Howerton
   Mrs. John L. 2249
Howery 670
Rev. 412
Hoyle 595, 596
   Fred 2139
   Miss Laura 497
   Robert 2139
   Robert B. 639
   William. 498, 595, 596, 656, 2140
Hritz
   Andy 358
   Father 408
Hronec
   Steve 358
Hrosmond 2312
Hubbard 1065, 1066
   William 1060
   William B. 73, 824
Hubert 41
   Andrew 270
   Daniel 457, 2062
   Daniel (Heirs) 646
   Mary ... 41, 2283, 2284
   Widow 2283
Huddleston 833
Hudnall
   Frank Perry 366
Hudson
   Benjamin 1030
   James 277, 283
   Shepherd 938
   William 247
Huff
   John 2009
Huffman 884
   Abraham 824
   Benjamin 893
   Colonel 303

George . 746, 893, 938, 1017
   H. B. 88
   Hugh B. 157
   Jack 616
   Jacob 746, 834
   John 798, 2196
   John W. 621
   Mary 507
   Ralph E. 358
   Robert F. 834
   Stewart 606
Hufford
   Mary 923
Huggins
   Andrew (Heirs) 994
   John 994
   Thomas 996
Hughes 949, 2073
   Aaron 1012, 1017
   Charles E. 176, 177, 2149
   Eugene 351, 358
   Henry P. 798
   Jesse 746, 748
   John 279, 621
   John G. 507
   John W. 277
   Joseph 938
   Joseph C. 278
   Levi 1030
   Lizzie 507
   Thomas 893
   Willard F. 358
   William 370
Hughey
   H. O. 2026
Huhn
   Jacob 994
   John 994
   William H. 358
Hujdick
   Frances 513
Hulbert
   Daniel 112
Hull
   David 869

ALL NAMES INDEX

George R. 276
John 198
Joseph M. 276
M. C. 462
M. R. 548
Madison 276
Mrs. 965
Hulse
   A. P. 657
Humble
   John 278
Humphrey
   Allen 265
   David 2170, 2172
Hunchak
   Father 408
   Father Joseph 408
Hunnell
   William M. 358
Hunt
   Austin 854, 859
   David 746, 798
   Dr. S. P. 126
   Dr. Samuel 701
   Dr. Samuel P. 123
   H. F. 2168
   John 867
   Joshua 498
   Lewis 502
   Mrs. Sarah 865
   Raymond D. 358
   Reuben O. 358
   Rufus 2137
   S. P. 698
   Samuel P. 646
   Thomas 965
   W. D. 183
   Willard S. 358
Hunter 21
   C. F. 508
   Dr. C. L. 2260
   J. C. 261, 568
   James 2206
   John 283, 501
   Maggie 501
   Martha 2206
   O. L. 655

Robert 2092
W. 601
William .. 66, 673, 1026
William F. 278
Huntsman
   Herman H. 358
   Howard J. 358
   Joseph 913
Hurd
   Luman 501
   Lyman 996
Hurford
   David 278
Hurley
   Cornelius 276
Hurst
   James 919
   John 798
   Joseph W. 153
   William 974, 1062
Huseham
   Mary 1062
Huston 833
   Charles E. 358
   James 198
   Mary 893
Hutcheson
   Earl R. 358
Hutchinson 48
   Wyatt 676
Hutchison 9, 223, 226,
   520, 521, 532, 533,
   547, 548, 549, 553,
   568, 669, 887, 2059,
   2060, 2068, 2069,
   2070, 2081, 2098,
   2114
   A. C. 88
   A. J. 499, 500, 652,
   656, 2185
   A. U. 656
   Al 176, 185
   C. B. 447
   C. M. 656
   Corbin 57, 798
   David W. 283
   Enoch 798

Fanny 2068
George W. 258
Hayes 981
James 867, 1000
James C. (Heirs) 790
James E. 358
John 110, 247, 574,
   695, 849, 855,
   2068, 2069
John C. 955
Joseph 279
Lieut. Wyatt 574
M. W. 518
Mary 375
Matilda 2068
Mrs. A. J. 2235
Nathan 124, 790
Ralph M. 358, 368, 626
Richard 601, 675
Robert (Heirs) 798
S. M. 390
Samuel 649, 947
Stephen 824
Thomas .. 21, 258, 279,
   358
Watt 595
Watt M. 346, 639
Wyatt ... 32, 35, 39, 67,
   72, 73, 87, 123,
   245, 260, 373, 375,
   495, 548, 549, 550,
   566, 574, 580, 646,
   762, 795, 2068,
   2113, 2194, 2195,
   2196, 2197
Wyatt M. 2047
Hutton 482
   Alice 510
   Solomon 1000
   Wesley F. 358
   William 824, 827
Hyatt
   A. G. 467
   C. M. 621
   Charles 617
   Charles S. 358
   Ellen Grimes 2099

ALL NAMES INDEX

Florence 508
Grim 604
H. S. 258
Hezekiah 277
Miss Rebecca 81
N. 559, 560, 678
Noah 123, 151, 695, 782, 798, 800, 2099
Hyde 8, 321, 322, 323
A. D. 876
Andrew 865, 867
Ellis 358
Mrs. A. D. 871
Mrs. A. D. (Carpenter) 876
Robert 649, 1060
S. M. 498, 499
Thomas 153, 247, 811, 814
Thomas (Heirs) ... 1060
William 919
Hyers 2246
Hyman
Rev. S. B. 402

I

Ihnat
Antonia 513
Imlay
Annie 988
Joseph 995, 1009
Immortal J. N. 9, 536, 537
Imrie
Col. Norman 185
Indian 966
Jim 966
John 966
Ingalls
David S. 183
Ingersoll
Robert G. 525
Ingle
Amelia 988
Hiram 988
Mrs. 865

Inglish
George W. 105
Richard 955
Ingram
Murrell 358
W. C. 88
Wilbur 178
Inskeep
John M. 115
Joseph 956
O. D. 487
Otis 358
Inskip
Phineas 498
Ireland
Jonathan 974
Irons
Joseph 867
Irwin
George 762
Joel T. 2106
William 893, 995
Isaac 670
Andrew 390
Neb 671
Israel
Basil 242
Col. Basil 128
Priscilla 128
William ... 90, 106, 113, 122, 123, 128, 245, 974

J

Jack 2259
Capt. James .. 242, 574, 2259, 2260
Capt. John 570
Edward 125, 938, 1012
James 2260
Patrick 2260
Robert 2260
Samuel 2260
Sarah 2260
Jackman
Mary 965

Jackson .. 196, 1004, 2026, 2027
A. W. 173
Andrew 676
Bamford 616
Benjamin 955
Bert 604
Billy 671
Charles 515
Charles L. 514
David 112
Forrest W. 358
General 949
General Andrew ... 519, 520, 534
'General' Samuel ... 226
George J. 67
George S. 358
Henry .. 800, 824, 2158
Israel 662, 697
Jacob 2158
James 824
Jennie A. 2247
John 302
John M. 275
Lewis 669
Margaret 375
Miss Sadie 443
Mrs. Ida B. 1070
Peter 669, 2069
President Andrew 8, 101, 111, 112, 113, 114, 117, 144, 175, 182, 198, 230, 460, 461, 462, 519, 520, 530, 534, 624, 720, 727, 968, 1026, 2055, 2156, 2167, 2172, 2178, 2244, 2296
Rev. J. J. 2203
S. 269
Samuel 226, 278
Tempy Mitchell ... 2069
'Tempy' Mitchell ... 669
Theodore 604
Thomas 604

ALL NAMES INDEX

William.. 285, 286, 289
William E. 358
Jacob G. Metcalf, ... 2106
Jacobs
   Charles 358
Jacquet
   Father 406
Jaggar
   Bishop 405
Jakubisin
   Steve F. 358
James
   Edward E. 366
   George 868
   George, Esq. 206
   Hollis 2134
   Jesse O. 358
   Judah 923
   Rev. 412
Jameson
   David 923
   John 746
   John B. 868
   Samuel 1030
Jamieson
   William S. 279
Jamison
   Alexander 2062
   Thomas 649
Jarvis
   John 277, 811
   Mely 956
Jaynes
   Dr. 2103
Jefferies
   David 2107
   John 2156
   Joseph 974
   Mifflin 974
Jefferson 160, 2256
   Belle Patterson 642
   Catherine Keil 970
   Charles Frederick .. 643
   Dr. 2264
   Dr. Charles E. ... 9, 640, 641, 642, 643, 644, 2186, 2187, 2264

Dr. Milton 640, 641
Franklin 696
Jeremiah 646, 696, 970, 2186
Milton 696
President Thomas .. 35, 530, 624, 739, 740, 2055, 2085, 2149
Ralph 643
Thomas 896
Jeffrey
   John W. 279
   William M. 277
Jeffries
   D. T. 511
   David T. 280
   Joseph B. 280
Jenkins
   David 632, 2178
   Edward 824
   Eleazer 893
   Henry 723
   James 674, 1062
   John 73
   Mrs. H. M. 516
   Sidney 337, 358
   Thomas 746, 834
   Warren 886
   William 834
   William M. 886
Jenning
   F. H. 498
Jennings
   David 105, 112, 120, 457, 2154
   Dr. M. L. 394
Jester
   T. E. 972
Jetto
   Norman Bennem .. 366
Jewell
   Charlie 358
   T. H. 2168
Jewett
   Hon. Hugh J. 713
   Hugh J. 462
   Judge 147

Jinkens
   Charles W. 358
   Ross L. 358, 368
Jirles 2186
   Oscar F. 358
John
   Miss Helen W. 180
Johns
   George 358
   John A. 499
   Llewellyn James 358
Johnson 431, 508, 833, 871, 989, 1038, 1053
   A. M. 470
   Abraham 790
   Al 81
   Alex 697
   Alexander 145
   Alfred 160
   Anderson 278
   B. C. 1010
   Bob 771
   C. L. 509
   C. R. 174
   C. V. 185
   Catherine .. 2087, 2088
   Charles R. 358
   Colonel R. M. 114
   Daniel 507
   David 114, 894, 923, 953, 954, 976, 1006, 1007, 1038, 1039
   E. 1038
   Edward 974
   Ethel 370, 503
   Ezekiel 1048
   Ezra 358
   Ferdinand S. 280
   Forest 509
   Frank 358
   Frank H. 639
   Frank T. 179
   George . 747, 814, 938, 995
   George R. 2158
   Gershon 906

ALL NAMES INDEX

Harry C. 186
Harry Wilbur 366
Helen Elizabeth 367
Henry 894
Herman D. 358
Herschel V. 145
Hiram W. 174
J. 457
J. R. 654, 932
James 258, 431, 790
James E. 358
James R. 121, 128, 142, 649, 919, 923
Jesse 381, 656, 798
John 649, 747, 923, 938, 939, 940, 995
John A. 277
John B. 955
John W. 358
Joseph 94, 261
Joseph R. 2106
Lambert 616, 617
Levi F. 277
Mary 988
Matthew 936, 938, 939
Mr. 228
Mrs. C. R. 178, 516
Mrs. Mary 886
Mrs. Ward 2209
Nancy 2114
Nathaniel 277
O. C. 503, 504
'Old Uncle Billy' ... 1009
Paul 370
Paul S. 358
Philander 276
Polly 2300
President Andrew 152, 154, 625, 1040
Priscilla 919
Priscilla Israel 128
Ralph R. 358
Rev. A. B. 1010
Rev. Samuel 404
Rev. Samuel F. 1010
Rev. William T. 1010
Richard M. 65

Robert 67, 88, 110, 265, 974, 1058
Robert (Bob) 771, 772, 773, 774
Robert B. 280
Rufus 391
S. M. 467
Salem 278
Samuel .. 265, 280, 695
Samuel B. 326, 327
Sarah 503
T. H. 509
T. M. 95, 264, 654, 706, 917
Thomas 283, 748, 867, 894, 938
Thomas M. 722
Thomas, Sr. 868
W. B. 173
William. 155, 258, 494, 675, 894, 974, 989, 995, 996, 1009
William G. 278
William J. 412
William of Robert.. 974
William, Jr. 995
Winnie 504
Johnston.... 48, 538, 2073, 2086, 2087, 2139, 2176, 2178
Alexander........ 90, 261
C. A. 652
Catherine Johnson
.... 2087, 2088
Colonel 1026
J. 269
J. G. 595
J. P. 2168
J. Press 639
J. Preston 499
James ... 276, 607, 740, 741
James R. 358, 367
Jane B. Smith 2088
Jim 2072
John 2072
John A. 2087

John A., Jr.. 2088, 2089
John A., Sr. 2088, 2089
Joseph E. 2077
Judge 153
Matthew 2072
Miss Hannah 623
Miss Sallie J. 268
Orin 2072
Orin M. 640
Pres 2072
Rev. 263
Robert 110, 111
Thomas 651
W. B. 87, 629
W. B. (Beverage) .2088
W. F. 2141
William .. 390, 391, 964
Jones 833
A. F. 621
Abraham 974
Andrew 1061
Anthony 997
Aunt Delphi 671
Charles G. 1048
Charles S. 276
Dick 1028
Dr. O. R. 606
Edward 1031
Enoch 848, 1048
G. W. 621
Garrett E. 276, 283
George 603, 800
Hattie 500
James 358
James L. 1048
John 299, 515, 886
Joseph W. 279
Josephus 283
Llewellyn 366
Mrs. Josiah 516
Paul L. 652
Professor 2111
Raymond 606
Rev. J. S. 399
Rev. James 528
Rev. L. S. 402
Robert C. 279

ALL NAMES INDEX

Stephen 428
Thomas 649
Tressie 965
William, Jr. 995
Wilmuth................957
Jordan 2159
   Adam 2160
   Elizabeth 402
   Jacob......... 2159, 2160
   Joshua..................995
   Mrs. 2160
   Peter 2160
   Rebecca Albin 2160
   William..................278
Joy
   John 2156
   William B. 358
   William Basil 338
Joyce
   James... 104, 105, 106,
      169, 172, 173, 174,
      175, 176, 514
   James E. 358
   Michael 279, 988
Juillerat
   Paul E. 358
Julian
   W. A. 179
Justice
   Elmer E..................358
Justus
   Charles A...............358
   Earl L. 358

K

Kackley......................970
   Baylis D. 402
   Belle......................510
   Elizabeth A. 402
   Ellis D. 358
   H. W. 470
   Isaac....................2158
   J. A. 402, 1005
   J. R. 501
   John .. 242, 2158, 2159
   Lura......................502

Oliver C. 358
Owen R. 358
Paul......................784
Samuel 2158
Vernon O. 507
Willard H. 358
Kahn
   Harry 2168
Kaho 972
   James 87
Kalt
   Oscar Charles 366
Karnahan
   William 868, 893, 1048
Karns
   L. D. 601
Karr
   Andrew 868
   James (Heirs) 824
   John 868, 995
   Thomas H..............278
   Thomas W.............358
   William..................370
Kase
   John 974
Kavulis
   Stephen R. 358
Kays...........................435
   Martin........... 279, 675
Kear
   Albert T. 358
Keenan
   Amy......................503
   Captain Thomas 310
   Emmett.................509
   James 279, 924
Keene
   Jesse.....................835
Keepers 2073
   George 835
   John 198, 887, 893,
      894
   Joseph. 834, 894, 2196
Keeran
   John (Heirs)...........790
Kegley
   William................1061

Keil
   Catherine 970
   Conrad 970
   Elizabeth 970
   John 698
   Mary Ann 970
   Philip 970
   Rebecca................970
   Rev. W. G. 128, 317,
      2098, 2193, 2263
   Rev. William G......400,
      402, 413, 704, 711,
      969, 970, 971, 974,
      2233, 2234, 2293,
      2295
   W. H. 447
   William G. 649, 965
Keiser
   William..................509
Keith
   Alva 358
   Andy R...................358
   Earl E. 358
   Roy W. 358
   William..................358
Kell
   Andrew 995
   John 869, 996
   John (Heirs).812, 1062
   Robert 995
Kellackey 618, 619
Kellar
   Thomas 110, 111
Keller
   Captain..................263
   J. W. 652
   John W. 181
   Levi.....................2154
Kelley
   Alfred 719
   James 574
   Joseph 1025
   Lyman 621
Kelly
   J. C.......................707
   Joseph 1030, 1031
   William E...............358

ALL NAMES INDEX

Kelsey
- J. H. 509
- John H. 509
- Rev. H. A. 342, 489, 490

Kelso
- John 748
- Mark 811

Kemp
- Athol 358
- David.................... 43
- Perry 980
- William.................. 278

Kendall
- Andrew I. 276
- Homer.................... 366
- John 124, 869
- Mary 807
- Zebedee................. 811

Kendrick
- Dr. J. M. 405

Kendzicky
- Joe 358

Kennedy 618, 765
- A. 269
- Amanda Howell 274
- Andrew 848, 856
- Ben 2004
- Benjamin.............. 2003
- D. B. 124
- David B................. 834
- J. J. 514, 515
- James 989, 1062
- John 790, 848, 1048
- Joseph B................ 280
- Joseph R................ 265
- M. B. 265
- Moses 746, 938
- Moses B. 280
- Nathaniel 798
- Tom....................... 619
- William... 87, 261, 938, 2107

Kennin
- John 944

Kennon.. 957, 2099, 2309, 2311, 2312

Abner 2309
Congressman William 2257
D. C. 107, 164, 2257
David.................... 2310
David C................ 2138
Eliza L. 2305
Elizabeth Withney ... 2309, 2310, 2311
Grace 504
Henry 2310
Hon. David C. 2138
Hon. Henry.......... 2137
Hon. Newell 2137
James 955, 1019, 2305, 2310
James H..... 2310, 2311
John 100, 125, 775, 955, 2258, 2309, 2310, 2311
John, Jr....... 953, 2309, 2310
John, Sr. 953
Judge Newell........... 80
Margery 2309
Miss Verna 2310
N. 2099
Nancy.................. 2309
Newell.. 76, 80, 94, 95, 125, 956, 2138, 2208, 2258, 2310
Rose A. 2305
Ruth 2309
Thomas 2310
William 66, 67, 69, 101, 105, 114, 115, 676, 2127, 2257, 2309, 2310

Kent
- Governor............... 131
- Kenton 875
- Kenworthy................. 848
  - Charles 358, 621
  - Fred F. 358
  - John W. 279
  - Joseph E. 274
  - William.......... 844, 848

Kern
- John W. 172

Kerns
- William.................. 245

Kerr
- Adam 358
- Alfred 358
- Daisy 508
- Isaac W.................. 283
- Jonathan 276
- Robert................... 856

Kesler
- John 276

Kesselring
- William H. 2137

Kester
- Dr. 913
- John 157, 494, 923
- Priscilla................ 1061
- William.................. 923

Keyes
- Dr. J. R. 2203
- Raymond Stedman 366
- Zail R. 358

Keylor
- Chancey R. 358
- Cletus P. 358

Keyser
- William.................. 604

Keysor
- Louella Bay............ 501

Kidd
- Captain........ 827, 2035
- Captain William.... 234, 2031
- Russell................... 606

Kidwell
- Edward................. 995

Kilbourn
- Thomas 278

Kilburn
- Thomas 258

Kilgore
- Daniel.................... 790
- William................ 2172

Killbreath
- William C............... 278

ALL NAMES INDEX

Killburn
- James 283
- Thomas 283

Kilpatrick
- Francis 848
- General Judson 158

Kimball 2087
- George 277, 936
- George W 277
- Mary 2262
- Mrs. 832
- Nathan .. 242, 829, 830
- Rebecca 509, 511, 513
- Robert 277
- William 277, 940
- William C 279

Kimble 2073
- Adam 834, 938
- Fred 358
- James V 265, 280
- John 834, 938
- Nathan 265, 280
- Washington 938
- William 283

Kimmey
- Amos 669
- Delitha Mitchell .. 2069
- Sol 671, 2069

Kimney
- Melford R 358

Kincaid 198
- David 124, 808, 811, 813

Kincaide
- I. T. 696

Kindle
- John 813

King ... 408, 409, 477, 833, 2070
- A. L. 45
- Benjamin 277
- Frank 621
- Frank E. 358
- General Adam E. ... 525
- Harley B. 358
- James B. 283
- James R. 275

Joe 672
John S. 856
Michael ... 86, 910, 944
Morris M. 358
Pete 358
Samuel 426, 910
William 834

Kingman
- Peter 522

Kingsberry
- Lewis B. 1017

Kingsbury
- L. B. 2107
- Lewis B. 1012, 1014

Kinkead
- David. 893, 2097, 2098
- Isaac 856
- J.   203, 2075
- Joseph 2191

Kinley
- Rachel 646

Kinney
- David 995

Kinsey
- Sade 510

Kip 446
- John D. W 445
- John W. 426

Kipling 477
- Rudyard 477

Kipp 96

Kirby
- Josiah 106

Kirk
- Edward 691
- J. B. 887
- Joel 865
- Lyde 510
- Mrs. J. 865
- William 245, 868

Kirkbride
- William M. 358

Kirke
- Harry E. 368

Kirkham 2095, 2220

Kirkpatrick
- Alexander 71, 956

David 110, 111
James 695, 1062
John 81, 157, 464, 500, 586, 811, 1029, 2138, 2187
John K. 358
Judge 953
R. 653
Richard 955
Roger 499, 2187
Samuel 1007
Thomas 955
Thomas B. ... 66, 67, 81, 85, 550, 952, 2009, 2061, 2257
William 824

Kirkwood 127
Iva 512
- James T. 283
- Miss Margaret 3
- Robert .. 127, 703, 829, 835
- Samuel J. 441, 442
- William C. 358
- William Clyde 339
- William R. 283

Kisling
- S. E. 503
- Stella 503

Kissinger
- Benjamin B. 359

Klass
- Leonard C. 359

Kline
- John W. 359
- Matthew 824

Klineknecht
- Earnest L. 359

Klingman
- George 258, 275
- John 575

Kmits
- Paul 359

Knapp
- Mrs. Ellen 399

Knapper
- Harold C. 178

2379

ALL NAMES INDEX

Knerler
- Charles 504
- Eva 504

Knight
- Frank T. 359
- Hiram 2160
- Jonathan 553, 2075, 2077
- Karl K. 503
- Ora 510
- Stewart 956

Knott 508, 515
- Nellie 513

Knouff
- Pat 605
- Robert 610
- S. C. 324, 325
- Samuel C. (Craig) . 902, 903, 904
- Samuel C. 'Craig' . 2263
- William 902
- William A. 279

Knowles
- C. E. 501
- Samuel F. 835

Knowls 2059, 2166
- John 621
- Samuel F. 1048
- Sheriff Thomas 86
- Thomas 67, 89, 90, 552

Knowlton
- I. N. 989
- Josiah 995, 996
- Warren 649, 996

Knox 833
- Frank 184, 185
- George 279
- James 790, 2100
- Jane Miller 786
- John 1059
- John T. 176, 181
- M. 80
- Matthew 844
- Rev. 324
- Rev. E. W. 412
- T. C. 87, 106, 176, 177, 178, 180, 181

Thomas 786, 790
Thomas C. 186
Thomas E. 412
Tom C. 185
William 2191

Kocheary
- Anna 513

Kochera
- Andrew 359
- Mike 359

Kochur
- John 359

Koich
- Jack 359

Kokos
- Steve 359

Kolasky
- Andy 359

Komnenich
- Obrad 359

Kondicko
- Susan 513

Koontz
- Israel 996

Koren
- Joseph 656

Korte
- Frank 359

Koshock
- Peter 359

Koval
- John 359

Kovalchick
- John 359

Kovalchik
- Sue 513

Kratz
- Rev. W. J. 403

Kreider
- Henry 1048

Kreikenbaum
- Charles E. 359

Kreitzheimer
- John C. 747

Krivonak
- Father 408

Kromi

George 350, 359
John 359

Kugler
- Joseph 230

Kuhn
- Arthur R. 359
- Homer B. 359
- Hugh A. 359

Kuhns
- Daniel 923
- Samuel 924

Kyle
- David 2187
- Harold 640
- John 1048

L

La Rive
- Dr. 697

La Rue
- Mary 2297

Lacey 670
- Lewis 412

Lacham
- James 853

LaChat
- I. W. 335, 605
- Prof. I. W. 422

Lackney
- Paul M. 359

Lady
- A. F. 507, 510

LaFayette 457
- Marquis de 458

Lafferty
- Curtis 529

Laffin
- Father 406

Lafollett
- William 1007

LaFollett
- Jacob A. 95, 99

Lafollette
- Camelia 510

LaFollette
- Isaac 315, 316

2380

ALL NAMES INDEX

J. A. 171
Mary J. 315, 316
Robert M. 179, 180, 2150
William.......... 315, 316
Lagneaux
   E. Maurice............. 359
   Nexter.................. 359
   Peirre 359
Lahue
   Darl 349, 359
Lair
   Russell.................. 359
Laird
   David............ 232, 790
   James................... 812
   John 1061
Laisure
   Oscar.................... 359
Lake
   Charles L. 359
   Fred M. 359
   Freda.................... 369
   John 829, 835
   Newton.................. 621
   William.. 277, 283, 833
Lamb
   Isaac..................... 279
Lambert
   James A................. 621
   Lewis.................... 245
Lamon
   James................. 1031
Lancaster
   Rev. Samuel 940
Landman
   John W.................. 359
Landon
   Alfred M....... 184, 185, 2149
Landrith
   Ira 177
Landy
   W. 258
Lane 2256
   Dr. 2103
   Dr. Fred W. 2140

Fred W. 359, 368
Joseph.................. 145
W. G..................... 652
William.................. 956
Langell
   A. 601
Langley 41
   J. A. 655
   Peter 1009
Langlois 2050
   Peter 995
Langloise
   Peter 41
Lanick
   George F. 278
Lanley
   J. A. 656
Lanning
   Abraham 938
   Elizabeth 832
   Isaac...... 125, 829, 835
   Isaac M.......... 835, 938
   Jacob.................... 830
   John .. 125, 1017, 1048
   John M. 339, 359
   Joseph.................. 938
   Lydia 936
   Robert......... 938, 1017
   Russell.................. 359
Lansing
   Robert.................. 245
Lard
   Andrew 245
Larimer
   Benjamin............... 974
Larison
   John 858
LaRive
   Dr. 697
Larne
   William.................. 974
Larrick 970
   Byron M. 359
   Caroline 502
   Casper 400
   Charles E. 359
   Ellis B................... 359

Harvey........... 370, 503
Jacob..................2158
John 2158
John H. 501
Jonas 502
Mable................... 502
N. H. 1005
W. A. 185, 186
W. H. 502
William.................. 502
William T. 501
Larrison
   Howard 359
   Robert................... 276
Larry
   Harrison F. 2160
Larue
   David..................1061
   James (Heirs).........974
   John 1061
LaRue 1056
   Benjamin............... 278
   Elias J................... 278
   John 114
   John D. 41
   L. 435
   Laban 965
   Margaret............... 965
   Mrs. D. 819
Lashley
   Charles G............... 359
   Howard G.............. 359
   Oscar S. 359
Latchic
   Andrew S............... 359
   Joseph A................ 359
Latimore
   William.................. 790
Latta
   John 985
Laughlin. 637, 2192, 2224, 2278, 2279
   Alex 80, 125
   Alexander....... 87, 974, 2278, 2279
   Arthur J. 359, 370
   Captain................. 306

Captain James B... 327, 328, 329
Captain John . 318, 320
Charles C. 2279
Colonel James 494
Deborah... 2056, 2057, 2278, 2279
Deborah Wilson . 2278, 2279
Hugh 2278, 2279
J. 269
James... 264, 265, 280, 492, 2278, 2279
John 380, 691, 812, 965, 967, 2056, 2057, 2278, 2279
John W. 280, 2279
John, Sr. 965
Justice 176
Justus 87
Margaret... 2278, 2279
Mary B. 2278, 2279
Miss Emma E. 2279
Mrs. A. 965
Ralph A. 359
Samuel 656
Thomas W. 2278, 2279
William.................. 621
Laughman
　Dennie J. 359
Launtz 837
　George . 245, 250, 252, 746, 748, 835, 836, 837, 856, 2291
　Jacob..... 832, 833, 835
　William. 829, 830, 835, 889, 2291
Laurenson
　Rev. R. M................ 405
Laverty
　S. A....................... 499
Law.......................... 1056
　Andrew M. 277
　Frank............ 588, 589
　James 868, 2152, 2154
　John 125, 1061
　John (Heirs)........... 849

John G. 277, 283
Jonathan (Heirs).. 1061
Thomas 849
Willard 359
William.................. 790
Lawn
　Edward................ 1062
　William.................. 673
Lawrence... 11, 103, 1035, 1056, 2224, 2242
　A. 269
　A. G. 673
　Albert 492, 1072, 1073, 1074
　Albert G. 381, 1071, 2105
　Alex 746
　Alexander...... 868, 869
　Attorney Keith 1074
　Bert 1074
　Capt. James........... 248
　Charles C. 359
　Clarence B. 359
　Eleanor Beymer .. 1074
　Hon. William . 80, 2138
　J. E.................. 81, 656
　Jacob..................... 849
　James... 123, 127, 747, 868, 869, 1025, 1074
　James E. 628, 629
　John 359, 492, 498, 559, 673, 1062, 1072, 1074
　Kathryn 1074
　M. S............... 502, 657
　Mr. 320
　S. B. 492, 1059
　Samuel 54, 87, 461, 1061, 1062, 1072, 1074
　Samuel B. 650
　Simon B.............. 1074
　Thomas 574
　W. 269
　W. A. 95, 653, 1059

William... 81, 103, 105, 106, 107, 108, 115, 125, 131, 144, 146, 153, 155, 157, 158, 161, 164, 209, 242, 255, 256, 329, 381, 463, 487, 492, 674, 1072, 1073, 1074, 2105
William, Jr. 1074
William, Sr........... 1074
Laws
　William.................. 247
Lawton
　David 359
Lawyer
　Deborah 2032
　E. C. 106, 447
　E. W.. 95, 96, 174, 183, 185
　Elza C..................... 178
　James 812
　John 813
　Ruskin B. 359, 368
　W. M. 176
　William Everett 186
Lazear
　Amos 2158
　Francis................... 995
Le Lacheur 2050
Le Lecheur
　William................ 2184
Le Page 2050
　C. A........................ 506
Leach
　Harvey................... 359
Leaman
　Nicholas 1030
Leas
　John 893
Leasure
　Charles 185
Leath
　Samuel 965
Leatherwood God 729
Lebold
　W. R. 499

ALL NAMES INDEX

Lecabaugh
- John 127

Ledlie 678
- Sarah J. Rea 2243
- William H. 2243

Ledman
- Carl 504
- Catherine 965, 976, 977
- Henry 965, 976, 977
- Ida 504
- John 242, 974, 976, 977

Lee
- General 2123
- General Robert E. 2287
- J. J. 671
- Mrs. S. 787
- N. H. 712
- Samuel . 127, 129, 787, 849
- T. J. 821, 2113, 2133
- W. B. 2137, 2138
- Walter W. 498

Leech
- John 787, 790
- Matthew 124, 790
- Matthew, Jr. 1030
- Robert 108, 463

Leeper 230, 2224
- Alexander 292, 787, 790
- Alexander W. 966
- Charity Wines 292
- David 275
- Dr. John A. 293
- Edward 293
- George 153
- George B. 127, 651, 853, 856
- Harry F. 359
- James 66, 112, 115, 720, 995
- James M. 279
- James, Jr. (Heirs) ... 856
- John 832, 835, 856
- John A. 265, 280

John H. 293
Judge 719
Mary Jane 292
Robert 142, 2107, 2108
Robert E. 292
Robert, Jr. 1061
Robert, Sr. 1061
Samuel 790, 1030
William 790

Leggett
- General M. D. 166, 300

Legree
- Simon 2246

Lehman
- Daniel 359

Leland
- Judith 996

Lemke
- William 185

Lemmon
- Carl M. 359
- Hannah 1054
- John 868
- Lorain 621

Lemon
- Hannah 1018

Lenfestey 41

Lenfesty 574
- Mrs. C. 886
- Thomas 198, 566, 567, 798, 804, 888, 893, 894, 2167
- Thomas M. 91, 145, 261
- Thomas, Jr. 682
- W. H. F. 261, 459
- William 653

Lening
- Phebe 2262

Lenington
- Mr. 2244
- Rev. 380

Lennon
- Matthew 279

Lennox
- Sally 946

Lent

Irven 359
Ludlow 849
Mrs. Samuel 965
Samuel 965, 974
William H. 349, 359

Lenton
- Samuel 277

Leonard 435
- C. O. 487
- J. F. R. 168
- J. W. 171

Lepage
- Clarence P. 359
- Cornelius 278
- Frank A. 359
- Thomas 798

LePage 41, 972
- Adam 966
- Harriet 511
- Howard 1010
- Rev. Frank A. 1010
- Rev. Herbert 1010
- Rev. John E. 1010
- Rev. Samuel Maynard 1010
- Thomas 651, 2199

Lerner
- Ethyl 512
- Ethyl D. 512

Leverick
- John 246

Leverson
- Richard 1038

Levicky
- Father 408

Lewelman 712

Lewis
- A. S. 276
- Amos 359
- Dr. Dio 659, 660
- Everett H. 359
- George 856
- Gomer 2134
- John 242
- Levin 245
- T. H. 87, 203, 488

ALL NAMES INDEX

Thomas 178, 1017, 1048
Watson 799
William.................. 359
William T. 359
Leybrand
   Charles C. 2191
Leyshon 2178
   Frank 480, 499
   Frank C. 639
   John 84
   John A. 176
Libby 2205, 2249
Liggitt
   Earle O. 359
Likes
   Arthur 662
   C. E. 509
   Charles 621
   H. 621
   James 1017
   Lemuel 621
   Mrs. James 268
Lile
   Samuel 114
Lilly
   Rev. 399
   Rev. C. H. 400
   Robert 71, 868
Lincoln
   Abraham 727
   President Abraham .. 8, 102, 145, 146, 147, 148, 152, 154, 260, 293, 334, 368, 527, 529, 532, 535, 625, 2014, 2015, 2017, 2056, 2095, 2229, 2236, 2285
Linder
   Harvey H. 579
Lindley
   Ziby 699, 987
Lindsay
   Thomas 258
Lindsey 873
   Abraham 923

James 73
John 131, 551
John A. 280
John R. 265
Joseph 124, 893
M. L. 265
Martin T. 280
Mary Jane Tingle ... 551
Mollie 268
Mrs. M. 886
Robert 142, 894
Samuel . 131, 495, 646, 886, 893
Thomas 868
William, Sr. 131
Linehardt
   Ervin 359
Lingenfelter
   Florence 507
   Mrs. C. A. 516
Lingo
   Laura 503
   Laura M. 503
   Wayne W. 359
Linkhorn 819
   L. S. 95, 173
Linn 166, 1028, 2064, 2066
   A. F. 833
   A. J. 171
   Aaron 2065
   Adam 71, 127, 198, 242, 829, 835, 887, 2065
   Andrew F. 127, 283, 886, 2065
   Andrew J. 91
   Ann Hefelbower .. 2065
   Anna 509
   Augustus 127, 2065, 2066
   Benton 174
   Caroline 2065
   Cyrus . 127, 2065, 2107
   Elizabeth 2065
   Finley 833
   Francis 919, 923

George . 112, 115, 127, 649, 746, 830, 835, 887, 2065, 2066
'Gus' 2066
Harriet 2065
James A. 359
John 73, 242, 574, 835, 2065
Joseph 245, 2065
Margaret 2065
Mary 2065
Mr. 24, 25
Nancy 2065
Pamelia Matthews
   2065
Rebecca 2065
S. S. 494
Samuel 1030, 2065
Samuel M. 277
Sarah 2065
William. 246, 646, 835, 2065
William H. 359
Linton 863
   Bengemen 805
Lipardi
   Domminick 359
Liseton
   George 835
Lisetor
   George 938
Lisle
   John 812
Lister
   James 265, 280
Litesky
   Steve 359
Little 2073, 2087, 2290
   Archibald 746, 934, 940, 941, 2003
   Archibald, Jr. 936
   Carrie 509
   Davis R. 126
   Edward 938, 941
   Ellen 941
   Francis ... 283, 938, 941
   Inglis 512, 513

ALL NAMES INDEX

Isabel 940, 941
Isabelle 938
James 790
John 395, 649, 938, 940, 941
John W. 2186
Joseph 938, 941
Mary 941
Rebecca 941
Sidney 936
Walter 88, 186
William. 395, 938, 940, 941
William G. 938

Littlefield
Herbert 359

Litton
John 369

Livi
Joe 359

Livy 439

Llewelln
Henry 245

Llewellyn 618, 619
William 995

Lloyd
David 359
H. R. 629
Herbert R. 498
J. R. 367, 368, 518, 624, 625, 626
James 110, 2009
John R. 359
Mrs. H. R. 2308

Lochary
Almeta 503
P. 87, 502
Patrick. 75, 76, 80, 160

Locke
J. L. 164, 498, 499
John L. 93, 166, 169, 170, 296, 298, 496, 499, 500
Rev. W. H. 81

Loder
James 762

Lofland 552, 574, 2039, 2235
Boaz 34, 695
Col. Gordon.. 126, 206, 272, 273, 291, 762, 2108, 2109, 2235, 2236
Colonel 131, 301
Colonel Gordon 659
Gordon 24, 34, 126, 495, 566, 798, 2039
Joseph 574
Miss Caroline 268
Mrs. Sarah P. Gomber Metcalf 2235
Sarah P. Gomber Metcalf 34
Susan M. Metcalf 34
William 695

Logan 2214
A. C. 84, 447
Edward 1013, 1017
James 1017
John 865
John A. .. 162, 525, 599
John, Jr. 868
John, Sr. 868
Mrs. A. 865
Mrs. Edward 1013
Mrs. James 1013
R. M. 626
William 746

Logee
Daniel 689, 2108

Loggins 670
Oscar J. 359
W. A. 671
William T. 412

Long
Beatty M. 279
Braden 292
C. C. 629
Chief of Police John A. 421
Dr. 913
Dr. G. A. 528
Emma 503
Eunice 513
Fire Chief C. C. 585
Frederick (Heirs) ... 790
George C. 359
Howard 359
Iona 507
Ira Oliver 367
Isaac 276, 278
Jacob 798, 800
John 923
John J. 923
Jonathan 893
Lucian E. 349, 359
Lucian Edward 339
Martha 507, 2308
N. B. 632, 678, 2178
Samuel 703
Samuel A. 278
Sumpter 917
W. H. 917
Willis H. 502

Longfellow 330, 2126

Longley 70
J. B. 115
Jefferson 673
John B. 703

Longstreth
James 1048

Longsworth 1019
Basil ... 395, 1012, 1017
J. C. 629, 630
Mayor John C. 347
Peter 1000
William C. 359

Looker
William 1030, 1031

Looman
Mina 511

Loomis 478
E. G. 476
Harry 476
James P. 476
Prof. Elias 1035

Lorain
Alfred H. 2191

Lord 462

ALL NAMES INDEX

A. D. 439
Lorentz
  F. V. 509
Lorimer
  Joseph 966
  Miss N. M. 268
  Rev. William .. 440, 789
  S. W. 391
  William 114, 390
Lott
  Samuel 995
Lotton
  Kate 510
Louvell
  J. W. 696
Love
  David 359
  Thomas 503
  Thomas W. 359, 370
Lovejoy 1059, 2120
  Elijah 2119
  W. A. 1059
Lovewell
  J. W. 696
Lowe
  Benedict 923, 932
  Henry 923, 932, 955
  Ralph L. 359
  Ray 509
  Samuel 923
  William T. 359
Lowell 2119
Lowery 972
  Dr. O. F. 491
  Elijah 649, 691, 967, 2278
  Elizabeth 2267
  James 2155
  Lydia 965
  Margaret 965
  Mary 511
  Richard 972
  Robert 246
  William ... 87, 114, 649, 2152, 2158
Lowrey
  John A. 278

Lowry
  Alexander L. 280
  Elijah 974, 1061
  Haven S. 349, 359
  James 923, 974
  John 128, 974
  Newton 279
  Ray Smith 366
  Richard 279
  Robert 974
  Russell S. 359
  Stephen 976
  William 128, 974
Lucas 719
  'Aunt Edie' 669
  Bennett 812, 813
  David 606
  Edith Simpson 631, 669
  James 669
  John 813
  Mike 359
  William 669
Luccock 678
  Attorney H. W. 528
  H. W. 94, 166, 169, 173, 335, 343, 491, 629
  Hon. Thomas S. 80
  Howard W. 636
  Judge H. W. 298, 530
  Maria 2084
  Mayor H. W. ... 169, 296
  N. 115
  Naphtali 120, 123, 127, 646, 853, 854, 855, 856, 970
  Rebecca Keil 970
  S. C. 160
  S. W. 81, 269, 696
  Samuel W. 854
  T. S. 269, 854
  Thomas S. 106, 272, 662, 854
Luch
  James 956
Lucus
  Francis 805

John 805
Lukens
  Charles 2160
Lundy
  Benjamin 702, 2119
Luse
  Charles 992
Lute
  Philip 806
Luzadder 2031
  Abraham 242, 2031, 2032, 2296
  Abraham (Heirs) 812
  David G. 2032, 2033
  Deborah Lawyer .. 2032
  Isaac 2032
  Jacob 2032
  John 807, 2032
  Leah Hogue 2031
  Martha 2296
  Patty 2032
  William E. 2032
Lydick
  D. L. 509
  J. B. 917
  John B. 502
Lykes
  A. J. 467
Lynch
  Al 603, 604
  John 849
  Thomas 849
Lyndon 588, 589
Lyne
  Paul R. 359
Lyon
  Dr. Milford H. 8, 422, 423, 424
  James (Heirs) 849
  Miss Emma 491
Lyons
  Bill 21, 1049
  Jacob 87
  Jim 21, 1049
  John 835
  Levi 2158
  Mrs. Sallie G. 268

ALL NAMES INDEX

William 440
William M. 441
Lytle
   David 839
   G. 886
   John, Sr. 1038
Lyttle
   Alfred W. 498, 499
Lyzer
   John 814

M

Macbeth 151
MacConkey
   Sam F. 94, 186, 639
   Samuel F. 185
Mack
   James 868
   John 868, 2128
   Mrs. E. 865
Mackey
   Alexander 73, 995
   Belle Conner 2237
   David L. 278
   Frank C. 359, 367, 2237
   Glessner 2237
   J. H. ... 74, 93, 164, 166,
      169, 2216, 2239
   James T. 280
   Judge J. H. 653
   Judge Justus H.
      'Howard' 2236,
      2237
   Mrs. J. H. 491
   Mrs. Laura Hobbs 2237
   Richard 790
   Robert 790
   T. C. 87
   William 995
Mackley
   Foster 369
   Foster E. 366
   William 2134
Macomber
   George 522
Madden

James G. 359
Melville 279
Mrs. S. 865
Robert 865, 868
Maddox
   Rev. J. Stewart 410
Madison
   C. L. 77, 139, 143, 144,
      261, 601, 625, 628,
      2056, 2099, 2106,
      2109
   Charles L. 498, 601,
      605
   James 740
   President James ... 110,
      111, 931, 2149,
      2271
Maffett
   Mella 507
Maffit
   Robert 806
Maffitt
   Robert 798
Magee
   Andrew 430, 495, 649,
      801, 802, 2237,
      2238
   Jackson 1030
   Rev. Andrew 379
Magers
   Marjorie 629
Magiffin
   John 232
Magill
   Stewart 1017
Maginnis
   F. J. 153
Mahaffey
   Frank 2136
   G. F. 514
   J. P. 76, 80, 81, 91, 107,
      467, 507, 508, 514,
      2207
   J. P. 'Perry' 467
   John 2239
   Perry 616, 662
Mahan

John 1017
Mahanney
   William 1062
Maharry
   Isaac 835
Mahoney
   John 24, 985
   Mr. 552, 2043
   William 981
Maitland
   M. S. 2107
Major
   Col. John O. 289
Majors
   E. A. 254
Maldoth
   Joseph 359
Mallett
   Fred Wesley 367
   Leon H. 359
Malloney
   Joseph F. 168
Malone
   Alcava 976
   Alfred 283
   David 1048
   Elias 283
   James 856
   Reuben J. 283
Mancup
   John 790
Maney
   General 161
Mankaps 232
Mann
   Erma 508
   Guy 359
   Thomas O. 989
Manypenny
   George W. 461, 462
Maple
   Jacob 824, 995
   William 246, 1037
   William B. 1048
Mardis
   Samuel 1048
Marion

ALL NAMES INDEX

General 804
Maris
  F. L. 770
  Francis L. 639
  Sidney 800
Marker
  Percey 279
Markle
  Nora Carpenter .. 2029, 2030
  Oliver ... 350, 351, 359, 2028, 2029
  Oliver, Jr. 2029
  Oliver, Sr. 2029
  Pfc. Oliver, Jr. 2030
Markley
  George J. 656
Marks
  Charles 982, 983
Marland
  Gilley 603, 604
  Gilly 616
Marlatt
  Abraham 1048
  Jacob 844, 849
  John 1048
  Richard 923
Marlett
  William 279
Marling
  John 112, 247, 457, 798, 839
  Matthew 762
  Matthew (Heirs) ... 812
  Sarah 795, 796, 797, 2053, 2054
  Vincent 603
  William 275
Marlow
  Peter 939
  Samuel 945
Marlowe 2302
  Miner 284
  Samuel 955
  William 923, 932
Marquand ... 41, 719, 803, 804, 2050, 2186

Charles E. 2186
John 41, 651, 803, 856
John W. 636
Mary 45
Peter 1048
Marsh 226, 559, 595, 2130
  Albert 603
  C. S. 204
  Charles 178
  Charles S. 100, 180, 514
  David C. 275, 276
  Eli 2069, 2098
  Enoch 944
  Frank 337
  Frank N. 359
  Harry R. 359
  Jesse 2009
  Jonathan 1017
  Moses 88, 142, 153, 261
  Rucker 621
  Ruckie 616
  T. C. 507, 508
  Thomas 499
  Thomas C. 2130
  William 502
  William P. 279
  Yvonne 508
Marshall 129, 523
  Andrew 67, 574, 2060, 2063
  Benjamin. 71, 868, 893
  David 2196
  Elizabeth 995
  John 390
  John R. 283
  Joseph M 995
  Joseph W. 747
  Judge 1028
  Robert 67, 69, 87, 114, 123, 1030, 2106
  Samuel 115, 129, 1030
  Thomas R. 175
  W. M. 447
  William 790, 923, 2199
  Martel 2050

Nicholas 647, 812, 2190
Martin 889
  Absalom 67, 85, 87, 122, 128, 244, 245, 250, 838, 884, 887, 889, 896, 2061
  Capt. Absalom 70, 836, 2296
  Captain Absalom .. 549, 2300
  Elizabeth 649
  Emma 2255
  Hugh 2009
  J. F. 106
  J. W. 391
  James 696
  Joel 923, 932
  Joel F. 123, 124, 649
  John . 9, 110, 434, 649, 726, 727, 728, 729, 832, 835, 856, 939
  John (Heirs) 812
  Joseph A. 278
  Joshua 703, 1059, 1061, 1062
  Nicollas 2050
  Rev. A. C. 402
  Robert 574
  Samuel 86
  Victor 501
Masefield 798
Mason
  Clifford H 498
  Edgar O. 797, 2054
  James 90, 696
  Mary Ethel 2054
  Mrs. Clara E. Oldham 797
  Mrs. Clara Oldham 2054
  Rev. 412
  William 279
Mast
  Charles 2168
Masters 718

ALL NAMES INDEX

Benjamin...... 741, 945, 949, 950, 951, 956
Cory M. 504
Daniel............ 819, 955
Hannah McPeek.... 951
Henry 279, 893
Richard.... 69, 951, 955
William.................. 955

Matheny
  H. E. 88, 185
  Henry E. 183
  Mrs. 596
  Willard F. 359

Mather
  Madeline............... 512

Mathers
  Henry 856
  Samuel (Heirs) 856

Mathews 570
  Alfred W. 359
  Amelia Haynes.... 2240
  Anna Means........ 2240
  E. 261
  E. W. 74, 81, 157, 161, 162, 164, 498, 586, 629, 696, 704, 1029, 2117, 2128, 2129, 2174
  E. W., Sr. 498
  Edward W. 2216, 2217
  Edward W., Jr...... 2239
  Frank.................. 2196
  Fred C. 360
  George 360
  Gnomar................. 247
  Ill. E. W 500
  Judge E. W. . 590, 2307
  Judge Edward W. 2238, 2239, 2240
  Mary 512
  Ralph.................... 515
  Robert................... 423

Mathias
  Lizzie 510

Mathieu
  Charles E. 360

Matson

Mark 1031
Matthews......... 207, 2004
  Abraham 829
  Archdeacon John R. 405
  Donald C. 360
  Donald Cameron... 367
  Garrett 242
  Henry 853
  Mary 504
  Newman 830
  Pamelia 2065
  Paul 1017
  Samuel 504

Mattingly
  George 515

Mawhorr
  William.......... 839, 896

Max
  C. A....................... 509
  Charles E. 506
  Kenneth I. 360

Maxfield
  Allen..................... 140
  James 647
  Kinsey 498
  Thomas 498

Maxwell 262, 2178
  Charles 278, 284
  David............ 799, 800
  Mrs. 787
  Mrs. Robert......... 1013
  Robert....... 1013, 1017
  Samuel 787

May
  George W.............. 278
  Margaret............. 1017
  Mr. 985

Maynard
  Rev. Washington. 2102
  W. 577, 2106
  Washington 505

Mays
  T. E. 157, 783

Mazenko
  Mike George 366
McAbee..................... 833

McAdams
  S. 678
McAllister
  Corwyn................. 956
McArthur
  Samuel 391
McBride.................... 884
  Alexander............. 995
  Arthur C. 360
  Christine............... 511
  Everett F............... 360
  Franklin Russell 367
  James 866
  John 746, 868
  Lawrence A. 360
  Pauline 509, 512
  R. W. 390
  Ramsey 88
  Roy E. 360
  Roy N. 360
  T. B. 87, 174

McBurney
  Charles 277
  Dorman 325, 326
  Dr. John 442, 468, 469, 789, 801, 2221, 2237
  Grandmother 326
  Hazel 503
  Helen............. 500, 516
  Ida 326
  Isaac 258
  James 277, 603, 812
  John 279, 441, 444, 447, 653, 974, 2129, 2130
  John B. 360
  Lenna 326
  Miss Anna 801
  Mrs. Helen 181
  Robert 654
  Russell.................. 503
  William. 265, 277, 280, 283, 1061
  William W. 360

McCaffrey
  Father 407

ALL NAMES INDEX

McCall
- Alex 603, 604
- Dr. 330
- Dr. J. H. 586
- Fred 360
- J. H. 989
- Miss Maggie.. 443, 623

McCandless
- John 893

McCann
- Jones 242, 966

McCarrell
- John 868

McCartney . 556, 557, 873
- Andrew 153
- Captain 263
- Estella 556, 2098
- Harriet N. 557
- Henry 80, 87, 337, 360, 434, 640, 649, 651, 1043, 1048
- Henry of William. 1048
- Henry, Jr. 939, 1048
- James 868
- John 166, 955, 2076
- Margaret 728
- Provost Marshal... 305, 310
- Stella 132, 2048
- W. C. 707
- W. S. 518, 656
- William.................. 747
- William (Heirs) 1048
- Winfield S. 166

McCarty
- C. H. 2197
- C. R. 2196

McCaskey
- Hugh 1017

McClain
- James 441
- M. 923
- Mrs. Marie 370

McClanahan
- Robert 868

McClary 647, 2080
- Andrew 1061

Henry 974
Margaret 2081
R. J. (Heirs) 647
Robert J. 495
Thomas 2062, 2080, 2081

McClaskey
- Charles 923

McCleary ... 449, 767, 830, 831, 833, 2064, 2218, 2219, 2220
- Alexander 1062
- Almira 965
- Andrew 80, 87, 169, 1059, 2009
- George 2009
- H. 856, 1062
- Henry .. 832, 856, 2218
- Herman 618
- J. 856
- James 2024
- James A. (Heirs) .. 1062
- Jane W. 2267
- Joseph 863
- Julius 862, 863
- Loney Leo 366
- Mary 832
- Thomas 975
- William 57

McClellan
- General George B. 152, 154

McClelland 304, 331, 770, 989
- Alexander 330
- Alta 330
- Dick 330
- General 147
- George 153, 464
- George W. 278
- Grandmother 330
- H. D. 518, 770
- J. A. 330
- J. C. 157
- J. E. 84, 165, 655
- J. P. 498
- James 330, 331, 995

Laura 501
Lydia 501
Mary . 8, 329, 330, 331
Mattie 952
Mrs. James 330
Nancy 988
Paul T. 770
Sylvester 501
Thomas 330
W. W. 936, 2073
William 988

McClenahan
- D. A. 964
- Dr. Frank 789
- James M. 275
- John 67, 110, 275, 442, 447
- John G. 284
- Mrs. James 268
- Mrs. Sarah 426
- Rev. John 789
- Rev. William 789
- Robert S. 275
- S. W. 283
- Sarah 2167
- Stewart 964
- Thomas 110
- Uray 964

McClenehan
- James 160
- John 955
- Mr. 263

McCluney
- William 805

McCluny
- Nichols 798

McClure
- George 2160
- George A. 2160

McClurg
- Jim 850, 851
- Joe 850, 851
- Joseph 812
- William 812

McCluskey
- Joseph 280

McClusky 819

2390

Henry 790
Kate 440
McCollum .. 194, 195, 587, 588, 2224
   Casper 893
   E. R. 595
   Ezekiel 2196
   Isaac 115, 126, 276, 381, 649, 807, 808, 812, 813
   John (Heirs) 835
   Miller 494
   Nancy 807
   Paul 432
McColough
   Liley 806
McComb
   Hugh 868, 869
McCombs
   Hugh 461, 870
McCon
   Jane 703
   Thomas 703
McConahay
   James 258
McConahey
   Mary Gillett 2099
   Robert 2099
McConaughey
   John 762, 763
McConaughy
   Andrew 835
   David 894
   John 798
McConauhy
   James 798
   Nancy 798
McConegle
   Joseph 463
McConehay
   Andrew 574
   Dave 616
   Horace 616
McConehey
   Robert 261
McConkey
   Belle 832

James 360, 812
John 283, 812
Samuel 798
McConn
   William 142
McConnaughy
   Duncan 278
McConnell
   J. 269
   James 245, 1062
   Joe 515
   Joseph 70, 649, 812, 1061
   Mary 939, 2072
   Palmer 656
   Pierre C. 181
   Rev. 294
   Thelma 369
   Thomas 812, 955
   Thurman 360
   V. D. 180
   William 278, 649, 1061
McConnelsville 165
McCord
   John 1017
McCormick 431, 2289
   Cyrus 778
   Dr. W. L. 422, 424
   George .. 522, 886, 893
   James 277
   Robert ... 432, 923, 932
   Robert M. 360
   Robert N. 339
   Robert, Sr. 917
McCortle 989
   Mary 501
   Mary M. 501
   William 989, 1031
McCotter 873
McCown
   Thomas 812
McCoy 377, 866, 2191
   Alex 80, 87, 261
   Alexander 145, 2126
   Anna 511
   Benjamin 1061
   Cornight 1061

Daniel 798
Henry C. 824
Hugh 246, 824, 995, 1009, 2158
James 868, 944
James H. 278
Steven 278
William H. 894
McCracken .. 55, 262, 644, 647, 653, 806, 2106, 2154, 2181, 2184, 2211, 2224
   Addie 514
   Alex 781
   Alexander 575, 647, 712, 820, 893, 2250, 2263
   C. F. 514
   Ella 2249
   H. 269
   H. M. 87, 174
   Henry 494
   Jane 2222
   John H. 360
   John M. 302
   Margaret McClary
      2081
   Orville 360
   Rev. Charles 972
   William ... 87, 110, 111, 112, 123, 247, 249, 387, 457, 495, 563, 564, 565, 566, 567, 574, 647, 670, 799, 2081, 2085, 2184, 2185, 2203, 2222, 2250
McCrea 873
   David 955
   Edward 1061
   James 964
McCreary 2224
   Alexander 1030
   Dr. Henry 1027
   George 1030
   Hugh 494, 812

ALL NAMES INDEX

James ... 381, 492, 649, 2279
John 812
John L... 106, 173, 174, 265, 280
Loney 369
Margaret Laughlin 2279
Mint 360
Sarah Mills 1028
Thomas 360
Walter Haven 360

McCrory
   Lavinia 798
   William 798

McCuen 972

McCulley 589
   Byron 606
   Charles 603, 604
   Gilbert 127
   Gilbert, Jr. 856
   Gilbert, Sr. 856
   James 142
   John 696
   Matthew 849
   S. J. 657
   S. M. 262
   Samuel J. 514
   William. 153, 610, 657, 787

McCulloch 589, 2143
   A. R. 177, 178, 180, 181, 183, 184, 186, 296, 335, 491, 657
   Attorney A. R. 496, 497, 664
   William 192, 247

McCullock
   David 434

McCullough 21, 2280, 2281
   Abraham 2280
   Capt. John 26, 2235
   David ... 127, 939, 2280
   Davis 835
   Dr. J. 56
   Dr. P. H 56

Elizabeth 2280
George 2280
Hugh 73, 360, 746, 868
J. C. 698, 699
Jane Forsythe 2280, 2281
John 649, 829, 830, 835, 1031, 2280, 2281
John M. 746
Major Samuel 2280, 2281
Raymond M. 360
Robert 939, 2280, 2281
Samuel 2280
Silas 812
Thomas 115, 124
Thomas J. 635
William 24, 25
William A. 840, 842

McCully
   James 856

McCune 128, 833
   Clark 813
   Hugh 856
   James 1048
   John 746, 893, 894, 1062
   John B. 280
   John T. 275, 283
   M. 124
   Michael 115, 813
   Robert 976
   Willam T. 279

McCurdy 2224
   J. M. 270
   John 121, 123, 381, 649, 650, 1061, 1062
   Mr. 320

McCusky
   Joseph 265

McCutcheon
   Rev. R. 405

McDaniel
   Jackson 966
   Joseph 939, 2072

McDonald. 587, 588, 2143
   Annie 936
   Archibald 1030
   Daniel 798
   Finley 277
   H. F. 295
   Hannah 2267
   Hugh 90, 511
   Hugh F. 279
   Isaac 278
   James 616
   James M. 978
   James T. O. 634
   John 24, 124
   Margaret 978
   Mary M. 978
   Meade 605
   Robert ... 605, 977, 978
   Thomas 1031
   Waite M. 360
   William. 232, 261, 553, 554, 625, 849, 923, 924, 2023
   William, Jr. 1030

McDonough
   Andrew F. 360
   Patrick 790
   Thomas 360

McDowell
   Captain 274
   F. M. 258
   Hugh C. 279, 284
   James 494, 812
   James C. 275
   James E. 283
   Jefferson 283
   John ... 115, 813, 1048, 2107
   Mark 893
   Milton 275
   T. C. 488

McElhaney
   Henry H. 360

McElhany
   Robert 399

McElhenry
   William 835

ALL NAMES INDEX

McElheren
   Joseph 849
McElroy 2159
   Archibald 2191
   Earl R 360
   John 868
   Larry 360
   Mrs. S 865
   Rev 552
McElwee
   George 824
McEwen
   J. A. 161, 164, 502
McFadden
   Margaret 2182
   William H. 360
McFaren
   John 559
McFarland 563, 578, 2048, 2081
   Dr. 528
   Dr. John 977, 1062, 2242
   Dr. W. H. .. 80, 296, 726
   J. 699
   J. M. 652
   James 490
   James Farrar 367
   James H 278
   James M. 517, 518, 572
   Jeanette 12
   John 123, 649, 650
   Miss Grace 623
   Rev. 261, 298, 302, 524
   Rev. W. H. 257, 262, 571, 643, 2016, 2124, 2204
   Rev. William H. 388, 389
   Robert W. 439
   Thomas 563, 932
   W. H 391
   William H. 277, 283
McFarran
   John W 522
McFarren
   John 2172

McFee
   Craig B 360
McGarraty
   Henry 72, 73
McGaw
   James 128, 976
McGee 833
McGeorge
   Dr. C. K. 389
McGiffen
   David 747
McGiffin
   George 522
   John 800, 1030
McGill 646
   J. M. 80, 81
   James 390, 391
   John 76
   John M. 160
   John N. 90
   Rev. James 56, 389, 437, 2203, 2204
McGilton 56
McGiven
   John 246
   William 246
McGlaughlin
   Peter 996
McGonagle
   James 790, 2107
McGowan
   Andrew 245
   George 522
   Wilson 70, 71
McGrath 872
McGraw
   Bessie 513
McGregor
   Archie G. 360
   John 835
   Matthew 673
McGrew
   Finley 939, 1013, 2072
   Mrs. Finley 1013
McGuffey 8, 431, 444, 446, 450, 451, 452, 2059, 2220

   Beulah 500
   John G. 499
   William H. 451, 452
McGuire
   C. J. 761
   John 868
   Patrick 849
   Thomas 291
McHenry
   Carl W. 360
   Fred T 360
   Fred Thomas 339
   Joseph E. 360
McHugh
   Jack 360
McIllyar
   Ellen 375
   J. O. 379
McIlvaine
   Andrew 1030
McIlyar 262, 833, 2180
   C. C. 508
   C. R. 514
   Clyde R. 635
   E. J. .. 2033, 2034, 2035
   Isaiah 560, 624, 629, 647, 2097, 2190
   Isaiah M. 123
   J. O. 298, 586, 653
   James 276
   James O 153
   Maurice 616, 617
   Mrs. 800
   Rev. J. L. 2203
   Thomas 393, 790, 2192, 2198
   W. H. H. 166, 279, 300, 507, 508, 625, 662, 2180
   William 798
McIntire
   John 192
McIntyre
   John 29, 30
McKahan
   J. 106

ALL NAMES INDEX

Robert.. 100, 142, 160, 2196
Thomas 278
McKain
    Charles L. 360
    Elisha 913
McKee
    Annie 661
    Eleanor 798
    Harold L. 503
    Jacob 270
    John 246, 574, 798
    Joseph 278
    Miss M. 268
    Robert 798
    Rodrick 976
    Samuel 1031
    Thomas . 125, 856, 955
McKelvey
    John 695
    William 988, 1062
McKendree
    Bishop 570
McKennon
    William 505
McKewen
    Peter 812
McKim
    Catherine 270
    Elizabeth 270
    George 270
    George W. 258
    Hiram 270
    James 270, 276
    John 258, 270, 275
    M. V. 275
    Martin 270
    Rebecca 270
    Widow 269
    William 270
McKinley 477
    Governor William . 166
    Hon. William 527
    President 295, 932
    President William 8, 166, 167, 168, 170, 171, 467, 468, 521,

525, 526, 527, 528, 625, 631, 637, 711, 2148, 2214, 2263, 2310
    William 597, 599
McKinney
    Alex 1028
    Alexander 276
    Ham 617
    J. F. 158
    J. K. 588
    John 1031
    John (Heirs) 1030
    John B. 275
    Joseph 1030
    Mary 1030
    Matthew 1030
    Miller 1028
    Mrs. A. M. 1013
    Mrs. S. 1013
    S. F. 125
    Spear 697
McKinnie
    Samuel 1017
McKinsie
    Samuel 868
McKisson
    William L. 277
McKitrick 873
    A. M. 127
    Alexander 868
    Ebenezer 800
    J. M. 76, 81, 90, 99, 157, 158, 754, 755, 2207
    James 800, 1017
    John 1061, 1062
    Joseph 868
    Mrs. James 800
McKnight
    Jacob A. 790
    Samuel 790
McLane
    Rev. Daniel 495
McLaughlin
    John 69, 230
    Patrick 247

Peter R. 501
McLean
    Daniel 390
    Judge John 1016
    Rev. Daniel .. 389, 2203
McLeod
    Mildred 504
McLeran 693
McMahan
    James 87, 995
McMahon.. 126, 454, 573, 576
    Ada Rea 2243
    C. S. 652
    Charles S. 343, 518
    Fulton 576, 577
    M. G. 2243
    Mary C. 576
    Ruth 298
    S. J. 383, 524, 652
    Samuel J. 498, 652
McManaway
    Thomas 258
    William 800
McManus
    Earl 515
    Earl J. 368
McMichael
    Eleanor 790
McMillan
    Laura 511
McMillen 2302
    David 277, 283
    Edwin L. 460
    George 494
    James .. 434, 893, 1048
    John 57, 939, 1048
    John C. 90
    Margaret 513, 856
    Nancy 832
    S. B. 498
    Samuel 283
McMilligan
    Alex 270
McMorris
    Elizabeth 513, 514
McMullen

Alex 265
Alexander 270, 280
Elizabeth 2121
J.   126
James 246, 812, 835
John 270, 849
Joseph .. 283, 284, 852, 856
Mack 270
Robert 283
McMullin
Elizabeth 318, 320, 321, 327
Noah 1059
McMunn
J. S. 391
O. C. 183
McMurray 762
Bill 540
Robert 566, 763
McMurry 531, 532
James 798
Peter 798, 824
Robert 232, 798
William 799
McNabb
James H 360
Peter E. 360
McNary
Alex 696
Charles L. 185
Thomas (Heirs) 798
McNeal
Malcolm 339
McNeel
Ralph C. 351, 360
McNees
Arthur P. 498
McNeil
Archie 221
Malcolm 360
Robert 360
McNutt 1056
Benjamin ... 2060, 2061
Isaac 302
Isaac N. 276
John 284

John M. 277
Samuel 1061
William H. H. 276
McPeek 951
Albright 375
Daniel 951, 955
Daniel, Sr. 868
Ezekiel 893, 951
Hannah 951
James A. 360
John 868, 951, 955
Joshua ... 258, 276, 284
M. 2196
Mordecai 276, 375
Patrick 951
Richard 868, 951
Samuel 957
William 951
McPherson 2164
D. M. 458
Daniel 868
Dr. J. T. 1029, 2138, 2162, 2164
Dr. T. J. 81
J. T. 654
John 868
Lewis 671
Mary 868
Miss Jennie 81
McQuaide
Charles 923
McVey
Resin 975
McVicker
Alexander 280
Alexander H. 649
Harvey F. 649
James H. 279
Samuel 279, 976
McWilliams
Abraham 975
Daniel 835
Philip 246
Robert 939
Samuel 955
Thurman 360
Meacham

Carlo C. 279
Hun 502
James M. 279
Mead
B. L. 264
Benjamin F. 913
Benjamin L. 87, 144, 649
Daniel 923
Miss Clara 264
Phineas W. 649
Meade
Benjamin L. 924
Daniel 2154
Meagher
J. C. 270
Meaher
John C. 258
Mealman
John 246
Means
Anna 2240
Mears
Elder 373, 375
Peter 2196
Rev. William 2195, 2196
Medill
William 462
Medley
Eleanor 965
Francis 893
Mee
Rev. C. B. 405
Meek 819, 937, 2112
Carl O. 360
Charles C. 360
David 2196
Erastus F. 278
Isaac 819
J. D. 258
Jacob 824
James H. 279
John W. 258
Rev. John 1040
W. H. 2141
Meeks

ALL NAMES INDEX

David A. 375
Matilda 375
Mehaffey 756
Alice 756
Anna 513
James 278
James, Sr. 790
John 498, 646, 790, 798, 800, 2165
John O. 360
Joseph 278
Margaret Bingham 787
Rev. Samuel 438, 1059
Robert 790
Samuel .. 447, 756, 787
Samuel, Jr. 790
Samuel, Sr. 790
Mehanna
John 924
Mehling
Captain H. 411
Meighen
Hobart M. 360
Lilian Bell 513
Renwick H. 360
Meigs
Return J. 110, 111
Melching
Joseph 360, 368
Mellon
James 2154
Mellott
Clyde S. 360
Mendenhall
Isaac 2152
Menendez 554
Mercer 2096
Albert 360
Henry H. 258
James 1038
John 1017
John B. 258
Solomon 160
Win 619
Meredith 2073, 2200, 2282
Eleanor 2282

Eleanor Thomas .. 2282
Frances 2283
George 868, 2282, 2283
George W.. 2282, 2283
Georgia 2283
H. M. 90, 178
Isabella 2282
J. P. 936
James 370
John 2282
Jonathan 2282
Lettice 2282
Nathaniel 939
Owen 2282
Robert 2282
Sarah 2282
Thomas 2282, 2283
W. A. 936
W. F. 339
William 2282
William F. 360
Merrick
L. H. 466, 652, 1071, 1074
Lawrence H. 639
Mrs. Kathryn Lawrence 1074
Merrilees
Charles H. 639
Merriman 833
Merritt
Thomas 246
Merry
Gay 488
Merryman 2305, 2306
Benjamin 284
Hannah Stevens .. 2306
James . 447, 955, 2305, 2306
James E. 2306
Jane 2306
Kile E. 2306
Margaret 2306
Margaret Etzlar ... 2306
Rachel 2306
Thomas 2137

Merz
Charles W. 514
Messer 1028
Carlos 360
Israel 1030
James 800
Job 1030
Rezin 1031
Metcalf 118, 223, 521, 531, 611, 886, 2006, 2007, 2027, 2044, 2045, 2144, 2145, 2148, 2199, 2270
A. B. 559
Allen 34
Andrew 89, 90, 112, 114, 126, 198, 457, 495, 567, 762, 2059
Catherine Gomber 611, 626
George ... 7, 32, 34, 35, 37, 66, 67, 86, 88, 95, 99, 110, 111, 114, 115, 126, 260, 495, 546, 547, 550, 556, 557, 577, 579, 624, 647, 762, 795, 799, 2044, 2045, 2046, 2047, 2048, 2055, 2059, 2063, 2098, 2172, 2240
J. A. 55, 559, 647, 2172
J. G. 55, 647, 666, 693, 2100, 2172
J. M. 666, 693
Jacob 126, 630
Jacob G. 34, 54, 88, 126, 647, 798, 2172
Jacob Gomber 2045
Jacob Gomber, II . 2045
Joseph A. 34, 601, 2172
Judge George 38
Margaret 34
Margaret W. 34

2396

ALL NAMES INDEX

Margery 34
Mr. 2091
Mrs. Sarah P. Gomber
 2235
Sarah 557
Sarah P. Gomber 34
Surveyor George 68
Susan Gomber . 32, 34, 2045, 2046
Susan M. 34
Thomas 34, 2235
Metcalfe 2045, 2046
 George 2044
 J. G. 2045, 2242
 Jacob Gomber 2240, 2241
 Mr. S. W. 2044
 S. W. 2046, 2241
Metheny
 Elihab 501
 Ephraim 501
Meton
 Stafford 868
Metsker
 Jennie 511
Mevey
 John 996
Meyer
 John 498, 500
Meyers
 James C. 360, 368
 Max P. 360
Michael
 Ray B. 360
Michaels
 Claude 515
Michenor
 Daniel 868
Mihelik
 Father 408
Miles
 David 265
 Harry T. 360
 Henry 360
 John 478
Miley 970
 Abraham 2158

J. R. 402
John 2154, 2158
Olive 502
Milhoan
 Harry 360
Millbourne
 Joseph 601
Miller . 386, 390, 391, 437, 569, 646, 728, 746, 786, 809, 810, 830, 855, 897, 898, 992, 1019, 2103, 2118, 2224, 2225
 Adam ... 712, 853, 856, 861
 Alexander 269, 389, 390, 391
 Anna 501
 Audrey 512, 513
 Audrey M. 513
 C. R. 499
 Charles 360
 Charles R. 498
 Charley 232
 Cuba 512
 Cuba Secrest 512
 David 868, 995
 Dr. Thomas 2221
 Francis 279, 2156
 Frank 2089
 George 246, 1061
 Howard 360
 Hugh 807, 809, 812
 James 790, 965
 Jane 786
 John 856, 1043
 John F. 1048
 Jonathan 956, 1061
 Joseph ... 127, 128, 856
 LaFayette 861
 Levi P. 2191
 Lewis 277, 280
 Louis 498
 Margaret 511, 861
 Marion 621
 Matthew 893, 894
 Matthew T. 279

Merle 371
Mrs. 809
Mrs. S. 268
P. T. 126
Paul E. 514
R. R. 852
Ray D. 360
Rev. Alexander 963
Rev. Leland M. 389
Rev. W. R. 972
Richard M. 360
Robert 1028
Robert R. 861
Thomas . 495, 647, 698
William 270
Millhone 970
 Elijah 974, 2158
 Enoch 969, 975
 Ethel 501
 Horace D. 360
 John .. 974, 2152, 2154
 Myron E. 360
 R. E. 447
 Waite 501
 William F. 360
Milligan
 A. P. 185
 Alexander 835, 856
 Alexander N. 127
 Alexander P. 277
 Ann 853
 Dr. 2215
 Dr. W. V. 296, 528, 676, 2168
 E. B. 489, 490
 John 115, 198, 682, 835
 Lacey 621
 Rev. 261, 272
 Rev. W. V. 81
 Rev. William V. 383, 384
 Robert 868
 Thomas 868
Milliken
 Edward 856
Milliner

ALL NAMES INDEX

Grammer 799
Millner
    Edward................ 939
Mills 2073
    David.................. 1030
    Elizabeth 919
    George S. 213
    J. 2191
    J. W. 886
    James R. 2201
    John 2155
    Joseph.................. 894
    Mrs. 268
    R. H. 655
    Rev. J. R. 379
    Rev. Jacob 378
    Sarah................... 1028
    Thomas 919
    William (Heirs) 1030
Millson
    John 956
Millwood
    of 2098
Milner
    Alonzo.................. 258
    Edward. 115, 121, 125,
        245, 522
    Jesse 112, 747, 936,
        2073
Minale
    Sam 350, 351, 360
Minor 833
Minos
    King..................... 2134
Minters
    William A. 280
Minto
    G. A. 515
    Richard................. 484
Miskimen
    Abraham............... 849
    George 499
    Hezekiah 279
    James 1038, 1050,
        1051
    Nelson.................. 849
    Susan 2274

Miskimmins
    Abraham 1048
    Harvey H. 1048
    Isaac 1048
    James, Jr. 1048
    James, Sr. 1048
    Nelson................ 1048
Mitchel
    Hance................... 292
Mitchell
    Alex 106
    Alexander....... 87, 115,
        123, 129, 685, 790,
        856, 1038, 1040,
        1042, 1048, 2108
    Asbury................ 2069
    Atkinson................ 246
    David............ 277, 938
    Delitha 2069
    Dr. F. M. 337, 339, 491
    G. J. 269
    George849, 856, 1040,
        1048
    Hans................... 1048
    Hugh 83
    James 856
    John B. 128, 856
    Joseph.................. 125
    Mrs. Alexander ... 1038
    Prof. Ralph E. 422, 423
    Rev. 399
    Singleton............... 868
    Temperance........ 2069
    Tempy................. 2069
    'Tempy' 669
    William................ 2191
Mitchener
    C. E. 157, 210
    Charles E. 464, 704
Mitner
    Alonzo.................. 275
    George 275
Moffatt
    George B. 360
    John 67
    Robert.................. 242
    Val514

Moffett
    Charles 360
    Mr. 762
Moffit
    John 889
    Thomas 621
Moirison
    Joseph.................. 939
Moland
    Jacob.................... 923
Molatt
    Richard................. 932
Molineause
    Thomas 923
Moll
    Mary 512
Mollineaux
    Thomas 812, 1061
Monahan
    John C. 360
Monk
    Harry R. 350
    Henry R. 360
Monnett
    Attorney General F. S.
        170
Monroe
    Charles 494
    Charles C. 360
    Clara..................... 511
    James 934
    President James ... 111,
        2031, 2282
Montag
    Father 406
Monteratti
    Ferdinando............ 360
Montgomery
    Edward Michael 366
    George E. 360
    Herbert Spencer.... 367
    James 955
    John 1061, 2128
    Levi............. 747, 1061
    Michael 242
    Robert................... 812
    Thomas 360

ALL NAMES INDEX

William 1058
Mooney
  W. C. 105, 176, 177
Moore 218, 223, 238, 562, 563, 576, 659, 688, 716, 720, 746, 889, 1065, 2073, 2097, 2224, 2268
  Aaron 995
  Andrew .. 34, 194, 227, 230, 556, 557, 671, 714, 800, 889, 1061, 2098, 2210
  Andrew B. ... 601, 1064
  Andrew, Jr. 2211
  Andrew, Sr. ... 668, 716
  Azor 868
  Blanche 511
  C. E. 507
  C. Ellis 93, 104, 105, 176, 178, 179, 180, 181, 182, 183, 421, 639, 652, 952, 2258
  C. R. 88, 2107
  Capt. James W. ... 2124
  Catherine B. Gomber 34
  Catherine G. 34
  Chalmer Elvin 366
  Charles H. 258, 278, 670
  Charles L. 186
  Congressman C. Ellis 184, 2257
  Cyrus 34
  David 245, 995
  Donald 506
  Dorothy 503
  Dr. David H. 1010
  Edward 955
  Eliza 2210, 2211
  Elizabeth B. 34, 557
  Elizabeth Bines ... 2210, 2211
  F. M. 601
  Flora 503

Frank R. 360
Fred W. 464
Frederick E. 360
Frederick W. 360
G. W. 171
Gen. R. B. 132
General Robert B. . 659
George 34
George A. 276
George W. 284
H. K. 90, 173
Hannah M. Carlisle 260
Harriet 34, 1064, 2210
Harrison 571
Harrison C. 279
Hezekiah 936, 939
Hiram 280
Horace C. 278
Isaac 995, 1009
J. B. 559
J. G. 503, 695, 698
Jacob 2210
Jacob G. 34
James 995, 1030
James B. .. 34, 495, 647, 798, 800, 2059, 2210
James L. 278
James W. 258, 277, 2015
James, Jr. 995
Jane 557, 936
John 81, 835, 955, 995, 1030, 2107
John A. 278
John of David 995
Joseph 399
Joseph D. 360
L. P. 87, 171, 2258
Lycurgus 494
Mahala 400
Major J. W. 494
Major James W. ... 259, 260, 2016
Malvina 714
Margaret M. 556
Maria 34, 2210

Maria A. Gomber 34
Mary A. 2211
Mary Jane 2253
Mordecai 868
Mrs. Charles 800
Mrs. Samuel 2196
Peter 1017
R. B. 54, 106, 126, 439, 559, 568, 574
R. R. 1025
Rev. James 988
Rev. L. B. 726
Robert ... 675, 687, 688
Robert B. 34, 73, 84, 112, 113, 457, 495, 557, 562, 566, 567, 647, 762, 798, 1066, 2090, 2098, 2210
Samuel 849
Sarah 936
Susan 34
T. I. 1010
Thomas .. 34, 156, 605, 654, 722, 913, 914, 917, 936, 939, 995, 1006, 1030, 2210
Thomas I. 936
W. O. 447, 460, 467
Walter 2199
William. 129, 227, 230, 246, 381, 575, 670, 746, 747, 955, 1061, 2210, 2211
Wilmer D. 360
Zula 507
Moorehead
  Al 604
  Alexander 975
  Cummins 1030
  Dwight L. 100, 176
  Joseph 1030
  Leander 976
  Leona 500
  Ray 499
  T. S. 466, 639
  T. Stanley 517

ALL NAMES INDEX

Thomas 1031
William 1030
Moorhead
   Alexander 966
   Earl W. 360
   George H 360
   William 360
Moose
   Everett E. 360
Mophett
   John 110
Morehead
   Senator 548
   William 246, 360
Moreland
   James 491, 980
   Joseph 601
   Thomas 621
Morgan 214, 232, 381, 1006, 2018, 2022, 2122, 2296
   C. F. 503
   Elizabeth Conner 1024
   Emma 500
   F. A. 469
   Fred 337
   Fred H. 360
   Gen. George W. 141
   Gen. John H. 303, 304, 305, 306, 307, 308, 309, 310, 311, 312, 313, 314, 315, 316, 317, 318, 319, 320, 321, 322, 323, 324, 325, 326, 327, 328, 329, 330, 331, 332, 333, 513, 670, 810, 993, 2020, 2121
   General John H. 8
   George 242, 370
   George B. 360
   Harvey 646
   Hon. John H. 299
   John 670, 938
   John H ... 107, 499, 888
   Josiah 696
   Levi 547

Mildred 369, 500
Moman 2069
Mrs. 332, 333
N. R. 81
Pink 2070
Stanley A. 368
Susan 507
Treva 369
William 606
William F. 360
Zilda 611
Morganstern
   Leonard G. 360
Morrell
   Abraham 1048
   Joseph 748
Morris 473, 477, 479, 982, 989, 2073
   Aaron 2154
   Allen Edgar 367
   Argus 245
   Arthur C. 498
   Benjamin 2134
   Bishop 65
   D. E. 447
   Earl 360
   Henry 2154
   Isaac 824
   Isaac Q. 2154
   J. H. 503
   James E. 145, 146
   John 939
   Jonathan 835, 2154
   Lillie 504
   Orea 511
   Rev. 570
   Samuel 265, 280
   Sarah 510
   Thomas A. 2191
   Willie E. 360
Morrison 24, 449, 2186
   Abraham 974
   Agatha 511
   Andrew 115, 125, 966, 976
   Andrew J. 280
   Benjamin 675

C. L. 652
Charles 2267
Clarence L. 639
E. M. 258
Earl 360
George .. 242, 651, 966
George W. 279
Holmes 975
James 976
John 675, 923
John, Jr. 976
John, Sr. 976
Joseph .. 674, 675, 893, 894, 939, 956, 1048, 2072
Joseph D 280
L. B. 515
Mary 965
Matilda 860
Mrs. H. O. 2302
Perry A. 276
Samuel 798
Samuel H. 279, 284
Squire 50
Thomas C. 279
Victor E. 360
William 498, 956
Morrow 847
   Bert 605
   Edna 514
   Gov. Jeremiah 2235
   Governor Jeremiah 457
   H. A. 621
   Harland H. 360
   Harry 605
   Hiram 603
   James 621, 812, 849
   James R. 105
   Jeremiah 105, 112
   John 696
   William . 106, 381, 494, 849, 865, 868, 1061
Morse
   Rev. Intrepid 404
Morton 526, 582, 599, 631, 632, 636, 637,

659, 863, 873, 957, 2178, 2311
Annie 2311
David 575, 2311
E. C. 2138
Edward.. 746, 945, 956
Edward (Heirs) 955
Georgeanna 500
Hon. Isaac 81
Isaac. 76, 80, 261, 575, 636, 651, 781, 1061, 2149, 2311, 2312
J. T. 2137, 2138
Jacob G. 2311
James 2311
John 100, 142, 470, 2107, 2258
Joseph. 631, 632, 2178
Levi P. ... 163, 164, 165
Lydia 2311
M. 269
Margaret... 1064, 2311
Mary 2311, 2314
Mary Girtler 2311, 2312
Miss Mame 492
Miss Nannie 623
Miss Nannie E. 443
Morris 80, 87, 261
Moses 746, 955
Robert B. 2311
Sarah 2311
William 278, 852, 2137, 2254, 2311
William H. 278
William, Jr. .. 945, 2311, 2312
William, Sr. 945, 2311, 2312
Mosely
Marion A. 280
Moser
Conrad 974
John 974
Moses
Daisy 513

Geologist 2038
Michael 360
Mosier
John 965
Mosko
George H. 360
Moss 478
Anna 268
Aunt Annie 670
Aunt Jane 670
Bernard O. 360
Dr. Naldo 2250
Fred 360
Great-grandfather 326
Henry 476, 808
Herbert 1030
Isaac 411, 412, 669, 671
J. B. 502
J. R. 198, 886
James 476
James R.143, 800, 893, 894
Jane 2172
John F. 280
John R. 142
John W. 361, 368
Maj. Charles W. 289
Miss Anna 325, 326
Nell 502
Nelle 369
Robert G. 280
Sarah Jane 671
Thomas 476
U. F. 411
Will 325
Mosser
Mrs. John F. 180
Mote
William E. 361
Mott
William 426
Motte
Daniel 644, 645
James 56, 645
Jesse 601
Os 616

William D. 647
Motter
John 279
Moxley
John D. 280
Muha
Father 408
Muhlbach
A. P. 656
Mullen
Joseph 856
Thomas 245
Mullins
Albert L. 361
Priscilla 2283
Mulvane
Jenkin 695
John 696
Murdock
Andrew 276
Murdough
J. F. 2168
Murgatroyd
Margaret 508
Murphy 618, 619, 661, 662
Basil 278
Belle 989
Francis 661, 662
George 697
Isaac C. 258
J. W. 2160
John H. 258
Lafayette 277
Mr. 1031
Patrick 361
S. L. 656
William 258
Murray 446, 473, 477, 2149
A. R. 498, 500, 652, 2312
Edwin M. 361
Elder James 375
Isabel 375
John 515, 662
John R. 276

ALL NAMES INDEX

Lindley 444
William 2156
Murry
James 856
Musgrave
Mr. 50
Musselman
Mr. 562
Mustard
John 893
Muzzey
David Saville 2119
Muzzy
Jeremiah D. 279
Larinda 988
Thomas N. 129, 426, 522, 985, 987, 988, 989, 995, 996
Myers
Clarence P. 361
George L. 361
Jacob 2199
John B. 361
Louis 1013
Margaret 1030
Mrs. Louis 1013
Rev. J. C. 301
Rev. Jacob 393
William 1012

N

Nace
Samuel 955
W. L. 503
William L. 502
Naftel 41
Daniel 2186
T. 2106
Thomas 41, 2186
Naftle 55
Nagel
Elizabeth 504
Martin 504
Nagle
Martin F. 504
Naphtali 840

Nash
J. H. 391
Joshua 856
Rev. J. H. 488
Rev. R. K. 405
Nation
Carrie 660
Nations
Gilbert O. 179
Naylor
Millard F. 361
Naymik
Pete 370
Neal
Dudley I. 361
Dudley Irwin 339
James 936, 939
John 936
Sarah 868
William 939
Needham
David 90, 975, 2107
James 800
James W. 276
John 2161
Mrs. Rhoda 2106
Rhoda 647
Seneca 495, 574
Seneca (Heirs) 647
William 302
Neel
A. H. 941
Samuel M. 2103
Neeland
Ada 369
E. E. 337, 402
Harold R. 361, 368
Jay W. 361
Joseph 799, 2190
Joseph W. 361
Nathan 275
Nathaniel 696
Thomas M. 276
Neeley
Magee 284
Neil 218, 223, 238, 659
Dius 703

Dr. Solomon 129
Solomon 995, 996
William. 238, 239, 240, 956
Neilley
Fred B. 361
Neiswanger
David 812
William 975
Nelson 231, 767, 837
Andrew 2099
Benjamin 799, 824
Charles R. 361
J. M. 588, 589
James 651
James M. 839
John 258, 799
John A. 280
John S. 278
Matilda Talbert ... 2099
Owen 87, 174
Peter 995
Samuel 272, 277
Thomas 868
Welcome B. 278
William M. 280
Neremer
A. L. 499
Nesbit
John M. 662
Nethers
Walter 361
Neuhart
Charles 361
Neusbaum
Miss M. A. 441
Nevin
John D. 799, 824
Newbern
Thomas 939
Newberry
Viola 512
Newell 859
Charles 124, 856
David 906
Eli 747
Margaret 551

ALL NAMES INDEX

Samuel 746, 856
Newland
  Asa 276
  Daniel.................... 995
  Elza 276
  John 824
  Joseph................... 995
  Stephen 276
Newman
  John 799
Newmon
  Ralph.................... 174
Newnom
  John 824
Neyman
  Guy W. 183, 498
  Harry A................. 361
  I. L. 972
Nichol
  Dr. 56
  T. 699
  Thomas 868
  William................. 868
Nicholas 670
Nichols
  Albert 361
  Elmer 367
  Eva 504
  George (Heirs) 1061
  George S. 1000
  Henry 886, 893
  J. C. 505
  J. S. 508
  Jacob........... 579, 2199
  John 1061
  Lizzie 508
  Mrs. S. 886
  Oran............. 349, 361
  Perry 649
  Rev. J................... 2099
  Sade 510
  W. G. 470, 501
Nicholson .. 483, 485, 833, 2060
  A. W. 75, 76, 81, 87
  Andrew W............. 483
  Benjamin............... 725

Carl S..................... 361
D. W. 272
Dwight 369, 370
Dwight R. 361
E. H. 265
Erastus H............... 280
George D....... 490, 518
James A................. 498
John 128, 495
John L. 180
John R. 726
June 509
Nancy 510
Robert ... 647, 799, 819
S. W. 635, 2164
T. S. 402
Thomas 2158
W. F. 258
W. H. 499
William.................. 166
Nicols
  Sylvester 703
Niswander
  Anna 514
  Isaac 2101, 2174
  'Peggy'................. 2174
Nixon
  Harvey E................ 361
Noah
  Joshua 1048
Noble 798
  Andrew 1030
  Ernest L. 361
  George 275, 662
  George W............. 279
  James .. 246, 686, 1030
  John 361
  John W. H....... 265, 280
  Joseph.................. 124
  Thomas 799
  William......... 747, 1030
Nordhause
  Emma................... 507
Norris . 471, 476, 477, 480
  Carey.................... 706
  Fred...................... 361
  J. H. 2117

Joseph 1048
Thomas (Heirs)...... 835
William.......... 476, 809
Northgrave
  William .. 832, 833, 835
Northwood
  Arnold 361
Nossett
  Joseph................... 824
  Samuel 799
Nowell
  George F. 361
  W. T...................... 498
  Will T. 361
  William T. 498
Nugent
  L. E. 515
Null
  William 742
Nunley
  William H. 361
Nyce 207, 232, 262
  E. 653
  E. R. 2239
  Edwin R. 625
  John 812, 814

O

O'Brien
  Father 407
O'Conner
  Harry B. .. 349, 351, 361
O'Ferrell
  Dick 669
  Dr. Ignatius............ 669
  I. 698
  Milly 669
O'Haner
  Jacob 375
O'Hara
  George 682, 1026
O'Haven
  Mary 375
O'Haver
  Nathan 799
O'Malley

Paul 515
W. T. 652
Walter................... 515
Walter T. 361, 368
O'Morrow
    Lloyd 361
O'Neal
    C. E. 500
    Howard Dudley 339
    Ralph 361
O'Neil
    Howard D. 361
Oakley
    Samuel 339, 361
Obenour
    S. W., Jr. 2040, 2053
Oburn
    Charles 258
Odell
    Joseph 1000
    Stephen 955
Odle
    Stephen 746
Ogan
    E. 995
    Peter 995
    Philip M. 275
Ogier 7, 41, 42, 43, 45, 55, 2106, 2221
    C. T. 514
    J. M. 157, 2164
    James 41
    John 45, 653
    John M. .. 508, 617, 657
    John, Jr. 651
    Mary Marquand 45
    Mr. 43
    Mrs. Judith 800
    Peter 145, 262, 586, 800, 2055, 2056, 2221
    Sarepta Bonnell 45
    T. W. 81, 514
    Thomas 43, 44, 45, 46, 566, 799, 995, 2071
    Thomas W. 467

William 41, 45, 46, 647, 799
Ogle
    Rev. 261
Oglebay
    James 54, 87, 115
Ohaver
    Nathan 647
Old Pete 10, 982, 983, 984, 2134
Olden
    James F. 361
Oldham 57, 554, 746, 752, 802, 2054, 2071, 2106
    Chauncy 784
    George E. 181
    I. A. 81, 298, 704
    Isaac ... 20, 21, 54, 247, 554, 566, 569, 720, 795, 796, 797, 799, 2010, 2047, 2053, 2054, 2071
    Isaac (Heirs) 799
    Isaac J. .. 554, 797, 2054
    J. T. 1000
    James 247, 856
    Marling 651, 797, 2054
    Mrs. I. A. 81
    Rebecca 302
    S. 269
    S. M. 696
    Samuel .. 151, 649, 800
    Samuel H. 799, 2165
    Samuel M. ... 696, 2099, 2103
    Samuel of Isaac 647
    Sarah Marling 795, 796, 797, 2053, 2054
    Thomas .. 67, 106, 112, 124, 153, 157, 261, 381, 461, 781
    Thomas (Heirs) 799
Olds
    Mr. 469
Oliver 323, 2082
    Albert W. 361

Elizabeth 965, 2084
Harold N. 361
Henry 923
Hiram 68, 99, 286, 289, 290, 709
Homer E. 351, 361
J. H. 621
Jane Black 2084
John ... 799, 812, 2082, 2084
John W. 178, 361, 812, 2082
Joseph 621
L. B. 156
Meta 504
Mrs. Ruth 896
Roy H. 361
Samuel 494
Thomas 1017
Wayland W. 361
William 747
Wilmer O. 95
Olmstead
    J. D. 469
Olney
    John 824
Olnhausen
    R. H. 514
Oloff
    Frank 361
Opperman 479, 1006
    J. H. 1002
Orme .. 126, 141, 548, 595
    Chairman W. L. 367
    Mrs. Wilber 497
    R. V. 583, 603, 604, 652, 2114, 2115
    Verner E. 361
    W. L. 518, 652, 657, 707
    Wilber L. 361, 367, 639
    William C. 639
Orr 934, 2087
    Captain John 940
    Carl F. 361
    Colonel 230, 742
    Guy 361

Isa 500
J. C. 87
J. F. 498
James 173
James C. 2134
John 277, 395, 2134
John (Heirs) 939
John, Jr. 939
Matthew, Jr. 939
Matthew, Sr. 939
Philip 284
Robert 650, 893
Robert (Heirs) 868
Thomas 939, 1048
Watson 824
William... 71, 945, 952, 955
William A. 868
Osborn
Charles 702
Covey 955
Emmett E. 361
William 955
Osborne
Charles 276, 2119
Oshe
Carl M. 518, 629
Osler
George N. 278, 284
John H. 276
Ostler
Charles E. 280
Ourant
Kirby K. 361
Outland
James 280
Josiah 919
Owen
Lum W. 900, 901
Mary 900
Rebecca 901
Owens
Dr. 524
John 395
Rachel 502
Oxley
Agnes M. 792

J. H. 941
Oyler
William 246
Ozanne
Lady 43

P

Paber 719
Pace 769
Will 603
Pack
Charles T. 2023
George T. 361
Harry S. 2023
Ross C. 2023
Thomas K. . 2022, 2023
Padden
Dick 619
Paden
Charley 361
David H. 812
James 762, 812
John 763, 812
Thomas 499
Padgett
Enoch K. 361
W. F. 88
William 606
Padgitt
Jim 324
W. F. 447
Page 670
Amos 669, 670
Paine
John W. 276
Paisely
James 995
Paisley 2242
Benjamin 868
Captain George 411
John 575
Robert . 747, 748, 1013
Pallet
Betty 2007, 2008
Palmater
Benjamin 996

Palmer 1028
Charles F. 361
George 919, 1049
George, Jr. 1049
John 1049
John McAuley 167, 168
Lot 975
Rev. Thomas 438
Richard 868
William 800, 1030
Panjak
Father 408
Park 166, 595, 2178
Dr. 206
Parker
Alton B. 171
G. C. 269
George W. 280
Isaac 809
John 835
Lenora 512
Mrs. F. 886
Theodore 2119
William 80
William T. 180
Parkerson
William 813
Parkhill
James 246, 277, 284
James (Heirs) 790
John 1031
Parkinson
Edward.. 626, 748, 799
William 762, 812, 2107
Parkison
Edward 126
Parks
Hugh 790, 956
Joseph 2189
Parlett
Isaiah 227
Stewart 606
Parlott
Isaiah 1061
Parmele
Rev. James H. 383
Parr

ALL NAMES INDEX

Thomas 723
Parrett
    Ross 514
Parrish
    Adonijah 997, 998
    Atty. 56
    E. E. 2161
    Evans 995, 996
    Isaac. 66, 93, 102, 105, 106, 115, 121, 122, 131, 137, 495, 498, 647
    Jesse 995
    Parker 995
    Solomon 7, 71, 72
Parrott
    Abraham 939, 2107
    William.................. 939
Parry
    Gibbons 955, 956
    John H. 361
Parsons
    Charles L. 939
Pastorius
    Harvey 619
Patrick
    J. T. 400
    John 746, 848, 849
    Luther H. 361
Patter
    Samuel 124
Patterson 644, 762, 1056, 2224
    Aaron ... 230, 292, 494, 696
    Alexander 894, 964
    Alfred 995
    Andrew . 106, 381, 699
    Andrew D. 1062
    Andrew Jackson 367
    Belle 642
    Captain 262
    Captain R. M. 719
    Captain R. M. G. 700
    Charles 503
    Daniel.................... 762
    Dr. 913

Dr. A. 80, 256
Elias...................... 856
Elias G. 361
Elijah 995
Gay........................ 361
George 124, 939
J. M. 886
J. T. 269
James 642, 812, 848
James (Heirs) 1062
James C. 361
James M................ 278
Jeremiah (Heirs)... 799, 1030
John 67, 105, 112, 139, 390, 391, 434, 457, 647, 856, 1030
John D. 95, 98, 99
Jonathan 812
Joseph ... 790, 848, 995
Josiah 276
L. H. 174
M. R. .. 76, 81, 93, 164, 499, 500, 502
Mabelle.................. 500
Mark 975
Martha 807
P. C. 608
Robert E. 498, 499
Samuel .. 787, 835, 856
Stewart 647
Stout 124, 762, 807, 812, 813
Sylvester 274, 810
W. N. 643, 652
William.................. 955
Zaccheus (Heirs).... 812
Pattison
    Samuel 829
Patton
    Frank..................... 656
    Hugh 995
    James 277
    James D................. 277
    Lulu 504
    Willard 84, 2208
    William.................. 790

Paul
    Andrew 955
    David..... 391, 952, 964
    Dr. 2137
    Dr. David ... 2230, 2231
    Ella 2230, 2231
Paulos
    Carl........................ 361
Paulsen
    Rev. Mark G. 405
Paxon
    Elizabeth 703
    Isaac 703
Paxton
    James 835
    John (Heirs) 790
    Mary 2314
    Samuel 995
    William.................. 790
Payne
    Mrs....................... 965
Payton
    Theodore 361
Peach
    Dick 506
    Frank..................... 361
    William.................. 361
Peacock
    T. W............... 143, 209
    Thomas W.66, 91, 463, 939, 2106, 2172
Pearson
    Orin 500
Peck
    James 955, 956
    John 956
Pedwin
    Nicholas 824
Pekalla
    Father 408
    Rev. Father Stephen J. 408
Pelt
    Rev. R. A. 395
Pendleton
    George H. 152
Penman

ALL NAMES INDEX

James 361
Penn
   Greenberry .. 230, 950, 956
   William 2282
Pennell
   Clifford A. 361
Penrose
   John S. 275, 284
   Mahlon 824
   Mrs. C. 268
Pentecost
   Rev. Tom 410
Peoples
   William 939
Perdue
   Jonathan 1017
Perego
   Sarah 919
Perhacs
   George O. 361
Perigo
   Enoch 502
Perkins
   Captain 262
   James 995
Permar
   S. B. 699
Perrigo
   Isaac 923
   James 923, 932
Perry 11, 996
   Captain Oliver Hazard 564
   Gibbons 125
   J. A. 917
   John 1026
   John, Jr. 995
   Jonathan 1061
   Nathan 647
   Oliver H. 243, 248, 249, 250
   Oliver Hazard 111
   Robert 1061
   Thomas 1061, 2126
   Walter G. 997, 998, 2024

Persons
   Charles H. 361
Peters 819
   Denver 361
   George 923, 970, 2155
   Gladys 500
   James 500
   James B. 498, 499, 500
   James P. 2168
   John 498
   Kenneth W. 361
   Raymond H. 361
   Reuben 824
   Solomon 124, 819, 824
   William 606
Peterson
   Edward 213
Petros
   August C. 361
Pettay
   Daniel 969
   Orange 1000
   Rev. Daniel 704
Petter
   Elisha P. 278
Petticord
   Lias 671
Petty 833
   Dr. A. L. 2203
   Francis 501
   L. D. 502
   Lizzie 501
   Travis 501
Phelps
   Elijah 853
   H. R. 2026
   Walter 2026
Philip
   John M. 184
Philips
   David (Heirs) 975
   Thomas 856
Phillipe
   King Louis 548
Phillips
   Albert D. 361
   Alex 361

Enoch 247
   George 858
   George W. 1042
   Herbert C. 339, 361
   John 247
   Milligan 270
   Moses 270
   Mr. 1041
   Theodore L. 361
   W. H. 258, 377
   Wendell 2119
   William 522
   William M. 514
Phillis 1036
   Charles 995, 1026, 1030, 1031
Philpot
   Ann 654
   Maria 654
   William 649
Phipps
   Clay 2263
Piatt
   Gen. A. S. 157
   Homer 621
   Lloyd 302
   Robert L. 349, 361
Pickens
   Evan 747
   General 804
Pickering
   Greenberry 835
   Lot 835
Pierce
   A. C. 506
   Franklin 813
   President Franklin 120, 142, 143, 462, 625
   Robert 279, 284
Piersol
   George W. 361
Piggott
   John 923
Pilcher
   Thomas 115
Pine
   Harry L. 361, 639

ALL NAMES INDEX

Pitman
  Uriah 868
Place
  Capt. Samuel 289
Plant
  Thomas 812, 956
Plattenburg
  George 956
Plattenburgh
  George 2137
Plodvin
  Nicholas 41
Plummer
  Benjamin 695
  John R. 696
  Mrs. M. A. 441
Podwin 2050
Poe 723
  Edgar Allan 2031, 2032
Poland
  Freeman 504
  Grant 361
  William H. 1048
Polen
  James L. 278
Polk
  James K. 254, 674, 675, 813
  President James K.
    .... 139, 140, 625, 2055, 2102
  Rev. David 381, 972, 2194
  Samuel 246
Pollard
  James 697
  William (Heirs) 647
Pollock
  A. 1030
  Abraham 57
  Carl B. 361
  Col. John 129
  James W. 284
  John 97, 1031
  John W. 275
  Joseph ... 97, 135, 1031

Rev. Thomas C. 389, 528
  Sarah 1030, 1031
  Stephen 939
  Stephen A. 278
  Thomas 939, 955
  William 941, 2009
Pontius
  Carl 361
Pool
  Thomas 800
Poole
  George 284
Poorman
  C. L. 156
Pope
  Dr. R. B. 2201, 2203
  Dr. Russell B. 296
  Rev. 298
Popham
  Henry 965, 968, 976
Porter
  Burt R. 361
  Charles 854, 856
  Elizabeth 507
  Flora 513
  Harrison 270
  Harry 504
  Hugh 242, 893
  J. N. 799
  James 790, 847
  John 73, 121, 127, 856
  Martha 504
  Rev. R. B. 972
  Stewart 893
  W. W. 277
Pott
  Stephen 2258
Potten
  James 2105
Potter 2055
  Chester 500
  Fred K. 514
  Ill. M. R. 500
  M. R. 499, 566, 569, 765
  Maurice R. 498

Mrs. Irene Anderson
  2206
Potts 435
  Belle 302
  General 522
  Israel 975
  John 124, 748, 965, 969
  Joseph 975, 995
  Mrs. Eliza 293
  Mrs. Stephen 268, 800
  Roland 808
  Stephen 80, 95, 381, 660, 739, 782, 800, 2105, 2126
  William 965
Potwin
  H. W. 139
  J. W. 55, 693, 2098
Pounds
  William 893
Powell
  Abel 747
  William 824
  William B. 279, 2062
  William H. 249, 250
  William S. 790
Powelson
  I. N. 279
Powers
  Miss Adelphia A. ... 439
  William 856
Pratt
  Edward W. 814
  George W. 276
  James T. 276
  Philip 814
  Stella 512
Pressley
  William, Jr. 856
Prestley
  William 696
Preston
  Elijah 939
  J. E. 507
Presty
  Joseph 434

ALL NAMES INDEX

Priaulx
  John 790, 2100
  Nicholas 651, 790
  T. F. 2049, 2050
  William...... 2138, 2139
Price 618, 619, 2073
  Benjamin............... 278
  C. H. 2073
  J. P. 936
  James W. 361
  John 278
  Oscar.................... 361
  Robert................... 649
  W. 936
  William................ 2019
Priestly
  David.................... 284
Pritchard
  L. J. 367
  Leroy J.................. 361
  Lutitia................... 509
  Mrs. E................... 886
  Roy....................... 337
Proctor
  Floyd 361
Prometheus 439
Prosser 833
Proudfit.................... 1043
  Andrew 1030
  David............ 391, 787
  Dr. Charles P. 389, 789
  Patterson 1030
  Rev. David............. 386
  Robert................. 1030
  Thomas P. 789
Prouse
  J. S. 81, 488, 499
  John S. 498, 500
  Mrs. Hannah 516
  Mrs. J. S. 488
Prouty
  Russell. 987, 988, 2108
Pryor
  James M................ 280
Pugh
  George E. 151, 152, 462

Hon. Geo. E. 151
Josephus 956
Pulley 917, 2200, 2289
  Adam 868
  Dwight M. 91, 183, 185, 186, 515
  James 835
  Samuel 746
Pullman 221
Pultney 930
Pumphrey
  Absalom................ 956
  Beale 955, 956
  Horace 956
  Isaac............. 121, 956
  J. M. 956
Purcell
  Bishop 406
  Frank.................... 621
  John B. 977
Purdum
  E. G. 494
  N. C. 515
  R. C. 1059
Purely
  Dixon.................... 805
Purkey
  Daisy 501
  Joseph........... 160, 989
Putnam
  Israel 929
Putteron
  Collette de 2050
  George de 2050
  Jeremye de 2050
  Thomas de 2050
Pyle
  T. H...................... 1028
Pyles
  James 913, 924
  Nathaniel 2156
  Sadie 513

Q

Queen
  Hugh 279

  James 279
Quick
  Jonathan 1030
  Moses 1061
  Mrs....................... 989
Quillen
  George 361
Quinn
  Hughie.......... 616, 617
  James 302
  Steve 616, 617
  William................. 499

R

Rabe
  Bryan.................... 276
  Charles 63
  Goodhalt 603
  Herman 603, 604
  Noah H. 361
  Sarah 988
  William................. 988
  William M. 695
Race
  Sergeant Henry M. 290
Racey
  Winifred 369
Rachel
  Alex Alowoyish...... 366
  Michael B. 361
Racy
  Port E. 368
Radcliff
  William E. 499
Radcliffe
  S. B. 761
Rae
  S. 504
Ragan 2161
  J. W. 2199
  Rev. John W. . 393, 394
Rahl
  Colonel................ 2287
Rainey 164, 559, 2099, 2112, 2180
  Abraham 206

ALL NAMES INDEX

Ed 617
Edward 337
Edward S. 361
Ellen Elizabeth 2230
Flora 512
J. T. 81, 2117
James 693, 696
James H. 66, 2108
John 245, 800
John T. 258, 277, 2014, 2015
Major J. T. 662
Major John T. 2015, 2230
Maurice L. 499
Mrs. 819
Mrs. Annie 268
Samuel 746
Sue 367
W. S. 272
Walter B. 361, 499
William. 261, 269, 586, 651, 800, 819, 824, 976, 1017, 2180, 2181, 2221
William A. 704
William, Sr. 726
Rainie
J. M. 675
Joseph M. 156
Rainy
J. T. 261
Ralston 2004
Jacob 278
Joseph 1061
Mrs. Ella 268
Ramage
Mr. 120
Ramsey
Dr. W. T. 595
Dr. William T. 405
Hon. William M. 80
James 894
Joseph 277
Rev. A. 405
Sample 391
W. T. 498, 499

William T. 498, 500
Randall
Ananias 939
Aneas 936
Hunter 939
James R. 361
Rankin
Adam 522
Bobby 616, 617
D. L. 498, 499, 500
Dr. D. L. 530
F. C. 514
George 361
J. 618
Jacob 833
James 849
John 276, 278, 790, 869, 1030
John O. 361
Martha 512
Mrs. E. 800
Robert 647, 800
Simeon .. 604, 605, 606
William 367
Rankins
Mrs. E. 865
Rannels
William 987
Ransom
Bishop Reverdy ... 2246
James 1062
John 671
Nellie V. 2246
Rev. McCoy 412
Rev. Revedy 672
Ransome 2070
Charles G. 361
John F. 361
Rasey
H. B. 377
Ratcliffe
John 868
William 868
Ratliffe
John Reid 367
Willard P. 361
Ray 446

Archie R. 361
Dr. Joseph 899
Joseph 439
Kenneth C. 184
State Director of Education Kenneth 2302
Thomas 125, 434, 1049
Raymond 617, 618
Frank 617
Fred 617, 652
Ill. Fred M. 500
Razor
George 1061
Rea 2224, 2242
Ada 2243
Andrew G. 275
David E. 2243
Dr. Francis 1059, 2242, 2243
Elizabeth J. 2243
Francis... 381, 649, 650
George W. 284
Mary F. 2243
Mary H. England 2242, 2243
Rev. John 2242
Sarah J. 2243
William P. 2243
Read
George 2094
George (Heirs) 1017
James 1012
James (Heirs) 1017
John 1017
Susannah 2094
Reasoner 1036
Benjamin 115, 126, 787, 790, 1024
Catherine 1024
Elizabeth Wilson Thompson 1018, 1024, 1031
Garret 246
Harry 1031

John 87, 566, 1018, 1024, 1025, 1030, 1031, 1033
John C. 1030
Joseph 1030
Katy 1018, 1019
L. S. 498
Mrs. Benjamin 1024
Peter 242, 1018, 1019, 1024, 1028, 1030
Solomon ... 1024, 1030
William 1024
Reaves
  Joshua 246
Rech 514
  C. J. 2141
  Carl 2092
  Carl J. 3, 260, 2035, 2038, 2070, 2074, 2162, 2165, 2167, 2170, 2173, 2176, 2179, 2184, 2186, 2188, 2214, 2235
  Glessner Mackey 2237
  Mrs. Carl J. ... 347, 2237
Redd 1028
  Clarkson 279
  Isaih 923
  Peter 995
  Solomon 265, 280
Redman
  Robert 939
  William 1017
Reece
  Ford 989
  William 2019
Reed 2086
  Dorcas 440
  Ellen Broom 2086
  'Fighting Bill' 249
  J. E. 75, 80
  James . 278, 975, 1030, 2155, 2156
  Jesse E. 80, 87
  John 246, 270, 886, 923, 996, 2086, 2155

John M. 284
Joseph 245
Judge 128
Maggie 2086
Mr. 968
Rev. Joseph 381
Robert.. 54, 67, 69, 87, 123, 125, 2106
Robert, Jr. 1017
Robert, Sr. 1017
Samuel 696
Stephen 806
Thomas 246
Thomas B. 525
William. 110, 111, 243, 247, 248, 249, 250, 563
William 'Fighting Bill' 111, 564, 565, 2222
Reedle
  W. A. 469
Rees
  Rev. 375
  Rev. T. D. 375
Reese
  Armine .. 956, 995, 996
  Capt. John 2282
  Ford 258
  Rev. Theodore I. 405
Reeves.. 2151, 2152, 2269
  Joseph 2151, 2269
  Joshua 858
  Manesseh (Heirs) .. 799
  Rev. W 990
  William 975
Regan
  Thomas 306
Reicher
  Walter J. 361
Reid
  A. C. 391
  Duncan 361
  E. H. 784
  Jesse E. 157
  S. C. 391
  Whitelaw 165

Reimer
  John 924
Reinsch
  Robert 278
Reitler
  Hattie 513
  Sylvester 362
  William 362
Remer
  Edmond 362
Repasky
  John 367
Reppert
  Barney 618
Revenaugh
  Blanche 501
Revere
  Paul 330, 2014
Reynolds
  Abner 924
  David 995
  David J. 362
  Father 407
  Jeremiah 647, 2196
  Joseph 995
  Joseph H. 362
  Manford 362
  Rev. 940
  Rev. Fred 410
  Robert 278
  Rosaline T. 367
  Thomas 362
Rhinehart
  Enos 2154
  Ernest W. 362
  James 574, 649
  Joseph 2104
  Raymond C. 362
Rhoads
  John 280
Rhodes 833
Rice
  Capt. J. H. 289
  Christopher 606
  George 278
  Harry B. 362
  Mary 504

ALL NAMES INDEX

Rev. Paul V. 411
Richard 280
Thomas 856
William 362
Rich 833
  Abraham ... 2154, 2158
  Dallas G. 362
  Daniel 975
  George 2158
  J. W. 656
  John 2158
  O. K. 656
  P. E. 656
  Parmer E. 980
Richard
  William 956
Richards 2073
  A. 936
  Amos 936
  Benjamin 675
  Fred 337, 362
  John 276, 284
Richardson
  F. N. 657
  Floyd H. 505
  Frank 504
  Frank N. 504
  J. M. 589
  James 956, 972
  Jerry 503
  John 923
  John M. 603
  Miss Melissa 441
  Miss Mollie 268
  Robert D. (Heirs) ... 799
Richey
  George 971
  H. E. 1072
  John 1031
  John W. 276
  Lilian 508
  Robert 522
  Thomas 649, 971
Richie
  Andrew 2152
  Thomas 2152
Richmond

William 278
Richtarick
  Father 408
Ricker
  Isaac 886
  John 362
  Mrs. Amy 886
Rickey
  Isaac 1017
  Urban 362, 368
Riddle
  Belle 2129
  G. V. 623
  J. S. 1000
  Rev. 887
  William 621
Ridgeway
  Basil 868
Ridgley
  Cecil V. 504
  Everett C. 362
Riecher
  Jacob 515
Riemenschneider
  John W. 770
Riffle
  Lonie H. 362
Rigby . 473, 476, 477, 478,
  808, 966, 2302
  Bert 498, 499
  John 478
  John W. 514
  William, Jr. 337, 362
  William, Sr. 476, 478
Rigdon
  Eli 114
Rigel
  Arlie L. 362
  C. D. 507
  E. L. 370
  Everett L. 362
  I. T. 502, 507
  Irene 370
  Isaac T. 506
Rigg
  William 697
Riggle

Isaac 956
William H. H. 284
Riggs
  Bert 605, 606, 618
  Charles 616
  Daniel 975, 2154
  E. C. 91, 704, 2127, 2129
  Evan 799, 812
  Harry 603
  John 1062
  Joseph 975
  S. 623
  S. O. 470, 515
  Simeon 616, 976
  Simon 623
  Will 618
  William 95
  William A. 362
Riker
  Dr. 2203
Riley
  Captain F. 411
  John 2099
  Rebecca Agnew ... 2099
Rimer
  John 919
  Solomon 276
  William 276
Rinehart
  James 976, 2107
  Joseph 647, 1061
  Levi 495, 799
  Mrs. Alena Harford 891
Ringer 603, 604
  A. G. 173
  Alpheus 276
  T. B. 603, 604, 605
Ripley 1019
  Father 1020, 1021
  John ... 395, 747, 1017, 1019, 1020
Risk
  William 887
Ritchey
  Thomas 975
Ritchie

ALL NAMES INDEX

James 362
Ritter
   A. F. 498, 499
   Adam F. 499
   Frank L. 362
   Frank R. 368
   George D. 362
Roach
   James 746
   John 923
   W. 124
   William 868
Roache
   Edward 894
Roak
   William 246
Robb 380, 2224
   David .. 70, 71, 90, 107, 380, 460, 461, 462, 2104, 2243, 2244
   Hamilton 95, 96, 97, 98, 445, 470, 495, 690, 855
   Joseph 1030
   Joshua 112
   Josiah 856
   Oliver H. 278
   Samuel 1030
Robbin
   John 849
   John (Heirs) ... 824, 995
   Martin 995
Robbins 970
   Charles 518
   Charles C. 639
   John 566
   Peter 1007
Robe 1056, 2192, 2224
   David F. 956, 1062
   Joseph W. 362
   Joshua 247, 381
   Josiah ... 380, 461, 486, 747, 1061
   Josiah P. 276
   Robert T. 279
   Thurlow S. 362, 368

William 381, 989, 1061, 2126
Robert
   Paul 41
Roberts
   Charles 856
   John C. 362
   Samuel M. 695, 696
   Thomas 2009
Robertson
   Arthur 362
   Edward C. 362
   Herman W. 362
   Homer W. 362
   James 258
   Rev. C. W. 412
   Thomas 849
Robey
   S. S. 400
Robin 41, 2050
   D. J. 515
Robins 395, 480, 670, 1003, 1004, 2283, 2284
   Alexander S. 672
   Carl H. 362
   Deborah M. 400
   E. A. 1010
   J. E. 181, 183
   James T. 279
   John 41, 63, 670, 1003, 1009, 2283, 2284
   John H. 808, 1010
   Madison D. 670, 672
   Mary Hubert 2283, 2284
   Miss Lela F. 1009
   Miss M. Grace 497
   Mr. 469
   P. D. 269
   Peter C. 279
   Peter D. 80, 87, 400, 2284
   Rev. Harrison T. .. 1010
   Rev. James W. 1010
   W. W. 506
   William W. 280

Robinson 2156, 2224
   Alexander 853
   C. G. 655
   Capt. J. H. 263, 264
   Christopher 939
   Elizabeth 939, 2072
   George W. 276
   Hallie 514
   Henry 650, 812
   J. A. 412
   J. H. 264, 506
   James ... 606, 812, 813, 835, 1061, 2220
   John 76, 126, 381, 673, 824, 1061
   John (Heirs) ... 647, 799
   John H. 362
   John M. 280
   John W. 280
   Joseph T. 181
   Margaret 1061
   Rev. Alexander 972
   Robert 856
   Samuel 381, 835, 1049, 1061
   Samuel F. 276
   Thomas (Heirs) 856
   W. M. 129
   William 62, 87, 381, 649, 673, 856, 1062
   William B. 362
   William W. 280
Robison
   J. 124
   James 1046
Rochester
   Charles J. 362
Rockefeller
   John D. 2231
Rodecker
   Mrs. Capt. 2138
Rodgers 949
   Samuel . 124, 125, 913, 923, 924
Rodocker
   M. D. 161

ALL NAMES INDEX

Roe
  Elmer 362
  Ernest C. 362
  Lem 362
  Oliver 362
  Robert 362
Rogers 55, 819, 2106
  A. G. 515
  Benjamin 968, 976
  Bernie O. 362
  Clayton 504
  Eleanor 2098
  Everett 503
  Everit 369
  Everit C. 362, 370
  George L. 507
  Isaac N. 135
  John 125
  Joseph 910
  Lawson 819
  Lawson H. 279
  Mattie L. 507
  Michael .. 97, 626, 647, 790
  Newton 601
  Rev. 263
  S. P. 502
  Samuel 2098
  Siltburn 824
  Warner 278
  William B. 284
Rogos
  John C. 362
Roller
  Clyde A. 2040
  Clyde Addison 366
  James 946
  Sally Lennox 946
  Thomas E. 362
Rollingston
  John 799
Rollins
  John 824
  Jonathan 799
  William 2196
Rollston
  James 799, 849

  John 939
Roman
  Frank M. 362
Romans
  Dr. 913
  Dr. T. J. 264
  Evans 868
  Jacob 868
  Mrs. 865
  Viola D. 491
Romig
  C. E. 504
Roosa
  Clifford E. 362
Roosevelt
  President Franklin D.
    105, 177, 182, 183,
    184, 185, 626,
    2149, 2216
  President Theodore . 8,
    168, 169, 171, 172,
    173, 174, 175, 176,
    467, 528, 529, 530,
    531, 625, 2248
Root
  Sylvester 222
Rorick
  Edward 893
Rosamond 2312, 2313
  Dr. W. B. 2074
  Martin 2072
  William 2072
Rose 431, 663, 664
  Benjamin (Heirs) ... 975
  Benjamin F. 279
  Carl 362
  Cecil F. 362
  Charlie 362
  Clark 145, 654
  Elizabeth 654
  Ephraim 976
  George ... 97, 123, 800, 824
  Jessie 508
  John 790, 1049
  Jonathan .. 80, 87, 654, 2138, 2258

  Joseph 696
  L. S. 503
  Mary 976
  Nancy 976
  Robert T. 284
  Robertson 400
  Robinson 966
  S. 269
  Solomon 976
  Susanna 995
  Thomas 799, 824
  Thompson 258, 280, 956, 1061
  Victor H. 498, 517, 518, 639
  Vincent F. 265
  Vincent T. 280
  W. A. 862
  W. C. 169, 917
  W. E. 66
  Washington .. 923, 932, 956
  William. 433, 654, 919, 923, 975
  William C. 368
  William E. 362, 2107
  William P. 787
Rosecrans
  General 313, 314
Rosegrants
  Mrs. S. 865
  Simon 865
Roselle
  Mrs. Alice Anderson
    Hanna 2206
Roseman 989, 2312, 2313
  Bennett 75, 80, 156, 992
  Catherine 655
  Edward 54, 73, 647, 799
  James ... 268, 747, 939, 956
  James (Heirs) 647
  Martin . 939, 956, 2095
  Mary 956
  Morton 956

ALL NAMES INDEX

Philip 956
Sue 302
William .. 128, 265, 939
Rosemond 595, 957, 2256, 2312, 2313
   Attorney Fred L. ... 424, 640, 2313
   Captain 2016
   Ella Grimes 2313
   F. L. 498, 515
   Fred L. ... 164, 166, 169, 335, 346, 623, 642, 706, 2168, 2217
   James . 947, 949, 2067, 2223, 2313
   Martin 947, 949, 2067, 2223, 2313
   Morton M. 278
   Philip .. 945, 948, 2312, 2313
   Phillip P. 362
   William 280
   William E. 277
Rosenberg
   Harry E. 362, 2174
Rosengrant
   T. S. 2137
Rososco
   John 362
Ross 2191
   Albert 941
   Alexander C. 130
   Andrew 284
   Andrew S. 258
   Ezra 362
   Henry (Heirs) 995
   James, Jr. 939
   James, Sr. 939
   John 125, 2155
   John P. 277
   Mayor Vern 2302
   Mrs. 787
   Mrs. Vera 2302
   Randall 391
   Robert A. 790
   Robert S. 787
   Theodore 799

Thomas 995
V. F. 518
Vern 657
W. P. 143
Walter B. 277
William 844, 2199
William P. 80, 849
Rosseter
   Thomas 975
Rossiter
   Lindley 278
   Nathan J. 362
Rowan
   John 123
   Robert 812
Rowcliffe
   John 2199
   Rev. John 393, 394
Rowland
   Ivor C. 362
   James S. 280
Rowles
   Nicholas 956
   T. H. 174
Rowley
   George 868
Rubicain
   Jefferson 833
Rubincam
   David 835
Ruby
   John G. 362
   Johnson E. 362
   Lillian W. 629
   Samuel H. 924
Ruckle
   Mrs. 800
Rudolph
   John 975
Rule
   Gen. V. A. 185
Rush
   Rev. 399
   Rev. E. E. 399
Russell
   Joseph 975
   Richard J. 278

Robert 124
Senator Richard B. 187
Thomas 790, 824
Ruth 431
   Daniel 919
   Margaret 919
   Samuel .. 431, 923, 932
   Thomas .. 84, 124, 142, 143, 432, 919, 923, 2107
Ruthenberg 175
Rutherford
   John M. 362
Rutledge
   Harold 629
   Margaret 690
   T. R. 515
   William 849
Ryan
   Ebenezer .... v, 192
   Elwood E. 362
   Francis 498
   James Blackburn ... 366
   James F. 280
   Lemon 948, 956
   Thomas C. 265

S

Sadler 833
Sager
   George M. 362
Saire
   Edgar O. 362
Saive
   Emile 362
Sales
   Daniel A. 975
Salladay
   John 939
Salliday
   Elias 2158
   George 81
   Jacob 2158
Sallust 443
Salmon
   Charles 647

ALL NAMES INDEX

Charles M. 362
Fletcher 616, 662
Irma 369
J. F. 161, 623
Milton L. 275
R. 124
R. D. 629, 2098
Tom 616

Saltsgaver
  A. C. 2306
  Frederick 245, 893
  Jacob .. 747, 956, 1059, 1072
  Mary 893
  William 675

Saltsgiver
  Jacob 1061
  Jacob (Heirs) 1062
  Jane 1062
  Peter 1061

Saltz
  Edward R. 362
  Raymond C. 362

Sampson 295
Samson 2006

Samuel
  Garrett. 923

Sanborn
  George 324
  Mrs. C. C. 268

Sanderson
  Mrs. 884

Sandy 569

Sankey 873
  A. 886, 2128
  Alexander 144, 145, 279
  J. 800
  J. E. 81
  James 87, 115, 868, 869, 2189
  Jennett 893
  John E. 76, 95, 2189
  Mrs. J. 800

Santa Anna
  Antonio Lopez De 9, 232, 531, 532

Sarchet 40, 41, 56, 221, 449, 523, 557, 569, 570, 574, 786, 794, 848, 2086, 2144, 2185, 2231, 2270
  A. C. 296, 578, 587, 588
  Ann 627
  C. P. B. 164, 379
  Col. C. P. B. .....vii, 3, 26, 230, 378, 458, 505, 556, 569, 570, 782, 1042, 2006, 2068, 2080, 2144, 2270
  Colonel 554, 808
  Colonel C. P. B. 81, 122, 130, 140, 520, 533, 538, 547, 555, 563, 624, 625, 679, 719, 780, 849, 2052, 2145, 2174
  Colonel Cyrus P. B. 9, 713, 714, 716
  David 275, 495, 647, 692, 795, 799, 800, 803, 804, 856, 1043, 2085, 2144, 2251
  David, Sr. 482
  Fanny 512
  Hannah Jane 375
  Harold F. 362
  Hester Hill 2086
  J. C. 40
  James 621
  Jemima Dehart 2086
  John . 39, 40, 552, 803, 2145, 2170, 2173, 2174, 2176, 2269, 2270, 2271
  John H. 9, 161, 210, 275, 522, 596, 597, 598, 603, 2132, 2138, 2185
  John M. 696
  Joseph 696

Judith 2269, 2270, 2271
M. 577, 2099
Malvina Moore 714
Mary Torode 2086
Moses .. 54, 69, 80, 91, 121, 122, 123, 131, 255, 261, 458, 495, 555, 556, 560, 574, 626, 627, 629, 647, 660, 713, 782, 799, 2090, 2100, 2109, 2163
Mrs. John H. 598
Nancy 2027
Nicholas .. 39, 799, 803
Peter .. 39, 40, 73, 566, 569, 803, 2008, 2163, 2173, 2176, 2269, 2270, 2271
Peter B. 128, 495, 712, 713, 799, 2084, 2085, 2090
Peter J. 626
Prof. J. H. .. 81, 165, 166
Prof. John H. 169, 296, 524, 525, 597, 598, 599, 600, 958
Professor John H. .. 163, 662
Sarah Britten 2086
T. T. 2196
Thomas .. 9, 39, 40, 48, 52, 53, 54, 73, 378, 393, 413, 552, 566, 569, 570, 627, 690, 780, 799, 803, 804, 1043, 2027, 2028, 2085, 2170, 2173, 2176, 2190, 2192, 2198, 2199, 2260, 2269, 2270, 2271
Thomas, Sr. ... 700, 718, 719, 720
Thomas, Sr. (Heirs) 647
Tommy 1039
William 621

ALL NAMES INDEX

William C. 362
Sargent
   Jeremiah 965
Sarto
   Albert 362
Satan 732
Satterfield
   William 245
Satterthwaite
   Charles 975
   David 54, 704, 965, 967, 969, 970, 971, 975, 976, 2234, 2268, 2292, 2293
   Enoch 975, 976
   Joshua 674
Sattsman
   Thomas 377
Sausmares
   Jean de 2050
Sauter
   William F. 362
Savage
   A. R. 813
   Alexander 703
   George 603, 604
   Henry 703, 894
   Henry (Heirs) 868
   Robert 289, 2128
   Thomas 893, 894
Savely
   Eliza A. 402
   George 824
   John 824
Savers
   George 142
Savier
   Alice 512
Saviers
   George 835
   John 746, 884, 886, 893, 939
Sawders
   Elbert T. 362
Sawhill 1056, 2224
   A. J. 279
   Alexander J. 285

James ... 381, 649, 800, 1061
   Mrs. James 800
   Robert. 142, 703, 1061
Sayre 435, 2112
   Albina 919
   Harold 369
   Harold W. 362
   Leo 362
   William 767, 769
   William N. 362
Sayres
   David 975
   John D. 975
   Samuel 280
   Steven B. 278
Scantlan
   Thomas 995
Scantlin
   Thomas 996
Scarborough
   Joseph F. 276
   Rebecca 812
Scarr
   Cassius 302
Schafer
   Henry 515
Schaffer
   Jemima 2272
Schairer
   George 589
Schau
   William 589
Schick
   F. L. 498, 569
   Frank 337
   Frank W. 362
   H. T. 652
   Ill. Frank L. 500
Schley 295
Schlup
   Samuel 94, 181
Schmidt
   John A. 265
Schnebly
   Warner 265
Schneid

Esther 502
Frank 502
Schneider
   Ernest B. 171
Schofield
   Elijah 280
Schooley
   Joseph 1017
   Phineas 868
Schramm
   Elmer H. 362
Schrimpf
   Edythe 369
Schultz
   Harry H. 362
   William 337, 362
Schun
   Tacy 512
Schwyhart
   Isaac 277, 284
   Joseph 844
   William M. 349
Scott .. 262, 412, 471, 473, 474, 475, 476, 531, 565, 589, 595, 596, 603, 604, 605, 670, 671, 795, 833, 884, 2132, 2159, 2211, 2224
   A. G. 508
   Abraham 835
   Alexander (Heirs) .. 799
   C. A. 652
   C. H. 269
   Carl A. 362
   Charles . 112, 577, 579, 621, 696, 697, 799, 848
   Charles H. 1000
   Charley 232
   Cyrus 302
   David 956
   Dr. Winfield 2234
   Dred 713
   E. F. 515
   E. H. 577, 579
   E. M. 269

ALL NAMES INDEX

Elza 54, 151
Elza M. 586, 670, 2211
Francis 277, 790
G. J. 989
General Winfield. 2256
George 471
Hannah 919
Hannah Bainum 690
Harlan 337
Harlan M. 362, 367
Harry F. 362
Henry 616
Homer J. 362
Hugh 995
J. M. 1010
J. W. 498, 499
James... 277, 649, 690, 824, 956, 995, 1009, 1012
James R. 514
Jesse 924
John 380, 500, 868
John W. 499
Joseph 362
Josiah 258, 277
Leander 277, 284
Lizzie B. 508
Martha 868
Mary 799
Mary A. Moore ... 2211
Mary L. 656
Milton 603, 604
Mr. T. W. 368
Mrs. Ellsworth 2084
Nathan B. 280, 932, 952, 2256
Nora 369, 500
O. C. 652
O. F. 515
Orion 337
Orion C. 362
Otho 362
Pennington 914
R. T. 81, 178, 296, 335, 336, 337, 339, 346, 629, 634

Rev. James Harvey
 1010
Richard 246, 956
Robert B. 277
Robert E. 362
Russell 362
Samuel 849
Senator Nathan B.
 2257
State Grand Master
 W. M. 77
Stella 500
Sylvester ... 2159, 2160
T. H. 2199
T. W. 45, 529, 584, 595, 603, 604, 616
Thomas 110, 111, 362, 824, 833, 2159
W. M. 379, 704
William... 87, 107, 112, 115, 125, 844, 849, 886, 1012, 1017, 2081, 2085, 2107, 2211, 2272
William C. 887
William M. 498
William McK. 500
William T. 362
Wilson 972
Winfield 142, 532, 813
Scroggan
 William 944
Scroggins
 John 1061, 1062
Scudder
 Daniel C. 812, 824
Sealer
 John 246
Seals
 John 2113
Searle
 Carrington W. 67
Sears
 C. J. 2199
 Clark 270, 285
 Enoch 275
 Ephraim 107

Fred L. 596, 653
James 270
John 835
Seaton
 Robert 995
Secrest ... 970, 1003, 1004, 2112, 2287
 A. T ... 470, 1004, 2286, 2288
 Barbara 402
 Brodie G. 362
 Clifford 502
 Congressman Robert T. 187, 293
 Dalton 502
 Dr. Robert 606
 Elizabeth 400, 402
 Elizabeth Spaid 2287
 Ellsworth 502
 Emma 502
 F. M. 488
 Freda 502
 George 2154
 Harrison 304, 1005
 Harry E. 362
 Henry . 400, 976, 1003, 2287
 Herbert R. 362
 Hervy R. 362
 Ida 502
 Isaac 402
 J. H. 507
 J. L. 178
 J. M. 1005
 J. S. 95
 Jacob 501, 2158
 Jacob F. 501
 Jane 510
 Jay 362
 John ... 145, 247, 1003, 1006
 Levi 402, 501
 Mahala 402
 Margaret 501, 503
 Mary 402
 Melvin B. 362
 Minnie 502

Mrs. Angeline 293
Narwosta 512, 513, 514
Owen B. 362
R. J. 652
Ralph J. 518
Robert H. 503
Robert T. 105, 183, 184, 185, 186, 187
S. F. 1005
V. B. 502
W. B. 502
Will 510
William J. 362
Sedgwick
R. H. 498
Rev. George C. 568
Rev. William 373, 2179, 2195
William.. 436, 457, 568
Seeley
Henry 285
Seibe
Nellie 512
Seidel
Emil 174
Seins 819
Simon 258
W. M. 81
Selby 2112
Dr. J. A. 394
James 821, 2113
James S. 258
Lloyd 821
Milton 279
Prudence 819
Selders
John 275
Wilbur G. 363
Sell
Rev. A. 402
Sells 603
Serensun
George A. 363
Seresun
George 369, 370
Michael 369

Sergeant
Jeremiah 975
Seton
Robert 747
Severe
Joseph R. 363
Severn
Charles 621
Severns
John 261
W. B. 262
Seward
Isaac 854
John R. ... 95, 180, 363, 498, 499
William H. 156
Sewell 429
Arthur P. 167
Sexton
Lee 606
Seymour
Horatio 155
Shackelford 2121
Captain W. 411
General 317, 320, 321, 323, 324, 325, 326, 332, 513, 1006
General James 305, 306, 307, 309
Shadwell
Henry 2099, 2108, 2160
Shafer 747
Conrad 975
Hilda Long 513
Jacob 965, 975, 976
William 975
Shaffer 2128, 2247
Bishop 412
C. 972
Shaffner 262, 647, 678
A. P. 115, 124, 704
Alfred 687, 688, 976
Alfred P. 379
Jacob 97, 114, 122, 124, 624, 626, 682,

2055, 2063, 2172, 2176, 2178, 2190
Shairer
Leo 363
Louis 291
William 606
Shakespeare 623, 624
Shakler
Solomon 280
Shamhart
Henry 924
John 924
Shandrick
Paul 363
Shankland 2160
Shannon
Amon 853, 939
Charles 995
Gov. Wilson 2100
Governor Wilson ... 462
J. P. 203, 2075
Wilson 65, 105, 120, 121, 137, 140, 142, 143, 813
Sharon
Frank 621
Sharp
James 849
Sharrock
Eddie 363
Everett 247
James 242
Timothy 247
Shaw
David C. B. 363, 499
Franklin P. 363
George 976
George W. 280
J. C. 87, 178, 203
James A. 363
Jane 2286
John W. 265
Luke 812
Margaret 936
Mary 812
Mrs. Mary 886
Robert C. 498

ALL NAMES INDEX

Thomas 504, 656
Tobias R. 280
Virgil F. 363
W. D. 464, 2128
William.. 695, 856, 988

Shawver
Doyle M. 363

Shear
Joseph................... 280

Shearrow
Alexander R. 363
Glenn E. 363

Sheck
Effie 512

Sheehan
Ernest .. 363, 367, 466, 606
James................... 366
Joseph O. 363
Peter 100, 181, 183, 185, 204, 605, 606, 629, 2047
Peter P. 499
William 337, 363, 2134
William, Jr. 367

Sheeley
Christian 284
Clifford A............... 363

Sheely
Christian .. 1046, 1047, 1049
John 1046, 1047
Joseph.................. 1046
Samuel................ 1049

Sheen
Willa...................... 512

Sheerin
Elizabeth 512

Sheldon
George S. 503

Shelley
Charles................. 515

Shepard
Isaac W. 363
Rev....................... 524

Shephard
Hudson 868

Isaac W. 351
Shepherd
Col. David.......... 22, 23
Delbert................. 363
Shepler
Leda 502
R. I...................... 1010
S. D...................... 510
Samuel 502
Sheppard................... 961
B. F. 653
C. S. 169
Charles S. ... 74, 92, 93, 173, 186, 187, 335, 491, 529, 639, 2257, 2258
D. O...................... 499
John Charles.......... 186
Judge...................... 74
Mrs. B. Frank....... 2305
Mrs. William 268
Prosecuting Attorney
C. S.................. 664
Rev. A. M. 399
William.................. 247
Sherard
James.................. 141
Sherby
Elwin 363
Mike...................... 656
Sheridan 593
John 886
Sherman................... 593
Gen. William T. 273, 2167
General 274, 2122, 2123
Horace 975
James............. 83, 245
James S. 172
John 146, 155, 160, 161
Senator 65
Senator John 2148
William........ 245, 1017
Sherrard 449
Homer... 514, 629, 630

J. H. 678
James 787, 790
Mrs...................... 787
Richard W. 363
Will....................... 618
William.................. 790
Sherron
Jack 847
Sherrow
Hudson................ 1017
Solomon.............. 1017
Shers
Sol 1013
Sherwood
Kate B................... 511
Shevel
Samuel 245
Shewman
John 1061
Shields
John 799
William R............... 634
Shimp
Clarence W............ 498
Ernest E. 363
John 337
John M. 363
Myra 510
Shinn
R. M. J. 277
Shipe
Charles E. 363
Shipley...................... 449
A. 966
Carl H. 363
E. B. 629, 630
E. V. 2019
Ezekiel........... 246, 868
George .. 246, 250, 251
James 246
John 246
Lewis 124, 869, 870
Perry L.................. 675
Rezin 868
Talbert 956
Talbert R. 279
Shipman

ALL NAMES INDEX

George M. 265, 280
Homer 937, 938
Jacob 893, 894
John 76, 87
Samuel 1062
Samuel F. 363
Shirer 833
Shivel
  George 246
Shively
  Charles F. 363
  Henry 695
  J. W. 296
  Jacob 278
  John 996
  Mary 988
Shivers
  Archie E. 363
Shoaf
  Philip 246
Shoesmith
  Mrs. E. M. 2049
Shoff 2112, 2273
  John 1049
  Philip 824, 1037, 1040, 1049
  Washington 1038, 1049
Shonfield 262, 2059, 2174, 2214
Shook
  Rev. Isaac 990
Shope
  Jacob 939
Shoup
  George L. 2248
Shreves
  Samuel 258
Shrieves
  Rev. James 402
Shriver 2285
  Adam 247, 566, 824
  Adam G. 277, 284, 2286
  Adam, Jr. 818, 819, 2285, 2286
  Adam, Sr. 2285

Delila Gordon 2285, 2286
E. 269
Elijah ... 80, 2107, 2286
Elijah (Heirs) 824
Jacob 995
Jane Shaw 2286
John 2158
John F. 285
John S. 276
M. 269
Margaret Witten . 2286
Mark G. 363
Martha Woodson 2286
Michael 824, 2286
Samuel R. 276
Shrivers
  Rev. James 402
Shroyer
  David 975
  H. C. 514
  Howard 605
  Jacob D. 363
  Susan 965
Shry
  William E. 518
Shryock
  George W. 1038
Shuback
  George 265
Shultz
  R. I. 498
Shuman 431
  Clarissa 919
  Clyde W. 363
  John 919, 924
  Mrs. E. 886
Shun
  Adrian 276
Shutts
  Lieutenant 2017
Sickman
  Andrew 245
  John 245
  Presley 245
Sidlo
  John 518, 596

Sidwell 409
  Henry 909
Siegfried
  Carl 606
  Carl R. 363
  Clarence D. 363
  Frank B. 363
  Mrs. Mary J. LaFollette 315, 316
  Rev. B. Y. 375, 2196
Siegfrist
  Peter H. 276
Siens 2015, 2017
  Absalom ... 2015, 2016, 2017
  Christina ... 2015, 2016, 2017
  Edgar J. 363
  Elizabeth 2015
  Emma 2015
  George 2015, 2016
  Isaac 2015, 2016
  J. Jesse 339
  John 2015, 2016
  Leonard 2015, 2016
  M. H. 515
  Mary 2015, 2017
  Melissa 2015
  Peter 2015, 2016
  Peter R. 2017
  Sadie 2015
  Simon 2015, 2016, 2017
  Susan 2015
  Sy 2016, 2017
  William 2015, 2016
  William M. 145
  William S. 2128
Siffert
  Rev. W. O. 399, 400
Sights
  David 856
  Frazier 856
  William 856
Sigman
  Christine 513
  Edith 504

ALL NAMES INDEX

Florence 504
George 278, 799
Isaac.....................277
John 696, 799
Julia Ann 375
Laban 277
Luke 799
Philip....................276
Presley 278, 285
Richard..................279
Rollo.....................277
Thomas 275
Silliman
  Rev. W. W. 405
Sills 1038
  Henry 856, 1049
  James............265, 280
  Jonathan 280, 1049
Simcox
  O. A. 499
  Oscar A. 499
  Paul 606
  Paul C. 363, 499
  Richard...................606
Simms
  Absalom.................285
  Charlie 320, 2022
  Simeon...................285
Simon 2050
  A. 2007, 2055, 2059, 2101, 2144
  C. P........................508
Simons 262, 585, 2132, 2196, 2250
  Dr. C. P. 301
  Ella 302
  Howard 623
  Isaac.....................805
  John 2196
  John W..................575
  Miss Clara 268
  Mrs. H. 268
Simpkins
  Annas 1049
Simpson
  'Aunt Edie' 631
  Benjamin................807

Edith 631, 632, 669
Hon. W. L. 298
Jerry 669
Joseph...................790
Ned 669, 2070
Peter 9, 630, 631, 632, 962
Robert....................787
Thomas 412
W. L......................106
William..................509
William E..............363
Sims
  Earl.......................363
  Peter R. 278
Sinclair
  George H...............567
  William..................975
Sines
  Absalom..............1007
  William..................824
Singens
  Perry 276
Singer 670
  Carl T....................363
  Charles G..............363
  John 669
  Paul C. 363
  Perry 258, 284
Sinsabaugh
  Rev. George 402
Sipe 2188
  Al 616
  B. F......................2128
  Charles H.......363, 499
  Charles H., Jr. 518, 2189
  Manda 512
Sipes
  G. L.......................377
Siverd
  H. H. 265
  Hugh H. 280
Skinner
  Alfred 673
  Charles 868
  Dink......................617

H. 261, 2099, 2117
Harrison 280
Harry 616
Hiram 93, 143, 144, 157, 289
J. A. 469
John 893
L. B. 506
Leon 469
Perry 616, 617
Phineas 893
Samuel 1061
Sarah 288
William. 54, 66, 67, 69, 106, 112, 129, 457, 568, 650, 762, 1061, 1062
Sklener
  George 606
Skrapcansky
  Mrs.......................513
Sky
  Joseph 21
Slack
  Captain M. 411
Slaski
  John 363
Slasor
  Flora 502
  George (Heirs)....1061, 1062
Slater
  David 746
  Ellis 762
  Enoch 976
  Rev. C. C. 400
  Rev. S. E. 402
  Samuel 245
  West.....................813
Slaughter
  F. 976
  Frederick.............1061
  Philip . 747, 1061, 1062
Slay
  Burton 363
Sleeth
  David 790

ALL NAMES INDEX

James 284
Slevin
    Father 407
Slifko
    John 366
    Matt 363
Slingluff
    Jesse E. 514
Slocumb
    Linden H. 639
Sluter
    John 402
Slutts
    James 277
Small
    Charles T. .. 2245, 2246, 2247
    Jennie A. Jackson 2247
    Nellie V. Ransom. 2246
Smallwood
    J. W. 166, 169, 629
Smiley
    Andrew E. 284
Smith. 409, 431, 487, 559, 718, 833, 864, 873, 910, 951, 2087, 2115, 2116, 2224
    Aberneaser 805
    Addison T. 952
    Addison Taylor ... 2247, 2248, 2249
    Alexander 790
    Alfred E. 181, 182, 2150
    Alice 2288, 2290
    Amos, Sr. 868
    Andrew 381, 868
    Andrew (Heirs) 812
    Arthur 363
    Barney 806
    Benjamin 868
    Captain Thomas 298
    Charles 2115
    Charles E. 363
    Cleo 363
    Clifton 363
    Congressman Addison T. 2257
    David 956
    Denver K. 363
    Dr. 2103
    E. B. 2085
    E. E. (Hub) 2140
    E. W. 2133
    Ebenezer 73, 90, 95, 142, 495, 658, 869, 2060
    Elijah P. 279
    Elisha 1031
    Ernest 604
    G. W. 652
    Garrett 956
    George . 868, 992, 996, 2115
    Gilda L. 363
    Goldwin 612
    Green Clay 158
    Henry 824
    Hiram L. 350, 363
    Isaac 279, 2247
    Israel 278
    J. 269
    J. R 87
    Jacob 247, 284, 939, 2196
    Jacob (Heirs) 1017
    Jacob C. 276
    James ... 231, 320, 601, 649, 848, 939
    James H. 621
    Jane B. 2088
    Jane Forsythe 2247
    Jeremiah 1017
    Jerry 169
    Jesse. 399, 1012, 1017, 2107
    John 395, 654, 868, 886, 893, 924, 936, 939, 940, 941, 1028
    John H. 265, 280
    John L. 363, 746
    John M. 868
    Jonah 10, 128, 654, 911, 913, 924, 2107, 2115, 2289
    Jonas J. 278
    Joseph 49, 261, 736, 930, 1012, 1056, 1058, 1062
    Joseph B. 1049
    Joshua 832, 835
    Josiah P. 2187
    Judge Carl H. 771
    L. M. 507
    L. W. 469, 821, 2113
    M. 747, 886
    Margaret 367
    Mary 824
    Mayberry 747, 894, 902
    Minnie 512
    Mrs. Elizabeth 490
    Mrs. Mary 886
    Mrs. P. 1013
    Mrs. S. 865
    Mrs. S. B. 865
    Mrs. Sarah 268
    Mrs. W. 1013
    Nancy 2264
    Nathan 868
    Nathaniel 956, 1049
    Owen 790
    Pat 270
    Peter 812, 1031
    Reuben 501
    Rev. 405
    Rev. A. R. 402
    Rev. C. W. 2203
    Rev. James ... 381, 971, 2193
    Rev. Reuben 402
    Robert 868, 2156
    S. A. 879, 1016
    S. A. 'Amzi' 2094
    S. B. 865
    S. M. (Sam) 2115
    Sam 230
    Samuel ... 87, 125, 276, 868, 1061, 1062

ALL NAMES INDEX

Samuel M. 2115
Samuel T. 2249
Squire 2115
Squire F. 363, 370
T. H. 447
Thomas .. 84, 166, 245, 275, 747, 975, 2138, 2258
Thomas H. 441, 442, 443
Tom 452
W. A. 2133
Walter C. 265, 280
Washington 893
Will G. 95
William 63, 88, 122, 123, 245, 279, 621, 625, 659, 812, 913, 932, 2115
William (Heirs) 924
William B. 1030
William C. 1059
William H. ... 279, 2115
William M. 939
William N. 1049
William, Jr. 893

Smitley
   George W. 265

Smock
   E. E. 447
   Peter 996
   Philip S. 277

Smoots
   A. W. 509

Smyth
   John 1030

Smythe
   Collector 879

Snake-in-the-Grass.... 825, 826

Snaveley 1036

Sneddon
   Richard 363
   Robert B. 363

Snell
   Homer 370

Snider

Chester A. 498
Mrs. Tice 411
Rev. Tice 411
Thomas H. 180, 181, 183
Virgil Z. 363
Wayne L. 363, 368

Snodgrass
   Jesse 790, 849, 2103
   John 1027

Snow
   John 567, 568

Snyder
   C. W. 87, 181, 183, 186
   Fred 674
   Hal F. 363
   J. M. 939, 2072
   Lizzie 759
   Mark 653, 657
   Rev. Wayne 1010
   Thomas H. 91

Socolou
   Wasel 363

Soden
   Captain 263

Solomon
   Frank 621

Somers 477, 479, 833, 981
   Carl E. 363
   W. C. 391

Sothern
   Mr. 2069

Souders
   Jacob 799

Soukup
   Father 408

Soule
   Rev. 570

Sours
   Charles 956

Sousa 608

Spaht
   George N. ... 2286, 2287

Spaid 970, 1003, 1004, 2286
   Barbara Albin 2287
   Christina 2287

Elizabeth 402, 2287
Elizabeth Cale 2287
Frederick 2287
George 1003, 2158
George N.. 2286, 2287, 2288
George W. 363
J. H. 507
J. W. 402, 1005
James E. 1007
John 2287
John W. 402
Lizzie 510
M. L. 166, 973
Margaret 400
Mary 2287
Michael 1007, 2287
Nancy 2287
Richard 2287
W. H. 402
William 1007, 2287

Spangler
   C. H. 180

Spargrove
   John L. 363

Sparr
   Daniel 996

Spear 46
   A. S. 87
   Abraham 791, 2107
   Abraham S. 142
   Alexander 790
   Ernest 363
   Henry 277
   James A. 280
   Robert (Heirs) 1030
   Robert S. 277
   Robinson 893
   Stewart 791
   Thomas 1030
   Walter Clarence 367
   William S. 277

Spears 1019
   Jane 510
   Robert 835

Speck
   Augustus 1017

ALL NAMES INDEX

Samuel 1017
Speer 196
   Captain 262
   Henry 284
   John 442
   John S. 441
   Judge .. 125, 232, 1028
   Lieut. Henry 1028
   Robert.. 66, 67, 81, 85, 550, 2009, 2061
   Scott 126
   Stewart 54, 67, 125, 232, 245, 746, 786, 1033
   Stuart 66, 67, 566
   William R. 363
Speers
   Robert................... 832
Spence 1059
   David P.......... 265, 280
   James 807, 1059
   James, Jr. 812
   John (Heirs)......... 1017
   Rev. 399
Spencer 431, 914, 916, 917, 2018, 2019, 2025
   A. 269
   Asa 649
   F. M....................... 391
   Frank S. 279
   Henry 363
   Isaac..................... 919
   John W................ 1012
   Nathan 1030
   Rev. William........ 1040
   Richard.. 432, 924, 932
   Thomas R. 363
Spenia
   Alexander 363
   John A. 363
Speyer 2241
Sprague
   Ella 504
Spriggs
   Morris D.............. 2154
Spring
   Herman H. 500

Springer
   Clifford H............... 363
   Cornelius..... 579, 2191
   J. C........................ 265
   Jeremiah 579
   Rev. Cornelius 393, 2192, 2198
   Walter G. 363, 368
Sprinkle
   Betty 552
Sproat 487
   Alexander.... 812, 1061
   Elijah 494
   Samuel 494
Sprout
   Arthur H. 363
   L. H........................ 502
Spurgeon
   B. E. 503, 506
   Banks 503
   Harry P. 363
   Irene 507
Spurrier
   Lewis 502
Squibb
   John 965, 975
   Milton 435
   Mrs. John 965
Squier
   J. J. 272
   Odel 2160
   Rev. Ezra K. 991
Squiers 989
   Mr. 304
St. Clair 917, 920, 2288, 2290
   Alice Smith 2288, 2290
   Carl........................ 498
   Col. Arthur 2282
   Curtis 514
   David................... 996
   F. L. 655
   G. M. 917
   Gen. Arthur ... 752, 753
   General Arthur........ 24
   Gov. Arthur 2042, 2132
   H. T. 655

Henry 501
J. F. 494
James 649
Louella Bay Keysor 501
Margaret 996
Mathias R. 362
R. D. 917
Rosa 514
Scott H. 362
Silas R. 362
William. 689, 747, 989, 995, 2288, 2289, 2290
Staats
   Alexander A. 280
   Vance N................. 363
Stackhouse
   Amos 242
   Chauncey 363
   Homer F. 351, 363
Stafford
   Benjamin............... 893
   Rev. J. P. 972
Stage
   Herschel 363, 369
   John 800
   John R. 285
   Walter 585
   William M. 277
   William S. 503
Stagg
   Charles W.............. 289
Stahl
   Harry E. 2162
Stambaugh
   D. W. 151
Stamm
   Rev. J. C. 385
Stanberry
   E. M....................... 165
   Howard 849, 1049
   Jonas 824, 975, 996, 1049
   Thomas 956
Stanbery
   Henry 2167
Stanies

ALL NAMES INDEX

George 835
Stanley
    Allen 363
    D. F. 1041
    Harry 363
    Nathan 621
    T. C. 621
    Walter P. 605
    William 621
Stark
    Major George 411
    Rev. Langdon 972
Starr
    Edward 363
    J. Oras 363
    James .. 954, 995, 1061
    James H. 278
    John 2155
    John N. 276
    John W. 276
    M. D. 258
    Moses D. 276
    Samuel G. 363
State
    Ohio 647
Stauffer
    E. E. 377
Steadman
    Fred M. 363
    Samuel 703
Stears
    Peter 574
Steck
    Rev. J. 402
Steele 595, 623
    Alexander 996
    C. H. 503
    David 278
    Dewey G. 363
    E. 696
    Ernest L. 363
    Frederick G. 280
    Henry 276, 2154
    Herbert 605
    Herbert M. 635
    I. P. 502, 503, 654

J. C. 81, 93, 99, 595, 999, 1000
J. Homer 654
James 1030
John 790
John B. 276
John H. 363
Joseph 278
Lawrence S. 363
Lieutenant 411
Maggie 503
Ollie 514
Samuel 824
William. 265, 276, 280, 285
Steeth
    James 868
Steffey
    William 278
Stegler
    Benjamin 975
Steinhoure
    Captain J. 411
Stener
    Nicholas 1049
Stephens 2073
    Adam 278
    Albert 295
    Alton D. 503
    Arthur Linn 366
    F. R. 503
    John 824
Stephenson
    Moses 245
    R. G. 439, 886
Sterling
    James 1025
    James F. 277
    Mrs. 1025
Sterling T. 9
Stevenard
    Gustof 363
Stevens 989, 1036
    A. L. .. 93, 106, 169, 625
    Aaron 278, 1014
    Adam 276, 827
    Adeline 501

Daniel G. 278
Dewey K. 363
Eddie 2137
Elijah 996
Elizabeth 501
Ernest R. 363
George 278
Hannah 2306
Harry 606
Henry S. 363
James ... 121, 127, 618, 748
James J. 746
James, Sr. 868
John 1030, 2154, 2160
Joshua 956
Reuben 988, 995
Samuel 2159
Sophronia 149
Stanley E. 363
William 501, 996, 1030
Stevenson
    Adlai E. 165, 168
    Alexander 277, 284
    George 790, 800
    George W. 277
    Isaac 1049
    James 198, 231, 894
    John 127
    Moses (Heirs) 790
Stewart 833
    Andrew 363
    Charles 500, 975
    Charles W. 499
    D. C. 302
    David W. 276
    Dr. H. L. 514
    Edie 856
    Fred 337
    Fred L. 363
    G. N. 502
    Galbraith 812, 1061
    George 434
    George E. 350, 363
    H. L. 518
    Harry B. 363
    J. 269, 865

ALL NAMES INDEX

J. B. 106, 488, 494, 517, 518, 629, 630
J. Starkey............. 511
James... 126, 171, 649, 799, 856, 869, 956, 996, 1043
James B. 176, 177, 178, 784
James R. 187
James, Jr. 996, 1062
John 746, 856, 868, 893, 1049, 2107
John (Heirs)........... 956
John B. .. 265, 280, 299
John W. 180
Johnson 500
Joseph A................ 278
Joseph R........ 277, 284
Lizzie 268
Mary 510, 2084
Massy................. 1043
Miss M. 268
Ola 500
Pearl..................... 363
Rebecca 2219
Robert........... 924, 964
Samuel .. 124, 747, 832
Sarah..................... 512
Sheriff William 287
Thomas .. 57, 110, 111, 546, 799, 999, 1000
W. 258
W. W. 166, 169, 296
William... 90, 127, 153, 246, 270, 284, 621, 748, 835, 856, 888, 956, 988, 2127
William (Heirs) 1061
William A. 275
William B. 1025, 2148, 2187
William H. 363
William R. 275
Stiers 435, 977
Henry 245
Isaac..................... 114

Jacob.................... 276
John 276
Joseph H. 278
Joshua 278
Joshua M.............. 258
Mrs. 965
Raphael................ 965
Reason 976
Robert................... 278
Robert E. 258
Samuel 71, 246, 747
Samuel, Jr. 975
Samuel, Sr. 975
William M. 278
Stiles..... 2290, 2291, 2292
Andrew 832, 835, 2291
Clemma................ 512
Deborah 2291
Eliza..................... 2291
Fanny 832
Frank.................... 565
George 2291
George L............. 2291
Hiram 887
J. 856
Jacob........... 835, 2291
John 842, 956, 2291
Jonathan 124, 829, 832, 835
Jonathon ... 2290, 2291
Jonathon, Jr. 2291
Lewis.................. 2291
M. W. 653
Margaret............. 2291
Mary 2291
Miss Jessie V. 2290, 2291
Mrs. William 517
Roy....................... 363
Simon.......... 835, 2291
Stephen....... 832, 2291
Thomas 835, 2291
William............... 2291
Stillion
Earl D. 364
Stillions
Fred R................... 364

John J. 278
Stillwell
John W. 280
Judge.................... 70
Stilts
C. A...................... 447
Claude A............... 364
Stilwell
Herbert S.............. 364
Stins
John 400
Stires
Samuel 927, 928
Stitt
Anthony 364
John 2129
Stock
Albert E. 364
Stockdale . 873, 884, 2200, 2261, 2302
C. S. 88, 2258
Charles S. 173
Elias................... 2262
Elizabeth 2262
Hugh 2261
J. 269, 886
J. F. 169
James ... 127, 886, 893, 2107, 2261, 2262
James G. 166
James, Jr.............. 2262
James, Sr. 2262
Jane................... 2262
John 868, 886, 893, 2261, 2262
John F................... 164
Lizzie 315
Lydia.................. 2262
Maggie 268
Margaret............ 2262
Martha 2262
Mary 2262
Moses 258, 893, 2014, 2015, 2261, 2262
Mrs. M. 886
Phebe Lening 2262
Robert . 868, 894, 2261

ALL NAMES INDEX

S. W. 886
Sylvanus 2262
Thomas 853, 2262
Walter 364, 370
William 2261
Stockum
　Emmet L. 364
Stockwell 2110
　George 989
Stoddart
　Nancy 375
　Philo 375
Stoebe
　F. W. 514
Stoey
　William 674, 675
Stoffer
　Clancy A. 364
Stokely
　Mr. 120
　Samuel 647, 799
Stokley 513
　Max W. 364
　Rex 515
Stokol
　John N. 364
Stone
　Alexander C. 277
　Anna Asbury 516, 577, 2032
　Dalton 364
　Dr. 304, 993
　E. D. 87, 106, 173, 181, 494
　E. Thoburn 501
　Frazier 790
　James E. 629
　John 494
　Junietta 988
　Lemuel 1030
　M. F. 507
　Miss Mary 81
　Miss Mary A. 516, 613, 2049
　Solomon 799
　William H. 894
Stoneburner

Henry 975
Stoneking
　Jacob 2159
Stoner 547, 550, 552, 554, 2166
　Francis A. 276
　John 696
　Joseph .. 123, 124, 278, 647, 696, 2098
　Joshua 285
　Mr. 644, 645
　Nicholas 246, 747, 893
　Samuel 696
Storer
　Judge Bellamy 139
　S. T. 499
Stotler
　D. N. 696
　John B. 123
　W. B. 686
Stottlemire 505
　Ervin W. 276
　Frank E. .. 393, 569, 607
　George H. 278
　H. J. 693
　Wilbur F. 364
Stotts
　John 919
　Johnny 2152
　Joseph 812, 956
Stottsbury 2302
Stouppe
　Hugh 377
Stout 1028
　Dr. G. H. 494
　German 129
　Isaiah 2128
　James 1030
Stover
　Rev. F. R. 423
Stowe
　Harriet Beecher ... 702, 1070, 2119
Strahl
　David 995
　Jess 610
Strahn

William 2011, 2012
Strain
　James 830
Stranathan 970
　C. L. 470
　George 989
　Harry P. 364
　James 87, 965, 975, 976, 2107
　John 2152
　Miss May 470
　Octa 510
　S. 269
　Samuel . 129, 209, 651, 996
　Thomas 975
　William. 364, 502, 992, 2154
Strange
　John 2191
　Rev. John 378
Stratton
　Charles S. 534, 535
　Lavinia Warren 535
Strayer
　Samuel C. 280
Strong
　Albert 975, 2152
　Clarence F. 364
　Norville B. 280
　Thomas 975
Stroud
　Charles 364
　Jack 618
　John A. 364
Struble
　James 975, 976
Stuart
　General J. E. B. 308
　Mrs. Johnson G. 871
Stubbs
　Elbert E.. 364, 367, 368
　I. E. 93
　Iris 370
　Iris E. 364
　Isaac E. 181
　John 364

Leo 364
Lourie 503
Robert 364
Theo. J. 186
Theodore J. 185
Stull
  George W. 258
  Henry 73, 830
  John 856
  Jonathan 246
  Martin 829, 2291
Stump
  Black 552
Sturges
  Hezekiah 1049
  Solomon 939, 995
Stuth
  William M. 276
Stutts
  Joseph 814, 815
Styles
  Isaac 246
Sudden
  George 245
Suediker
  Josiah 995
Suhart
  Andy C. 364
Suite
  Miss Dolly R. 443
Suitt 2302
  Helen 375
  John S. 375
  Miss D. 623
  Miss Mary 623
  P. T. 81, 88
  Philip 790
  Wallace W. 755
  William C. 755
  Z. 626
  Z. C. 302, 505, 2098
  Zephaniah 647
  Zephima 2199
  Zephima C. ... 393, 2192
Sulen
  Mike 364
  Pete 364

Sullivan
  Charlie 617
  John 616
  Sul 603, 604
Sumner
  Senator Charles 156
Sumter
  General 804
Sunafrank
  Jacob 790
  John, Jr. 790
  John, Sr. 790
Sunday
  Billy 420, 422
Sunnafrank
  Helen 497
  J. 269
  J. E. 515
  John 695, 787
  John, Jr. 647
  John, Sr. 647
  Mable 513
  Solomon 695
Sunon
  Catherine .. 2299, 2300
Surmay
  Joseph 364
Sutton
  Christopher 1061, 1062
  Jacob 1062
  Philip 1061
  William 276
Svejkovsky
  Andrew 364
Swaim
  Cy 619
  Daniel 1017
Swain
  Benoni 278
  Matthias 824
Swan 230, 848, 2222
  George F. 639
  George Forney 366
  Harvey 2207, 2208
  Helen 2262
  John 844
Swaney 833

Swartz
  Alvah R. 364
Swayne
  Samuel 924, 2103
Swearingen
  E. B. 559
Sweeney
  Charles E. 498
  Winnie 503
Sweet
  C. T. 989
Swiedeski
  Johanna 982, 983
  Old Pete . 10, 982, 983,
    984, 2134
Swingle
  George I. 280
  George J. 265
Swope
  Christopher 1061
Swormstedt
  Leroy 2191
Symmes
  John Cleves 60
Szadinski
  Father 408

T

T.
  Sterling 610
Taber
  L. J. 184
Tacitus 439
Taft
  President William H. 9,
    172, 173, 174, 175,
    521, 528, 529, 530,
    531, 625
  President William
    Howard 2248
Tagg
  Dr. F. T. 394
Taggart
  Max H. 364
Talbert
  Matilda 2099

ALL NAMES INDEX

Nathaniel 812
W. 67
William 889
Talbot
  J. D. 2138
Talbott
  John S. 178
  Lloyd 34, 67, 87, 95, 106, 567, 568, 2167
  Rodney 246, 574
  William 246, 574
Talley
  John F. 2159, 2161
Tallmadge
  General David 659
Tandy
  James B. 276
  William 275
Tannehill 2200
  Henry C. 280
  I. A. 81, 2200
  Lyle 2200
  R. H. 729
  R. P. 2200
  Rev. 2013
  Rev. I. A. 2168
  Rev. Robert 2200
  Samuel 886
  William 2200
  William H. 2200
Tanner
  John 996
Tanneyhill
  William S. 115
Tannyhill
  I. A. 447
Tappan
  Benjamin 66
Taylor 24, 77, 380, 511, 554, 570, 587, 611, 653, 833, 2056, 2109, 2167, 2249
  A. A. 84, 278, 279, 511, 653, 2258
  A. D. 128
  Alexander A. 2249
Alexander D. 123, 956, 2249
Alfred 506
Arthur 364
Attorney J. Sherman 702, 703
Byron 2249
C. P. 623
Capt. Alexander A. 'Ad' 2249
Capt. Alexander Addison 'Ad' .. 2250
Capt. J. D. 289
Capt. Joseph D. 290
Captain A. A. 298
Captain Alexander A. 2249
Charlie 81
Col. J. D. 575, 653, 669, 671, 2138
Col. Joseph D. 2148, 2167, 2203, 2206, 2248
Colonel 614
Colonel J. D. . 166, 548, 588, 662, 726, 903
Colonel Joseph D. 9, 162, 165, 708, 709, 710, 711, 2168
Congressman Joseph D. 2257
D. D. 81, 157, 161, 164, 166, 169, 302, 527, 625, 662, 2138, 2168
Daniel 280
David C. 285
David D. 106, 447, 459, 460, 708, 2056, 2182, 2249, 2257
Dory 920
'Dory' 2255, 2289
Edgar H. 364
Edward 2191
Elizabeth A. Hill ... 2167
Ella McCracken ... 2249
Eve 832
G. Kennon 2249
Gen. Zachary 141
General A. D. .. 254, 255
George . 265, 280, 835, 893
George K. 278
George M. 364
'Guernsey' 460
Hon. D. D. 298, 299, 2138
Hon. J. D. 80, 496
I. N. 505
J. B. 625, 2128
J. Byron 2249
J. C. 265
J. Clarkson 2249
J. D. 105, 155, 157, 161, 164, 300, 2128
J. W. 390
James C. 649
Jim 2004
John . 567, 1064, 1065, 1066
John S. 181, 364
John Sherman 368
Joseph . 434, 988, 1049
Joseph D. 93, 100, 103, 104, 163, 261, 279, 379, 447, 459, 952, 2129, 2249, 2258
Justice C. 966
Justus C. 280
Lakin C. 2168
Mary E. 833
Mrs. 832
Mrs. B. 268
Mrs. J. D. 495, 496
N. W. 265
Norville W. 280
O. R. 171
President Zachary 141, 142, 532, 625, 2104, 2256
Rev. Edward 972
Rev. J. E. 410
Robert 1007

ALL NAMES INDEX

S. H. 174
Samuel 829
Samuel (Heirs) 835
Sarah 703
T. Corwin 2249
T. T. 106
Theodore 919
Thomas . 973, 975, 976
Thomas J. 97
W. A. 87, 183, 347
William 567
William P. 2249
Wilson S. 279
Wilson Shannon .. 2249
Zachary 675, 813

Teaker
   Nelson 115

Teal
   L. T. 784

Tedrick .. 869, 2073, 2299, 2302
   Adam 247, 835
   Charles E. 364
   Damon S. 518
   Edgar B. 364
   Gladys 512, 513
   Ira J. 364
   Isaac 893
   J. M. 87, 178, 180, 203
   Jacob 246
   Jacob, Jr. 893
   Jacob, Sr. 893
   John 246, 250, 251, 647, 835, 2009
   John, Jr. 893
   Lawrence, Sr. 939
   Leroy 370
   Loraine L. 350, 364
   Michael 246, 893, 1017
   O. M. 2065
   Peter 939
   Ray R. 364
   Richard 748
   Ward B. 350, 364
   William. 746, 869, 894, 940
   William F. 2074

Teel
   Harry F. 364

Teele
   Arron 1031

Teener
   Frances 501
   Merrill 501
   Rachel 996

Teeter
   Dr. 316
   Dr. William 402
   William 501, 1005

Temple
   Benjamin 1013
   Edward 1049
   Ella 500
   Lafayette 87, 173
   LaFayette 861
   Mrs. Benjamin 1013
   Mrs. LaFayette 861
   Paul H. 364
   Thomas 258
   William 924

Templeton
   William F. 439

Tenney
   Judge 525

Terrall
   Jared 849

Terrell 2143
   Daniel L. 364
   David T. 280
   Jared 844

Teterick
   Elias 128
   Maggie 268

Tetirick 890, 891
   Douglas E. 905
   Elias 905
   John 905
   Mary Jane 905
   Reuben 890

Tetlow
   Percy 180

Tetrick
   A. W. 278
   Daniel 884
   Dennison 1000
   Elias 887
   Hezekiah 278
   Jacob 86
   John 829, 830
   Joseph 278
   Lawrence 830, 934
   Mrs. E. 886
   Pleasant 936
   William E. 278

Tettemer
   John 364

Thackeray 612

Thalheimer 595
   Otto 485, 499, 604

Tharp
   Raymond 364

Thatcher
   Frank O. 364
   William 364

Theaker
   John 856, 956
   John S. 832
   N. 125
   Thomas C. 105, 145, 146

Theran
   Maria 2070

Theret
   Gusta 364

Theseus 2134

Thomas 670, 833, 2050
   Andrew 936
   Ann 965
   B. 504
   Captain 310
   Catherine Gomber Metcalf 611, 626
   E. 269
   E. A. 821
   Eleanor 2282
   Enoch 247, 812, 975
   Enos 699
   Forest R. 364
   H. L. 2254
   J. Smith 610

ALL NAMES INDEX

J. Sterling 610, 611, 612, 613, 776
Jacob 245, 689
James 246, 574, 975
Jesse 833
John 833
John M. 364
Jonathan (Heirs) ... 869
Lambert . 54, 120, 458, 611, 612, 626, 647
Lewis A. 278
Louis 833
Maria 412
Milton B. 277
N. E. 478
Norman 181
R. 81, 457, 568
R. E. 517
Rev. 991
Richard 73
Rudolf 76
Rudolph 88, 276
Samuel 833, 840
Sterling 623
W. D. 696
Walter S. 158
William 280
William Adrain 364
Thompkins
Ethel 507
Thompson ... 50, 126, 970, 971, 1028, 2106, 2200, 2224, 2292
A. C. 698
A. W. 491
Abraham .. 69, 71, 402, 939, 2158
Addison 706
Agnes M. (Oxley) .. 792
Alexander 809
Alfred 601
Alva H. 276, 285
Andrew 956, 1017
Ben 616
Ben I. 364
Benjamin 275, 812
Bert M. 447

Betsey 2293
Betsey Finley 2292, 2293
C. M. 166
Charles 616
Charles A. 621
Charles M. 180
Charlie (Shorty) 603
Daniel 494
David 100, 270, 391, 649, 787, 791, 825, 924
David G. 792
David R. 277
Deborah Laughlin 2279
Dr. W. O. 952, 2236, 2237
E. A. 2026
Ebenezer 747, 975, 976, 2293
Edward 276
Edwin C. 364
Elizabeth Wilson 1018, 1024, 1031
Evan 2293
Francis S. 2057
Frank S. 364
Harriet 2293
Henry S. 280
Homer Roscoe 367
J. A. 87
J. C. 106, 652
J. E. 377, 498, 518, 637
J. Elliott 635
Jacob. 975, 2154, 2158
James ... 142, 447, 762, 975, 980, 2009, 2293
James C. 180, 494, 2057
James D. 280
Jane 2293
John 261, 662, 689, 971, 975, 1030, 1049, 1061, 2152, 2158, 2293
John Alex 492

John Alexander ... 2057
John B. . 430, 495, 647, 698, 801, 802, 2237
John E. 503
John F. 285
John K. .. 265, 270, 280
John, Sr. 1049
Joseph M. 1007
Judge William 711, 2263
L. M. 280
Lawrence 364
Lee 604
Leroy W. 280
Lizzie 510
Louisa Halley 2293
M. 2090, 2100
Marshal John 291
Martin 1049
Mary 939
Mary F. 791
Matthew 131, 135, 647, 2185
Miss Sallie 268
Moses 966
Mrs. 50
Mrs. E. A. 2026
Norval J. 364
Philip 278
Robert .. 107, 115, 426, 696, 956, 967, 968, 971, 975, 976, 1031, 2267, 2268, 2293
Rose 507
S. 129
Samuel . 123, 869, 957, 1017
Samuel A. 893
Samuel F. 835
Sarah 936
Solomon H. 412
Thomas R. 277
W. A. 656
Walter E. 364

ALL NAMES INDEX

William..... 54, 66, 106, 128, 302, 381, 426, 704, 746, 758, 807, 812, 936, 939, 965, 968, 969, 970, 976, 2268, 2279, 2292, 2293
William (Heirs) 975
William A. 280
William H. 285
William H. (Halley) 2293
William of Robert . 975
William of William 975
William Oxley... 9, 792, 793
Thorla 2159
   Forest.................... 513
Thornberry
   Charles H. 623
   G. B. 621
   Grace McFarland .. 623
   Mrs. Charles.......... 492
Thorne
   Dr. Thomas 2301
Thornton
   Black 2070
Thrap...................... 2159
   Mrs. John 2159
Thrapp
   Israel 2199
Thrift
   Mrs. T. B................ 2168
Thucydides 439
Thumb
   General Tom 535
   Tom................... 9, 534
Thurman
   Allen G. 155, 163, 164, 165, 599
   Senator 65
Thwaite
   James 865
Tickhill
   William.................. 364
Tidball
   A. B. 279

Andrew 279
Captain................. 263
Volney........... 279, 285
Tidrick
   Daniel.................... 893
   Daniel (Heirs) 869
   Leroy E. 364
Tignor
   John 160
Tilden
   Samuel J. 158, 159, 523
Tillet
   James 919
   James H................. 917
Tillett
   Augustus C. 276
   Charles 2137
   Charles E. 364
   James 956
   John 276
Tilley
   John 364
Tilton
   Earl........................ 364
   Josephine.............. 512
Timmins
   Samuel 81
Timmons
   Samuel 2009, 2010
Tingle 9, 549, 550, 551, 567, 574, 848, 2059, 2062, 2166, 2214
   Alfred 551
   Alfred H................. 130
   Amanda Clark 551
   Anne 2214, 2215
   Dr. 263, 2023
   Dr. J. P. 261, 2214
   Dr. John P............... 56
   Eldred D. 825
   Evaline 800
   Eveline 2039, 2170
   Eveline R. 551, 2043
   George B. 799
   George B. (Heirs) .. 647

George R. .. 68, 95, 540, 550, 551, 566, 2214, 2262
George T. 551
J. D. 678
J. P......... 261, 695, 698
John (Heirs)........... 825
John A. 825
John P. 551, 2098
Joseph D... 67, 84, 143, 144, 577, 800, 2100
Margaret Newell ... 551
Mary Jane 551
Sarah 551, 647
Susan 551
Tom....................... 623
William.................. 551
Tipton 833
   J. W. 106, 2257
   John 1061
   Lucille 508
   Senator T. W. 2257
   Senator Thomas W. 2253
   T. W................ 66, 2106
   Thomas Corwin ... 2256
   Thomas W. 2099, 2256
   William.................. 956
Titrick
   Enoch 285
Titus
   John 1017
Tivis
   John 2191
Tobin
   Isaac 242, 939
   John 1049
   Nathaniel 939, 1049
   Wesley 939
   William.................. 939
Toby
   Uncle 25
Tod
   Gov. David... 260, 1007
   Governor..... 303, 2236
Todd

ALL NAMES INDEX

Charles H. 364
David............. 276, 813
George M.............. 280
Governor 714
John (Heirs)........... 939
Samuel A.............. 278
Stella 504
Thomas 869
Toland
    Orville J. 364
Tolbert
    William.................. 110
Tolle
    C. C....................... 887
Tom
    Edna..................... 501
Tomepomehala.......... 192
Tomlinson
    Wilbur H. 364
Toner
    Charles.................. 791
    John 1030
Toole
    John 1049
Tooley
    Mrs. Florence........ 411
Tope
    Marie 503
    W. H...................... 503
Topsy....................... 2246
Torade
    Mary 825
Toroade........................ 41
Torode 2050
    John 41
    Mary 2086
    Peter 41, 574
Torrence................... 1036
    G. W..................... 391
    Rev. George P. 405
Totten
    Harry 88, 90, 185, 186, 513, 514
Touvel
    Jackson 278
Touvell
    Alva C. 364

Edward J. 364
John 364
Touville
    Frank F. 364
    Mildred Secrest..... 513
Townsend
    Mr. 76
    Robert................... 825
    Veryl M. 364
Tracey
    Attorney W. W... 2180, 2229
    W. W...... 66, 560, 561, 574, 626, 629
    William.......... 458, 956
    William W. ... 93, 1062, 2187
Tracy 2106
    Mrs. Mary L......... 2223
    Sheridan................ 956
    W. W................... 2100
    William. 515, 647, 799, 812, 869, 893
    William W. ... 123, 495, 956, 2090
Travis
    William.................. 278
Treherne
    John A. 364, 368
    Joseph................... 364
    Steve 364
Trenner 1003, 1004, 2276, 2294, 2295
    Benjamin............. 2294
    Caleb 2294
    George S. 655
    Harriett 508
    Henry ... 242, 400, 825, 1003, 2158, 2277, 2294
    Henry, Jr..... 2294, 2295
    Henry, Sr. 2277
    Isaiah 2294
    Jennie................... 510
    John 2294
    Noah 2294

Sarah 400, 2041, 2277, 2278
Sarah Frye . 2294, 2295
William................ 2294
Tribbie
    Craig..................... 629
    Earl H. 183, 364
    Fred...................... 368
    Fred L.................... 364
    J. Craig................. 368
    John C. 364
Tribey
    James 832
Triem
    Dan W. 639
Trimble 848
    Allen.............. 112, 457
    Dr. Joseph M. 379
Triplett
    Jesse............. 649, 924
    Ralph 370
Tritt
    Earl....................... 771
Troette
    J. A. 81, 157, 161, 164, 169, 508, 623
Trott
    Allie 510
    Aura 501
    E. D............... 173, 504
    Elizabeth 502
    Elza D. 91
    F. 269
    Floyd S.................. 364
    G. F....................... 501
    P. A....................... 502
    Vivian 510
    W. F...................... 502
    W. G...................... 173
    William.................. 502
Troutman
    Clyde 364
Truax
    Phebe 510
Truce
    Matthias............... 849
True

ALL NAMES INDEX

Nettie 504
Trueman 833
Tsantes
   Stefano J. 364
Tuck
   Mary 504
Tucker
   Joseph 277
Tuckerman
   Henry T. 249
Tudor 2220
Tullis 980
   David 66, 87, 106, 112, 457, 746, 747, 975, 978, 979, 980
   Walter O. 350, 351, 364
Turkle
   John 956
   Joseph 956
Turnbaugh 514
   C. S. 499, 569, 2141
   Charles S. 74, 166, 173, 498
   Cyrus 279
   George W. 781
   Grant E. 364
   Grant H. 364
   John W. 696
   William 522, 805
Turner 670, 2251
   Albert C. 368
   Cornelius 669
   Eli 412
   Elza 81, 261, 262, 272, 629, 695, 2109, 2149, 2250
   George 124, 856, 1069, 1070
   Grover C. 364
   Hon. Milton... 298, 299
   J. P. 169
   James ... 258, 277, 285, 626, 1031, 2100, 2165, 2250
   James. 574
   John 242, 621

John P. 485, 491
Lester 515
Margaret A. 1070
Martha 412
Mary 2250
Milton 95, 164, 165, 166, 277, 298
Milton H. 74, 178, 180, 184, 335, 498, 514, 517, 529
Ross 364
Russell Corwin 366
Silky 11, 1070
Simon 669
Squire Elza 2251
Walter .. 364, 498, 606, 629
William 616
William E. 2145
William H. 364
Turner, Jr. 880
Turnifrend
   John L. 278
Turnipseed
   J. L. 917
   Louis 917
Tuttle 2200
   James 2154
   James H. 280
   John 280
   John A. 893
   Liale W. 364
   Lile W. 368
   Robert 337, 364
   William H. 368
   William N. 364
Twain
   Mark 2130
Tyler
   John 458, 547, 758
   President John 116, 118, 119, 129, 130, 131, 132, 133, 134, 135, 137, 138, 164, 187, 521, 625, 2055, 2067, 2102, 2218, 2274

Tyson
   Henry J. 364
   Ira 276

U

Uhleman
   William S. 364
Ulrich
   John Francis 364
Umstot
   Abraham ... 1061, 1062
   Jacob 1062
   Peter 1059
   Peter (Heirs) 1061, 1062
   Samuel 1049
   Solomon 1061, 1062
Umstott
   Abraham 115
   Justice Peter 674
   Peter 113, 114, 123, 682, 2299
   William 674
Unbour
   Owen 799
Underhill
   Elizabeth 2271
   Samuel 799
Unklesbay
   Mae 513
Updegraff
   J. T. 105
   Jonathan P. 160
   Jonathan T. 104
Urban
   Edward 656
   William G. .. 364, 2139, 2140, 2141

V

Valentine 951
   Benjamin 746
   Charles 364, 621
   Daniel 835
   Elizabeth 957

ALL NAMES INDEX

James 265
Jeremiah 869, 956
John 957
Raymond 364
Samuel 956, 957
Vallandigham 420, 591
   Clement .... iv, 314
   Clement L. 7, 146, 147, 148, 150, 151, 155, 2222, 2229, 2296
   Hon. C. L 151, 152
Van Buren
   President Martin 57, 114, 115, 117, 118, 119, 122, 125, 130, 132, 137, 141, 222
Van Buskirk
   W. G. 499
Van De Mark .. 2084, 2087
   C. C. 2038
Van Fossen
   Asa 2138
Van Horn
   Dr. 943
   William 246
Van Kirk
   Asher 515
Van Pelt
   John 245
Van Rensalear
   K. H. 498
Van Renselear
   Ill. K. H. 499, 500
   K. H. 498
Van Rensselaer
   Chief Marshal 151
   Marshal 263
Van Sickle
   George 270
Van Voorhis
   H. C. 104, 105, 166, 170
VanBuren
   President Martin. 2234
Vancamper
   John 835
Vance 932, 2073

Cyrus 276
Edward 364
Ezekiel .. 124, 924, 931, 945
Frederick E. 364
George A. 364
Ivan T. 364
James .. 924, 932, 1017
James (Heirs) 924
John 69, 1012, 1017
Joseph 115
Mrs. Robert 1013
Nancy 924
Robert 1012, 1013, 1017
Robert, Sr .. 1012, 1014
Ross E. 364
Samuel 275
Vandermark
   Peter 276
Vandervort
   John 1031
Vandruff
   Henry C. 278
Vanevey
   Isaac 893
   Mary 956
Vanhorn
   Bernard 893
   George T. 265
   William 125
Vanmeter
   Morgan 956
Vanpelt
   Daniel 856
   Robert 856
Vanrant
   A. H. 696
Vansickel
   J.   2073
Vansickle 2202
   A. W. 265
   Charles E. 365
   Leroy 365
VanSickle
   Augustus H. 280
VanVoorhis

H. C. 165, 169
Vaughn
   Charles 621
   John C. 879
Vermillion
   Joseph 1017
Vernon
   Abner 1017
   Floyd Raymond 366
   Phebe 1017
Vertican 833
Vessels
   B. E. 174
   Hayes H. 365
   James J. 365
   John A. 278
Vickers 55
Vickroy
   Jos. 703
   Joseph 975
Victor
   Henry 567
Victoria
   Queen 535, 2102
Vincent
   Jennie 514
   John 365, 791
   Thomas 351, 365
Vineall
   Captain 411
   Mrs. 411
Vining
   Henry W. 276
Virgil 414, 443
Virtue 2023
   David 128, 712, 939
   David S. 278
   Mary 936
   Mr. 2023
   Robert 939
   Samuel 939
   Samuel, Jr. 939
   William R. 365
Voght
   Ella 500
Von Scio
   E. E. 503

ALL NAMES INDEX

Fannie 503
Voon
    Burgess 703
Voorhies
    Eliza Warne 2296
    James 276
    Joshua 277
    Lewis 277
Vorech
    Stephen 365
Vorhes
    Joshua 285
    Lewis 285
Vorhies
    Albert 1061
    Charles E. 365
    Daniel 2152
    E. E. 107
    Ephraim 2154
    John 791, 849, 2152
    Lewis C. 1061
    Robert 791

W

Waddle
    James 246, 829
    Rev. Benjamin 787
    Samuel 391
Wade
    Senator 65
Waggoner
    Isaac 939
Wagner
    Father 407
    Floyd 515
Wagoner
    General 260
Wagstaff
    Arthur W. 365
    Captain Wm. R. 524
    Henry W. 277
    Hon. W. R. 2137
    Israel B. 349, 365
    James 849
    John 124, 856, 1049
    John K. 365

Mrs. William 800
Robert 849, 2107
W. H. 629
W. R. 463
William 791, 800
Waite
    Morrison R. 108
Wakefield 2160
    Rev. D. W. 412
Walgamot
    Mr. 1047
Walgamott
    David 1038
    Joseph 696
    Mrs. S. 1038
Walker 1039, 2209
    Annie 268
    David R. 279
    Dr. Francis 2112
    Elizabeth W. 2099
    Ellen 2274
    Frank 349, 365
    George 869
    George B. 1017
    Isaac 128
    James 799
    John 552
    John B. 1028
    John C. 1028
    M. 865
    Mrs. J. 865
    Robert 1017, 1031
    Sarah 599
Walkinshaw
    John 869
Wall 595, 1036
    Andrew 261
    Cory 616
    Dr. A. 81
    Dr. Andrew ... 505, 670, 2149, 2251, 2252
    W. 2117
    William 261
Wallace
    Alexander 799
    Arthur E. 365
    Carl R. 365

Colonel. 317, 318, 327, 328, 329
Dan R. 84, 171, 447
David 952, 956
David A. 964
E. B. 260, 2075, 2097
George 198
George H. 280
H. F. 964
Harry C. 365
Henry A. 185, 186, 2257
John 809, 956, 957
Maggie 268
Maria Bratton 2253
Miss M. 268
Miss Nancy 439
Mrs. E. B. 2097
Rev. Samuel 787
Rev. William ... 56, 383, 385, 495, 566, 996, 2085, 2099
Robert 996
Samuel 391
Secretary of Commerce Henry A. 2253
Stout P. . 258, 265, 280
Thomas 566, 956
William .. 242, 874, 996
William J. 179
Wallar
    Earl E. 365
    J. T. 1005
    Joseph 522
    N. G. 1005
    Oscar E. 365
Wallenfelsz
    John 498, 499
Waller 1036
    Andrew 258
    Catherine 2264
    Christopher 242
    David 247
    J. 1031
    J. F. 400
    Joe 1026

ALL NAMES INDEX

John 247
Joseph. 800, 996, 1031
Joseph S. 996
Lewis 247
Lucy 371, 501
Margaret 501
Oscar 371
Oscar E. 501
Phebe E. 2129
Roy 514
Samuel 1031
Samuel (Heirs) 799
Walter 501
Walter E. 365
William 244, 1031
William S. 825
William, Sr. 825
Wallis
  Thomas 799
Walls
  Thompson F. 280
Walraves
  John 975
  William 975
Walsh
  William R. 365
Walter
  Christopher 244
  Dennis 365
  John 244, 1062
  John D. 125
  Roscoe 365
Walters
  C. F. 377
  Christopher 110
  John 110
  Joseph 939
  Lieut. Thomas L. ... 1028
  Medad 812
  Mrs. William 800
  Thomas 285
  William 799, 800
  William G. 2128
Wantz
  John E. 365
Ward 2151, 2152, 2269
  Benjamin 280

Colonel 303
Edward 969, 2152
Edward, Jr. 2152
Edward, Sr. 2152
Elmer E. 351, 365
Frank H. 181, 182
Howard C. 365
Iva 512
James 975
John 924, 2152
Joseph 246
M. E. 265
Mark E. 280
Martin V. 498
William, Jr. 650
William, Sr. 649
Warden
  Craig 91, 186
  Delno T. 349, 365
  Forest C. 365
  Frank R. 365
  Isaac 856, 969, 975
  Isaac J. 856
  Isaac(Heirs), Sr. 856
  J. F. 509
  J. M. 854
  James R. 365
  John 849
  Maurine 508
  Robert 285
  Samuel 856
  Wayne W. 365
Wardeska
  C. S. 498, 771
Wareham
  Michael 975
Warehime
  D. T. 502
Warfield
  Dr. J. M. 470
  Miss Fanchion 784
Warne 762, 807, 810, 1043, 2295
  Anne 2295, 2296
  Clarence T. 365
  D. C. 2295
  DeWitt Clinton 2296

Dr. J. C. 498
Ernest 365
George 246, 835
J. C. 498, 499
James H. 840
James R. 350, 365
John H. 499
Jonathan 114, 198, 246, 649, 748, 762, 807, 812, 894, 957, 996, 1062, 2296
Martha Luzadder 2296
Mary Catherine ... 2296
Thomas 807, 2295, 2296
Warner
  A. J. 104, 105, 163
  Charles E. 365
  Col. A. J. 289
  Gen. A. J. 483, 2124, 2240
  General A. J. .. 162, 209, 210
  George, Jr. 365
  John 230
  Pearl 513
Warnock
  Clara 509
  Elizabeth Bratton . 838, 896
  James 746, 830
  James, Jr. 939
  Jane 936
  John 246, 939
  Robert .. 246, 250, 251, 838, 839, 896
  William 936, 939
Warren 718, 2106
  Jonethen 805
  Lavinia 535
  Rachel 510
Warrick
  Lester B. 365
Warwick
  Rev. Robert 386
Washer
  Hugh E. 498

ALL NAMES INDEX

Washington 670
  Booker T. 1070
  General 726, 906
  General George ... 458, 516
  George .. 759, 819, 873
  James 412
  President George . 294, 530, 896, 2045, 2046, 2057, 2094, 2132, 2225, 2227, 2266, 2287
Waterhouse
  Hiram 696
  William 244
Watkins
  A. E. 502
  Aaron S. 174
  Archibald 747
  Edward 365
  Isaac 365
  Jacob 894
  Keziah 2306
  Lizzie 510
  Nancy 513
  Ray 365
  Thomas W. 365
  Tom 671
Watson 821
  Alexander (Heirs) .. 894
  Clovis A. 365
  David 799
  David A. 501
  E. D. 514
  F. C. 500
  Frank C. 498
  G. 269
  George 87
  Harvey 109, 784
  Ilo 365
  Ira H. 90, 171
  James (Heirs) 799
  Jay F. 365
  John 515
  John T. 285
  Mrs. H. E. 2242

Mrs. Marguerite Metcalf 2045, 2046
Mrs. Marguerite Metcalfe 2044
Otis 365
Ralph H. 365
Rev. Joseph E. 1010
Robert 981
Wilber L. 368
Wilbur 509
Wilbur L. 365, 491
William 502, 809
Watt
  Dr. Joseph W. 265
  J. W. 106
  James 849
  James H. 278
  Joseph 1017
  Joseph W. 280
Watterman
  John 2191
Watters 833
Watterson
  Bishop 407
  Father 407
Watts
  Francis 278
  James 2191
  Joseph 894
  Rev. J. 2198
  Rev. James ... 378, 393, 413, 570
Waverly 612
Waxler
  Brice 365, 498, 499
  Fred G. 498
Way
  Jacob 1049
Wayble
  Bert P. 365
Wayes
  Jane Ambler 375
Wayne 719
  Gen. Anthony 2266
  'Mad Anthony' 1054
Weaver 670, 2297
  Anna Duncan 2297

  Carlisle 2297
  Deborah Williams 2297
  Don E. 2269, 2297
  Dora 2297
  Edwin 2297, 2298
  Grace 2297, 2298
  Hans ... 461, 567, 1062, 2297, 2298
  Hans, Jr. 2297
  Harriet Bigham 2297
  James 2297, 2298
  James B. 161, 165, 166
  John 2297, 2298
  Judith 2297, 2298
  Mary La Rue 2297
  Nellie 2297
  Preston 2297
  Rev. Jonathan 399
  Robert 649, 2297, 2298
  Susanna 2297, 2298
  William 276, 654, 2297, 2298
Webb 559
  J. C. 499
  James 893
  John 893
Weber
  Joseph 422
Webster 10, 409, 833, 913
  Abner 924
  Asbury 279
  Charles 924
  Daniel 131, 132
  E. H. 2128
  Eli 654, 924
  Herschel 280
  Isaac 919, 924
  J. G. 783
  John 276, 502, 746, 909, 910, 920, 921, 924
  John B. 244
  Nancy 31
  Phebe 909
  Stocton 280
  Thomas 924
  W. V. 100

ALL NAMES INDEX

Walter A. 341, 419, 910
William 924
Weedon
   Alfred 91, 275, 276, 511, 2149
   David T. 365
   Homer H. 100, 174
Wehr
   Henry 2156
Weidmer
   Raymond F. 839
Weinstein
   Charles W. 280
Weir
   J. C. 2099
   Jesse 956
   Jesse C. 947, 949, 2067, 2223
   John 2019
   Rev. W. H. 496
   Thomas 1061
Weirich
   C. E. 458
Weirick
   Christian 381
Weirs
   Benjamin 819
   John 821
Weisenstine
   Celia 507, 512
   E. M. 507
   Grover 365
   S. P. 337
   Vernie Burris 366
Welch
   Joseph C. 280
   Rev. 787
Weller 1062
   Jacob 1056, 1062
   John 1062
   John B. 140, 141
Wells
   Amanda Howell Kennedy 274
   Benjamin 115, 128, 819

Dr. W. L. 394
Edwin 276
Henry L. 365
Jacob 939
John 821
M. K. 652
Moses 279
Moses (Heirs) 825
Rev. Logan 410
Ross 2011
Samuel 787, 791
Theodore 273, 274
Welsh
   James 866
Welter
   Jacob 1062
   John 1062
Wendell
   Chester A. 365
   Daniel 2156
   F. H. 509
   Harrison 2156
   Lawrence 924
   Philip 2156
   Roy 339
Wendle
   Daniel 970
   Philip 970
Wenger
   A. W. 518, 656
   Arthur W. 365, 514
Wernwag
   L. V. 203, 2075
   Lewis V. 34
   Margaret W. Metcalf 34
Wesley 416
   Martin G. 498, 499
   Winnie 504
West
   Charles 185
   Dennis 365
   Dora 502
   Nathaniel 996
   William 1062
Westbroom
   Martin 996

Westcott
   Lawrence L. 365
Westlake
   Burris 2191
Wetzel 21, 2280
   John 232
   Katy 232
   Lewis . 22, 23, 232, 874
Weyer
   J. A. 498
   James 94, 886
   James A. 166, 169
   Miss Jennie 516
Weyers 884
Weymer
   William C. 278
Whalon
   Mrs. 819
Wharton 833
   Abner 270
   Andrew 987
   George L. 1007
   Jacob 276
   James 122, 129, 996
   John 697, 996
   Lewis 276
   Rev. D. 160
   Samuel 141
   William. 265, 280, 569, 629
Wheatley
   Elizabeth 819
Wheaton
   James 87
Wheeler
   A. R. 656
   Bess 512
   Bess Stewart 512
   Lawrence H. 365
   Leah 502
   Marshall D. 365
   S.   125
   Samuel 1062
   Warren B. 365
   William A. 158
Wherry 49, 957, 2067, 2223, 2252, 2253,

ALL NAMES INDEX

2301, 2304, 2312, 2313, 2314
Ann . 2252, 2253, 2313
David.... 244, 869, 944, 949, 952, 953, 956, 2252, 2253, 2313, 2314
David E. 2253
James 956, 2253
James A. 285
John 956
Joseph 956
Marilynn 2253
Mary Jane Moore 2253
Senator Kenneth S. 2252, 2253

Whetstone
Henry 246, 1062

Whetzel
John 24, 25

Whissel
Walter L. 365

Whitaker 2073
Obed 939
Reuben 1031
Rev. J. G. 821
William 649, 939, 2073

Whitcraft
Albin 739
Henry 924
James 919, 924, 932

White 647, 833, 1027, 2099
Albert 501
Alice 512
Attorney J. W. 992
C. E. 391
Captain 263, 309
D. 601
Daniel 894
Dr. J. W. 2254
Dr. W. A. 917, 920, 2254, 2255
Edward 996
Elias 940
Elihu 939
Emma Martin 2255

George . 104, 105, 172, 173, 174, 175, 176, 177, 183
Gertrude 501
Gov. George 184
Harry 1028
Hon. J. W. 81, 2217
Hon. Joseph W. 586
I. N. 390, 391
J. C. 258
J. W. 256, 261, 574, 575, 630, 713, 917, 2106, 2239
James 1028, 1031
John 1028, 1031
John W. 365
Joseph 1062
Joseph H. 365
Joseph W. 9, 66, 93, 103, 105, 146, 152, 153, 154, 155, 590, 591, 601, 626, 647, 687, 799, 849, 2128, 2190
Josiah 649
Maria 1025
Martha 2217
Matthew 924
Mr. 2125, 2126
Mrs. W. 268
Oliver 1028
Reece 277
Rev I. N. 2137
Rev. 399
Rev. W. S. 399
Robert Floyd 339
Samuel 244
Sarah 936
Senator 548
Silky 1068
Simon 270
Speaker of the House 548
T. C. 84, 174
Thomas 552, 1028, 1031
Thomas E. 365

Thomas, Sr. 110
W. A. 502
Walter ... 767, 769, 975
William 1028
William E. 365
William G. 277

Whitehill
Thomas 835

Whitis
Robert F. 365
William 270

Whitman
A. A. 158

Whitney
Luie 365

Whittaker
Reuben 2060
Rev. J. G. 2112

Whittier 2119
Andrew 9, 244, 725, 726, 819
John G. 702
Philip 825
Sarah 825
Thomas (Heirs) 825

Whittington
Betsy 878
William 876, 878

Whittle
William 869

Wickham
Brindle 887

Wiemer
Adam 2156

Wier
James 894
Jesse C. 956
Thomas 849

Wiers
Benjamin 825

Wilcox
H. R. 503
Homer 657
Homer R. 419, 503
Icel 503

Wiles
Dr. H. L. 402

ALL NAMES INDEX

Wiley
- Claire 504
- Clifford C. 365
- David 975
- Effie 510
- Freddie 504
- Hance 835
- Harris 832
- John 246
- Joseph 682
- P. J. 370
- Parley 365, 369
- William 244, 975
- William, Jr. 825

Wilford
- David 975

Wilfred
- Holling 358

Wilkerson
- Lonnie 365

Wilkey
- Joseph 246

Wilkin 872, 1015
- Hananiah 894
- J. S. 81
- John B. 169
- John S. 1000
- Mrs. S. 865
- R. 269
- Robert 80, 112, 156, 197, 864, 865
- S. 269
- S. W. 166
- Samuel 865
- William 494

Wilkins 873
- Archibald 278, 869
- Daniel 747
- H. 124
- J. S. 95
- John S. 160
- Robert 87, 869, 901
- Samuel 869
- Thomas 246, 869
- William 869

Wilkinshaw
- John 746

Wilkinson
- Samuel 975, 976
- Thomas 747

Willey
- Earl M. 365

William
- James Thompson of 976

Williams 415, 603, 819, 909, 2200, 2289, 2302
- Abner 908, 975
- Amos 247
- Anthony 908, 975
- Betsy 878
- Betsy Whittington . 878
- Charles 669
- Clarence O. 365
- Clem 365
- Constantine 908
- David 825, 2133
- Deborah 2297
- Dr. 56, 913, 2111
- Dr. E. 913
- E. J. ... 81, 444, 524, 603
- Ebenezer 258
- Edward 878
- Edward M. 365
- Edward Richard 366
- Elijah 246, 818
- Ephraim 924
- Francis 670
- Freda 508
- George 381, 1062
- George R. 365
- H. B. 444
- H. L. 81, 616
- H. L. (Pode) ... 603, 604
- Hannah Lemmon 1054
- Hannah Lemon 1018
- Henry ... 870, 876, 877, 878
- Henry G. 468
- Henry L. (Pode) 623
- Henry, Jr. 878
- Israel 1062
- Jack W. 365
- Jacob 908
- James 618
- James M. 696
- Jed 87
- Joel 975
- John . 110, 1013, 1017, 1018, 1019, 1054
- Joseph 10, 244, 649, 906, 908, 975, 1017, 1062, 2290
- Levi ... 11, 24, 196, 254, 985, 1012, 1017, 1018, 1054, 1056
- Margaret 908
- Maria 2305
- Miss Mollie 268
- Nancy Carpenter .. 877, 878
- Nehemiah 245
- Nimrod 908
- Paul E. 365
- Pearl 513
- Phebe 908
- R. D. 499
- R. W. 412
- Reese 365
- Rev. Matthew Henderson 788
- Richard A. 505
- Roy M. 365
- Sam 365
- Samuel 1049
- Sarah 908, 1017
- Sarah Cook 908
- Sarah Woodard 906
- T. F. 716
- Thomas 262, 291, 499, 559
- Thomas W. 278
- Thomas, Jr. 499, 606
- William 2156, 2158
- William K. 365
- William Kenneth ... 339
- Woodard 908

Williamson
- Alex 110
- Col. David 23, 874
- Hon. Samuel 879

ALL NAMES INDEX

Rev. 800
Thomas 559
Willis 2073
  Big Jim 943
  C. E. 498
  C. H. 498, 499
  C. R. 87
  Edward 835
  Frank B. .. 176, 177, 179
  George 835, 936
  Governor Frank B. .. 177
  Isaac 124, 835
  James 835
  Lizzie 507
  Lota 513
  Margaret 936
  R. E. 90, 180, 181
  Senator Frank B. ... 180
  W. W. 447
Willkie
  Wendell 2149
  Wendell L. 185, 187
Wills
  John 747
Wilson 559, 718, 833, 1028
  A. 269
  A. L. 621
  Alex 671
  Anna 512
  Basil W. 365
  Benjamin 747
  Charles E. 350, 365
  Charles R. 365
  Cyrus 2165
  David. 246, 1031, 1049
  David P. 365
  Deborah 2278, 2279
  E. W. 90
  Ed W. 181
  Edward 112, 1037
  Eli 2134
  Eliza 2004, 2005, 2006
  Eliza J. 2274
  Elizabeth 819, 1018, 1031
  Frank P. 365
  George 812
  George W. 277, 365
  H. 1031
  Heber H. 365, 368
  Henry 156, 1038, 1049, 2006
  Henry H. 2006
  Hiram 981
  Ida 369
  Ira P. 365
  Isaac 97, 649, 825, 1031
  Isaac, Sr. 825
  J. W. 501
  James ... 124, 381, 829, 1017
  James H. 276
  Jane 2006
  Jeremiah 1062
  Jesse 825, 1012
  Jesse, Sr. 1017
  John 956
  John A. 270
  John C. 365
  John J. 277
  John M. 97
  John R. 365
  John W. 507
  Joshua 1031
  Josiah 799
  Judge William 2009, 2010
  L. H. 762
  Lieut. E. E. 289
  Llewen 365
  Lucy 514
  Margaret ... 1027, 1062
  Mary 512
  Mrs. 1025
  Mrs. C. 1038
  Myrta 513
  Oth 670
  Otho 825
  Otto 365
  President Woodrow 175, 176, 177, 182, 530, 625, 2149
  Ralph M. 365, 367, 368
  Ralph W. 639
  Reed 366, 499, 502
  Rev. H. 440
  Rev. William 564
  Robert 791
  Rodman 606
  Roy P. 365
  Sam 2165
  Samuel 495, 2005, 2006
  Stephen 649
  Thomas 696, 819, 825, 996, 2005, 2006
  Thomas P. 276, 787
  W. G. 842
  W. W. 447
  Wayne L. 365, 368
  William 66, 81, 399, 865, 1026, 1049
  William C. 996, 1009
  William Craig 1010
  William D. 1049
  Z. A. 272
  Zachariah .. 1062, 2006
Winder
  General 725
Wine
  Christian .. 67, 945, 956
  Emanuel 799
  George 198
  John 799
Wines 559
  Charity 292
  George .. 245, 292, 887
Winiker 435
Winkler
  Fred H. 280
Winland
  Walter P. 365
Winlow
  Major General 206
Winn
  William 996
Winnett
  Benjamin 965, 975
  John 965, 975

ALL NAMES INDEX

Winniker
- George 156

Wires
- John H. 278
- William H. 276

Wirick 2300
- Andrew 246
- Michael 246
- Peter 246, 829

Wirrick
- Dr. Shellbrick 1067

Wirt
- William 113, 114

Wise
- Clarence K. 365
- John 894

Wiseman
- Joseph 278

Wiser
- Captain 2016
- Daniel K. 647
- J. C. 258, 302
- Miss Kate 441

Wishard
- James 703
- Jane 703
- John R. 894

Wishart
- Harry 349, 365
- J. R. 124

Wister
- D. K. 56

Withney
- Elizabeth .. 2309, 2310, 2311

Withrow
- Captain 263
- O. 2099
- Oliver 123, 142

Witt
- Professor 2111

Witten
- Arthur H. 503
- Fred 629
- Harry R. 365
- Margaret 2286
- Thomas 567

Wodich
- Milly 365

Wolfe 833
- Betty 503
- Ernest W. 365
- Fred J. 503
- Helen 370, 503
- Herbert 606
- Herbert C. 366
- John 285
- Mr. 985, 987
- W. G. 447, 654, 657
- William G. i, ii, iii, iv, v, vi, vii, 1, 2, 4, 5, 639, iii

Wolford
- Henry 245
- Mary 919

Wolgamott
- David 1049
- Floyd O. 366

Wolverton
- N. L. 695

Womeldruf
- Nanney 510

Wontz
- Fred W. 366

Wood 840
- Dr. 913
- J. M. 499
- James 1007
- John R. 366
- Joseph. 285, 812, 2190
- Margaret 1062
- Martha 2102
- William 805, 806

Woodard
- Isaac 426, 968, 2292
- Sarah 906

Woodbeck
- John 246

Woodburn
- Albert 100
- Alex 696
- Alexander 791, 844, 956
- Clarence 370

Clarence G. 366
Hugh 494, 791
William 447

Woodrow 763
- Henry 124, 819, 825
- John 232, 495, 2061
- Mary 819

Woods
- I. T. 160
- James 869
- Justice William Burnham 462
- Samuel 1049
- William 278

Woodson
- Martha 2286

Woodward
- J. M. 2199

Woodworth
- Ward W. 366

Wooley
- John J. 168

Wooten
- Charles 366
- D. P. 508
- Rev. Byron 410
- William 412, 669
- Willie 618

Worgan
- Stanley A. 366

Workman
- Effy 924
- Roy A. 498

Worthing
- Price 285
- R. 269

Worthington
- Thomas 285

Wray
- Esther 500

Wright
- Alma 503
- Amos 869
- Dr. 913, 2111
- Harry 509
- James 762, 799
- John C. 105

2444

ALL NAMES INDEX

Mary 819
May 503
Moses 245
Rev. J. B 410
Robert 669
Samuel H 349, 366
Silas 689
William 747, 869
Writt
   Thomas 411
Wyckoff
   Cora 514
   W. W. 784
Wycoff
   Charles M 366
   Elijah 1025
   Esta 502
   Ida 512
   Mary 1025
   Peter 275
   Samuel 278
Wylie
   Effie 500
   Jasper G. 366
   Oliver 1027
   Raymond 366
   William DeWitt 367
Wynn
   James B. 351, 366
Wyrick 2299
   Betsey 2300
   Catherine Sunon 2299, 2300
   Christian 855
   David 2300
   Fanny 2300
   George Washington 2300
   Mary 2300
   Michael 2300
   Mrs. 886
   Obadiah 835, 893
   Obadiah G. 1062
   Peter .. 198, 244, 2299, 2300
   Sarah 2299
   Sarah Johnson 2300

Susanna 2300
Thomas Jefferson 2300
William 1062, 2300
Wyscarver
   Annas 503
   George W. 507
   Jacob 2156
   Rachel A. 507
   Samuel 2156

Y

Yakey
   Joseph 975, 2108
Yaple
   Alfred 151
Yarnell 937
   George 835
   J. M. 444
Yates
   Robert 647
   Robert A. 647
   Thomas 601
   William 302
Yearsley
   Charles S. 366
Yeo 884
   Harley 832
   Ida 832
Yingling 833
Yoho
   Jacob 689, 2152
   Thomas C. 366
Yontz
   Fred W. 366
Yost
   J. W. 76
   John 894
   Vita 503
Young 2079
   Alexander 1062
   Carrie 501
   Charles 366
   Clair A. 186, 187
   Cy 619
   David 2191
   Elder W. L. 412

Elizabeth 988
F. C. 504
George 869
H. O. 447
Harry E. 366
I. C. 655
Isaac 996
J. A. 501
J. K. 639
Jeanetta 501
John 501
Nye D. 366
O. E. 502
Otto E. 502
Rev. William 378
W. H. 2143
W. T. 447
William . 674, 844, 849, 2191
William J. 501
Younger
   Jacob R. 280
Yunk
   Bennett 366

Z

Zahniser
   R. W. 499
Zahnizer 585
   M. 272, 2099, 2103, 2106
   R. W. 595
Zane .. 21, 700, 874, 2153, 2226, 2280
   Betty 2280
   Ebenezer ...... v, 29, 30, 192, 193, 544, 2156, 2225, 2226, 2280
   Elizabeth McCullough 2280
   Jonathan 22, 24, 30, 192, 2225
   Mr. 50
Zatkovich
   Father Theophil 408

ALL NAMES INDEX

Ziegfeld
- Billie Burke 2028
- Florenz 2028

Zillmer
- Captain A. 411

Zimmerman
- John 844

Zoller
- H. B. 989